DRIVING
UNDER THE
INFLUENCE OF
CHILDREN

Other Baby Blues® books from Andrews McMeel Publishing

Guess Who Didn't Take a Nap?
I Thought Labor Ended When the Baby Was Born
We Are Experiencing Parental Difficulties . . . Please Stand By
Night of the Living Dad
I Saw Elvis in My Ultrasound
One More and We're Outnumbered!
Check, Please . . .
threats, bribes & videotape
If I'm a Stay-At-Home Mom, Why Am I Always in the Car?
Lift and Separate
I Shouldn't Have to Scream More Than Once!
Motherhood Is Not for Wimps
Baby Blues®: Unplugged
Dad to the Bone
Never a Dry Moment
Two Plus One Is Enough
Playdate: Category 5

Treasuries

The Super-Absorbent Biodegradable Family-Size Baby Blues®
Baby Blues®: Ten Years and Still in Diapers
Butt-Naked Baby Blues®
Wall-to-Wall Baby Blues®

DRIVING UNDER THE INFLUENCE OF CHILDREN

A Baby Blues® Treasury by
Rick Kirkman & Jerry Scott

Andrews McMeel
Publishing

Kansas City

Baby Blues is syndicated internationally by King Features Syndicate, Inc. For information, write King Features Syndicate, Inc., 888 Seventh Avenue, New York, New York 10019.

 For information, write Andrews McMeel Publishing, an Andrews McMeel Universal company, 4520 Main Street, Kansas City, Missouri 64111.

05 06 07 08 09 BAM 10 9 8 7 6 5 4 3 2 1

ISBN: 0-7407-5005-4

Library of Congress Catalog Card Number: 2004114430

Find *Baby Blues* on the Web at
www.babyblues.com.

**To Stephanie Bennett—
Cheerleader, wrangler, and editor nonpareil**

—R.K and J.S.

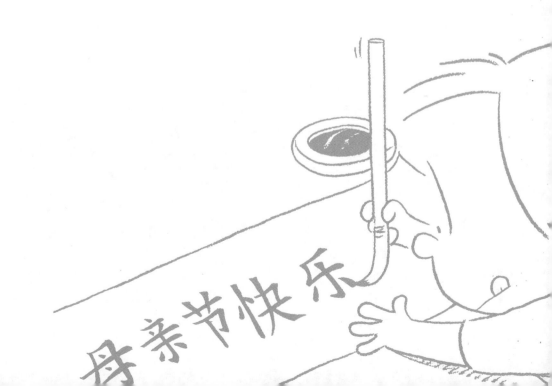

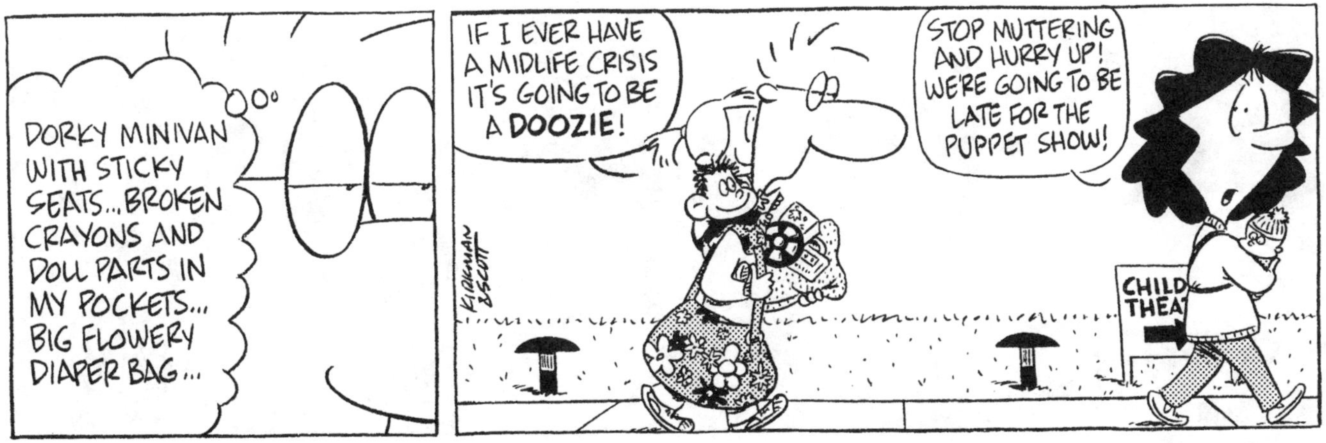
DORKY MINIVAN WITH STICKY SEATS...BROKEN CRAYONS AND DOLL PARTS IN MY POCKETS... BIG FLOWERY DIAPER BAG...
IF I EVER HAVE A MIDLIFE CRISIS IT'S GOING TO BE A **DOOZIE**!
STOP MUTTERING AND HURRY UP! WE'RE GOING TO BE LATE FOR THE PUPPET SHOW!

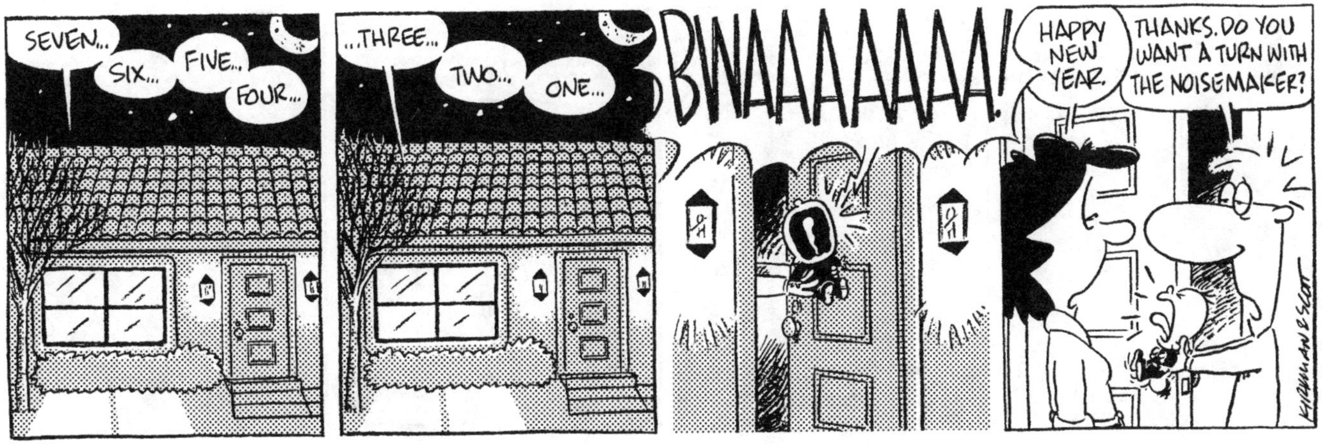
SEVEN...
SIX...
FIVE...
FOUR...
...THREE...
TWO...
ONE...
BWAAAAAAAA!
HAPPY NEW YEAR.
THANKS. DO YOU WANT A TURN WITH THE NOISEMAKER?

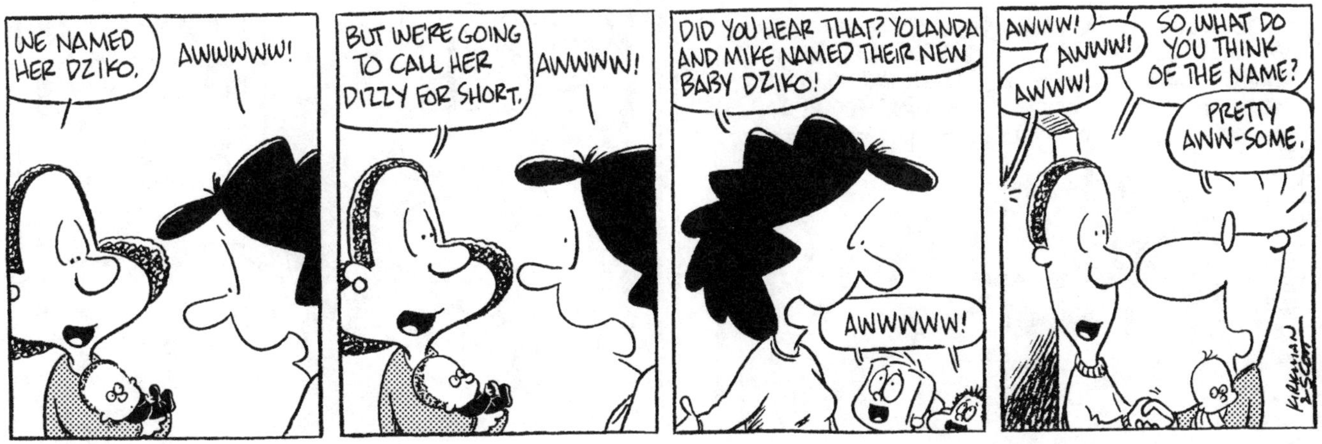
WE NAMED HER DZIKO.
AWWWWW!
BUT WE'RE GOING TO CALL HER DIZZY FOR SHORT.
AWWWW!
DID YOU HEAR THAT? YOLANDA AND MIKE NAMED THEIR NEW BABY DZIKO!
AWWWWW!
AWWW!
AWWW!
AWWW!
SO, WHAT DO YOU THINK OF THE NAME?
PRETTY AWW-SOME.

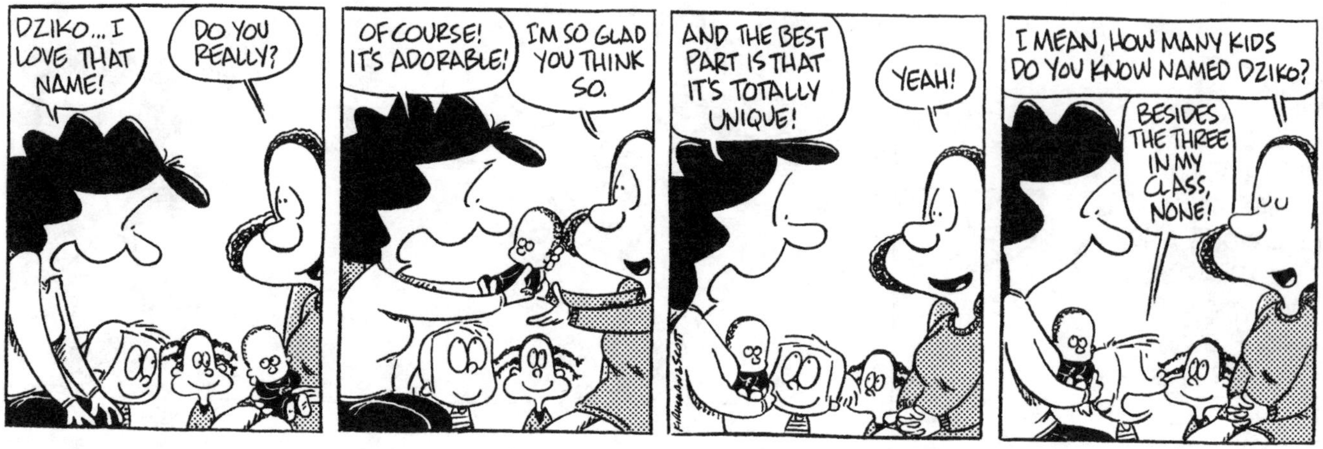
DZIKO... I LOVE THAT NAME!
DO YOU REALLY?
OF COURSE! IT'S ADORABLE!
I'M SO GLAD YOU THINK SO.
AND THE BEST PART IS THAT IT'S TOTALLY UNIQUE!
YEAH!
I MEAN, HOW MANY KIDS DO YOU KNOW NAMED DZIKO?
BESIDES THE THREE IN MY CLASS, NONE!

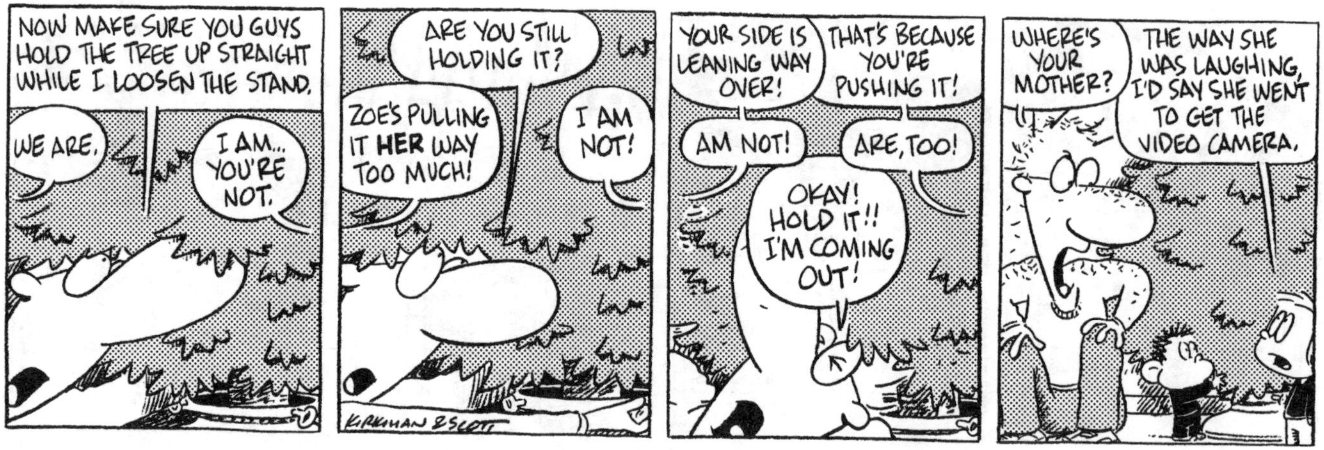
NOW MAKE SURE YOU GUYS HOLD THE TREE UP STRAIGHT WHILE I LOOSEN THE STAND.
WE ARE.
I AM... YOU'RE NOT.
ARE YOU STILL HOLDING IT?
ZOE'S PULLING IT HER WAY TOO MUCH!
I AM NOT!
KIRKMAN & SCOTT
YOUR SIDE IS LEANING WAY OVER!
THAT'S BECAUSE YOU'RE PUSHING IT!
AM NOT!
ARE, TOO!
OKAY! HOLD IT!! I'M COMING OUT!
WHERE'S YOUR MOTHER?
THE WAY SHE WAS LAUGHING, I'D SAY SHE WENT TO GET THE VIDEO CAMERA.

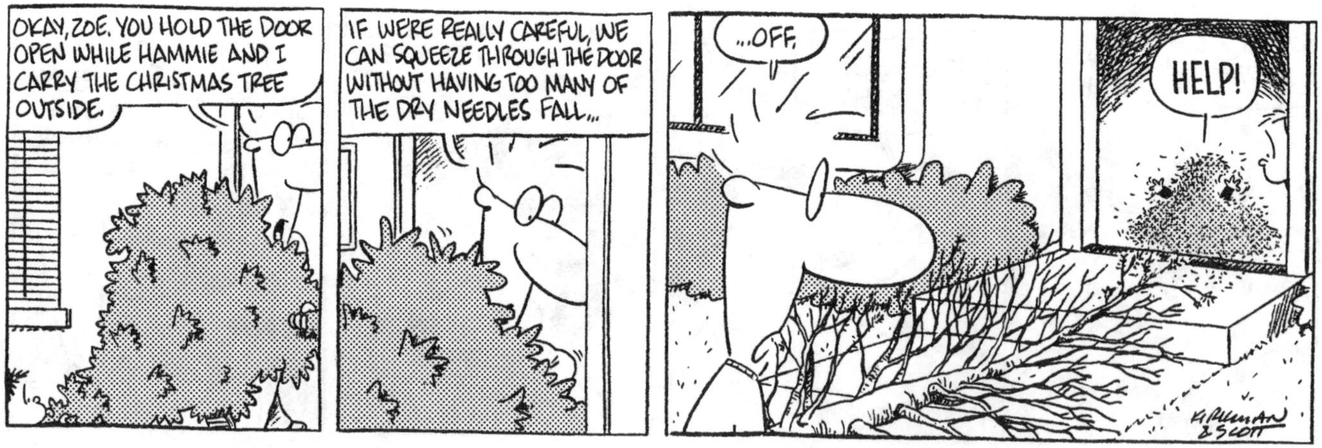
OKAY, ZOE. YOU HOLD THE DOOR OPEN WHILE HAMMIE AND I CARRY THE CHRISTMAS TREE OUTSIDE.
IF WE'RE REALLY CAREFUL, WE CAN SQUEEZE THROUGH THE DOOR WITHOUT HAVING TOO MANY OF THE DRY NEEDLES FALL...
...OFF.
HELP!
KIRKMAN & SCOTT

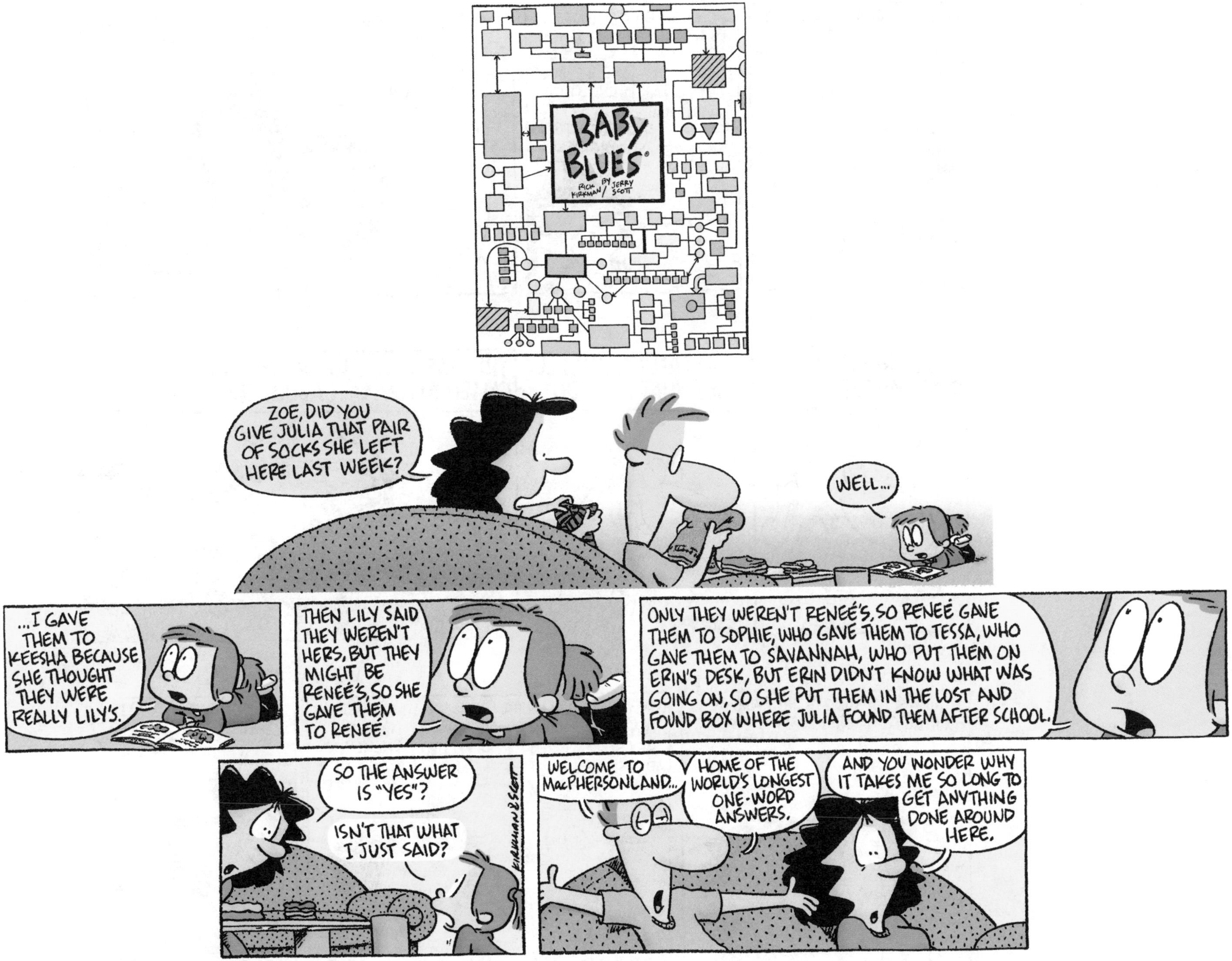
BABY BLUES®
RICK KIRKMAN / BY / JERRY SCOTT
ZOE, DID YOU GIVE JULIA THAT PAIR OF SOCKS SHE LEFT HERE LAST WEEK?
WELL...
...I GAVE THEM TO KEESHA BECAUSE SHE THOUGHT THEY WERE REALLY LILY'S.
THEN LILY SAID THEY WEREN'T HERS, BUT THEY MIGHT BE RENEÉ'S, SO SHE GAVE THEM TO RENEÉ.
ONLY THEY WEREN'T RENEÉ'S, SO RENEÉ GAVE THEM TO SOPHIE, WHO GAVE THEM TO TESSA, WHO GAVE THEM TO SAVANNAH, WHO PUT THEM ON ERIN'S DESK, BUT ERIN DIDN'T KNOW WHAT WAS GOING ON, SO SHE PUT THEM IN THE LOST AND FOUND BOX WHERE JULIA FOUND THEM AFTER SCHOOL.
SO THE ANSWER IS "YES"?
ISN'T THAT WHAT I JUST SAID?
KIRKMAN & SCOTT
WELCOME TO MacPHERSONLAND...
HOME OF THE WORLD'S LONGEST ONE-WORD ANSWERS.
AND YOU WONDER WHY IT TAKES ME SO LONG TO GET ANYTHING DONE AROUND HERE.

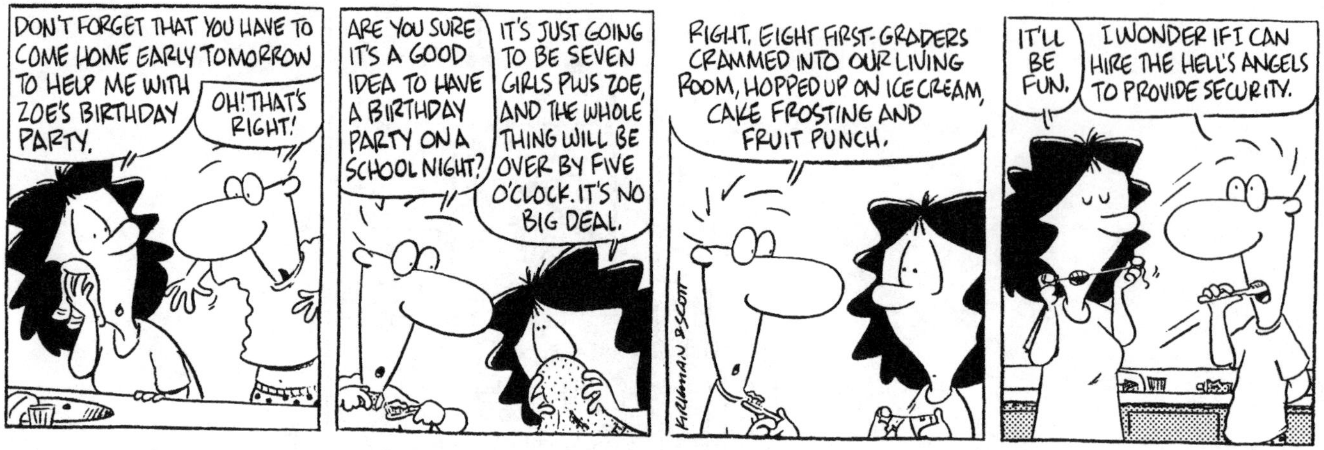
DON'T FORGET THAT YOU HAVE TO COME HOME EARLY TOMORROW TO HELP ME WITH ZOE'S BIRTHDAY PARTY.
OH! THAT'S RIGHT!
ARE YOU SURE IT'S A GOOD IDEA TO HAVE A BIRTHDAY PARTY ON A SCHOOL NIGHT?
IT'S JUST GOING TO BE SEVEN GIRLS PLUS ZOE, AND THE WHOLE THING WILL BE OVER BY FIVE O'CLOCK. IT'S NO BIG DEAL.
RIGHT. EIGHT FIRST-GRADERS CRAMMED INTO OUR LIVING ROOM, HOPPED UP ON ICE CREAM, CAKE FROSTING AND FRUIT PUNCH.
IT'LL BE FUN.
I WONDER IF I CAN HIRE THE HELL'S ANGELS TO PROVIDE SECURITY.

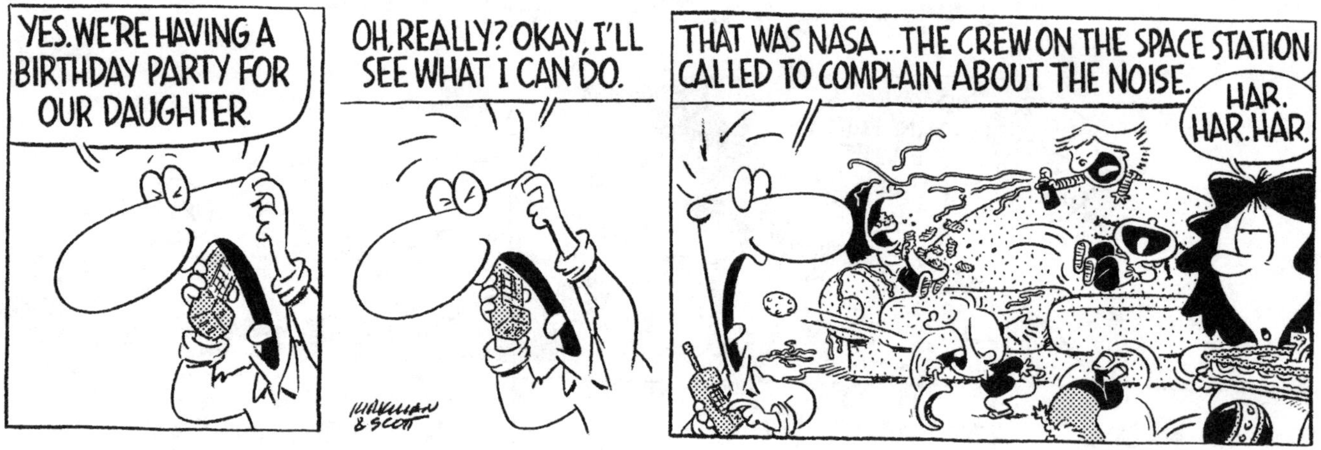
YES. WE'RE HAVING A BIRTHDAY PARTY FOR OUR DAUGHTER.
OH, REALLY? OKAY, I'LL SEE WHAT I CAN DO.
THAT WAS NASA...THE CREW ON THE SPACE STATION CALLED TO COMPLAIN ABOUT THE NOISE.
HAR. HAR. HAR.

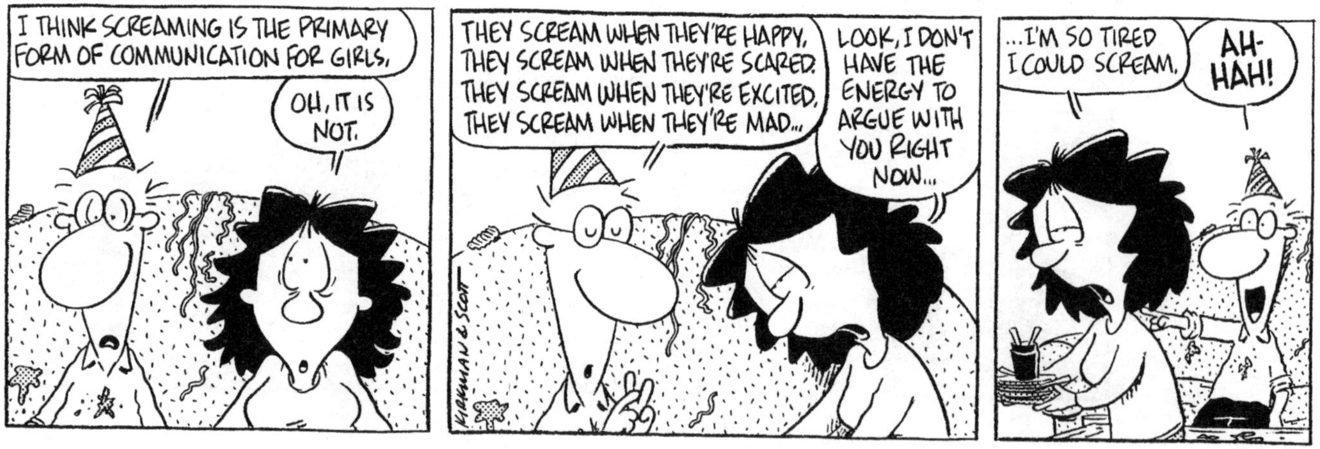
I THINK SCREAMING IS THE PRIMARY FORM OF COMMUNICATION FOR GIRLS.
OH, IT IS NOT.
THEY SCREAM WHEN THEY'RE HAPPY. THEY SCREAM WHEN THEY'RE SCARED. THEY SCREAM WHEN THEY'RE EXCITED. THEY SCREAM WHEN THEY'RE MAD...
LOOK, I DON'T HAVE THE ENERGY TO ARGUE WITH YOU RIGHT NOW...
...I'M SO TIRED I COULD SCREAM.
AH-HAH!

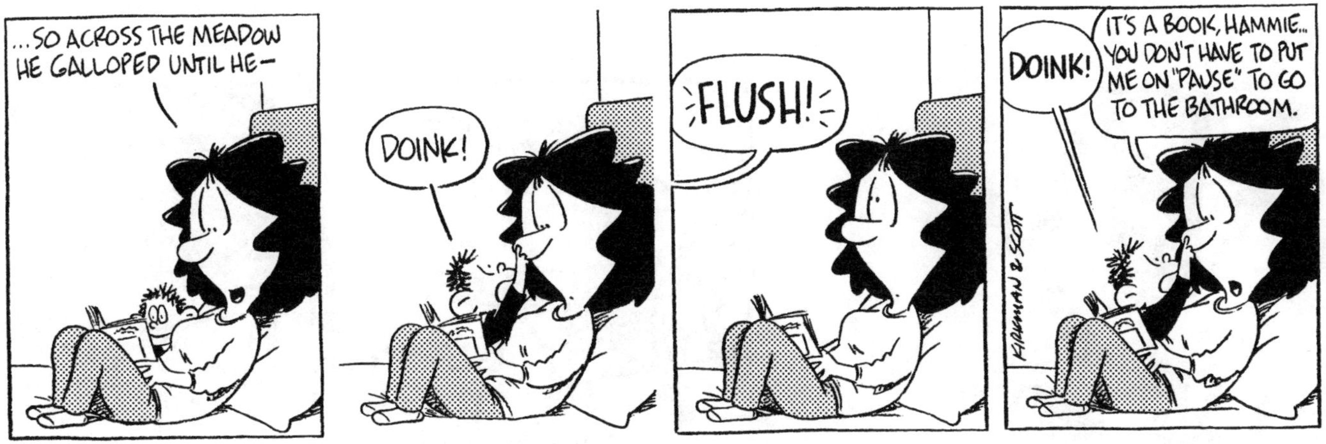
...SO ACROSS THE MEADOW HE GALLOPED UNTIL HE—
DOINK!
FLUSH!
DOINK!
IT'S A BOOK, HAMMIE.. YOU DON'T HAVE TO PUT ME ON "PAUSE" TO GO TO THE BATHROOM.

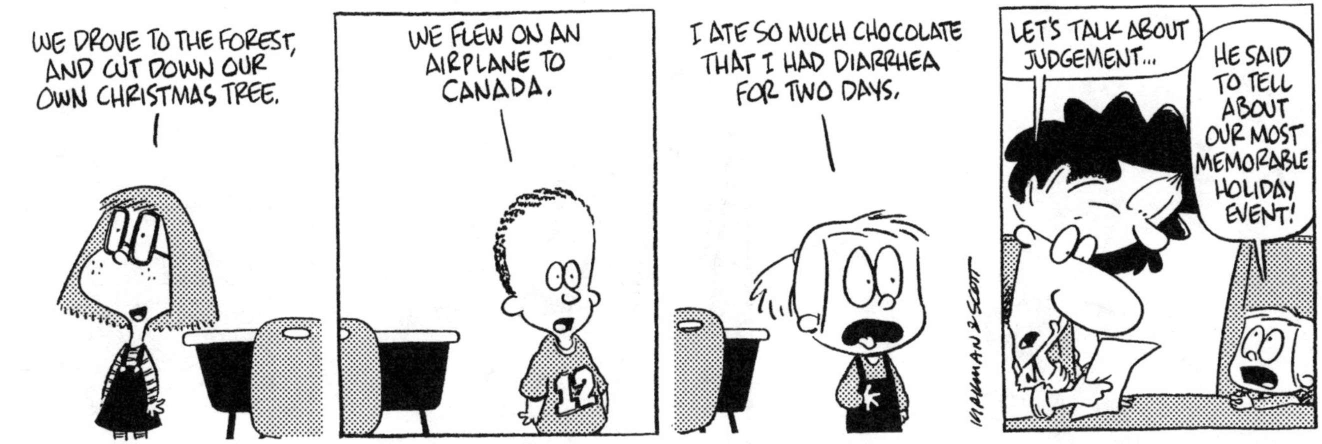
WE DROVE TO THE FOREST, AND CUT DOWN OUR OWN CHRISTMAS TREE.
WE FLEW ON AN AIRPLANE TO CANADA.
I ATE SO MUCH CHOCOLATE THAT I HAD DIARRHEA FOR TWO DAYS.
LET'S TALK ABOUT JUDGEMENT...
HE SAID TO TELL ABOUT OUR MOST MEMORABLE HOLIDAY EVENT!

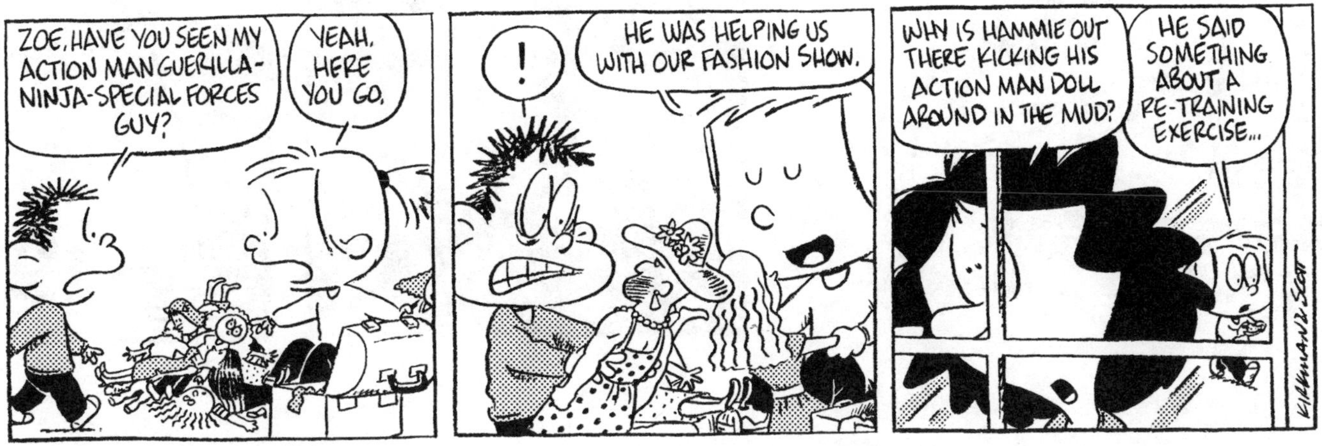
ZOE, HAVE YOU SEEN MY ACTION MAN GUERILLA-NINJA-SPECIAL FORCES GUY?
YEAH. HERE YOU GO.
!
HE WAS HELPING US WITH OUR FASHION SHOW.
WHY IS HAMMIE OUT THERE KICKING HIS ACTION MAN DOLL AROUND IN THE MUD?
HE SAID SOMETHING ABOUT A RE-TRAINING EXERCISE...

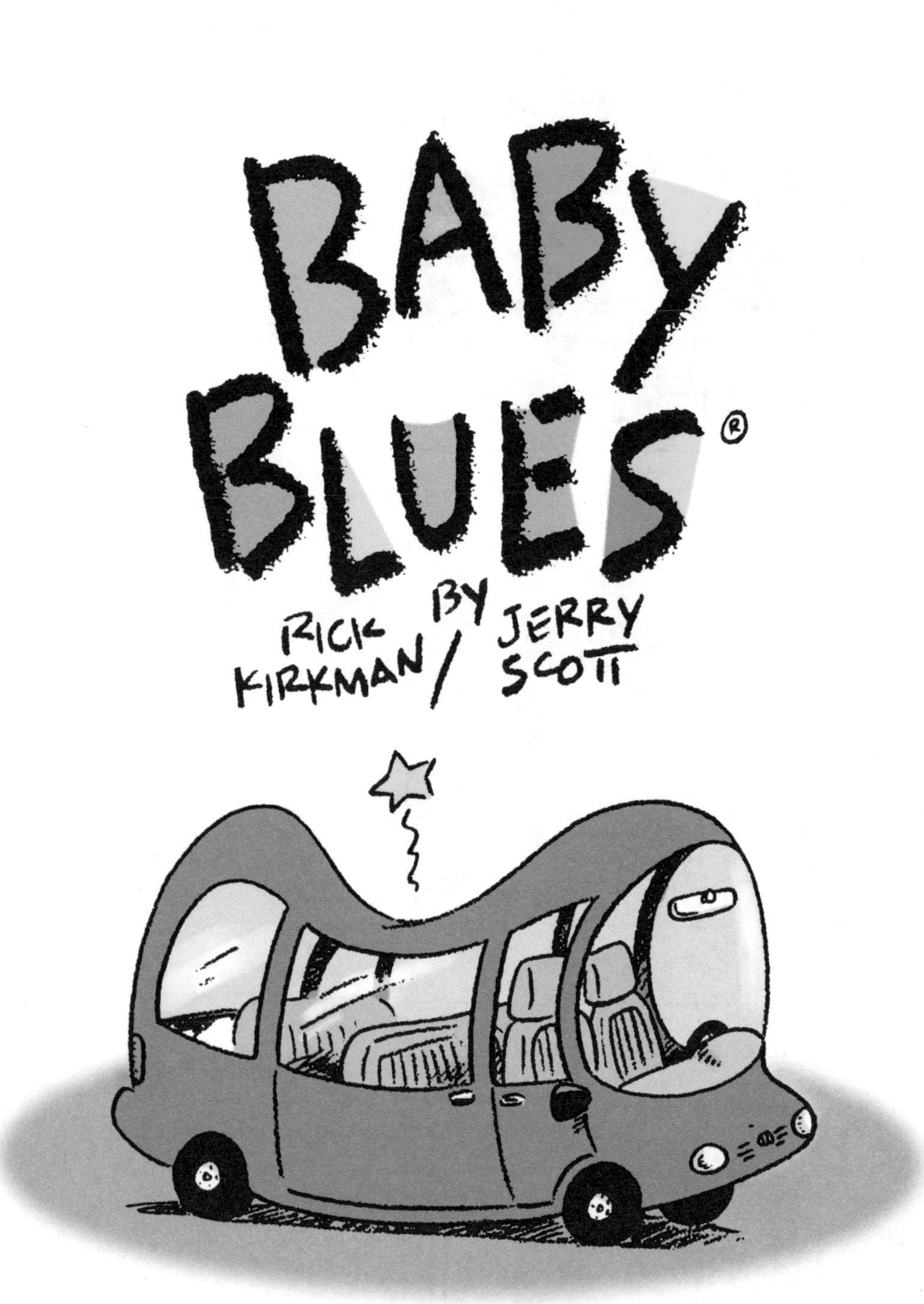
BABY BLUES®
BY
RICK KIRKMAN / JERRY SCOTT

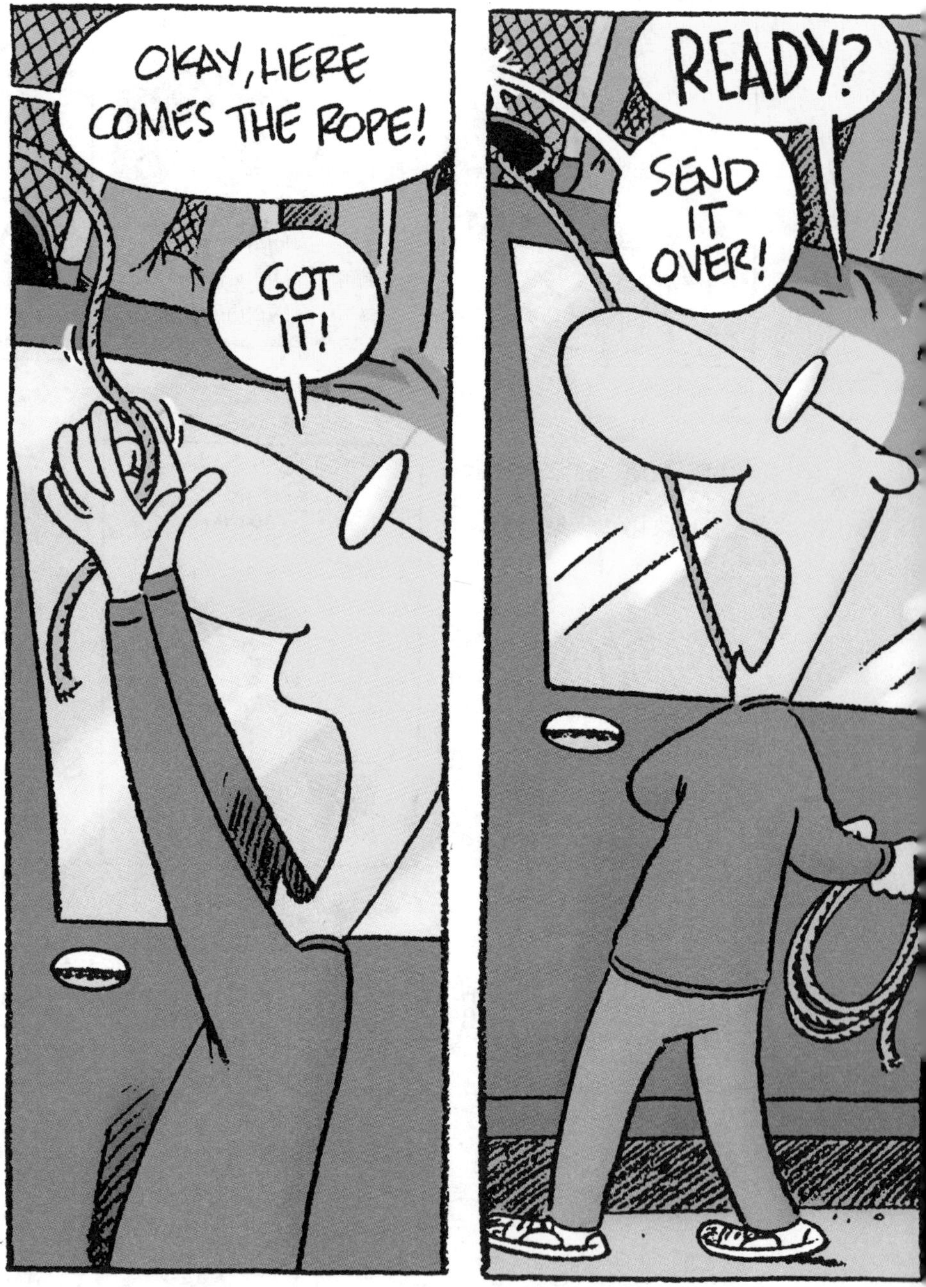
OKAY, HERE COMES THE ROPE!
GOT IT!
READY?
SEND IT OVER!

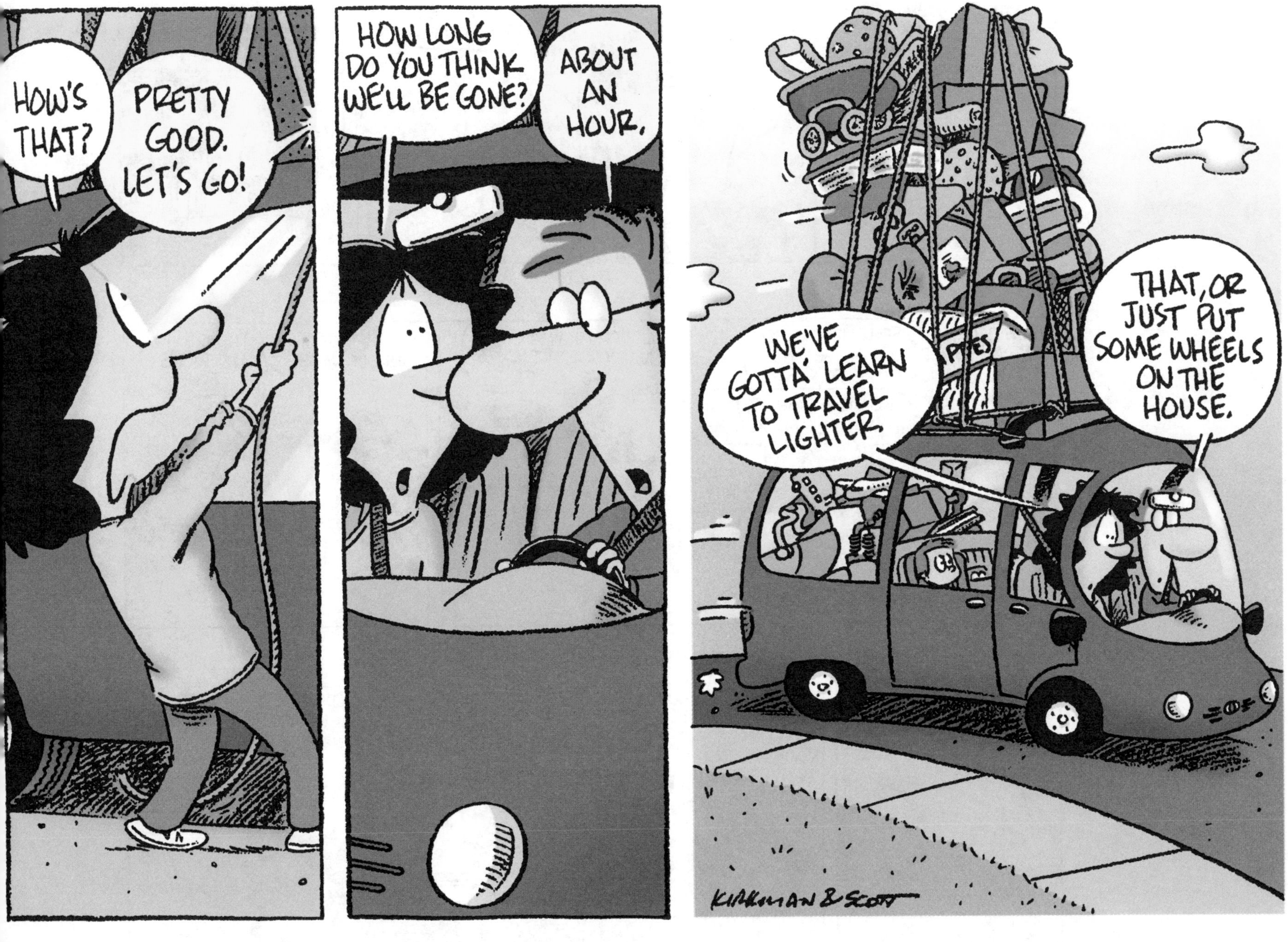

HOW'S THAT?
PRETTY GOOD. LET'S GO!
HOW LONG DO YOU THINK WE'LL BE GONE?
ABOUT AN HOUR.
WE'VE GOTTA' LEARN TO TRAVEL LIGHTER.
THAT, OR JUST PUT SOME WHEELS ON THE HOUSE.
KIRKMAN & SCOTT

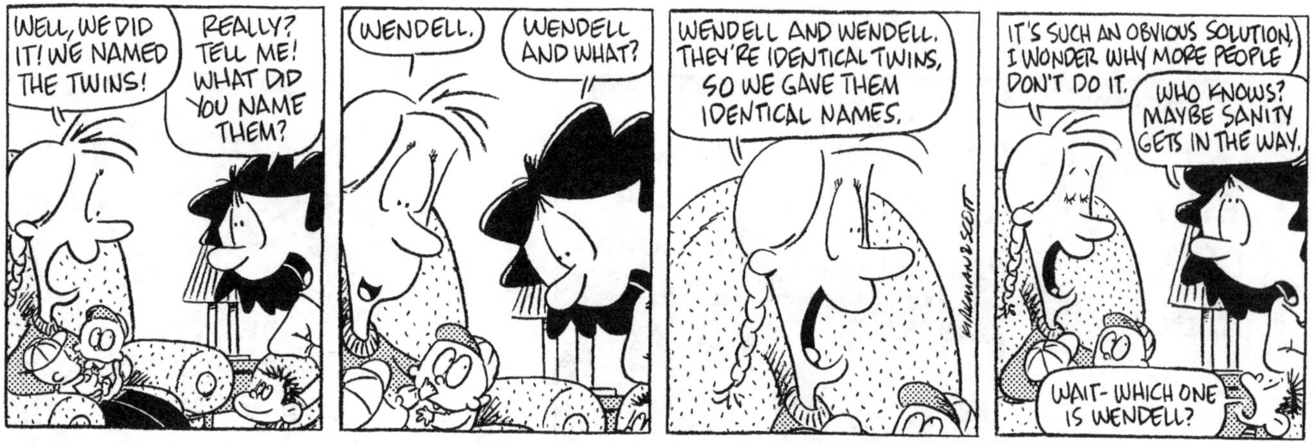
WELL, WE DID IT! WE NAMED THE TWINS!
REALLY? TELL ME! WHAT DID YOU NAME THEM?
WENDELL.
WENDELL AND WHAT?
WENDELL AND WENDELL. THEY'RE IDENTICAL TWINS, SO WE GAVE THEM IDENTICAL NAMES.
KIRKMAN & SCOTT
IT'S SUCH AN OBVIOUS SOLUTION, I WONDER WHY MORE PEOPLE DON'T DO IT.
WHO KNOWS? MAYBE SANITY GETS IN THE WAY.
WAIT- WHICH ONE IS WENDELL?

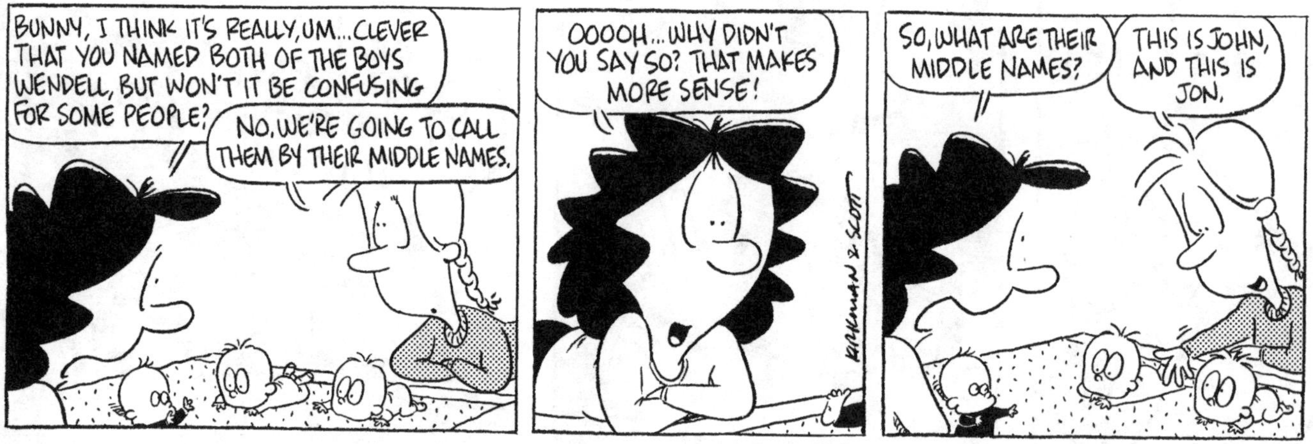
BUNNY, I THINK IT'S REALLY, UM... CLEVER THAT YOU NAMED BOTH OF THE BOYS WENDELL, BUT WON'T IT BE CONFUSING FOR SOME PEOPLE?
NO, WE'RE GOING TO CALL THEM BY THEIR MIDDLE NAMES.
OOOOH... WHY DIDN'T YOU SAY SO? THAT MAKES MORE SENSE!
KIRKMAN & SCOTT
SO, WHAT ARE THEIR MIDDLE NAMES?
THIS IS JOHN, AND THIS IS JON.

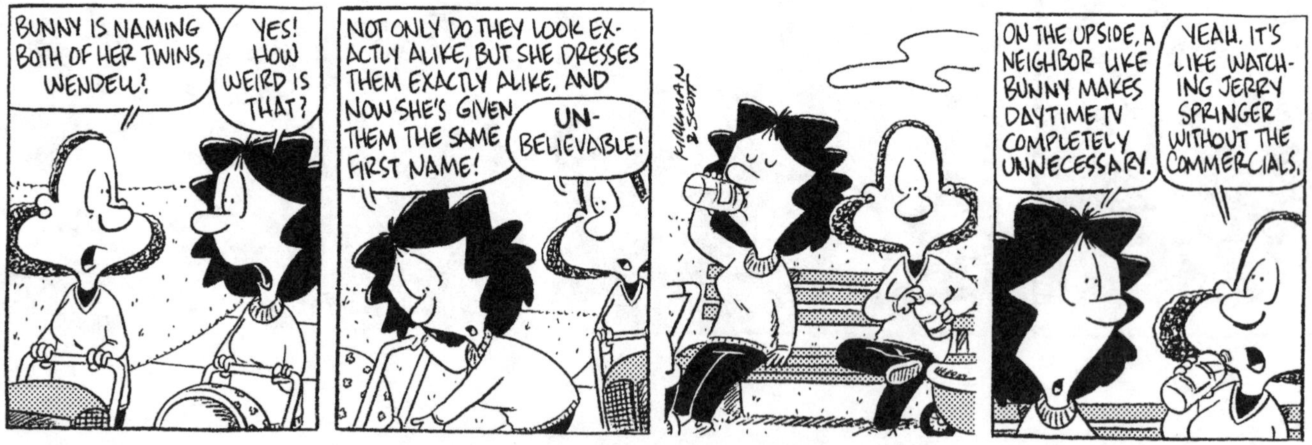
BUNNY IS NAMING BOTH OF HER TWINS, WENDELL?
YES! HOW WEIRD IS THAT?
NOT ONLY DO THEY LOOK EXACTLY ALIKE, BUT SHE DRESSES THEM EXACTLY ALIKE, AND NOW SHE'S GIVEN THEM THE SAME FIRST NAME!
UN-BELIEVABLE!
KIRKMAN & SCOTT
ON THE UPSIDE, A NEIGHBOR LIKE BUNNY MAKES DAYTIME TV COMPLETELY UNNECESSARY.
YEAH. IT'S LIKE WATCHING JERRY SPRINGER WITHOUT THE COMMERCIALS.

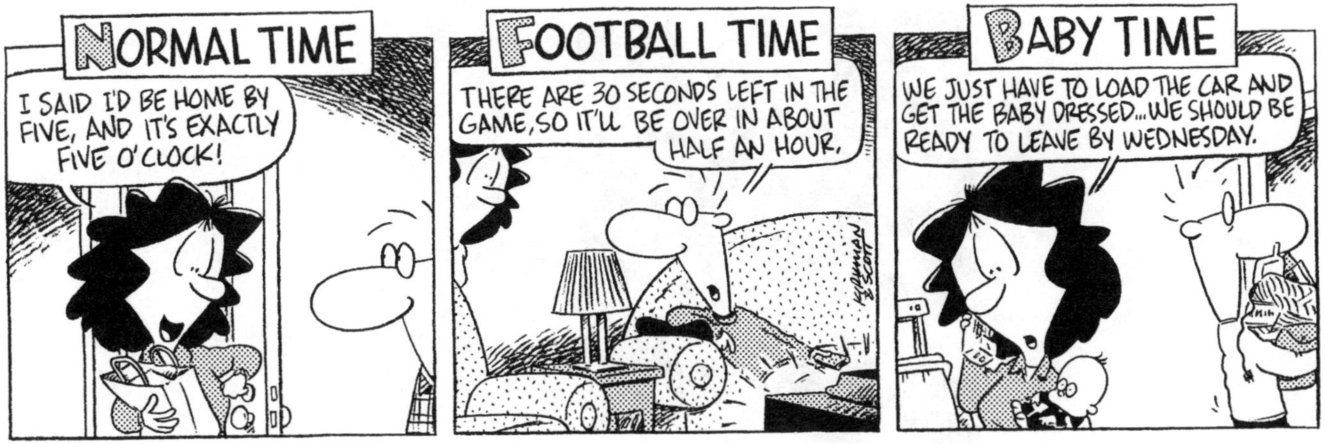
NORMAL TIME
I SAID I'D BE HOME BY FIVE, AND IT'S EXACTLY FIVE O'CLOCK!
FOOTBALL TIME
THERE ARE 30 SECONDS LEFT IN THE GAME, SO IT'LL BE OVER IN ABOUT HALF AN HOUR.
BABY TIME
WE JUST HAVE TO LOAD THE CAR AND GET THE BABY DRESSED... WE SHOULD BE READY TO LEAVE BY WEDNESDAY.

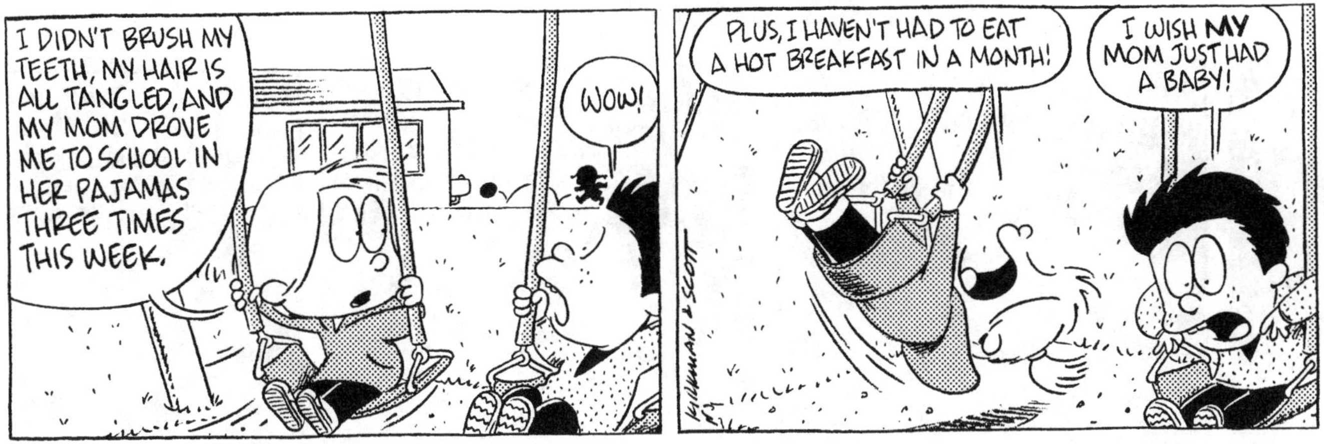
I DIDN'T BRUSH MY TEETH, MY HAIR IS ALL TANGLED, AND MY MOM DROVE ME TO SCHOOL IN HER PAJAMAS THREE TIMES THIS WEEK.
WOW!
PLUS, I HAVEN'T HAD TO EAT A HOT BREAKFAST IN A MONTH!
I WISH MY MOM JUST HAD A BABY!

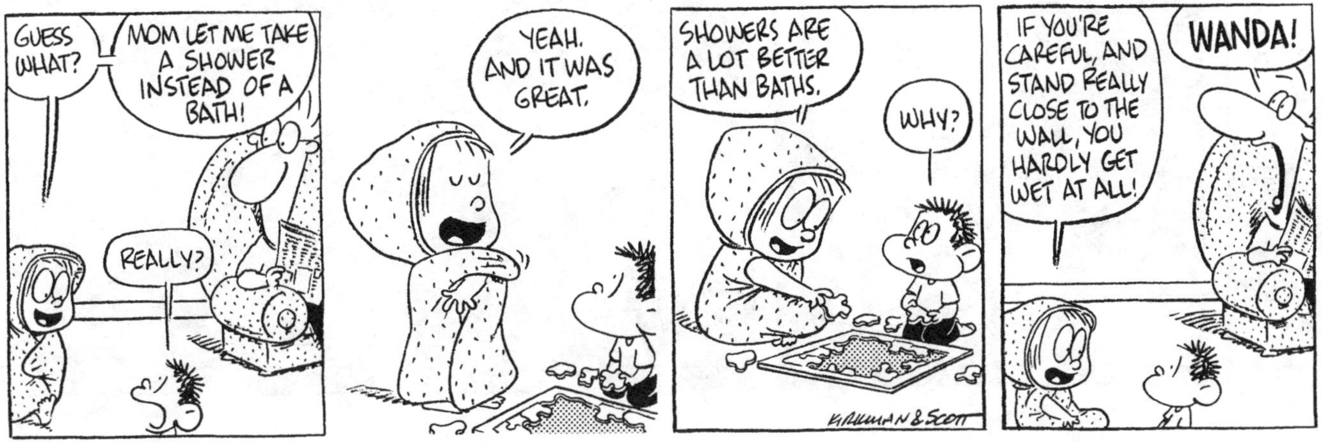
GUESS WHAT?
MOM LET ME TAKE A SHOWER INSTEAD OF A BATH!
REALLY?
YEAH. AND IT WAS GREAT.
SHOWERS ARE A LOT BETTER THAN BATHS.
WHY?
IF YOU'RE CAREFUL, AND STAND REALLY CLOSE TO THE WALL, YOU HARDLY GET WET AT ALL!
WANDA!

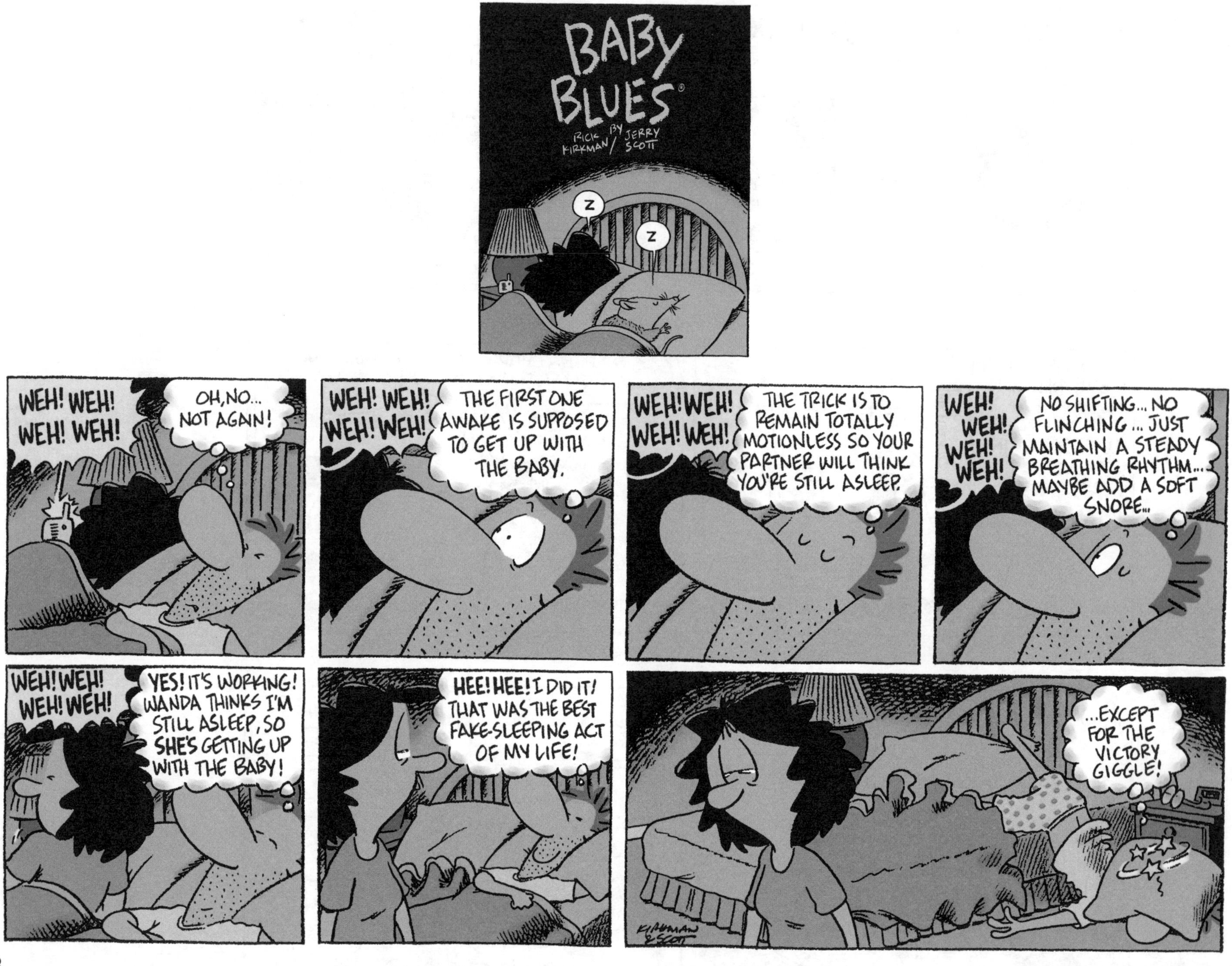
BABY BLUES®
RICK KIRKMAN / BY JERRY SCOTT
Z
Z
WEH! WEH! WEH! WEH!
OH, NO... NOT AGAIN!
WEH! WEH! WEH! WEH!
THE FIRST ONE AWAKE IS SUPPOSED TO GET UP WITH THE BABY.
WEH! WEH! WEH! WEH!
THE TRICK IS TO REMAIN TOTALLY MOTIONLESS SO YOUR PARTNER WILL THINK YOU'RE STILL ASLEEP.
WEH! WEH! WEH! WEH!
NO SHIFTING... NO FLINCHING... JUST MAINTAIN A STEADY BREATHING RHYTHM... MAYBE ADD A SOFT SNORE...
WEH! WEH! WEH! WEH!
YES! IT'S WORKING! WANDA THINKS I'M STILL ASLEEP, SO SHE'S GETTING UP WITH THE BABY!
HEE! HEE! I DID IT! THAT WAS THE BEST FAKE-SLEEPING ACT OF MY LIFE!
...EXCEPT FOR THE VICTORY GIGGLE!
KIRKMAN & SCOTT

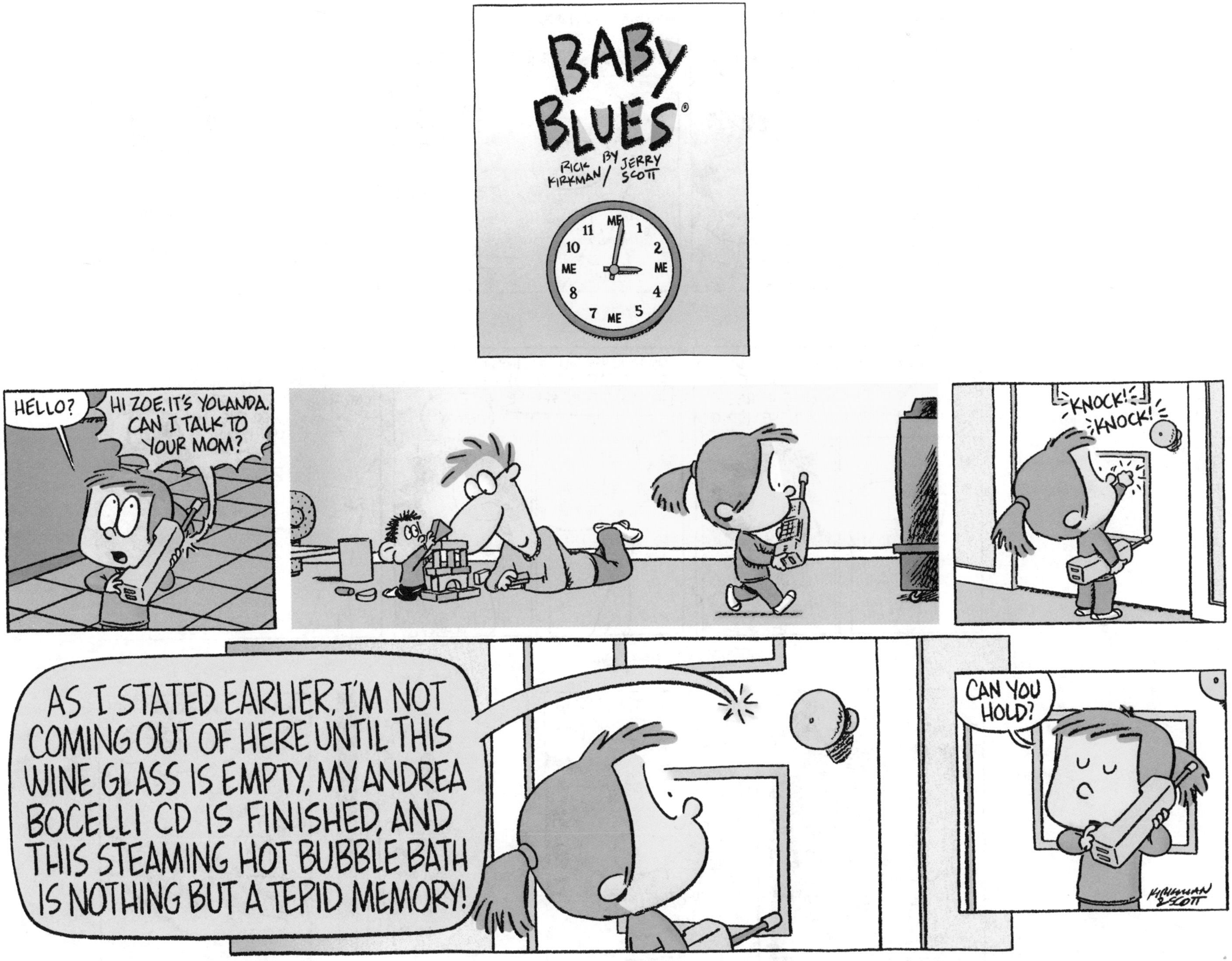
BABY BLUES®
BY RICK KIRKMAN / JERRY SCOTT
HELLO?
HI ZOE. IT'S YOLANDA. CAN I TALK TO YOUR MOM?
KNOCK! KNOCK!
AS I STATED EARLIER, I'M NOT COMING OUT OF HERE UNTIL THIS WINE GLASS IS EMPTY, MY ANDREA BOCELLI CD IS FINISHED, AND THIS STEAMING HOT BUBBLE BATH IS NOTHING BUT A TEPID MEMORY!
CAN YOU HOLD?

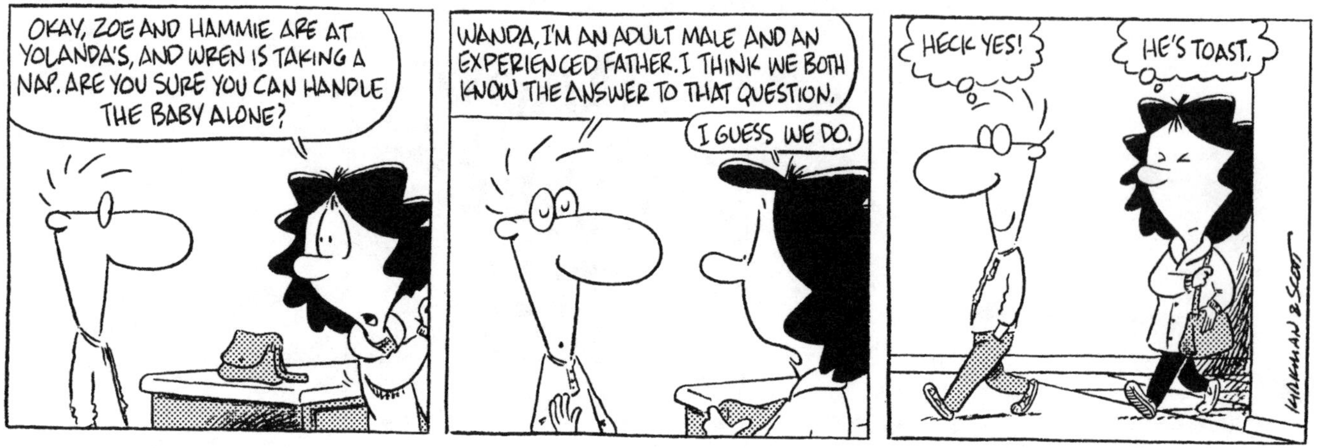
OKAY, ZOE AND HAMMIE ARE AT YOLANDA'S, AND WREN IS TAKING A NAP. ARE YOU SURE YOU CAN HANDLE THE BABY ALONE?
WANDA, I'M AN ADULT MALE AND AN EXPERIENCED FATHER. I THINK WE BOTH KNOW THE ANSWER TO THAT QUESTION.
I GUESS WE DO.
HECK YES!
HE'S TOAST.
KIRKMAN & SCOTT

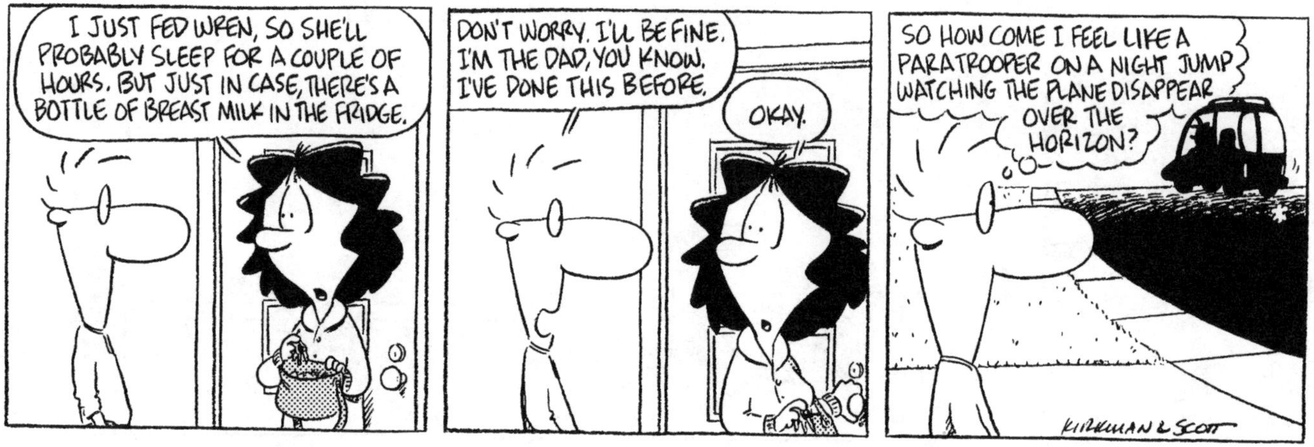
I JUST FED WREN, SO SHE'LL PROBABLY SLEEP FOR A COUPLE OF HOURS. BUT JUST IN CASE, THERE'S A BOTTLE OF BREAST MILK IN THE FRIDGE.
DON'T WORRY. I'LL BE FINE. I'M THE DAD, YOU KNOW. I'VE DONE THIS BEFORE.
OKAY.
SO HOW COME I FEEL LIKE A PARATROOPER ON A NIGHT JUMP WATCHING THE PLANE DISAPPEAR OVER THE HORIZON?
KIRKMAN & SCOTT

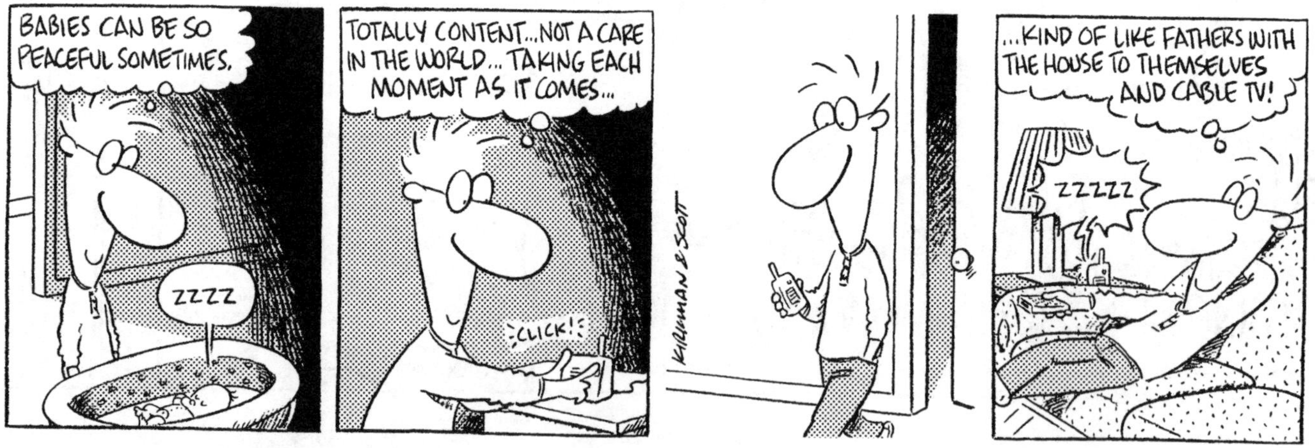
BABIES CAN BE SO PEACEFUL SOMETIMES.
ZZZZ
TOTALLY CONTENT...NOT A CARE IN THE WORLD... TAKING EACH MOMENT AS IT COMES...
CLICK!
KIRKMAN & SCOTT
...KIND OF LIKE FATHERS WITH THE HOUSE TO THEMSELVES AND CABLE TV!
ZZZZZ

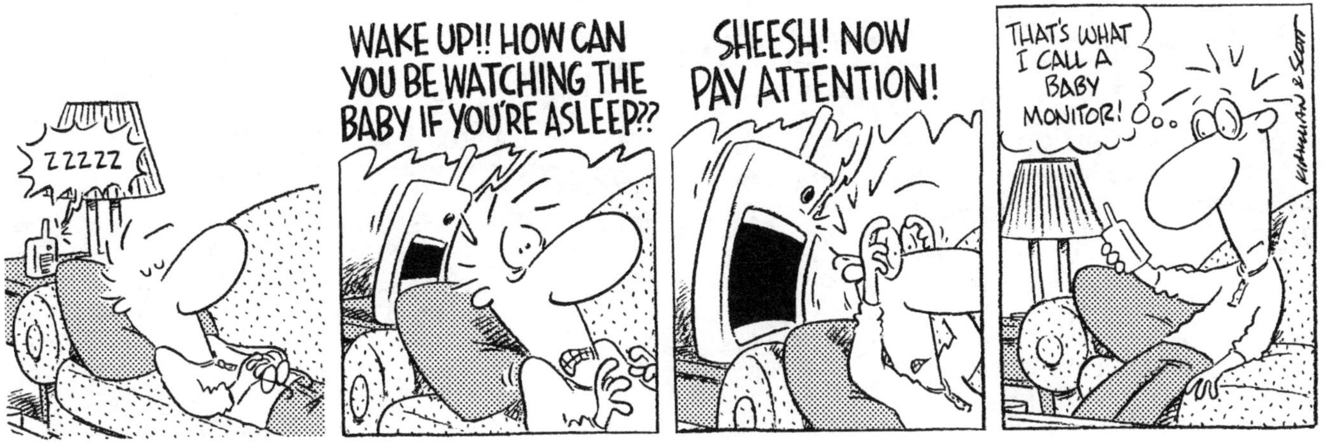
ZZZZZ
WAKE UP!! HOW CAN YOU BE WATCHING THE BABY IF YOU'RE ASLEEP??
SHEESH! NOW PAY ATTENTION!
THAT'S WHAT I CALL A BABY MONITOR!
KIRKMAN & SCOTT

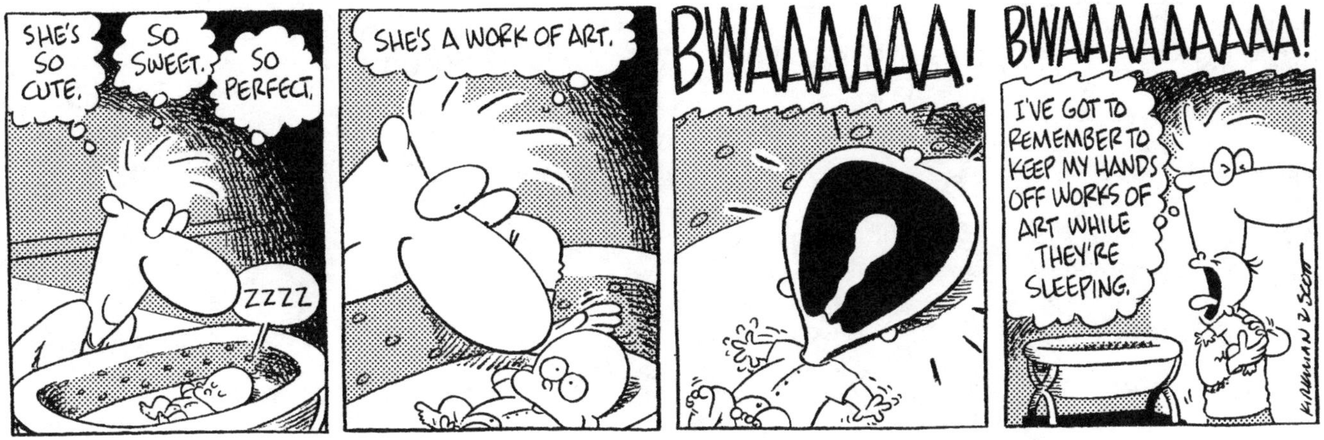
SHE'S SO CUTE.
SO SWEET.
SO PERFECT.
ZZZZ
SHE'S A WORK OF ART.
BWAAAAAA!
BWAAAAAAAAA!
I'VE GOT TO REMEMBER TO KEEP MY HANDS OFF WORKS OF ART WHILE THEY'RE SLEEPING.
KIRKMAN & SCOTT

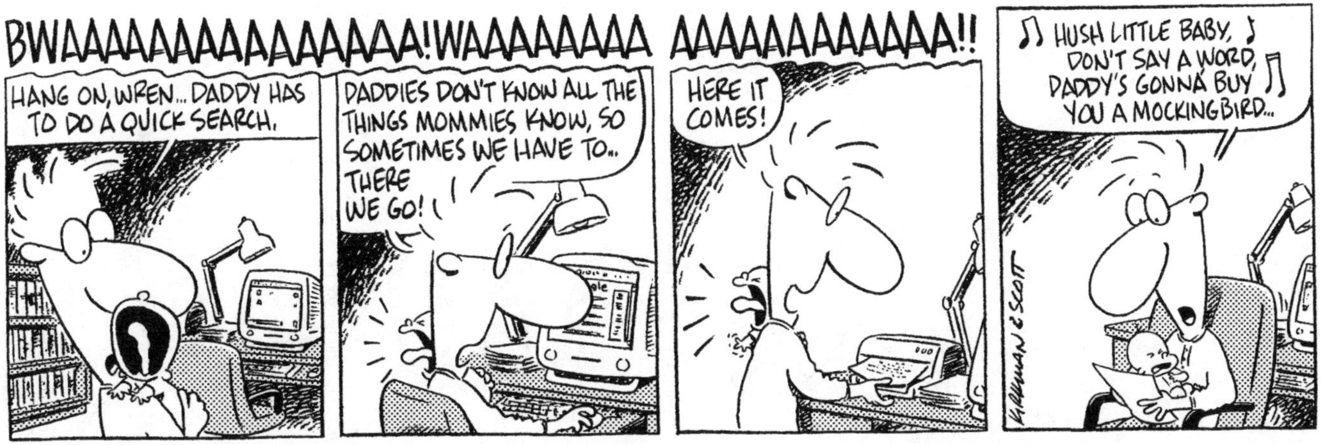
BWAAAAAAAAAAAAAAA!WAAAAAAAA AAAAAAAAAAAA!!
HANG ON, WREN... DADDY HAS TO DO A QUICK SEARCH.
DADDIES DON'T KNOW ALL THE THINGS MOMMIES KNOW, SO SOMETIMES WE HAVE TO... THERE WE GO!
HERE IT COMES!
KIRKMAN & SCOTT
♫ HUSH LITTLE BABY, DON'T SAY A WORD, DADDY'S GONNA BUY YOU A MOCKINGBIRD... ♫

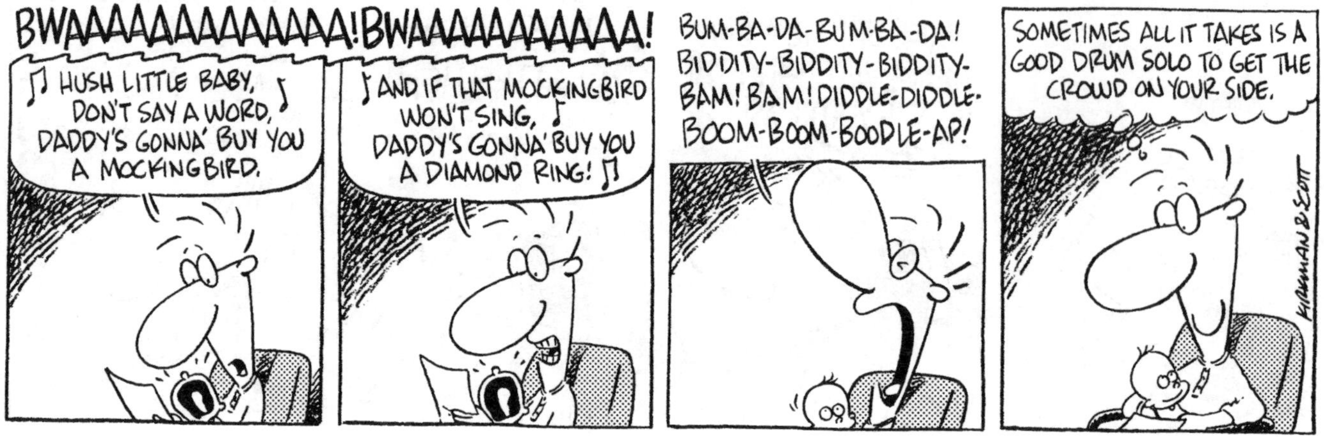
BWAAAAAAAAAAAAAA! BWAAAAAAAAAAAA!
HUSH LITTLE BABY, DON'T SAY A WORD, DADDY'S GONNA' BUY YOU A MOCKINGBIRD.
AND IF THAT MOCKINGBIRD WON'T SING, DADDY'S GONNA' BUY YOU A DIAMOND RING!
BUM-BA-DA-BUM-BA-DA! BIDDITY-BIDDITY-BIDDITY-BAM! BAM! DIDDLE-DIDDLE-BOOM-BOOM-BOODLE-AP!
SOMETIMES ALL IT TAKES IS A GOOD DRUM SOLO TO GET THE CROWD ON YOUR SIDE.
KIRKMAN & SCOTT

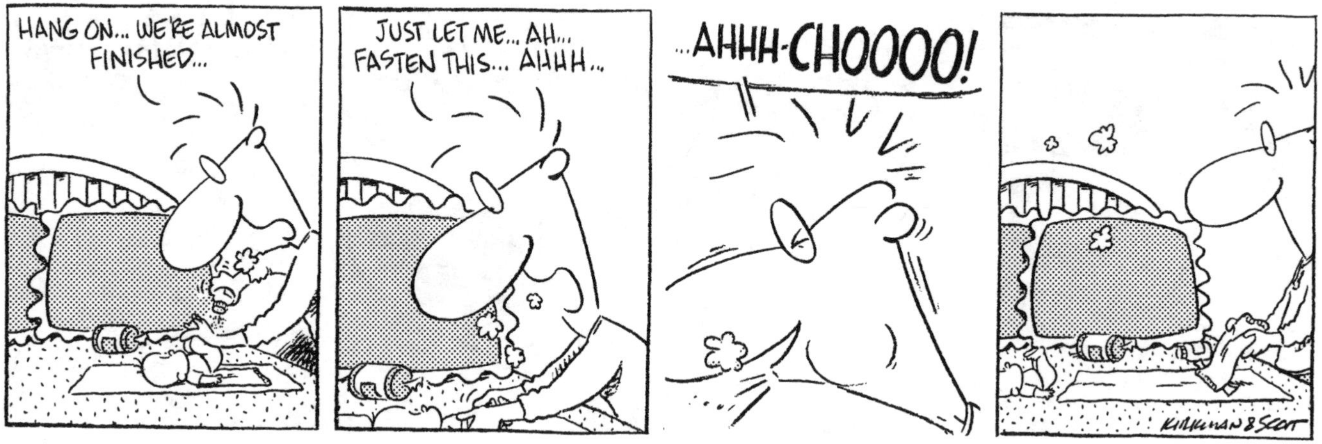
HANG ON... WE'RE ALMOST FINISHED...
JUST LET ME... AH... FASTEN THIS... AHHH...
...AHHH-CHOOOO!
KIRKMAN & SCOTT

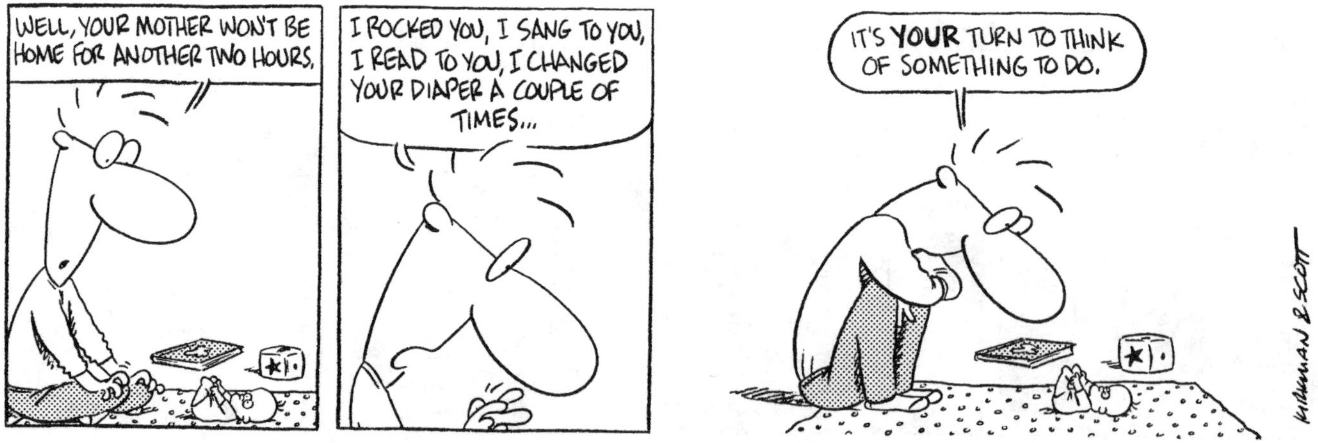
WELL, YOUR MOTHER WON'T BE HOME FOR ANOTHER TWO HOURS.
I ROCKED YOU, I SANG TO YOU, I READ TO YOU, I CHANGED YOUR DIAPER A COUPLE OF TIMES...
IT'S YOUR TURN TO THINK OF SOMETHING TO DO.
KIRKMAN & SCOTT

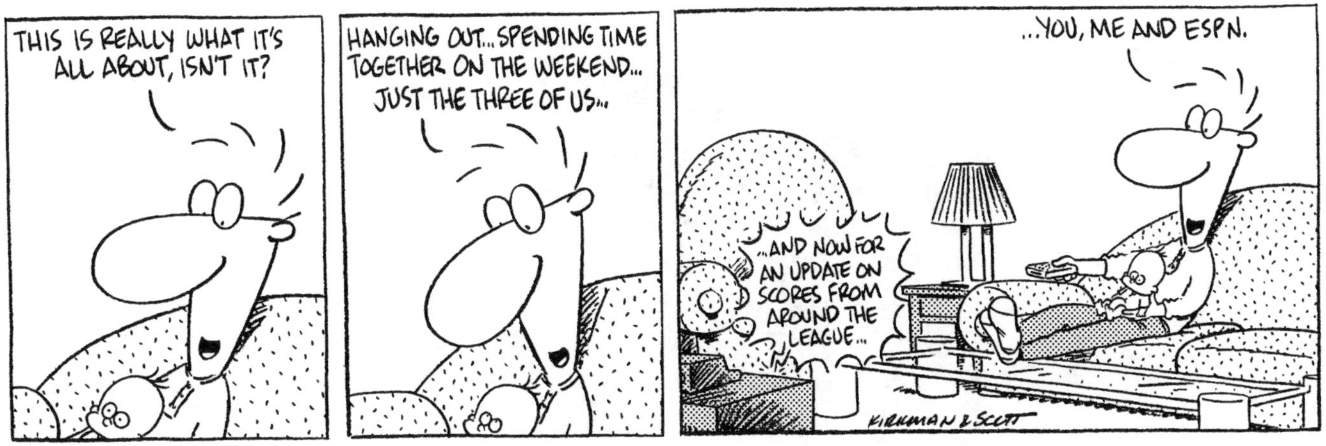
THIS IS REALLY WHAT IT'S ALL ABOUT, ISN'T IT?
HANGING OUT... SPENDING TIME TOGETHER ON THE WEEKEND... JUST THE THREE OF US...
...YOU, ME AND ESPN.
...AND NOW FOR AN UPDATE ON SCORES FROM AROUND THE LEAGUE...
KIRKMAN & SCOTT

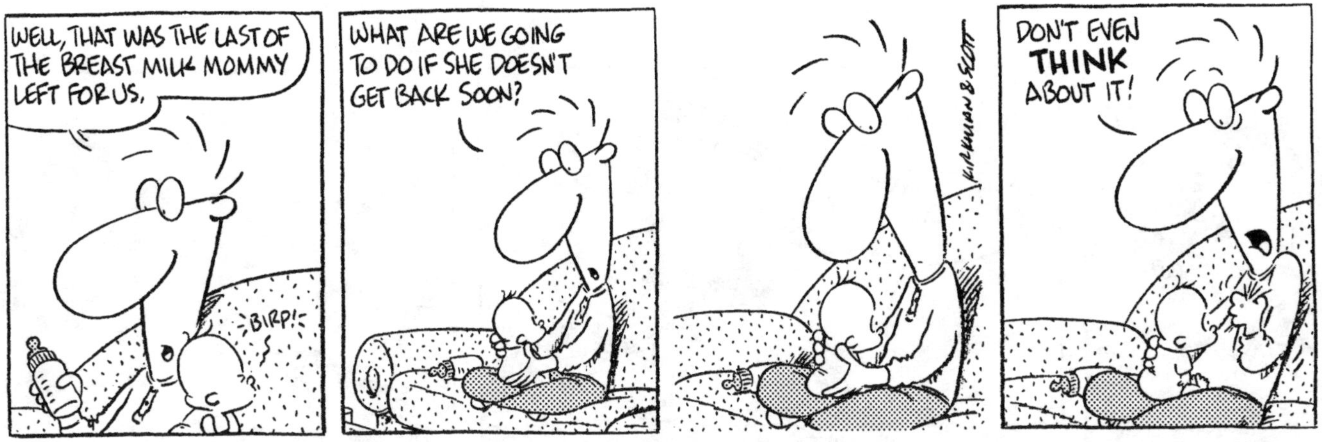
WELL, THAT WAS THE LAST OF THE BREAST MILK MOMMY LEFT FOR US.
BIRP!
WHAT ARE WE GOING TO DO IF SHE DOESN'T GET BACK SOON?
KIRKMAN & SCOTT
DON'T EVEN **THINK** ABOUT IT!

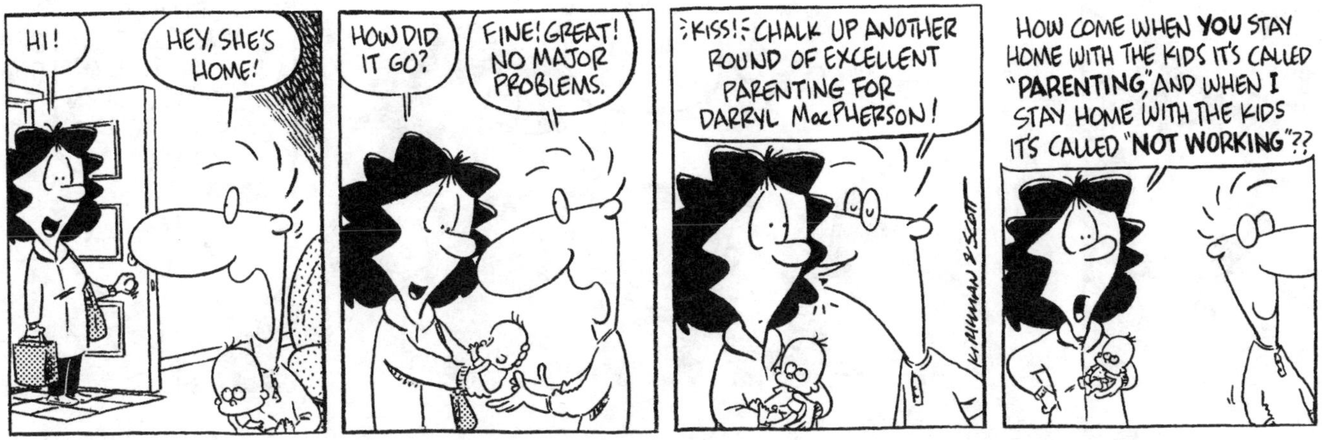
HI!
HEY, SHE'S HOME!
HOW DID IT GO?
FINE! GREAT! NO MAJOR PROBLEMS.
KISS!
CHALK UP ANOTHER ROUND OF EXCELLENT PARENTING FOR DARRYL MacPHERSON!
KIRKMAN & SCOTT
HOW COME WHEN **YOU** STAY HOME WITH THE KIDS IT'S CALLED "**PARENTING**," AND WHEN **I** STAY HOME WITH THE KIDS IT'S CALLED "**NOT WORKING**"??

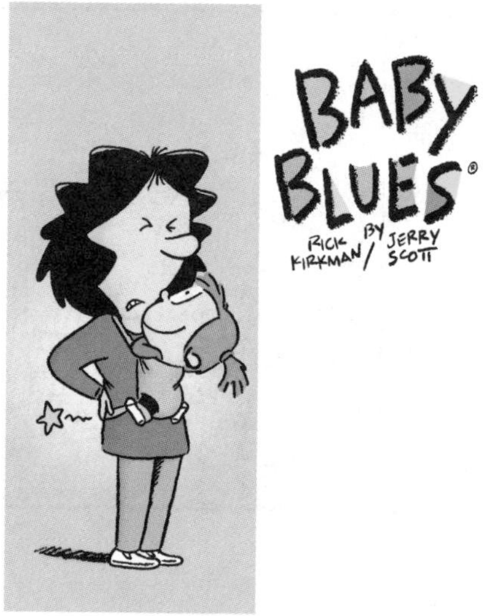
BABY BLUES®
RICK KIRKMAN / BY JERRY SCOTT

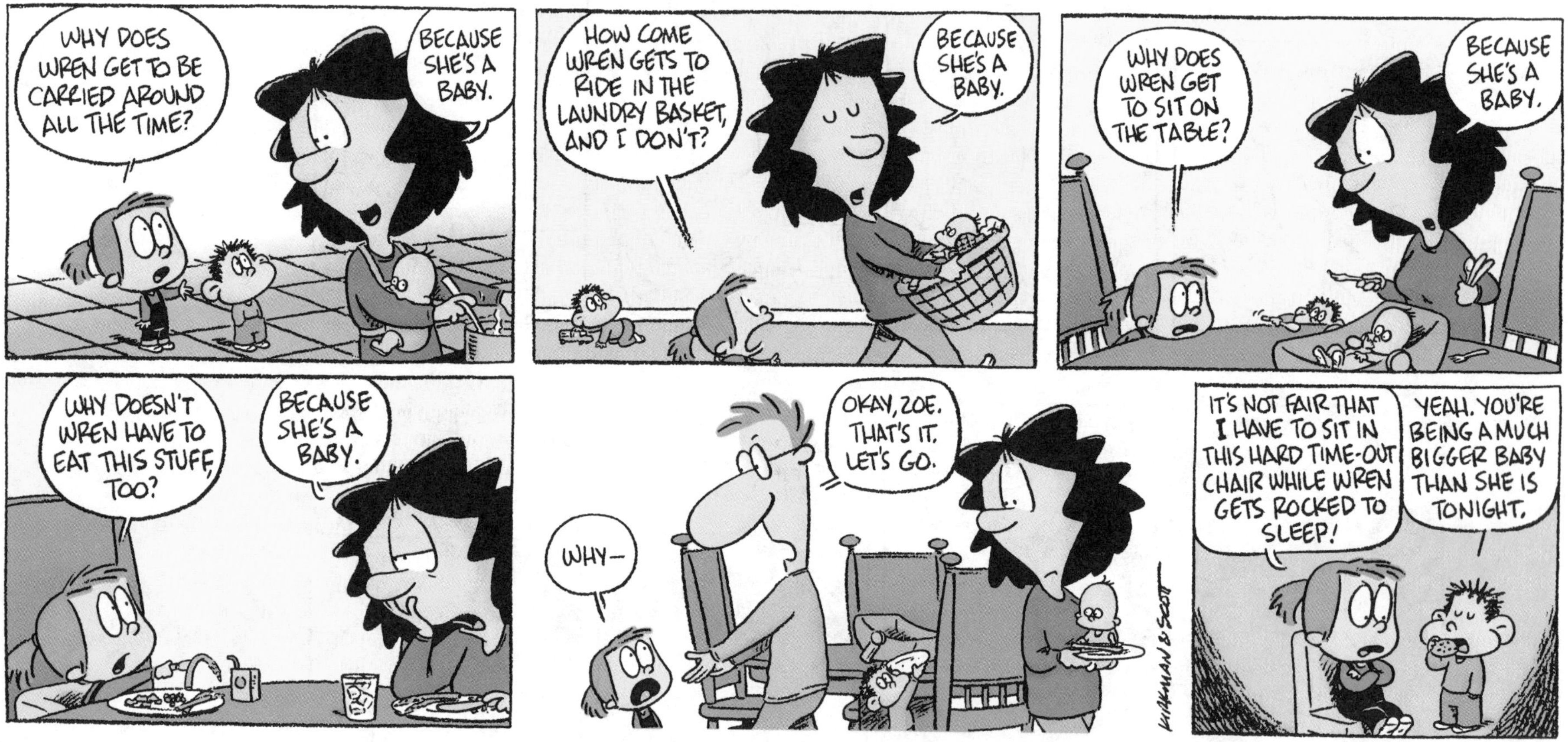
WHY DOES WREN GET TO BE CARRIED AROUND ALL THE TIME?
BECAUSE SHE'S A BABY.
HOW COME WREN GETS TO RIDE IN THE LAUNDRY BASKET, AND I DON'T?
BECAUSE SHE'S A BABY.
WHY DOES WREN GET TO SIT ON THE TABLE?
BECAUSE SHE'S A BABY.
WHY DOESN'T WREN HAVE TO EAT THIS STUFF, TOO?
BECAUSE SHE'S A BABY.
WHY--
OKAY, ZOE. THAT'S IT. LET'S GO.
KIRKMAN & SCOTT
IT'S NOT FAIR THAT I HAVE TO SIT IN THIS HARD TIME-OUT CHAIR WHILE WREN GETS ROCKED TO SLEEP!
YEAH. YOU'RE BEING A MUCH BIGGER BABY THAN SHE IS TONIGHT.

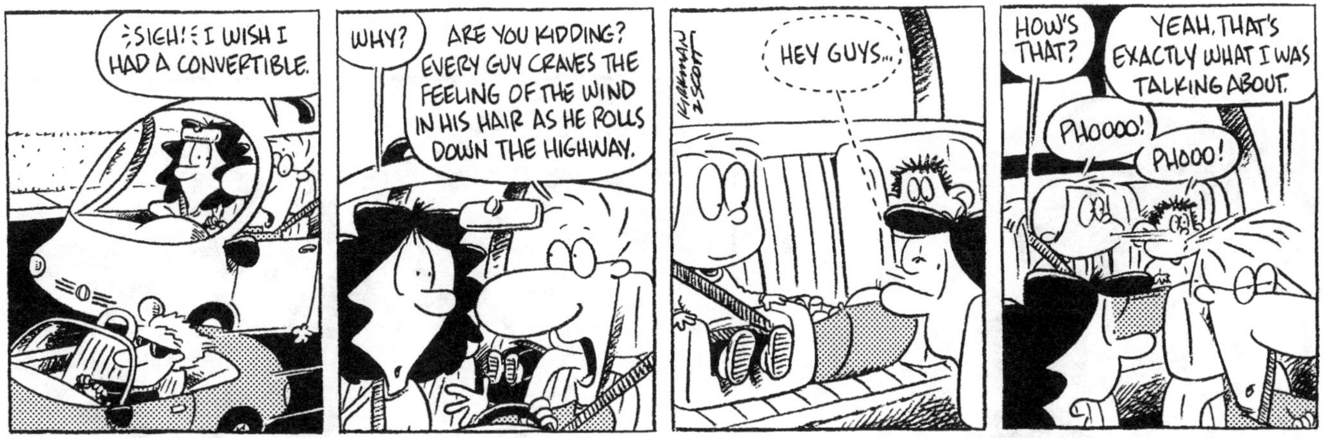

⁏SIGH!⁏ I WISH I HAD A CONVERTIBLE.
WHY?
ARE YOU KIDDING? EVERY GUY CRAVES THE FEELING OF THE WIND IN HIS HAIR AS HE ROLLS DOWN THE HIGHWAY.
KIRKMAN & SCOTT
HEY GUYS...
HOW'S THAT?
YEAH, THAT'S EXACTLY WHAT I WAS TALKING ABOUT.
PHOOOO!
PHOOO!

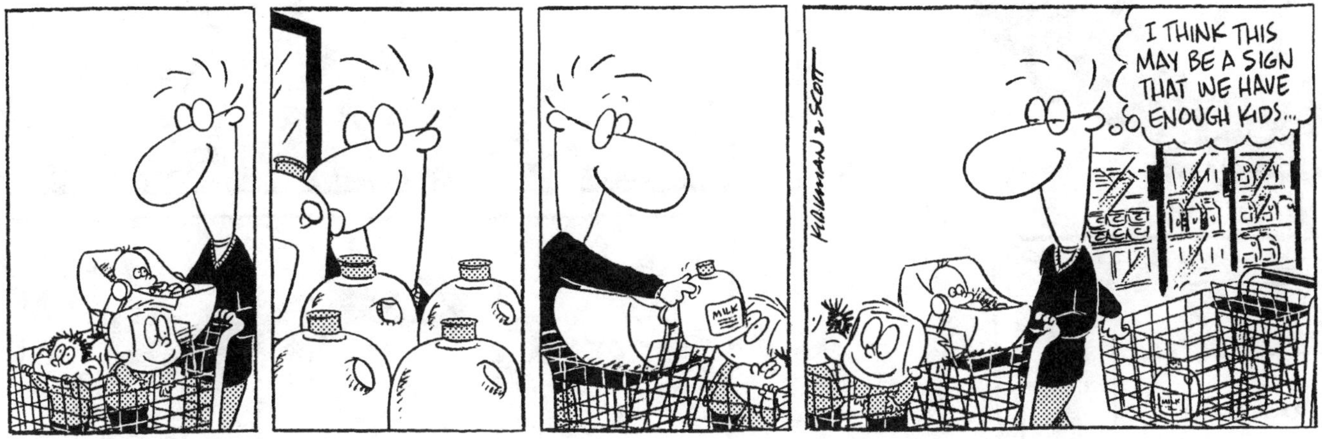

MILK
KIRKMAN & SCOTT
I THINK THIS MAY BE A SIGN THAT WE HAVE ENOUGH KIDS...
MILK

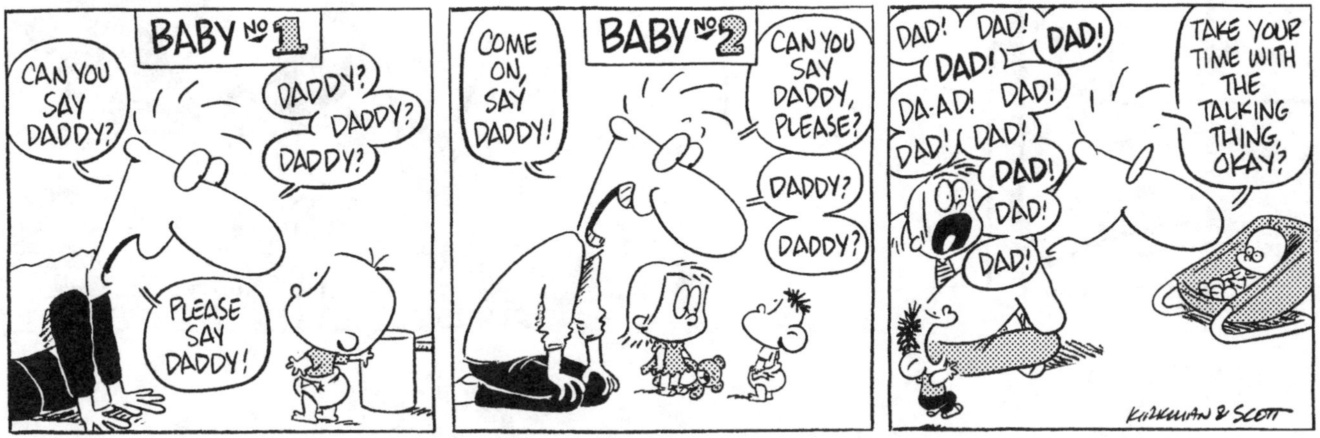

BABY No 1
CAN YOU SAY DADDY?
DADDY?
DADDY?
DADDY?
PLEASE SAY DADDY!
BABY No 2
COME ON, SAY DADDY!
CAN YOU SAY DADDY, PLEASE?
DADDY?
DADDY?
DAD!
DAD!
DAD!
DAD!
DA-AD!
DAD!
DAD!
DAD!
DAD!
DAD!
DAD!
TAKE YOUR TIME WITH THE TALKING THING, OKAY?
KIRKMAN & SCOTT

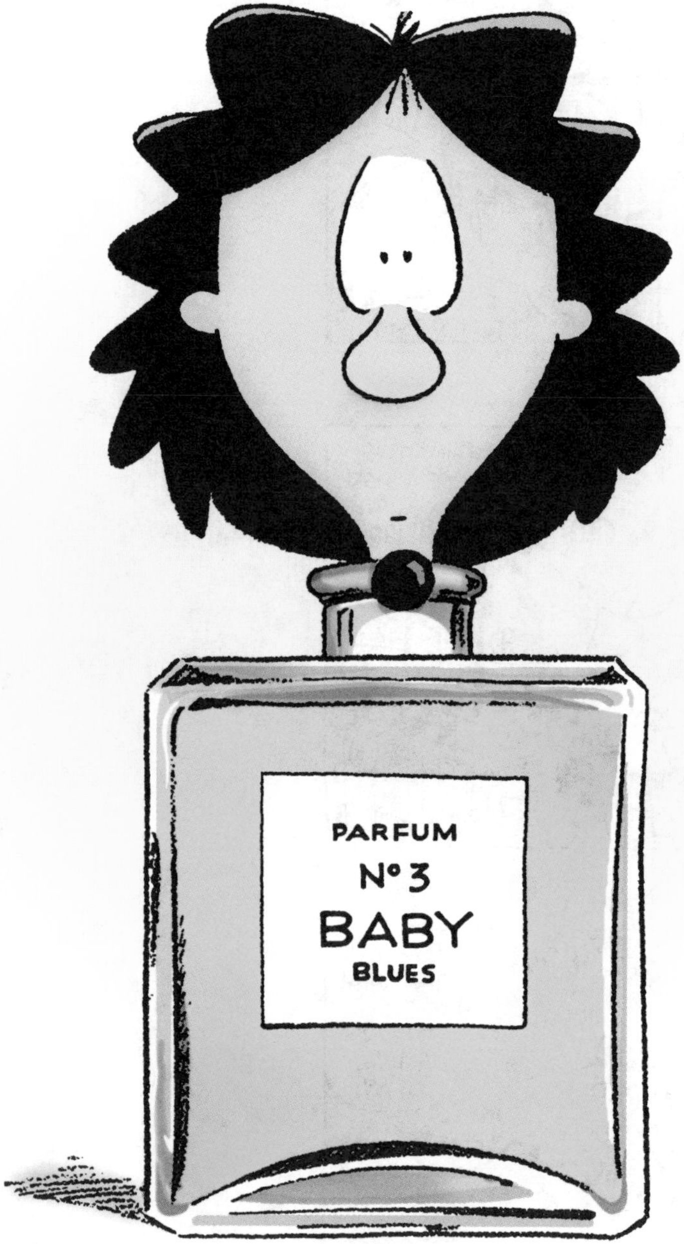
PARFUM
N°3
BABY
BLUES

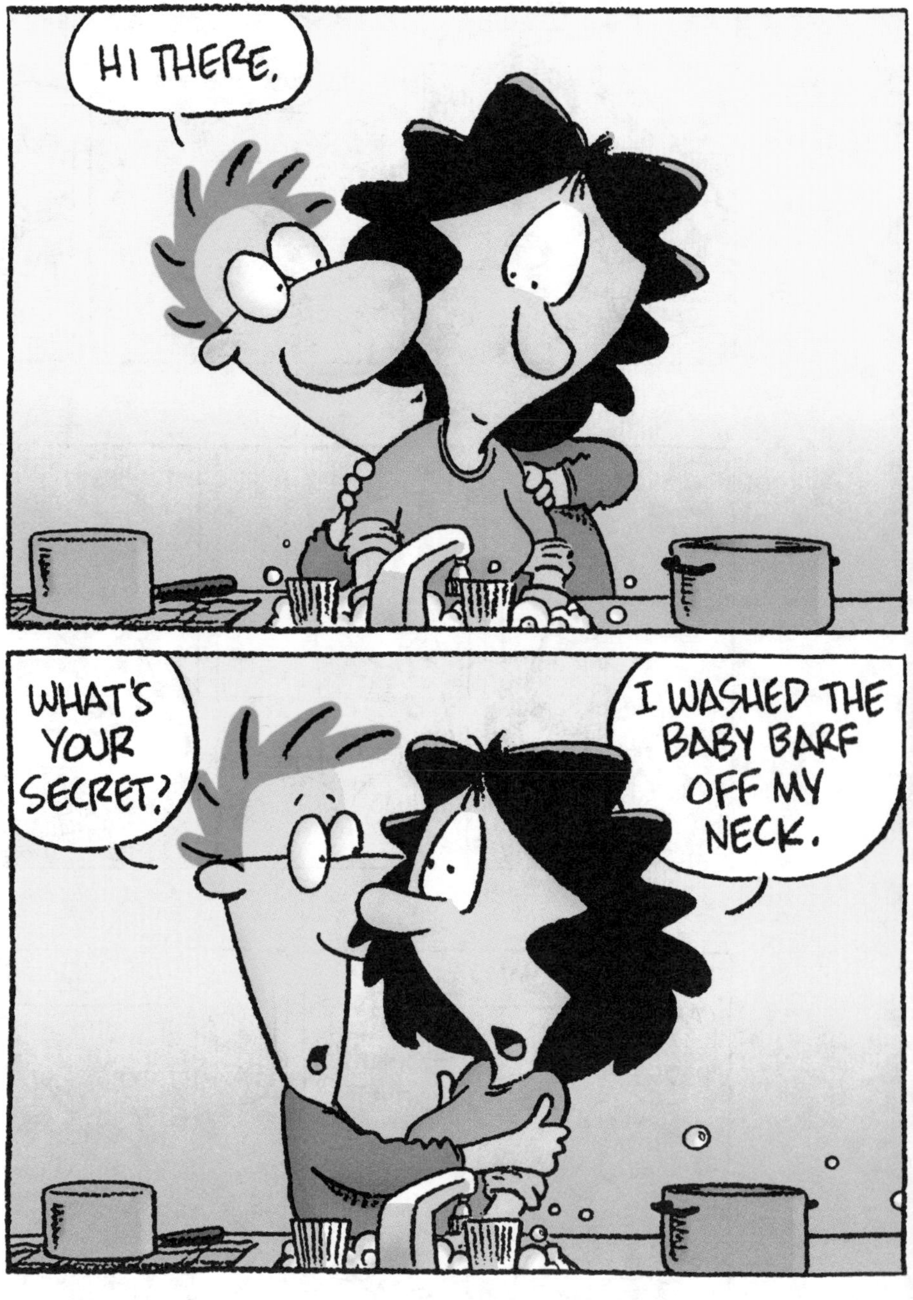
HI THERE.
WHAT'S YOUR SECRET?
I WASHED THE BABY BARF OFF MY NECK.

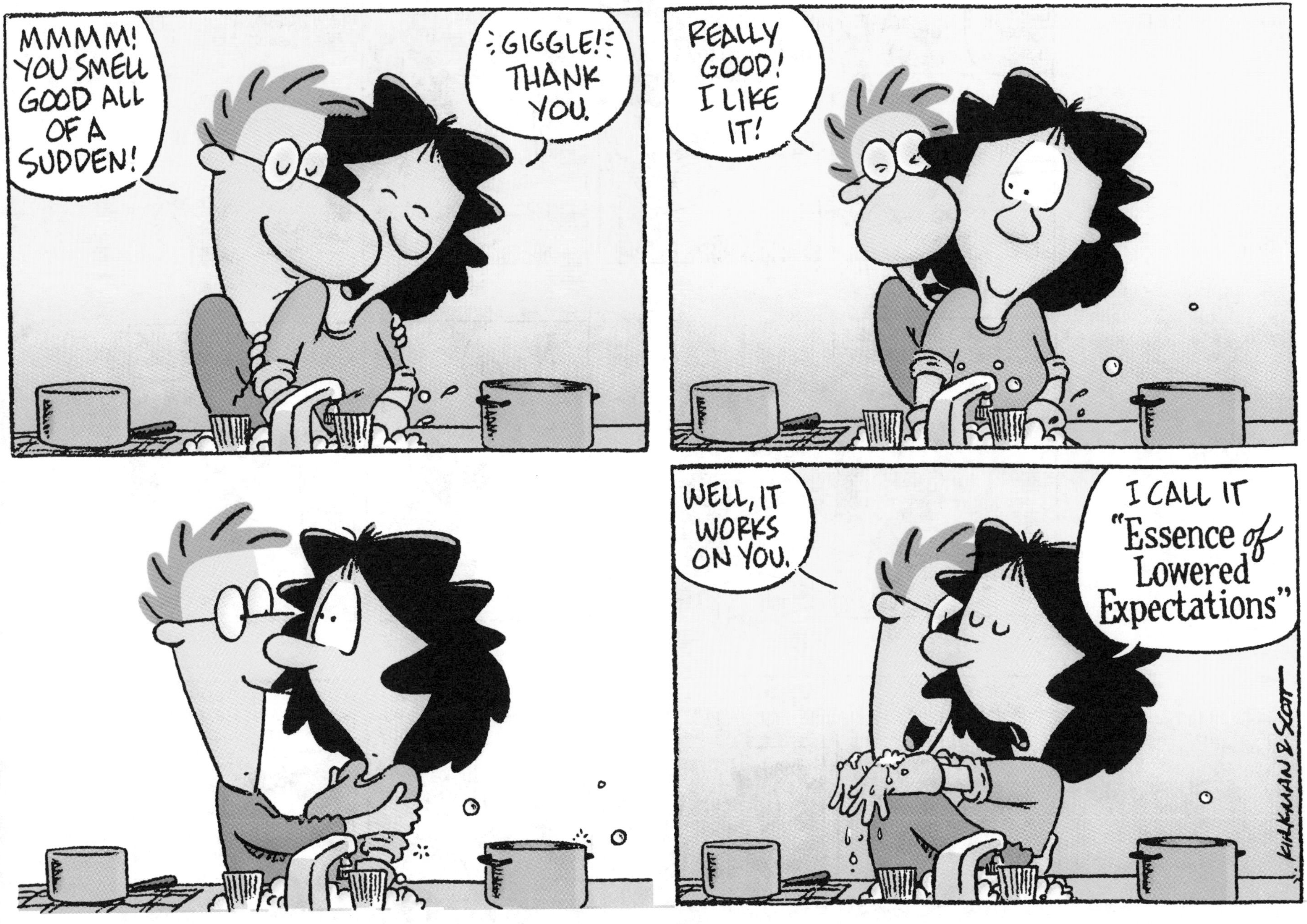
MMMM! YOU SMELL GOOD ALL OF A SUDDEN!
GIGGLE! THANK YOU.
REALLY GOOD! I LIKE IT!
WELL, IT WORKS ON YOU.
I CALL IT "Essence of Lowered Expectations"
KIRKMAN & SCOTT

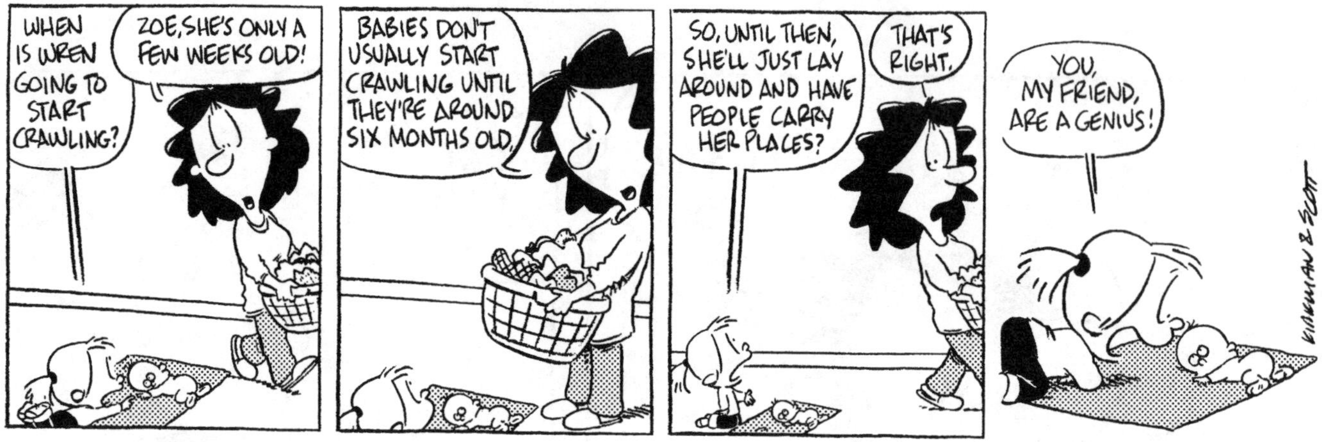
WHEN IS WREN GOING TO START CRAWLING?
ZOE, SHE'S ONLY A FEW WEEKS OLD!
BABIES DON'T USUALLY START CRAWLING UNTIL THEY'RE AROUND SIX MONTHS OLD.
SO, UNTIL THEN, SHE'LL JUST LAY AROUND AND HAVE PEOPLE CARRY HER PLACES?
THAT'S RIGHT.
YOU, MY FRIEND, ARE A GENIUS!
KIRKMAN & SCOTT

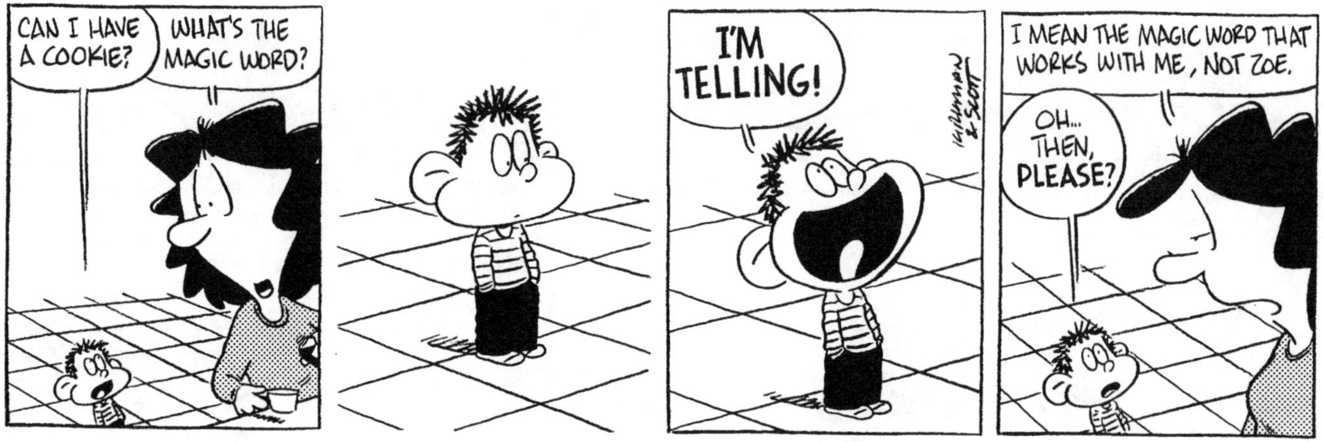
CAN I HAVE A COOKIE?
WHAT'S THE MAGIC WORD?
I'M TELLING!
KIRKMAN & SCOTT
I MEAN THE MAGIC WORD THAT WORKS WITH ME, NOT ZOE.
OH... THEN, PLEASE?

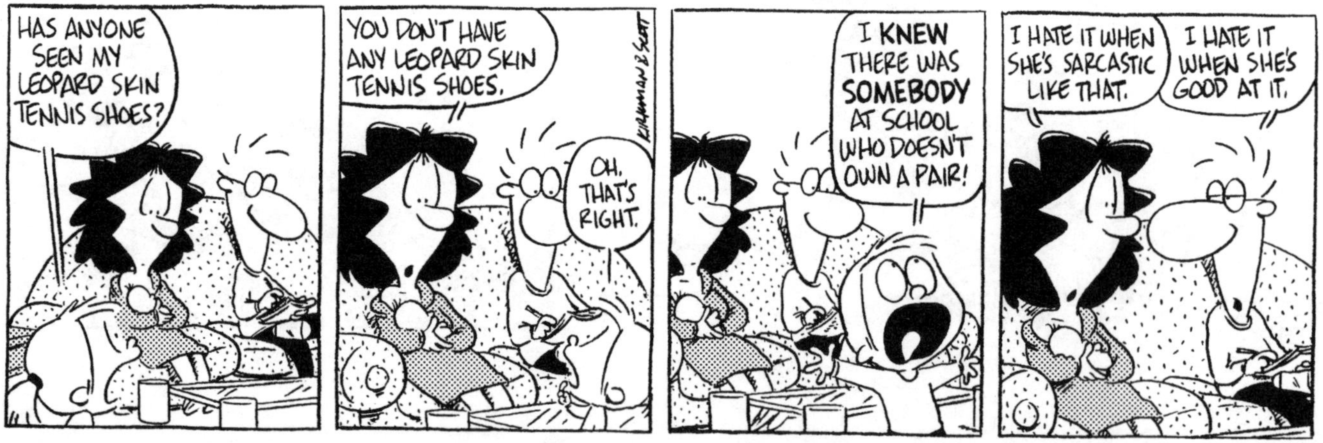
HAS ANYONE SEEN MY LEOPARD SKIN TENNIS SHOES?
YOU DON'T HAVE ANY LEOPARD SKIN TENNIS SHOES.
KIRKMAN & SCOTT
OH. THAT'S RIGHT.
I KNEW THERE WAS SOMEBODY AT SCHOOL WHO DOESN'T OWN A PAIR!
I HATE IT WHEN SHE'S SARCASTIC LIKE THAT.
I HATE IT WHEN SHE'S GOOD AT IT.

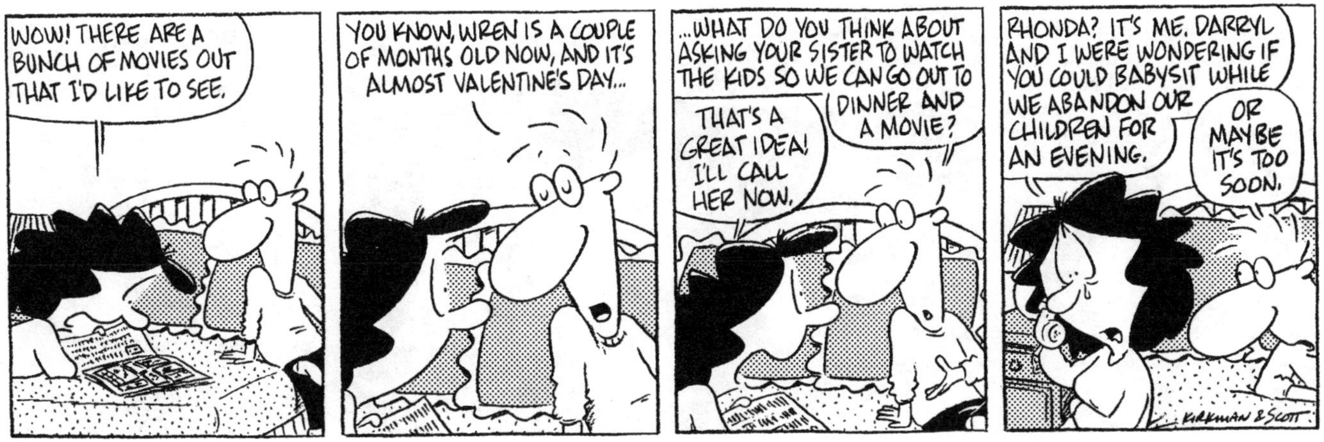
WOW! THERE ARE A BUNCH OF MOVIES OUT THAT I'D LIKE TO SEE.
YOU KNOW, WREN IS A COUPLE OF MONTHS OLD NOW, AND IT'S ALMOST VALENTINE'S DAY...
...WHAT DO YOU THINK ABOUT ASKING YOUR SISTER TO WATCH THE KIDS SO WE CAN GO OUT TO DINNER AND A MOVIE?
THAT'S A GREAT IDEA! I'LL CALL HER NOW.
RHONDA? IT'S ME. DARRYL AND I WERE WONDERING IF YOU COULD BABYSIT WHILE WE ABANDON OUR CHILDREN FOR AN EVENING.
OR MAYBE IT'S TOO SOON.
KIRKMAN & SCOTT

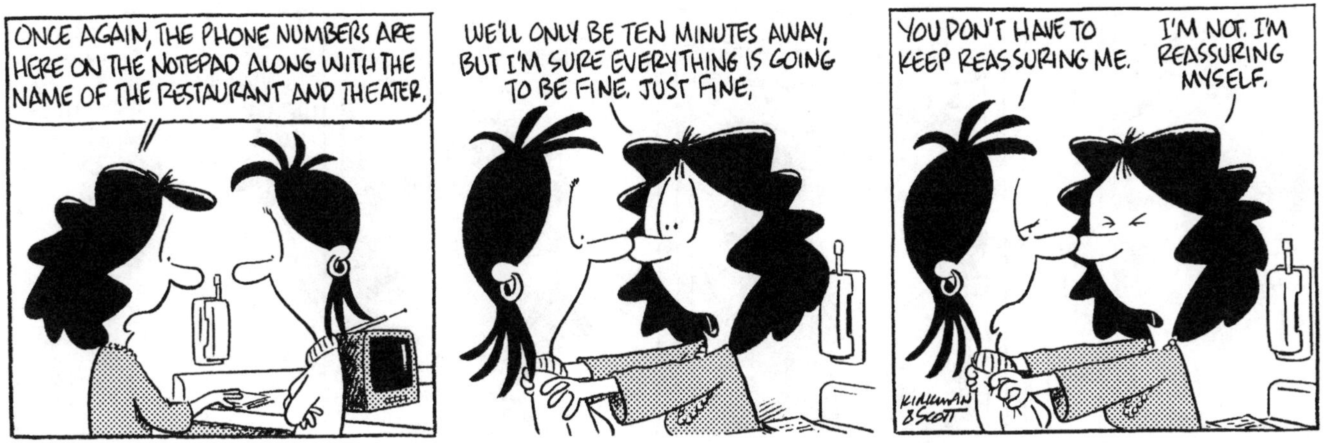
ONCE AGAIN, THE PHONE NUMBERS ARE HERE ON THE NOTEPAD ALONG WITH THE NAME OF THE RESTAURANT AND THEATER.
WE'LL ONLY BE TEN MINUTES AWAY, BUT I'M SURE EVERYTHING IS GOING TO BE FINE. JUST FINE.
YOU DON'T HAVE TO KEEP REASSURING ME.
I'M NOT. I'M REASSURING MYSELF.
KIRKMAN & SCOTT

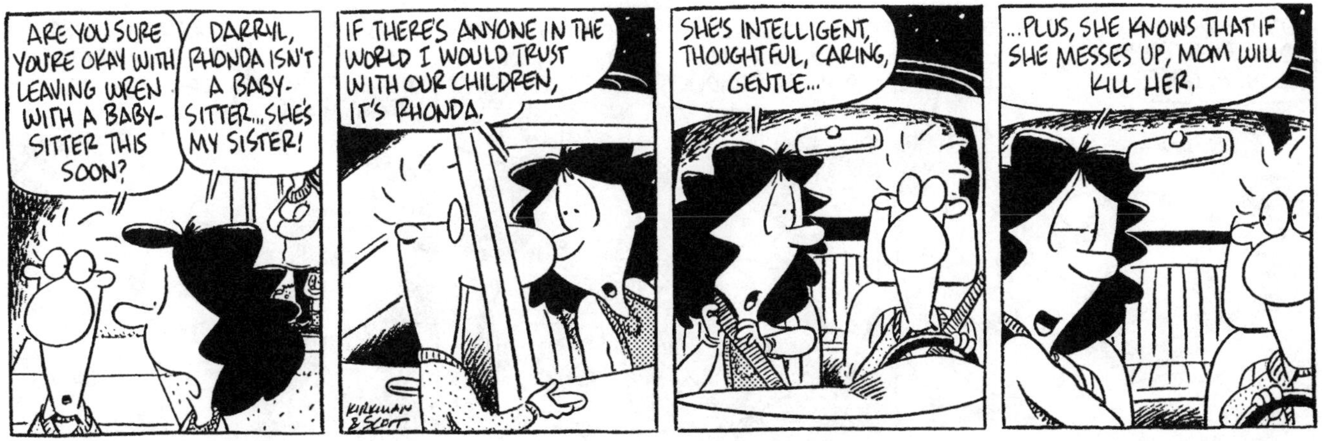
ARE YOU SURE YOU'RE OKAY WITH LEAVING WREN WITH A BABY-SITTER THIS SOON?
DARRYL, RHONDA ISN'T A BABY-SITTER...SHE'S MY SISTER!
IF THERE'S ANYONE IN THE WORLD I WOULD TRUST WITH OUR CHILDREN, IT'S RHONDA.
SHE'S INTELLIGENT, THOUGHTFUL, CARING, GENTLE...
...PLUS, SHE KNOWS THAT IF SHE MESSES UP, MOM WILL KILL HER.
KIRKMAN & SCOTT

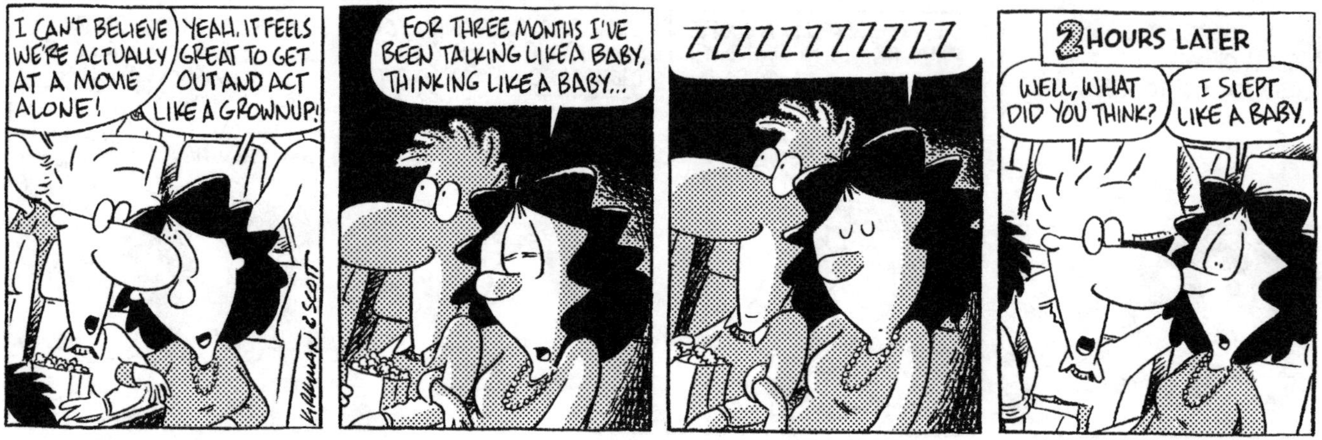
I CAN'T BELIEVE WE'RE ACTUALLY AT A MOVIE ALONE!
YEAH. IT FEELS GREAT TO GET OUT AND ACT LIKE A GROWNUP!
KIRKMAN & SCOTT
FOR THREE MONTHS I'VE BEEN TALKING LIKE A BABY, THINKING LIKE A BABY...
ZZZZZZZZZZZ
2 HOURS LATER
WELL, WHAT DID YOU THINK?
I SLEPT LIKE A BABY.

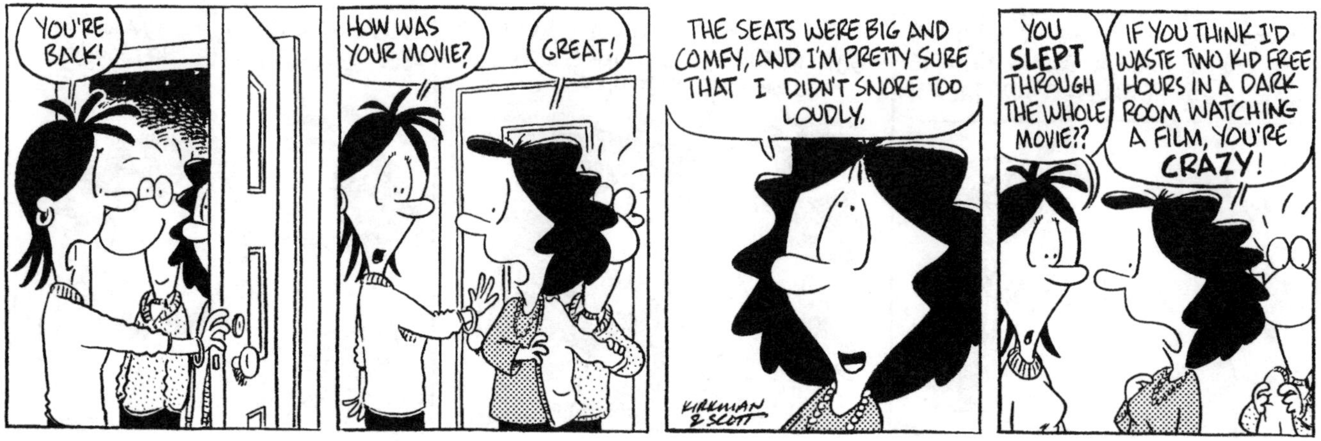
YOU'RE BACK!
HOW WAS YOUR MOVIE?
GREAT!
THE SEATS WERE BIG AND COMFY, AND I'M PRETTY SURE THAT I DIDN'T SNORE TOO LOUDLY.
KIRKMAN & SCOTT
YOU SLEPT THROUGH THE WHOLE MOVIE??
IF YOU THINK I'D WASTE TWO KID FREE HOURS IN A DARK ROOM WATCHING A FILM, YOU'RE CRAZY!

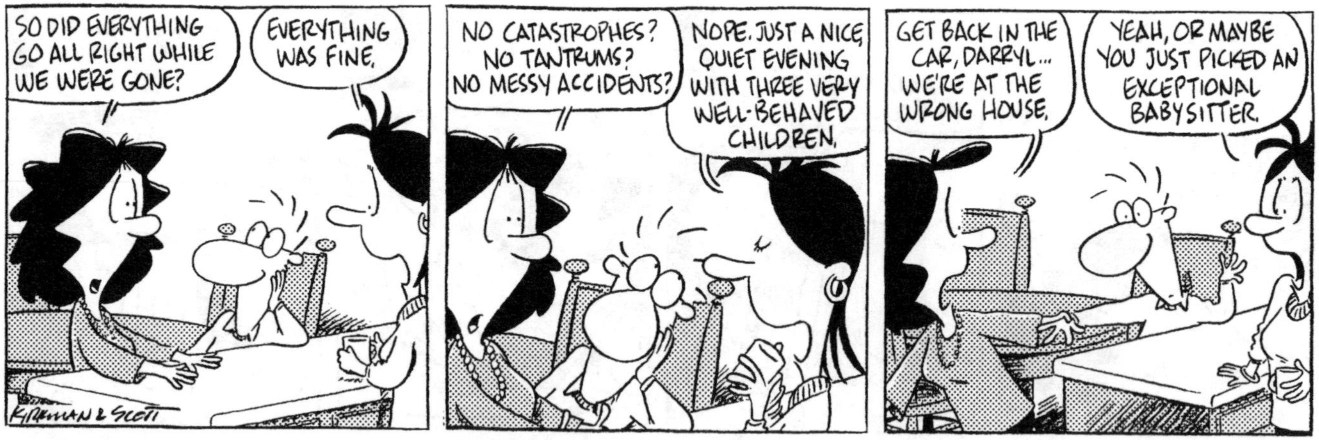
SO DID EVERYTHING GO ALL RIGHT WHILE WE WERE GONE?
EVERYTHING WAS FINE.
KIRKMAN & SCOTT
NO CATASTROPHES? NO TANTRUMS? NO MESSY ACCIDENTS?
NOPE. JUST A NICE, QUIET EVENING WITH THREE VERY WELL-BEHAVED CHILDREN.
GET BACK IN THE CAR, DARRYL... WE'RE AT THE WRONG HOUSE.
YEAH, OR MAYBE YOU JUST PICKED AN EXCEPTIONAL BABYSITTER.

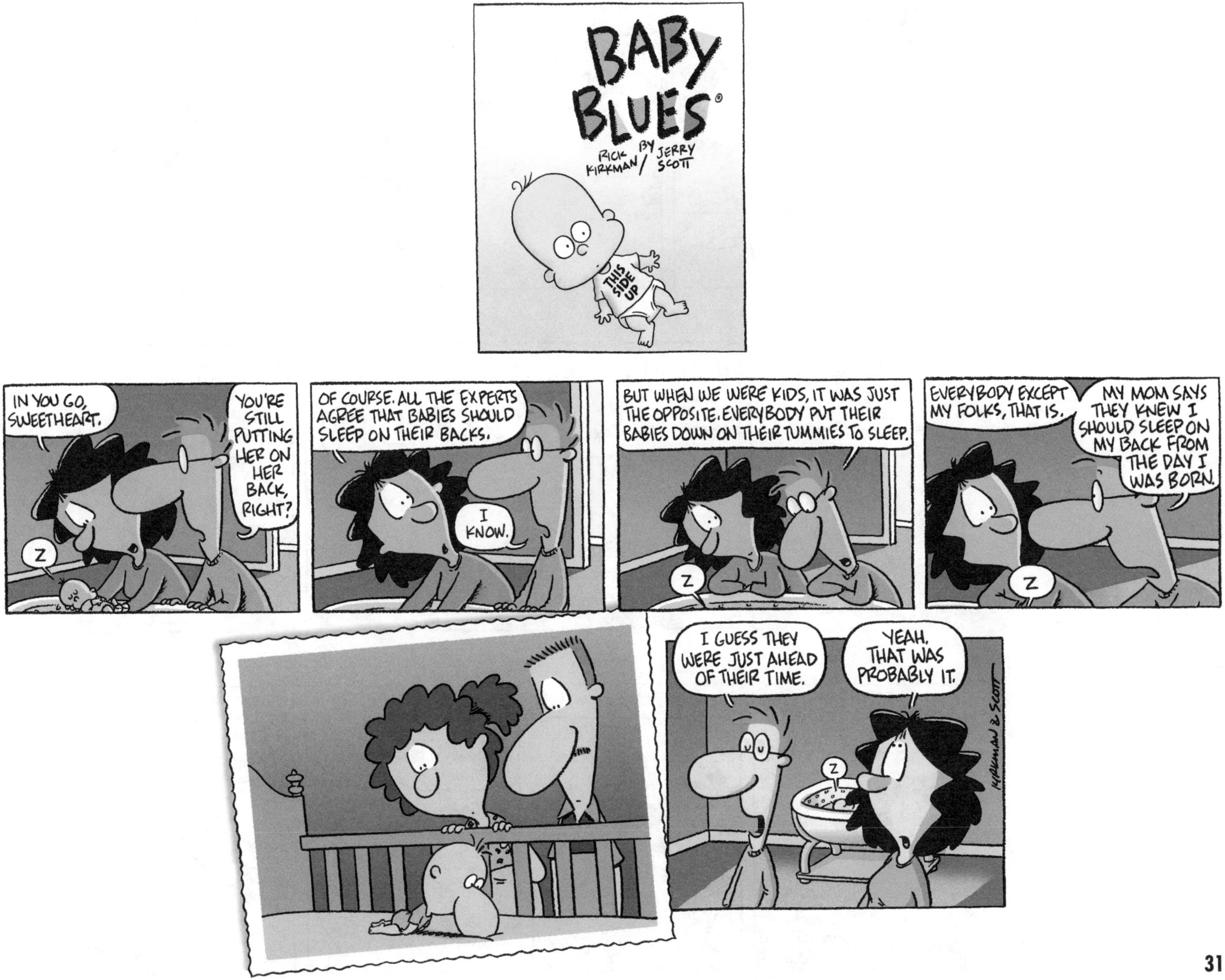
BABY BLUES®
BY RICK KIRKMAN / JERRY SCOTT
THIS SIDE UP
IN YOU GO, SWEETHEART.
YOU'RE STILL PUTTING HER ON HER BACK, RIGHT?
Z
OF COURSE. ALL THE EXPERTS AGREE THAT BABIES SHOULD SLEEP ON THEIR BACKS.
I KNOW.
BUT WHEN WE WERE KIDS, IT WAS JUST THE OPPOSITE. EVERYBODY PUT THEIR BABIES DOWN ON THEIR TUMMIES TO SLEEP.
Z
EVERYBODY EXCEPT MY FOLKS, THAT IS.
MY MOM SAYS THEY KNEW I SHOULD SLEEP ON MY BACK FROM THE DAY I WAS BORN.
Z
I GUESS THEY WERE JUST AHEAD OF THEIR TIME.
YEAH. THAT WAS PROBABLY IT.
Z
KIRKMAN & SCOTT

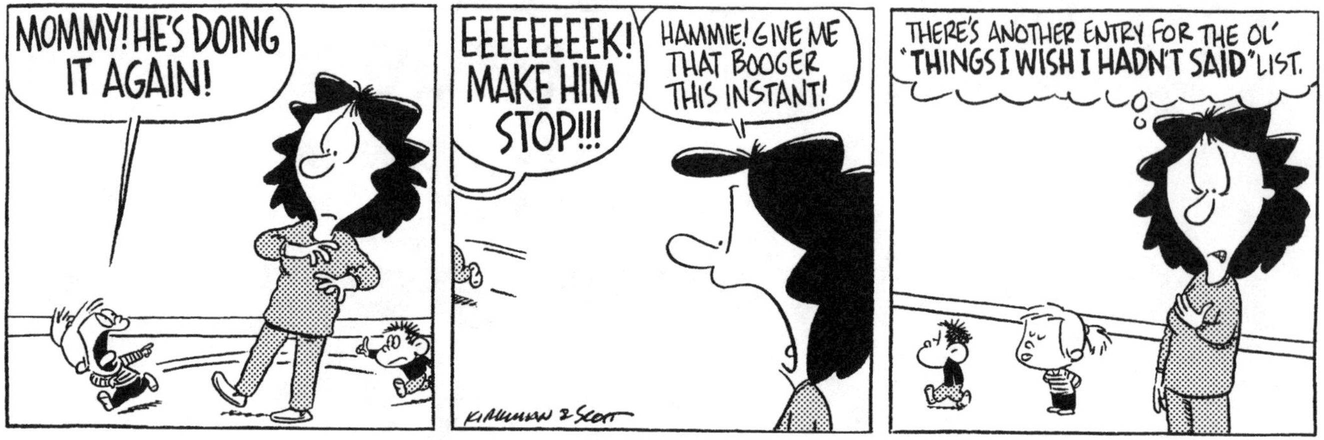
MOMMY! HE'S DOING IT AGAIN!
EEEEEEEEK! MAKE HIM STOP!!!
HAMMIE! GIVE ME THAT BOOGER THIS INSTANT!
KIRKMAN & SCOTT
THERE'S ANOTHER ENTRY FOR THE OL' "THINGS I WISH I HADN'T SAID" LIST.

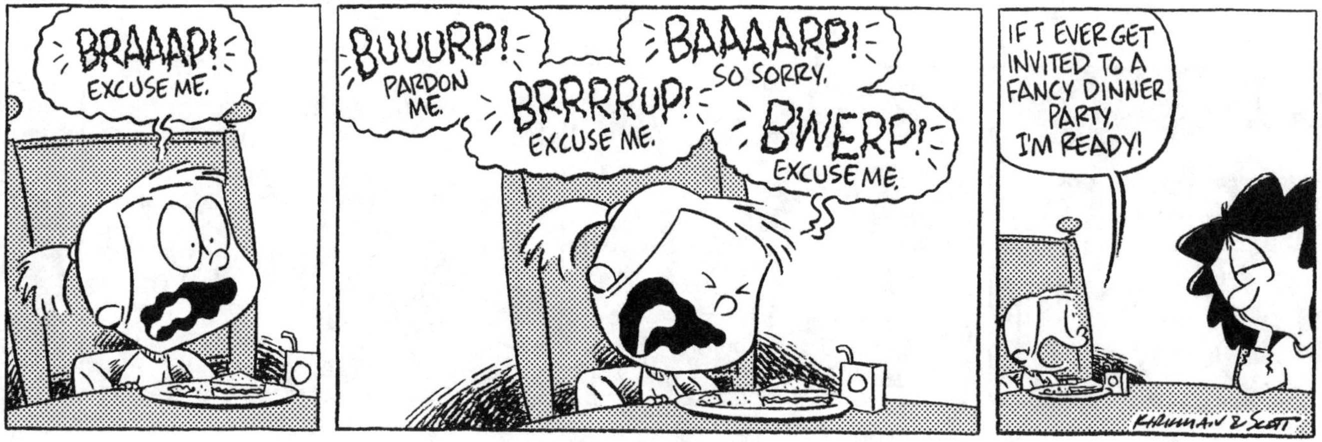
BRAAAP! EXCUSE ME.
BUUURP! PARDON ME.
BAAAARP! SO SORRY.
BRRRRUP! EXCUSE ME.
BWERP! EXCUSE ME.
IF I EVER GET INVITED TO A FANCY DINNER PARTY, I'M READY!
KIRKMAN & SCOTT

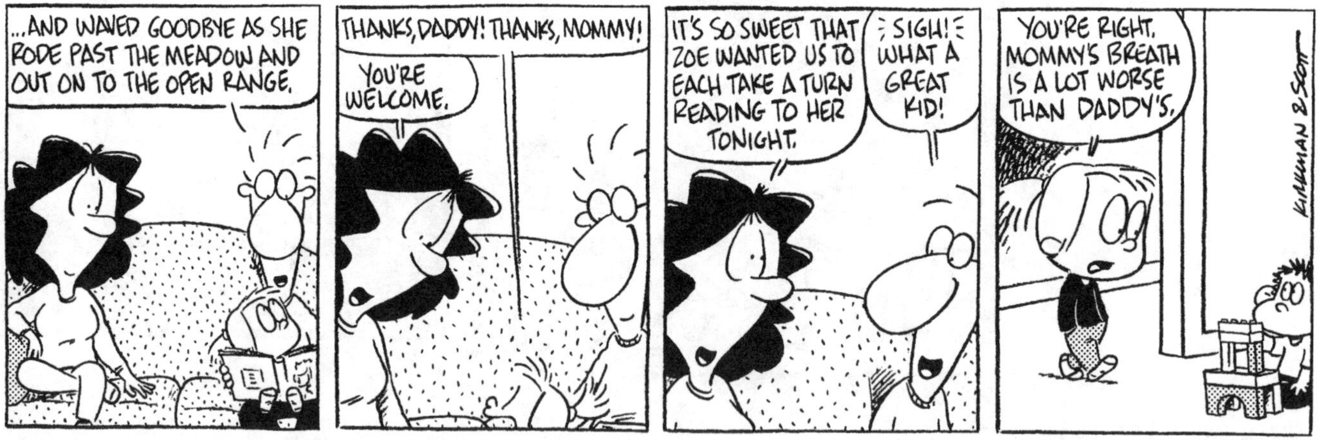
...AND WAVED GOODBYE AS SHE RODE PAST THE MEADOW AND OUT ON TO THE OPEN RANGE.
THANKS, DADDY! THANKS, MOMMY!
YOU'RE WELCOME.
IT'S SO SWEET THAT ZOE WANTED US TO EACH TAKE A TURN READING TO HER TONIGHT.
SIGH! WHAT A GREAT KID!
YOU'RE RIGHT. MOMMY'S BREATH IS A LOT WORSE THAN DADDY'S.
KIRKMAN & SCOTT

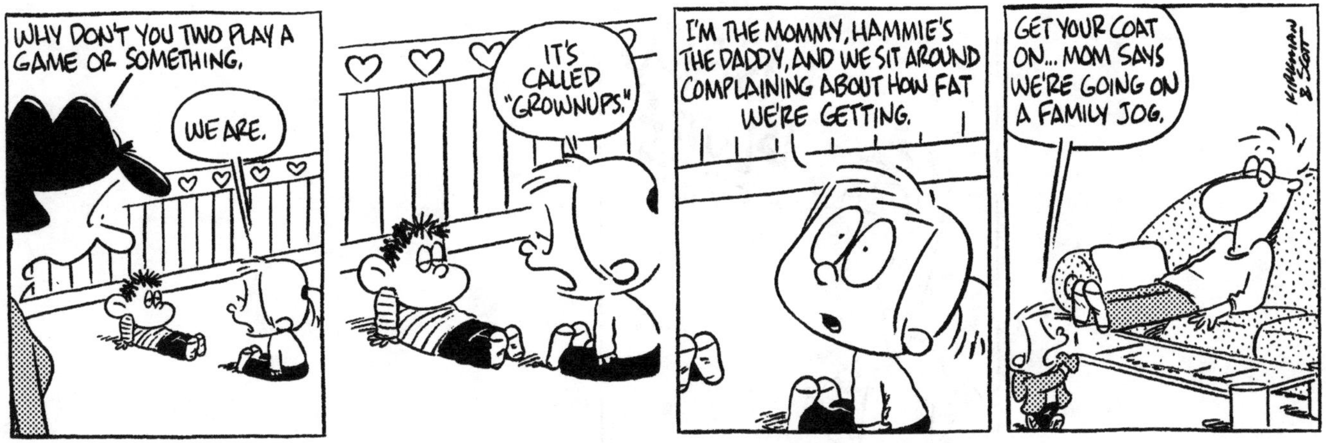
WHY DON'T YOU TWO PLAY A GAME OR SOMETHING.
WE ARE.
IT'S CALLED "GROWNUPS."
I'M THE MOMMY, HAMMIE'S THE DADDY, AND WE SIT AROUND COMPLAINING ABOUT HOW FAT WE'RE GETTING.
GET YOUR COAT ON... MOM SAYS WE'RE GOING ON A FAMILY JOG.
KIRKMAN & SCOTT

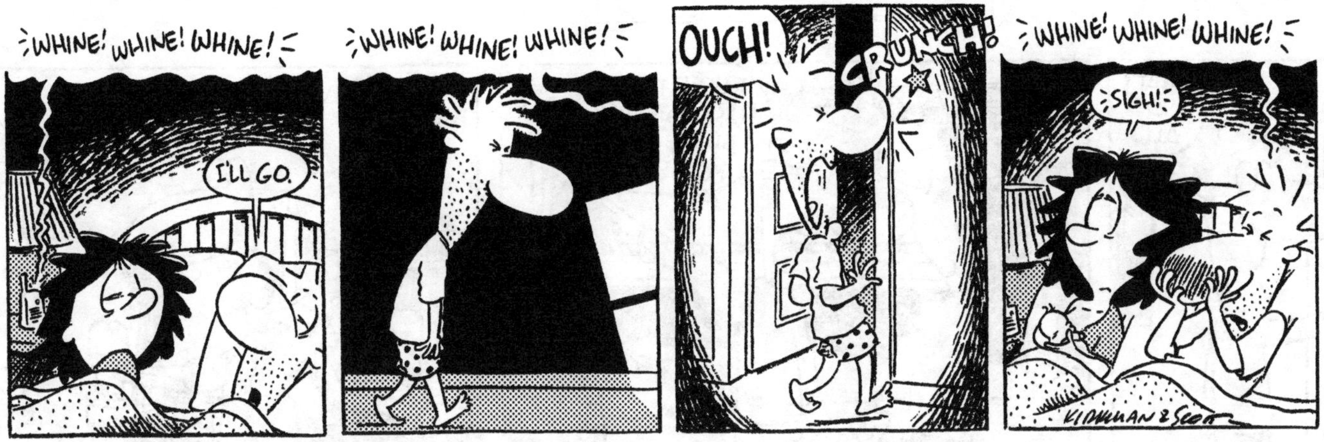
WHINE! WHINE! WHINE!
I'LL GO.
WHINE! WHINE! WHINE!
OUCH!
CRUNCH!
WHINE! WHINE! WHINE!
SIGH!
KIRKMAN & SCOTT

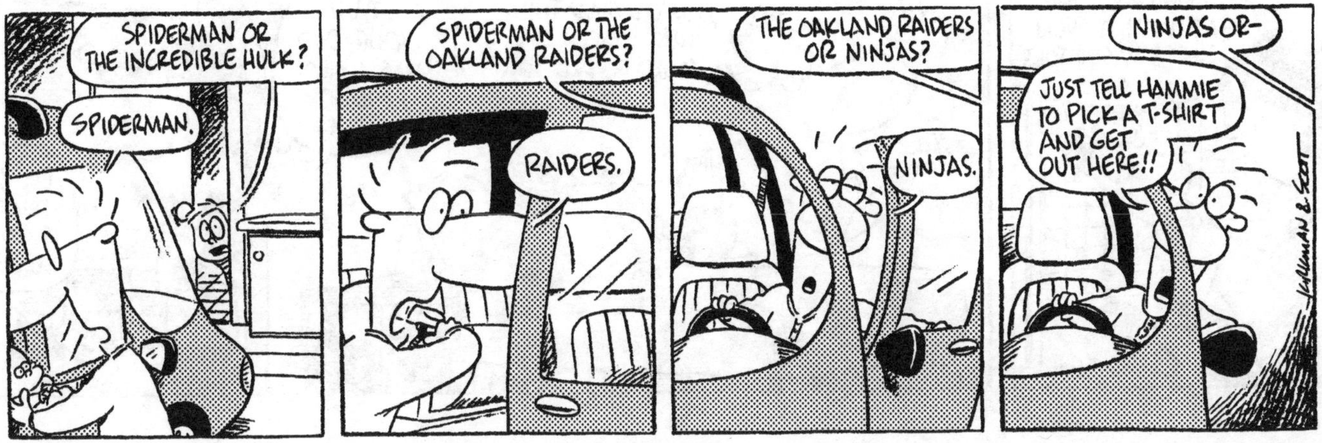
SPIDERMAN OR THE INCREDIBLE HULK?
SPIDERMAN.
SPIDERMAN OR THE OAKLAND RAIDERS?
RAIDERS.
THE OAKLAND RAIDERS OR NINJAS?
NINJAS.
NINJAS OR-
JUST TELL HAMMIE TO PICK A T-SHIRT AND GET OUT HERE!!
KIRKMAN & SCOTT

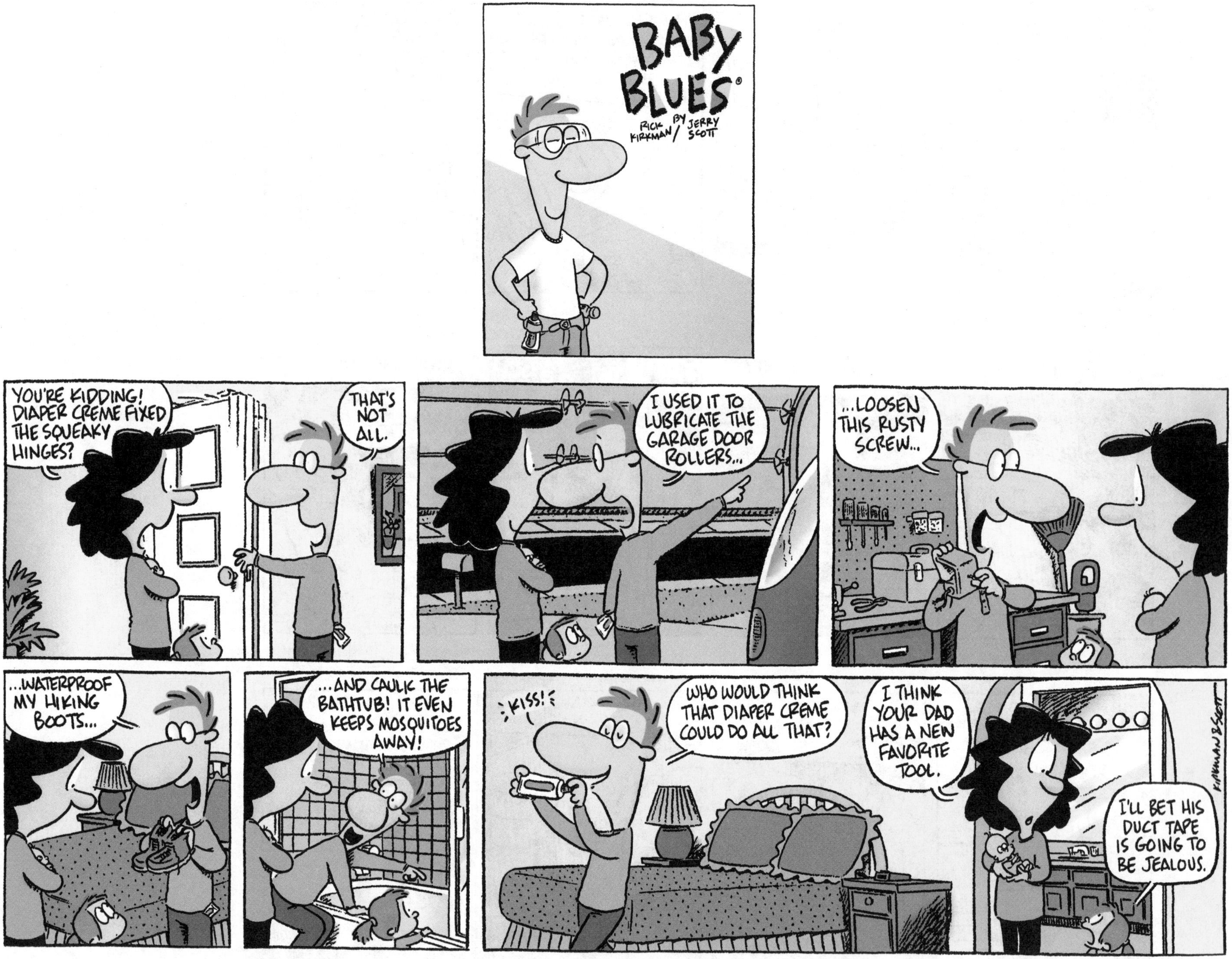
BABY BLUES®
RICK KIRKMAN / BY JERRY SCOTT
YOU'RE KIDDING! DIAPER CREME FIXED THE SQUEAKY HINGES?
THAT'S NOT ALL.
I USED IT TO LUBRICATE THE GARAGE DOOR ROLLERS...
...LOOSEN THIS RUSTY SCREW...
...WATERPROOF MY HIKING BOOTS...
...AND CAULK THE BATHTUB! IT EVEN KEEPS MOSQUITOES AWAY!
KISS!
WHO WOULD THINK THAT DIAPER CREME COULD DO ALL THAT?
I THINK YOUR DAD HAS A NEW FAVORITE TOOL.
I'LL BET HIS DUCT TAPE IS GOING TO BE JEALOUS.
KIRKMAN & SCOTT

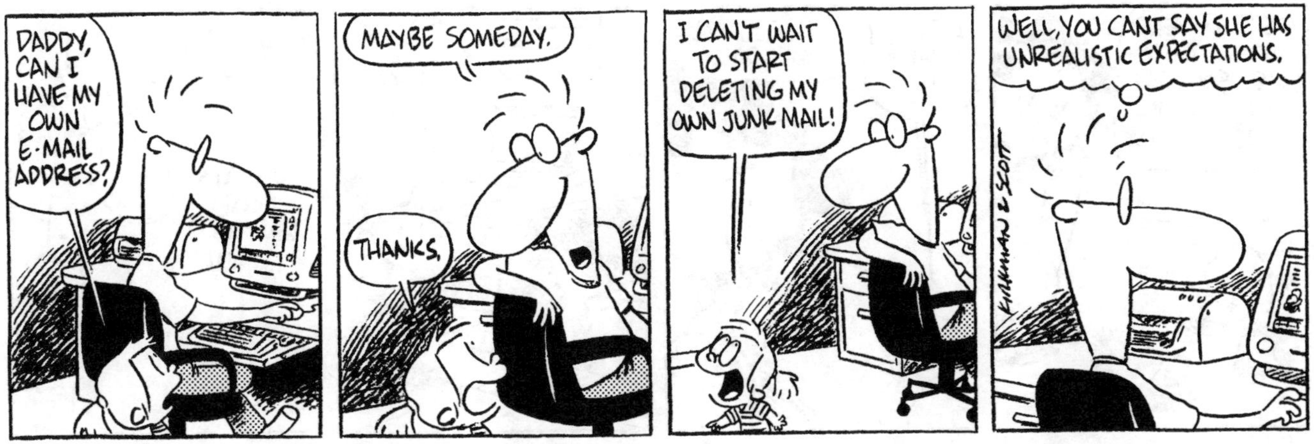
DADDY, CAN I HAVE MY OWN E-MAIL ADDRESS?
MAYBE SOMEDAY.
THANKS.
I CAN'T WAIT TO START DELETING MY OWN JUNK MAIL!
WELL, YOU CAN'T SAY SHE HAS UNREALISTIC EXPECTATIONS.
KIRKMAN & SCOTT

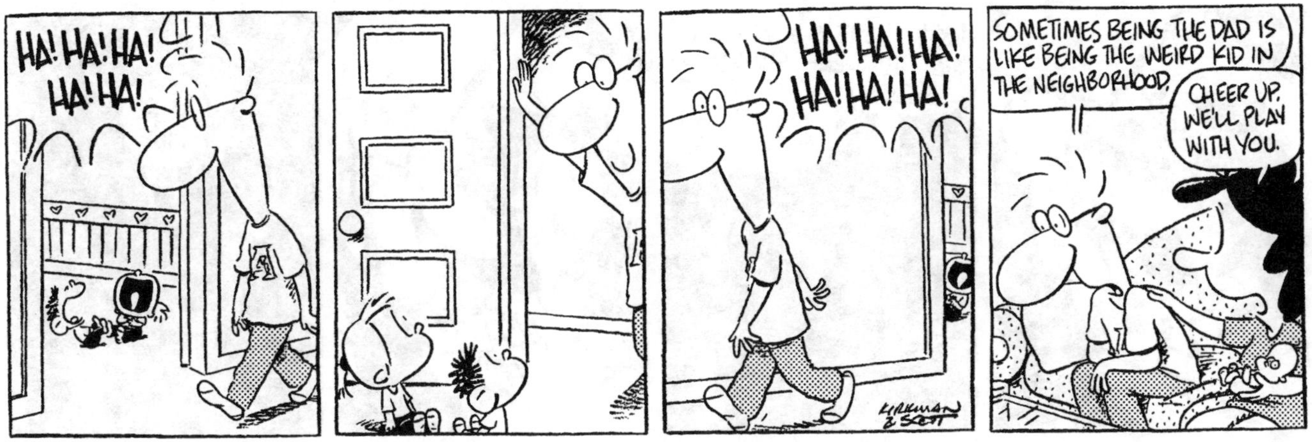
HA! HA! HA! HA! HA!
HA! HA! HA! HA! HA! HA!
KIRKMAN & SCOTT
SOMETIMES BEING THE DAD IS LIKE BEING THE WEIRD KID IN THE NEIGHBORHOOD.
CHEER UP. WE'LL PLAY WITH YOU.

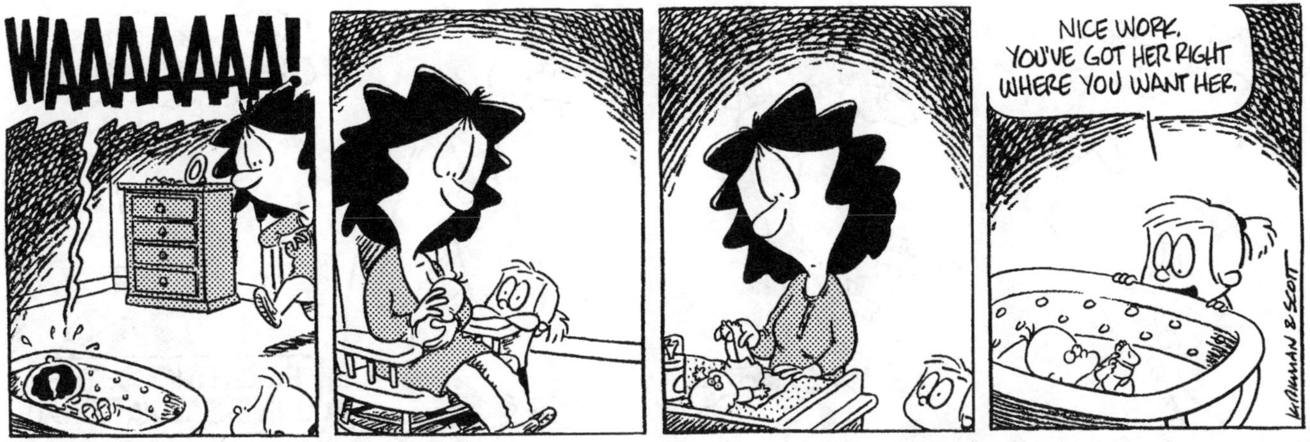
WAAAAAAA!
NICE WORK. YOU'VE GOT HER RIGHT WHERE YOU WANT HER.
KIRKMAN & SCOTT

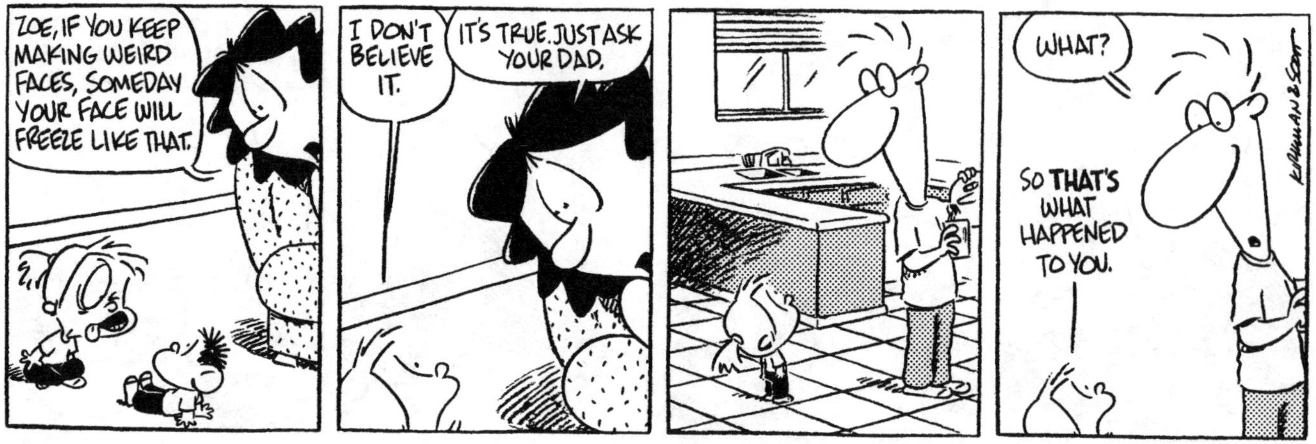
ZOE, IF YOU KEEP MAKING WEIRD FACES, SOMEDAY YOUR FACE WILL FREEZE LIKE THAT.
I DON'T BELIEVE IT.
IT'S TRUE. JUST ASK YOUR DAD.
WHAT?
SO THAT'S WHAT HAPPENED TO YOU.
KIRKMAN & SCOTT

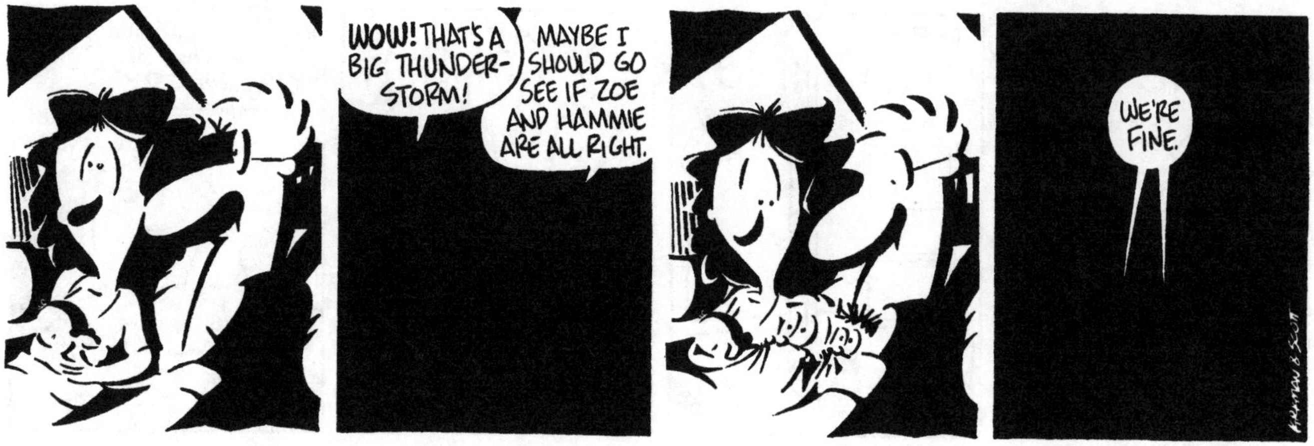
WOW! THAT'S A BIG THUNDER-STORM!
MAYBE I SHOULD GO SEE IF ZOE AND HAMMIE ARE ALL RIGHT.
WE'RE FINE.
KIRKMAN & SCOTT

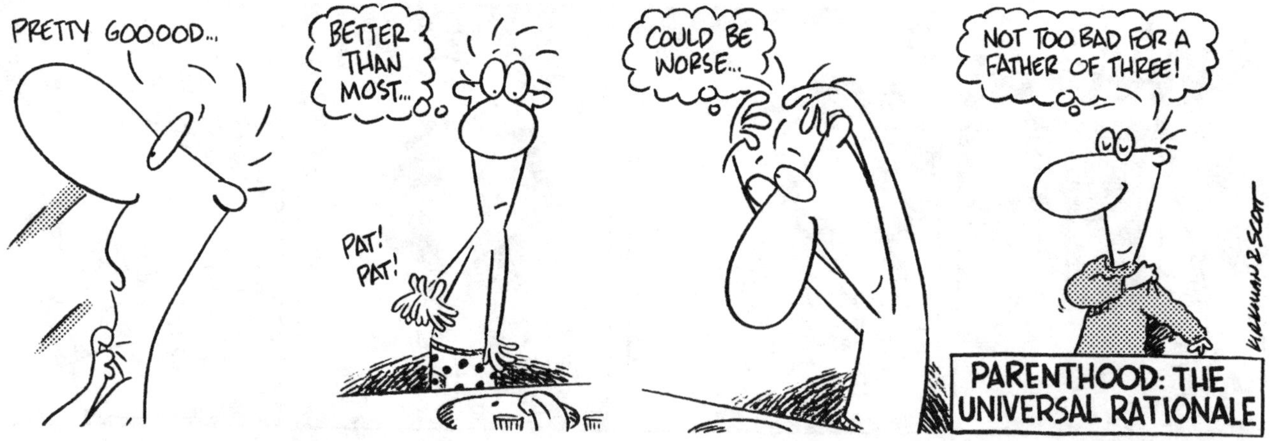
PRETTY GOOOOD...
BETTER THAN MOST...
PAT! PAT!
COULD BE WORSE...
NOT TOO BAD FOR A FATHER OF THREE!
KIRKMAN & SCOTT
PARENTHOOD: THE UNIVERSAL RATIONALE

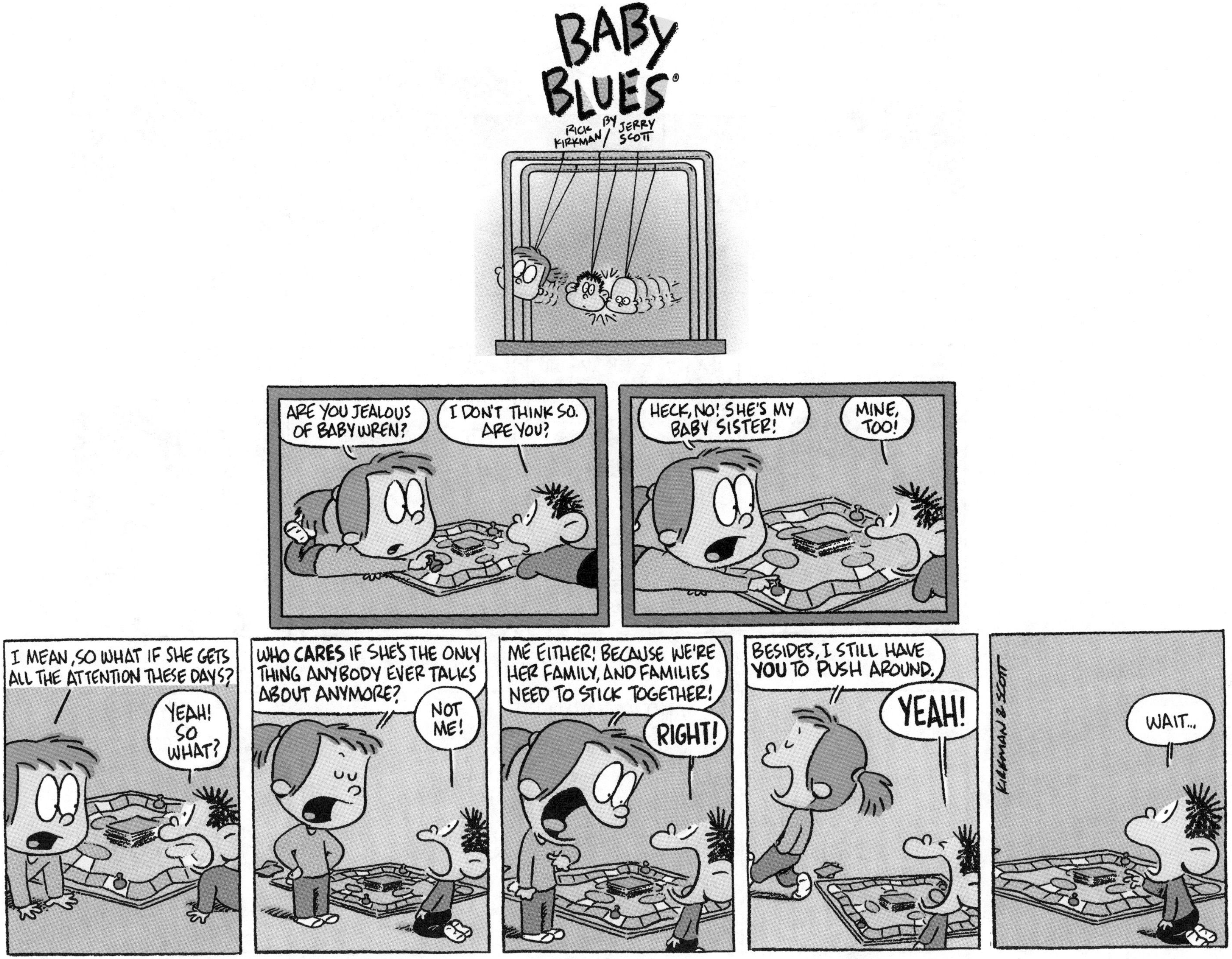
BABY BLUES®
BY RICK KIRKMAN / JERRY SCOTT
ARE YOU JEALOUS OF BABY WREN?
I DON'T THINK SO. ARE YOU?
HECK, NO! SHE'S MY BABY SISTER!
MINE, TOO!
I MEAN, SO WHAT IF SHE GETS ALL THE ATTENTION THESE DAYS?
YEAH! SO WHAT?
WHO CARES IF SHE'S THE ONLY THING ANYBODY EVER TALKS ABOUT ANYMORE?
NOT ME!
ME EITHER! BECAUSE WE'RE HER FAMILY, AND FAMILIES NEED TO STICK TOGETHER!
RIGHT!
BESIDES, I STILL HAVE YOU TO PUSH AROUND.
YEAH!
KIRKMAN & SCOTT
WAIT...

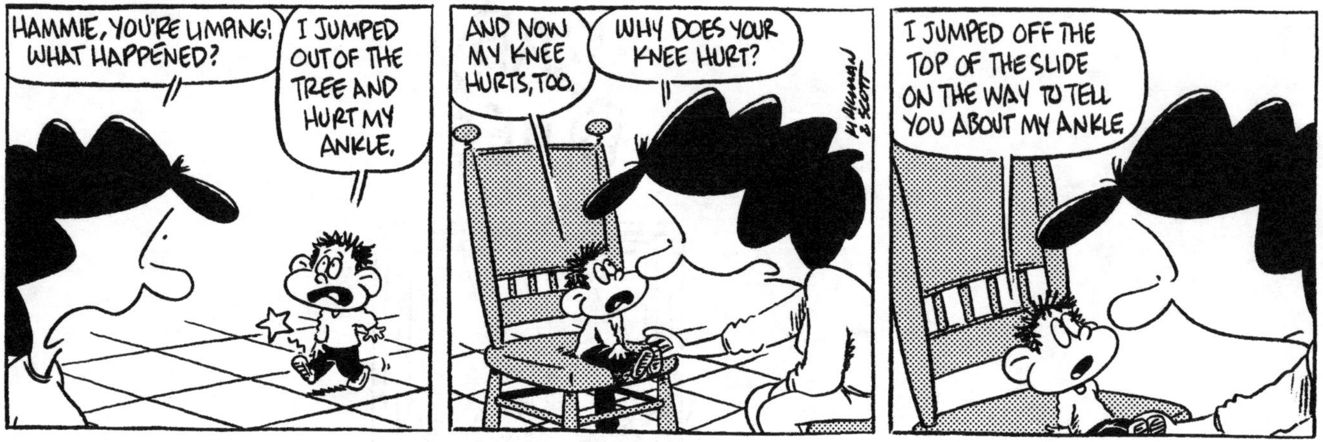
HAMMIE, YOU'RE LIMPING! WHAT HAPPENED?
I JUMPED OUT OF THE TREE AND HURT MY ANKLE.
AND NOW MY KNEE HURTS, TOO.
WHY DOES YOUR KNEE HURT?
I JUMPED OFF THE TOP OF THE SLIDE ON THE WAY TO TELL YOU ABOUT MY ANKLE.

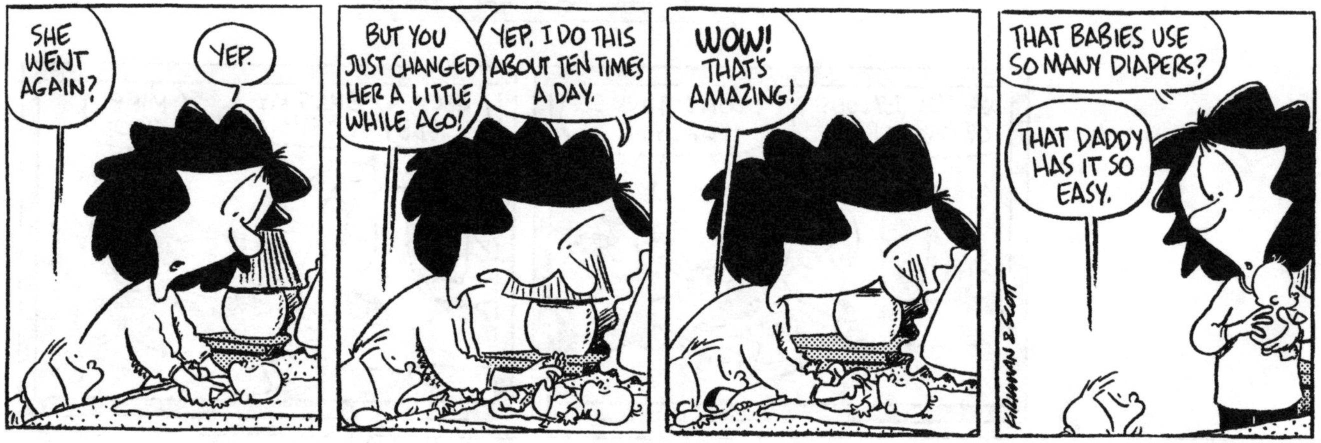
SHE WENT AGAIN?
YEP.
BUT YOU JUST CHANGED HER A LITTLE WHILE AGO!
YEP. I DO THIS ABOUT TEN TIMES A DAY.
WOW! THAT'S AMAZING!
THAT BABIES USE SO MANY DIAPERS?
THAT DADDY HAS IT SO EASY.

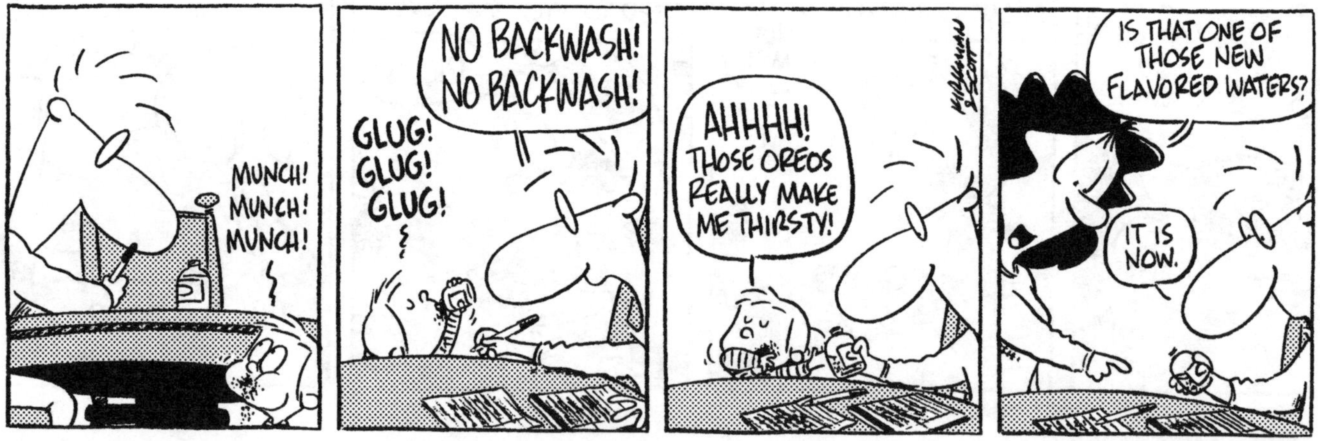
MUNCH! MUNCH! MUNCH!
GLUG! GLUG! GLUG!
NO BACKWASH! NO BACKWASH!
AHHHH! THOSE OREOS REALLY MAKE ME THIRSTY!
IS THAT ONE OF THOSE NEW FLAVORED WATERS?
IT IS NOW.

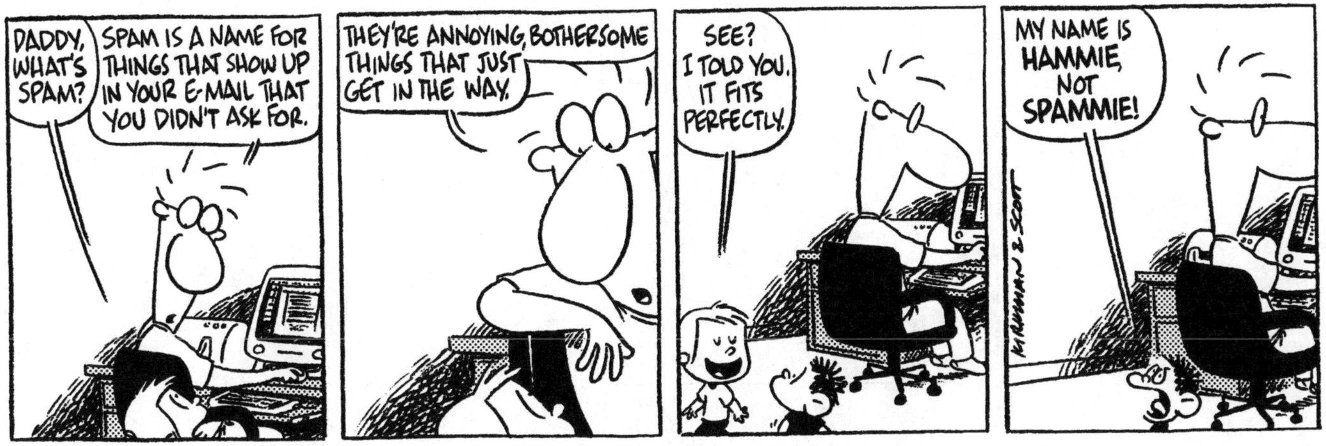
DADDY, WHAT'S SPAM?
SPAM IS A NAME FOR THINGS THAT SHOW UP IN YOUR E-MAIL THAT YOU DIDN'T ASK FOR.
THEY'RE ANNOYING, BOTHERSOME THINGS THAT JUST GET IN THE WAY.
SEE? I TOLD YOU. IT FITS PERFECTLY.
KIRKMAN & SCOTT
MY NAME IS HAMMIE, NOT SPAMMIE!

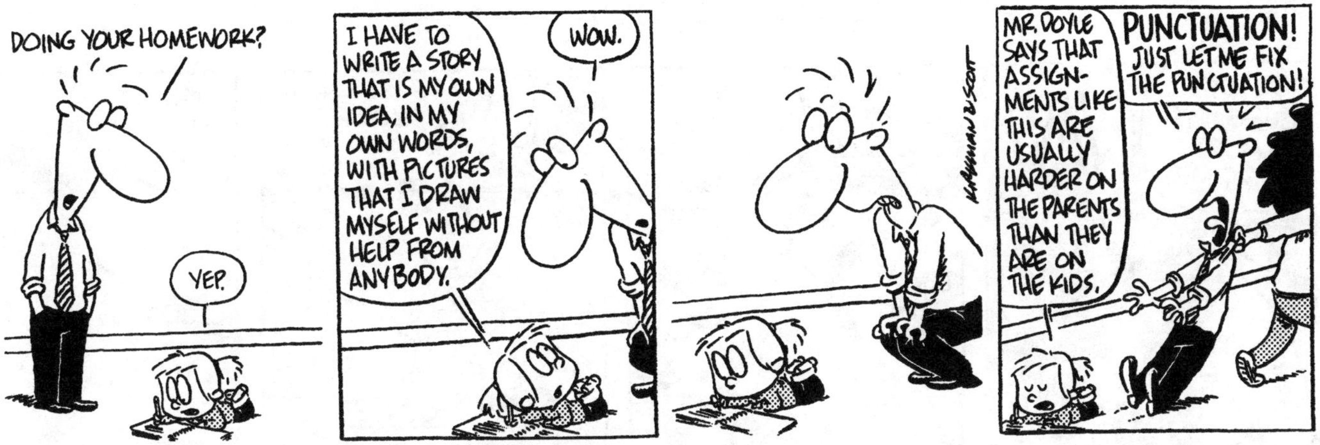
DOING YOUR HOMEWORK?
YEP.
I HAVE TO WRITE A STORY THAT IS MY OWN IDEA, IN MY OWN WORDS, WITH PICTURES THAT I DRAW MYSELF WITHOUT HELP FROM ANYBODY.
WOW.
KIRKMAN & SCOTT
MR. DOYLE SAYS THAT ASSIGNMENTS LIKE THIS ARE USUALLY HARDER ON THE PARENTS THAN THEY ARE ON THE KIDS.
PUNCTUATION! JUST LET ME FIX THE PUNCTUATION!

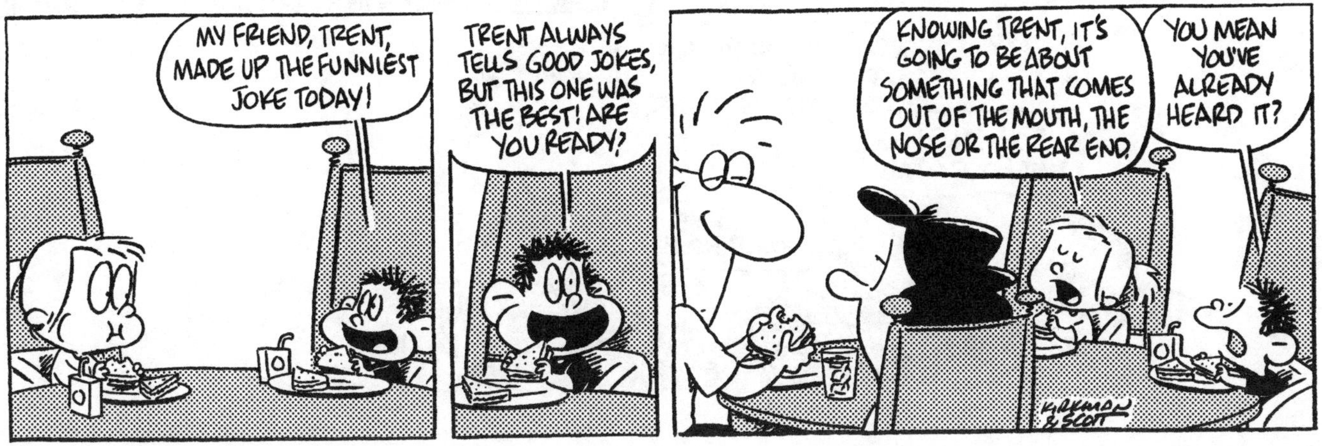
MY FRIEND, TRENT, MADE UP THE FUNNIEST JOKE TODAY!
TRENT ALWAYS TELLS GOOD JOKES, BUT THIS ONE WAS THE BEST! ARE YOU READY?
KNOWING TRENT, IT'S GOING TO BE ABOUT SOMETHING THAT COMES OUT OF THE MOUTH, THE NOSE OR THE REAR END.
YOU MEAN YOU'VE ALREADY HEARD IT?
KIRKMAN & SCOTT

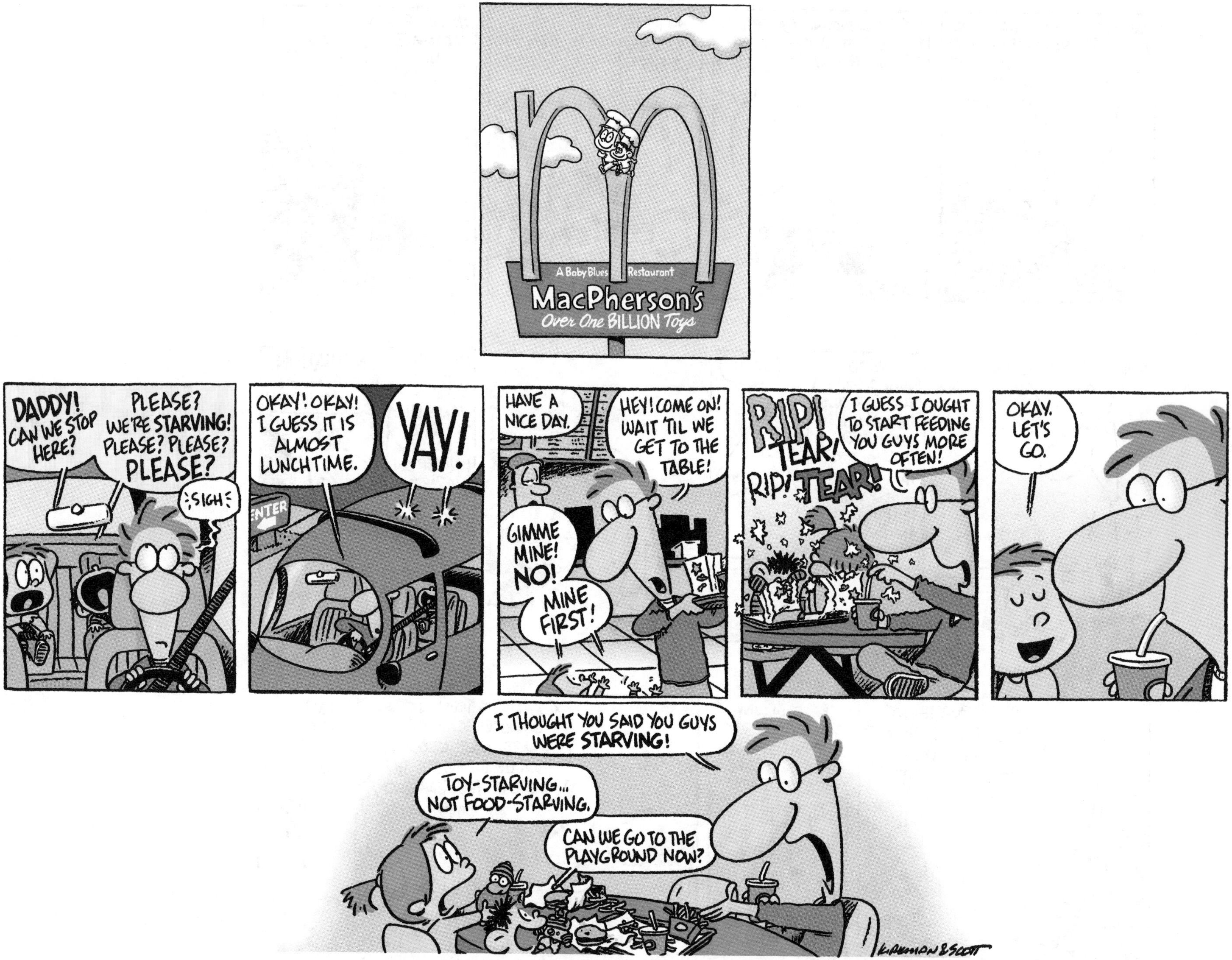
A Baby Blues Restaurant
MacPherson's
Over One BILLION Toys
DADDY! CAN WE STOP HERE?
PLEASE? WE'RE STARVING! PLEASE? PLEASE? PLEASE?
SIGH
OKAY! OKAY! I GUESS IT IS ALMOST LUNCHTIME.
YAY!
ENTER
HAVE A NICE DAY.
HEY! COME ON! WAIT 'TIL WE GET TO THE TABLE!
GIMME MINE! NO!
MINE FIRST!
RIP! TEAR! RIP! TEAR!
I GUESS I OUGHT TO START FEEDING YOU GUYS MORE OFTEN!
OKAY. LET'S GO.
I THOUGHT YOU SAID YOU GUYS WERE STARVING!
TOY-STARVING... NOT FOOD-STARVING.
CAN WE GO TO THE PLAYGROUND NOW?
KIRKMAN & SCOTT

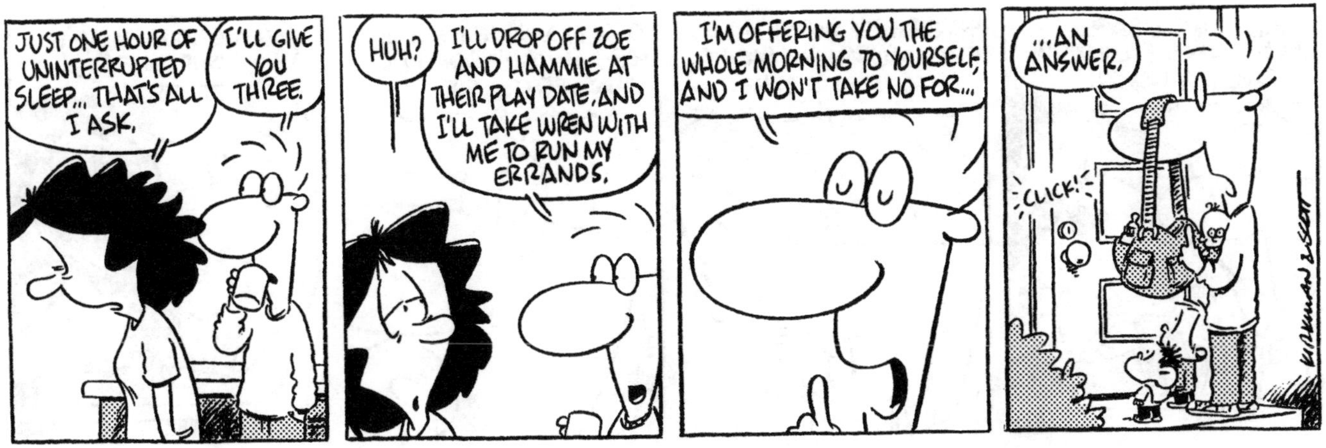
JUST ONE HOUR OF UNINTERRUPTED SLEEP... THAT'S ALL I ASK.
I'LL GIVE YOU THREE.
HUH?
I'LL DROP OFF ZOE AND HAMMIE AT THEIR PLAY DATE, AND I'LL TAKE WREN WITH ME TO RUN MY ERRANDS.
I'M OFFERING YOU THE WHOLE MORNING TO YOURSELF, AND I WON'T TAKE NO FOR...
...AN ANSWER.
CLICK!
KIRKMAN & SCOTT

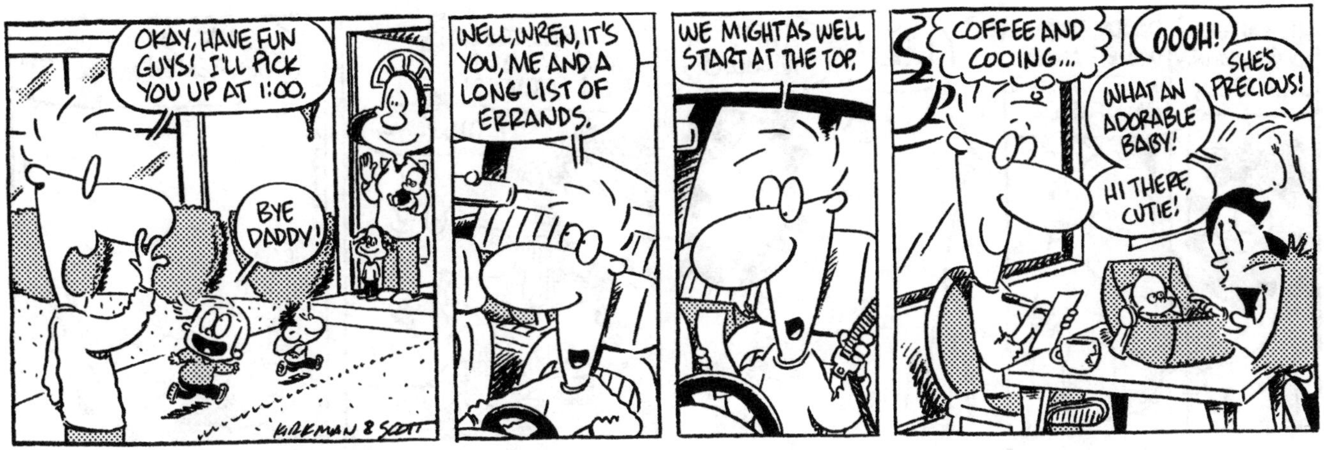
OKAY, HAVE FUN GUYS! I'LL PICK YOU UP AT 1:00.
BYE DADDY!
KIRKMAN & SCOTT
WELL, WREN, IT'S YOU, ME AND A LONG LIST OF ERRANDS.
WE MIGHT AS WELL START AT THE TOP.
COFFEE AND COOING...
OOOH!
SHE'S PRECIOUS!
WHAT AN ADORABLE BABY!
HI THERE, CUTIE!

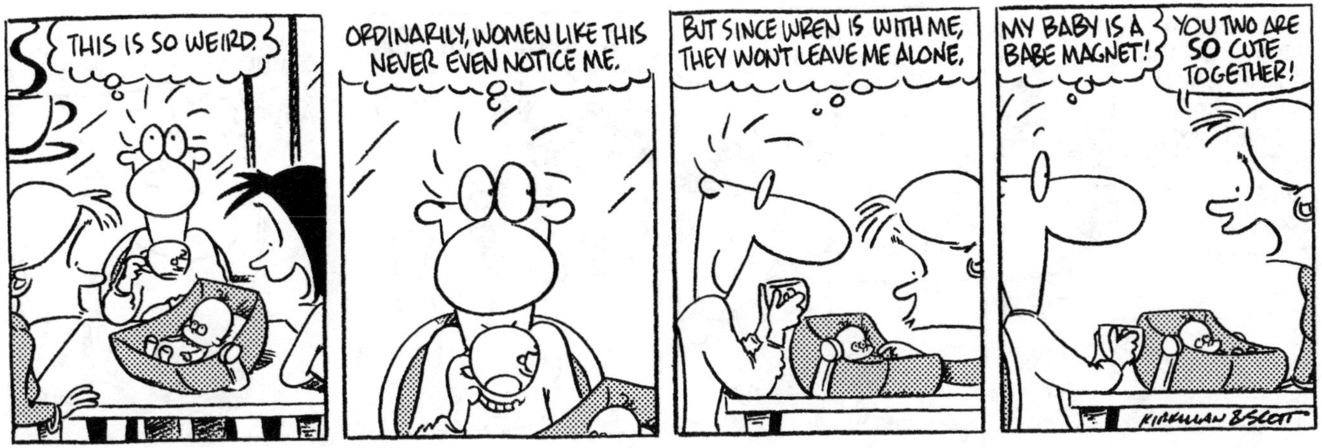
THIS IS SO WEIRD.
ORDINARILY, WOMEN LIKE THIS NEVER EVEN NOTICE ME.
BUT SINCE WREN IS WITH ME, THEY WON'T LEAVE ME ALONE.
MY BABY IS A BABE MAGNET!
YOU TWO ARE SO CUTE TOGETHER!
KIRKMAN & SCOTT

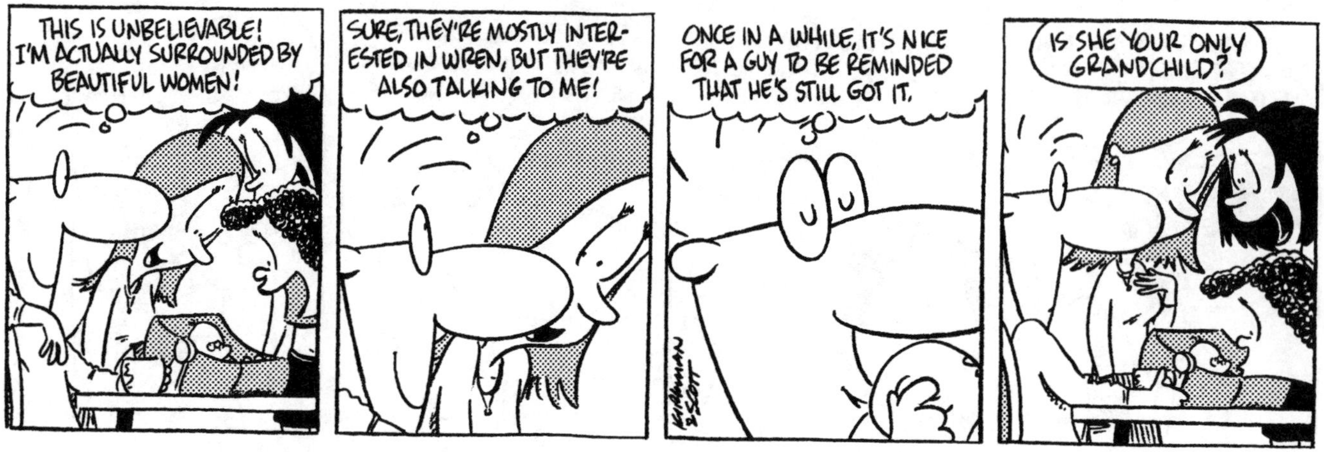
THIS IS UNBELIEVABLE! I'M ACTUALLY SURROUNDED BY BEAUTIFUL WOMEN!
SURE, THEY'RE MOSTLY INTERESTED IN WREN, BUT THEY'RE ALSO TALKING TO ME!
ONCE IN A WHILE, IT'S NICE FOR A GUY TO BE REMINDED THAT HE'S STILL GOT IT.
IS SHE YOUR ONLY GRANDCHILD?

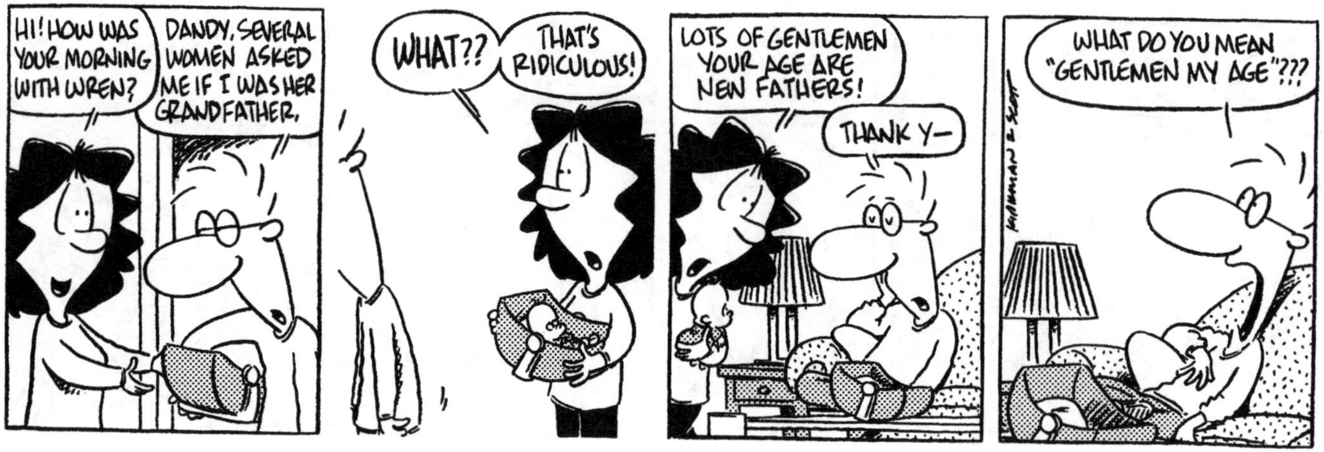
HI! HOW WAS YOUR MORNING WITH WREN?
DANDY. SEVERAL WOMEN ASKED ME IF I WAS HER GRANDFATHER.
WHAT??
THAT'S RIDICULOUS!
LOTS OF GENTLEMEN YOUR AGE ARE NEW FATHERS!
THANK Y–
WHAT DO YOU MEAN "GENTLEMEN MY AGE"???

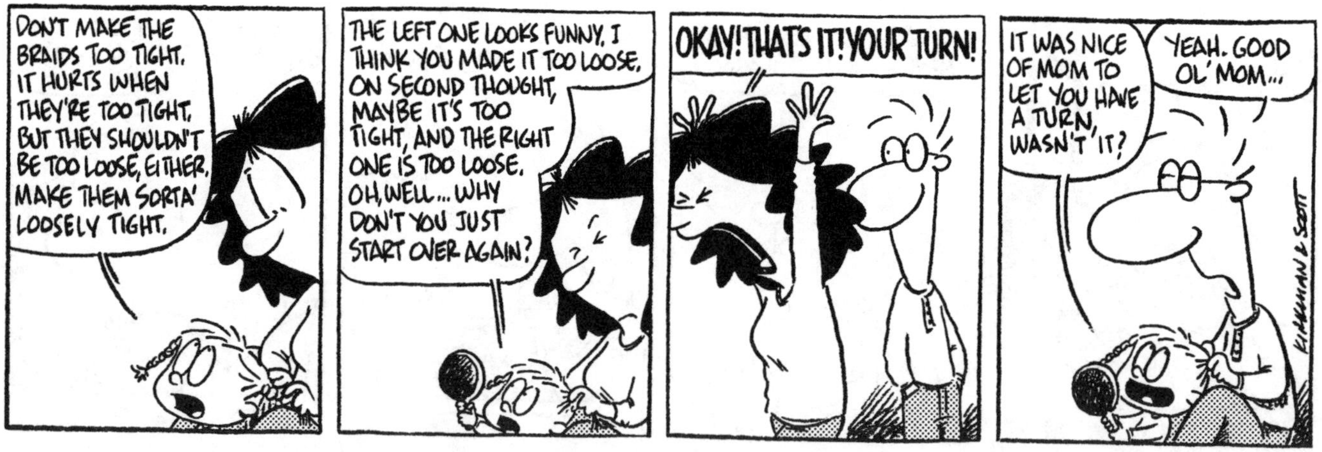
DON'T MAKE THE BRAIDS TOO TIGHT. IT HURTS WHEN THEY'RE TOO TIGHT. BUT THEY SHOULDN'T BE TOO LOOSE, EITHER. MAKE THEM SORTA' LOOSELY TIGHT.
THE LEFT ONE LOOKS FUNNY. I THINK YOU MADE IT TOO LOOSE. ON SECOND THOUGHT, MAYBE IT'S TOO TIGHT, AND THE RIGHT ONE IS TOO LOOSE. OH, WELL... WHY DON'T YOU JUST START OVER AGAIN?
OKAY! THAT'S IT! YOUR TURN!
IT WAS NICE OF MOM TO LET YOU HAVE A TURN, WASN'T IT?
YEAH. GOOD OL' MOM...

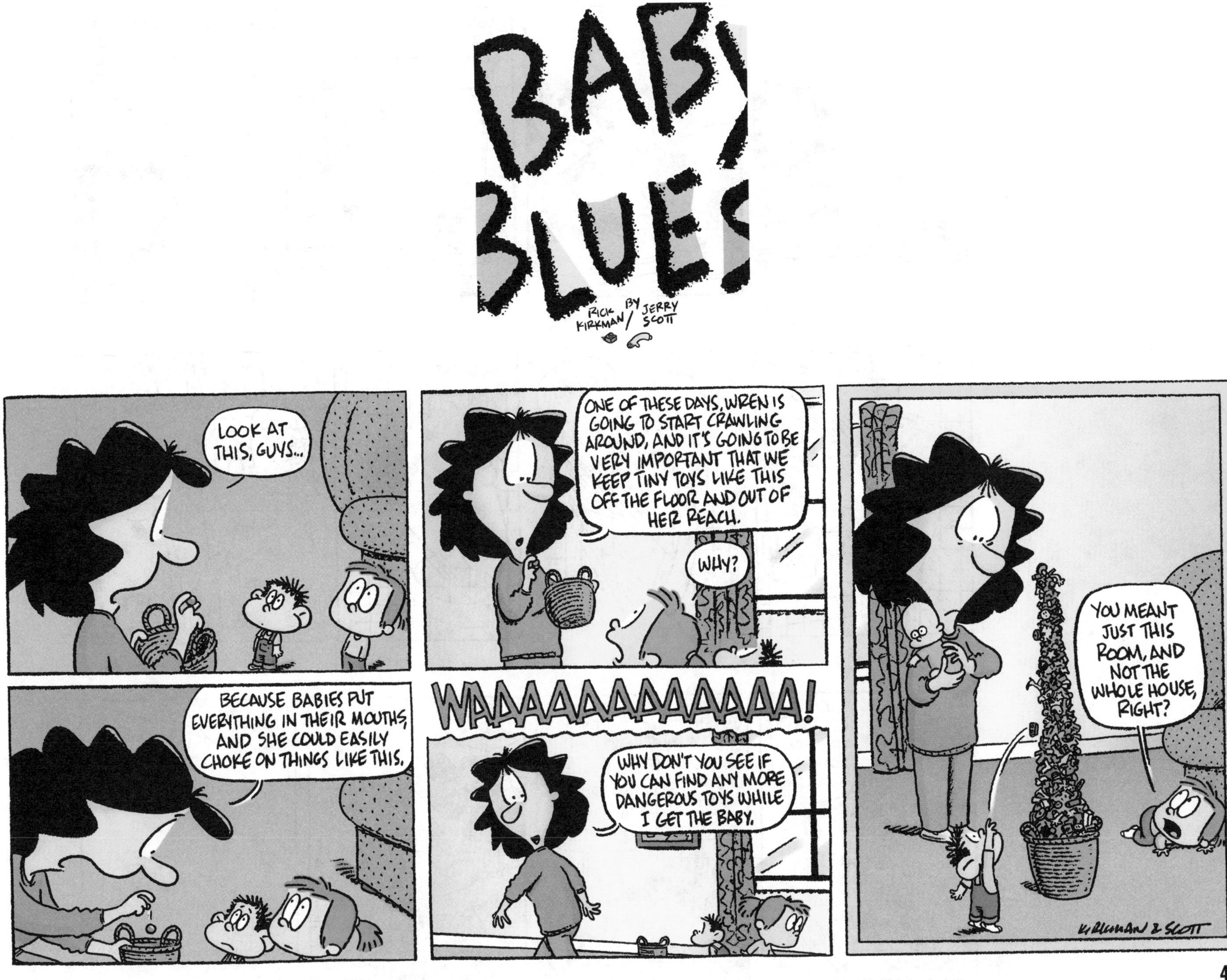
BABY BLUES
BY RICK KIRKMAN / JERRY SCOTT
LOOK AT THIS, GUYS...
BECAUSE BABIES PUT EVERYTHING IN THEIR MOUTHS, AND SHE COULD EASILY CHOKE ON THINGS LIKE THIS.
ONE OF THESE DAYS, WREN IS GOING TO START CRAWLING AROUND, AND IT'S GOING TO BE VERY IMPORTANT THAT WE KEEP TINY TOYS LIKE THIS OFF THE FLOOR AND OUT OF HER REACH.
WHY?
WAAAAAAAAAAAAA!
WHY DON'T YOU SEE IF YOU CAN FIND ANY MORE DANGEROUS TOYS WHILE I GET THE BABY.
YOU MEANT JUST THIS ROOM, AND NOT THE WHOLE HOUSE, RIGHT?
KIRKMAN & SCOTT

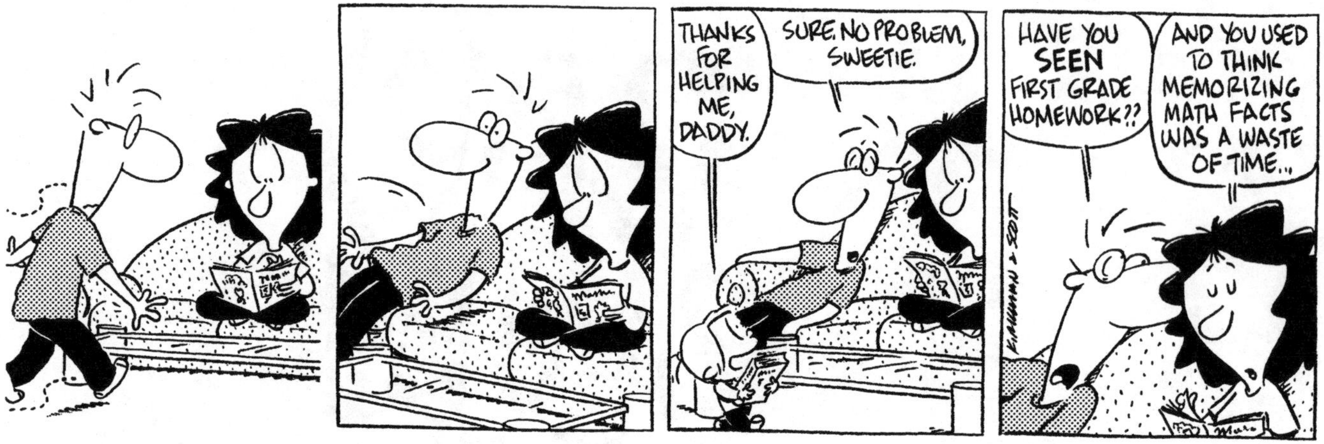
THANKS FOR HELPING ME, DADDY.
SURE. NO PROBLEM, SWEETIE.
HAVE YOU SEEN FIRST GRADE HOMEWORK??
AND YOU USED TO THINK MEMORIZING MATH FACTS WAS A WASTE OF TIME...
KIRKMAN & SCOTT

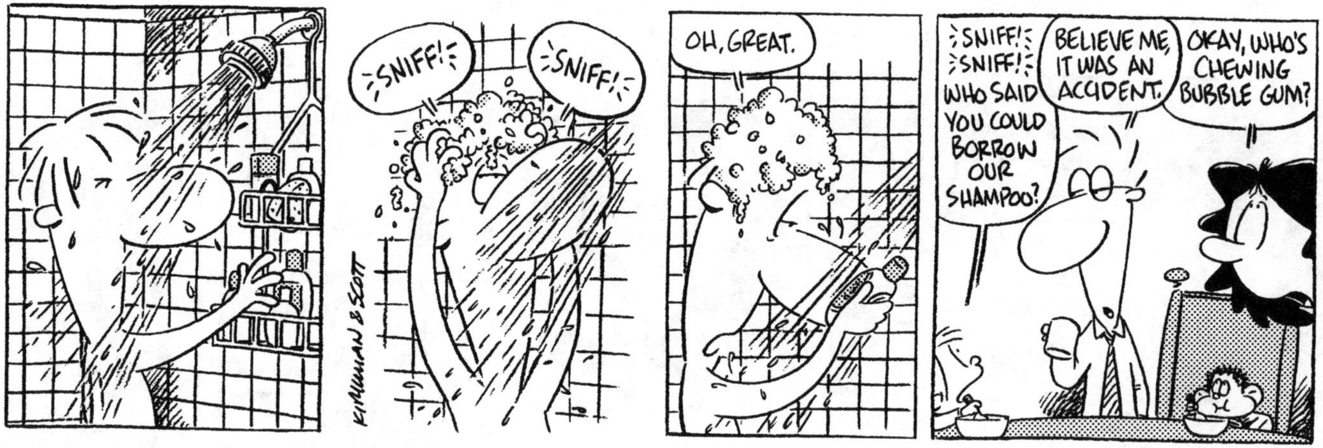
SNIFF!
SNIFF!
KIRKMAN & SCOTT
OH, GREAT.
SNIFF! SNIFF! WHO SAID YOU COULD BORROW OUR SHAMPOO?
BELIEVE ME, IT WAS AN ACCIDENT.
OKAY, WHO'S CHEWING BUBBLE GUM?

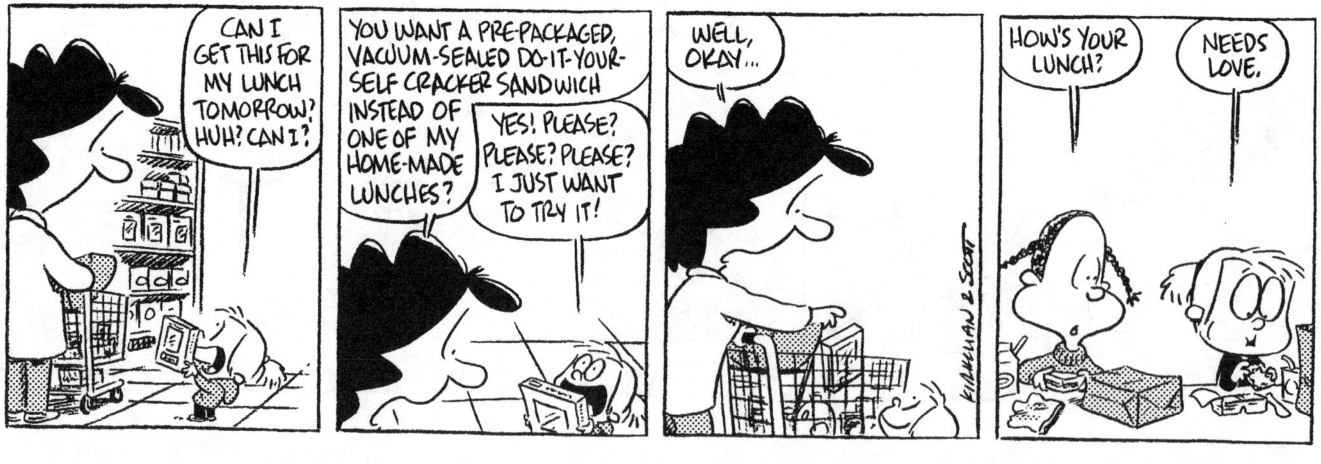
CAN I GET THIS FOR MY LUNCH TOMORROW? HUH? CAN I?
YOU WANT A PRE-PACKAGED, VACUUM-SEALED DO-IT-YOURSELF CRACKER SANDWICH INSTEAD OF ONE OF MY HOME-MADE LUNCHES?
YES! PLEASE? PLEASE? PLEASE? I JUST WANT TO TRY IT!
WELL, OKAY...
KIRKMAN & SCOTT
HOW'S YOUR LUNCH?
NEEDS LOVE.

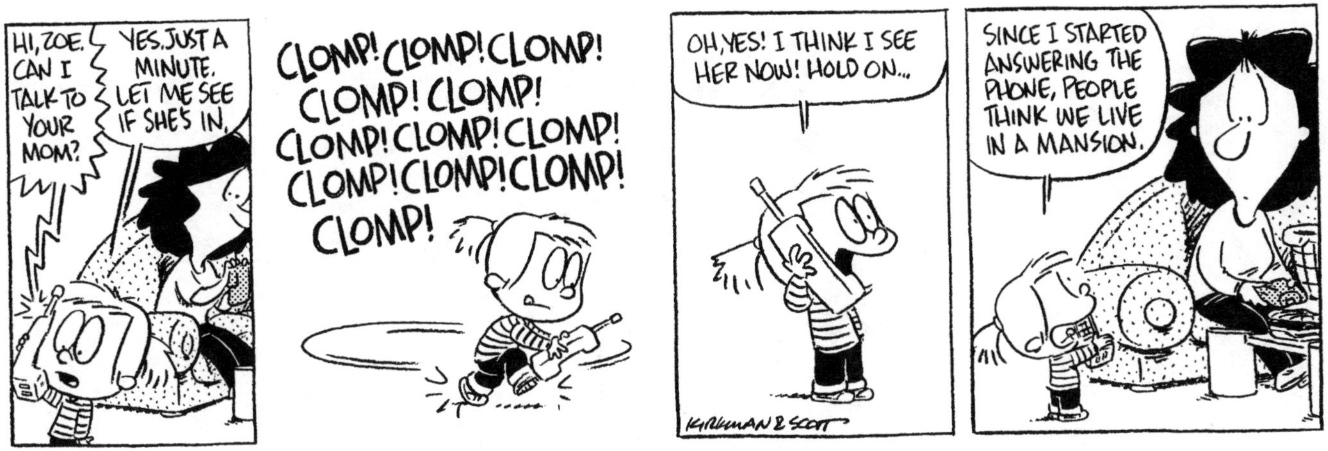
HI, ZOE. CAN I TALK TO YOUR MOM?
YES. JUST A MINUTE. LET ME SEE IF SHE'S IN.
CLOMP! CLOMP! CLOMP! CLOMP! CLOMP! CLOMP! CLOMP! CLOMP! CLOMP! CLOMP! CLOMP! CLOMP!
OH, YES! I THINK I SEE HER NOW! HOLD ON...
KIRKMAN & SCOTT
SINCE I STARTED ANSWERING THE PHONE, PEOPLE THINK WE LIVE IN A MANSION.

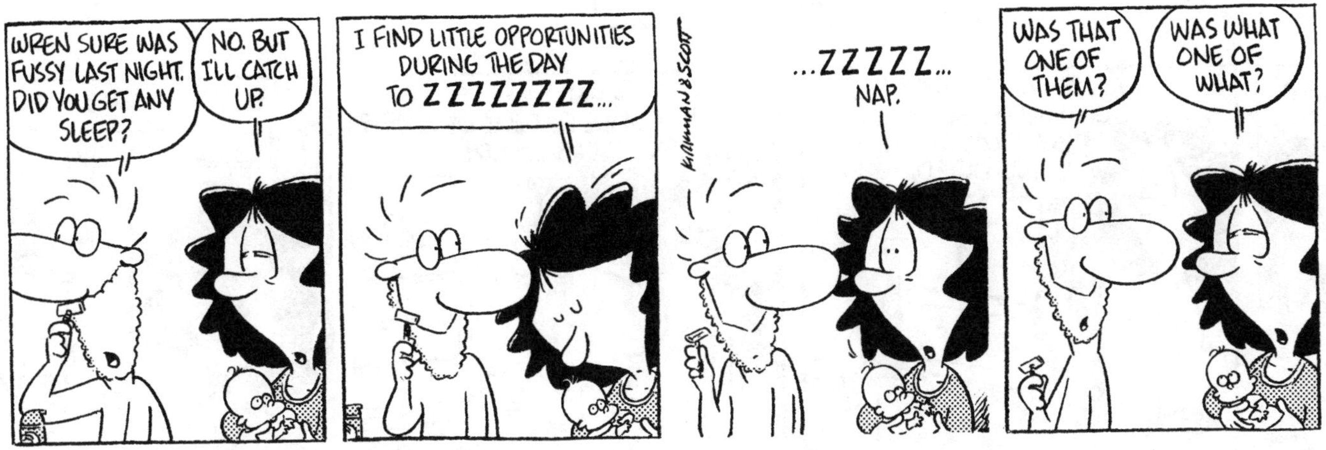
WREN SURE WAS FUSSY LAST NIGHT. DID YOU GET ANY SLEEP?
NO. BUT I'LL CATCH UP.
I FIND LITTLE OPPORTUNITIES DURING THE DAY TO ZZZZZZZZ...
KIRKMAN & SCOTT
...ZZZZZ... NAP.
WAS THAT ONE OF THEM?
WAS WHAT ONE OF WHAT?

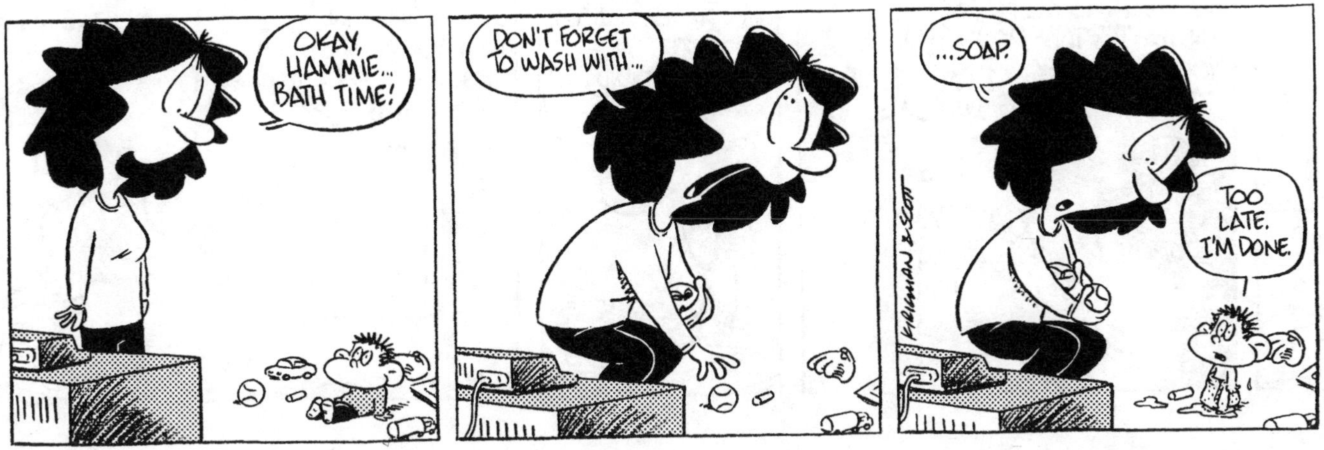
OKAY, HAMMIE... BATH TIME!
DON'T FORGET TO WASH WITH...
KIRKMAN & SCOTT
...SOAP.
TOO LATE. I'M DONE.

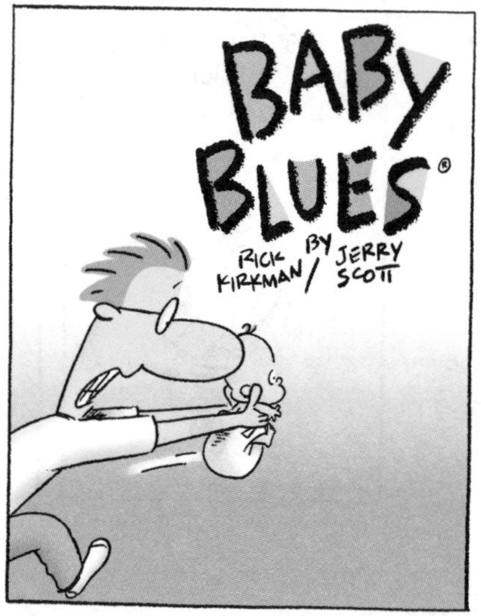
BABY BLUES®
BY RICK KIRKMAN / JERRY SCOTT

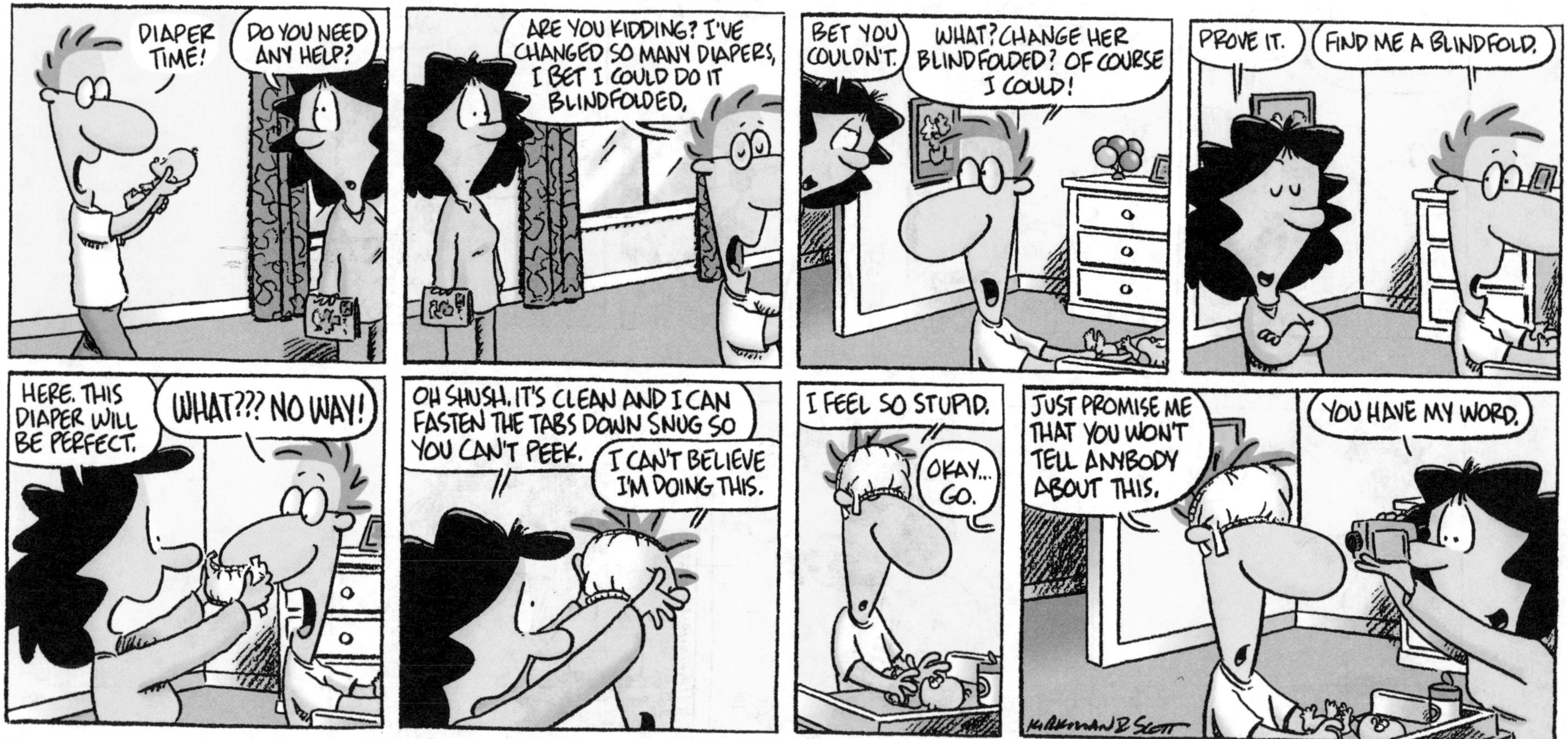
DIAPER TIME!
DO YOU NEED ANY HELP?
ARE YOU KIDDING? I'VE CHANGED SO MANY DIAPERS, I BET I COULD DO IT BLINDFOLDED.
BET YOU COULDN'T.
WHAT? CHANGE HER BLINDFOLDED? OF COURSE I COULD!
PROVE IT.
FIND ME A BLINDFOLD.
HERE. THIS DIAPER WILL BE PERFECT.
WHAT??? NO WAY!
OH SHUSH. IT'S CLEAN AND I CAN FASTEN THE TABS DOWN SNUG SO YOU CAN'T PEEK.
I CAN'T BELIEVE I'M DOING THIS.
I FEEL SO STUPID.
OKAY... GO.
JUST PROMISE ME THAT YOU WON'T TELL ANYBODY ABOUT THIS.
YOU HAVE MY WORD.
KIRKMAN & SCOTT

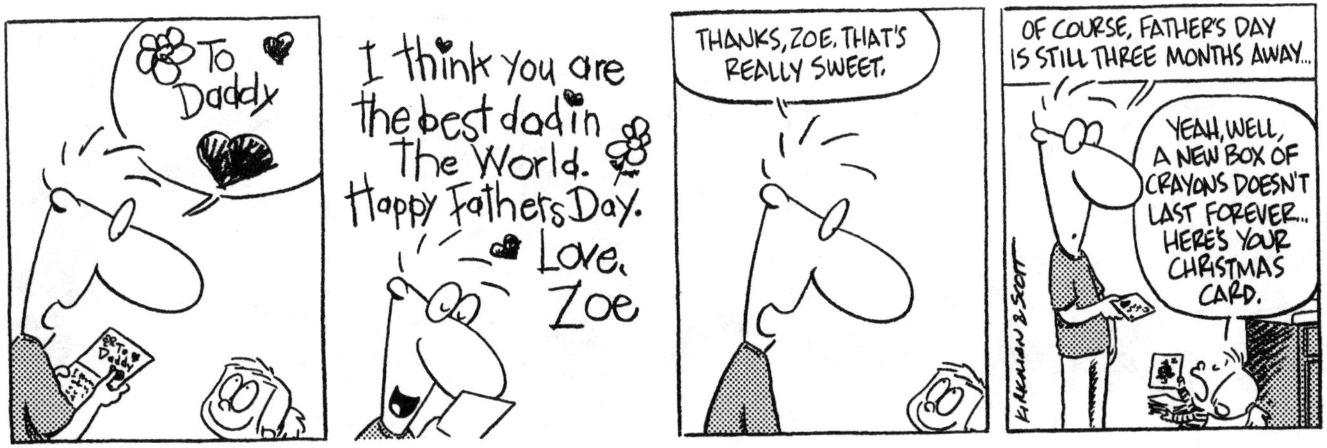
To Daddy
I think you are the best dad in The World. Happy Fathers Day. Love, Zoe
THANKS, ZOE. THAT'S REALLY SWEET.
OF COURSE, FATHER'S DAY IS STILL THREE MONTHS AWAY...
YEAH, WELL, A NEW BOX OF CRAYONS DOESN'T LAST FOREVER... HERE'S YOUR CHRISTMAS CARD.
KIRKMAN & SCOTT

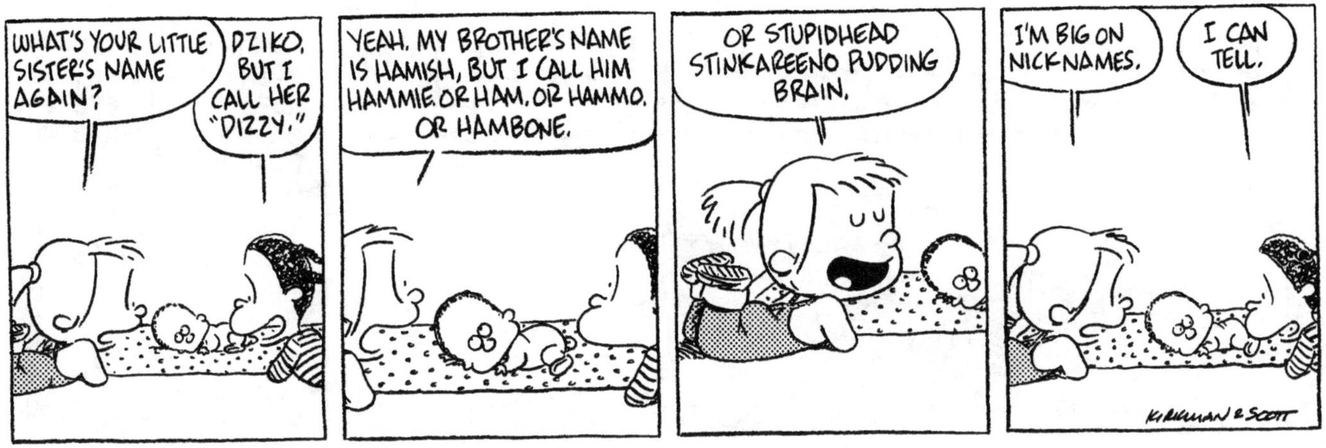
WHAT'S YOUR LITTLE SISTER'S NAME AGAIN?
DZIKO, BUT I CALL HER "DIZZY."
YEAH. MY BROTHER'S NAME IS HAMISH, BUT I CALL HIM HAMMIE OR HAM, OR HAMMO, OR HAMBONE.
OR STUPIDHEAD STINKAREENO PUDDING BRAIN.
I'M BIG ON NICKNAMES.
I CAN TELL.
KIRKMAN & SCOTT

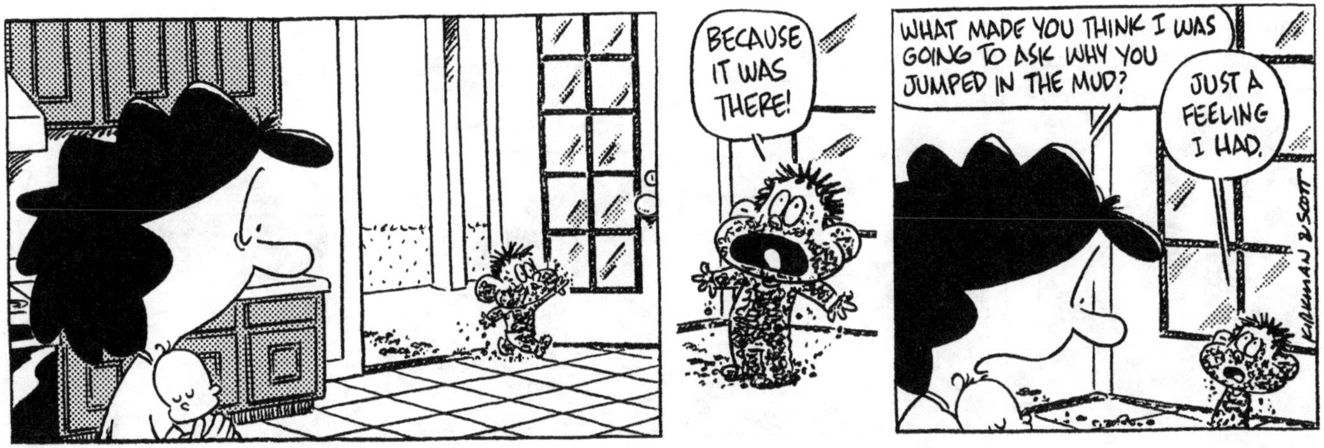
BECAUSE IT WAS THERE!
WHAT MADE YOU THINK I WAS GOING TO ASK WHY YOU JUMPED IN THE MUD?
JUST A FEELING I HAD.
KIRKMAN & SCOTT

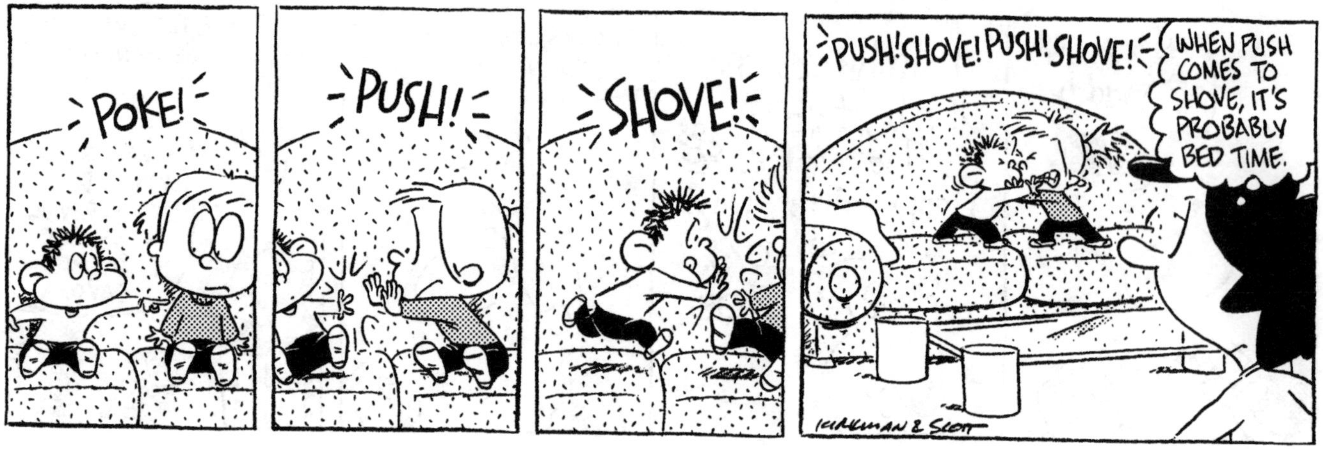
POKE!
PUSH!
SHOVE!
PUSH! SHOVE! PUSH! SHOVE!
WHEN PUSH COMES TO SHOVE, IT'S PROBABLY BED TIME.
KIRKMAN & SCOTT

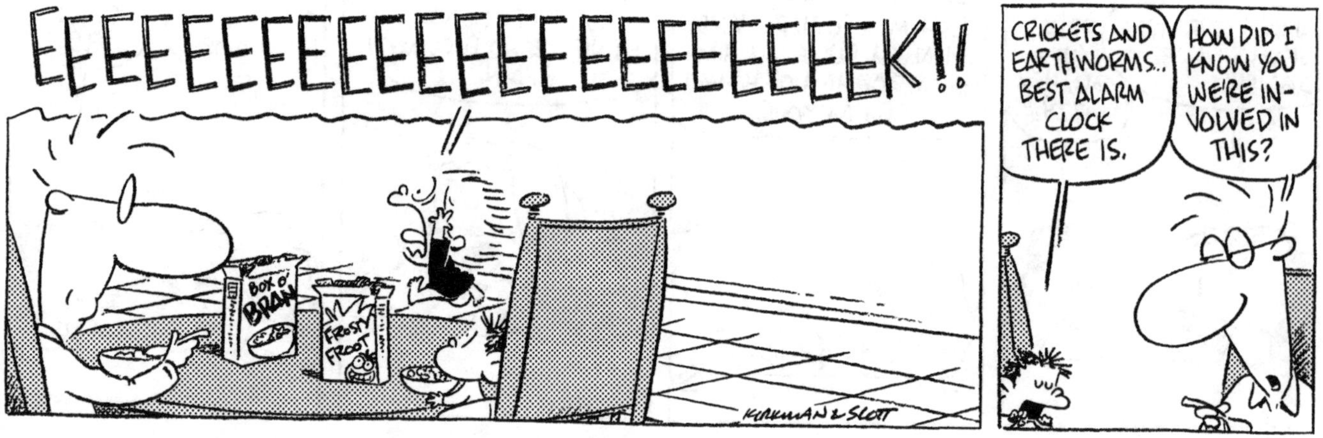
EEEEEEEEEEEEEEEEEEEEEEEEK!!
BOX O' BRAN
FROSTY FROOT
KIRKMAN & SCOTT
CRICKETS AND EARTHWORMS... BEST ALARM CLOCK THERE IS.
HOW DID I KNOW YOU WE'RE IN-VOLVED IN THIS?

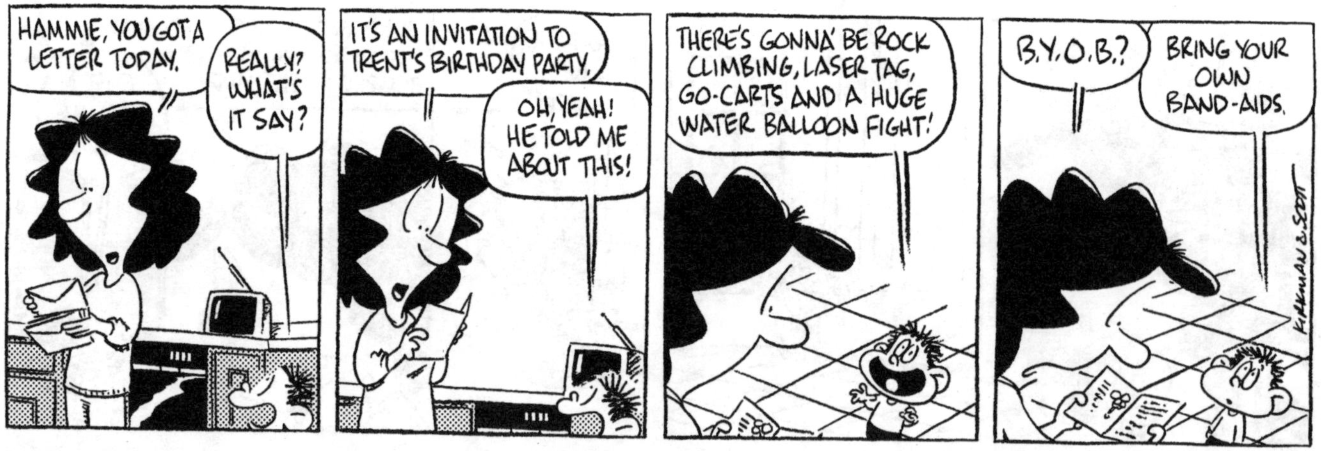
HAMMIE, YOU GOT A LETTER TODAY.
REALLY? WHAT'S IT SAY?
IT'S AN INVITATION TO TRENT'S BIRTHDAY PARTY.
OH, YEAH! HE TOLD ME ABOUT THIS!
THERE'S GONNA' BE ROCK CLIMBING, LASER TAG, GO-CARTS AND A HUGE WATER BALLOON FIGHT!
B.Y.O.B.?
BRING YOUR OWN BAND-AIDS.
KIRKMAN & SCOTT

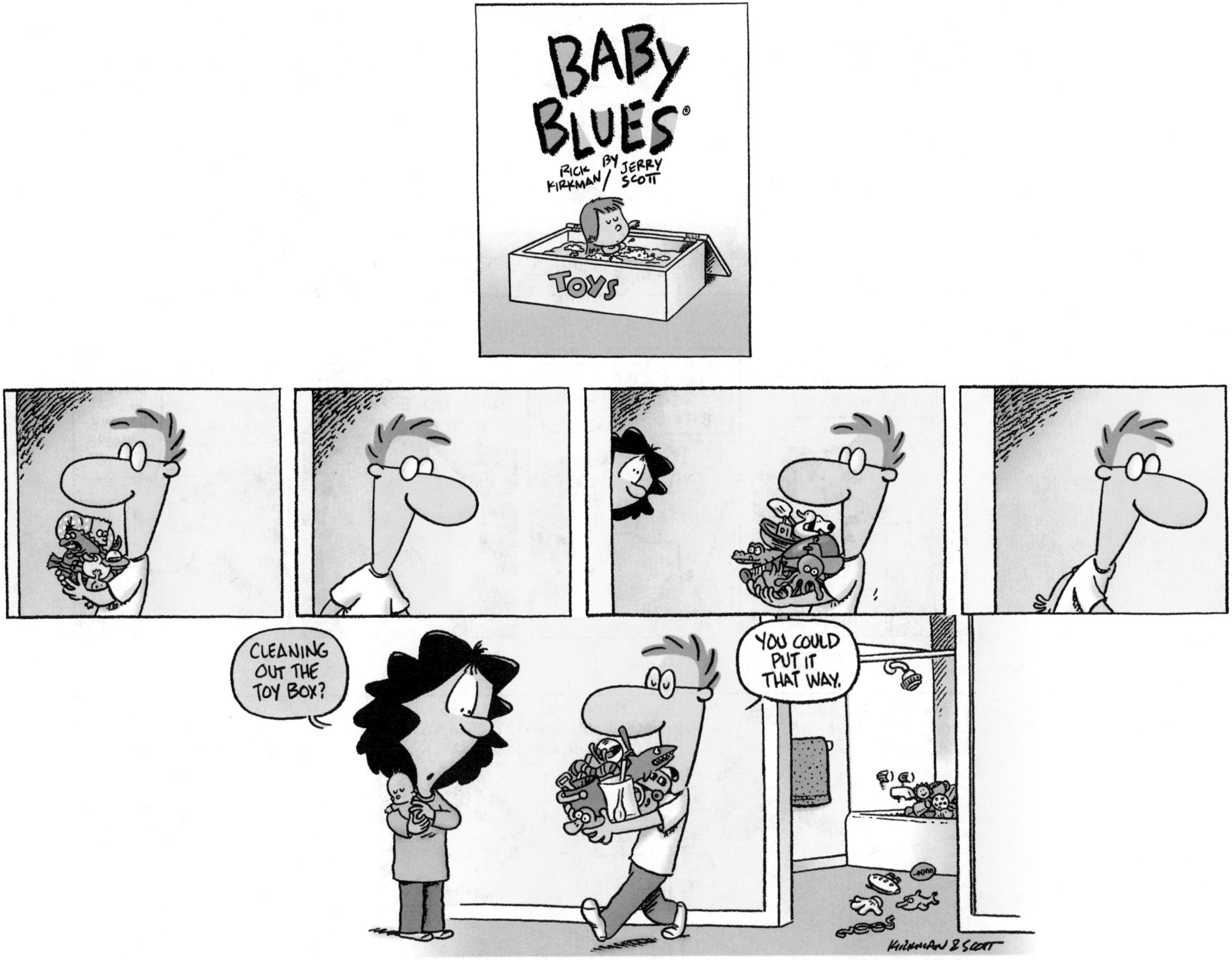
BABY BLUES®
BY RICK KIRKMAN / JERRY SCOTT
TOYS
CLEANING OUT THE TOY BOX?
YOU COULD PUT IT THAT WAY.
KIRKMAN & SCOTT

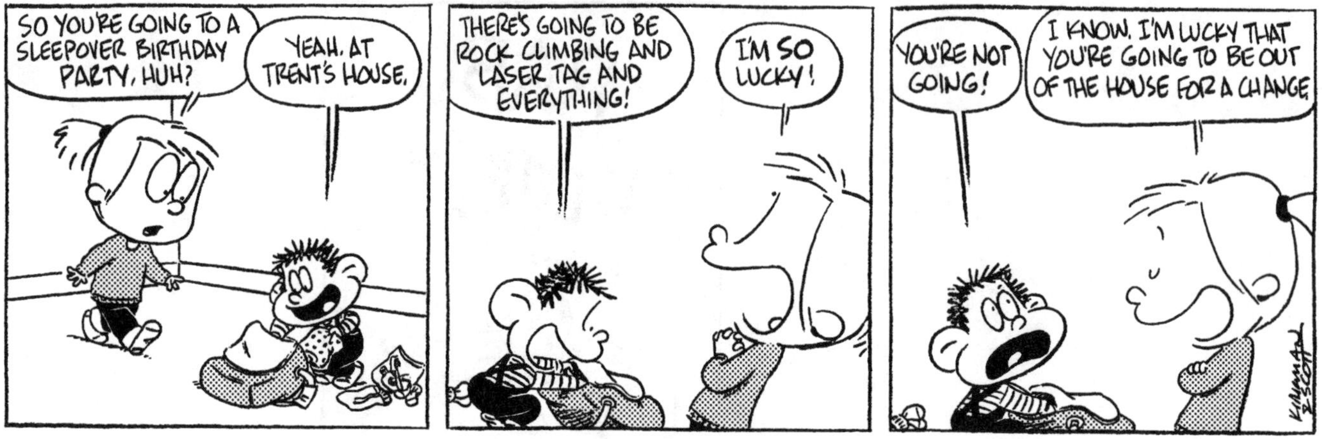
SO YOU'RE GOING TO A SLEEPOVER BIRTHDAY PARTY, HUH?
YEAH. AT TRENT'S HOUSE.
THERE'S GOING TO BE ROCK CLIMBING AND LASER TAG AND EVERYTHING!
I'M SO LUCKY!
YOU'RE NOT GOING!
I KNOW. I'M LUCKY THAT YOU'RE GOING TO BE OUT OF THE HOUSE FOR A CHANGE.
KIRKMAN & SCOTT

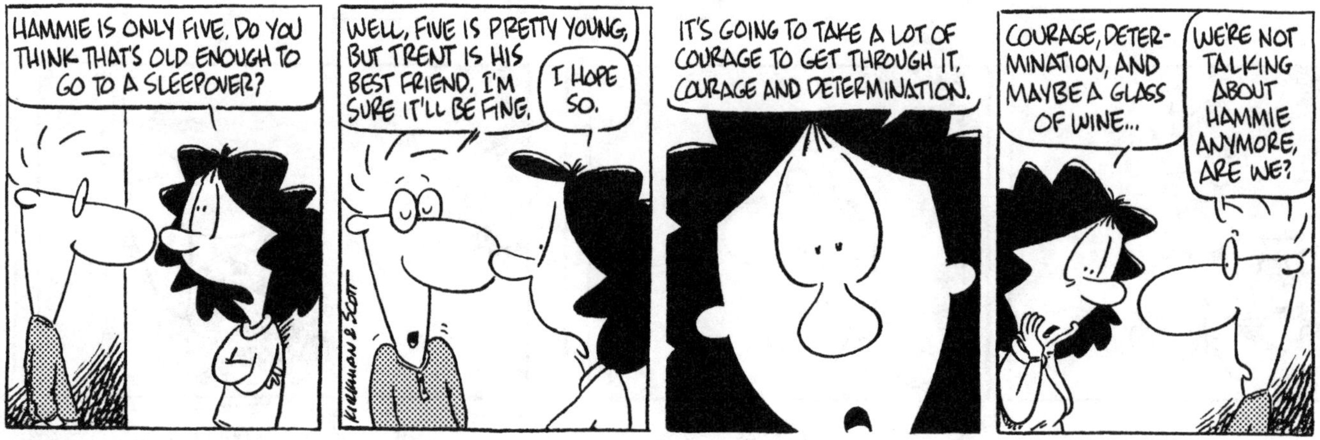
HAMMIE IS ONLY FIVE. DO YOU THINK THAT'S OLD ENOUGH TO GO TO A SLEEPOVER?
WELL, FIVE IS PRETTY YOUNG, BUT TRENT IS HIS BEST FRIEND. I'M SURE IT'LL BE FINE.
I HOPE SO.
IT'S GOING TO TAKE A LOT OF COURAGE TO GET THROUGH IT. COURAGE AND DETERMINATION.
COURAGE, DETERMINATION, AND MAYBE A GLASS OF WINE...
WE'RE NOT TALKING ABOUT HAMMIE ANYMORE, ARE WE?
KIRKMAN & SCOTT

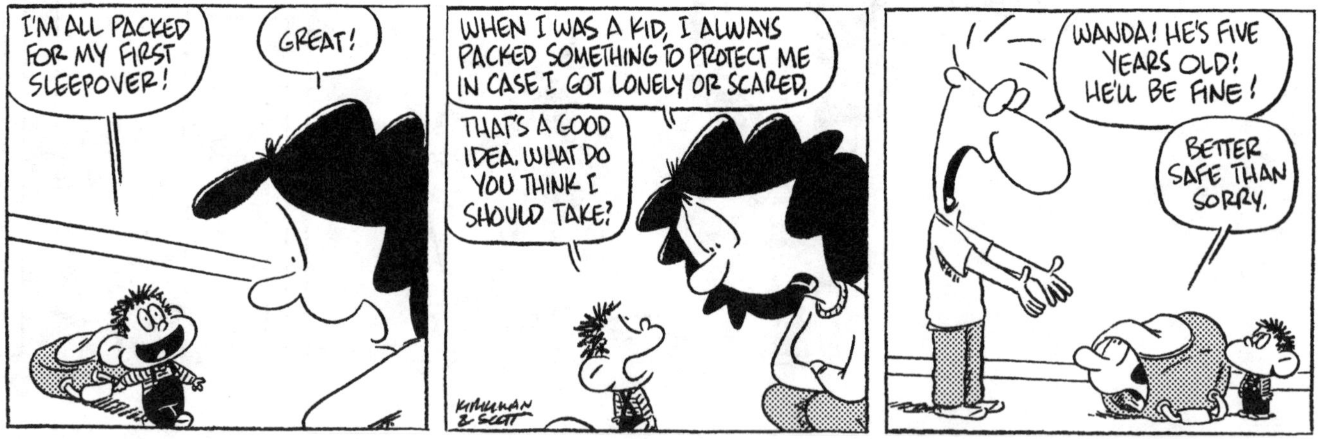
I'M ALL PACKED FOR MY FIRST SLEEPOVER!
GREAT!
WHEN I WAS A KID, I ALWAYS PACKED SOMETHING TO PROTECT ME IN CASE I GOT LONELY OR SCARED.
THAT'S A GOOD IDEA. WHAT DO YOU THINK I SHOULD TAKE?
WANDA! HE'S FIVE YEARS OLD! HE'LL BE FINE!
BETTER SAFE THAN SORRY.
KIRKMAN & SCOTT

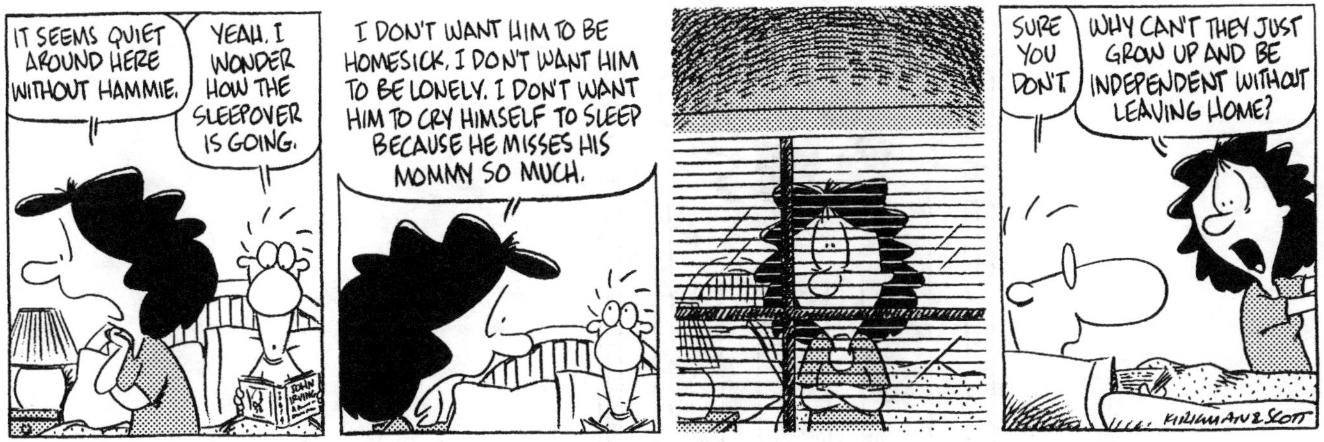
IT SEEMS QUIET AROUND HERE WITHOUT HAMMIE.
YEAH. I WONDER HOW THE SLEEPOVER IS GOING.
I DON'T WANT HIM TO BE HOMESICK. I DON'T WANT HIM TO BE LONELY. I DON'T WANT HIM TO CRY HIMSELF TO SLEEP BECAUSE HE MISSES HIS MOMMY SO MUCH.
SURE YOU DON'T.
WHY CAN'T THEY JUST GROW UP AND BE INDEPENDENT WITHOUT LEAVING HOME?
KIRKMAN & SCOTT

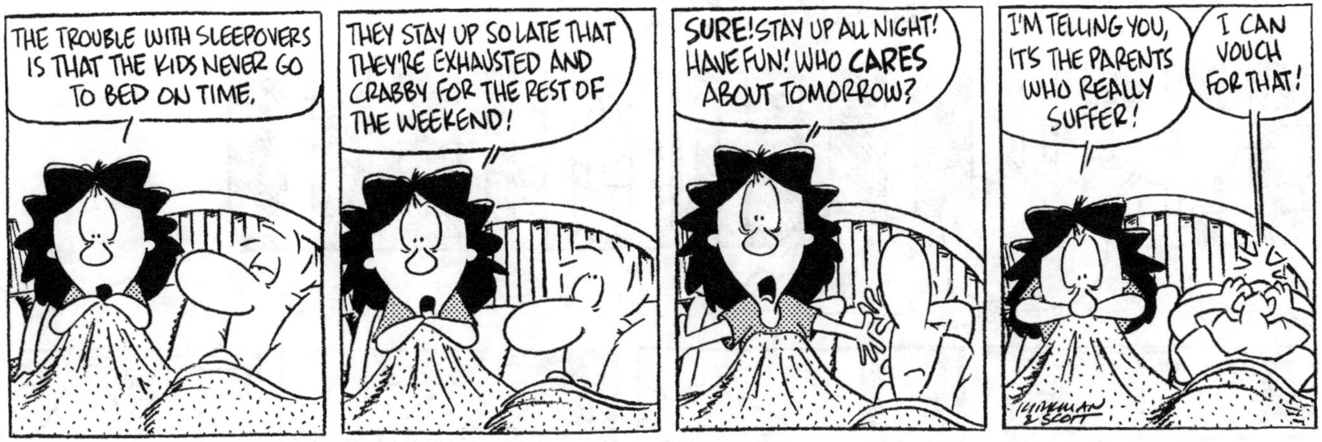
THE TROUBLE WITH SLEEPOVERS IS THAT THE KIDS NEVER GO TO BED ON TIME.
THEY STAY UP SO LATE THAT THEY'RE EXHAUSTED AND CRABBY FOR THE REST OF THE WEEKEND!
SURE! STAY UP ALL NIGHT! HAVE FUN! WHO CARES ABOUT TOMORROW?
I'M TELLING YOU, IT'S THE PARENTS WHO REALLY SUFFER!
I CAN VOUCH FOR THAT!
KIRKMAN & SCOTT

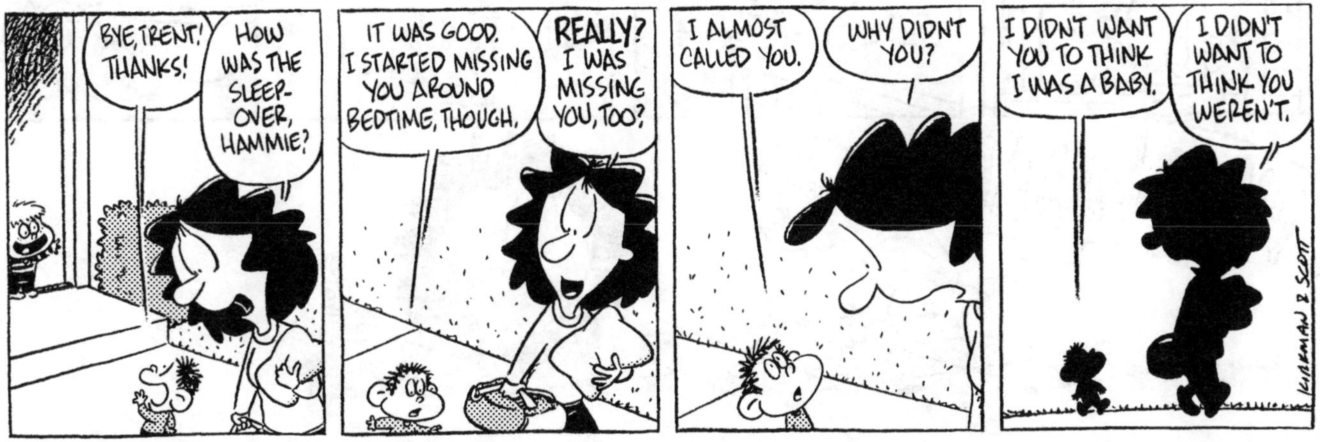
BYE, TRENT! THANKS!
HOW WAS THE SLEEP-OVER, HAMMIE?
IT WAS GOOD. I STARTED MISSING YOU AROUND BEDTIME, THOUGH.
REALLY? I WAS MISSING YOU, TOO?
I ALMOST CALLED YOU.
WHY DIDN'T YOU?
I DIDN'T WANT YOU TO THINK I WAS A BABY.
I DIDN'T WANT TO THINK YOU WEREN'T.
KIRKMAN & SCOTT

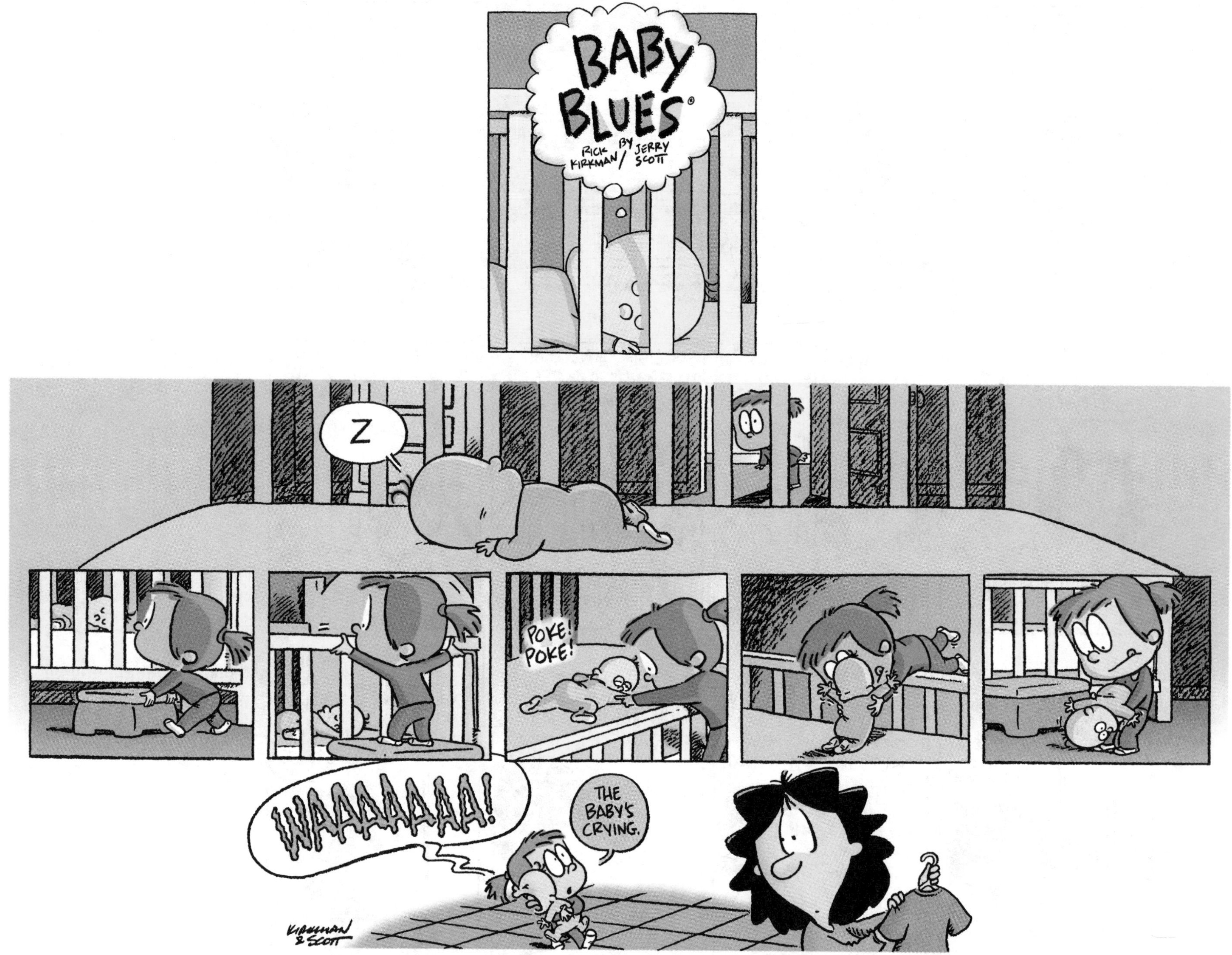
BABY BLUES®
BY RICK KIRKMAN / JERRY SCOTT
Z
POKE! POKE!
WAAAAAAA!
THE BABY'S CRYING.
KIRKMAN & SCOTT

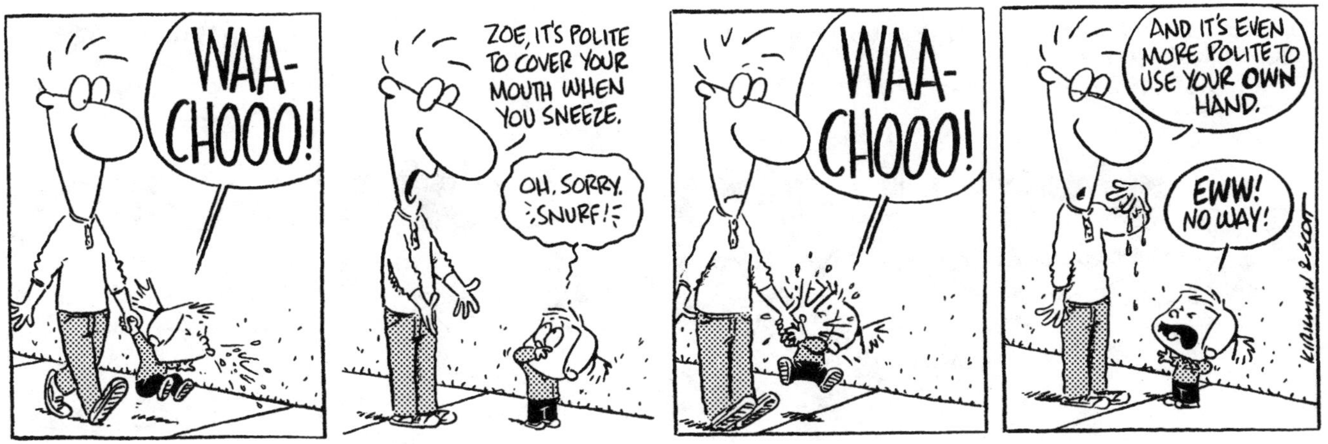
WAA-CHOOO!
ZOE, IT'S POLITE TO COVER YOUR MOUTH WHEN YOU SNEEZE.
OH. SORRY. SNURF!
WAA-CHOOO!
AND IT'S EVEN MORE POLITE TO USE YOUR **OWN** HAND.
EWW! NO WAY!
KIRKMAN & SCOTT

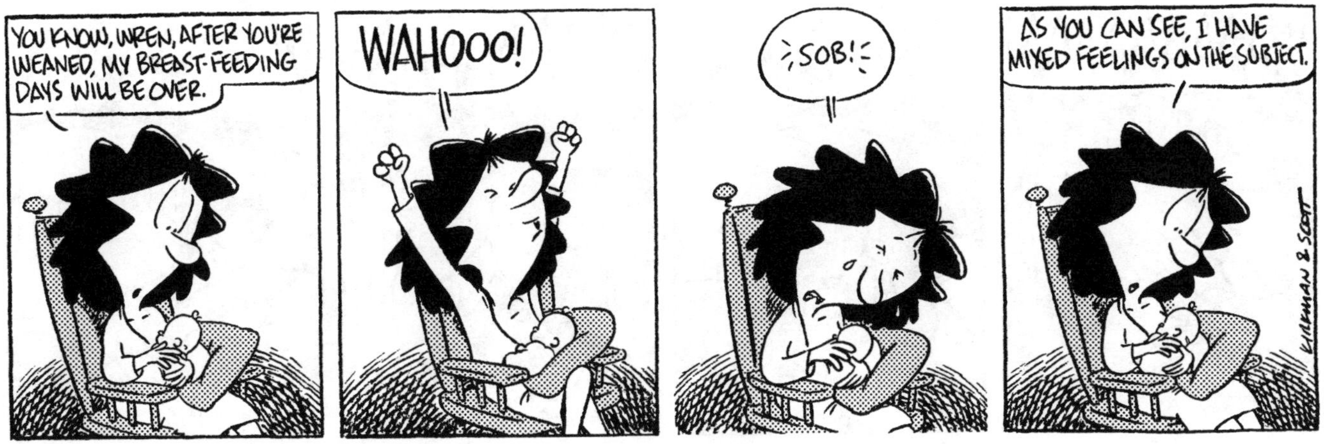
YOU KNOW, WREN, AFTER YOU'RE WEANED, MY BREAST-FEEDING DAYS WILL BE OVER.
WAHOOO!
SOB!
AS YOU CAN SEE, I HAVE MIXED FEELINGS ON THE SUBJECT.
KIRKMAN & SCOTT

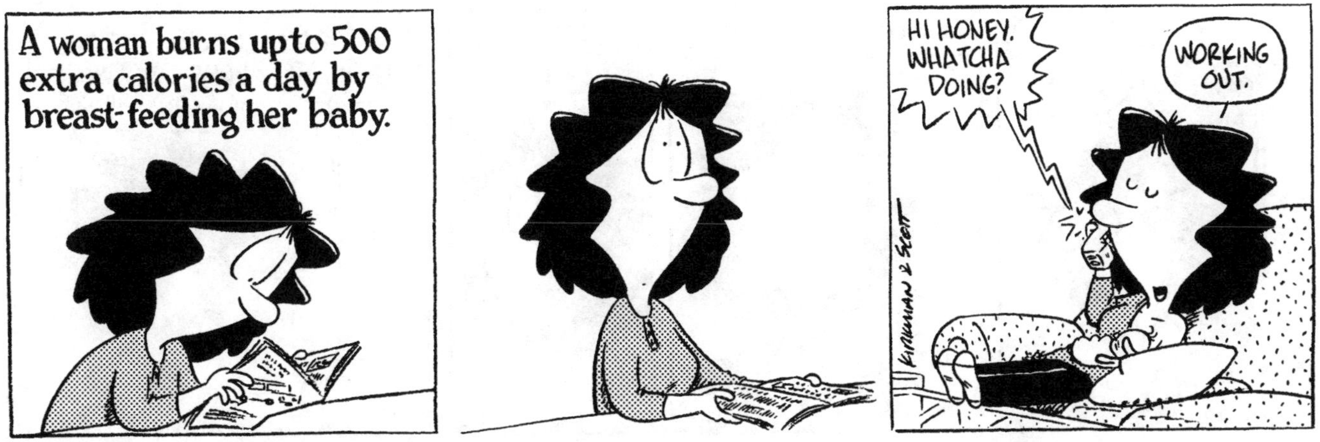
A woman burns up to 500 extra calories a day by breast-feeding her baby.
HI HONEY. WHATCHA DOING?
WORKING OUT.
KIRKMAN & SCOTT

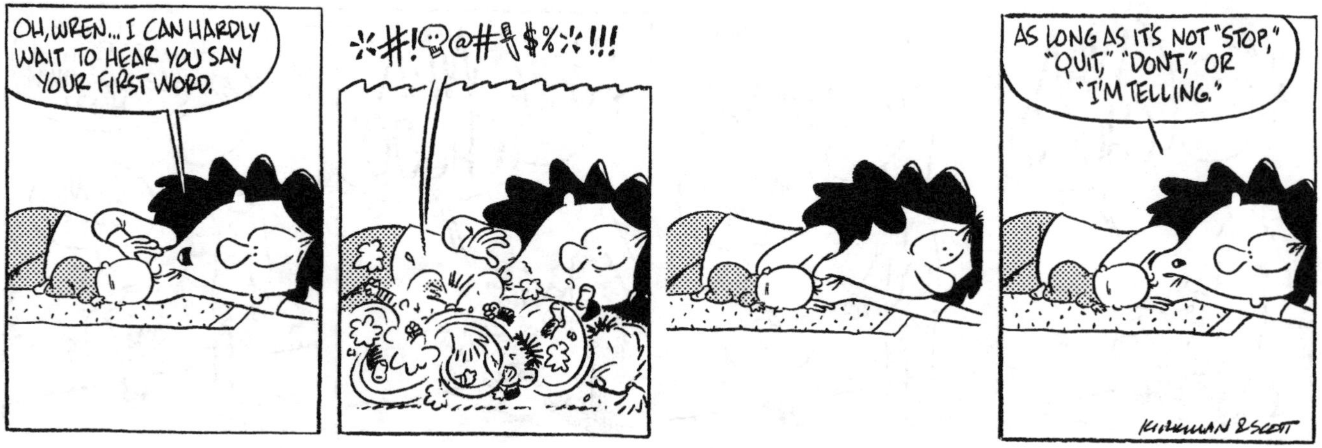
OH, WREN... I CAN HARDLY WAIT TO HEAR YOU SAY YOUR FIRST WORD.
#!@#$%!!!
AS LONG AS IT'S NOT "STOP," "QUIT," "DON'T," OR "I'M TELLING."
KIRKMAN & SCOTT

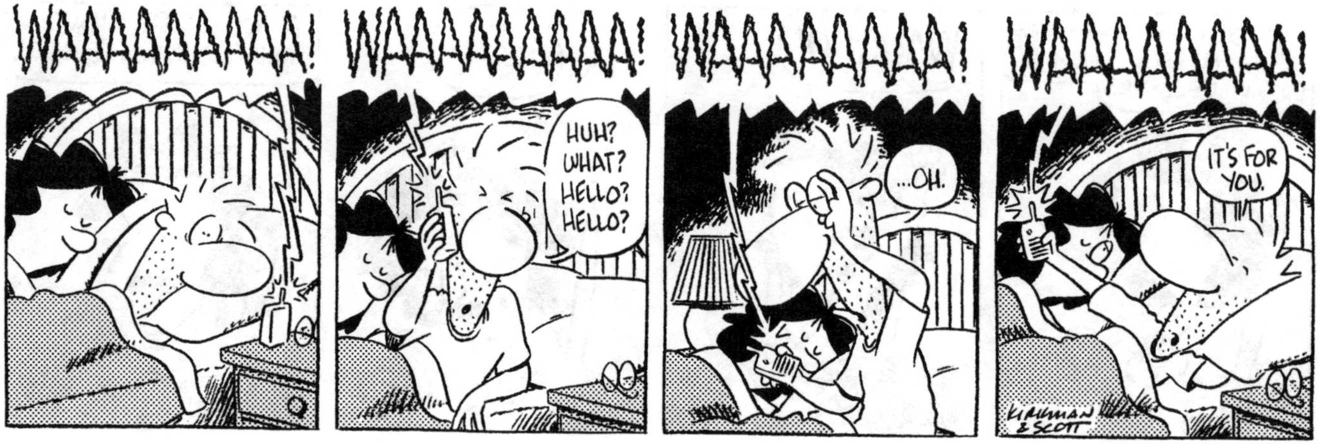
WAAAAAAAAA!
WAAAAAAAAA!
HUH? WHAT? HELLO? HELLO?
WAAAAAAAAA!
...OH.
WAAAAAAAAA!
IT'S FOR YOU.
KIRKMAN & SCOTT

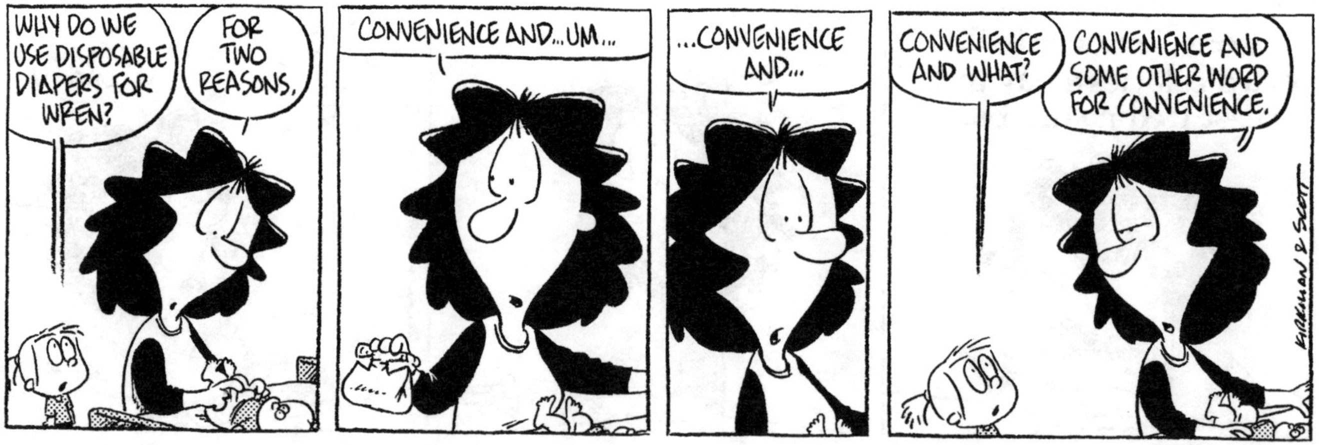
WHY DO WE USE DISPOSABLE DIAPERS FOR WREN?
FOR TWO REASONS.
CONVENIENCE AND...UM...
...CONVENIENCE AND...
CONVENIENCE AND WHAT?
CONVENIENCE AND SOME OTHER WORD FOR CONVENIENCE.
KIRKMAN & SCOTT

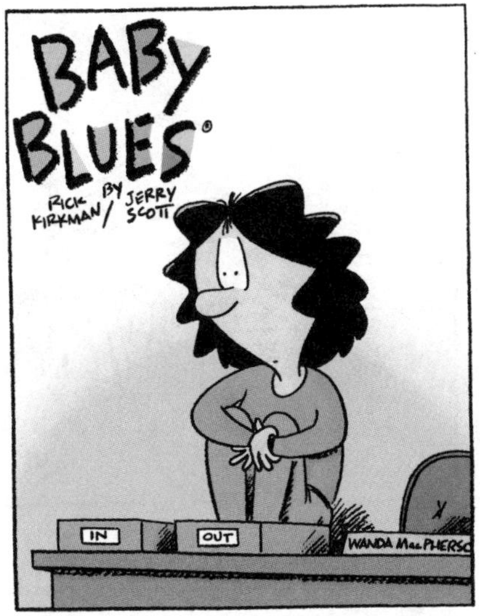
BABY BLUES®
BY RICK KIRKMAN / JERRY SCOTT
IN
OUT
WANDA MacPHERSO

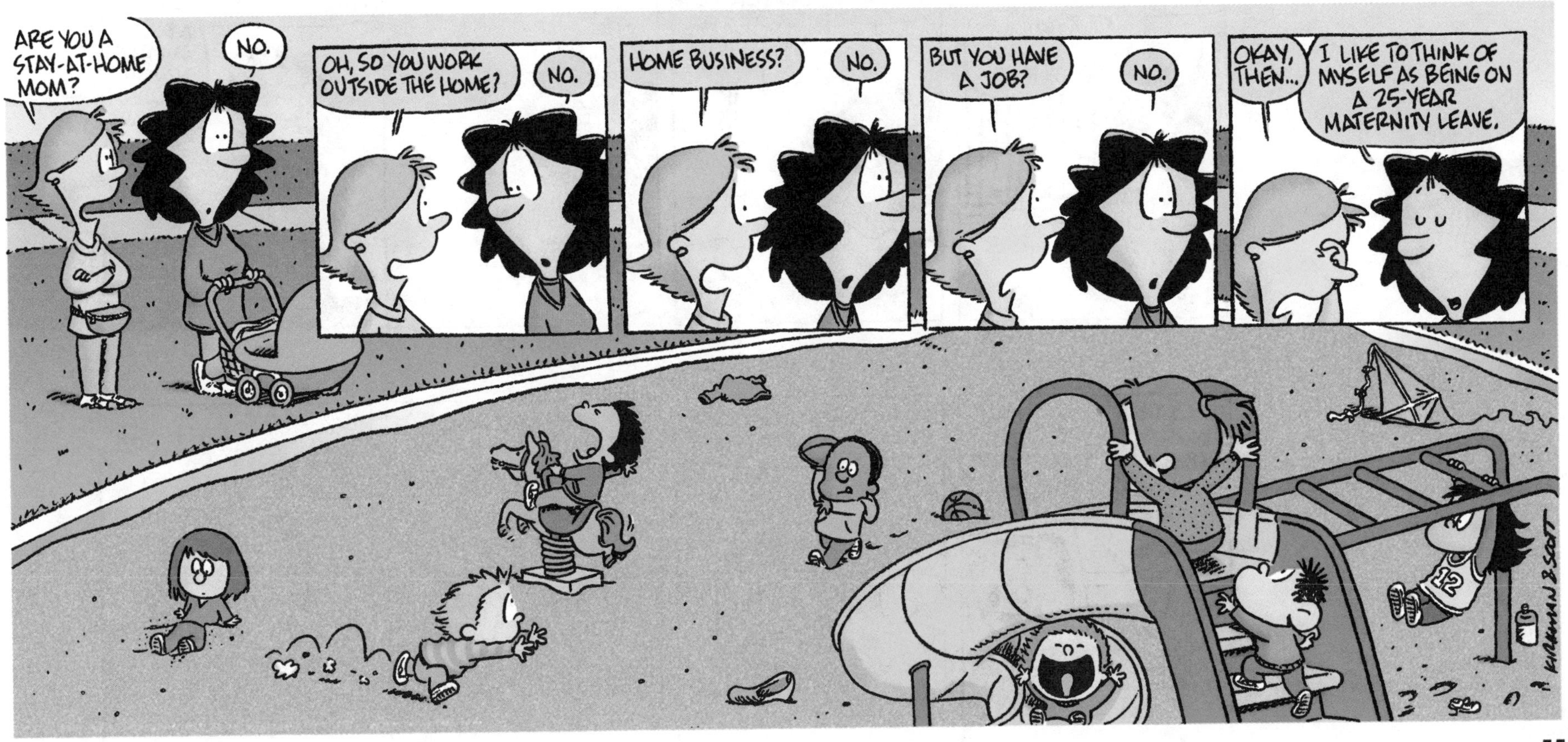
ARE YOU A STAY-AT-HOME MOM?
NO.
OH, SO YOU WORK OUTSIDE THE HOME?
NO.
HOME BUSINESS?
NO.
BUT YOU HAVE A JOB?
NO.
OKAY, THEN...
I LIKE TO THINK OF MYSELF AS BEING ON A 25-YEAR MATERNITY LEAVE.
KIRKMAN & SCOTT

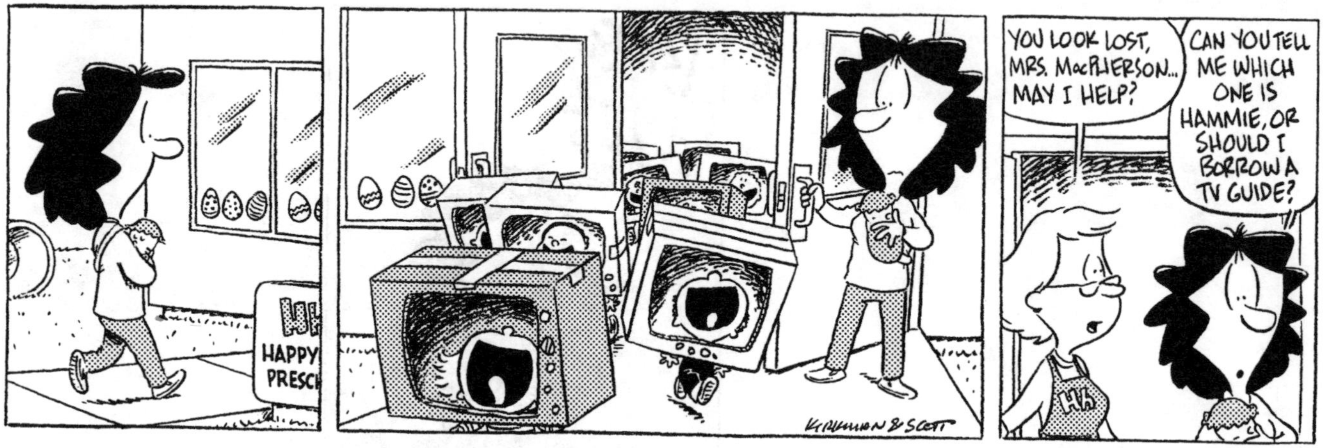
HAPPY
PRESCH
YOU LOOK LOST, MRS. MacPHERSON... MAY I HELP?
CAN YOU TELL ME WHICH ONE IS HAMMIE, OR SHOULD I BORROW A TV GUIDE?
KIRKMAN & SCOTT

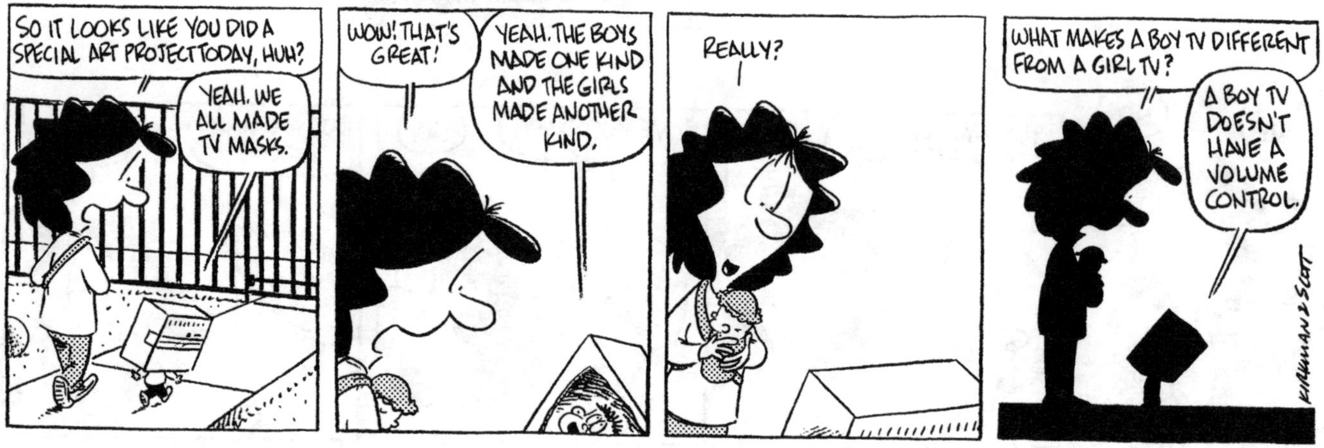
SO IT LOOKS LIKE YOU DID A SPECIAL ART PROJECT TODAY, HUH?
YEAH. WE ALL MADE TV MASKS.
WOW! THAT'S GREAT!
YEAH. THE BOYS MADE ONE KIND AND THE GIRLS MADE ANOTHER KIND.
REALLY?
WHAT MAKES A BOY TV DIFFERENT FROM A GIRL TV?
A BOY TV DOESN'T HAVE A VOLUME CONTROL.
KIRKMAN & SCOTT

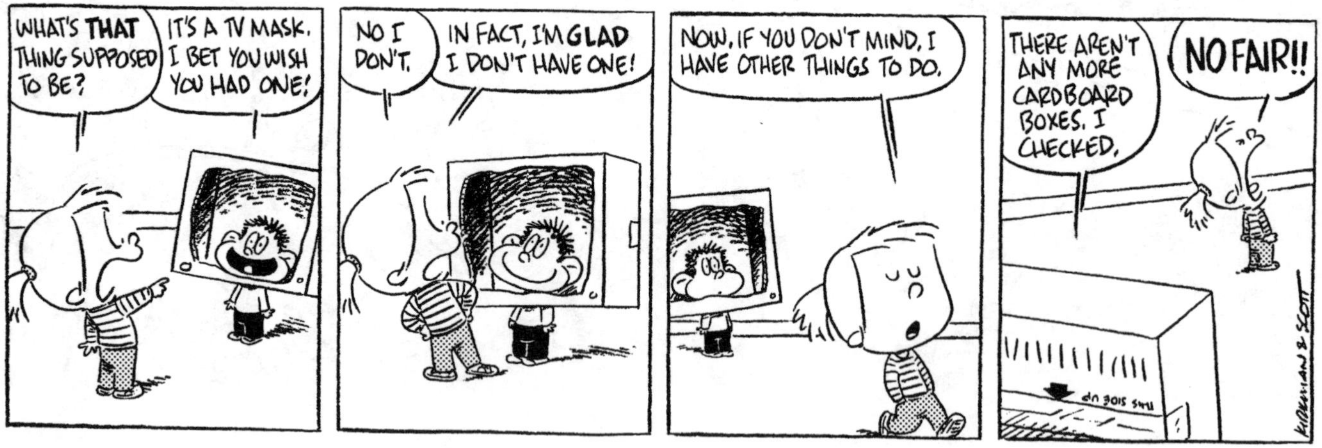
WHAT'S **THAT** THING SUPPOSED TO BE?
IT'S A TV MASK. I BET YOU WISH YOU HAD ONE!
NO I DON'T.
IN FACT, I'M **GLAD** I DON'T HAVE ONE!
NOW, IF YOU DON'T MIND, I HAVE OTHER THINGS TO DO.
THERE AREN'T ANY MORE CARDBOARD BOXES. I CHECKED.
NO FAIR!!
KIRKMAN & SCOTT

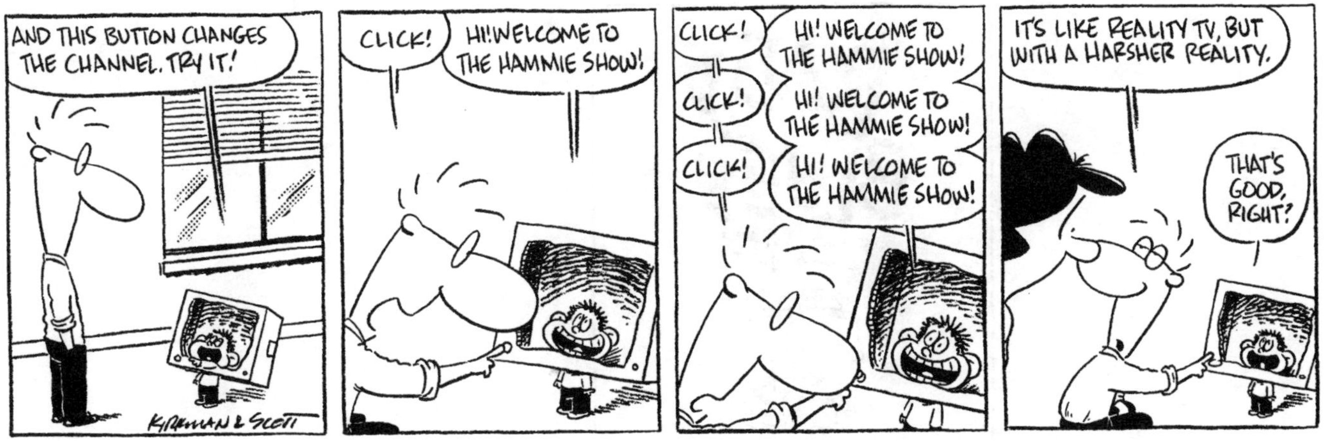
AND THIS BUTTON CHANGES THE CHANNEL. TRY IT!
KIRKMAN & SCOTT
CLICK!
HI! WELCOME TO THE HAMMIE SHOW!
CLICK!
HI! WELCOME TO THE HAMMIE SHOW!
CLICK!
HI! WELCOME TO THE HAMMIE SHOW!
CLICK!
HI! WELCOME TO THE HAMMIE SHOW!
IT'S LIKE REALITY TV, BUT WITH A HARSHER REALITY.
THAT'S GOOD, RIGHT?

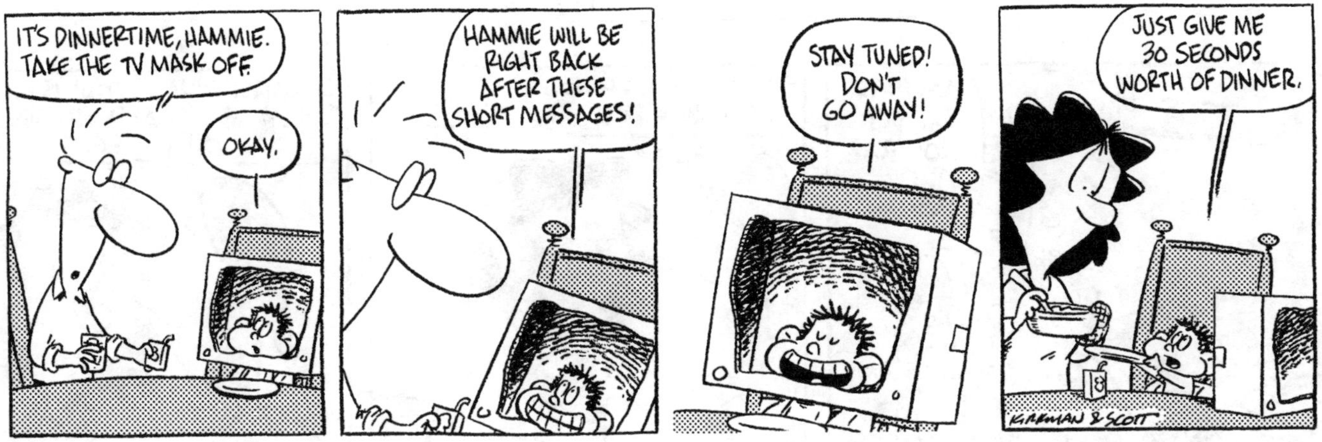
IT'S DINNERTIME, HAMMIE. TAKE THE TV MASK OFF.
OKAY.
HAMMIE WILL BE RIGHT BACK AFTER THESE SHORT MESSAGES!
STAY TUNED! DON'T GO AWAY!
JUST GIVE ME 30 SECONDS WORTH OF DINNER.
KIRKMAN & SCOTT

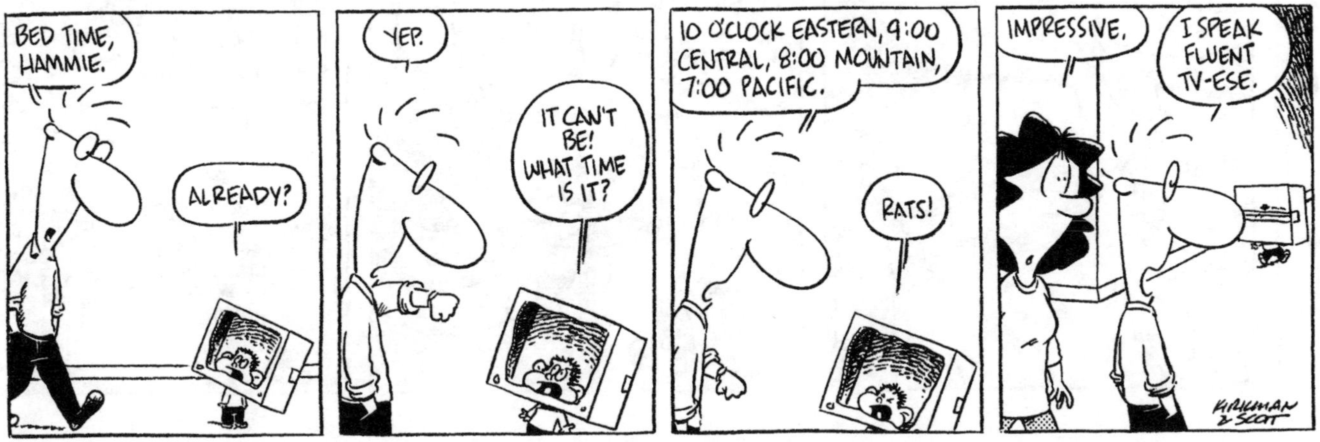
BED TIME, HAMMIE.
ALREADY?
YEP.
IT CAN'T BE! WHAT TIME IS IT?
10 O'CLOCK EASTERN, 9:00 CENTRAL, 8:00 MOUNTAIN, 7:00 PACIFIC.
RATS!
IMPRESSIVE.
I SPEAK FLUENT TV-ESE.
KIRKMAN & SCOTT

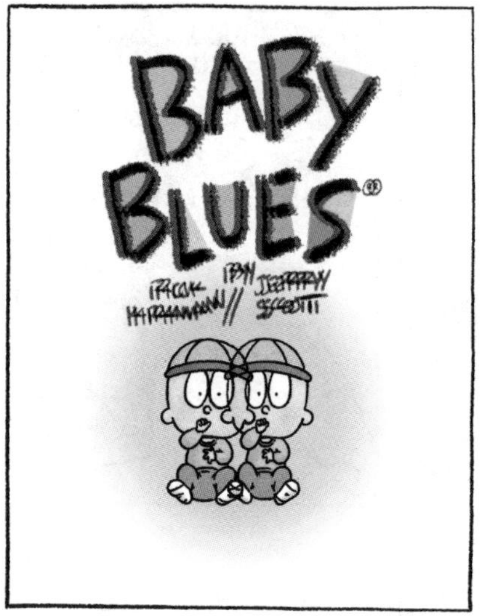
BABY BLUES®

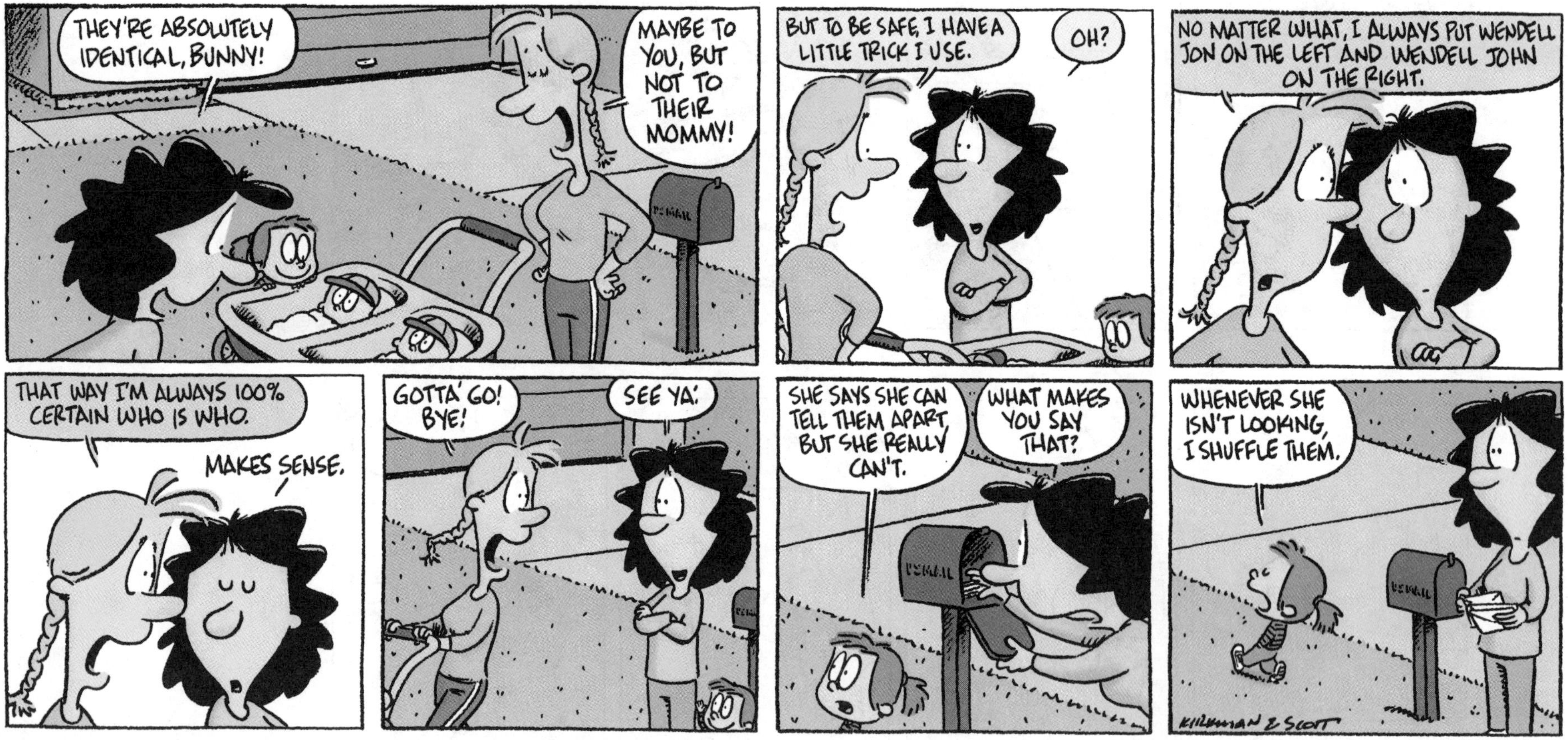
THEY'RE ABSOLUTELY IDENTICAL, BUNNY!
MAYBE TO YOU, BUT NOT TO THEIR MOMMY!
BUT TO BE SAFE, I HAVE A LITTLE TRICK I USE.
OH?
NO MATTER WHAT, I ALWAYS PUT WENDELL JON ON THE LEFT AND WENDELL JOHN ON THE RIGHT.
THAT WAY I'M ALWAYS 100% CERTAIN WHO IS WHO.
MAKES SENSE.
GOTTA' GO! BYE!
SEE YA!
SHE SAYS SHE CAN TELL THEM APART, BUT SHE REALLY CAN'T.
WHAT MAKES YOU SAY THAT?
WHENEVER SHE ISN'T LOOKING, I SHUFFLE THEM.
KIRKMAN & SCOTT

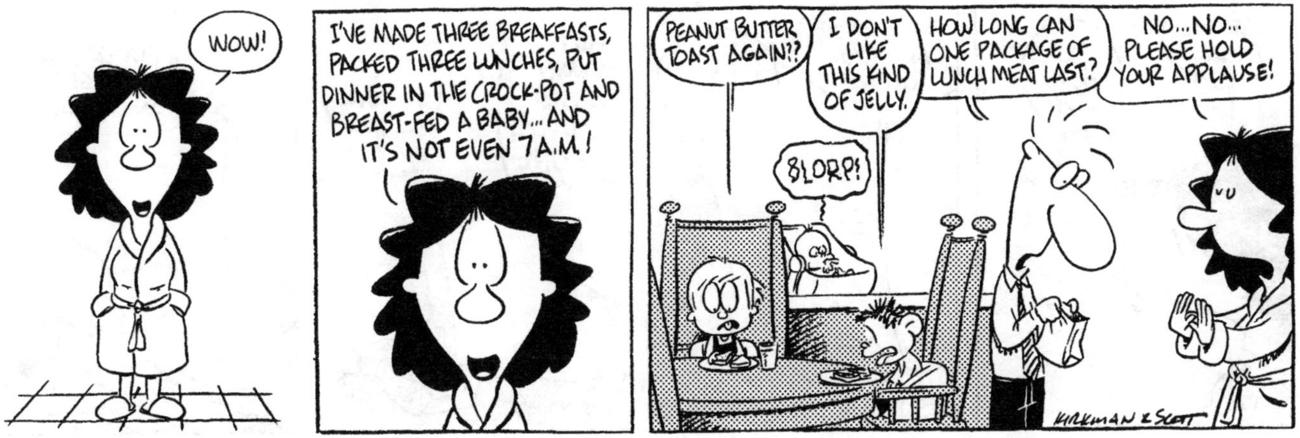
WOW!
I'VE MADE THREE BREAKFASTS, PACKED THREE LUNCHES, PUT DINNER IN THE CROCK-POT AND BREAST-FED A BABY... AND IT'S NOT EVEN 7 A.M.!
PEANUT BUTTER TOAST AGAIN!?
I DON'T LIKE THIS KIND OF JELLY.
BLORP!
HOW LONG CAN ONE PACKAGE OF LUNCH MEAT LAST?
NO...NO... PLEASE HOLD YOUR APPLAUSE!
KIRKMAN & SCOTT

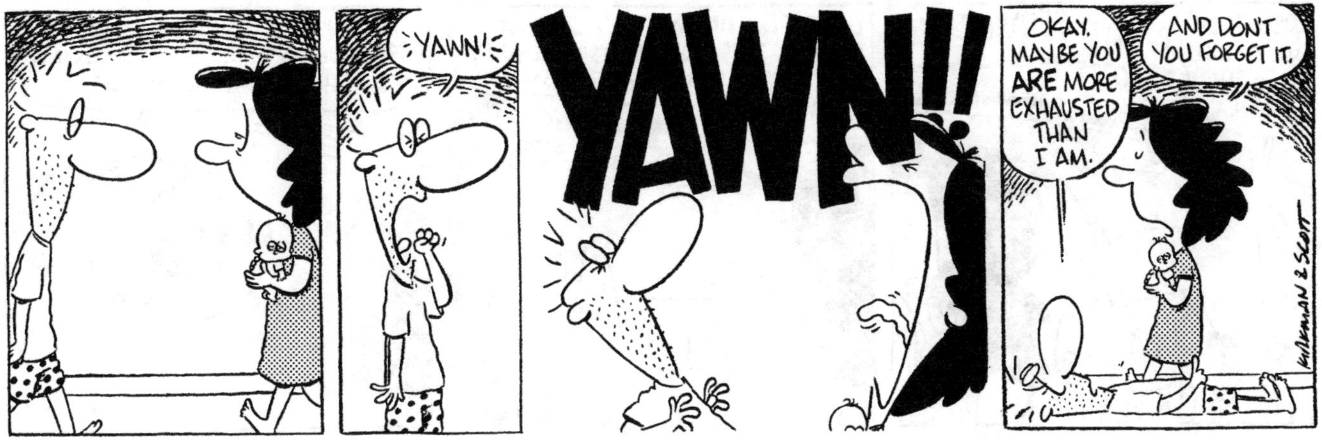
YAWN!
YAWN!!
OKAY. MAYBE YOU ARE MORE EXHAUSTED THAN I AM.
AND DON'T YOU FORGET IT.
KIRKMAN & SCOTT

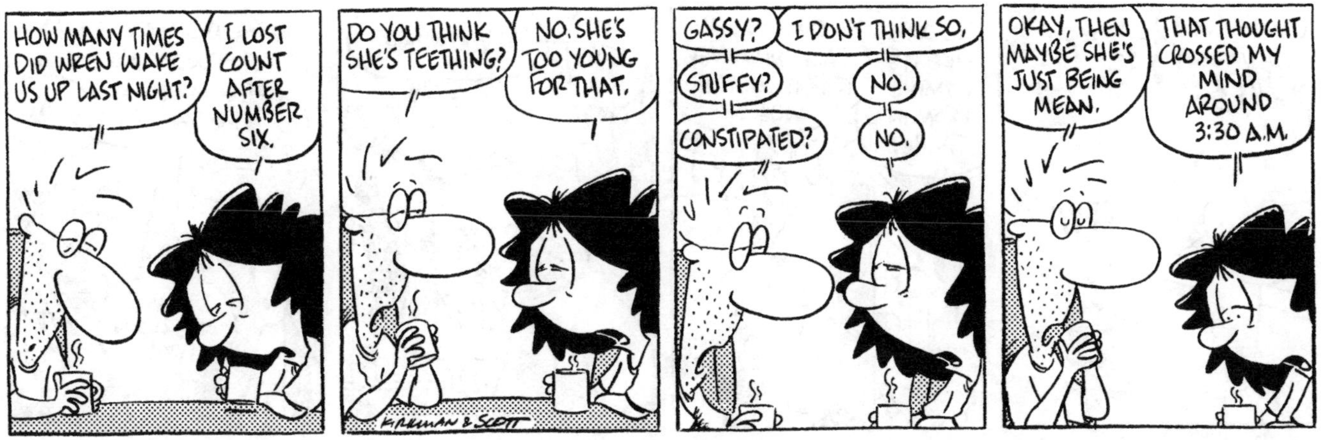
HOW MANY TIMES DID WREN WAKE US UP LAST NIGHT?
I LOST COUNT AFTER NUMBER SIX.
DO YOU THINK SHE'S TEETHING?
NO. SHE'S TOO YOUNG FOR THAT.
KIRKMAN & SCOTT
GASSY?
I DON'T THINK SO.
STUFFY?
NO.
CONSTIPATED?
NO.
OKAY, THEN MAYBE SHE'S JUST BEING MEAN.
THAT THOUGHT CROSSED MY MIND AROUND 3:30 A.M.

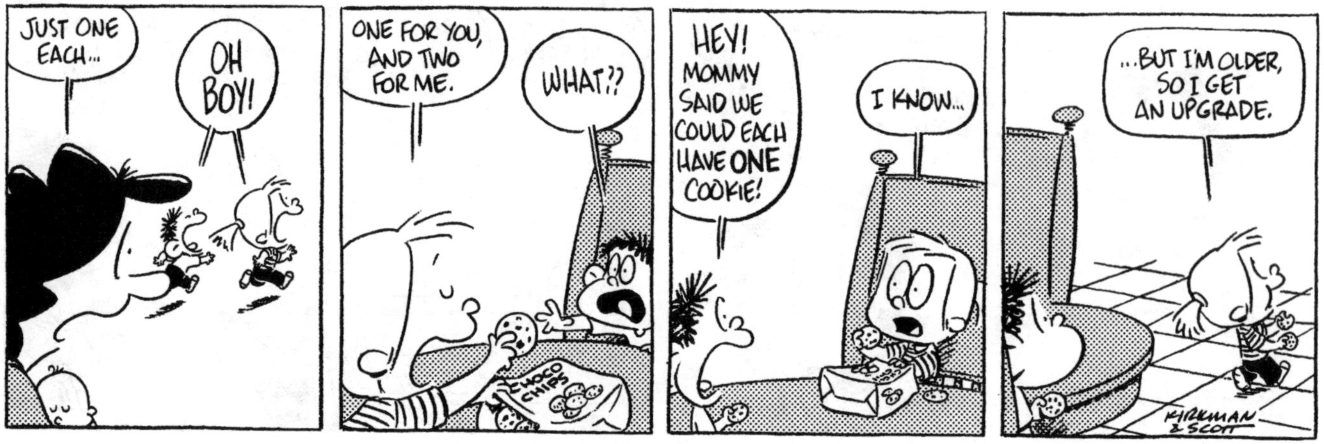
JUST ONE EACH...
OH BOY!
ONE FOR YOU, AND TWO FOR ME.
WHAT??
CHOCO CHIPS
HEY! MOMMY SAID WE COULD EACH HAVE ONE COOKIE!
I KNOW...
...BUT I'M OLDER, SO I GET AN UPGRADE.
KIRKMAN & SCOTT

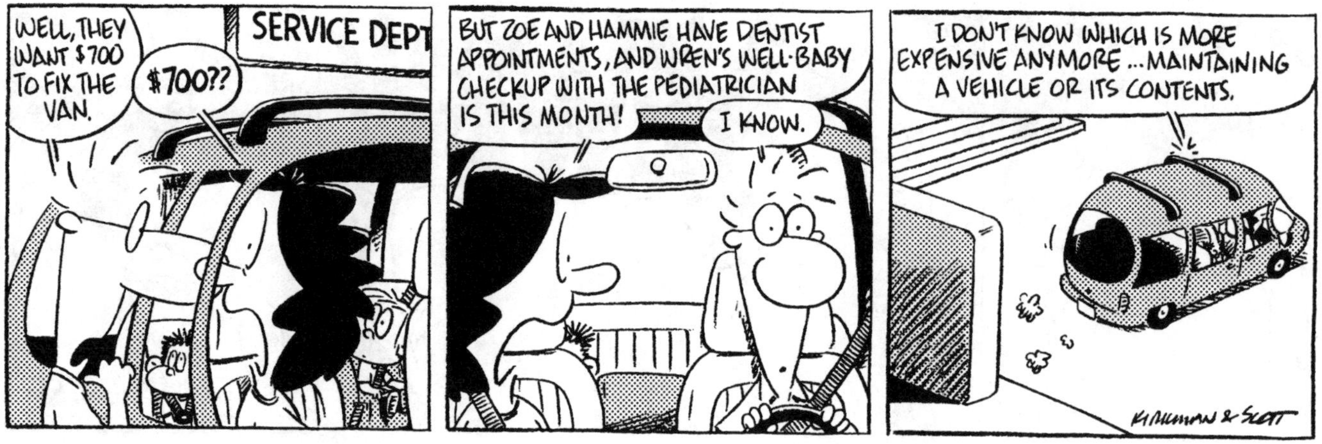
SERVICE DEPT
WELL, THEY WANT $700 TO FIX THE VAN.
$700??
BUT ZOE AND HAMMIE HAVE DENTIST APPOINTMENTS, AND WREN'S WELL-BABY CHECKUP WITH THE PEDIATRICIAN IS THIS MONTH!
I KNOW.
I DON'T KNOW WHICH IS MORE EXPENSIVE ANYMORE ... MAINTAINING A VEHICLE OR ITS CONTENTS.
KIRKMAN & SCOTT

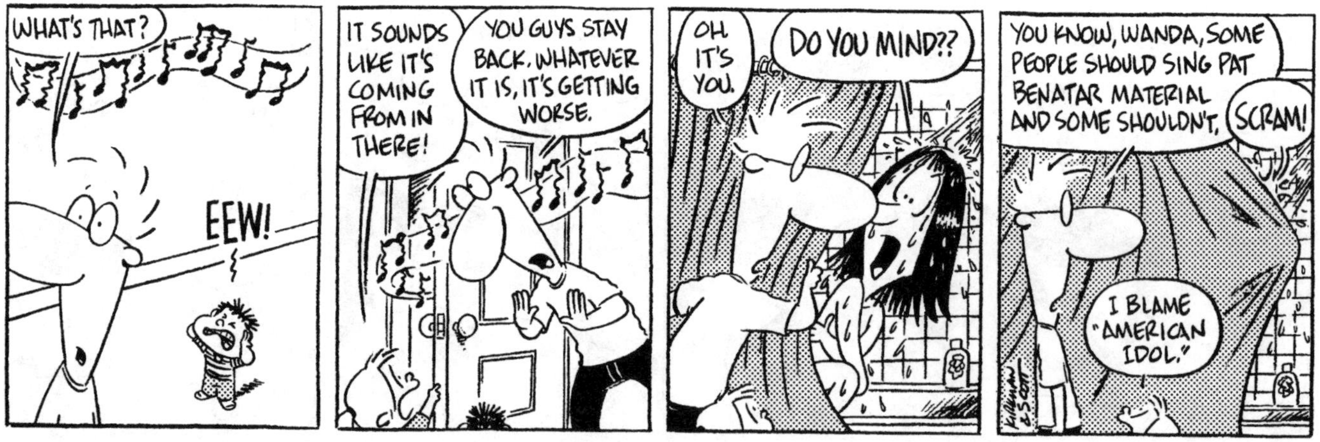
WHAT'S THAT?
EEW!
IT SOUNDS LIKE IT'S COMING FROM IN THERE!
YOU GUYS STAY BACK. WHATEVER IT IS, IT'S GETTING WORSE.
OH. IT'S YOU.
DO YOU MIND??
YOU KNOW, WANDA, SOME PEOPLE SHOULD SING PAT BENATAR MATERIAL AND SOME SHOULDN'T.
SCRAM!
I BLAME "AMERICAN IDOL."

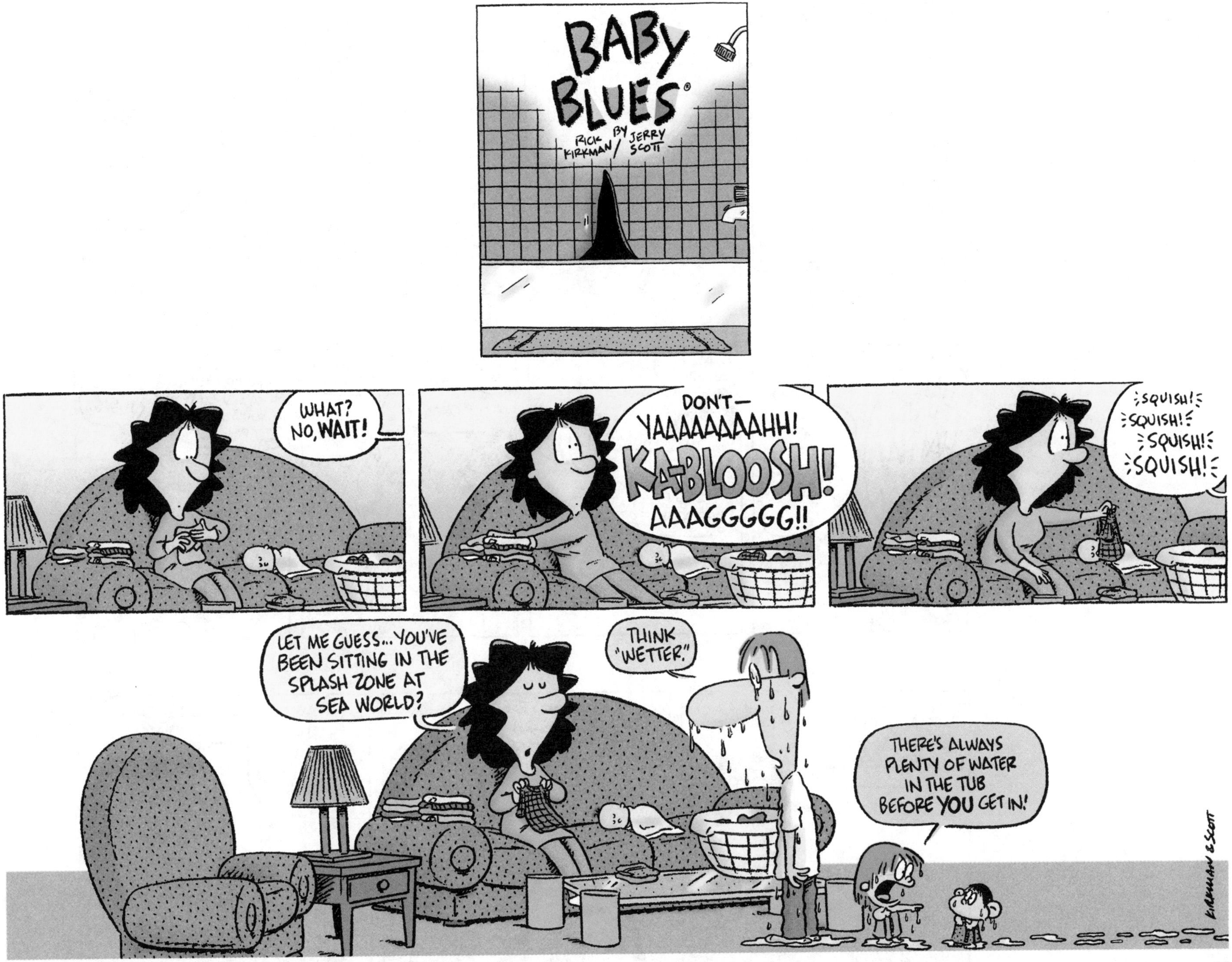

BABY BLUES®
BY RICK KIRKMAN / JERRY SCOTT
WHAT? NO, WAIT!
DON'T— YAAAAAAAAHH!
KA-BLOOSH!
AAAGGGGG!!
SQUISH! SQUISH! SQUISH! SQUISH!
LET ME GUESS... YOU'VE BEEN SITTING IN THE SPLASH ZONE AT SEA WORLD?
THINK "WETTER."
THERE'S ALWAYS PLENTY OF WATER IN THE TUB BEFORE YOU GET IN!
KIRKMAN & SCOTT

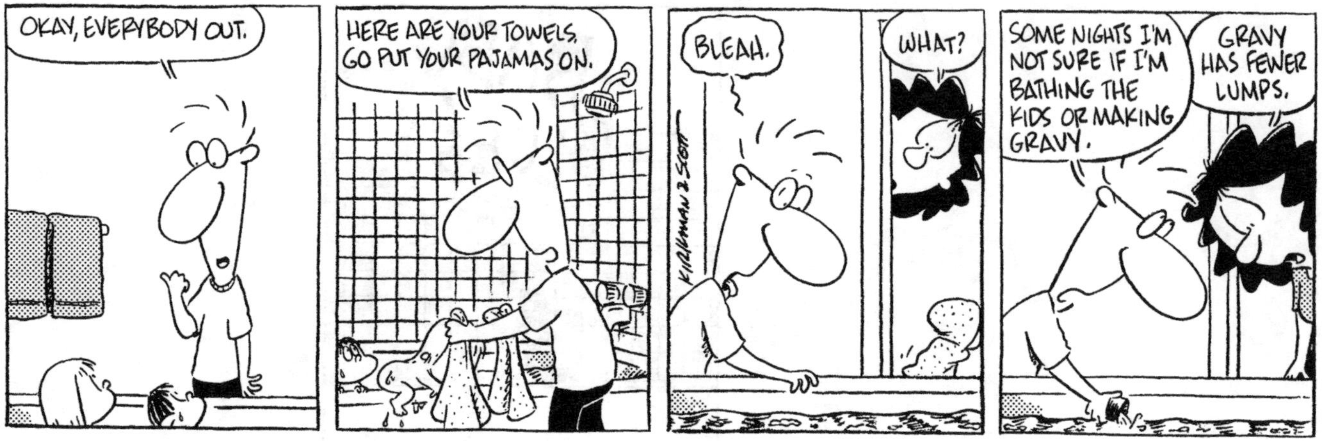
OKAY, EVERYBODY OUT.
HERE ARE YOUR TOWELS. GO PUT YOUR PAJAMAS ON.
BLEAH.
WHAT?
SOME NIGHTS I'M NOT SURE IF I'M BATHING THE KIDS OR MAKING GRAVY.
GRAVY HAS FEWER LUMPS.

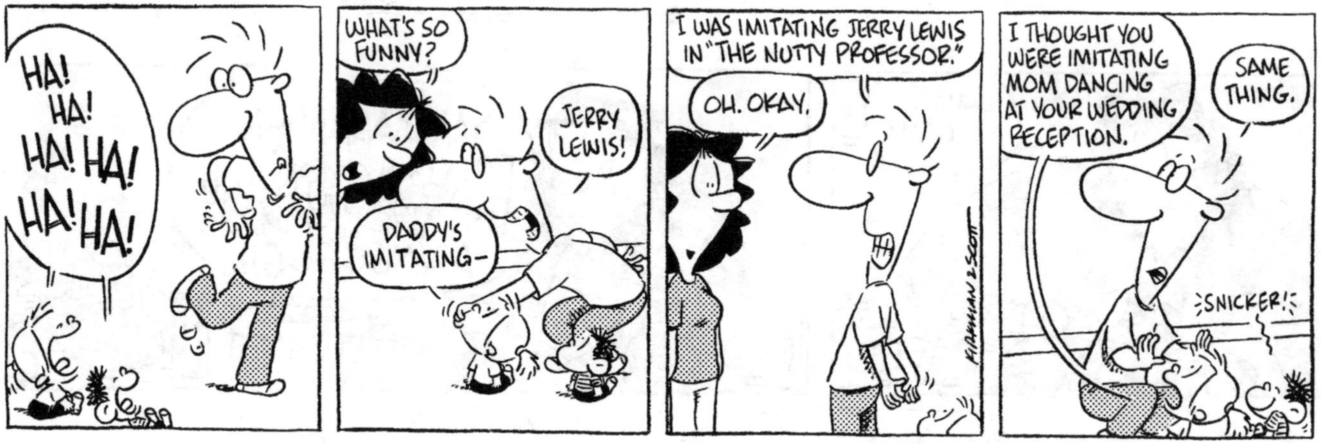
HA! HA! HA! HA! HA! HA!
WHAT'S SO FUNNY?
JERRY LEWIS!
DADDY'S IMITATING—
I WAS IMITATING JERRY LEWIS IN "THE NUTTY PROFESSOR."
OH. OKAY.
I THOUGHT YOU WERE IMITATING MOM DANCING AT YOUR WEDDING RECEPTION.
SAME THING.
SNICKER!

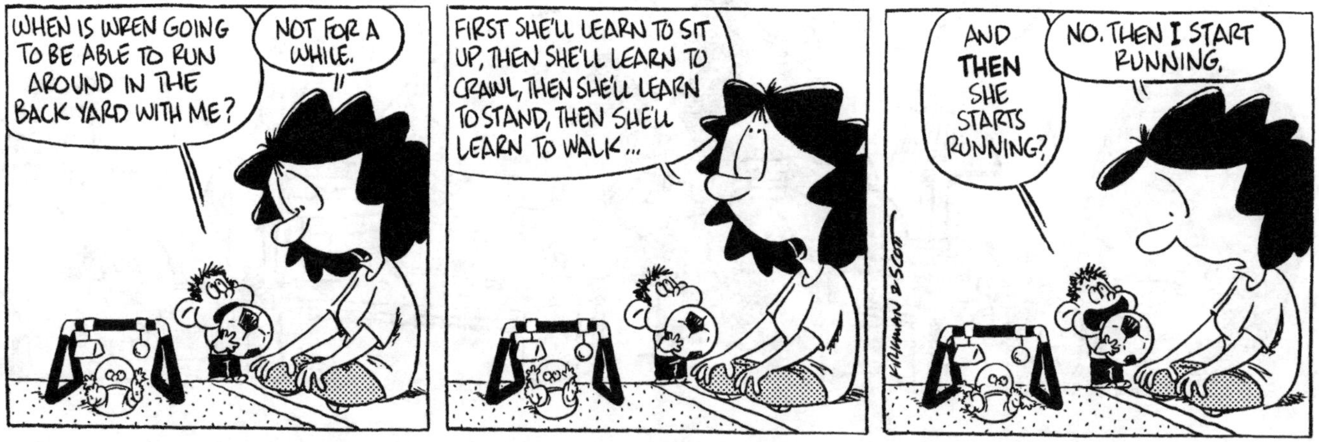
WHEN IS WREN GOING TO BE ABLE TO RUN AROUND IN THE BACK YARD WITH ME?
NOT FOR A WHILE.
FIRST SHE'LL LEARN TO SIT UP, THEN SHE'LL LEARN TO CRAWL, THEN SHE'LL LEARN TO STAND, THEN SHE'LL LEARN TO WALK...
AND THEN SHE STARTS RUNNING?
NO. THEN I START RUNNING.

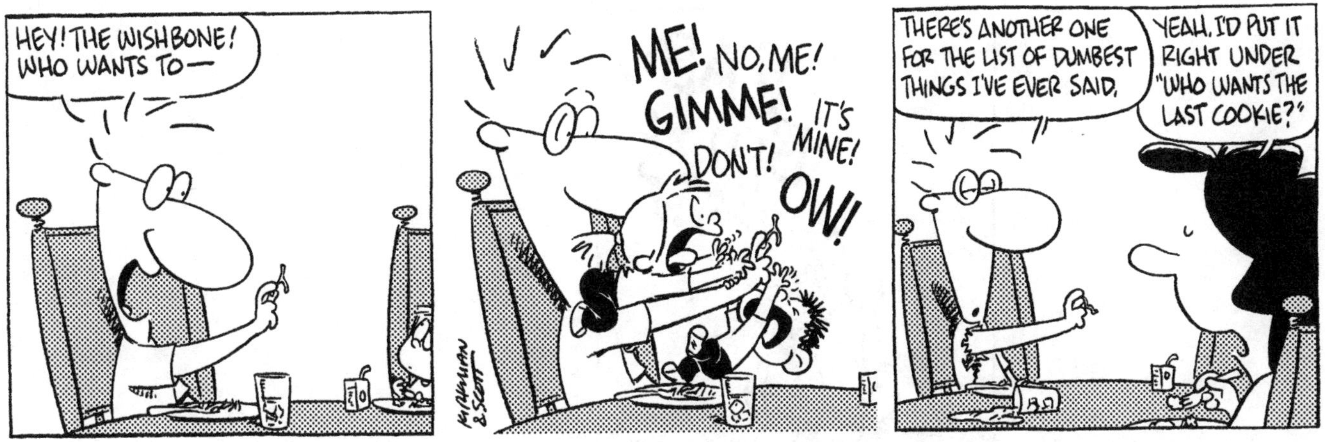
HEY! THE WISHBONE! WHO WANTS TO—
ME! NO, ME!
GIMME!
IT'S MINE!
DON'T!
OW!
KIRKMAN & SCOTT
THERE'S ANOTHER ONE FOR THE LIST OF DUMBEST THINGS I'VE EVER SAID.
YEAH. I'D PUT IT RIGHT UNDER "WHO WANTS THE LAST COOKIE?"

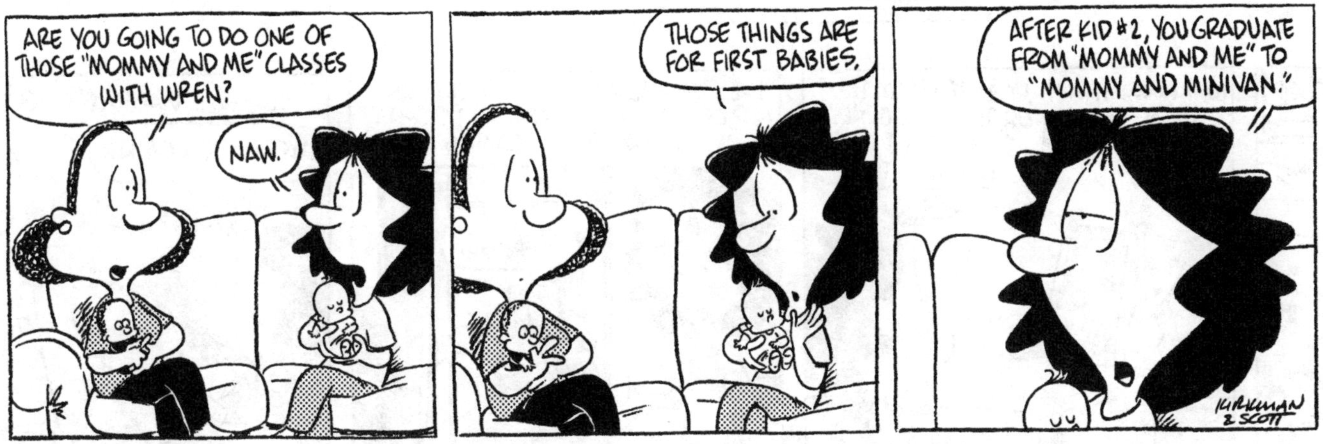
ARE YOU GOING TO DO ONE OF THOSE "MOMMY AND ME" CLASSES WITH WREN?
NAW.
THOSE THINGS ARE FOR FIRST BABIES.
AFTER KID #2, YOU GRADUATE FROM "MOMMY AND ME" TO "MOMMY AND MINIVAN."
KIRKMAN & SCOTT

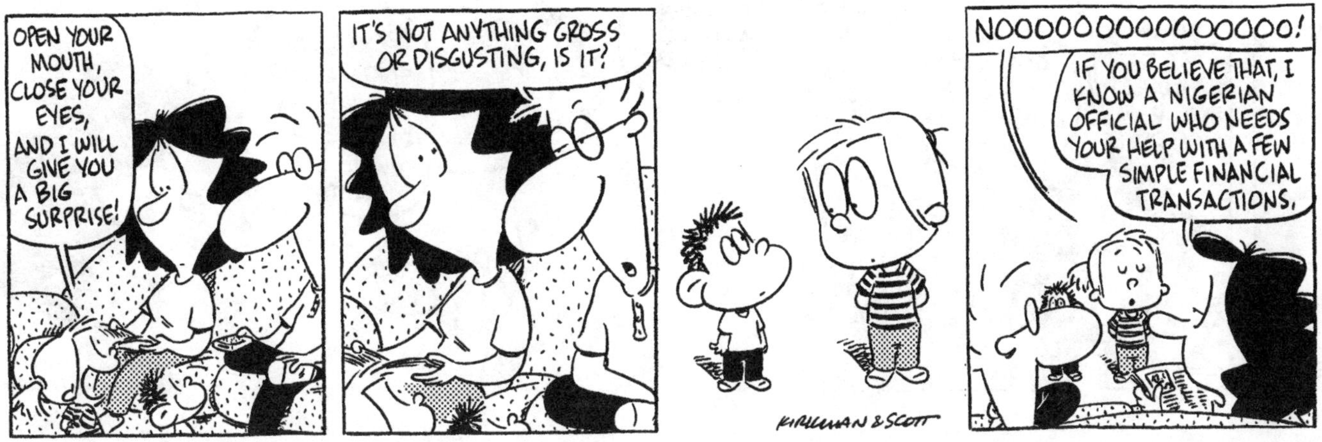
OPEN YOUR MOUTH, CLOSE YOUR EYES, AND I WILL GIVE YOU A BIG SURPRISE!
IT'S NOT ANYTHING GROSS OR DISGUSTING, IS IT?
KIRKMAN & SCOTT
NOOOOOOOOOOOOOOO!
IF YOU BELIEVE THAT, I KNOW A NIGERIAN OFFICIAL WHO NEEDS YOUR HELP WITH A FEW SIMPLE FINANCIAL TRANSACTIONS.

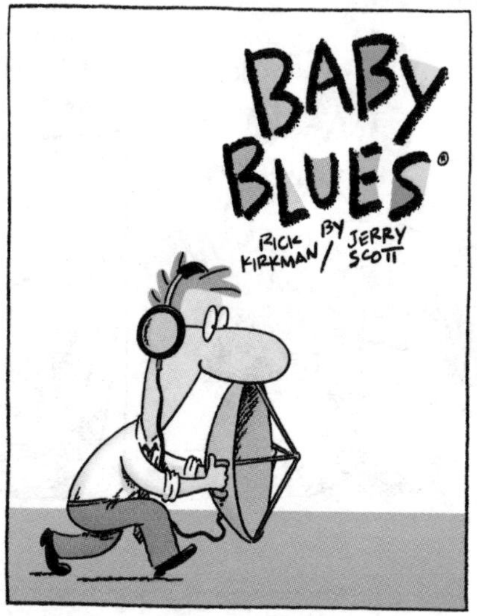
BABY BLUES®
BY RICK KIRKMAN / JERRY SCOTT

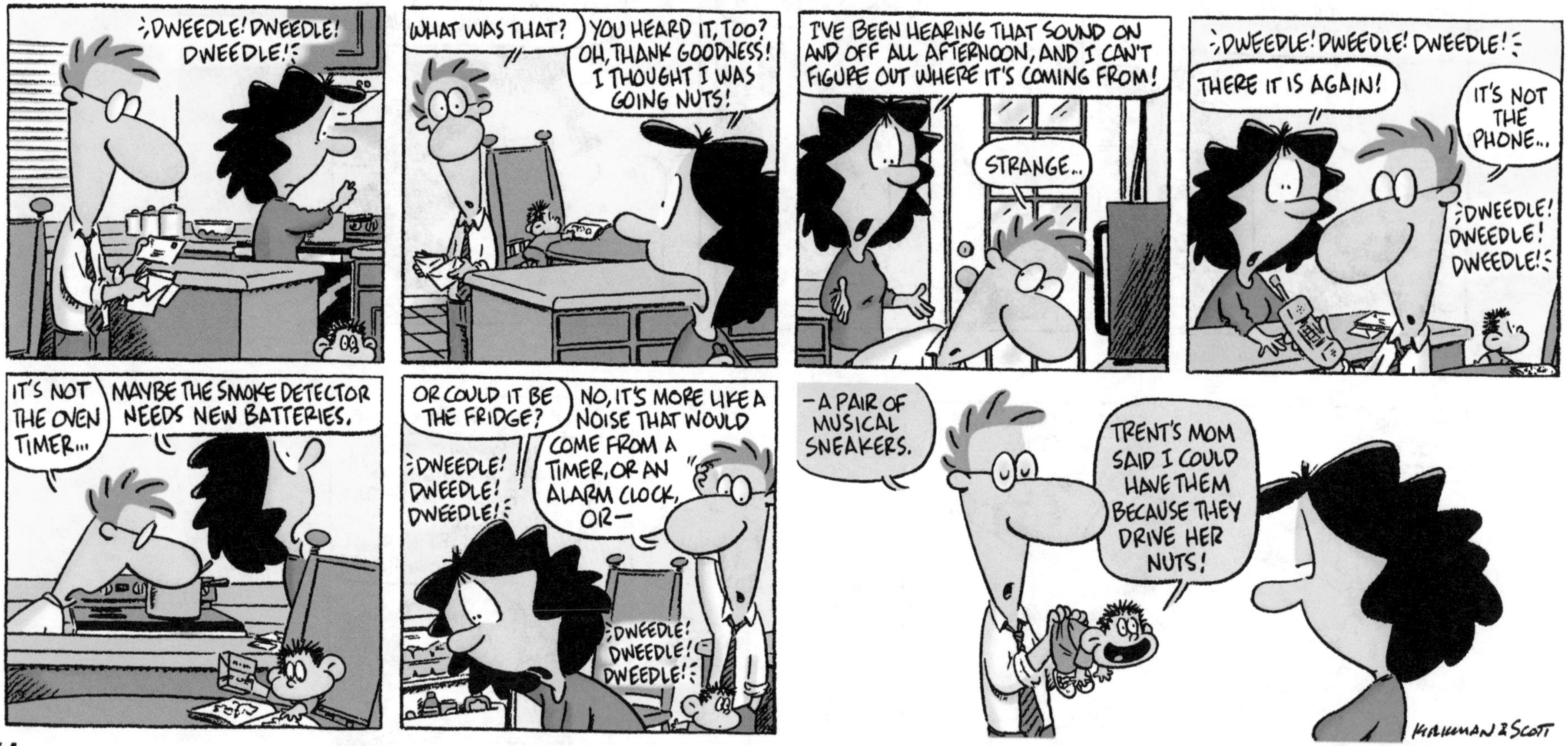
DWEEDLE! DWEEDLE! DWEEDLE!
WHAT WAS THAT?
YOU HEARD IT, TOO? OH, THANK GOODNESS! I THOUGHT I WAS GOING NUTS!
I'VE BEEN HEARING THAT SOUND ON AND OFF ALL AFTERNOON, AND I CAN'T FIGURE OUT WHERE IT'S COMING FROM!
STRANGE...
DWEEDLE! DWEEDLE! DWEEDLE!
THERE IT IS AGAIN!
IT'S NOT THE PHONE...
DWEEDLE! DWEEDLE! DWEEDLE!
IT'S NOT THE OVEN TIMER...
MAYBE THE SMOKE DETECTOR NEEDS NEW BATTERIES.
OR COULD IT BE THE FRIDGE?
NO, IT'S MORE LIKE A NOISE THAT WOULD COME FROM A TIMER, OR AN ALARM CLOCK, OR—
DWEEDLE! DWEEDLE! DWEEDLE!
DWEEDLE! DWEEDLE! DWEEDLE!
—A PAIR OF MUSICAL SNEAKERS.
TRENT'S MOM SAID I COULD HAVE THEM BECAUSE THEY DRIVE HER NUTS!
KIRKMAN & SCOTT

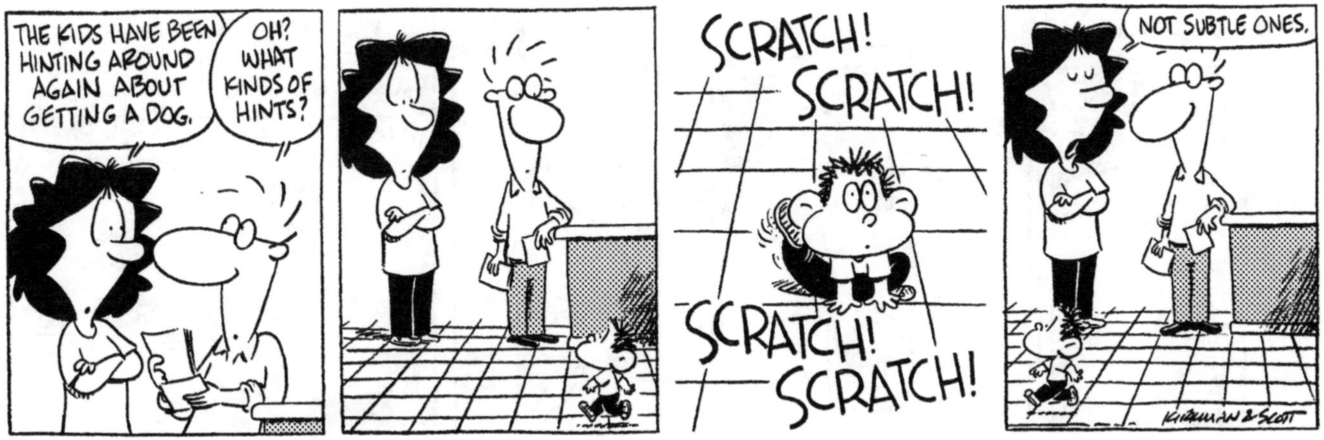
THE KIDS HAVE BEEN HINTING AROUND AGAIN ABOUT GETTING A DOG.
OH? WHAT KINDS OF HINTS?
SCRATCH! SCRATCH!
SCRATCH! SCRATCH!
NOT SUBTLE ONES.
KIRKMAN & SCOTT

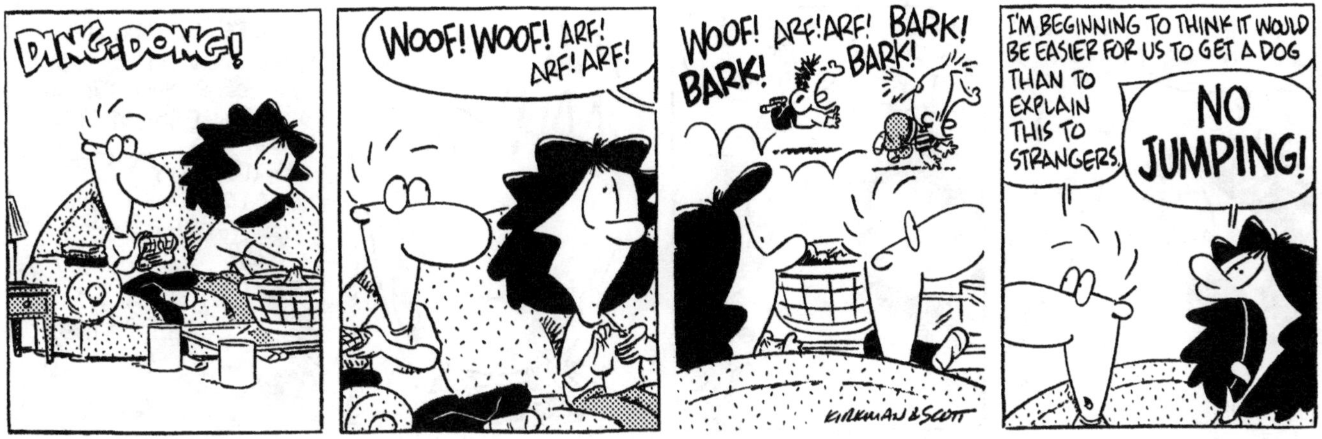
DING-DONG!
WOOF! WOOF! ARF! ARF! ARF!
WOOF! ARF! ARF! BARK!
BARK! BARK!
KIRKMAN & SCOTT
I'M BEGINNING TO THINK IT WOULD BE EASIER FOR US TO GET A DOG THAN TO EXPLAIN THIS TO STRANGERS.
NO JUMPING!

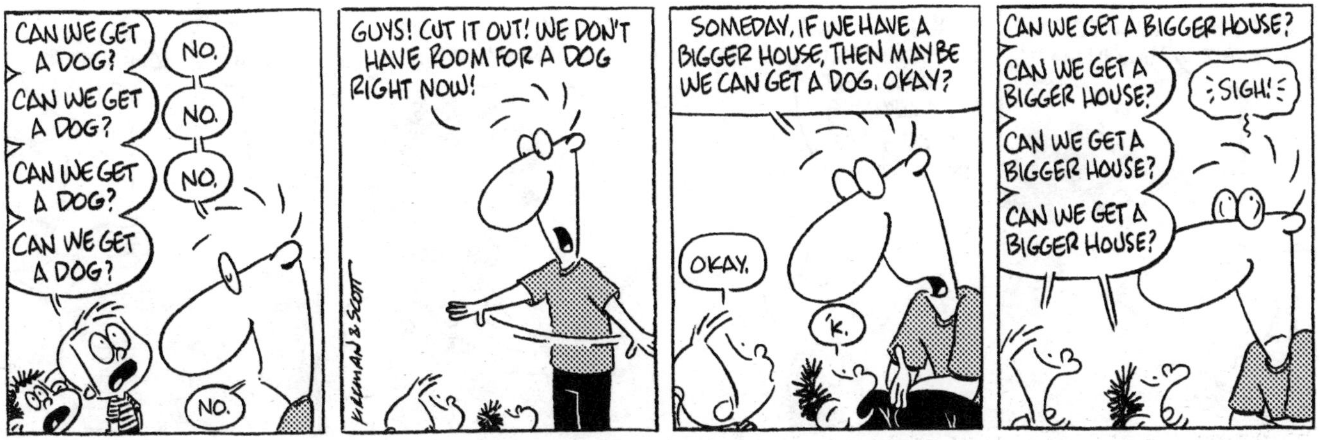
CAN WE GET A DOG?
NO.
CAN WE GET A DOG?
NO.
CAN WE GET A DOG?
NO.
CAN WE GET A DOG?
NO.
GUYS! CUT IT OUT! WE DON'T HAVE ROOM FOR A DOG RIGHT NOW!
KIRKMAN & SCOTT
SOMEDAY, IF WE HAVE A BIGGER HOUSE, THEN MAYBE WE CAN GET A DOG. OKAY?
OKAY.
'K.
CAN WE GET A BIGGER HOUSE?
CAN WE GET A BIGGER HOUSE?
SIGH!
CAN WE GET A BIGGER HOUSE?
CAN WE GET A BIGGER HOUSE?

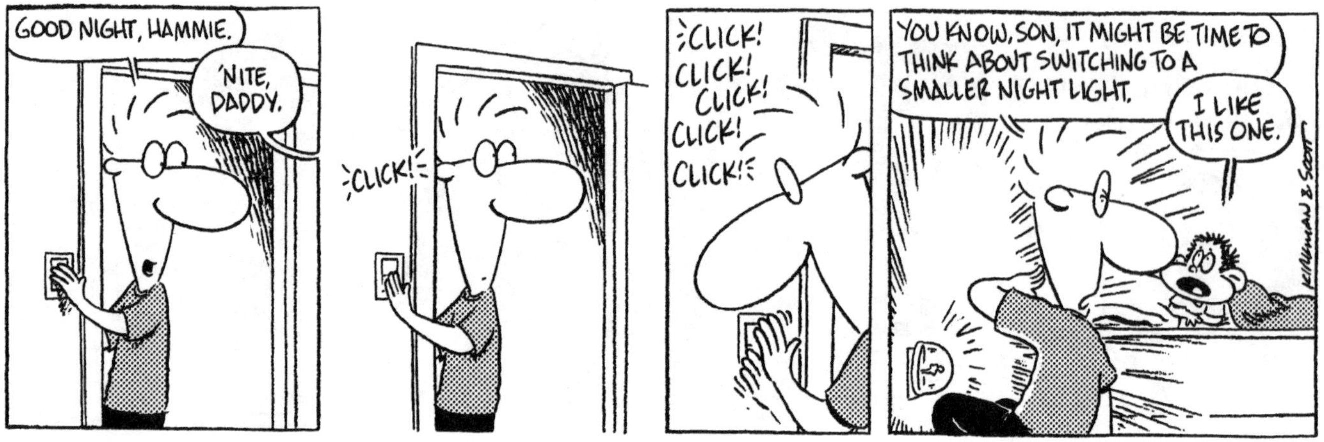
GOOD NIGHT, HAMMIE.
'NITE, DADDY.
CLICK!
CLICK! CLICK! CLICK! CLICK! CLICK!
YOU KNOW, SON, IT MIGHT BE TIME TO THINK ABOUT SWITCHING TO A SMALLER NIGHT LIGHT.
I LIKE THIS ONE.

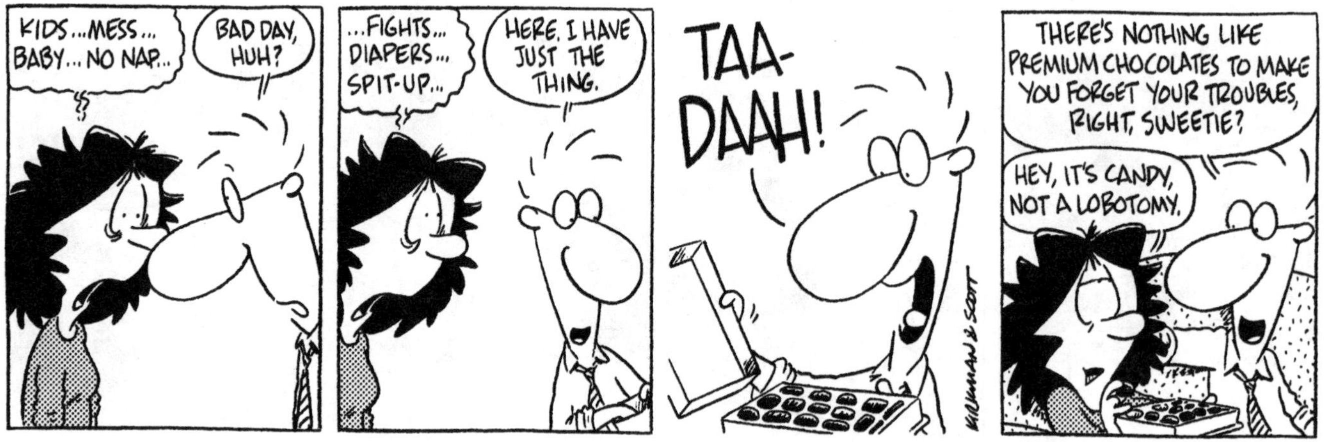
KIDS...MESS... BABY... NO NAP...
BAD DAY, HUH?
...FIGHTS... DIAPERS... SPIT-UP...
HERE. I HAVE JUST THE THING.
TAA-DAAH!
THERE'S NOTHING LIKE PREMIUM CHOCOLATES TO MAKE YOU FORGET YOUR TROUBLES, RIGHT, SWEETIE?
HEY, IT'S CANDY, NOT A LOBOTOMY.

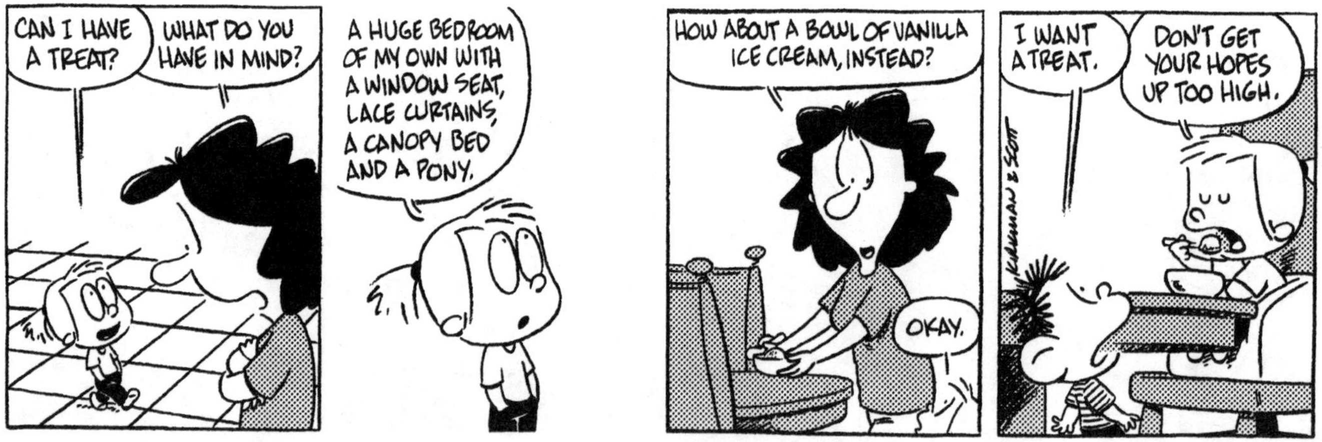
CAN I HAVE A TREAT?
WHAT DO YOU HAVE IN MIND?
A HUGE BEDROOM OF MY OWN WITH A WINDOW SEAT, LACE CURTAINS, A CANOPY BED AND A PONY.
HOW ABOUT A BOWL OF VANILLA ICE CREAM, INSTEAD?
OKAY.
I WANT A TREAT.
DON'T GET YOUR HOPES UP TOO HIGH.

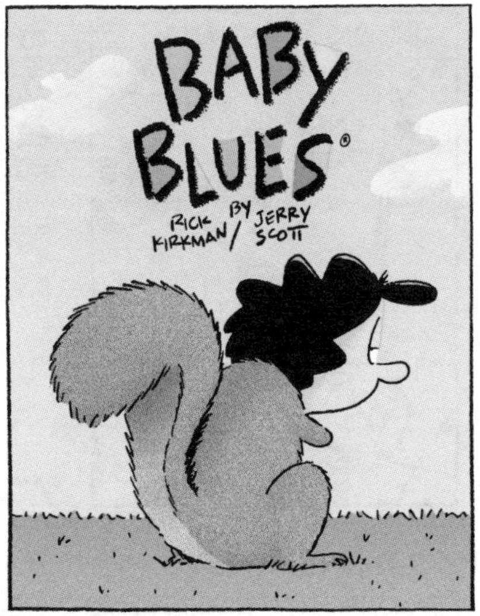
BABY BLUES®
BY RICK KIRKMAN / JERRY SCOTT

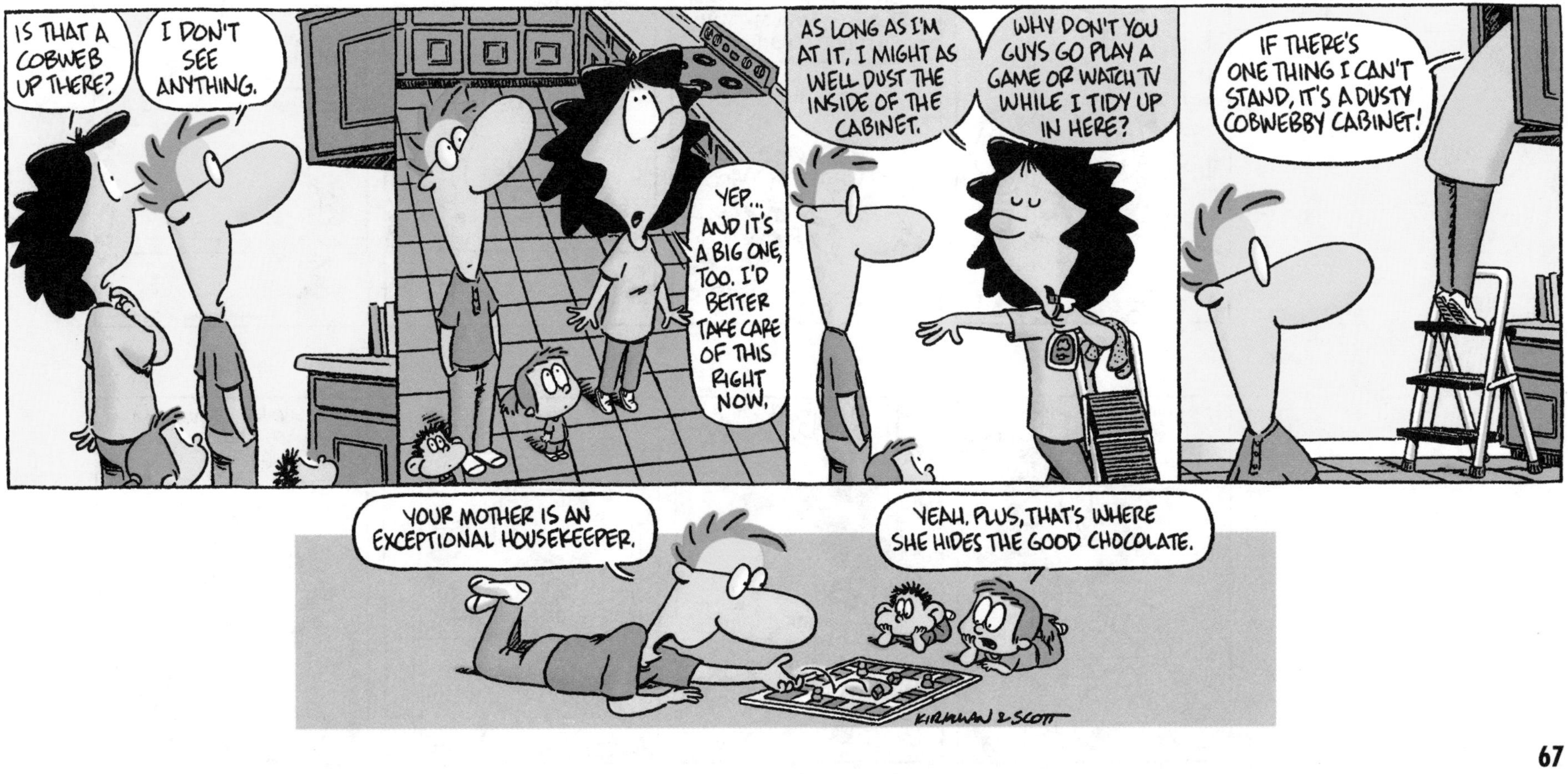
IS THAT A COBWEB UP THERE?
I DON'T SEE ANYTHING.
YEP... AND IT'S A BIG ONE, TOO. I'D BETTER TAKE CARE OF THIS RIGHT NOW.
AS LONG AS I'M AT IT, I MIGHT AS WELL DUST THE INSIDE OF THE CABINET.
WHY DON'T YOU GUYS GO PLAY A GAME OR WATCH TV WHILE I TIDY UP IN HERE?
IF THERE'S ONE THING I CAN'T STAND, IT'S A DUSTY COBWEBBY CABINET!
YOUR MOTHER IS AN EXCEPTIONAL HOUSEKEEPER.
YEAH. PLUS, THAT'S WHERE SHE HIDES THE GOOD CHOCOLATE.
KIRKMAN & SCOTT

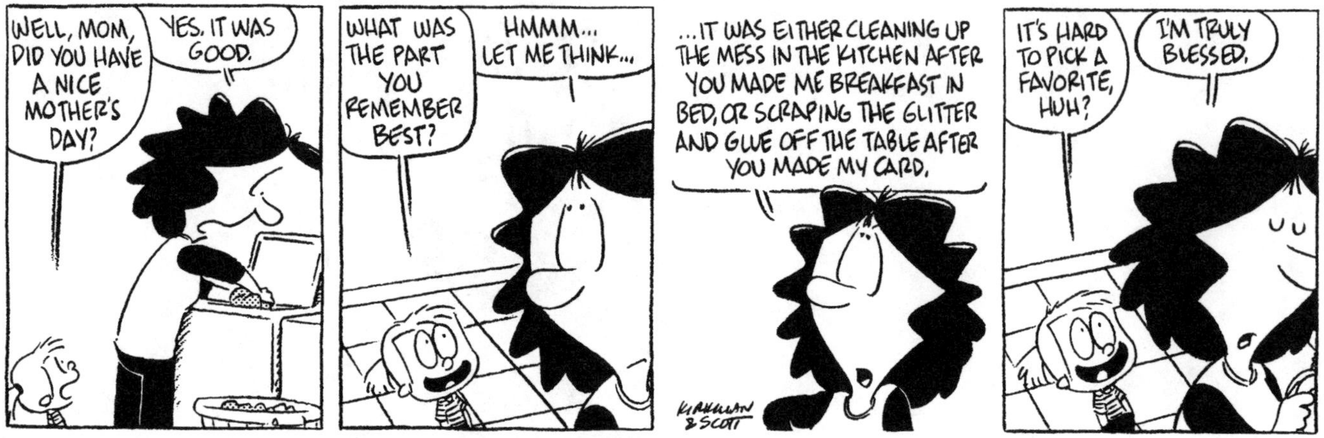
WELL, MOM, DID YOU HAVE A NICE MOTHER'S DAY?
YES. IT WAS GOOD.
WHAT WAS THE PART YOU REMEMBER BEST?
HMMM... LET ME THINK...
...IT WAS EITHER CLEANING UP THE MESS IN THE KITCHEN AFTER YOU MADE ME BREAKFAST IN BED, OR SCRAPING THE GLITTER AND GLUE OFF THE TABLE AFTER YOU MADE MY CARD.
KIRKMAN & SCOTT
IT'S HARD TO PICK A FAVORITE, HUH?
I'M TRULY BLESSED.

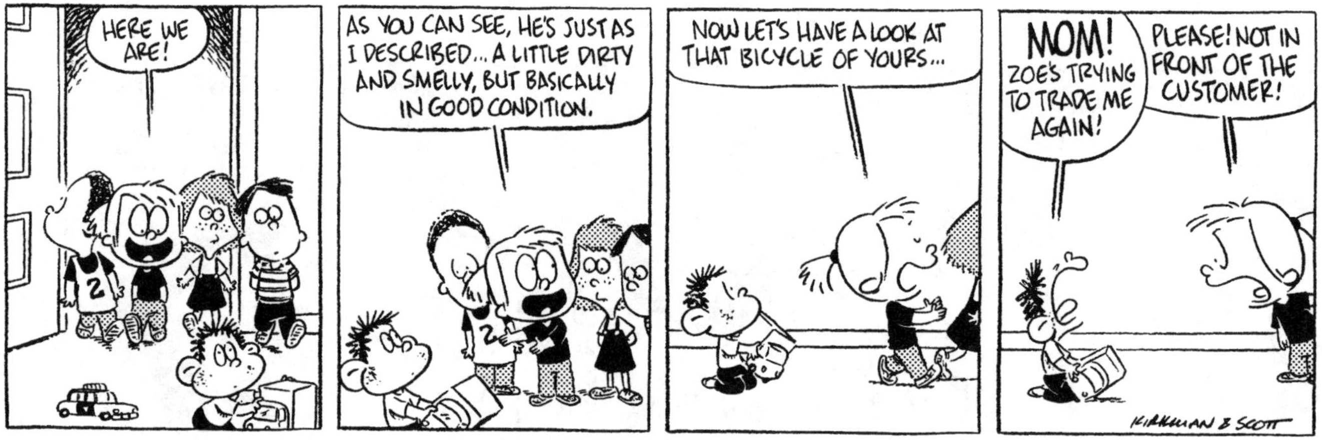
HERE WE ARE!
AS YOU CAN SEE, HE'S JUST AS I DESCRIBED... A LITTLE DIRTY AND SMELLY, BUT BASICALLY IN GOOD CONDITION.
NOW LET'S HAVE A LOOK AT THAT BICYCLE OF YOURS...
MOM! ZOE'S TRYING TO TRADE ME AGAIN!
PLEASE! NOT IN FRONT OF THE CUSTOMER!
KIRKMAN & SCOTT

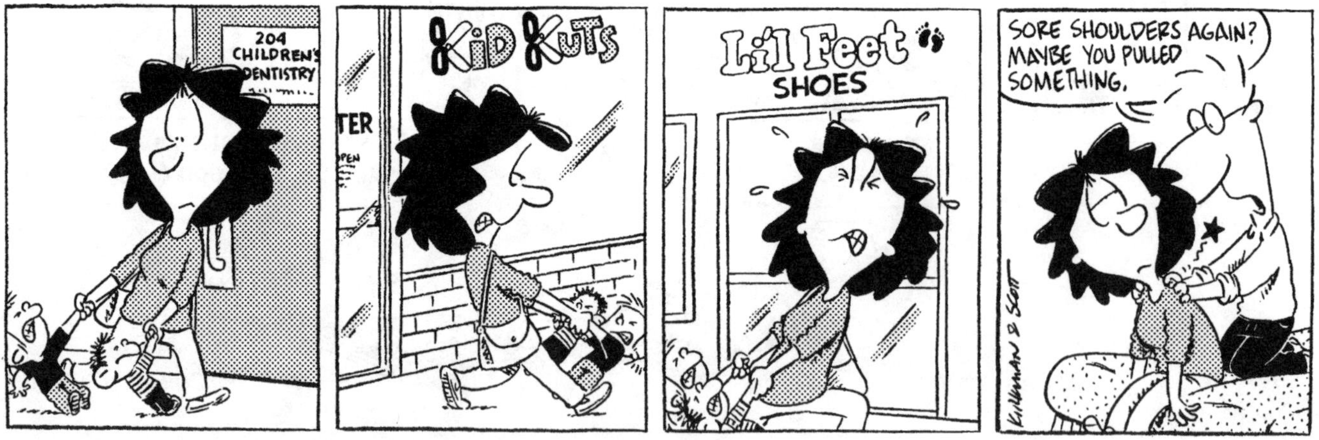
204 CHILDREN'S DENTISTRY
KID KUTS
TER
Li'l Feet SHOES
KIRKMAN & SCOTT
SORE SHOULDERS AGAIN? MAYBE YOU PULLED SOMETHING.

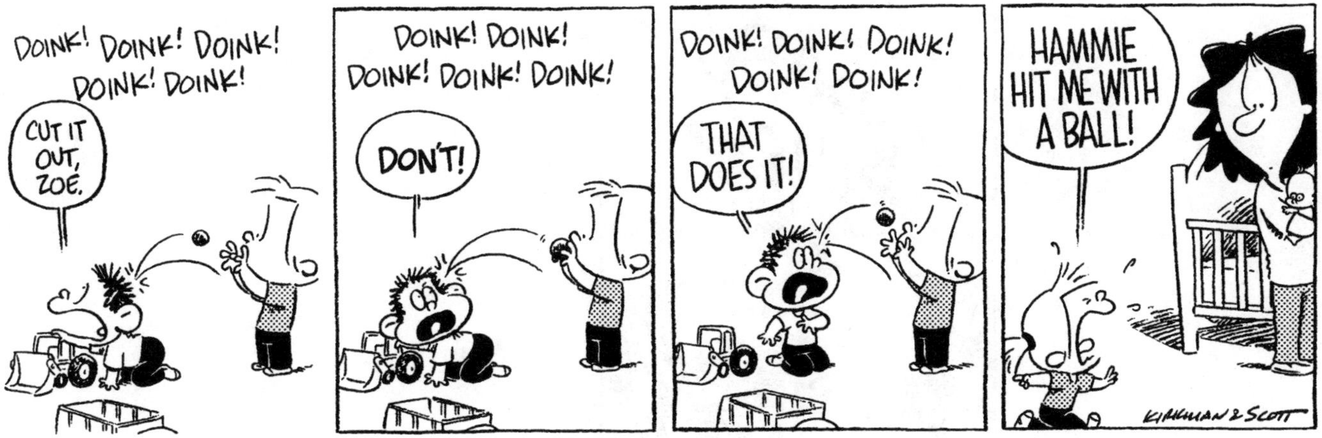
DOINK! DOINK! DOINK!
DOINK! DOINK!
CUT IT OUT, ZOE.
DOINK! DOINK!
DOINK! DOINK! DOINK!
DON'T!
DOINK! DOINK! DOINK!
DOINK! DOINK!
THAT DOES IT!
HAMMIE HIT ME WITH A BALL!
KIRKMAN & SCOTT

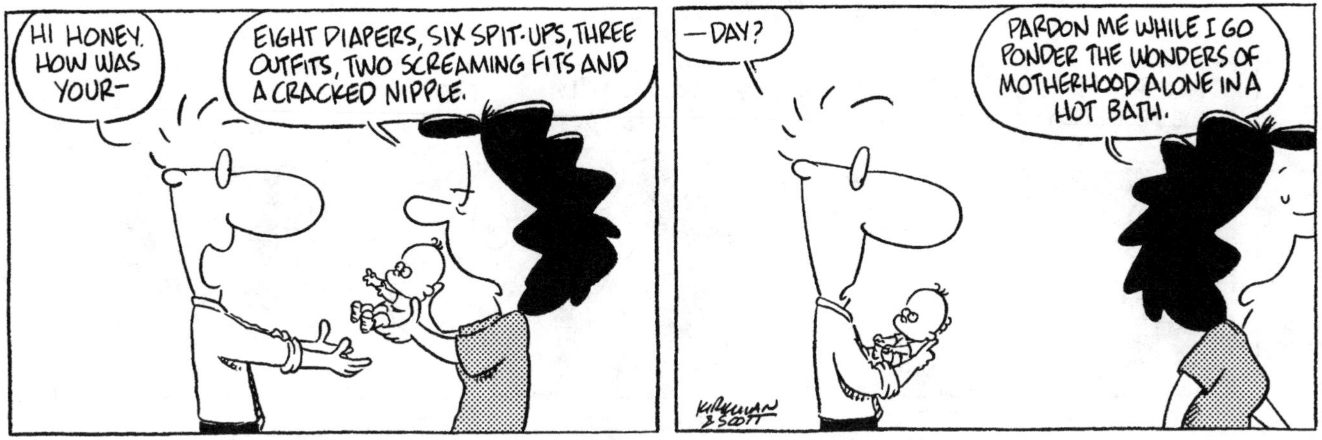
HI HONEY. HOW WAS YOUR–
EIGHT DIAPERS, SIX SPIT-UPS, THREE OUTFITS, TWO SCREAMING FITS AND A CRACKED NIPPLE.
–DAY?
PARDON ME WHILE I GO PONDER THE WONDERS OF MOTHERHOOD ALONE IN A HOT BATH.
KIRKMAN & SCOTT

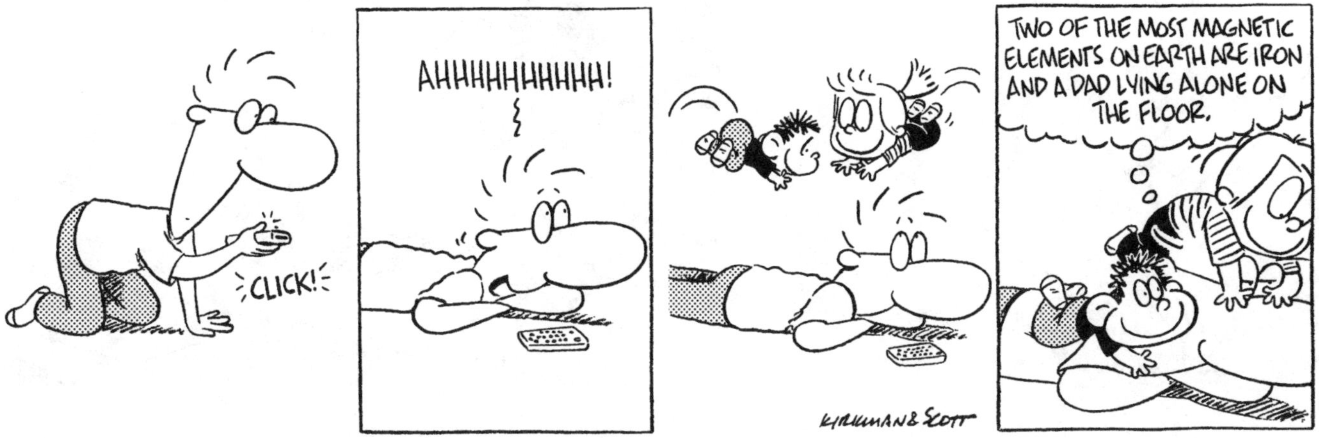
CLICK!
AHHHHHHHHHH!
TWO OF THE MOST MAGNETIC ELEMENTS ON EARTH ARE IRON AND A DAD LYING ALONE ON THE FLOOR.
KIRKMAN & SCOTT

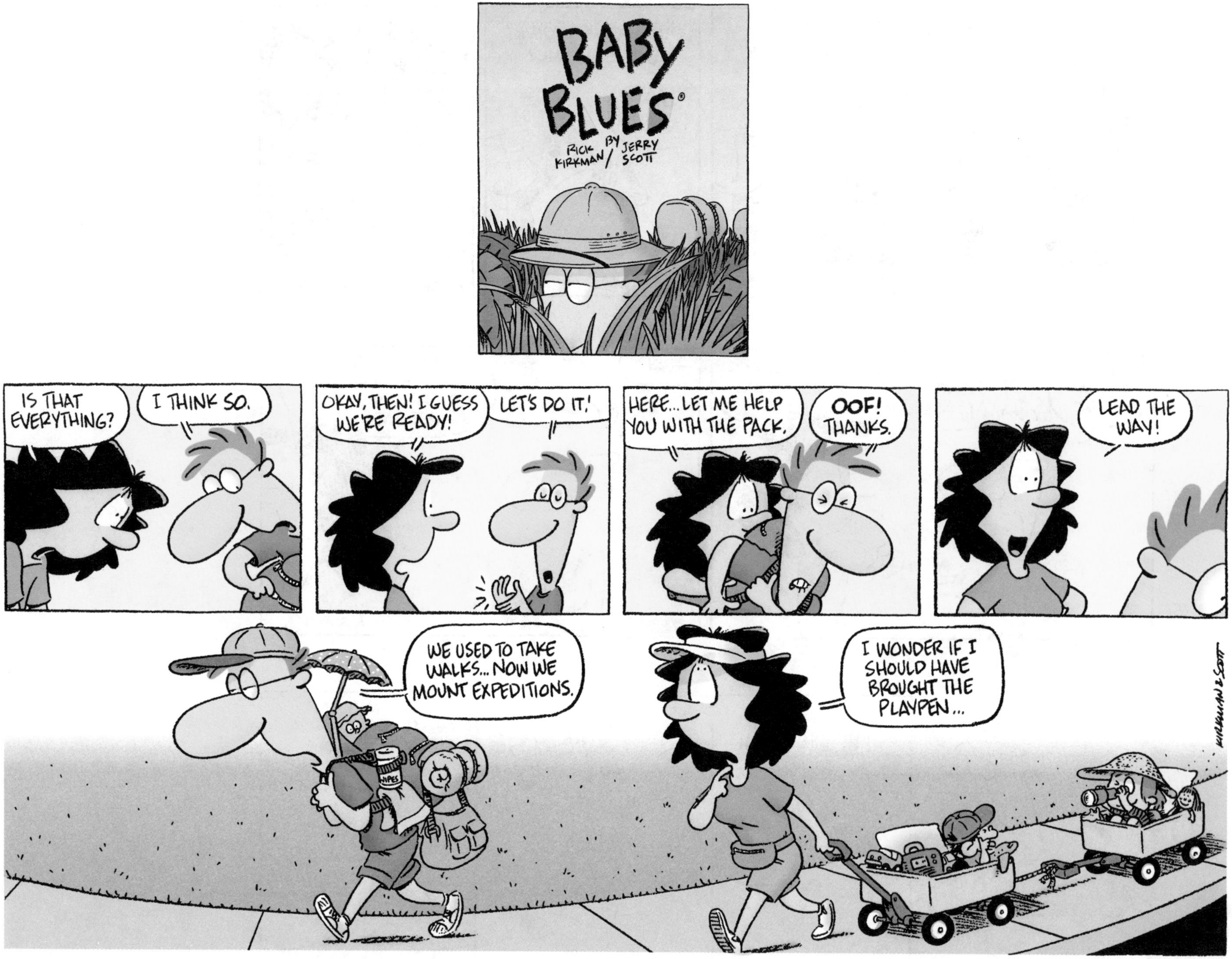
BABY BLUES®
BY RICK KIRKMAN / JERRY SCOTT
IS THAT EVERYTHING?
I THINK SO.
OKAY, THEN! I GUESS WE'RE READY!
LET'S DO IT!
HERE... LET ME HELP YOU WITH THE PACK.
OOF! THANKS.
LEAD THE WAY!
WE USED TO TAKE WALKS... NOW WE MOUNT EXPEDITIONS.
I WONDER IF I SHOULD HAVE BROUGHT THE PLAYPEN...
WIPES
KIRKMAN & SCOTT

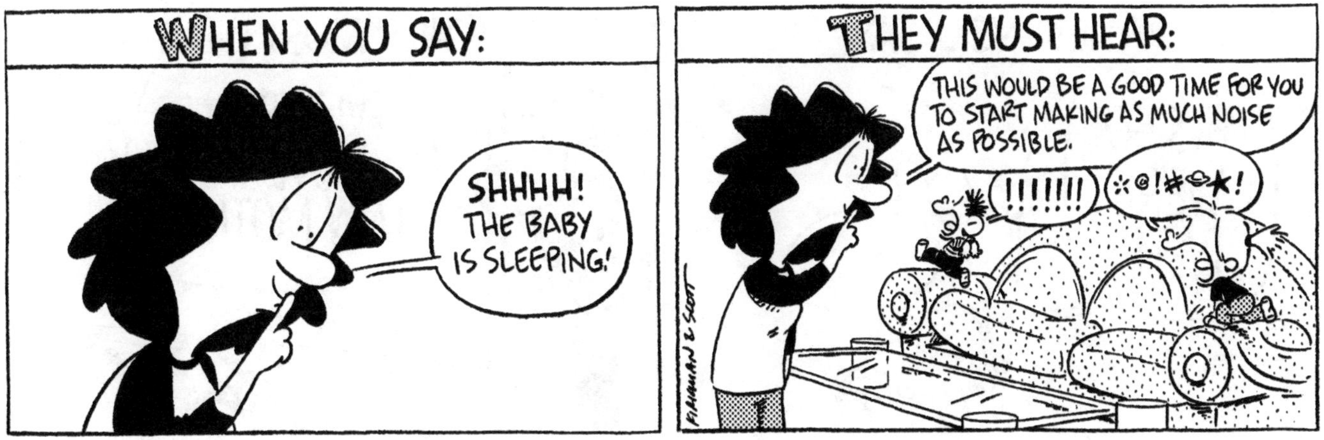
WHEN YOU SAY:
SHHHH! THE BABY IS SLEEPING!
THEY MUST HEAR:
THIS WOULD BE A GOOD TIME FOR YOU TO START MAKING AS MUCH NOISE AS POSSIBLE.
!!!!!!!

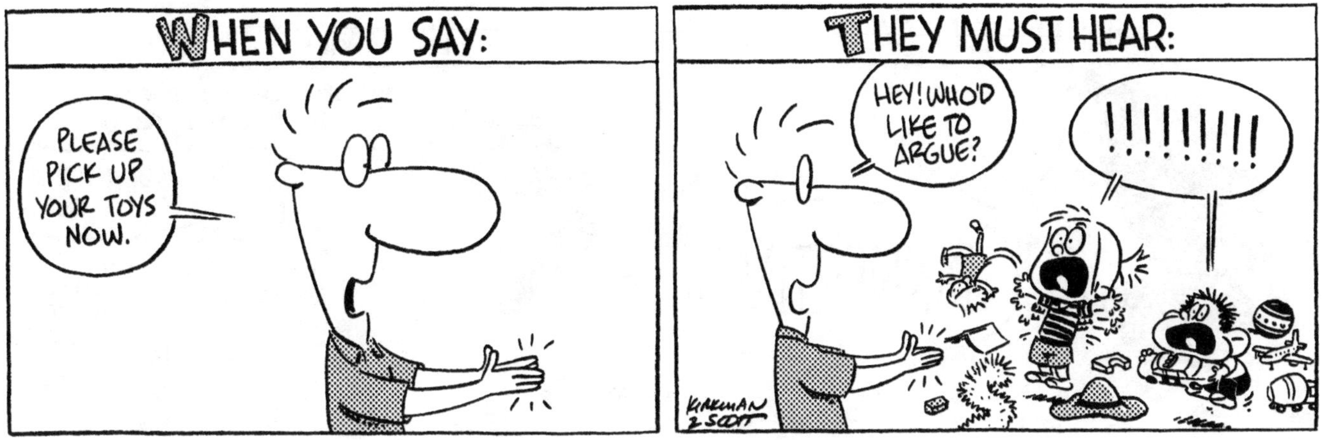
WHEN YOU SAY:
PLEASE PICK UP YOUR TOYS NOW.
THEY MUST HEAR:
HEY! WHO'D LIKE TO ARGUE?
!!!!!!!!!

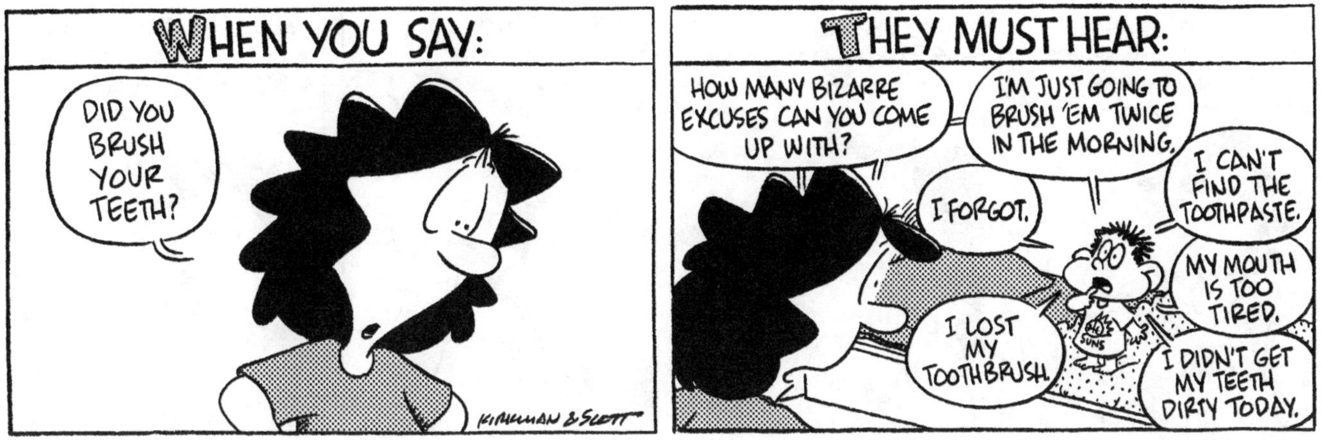
WHEN YOU SAY:
DID YOU BRUSH YOUR TEETH?
THEY MUST HEAR:
HOW MANY BIZARRE EXCUSES CAN YOU COME UP WITH?
I'M JUST GOING TO BRUSH 'EM TWICE IN THE MORNING.
I FORGOT.
I CAN'T FIND THE TOOTHPASTE.
MY MOUTH IS TOO TIRED.
I LOST MY TOOTHBRUSH.
I DIDN'T GET MY TEETH DIRTY TODAY.

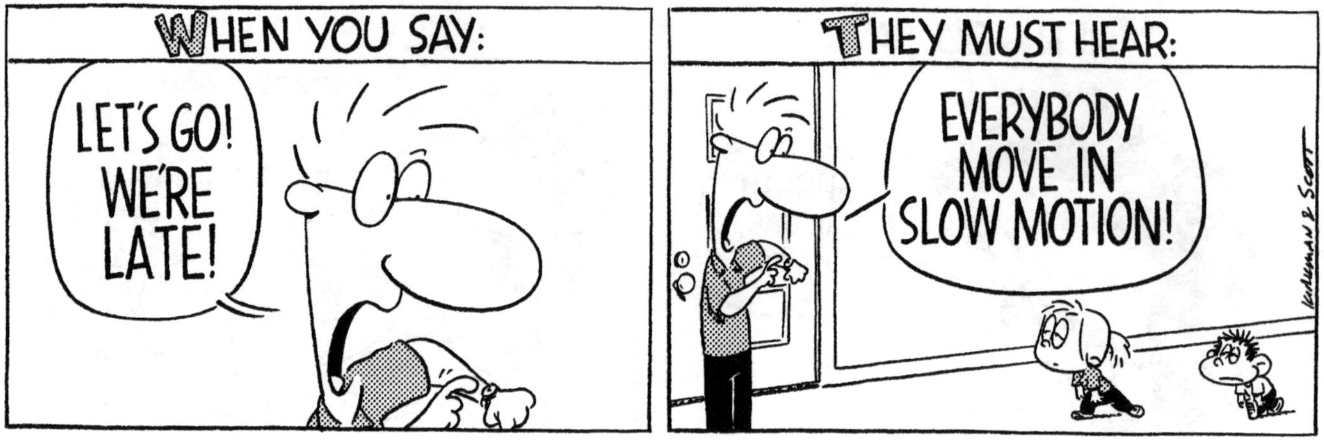
WHEN YOU SAY:
LET'S GO! WE'RE LATE!
THEY MUST HEAR:
EVERYBODY MOVE IN SLOW MOTION!
KIRKMAN & SCOTT

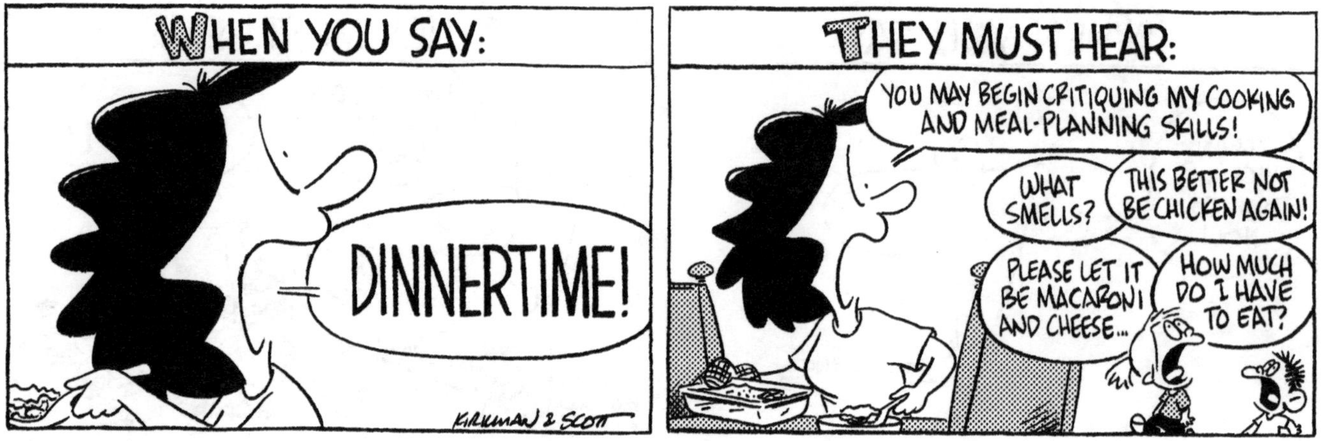
WHEN YOU SAY:
DINNERTIME!
KIRKMAN & SCOTT
THEY MUST HEAR:
YOU MAY BEGIN CRITIQUING MY COOKING AND MEAL-PLANNING SKILLS!
WHAT SMELLS?
THIS BETTER NOT BE CHICKEN AGAIN!
PLEASE LET IT BE MACARONI AND CHEESE...
HOW MUCH DO I HAVE TO EAT?

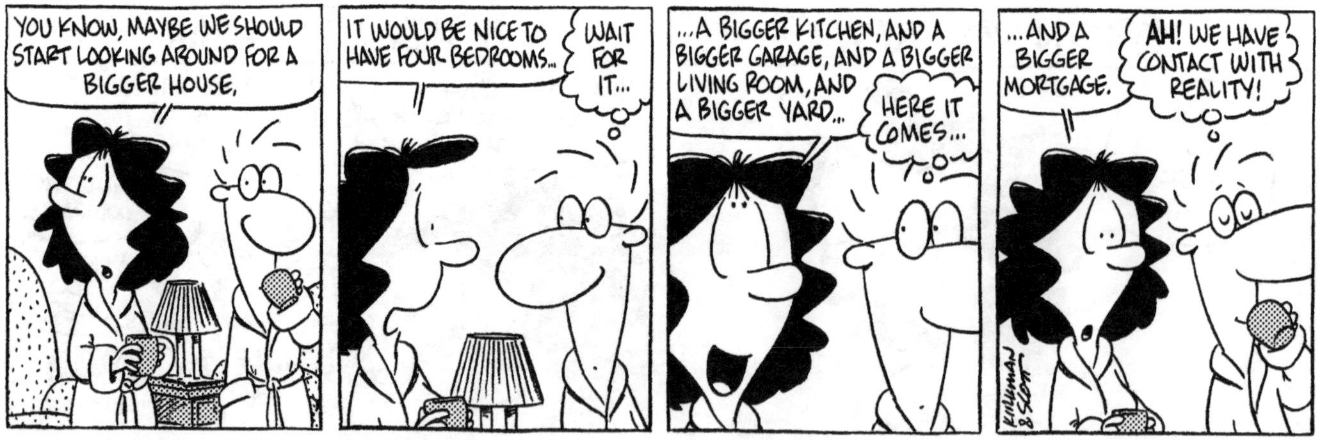
YOU KNOW, MAYBE WE SHOULD START LOOKING AROUND FOR A BIGGER HOUSE.
IT WOULD BE NICE TO HAVE FOUR BEDROOMS...
WAIT FOR IT...
...A BIGGER KITCHEN, AND A BIGGER GARAGE, AND A BIGGER LIVING ROOM, AND A BIGGER YARD...
HERE IT COMES...
...AND A BIGGER MORTGAGE.
AH! WE HAVE CONTACT WITH REALITY!
KIRKMAN & SCOTT

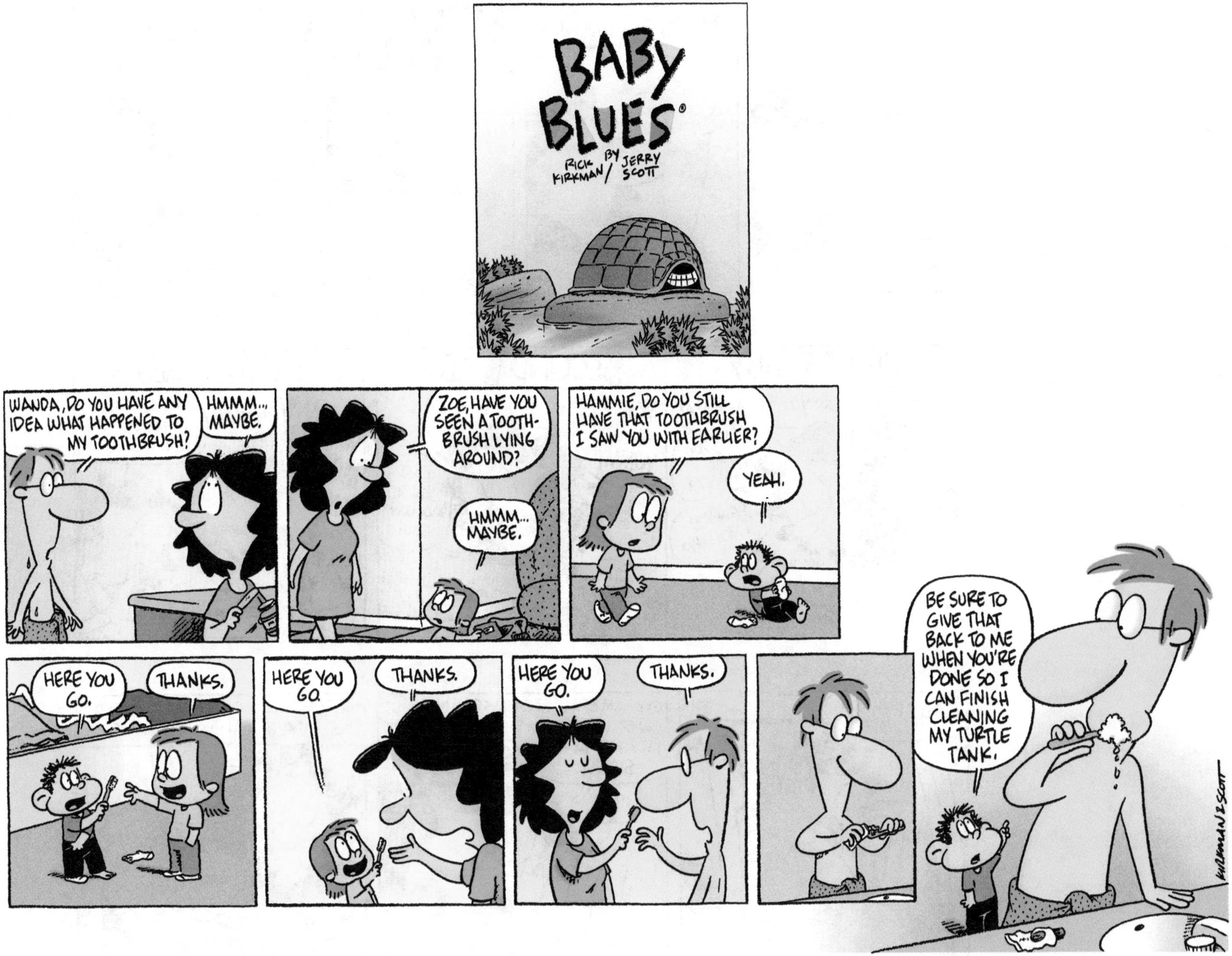
BABY BLUES®
BY RICK KIRKMAN / JERRY SCOTT
WANDA, DO YOU HAVE ANY IDEA WHAT HAPPENED TO MY TOOTHBRUSH?
HMMM... MAYBE.
ZOE, HAVE YOU SEEN A TOOTH-BRUSH LYING AROUND?
HMMM... MAYBE.
HAMMIE, DO YOU STILL HAVE THAT TOOTHBRUSH I SAW YOU WITH EARLIER?
YEAH.
HERE YOU GO.
THANKS.
HERE YOU GO.
THANKS.
HERE YOU GO.
THANKS.
BE SURE TO GIVE THAT BACK TO ME WHEN YOU'RE DONE SO I CAN FINISH CLEANING MY TURTLE TANK.
KIRKMAN & SCOTT

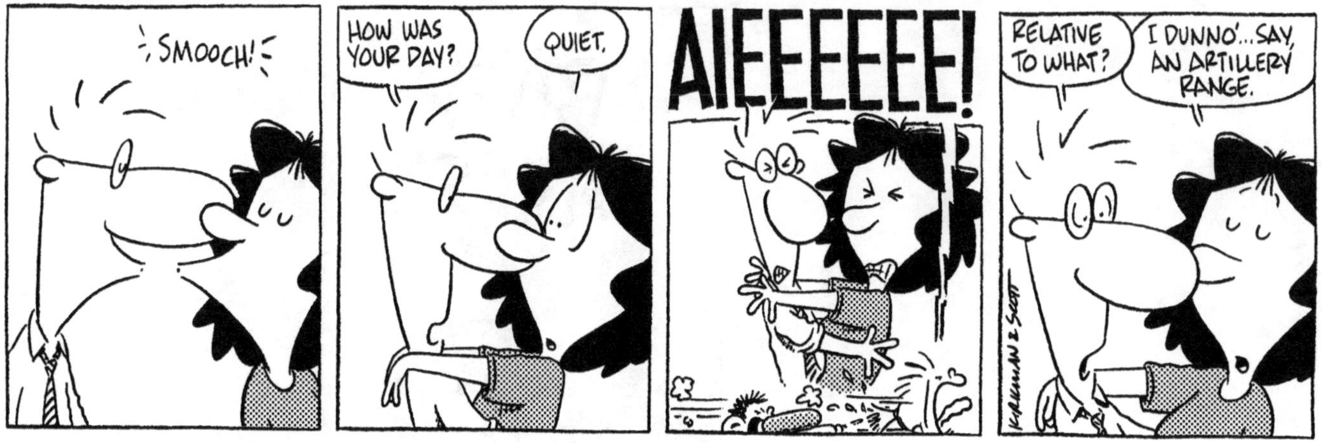
SMOOCH!
HOW WAS YOUR DAY?
QUIET.
AIEEEEEE!
RELATIVE TO WHAT?
I DUNNO'... SAY, AN ARTILLERY RANGE.
KIRKMAN & SCOTT

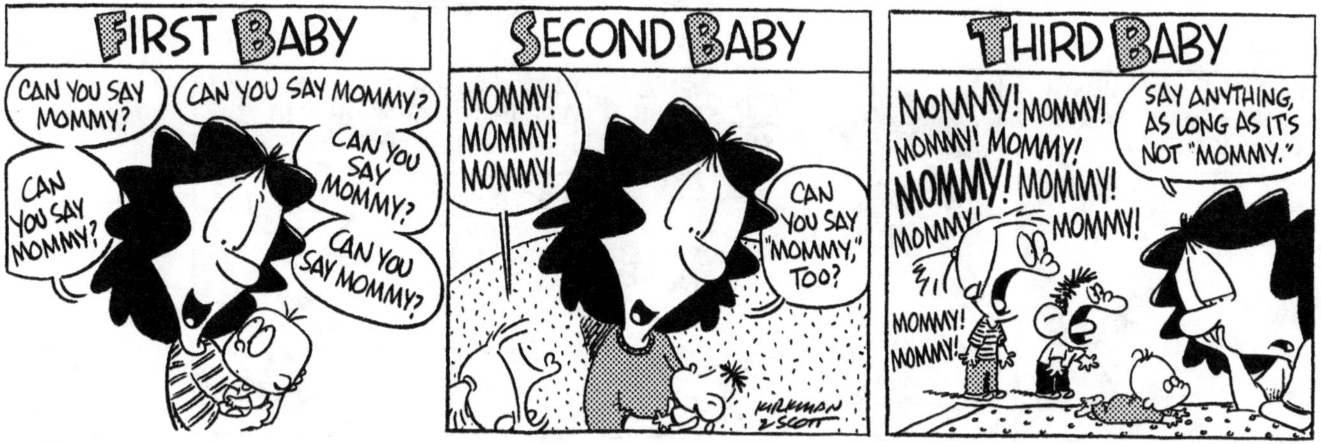
FIRST BABY
CAN YOU SAY MOMMY?
CAN YOU SAY MOMMY?
CAN YOU SAY MOMMY?
CAN YOU SAY MOMMY?
CAN YOU SAY MOMMY?
SECOND BABY
MOMMY! MOMMY! MOMMY!
CAN YOU SAY "MOMMY," TOO?
KIRKMAN & SCOTT
THIRD BABY
MOMMY! MOMMY! MOMMY! MOMMY! MOMMY! MOMMY! MOMMY! MOMMY! MOMMY! MOMMY!
SAY ANYTHING, AS LONG AS IT'S NOT "MOMMY."

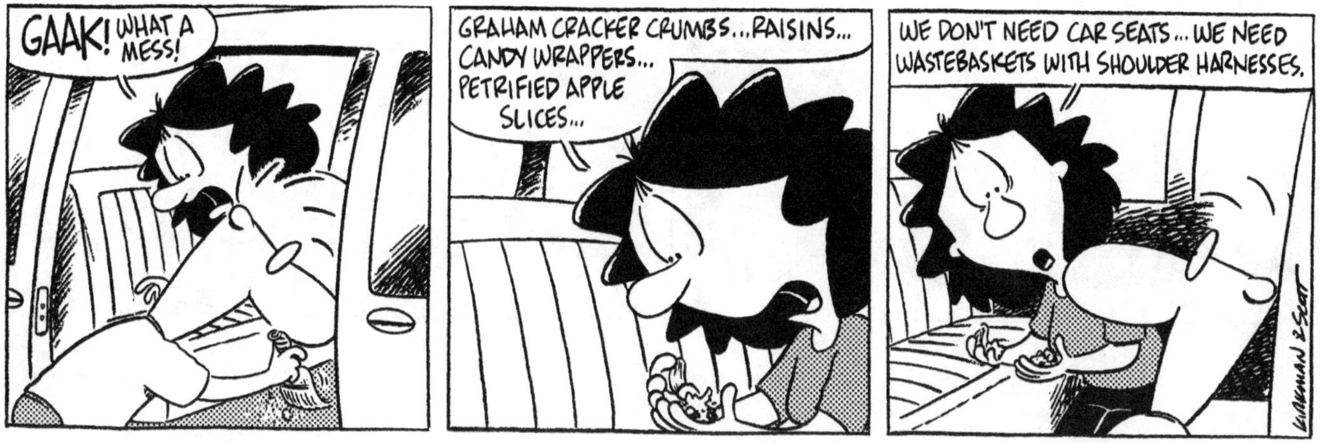
GAAK! WHAT A MESS!
GRAHAM CRACKER CRUMBS... RAISINS... CANDY WRAPPERS... PETRIFIED APPLE SLICES...
WE DON'T NEED CAR SEATS... WE NEED WASTEBASKETS WITH SHOULDER HARNESSES.
KIRKMAN & SCOTT

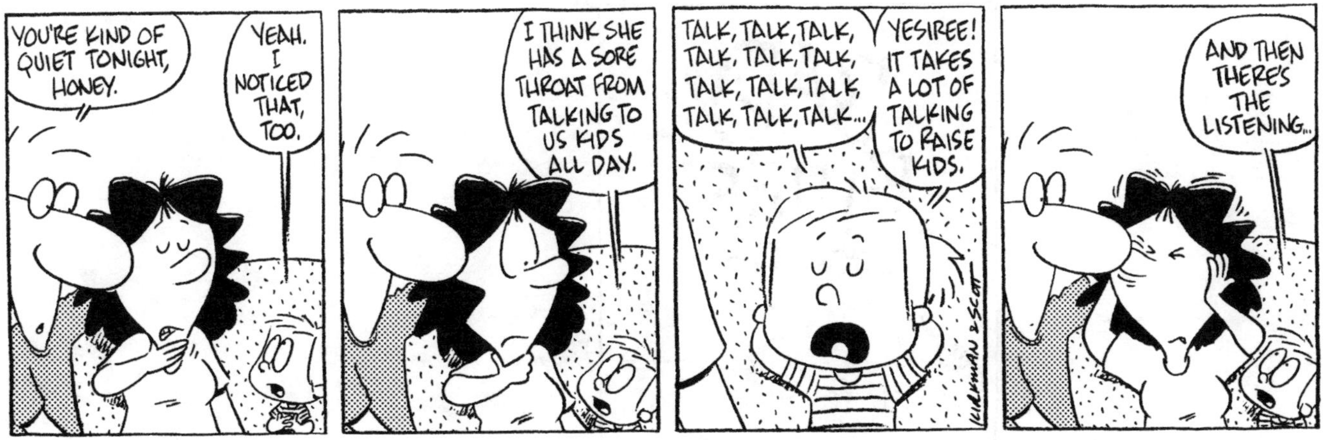
YOU'RE KIND OF QUIET TONIGHT, HONEY.
YEAH. I NOTICED THAT, TOO.
I THINK SHE HAS A SORE THROAT FROM TALKING TO US KIDS ALL DAY.
TALK, TALK, TALK, TALK, TALK, TALK, TALK, TALK, TALK, TALK, TALK, TALK...
YESIREE! IT TAKES A LOT OF TALKING TO RAISE KIDS.
AND THEN THERE'S THE LISTENING...
KIRKMAN & SCOTT

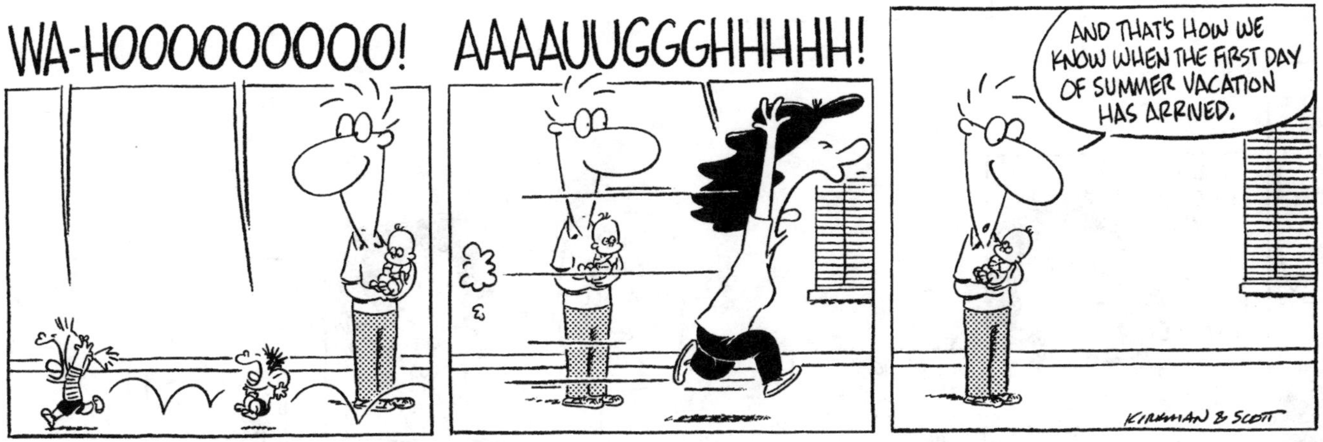
WA-HOOOOOOOOO!
AAAAUUGGGHHHHH!
AND THAT'S HOW WE KNOW WHEN THE FIRST DAY OF SUMMER VACATION HAS ARRIVED.
KIRKMAN & SCOTT

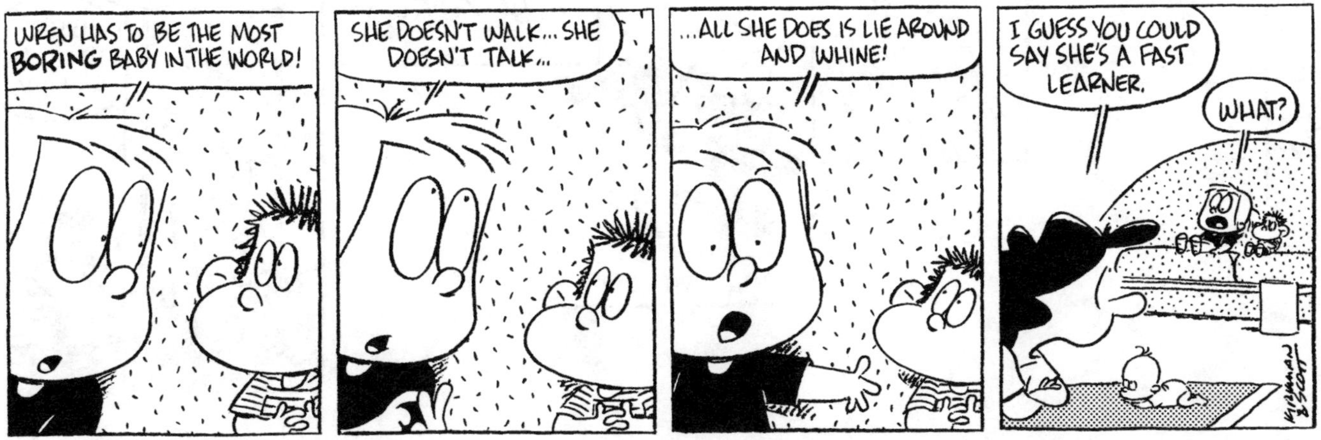
WREN HAS TO BE THE MOST **BORING** BABY IN THE WORLD!
SHE DOESN'T WALK... SHE DOESN'T TALK...
...ALL SHE DOES IS LIE AROUND AND WHINE!
I GUESS YOU COULD SAY SHE'S A FAST LEARNER.
WHAT?
KIRKMAN & SCOTT

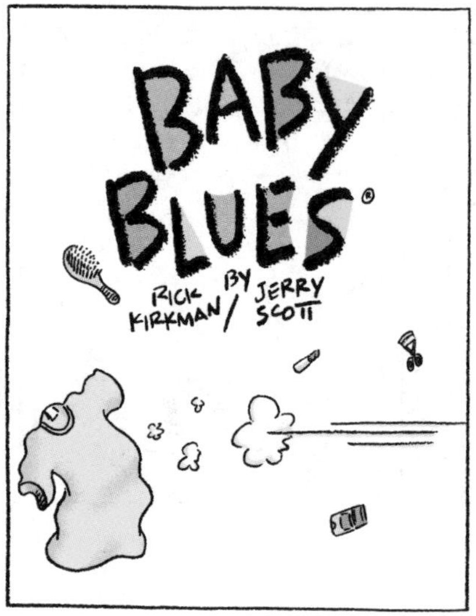
BABY BLUES®
BY RICK KIRKMAN / JERRY SCOTT

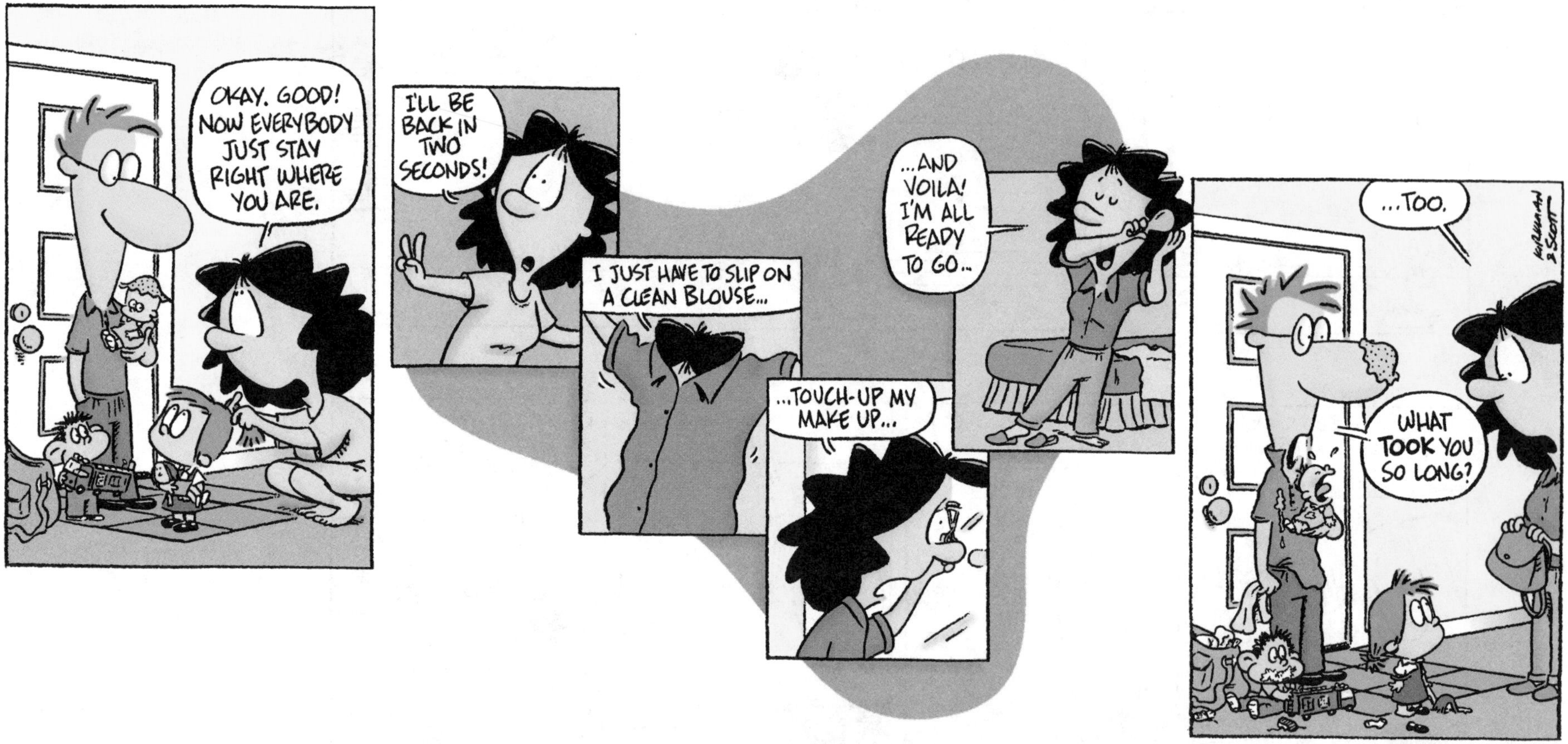
OKAY. GOOD! NOW EVERYBODY JUST STAY RIGHT WHERE YOU ARE.
I'LL BE BACK IN TWO SECONDS!
I JUST HAVE TO SLIP ON A CLEAN BLOUSE...
...TOUCH-UP MY MAKE UP...
...AND VOILA! I'M ALL READY TO GO...
...TOO.
WHAT **TOOK** YOU SO LONG?
KIRKMAN & SCOTT

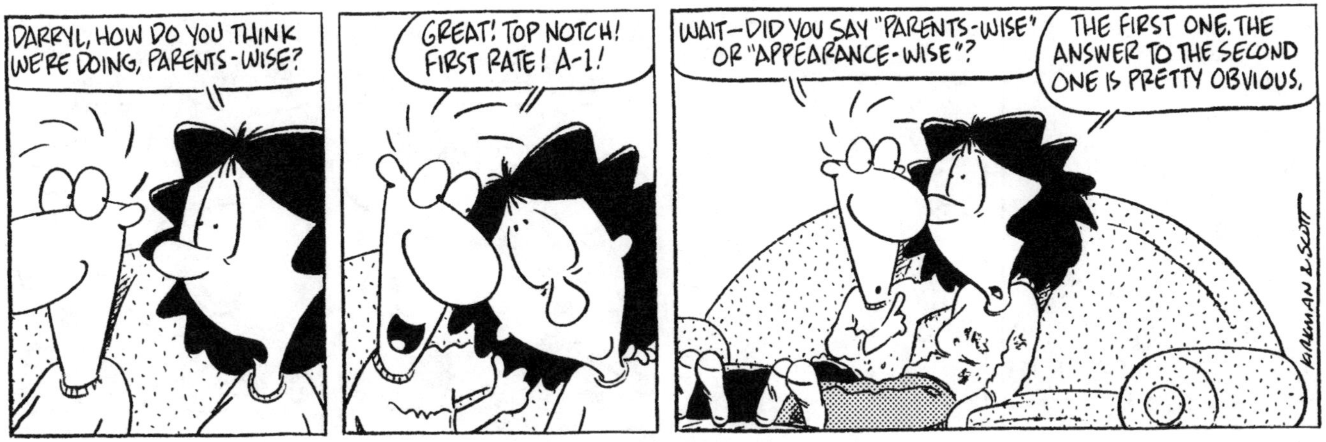
DARRYL, HOW DO YOU THINK WE'RE DOING, PARENTS-WISE?
GREAT! TOP NOTCH! FIRST RATE! A-1!
WAIT—DID YOU SAY "PARENTS-WISE" OR "APPEARANCE-WISE"?
THE FIRST ONE. THE ANSWER TO THE SECOND ONE IS PRETTY OBVIOUS.
KIRKMAN & SCOTT

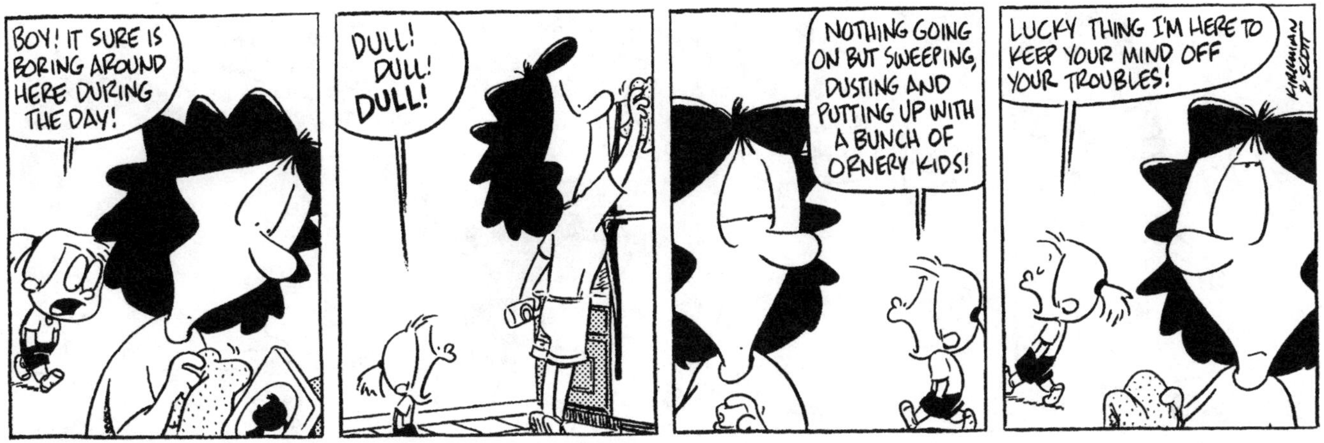
BOY! IT SURE IS BORING AROUND HERE DURING THE DAY!
DULL! DULL! DULL!
NOTHING GOING ON BUT SWEEPING, DUSTING AND PUTTING UP WITH A BUNCH OF ORNERY KIDS!
LUCKY THING I'M HERE TO KEEP YOUR MIND OFF YOUR TROUBLES!
KIRKMAN & SCOTT

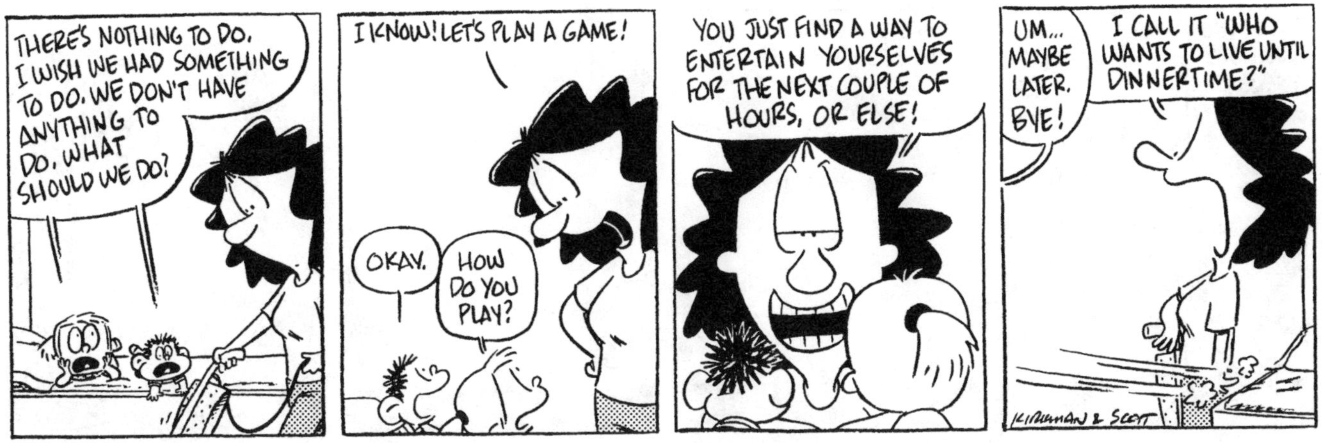
THERE'S NOTHING TO DO. I WISH WE HAD SOMETHING TO DO. WE DON'T HAVE ANYTHING TO DO. WHAT SHOULD WE DO?
I KNOW! LET'S PLAY A GAME!
OKAY.
HOW DO YOU PLAY?
YOU JUST FIND A WAY TO ENTERTAIN YOURSELVES FOR THE NEXT COUPLE OF HOURS, OR ELSE!
UM... MAYBE LATER. BYE!
I CALL IT "WHO WANTS TO LIVE UNTIL DINNERTIME?"
KIRKMAN & SCOTT

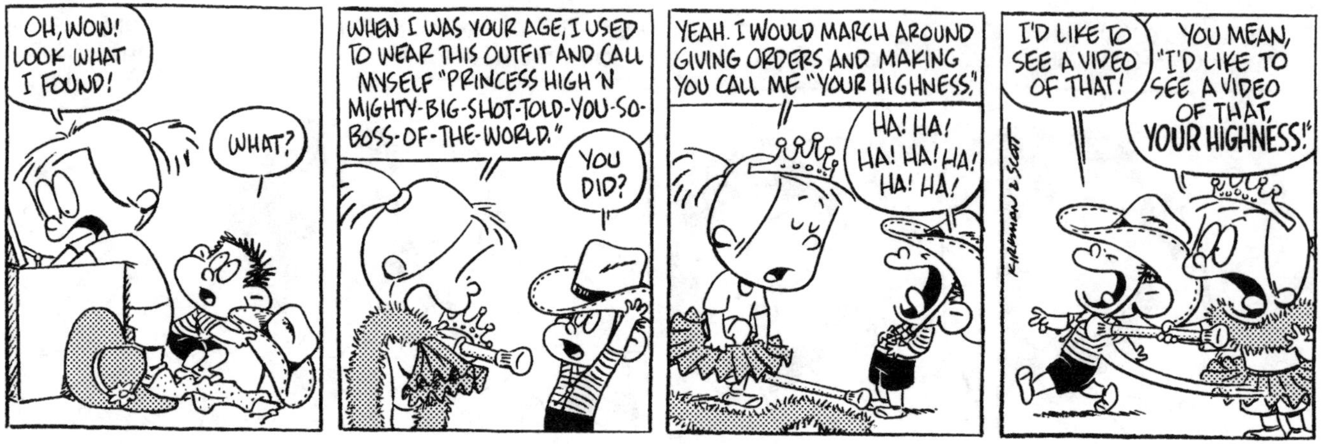
OH, WOW! LOOK WHAT I FOUND!
WHAT?
WHEN I WAS YOUR AGE, I USED TO WEAR THIS OUTFIT AND CALL MYSELF "PRINCESS HIGH 'N MIGHTY-BIG-SHOT-TOLD-YOU-SO-BOSS-OF-THE-WORLD."
YOU DID?
YEAH. I WOULD MARCH AROUND GIVING ORDERS AND MAKING YOU CALL ME "YOUR HIGHNESS."
HA! HA! HA! HA! HA! HA! HA!
I'D LIKE TO SEE A VIDEO OF THAT!
YOU MEAN, "I'D LIKE TO SEE A VIDEO OF THAT, YOUR HIGHNESS!"
KIRKMAN & SCOTT

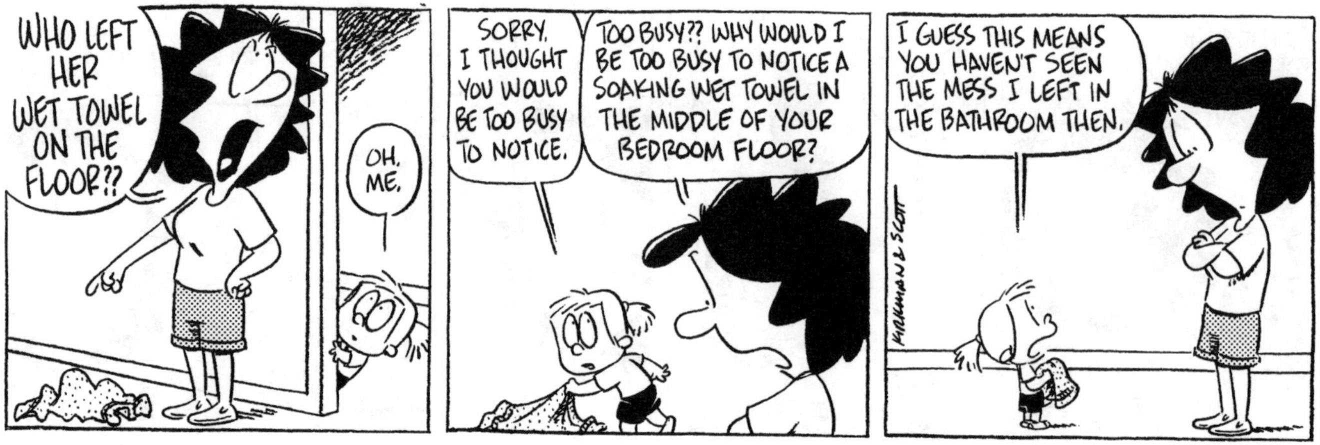
WHO LEFT HER WET TOWEL ON THE FLOOR??
OH. ME.
SORRY. I THOUGHT YOU WOULD BE TOO BUSY TO NOTICE.
TOO BUSY?? WHY WOULD I BE TOO BUSY TO NOTICE A SOAKING WET TOWEL IN THE MIDDLE OF YOUR BEDROOM FLOOR?
KIRKMAN & SCOTT
I GUESS THIS MEANS YOU HAVEN'T SEEN THE MESS I LEFT IN THE BATHROOM THEN.

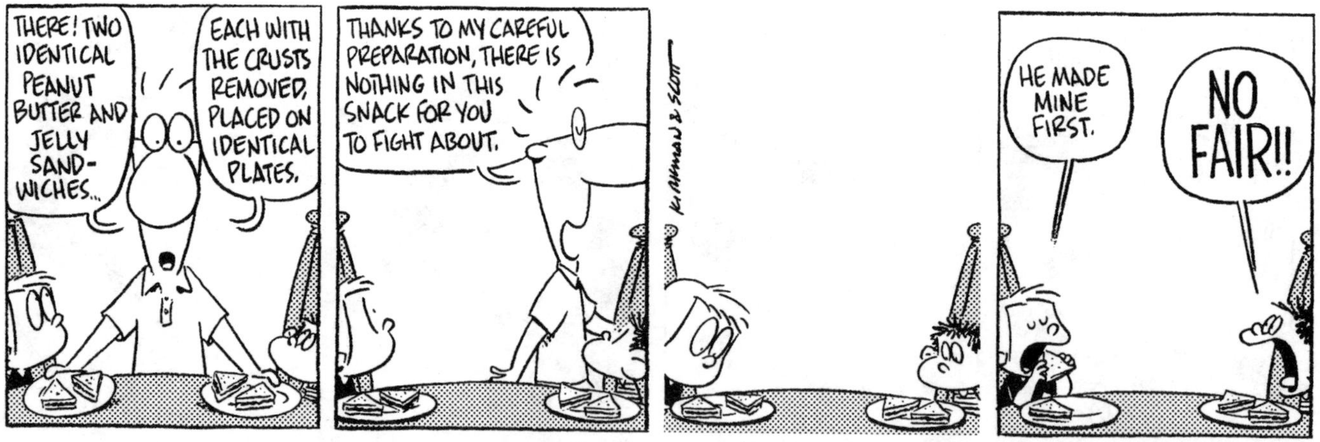
THERE! TWO IDENTICAL PEANUT BUTTER AND JELLY SANDWICHES...
EACH WITH THE CRUSTS REMOVED, PLACED ON IDENTICAL PLATES.
THANKS TO MY CAREFUL PREPARATION, THERE IS NOTHING IN THIS SNACK FOR YOU TO FIGHT ABOUT.
KIRKMAN & SCOTT
HE MADE MINE FIRST.
NO FAIR!!

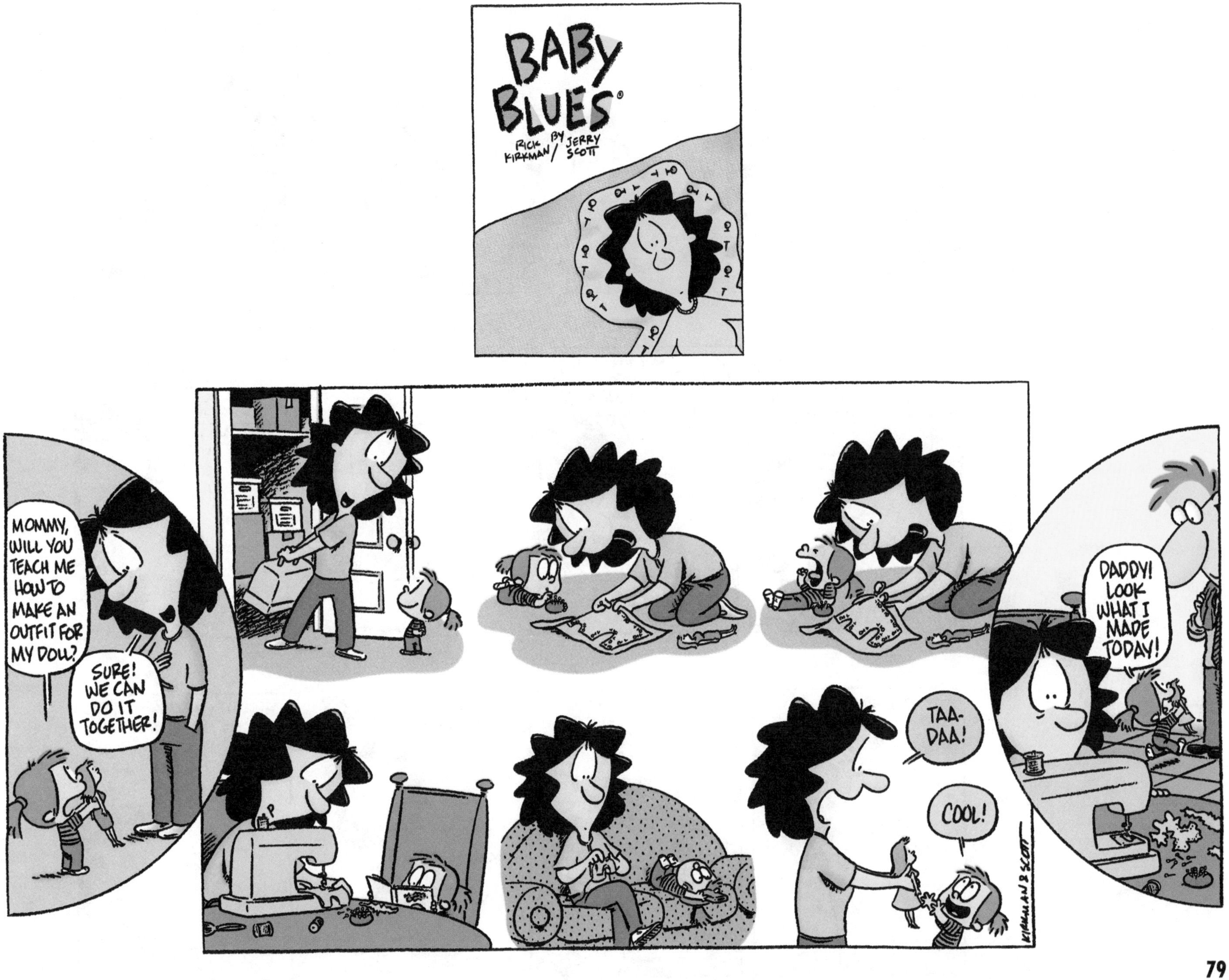
BABY BLUES®
BY RICK KIRKMAN / JERRY SCOTT
MOMMY, WILL YOU TEACH ME HOW TO MAKE AN OUTFIT FOR MY DOLL?
SURE! WE CAN DO IT TOGETHER!
TAA-DAA!
COOL!
DADDY! LOOK WHAT I MADE TODAY!
KIRKMAN & SCOTT

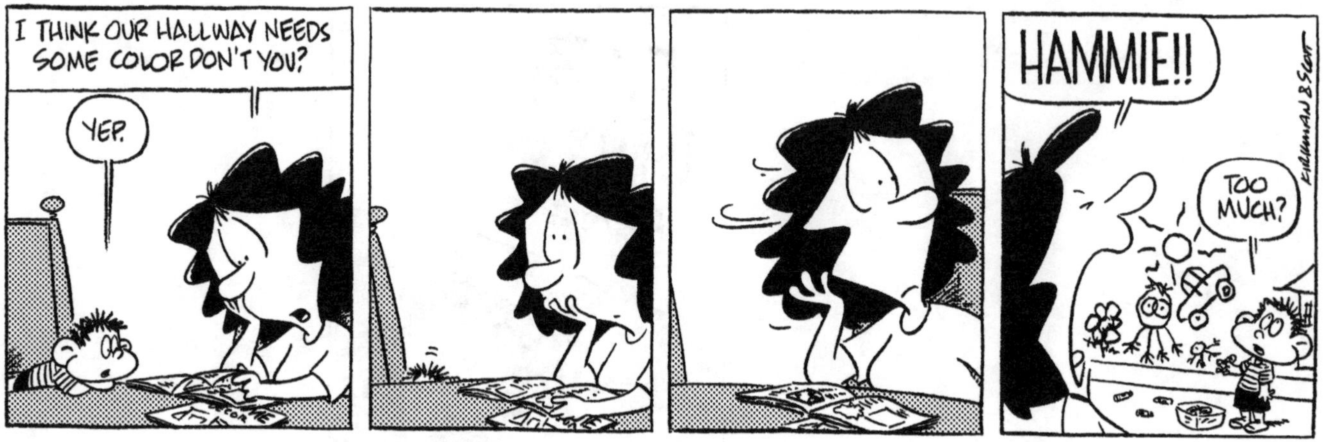
I THINK OUR HALLWAY NEEDS SOME COLOR DON'T YOU?
YEP.
HAMMIE!!
TOO MUCH?
KIRKMAN & SCOTT

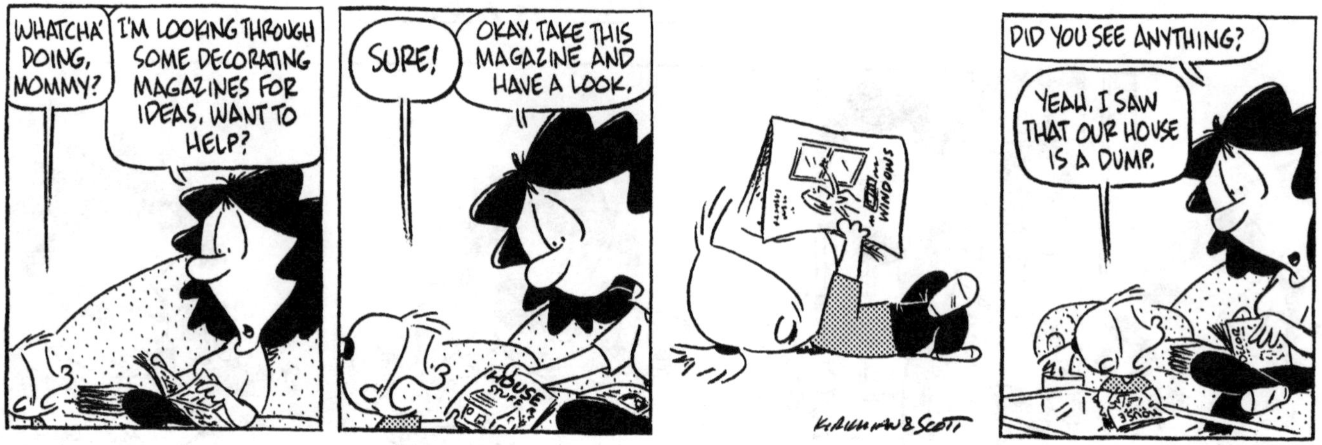
WHATCHA' DOING, MOMMY?
I'M LOOKING THROUGH SOME DECORATING MAGAZINES FOR IDEAS. WANT TO HELP?
SURE!
OKAY. TAKE THIS MAGAZINE AND HAVE A LOOK.
WINDOWS
DID YOU SEE ANYTHING?
YEAH. I SAW THAT OUR HOUSE IS A DUMP.
KIRKMAN & SCOTT

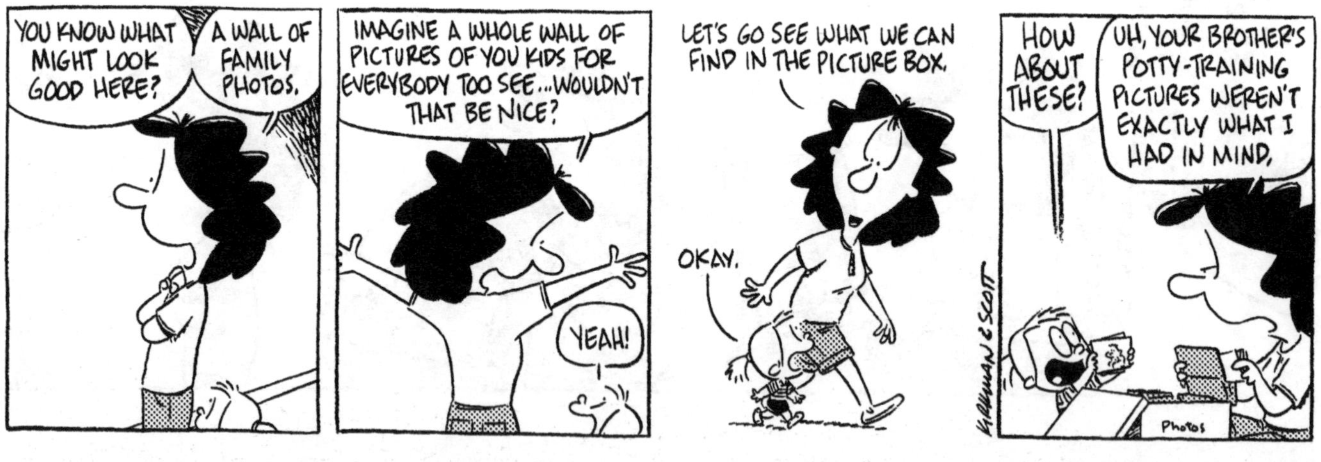
YOU KNOW WHAT MIGHT LOOK GOOD HERE?
A WALL OF FAMILY PHOTOS.
IMAGINE A WHOLE WALL OF PICTURES OF YOU KIDS FOR EVERYBODY TOO SEE...WOULDN'T THAT BE NICE?
YEAH!
LET'S GO SEE WHAT WE CAN FIND IN THE PICTURE BOX.
OKAY.
HOW ABOUT THESE?
UH, YOUR BROTHER'S POTTY-TRAINING PICTURES WEREN'T EXACTLY WHAT I HAD IN MIND.
PHOTOS
KIRKMAN & SCOTT

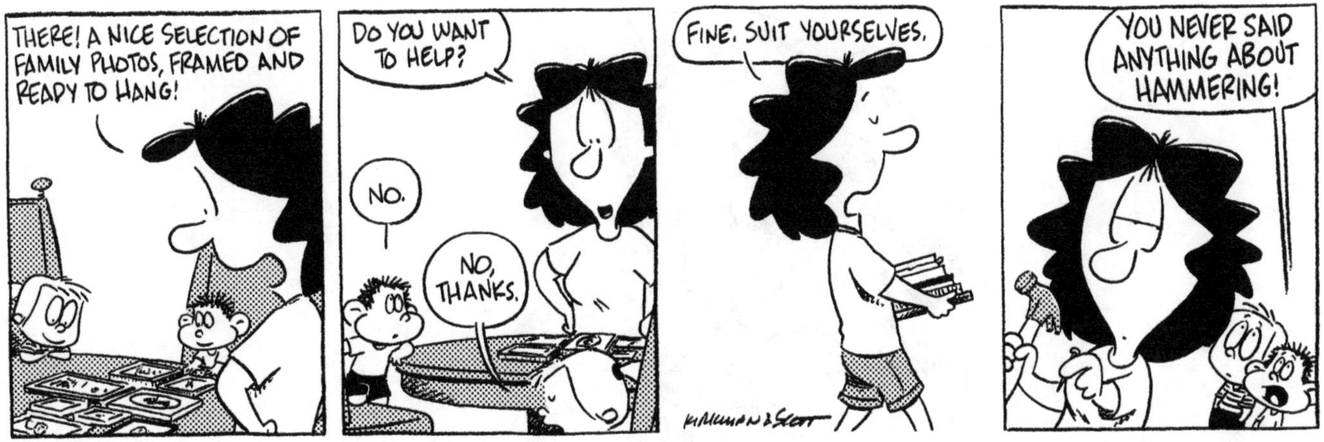
THERE! A NICE SELECTION OF FAMILY PHOTOS, FRAMED AND READY TO HANG!
DO YOU WANT TO HELP?
NO.
NO, THANKS.
FINE. SUIT YOURSELVES.
YOU NEVER SAID ANYTHING ABOUT HAMMERING!

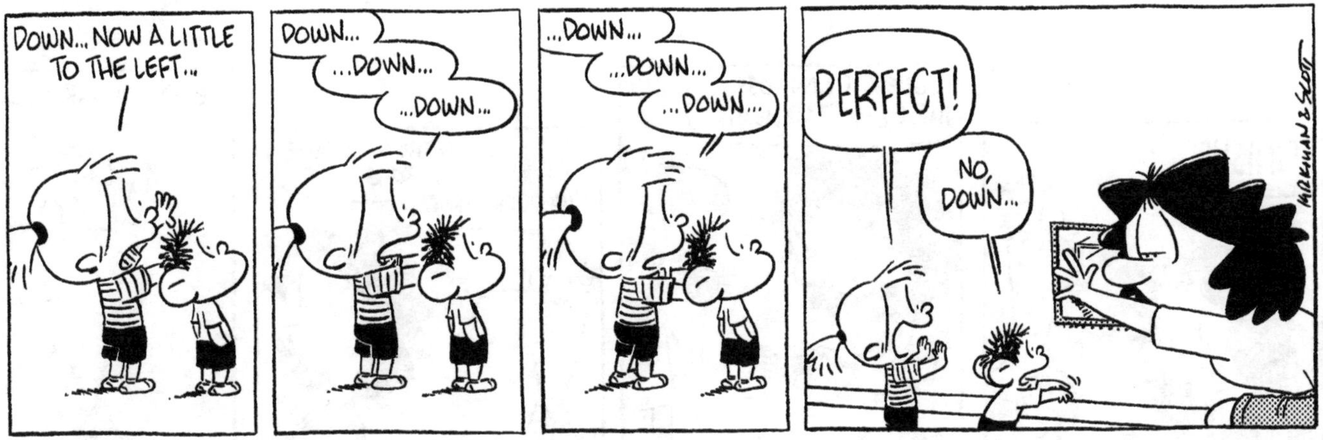
DOWN... NOW A LITTLE TO THE LEFT...
DOWN...
...DOWN...
...DOWN...
...DOWN...
...DOWN...
...DOWN...
PERFECT!
NO, DOWN...

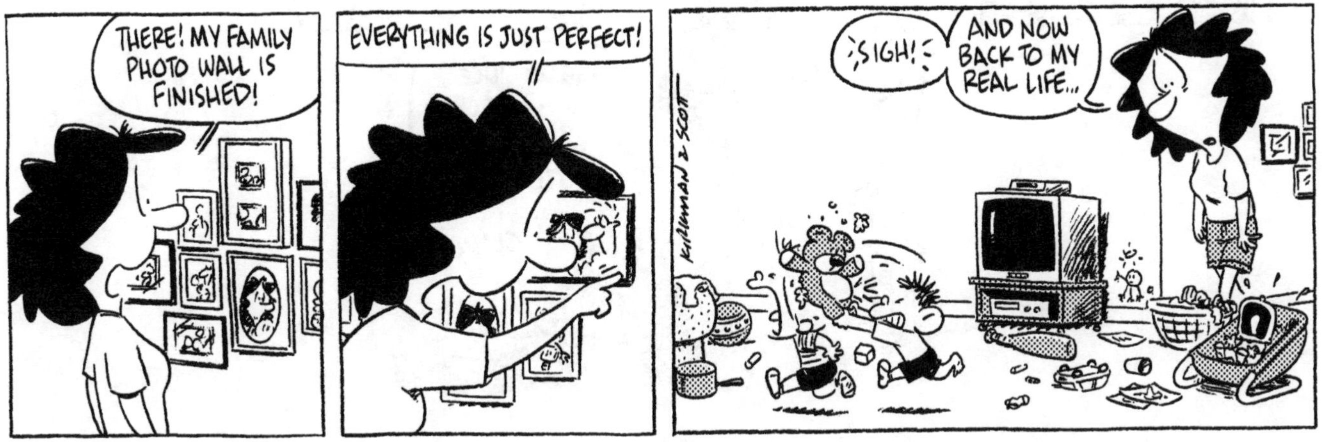
THERE! MY FAMILY PHOTO WALL IS FINISHED!
EVERYTHING IS JUST PERFECT!
SIGH!
AND NOW BACK TO MY REAL LIFE...

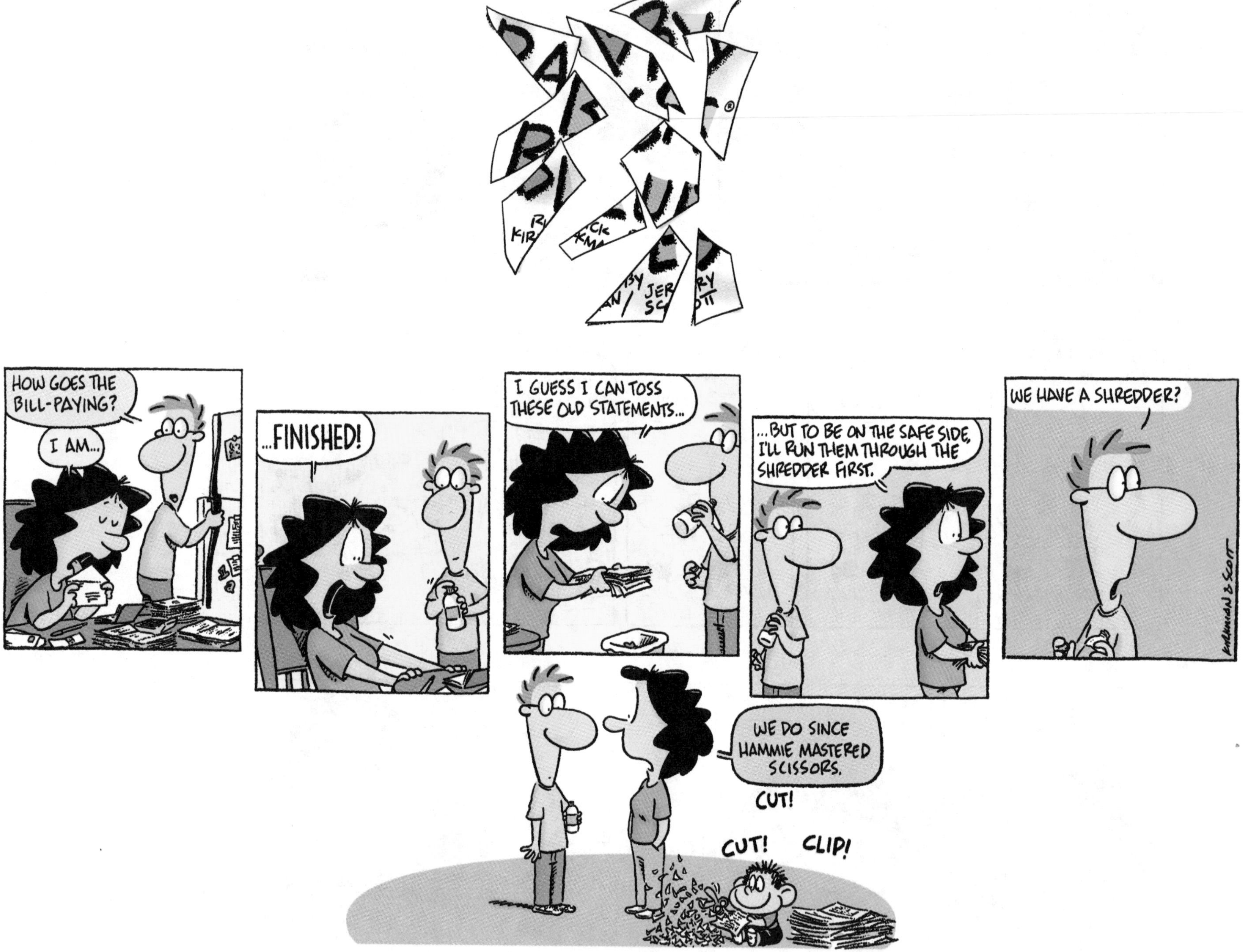
HOW GOES THE BILL-PAYING?
I AM...
...FINISHED!
I GUESS I CAN TOSS THESE OLD STATEMENTS...
...BUT TO BE ON THE SAFE SIDE, I'LL RUN THEM THROUGH THE SHREDDER FIRST.
WE HAVE A SHREDDER?
WE DO SINCE HAMMIE MASTERED SCISSORS.
CUT!
CUT!
CLIP!

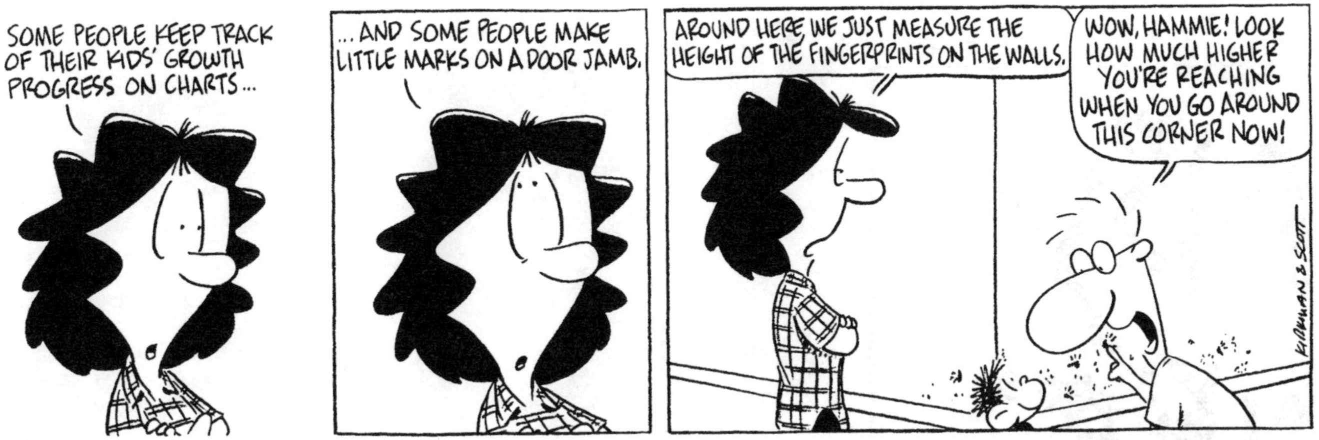
SOME PEOPLE KEEP TRACK OF THEIR KIDS' GROWTH PROGRESS ON CHARTS...
...AND SOME PEOPLE MAKE LITTLE MARKS ON A DOOR JAMB.
AROUND HERE, WE JUST MEASURE THE HEIGHT OF THE FINGERPRINTS ON THE WALLS.
WOW, HAMMIE! LOOK HOW MUCH HIGHER YOU'RE REACHING WHEN YOU GO AROUND THIS CORNER NOW!
KIRKMAN & SCOTT

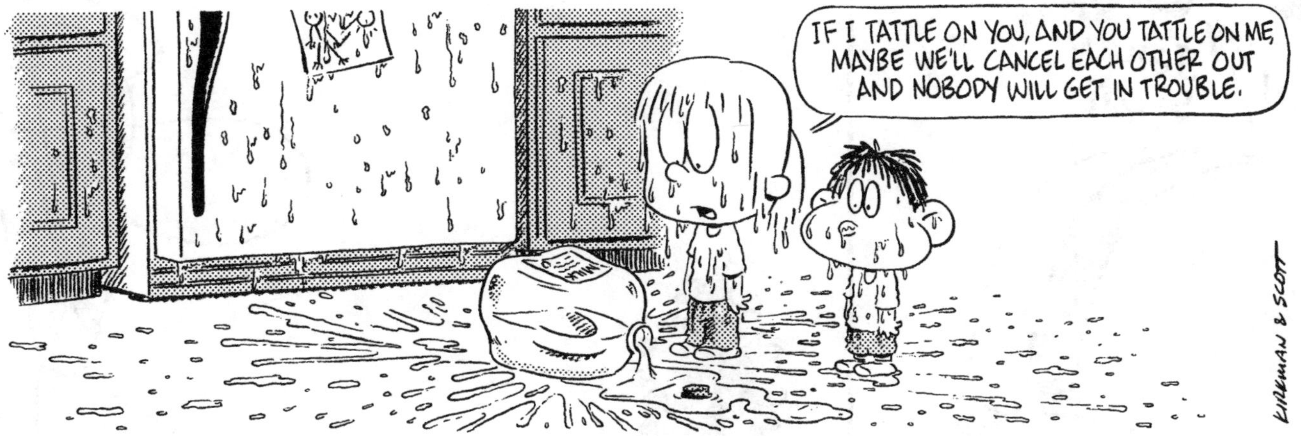
IF I TATTLE ON YOU, AND YOU TATTLE ON ME, MAYBE WE'LL CANCEL EACH OTHER OUT AND NOBODY WILL GET IN TROUBLE.
KIRKMAN & SCOTT

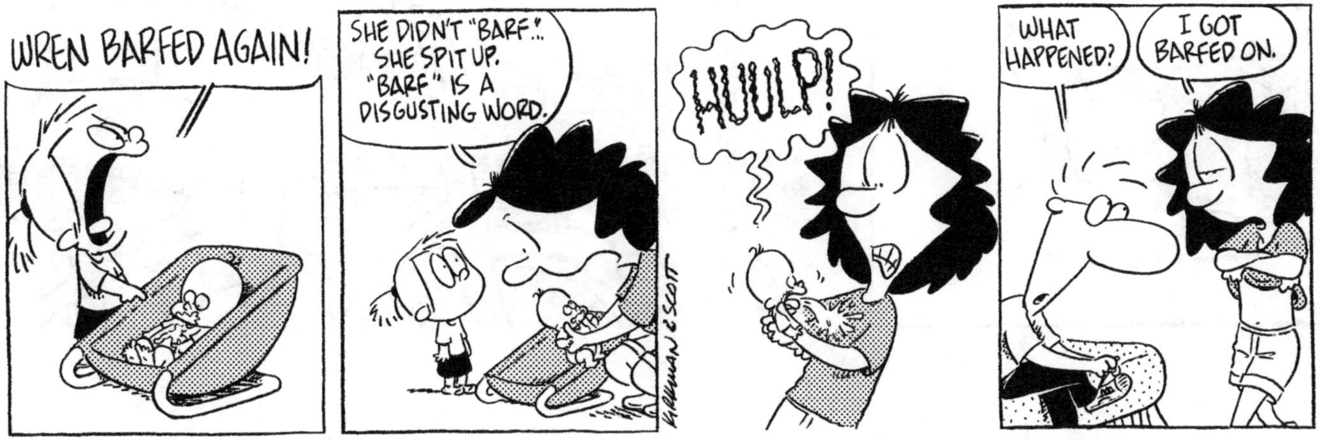
WREN BARFED AGAIN!
SHE DIDN'T "BARF." SHE SPIT UP. "BARF" IS A DISGUSTING WORD.
HUULP!
WHAT HAPPENED?
I GOT BARFED ON.
KIRKMAN & SCOTT

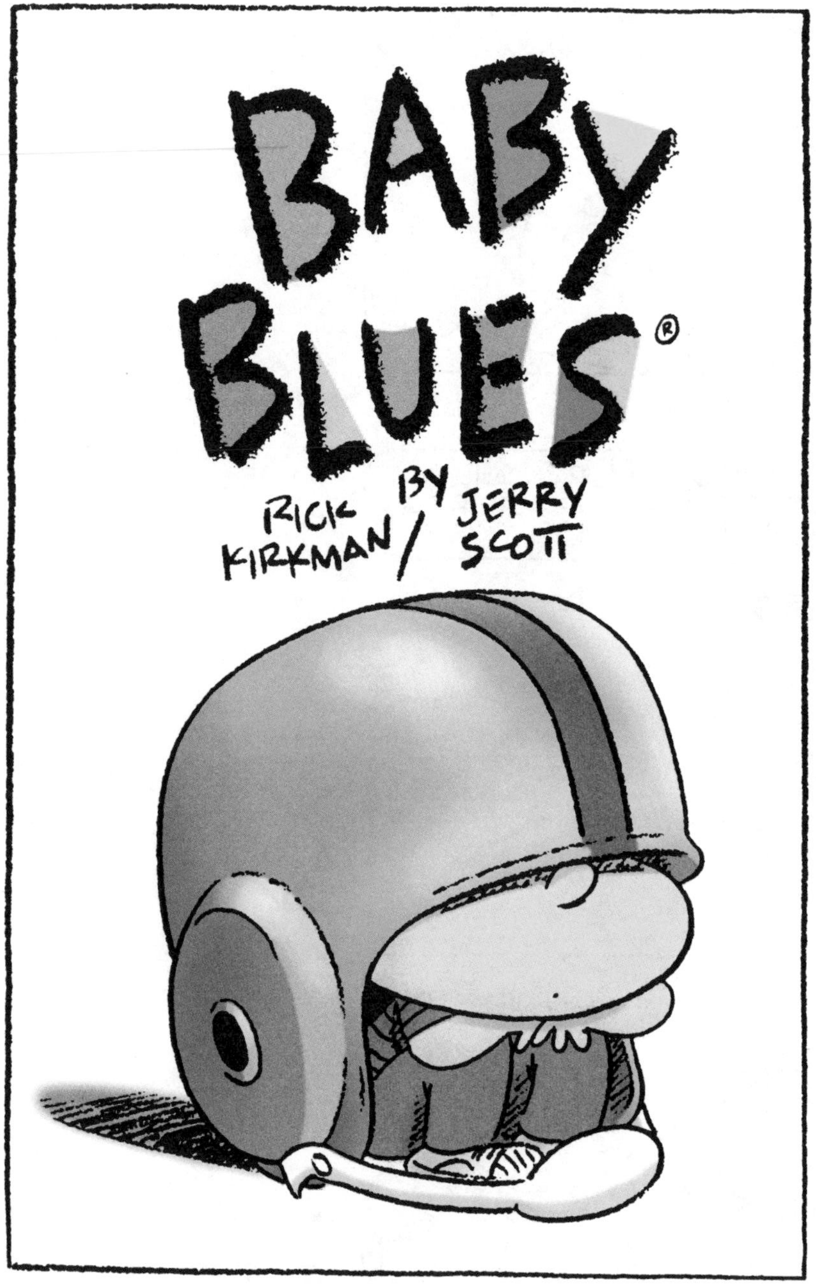
BABY BLUES®
BY
RICK KIRKMAN / JERRY SCOTT

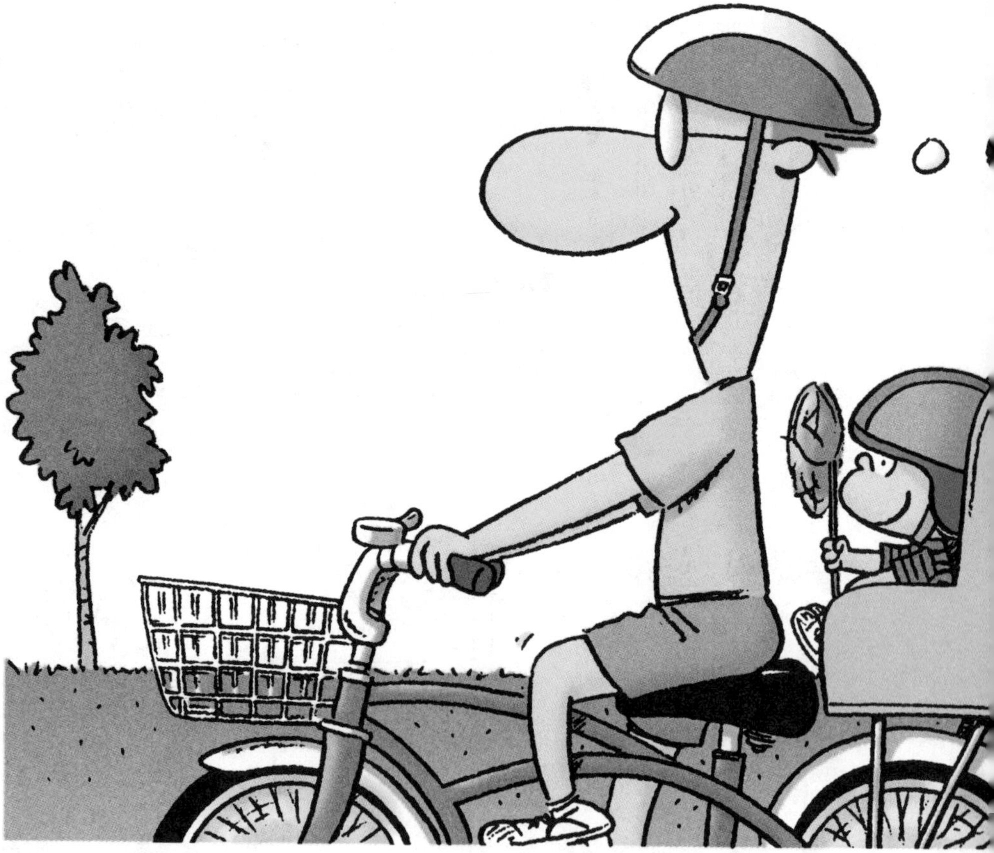

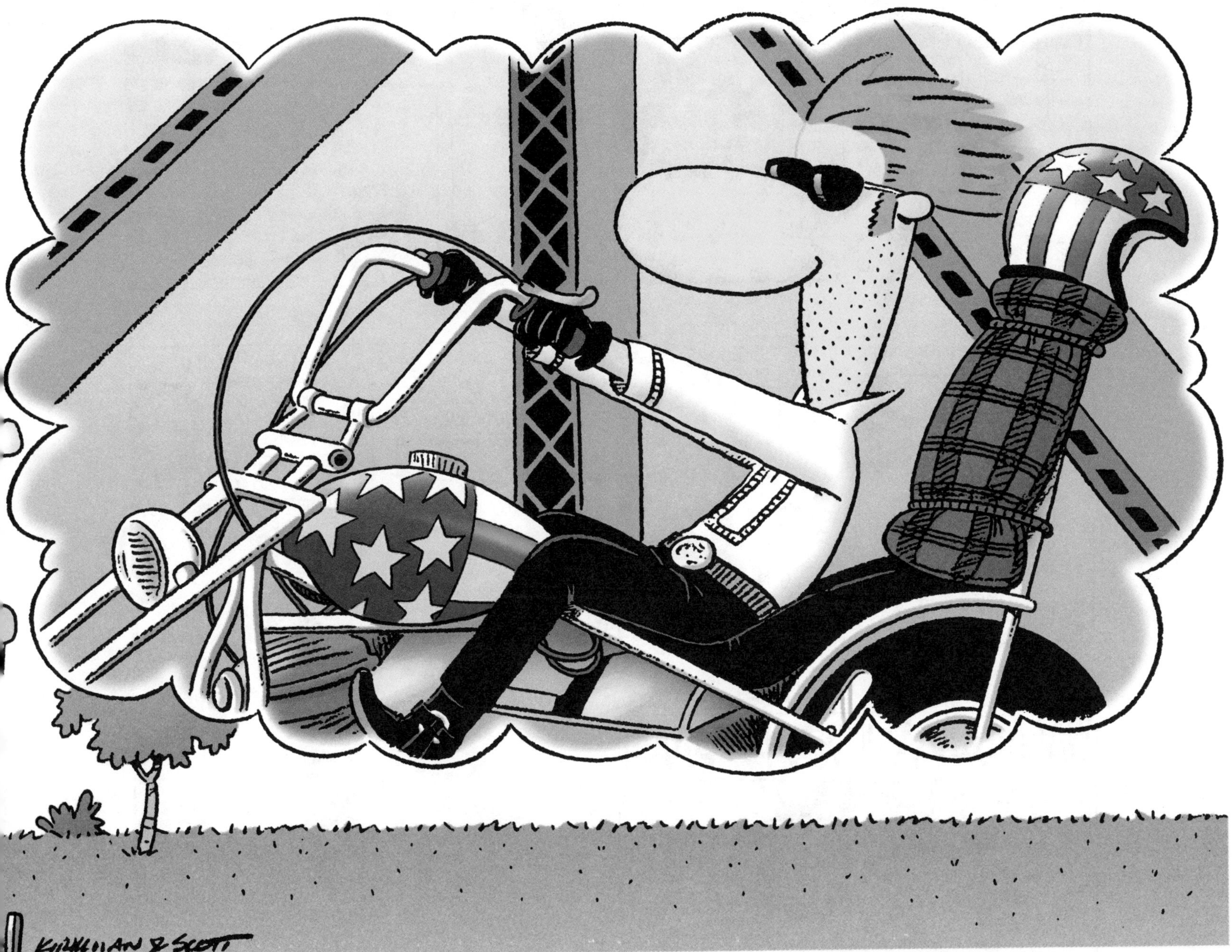
KIRKMAN & SCOTT

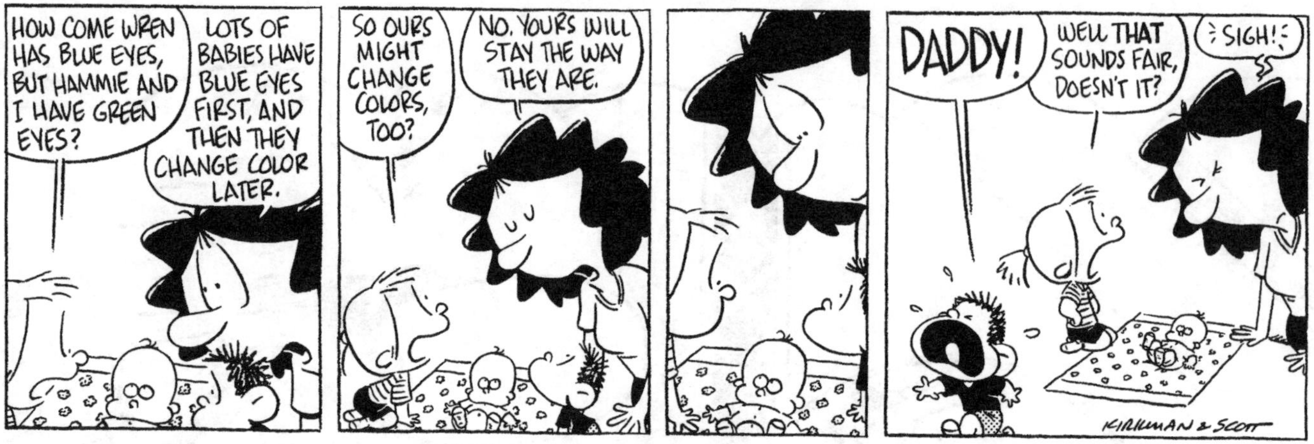
HOW COME WREN HAS BLUE EYES, BUT HAMMIE AND I HAVE GREEN EYES?
LOTS OF BABIES HAVE BLUE EYES FIRST, AND THEN THEY CHANGE COLOR LATER.
SO OURS MIGHT CHANGE COLORS, TOO?
NO. YOURS WILL STAY THE WAY THEY ARE.
DADDY!
WELL THAT SOUNDS FAIR, DOESN'T IT?
SIGH!
KIRKMAN & SCOTT

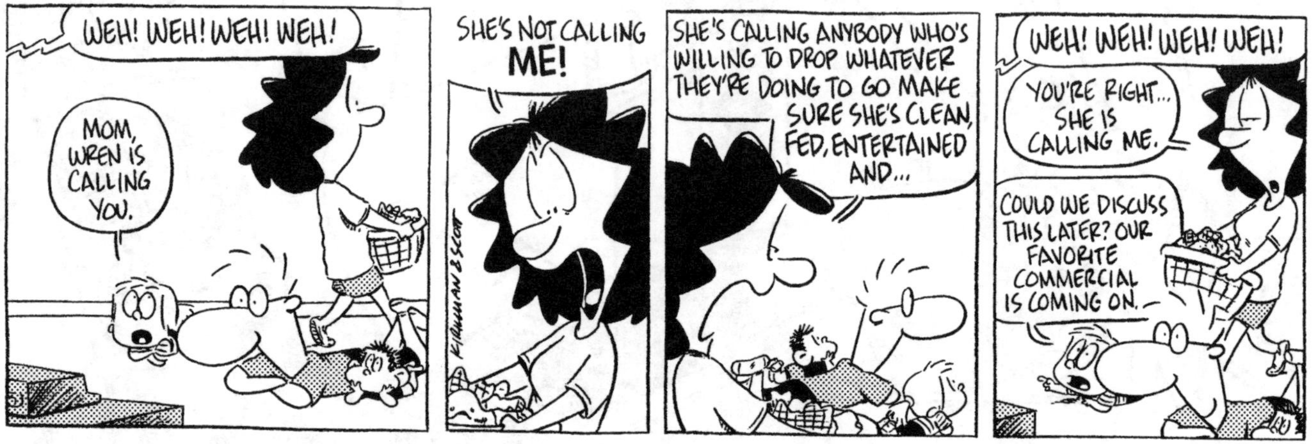
WEH! WEH! WEH! WEH!
MOM, WREN IS CALLING YOU.
KIRKMAN & SCOTT
SHE'S NOT CALLING ME!
SHE'S CALLING ANYBODY WHO'S WILLING TO DROP WHATEVER THEY'RE DOING TO GO MAKE SURE SHE'S CLEAN, FED, ENTERTAINED AND...
WEH! WEH! WEH! WEH!
YOU'RE RIGHT... SHE IS CALLING ME.
COULD WE DISCUSS THIS LATER? OUR FAVORITE COMMERCIAL IS COMING ON.

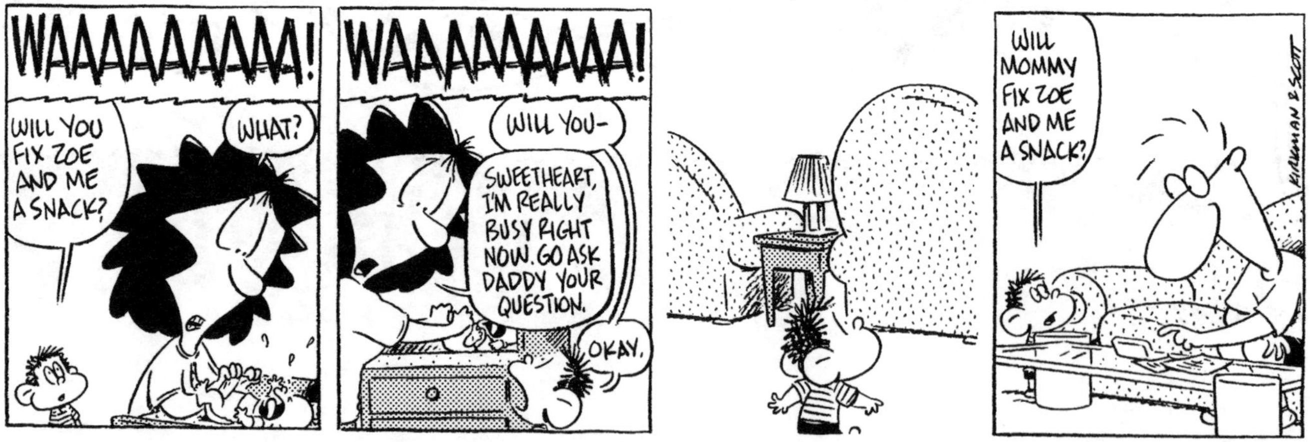
WAAAAAAAA!
WILL YOU FIX ZOE AND ME A SNACK?
WHAT?
WAAAAAAAA!
WILL YOU-
SWEETHEART, I'M REALLY BUSY RIGHT NOW. GO ASK DADDY YOUR QUESTION.
OKAY.
WILL MOMMY FIX ZOE AND ME A SNACK?
KIRKMAN & SCOTT

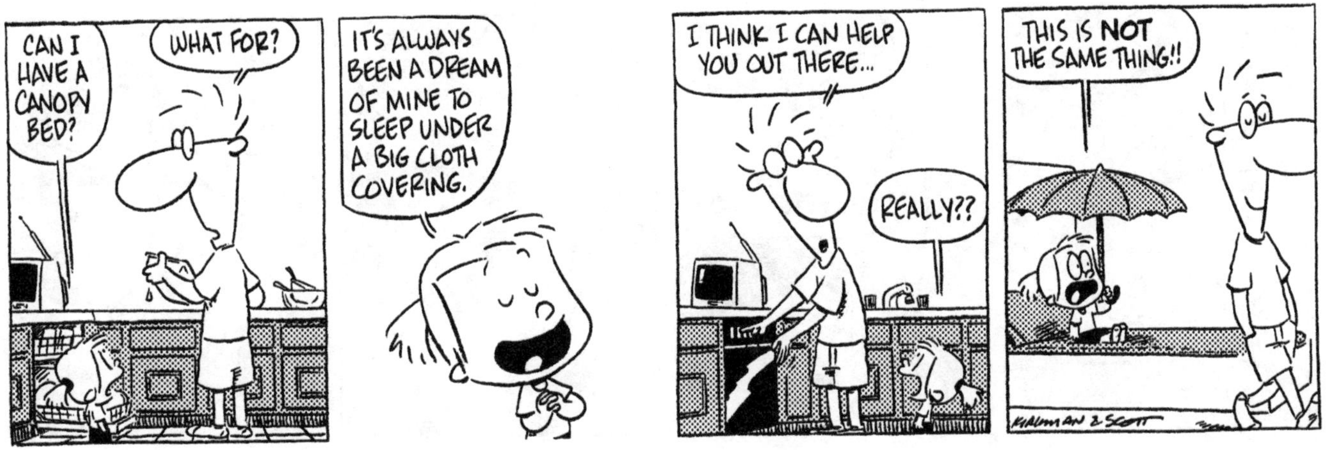
CAN I HAVE A CANOPY BED?
WHAT FOR?
IT'S ALWAYS BEEN A DREAM OF MINE TO SLEEP UNDER A BIG CLOTH COVERING.
I THINK I CAN HELP YOU OUT THERE...
REALLY??
THIS IS **NOT** THE SAME THING!!
KIRKMAN & SCOTT

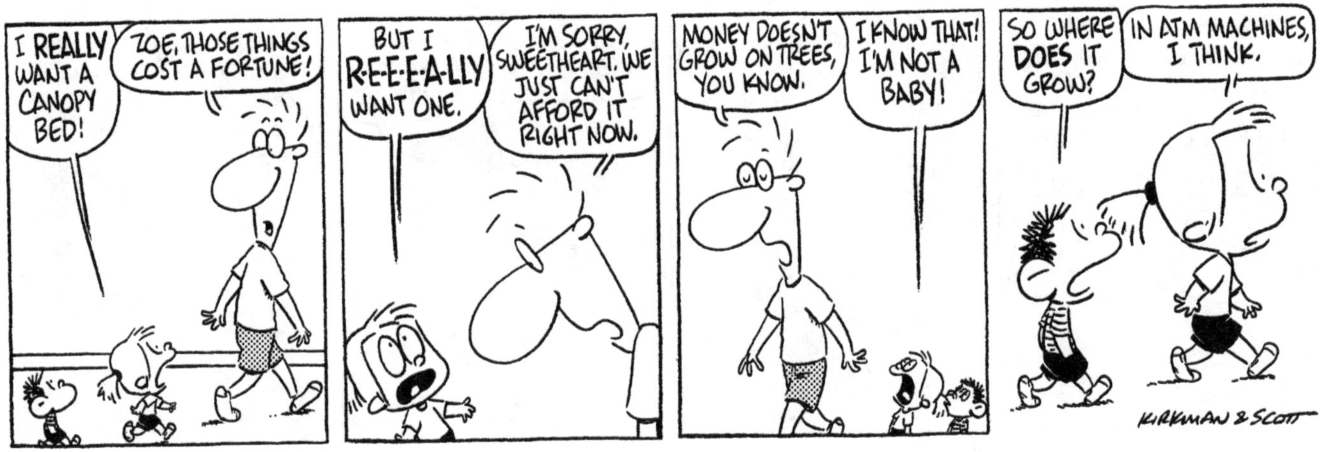
I **REALLY** WANT A CANOPY BED!
ZOE, THOSE THINGS COST A FORTUNE!
BUT I **R-E-E-E-A-LLY** WANT ONE.
I'M SORRY, SWEETHEART. WE JUST CAN'T AFFORD IT RIGHT NOW.
MONEY DOESN'T GROW ON TREES, YOU KNOW.
I KNOW THAT! I'M NOT A BABY!
SO WHERE **DOES** IT GROW?
IN ATM MACHINES, I THINK.
KIRKMAN & SCOTT

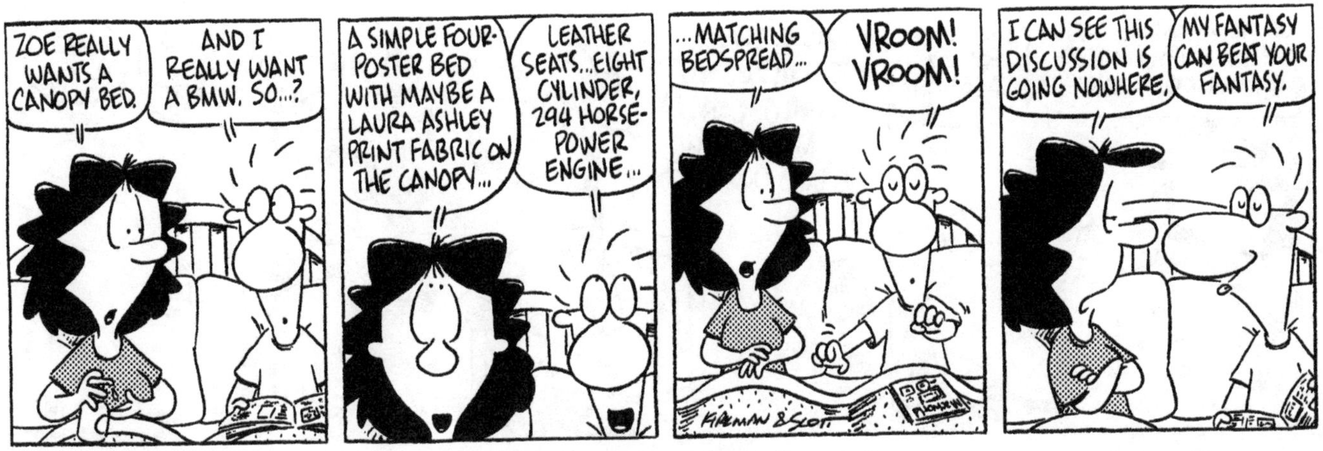
ZOE REALLY WANTS A CANOPY BED.
AND I REALLY WANT A BMW. SO...?
A SIMPLE FOUR-POSTER BED WITH MAYBE A LAURA ASHLEY PRINT FABRIC ON THE CANOPY...
LEATHER SEATS...EIGHT CYLINDER, 294 HORSE-POWER ENGINE...
...MATCHING BEDSPREAD...
VROOM! VROOM!
KIRKMAN & SCOTT
I CAN SEE THIS DISCUSSION IS GOING NOWHERE.
MY FANTASY CAN BEAT YOUR FANTASY.

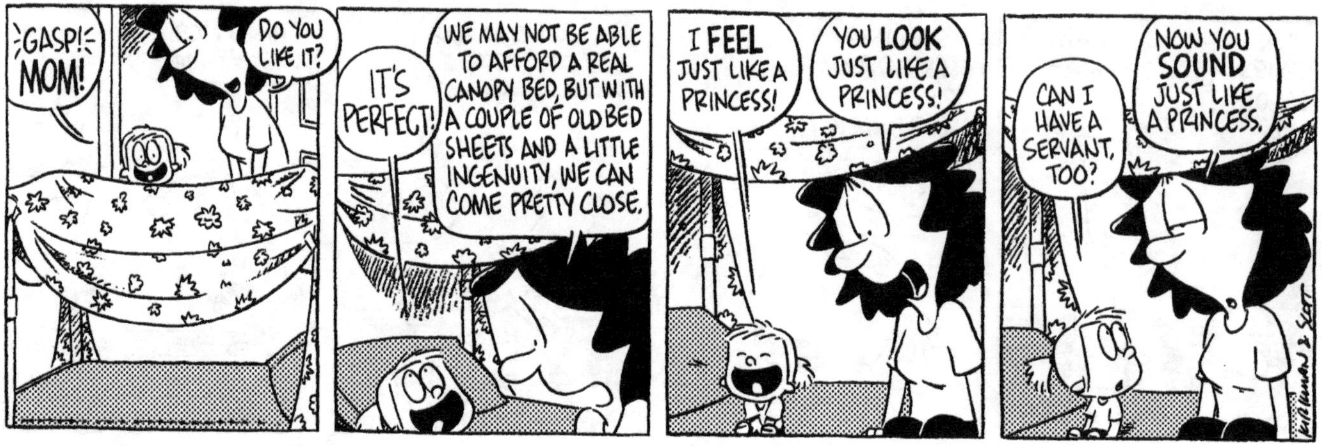
GASP! MOM!
DO YOU LIKE IT?
IT'S PERFECT!
WE MAY NOT BE ABLE TO AFFORD A REAL CANOPY BED, BUT WITH A COUPLE OF OLD BED SHEETS AND A LITTLE INGENUITY, WE CAN COME PRETTY CLOSE.
I FEEL JUST LIKE A PRINCESS!
YOU LOOK JUST LIKE A PRINCESS!
CAN I HAVE A SERVANT, TOO?
NOW YOU SOUND JUST LIKE A PRINCESS.
KIRKMAN & SCOTT

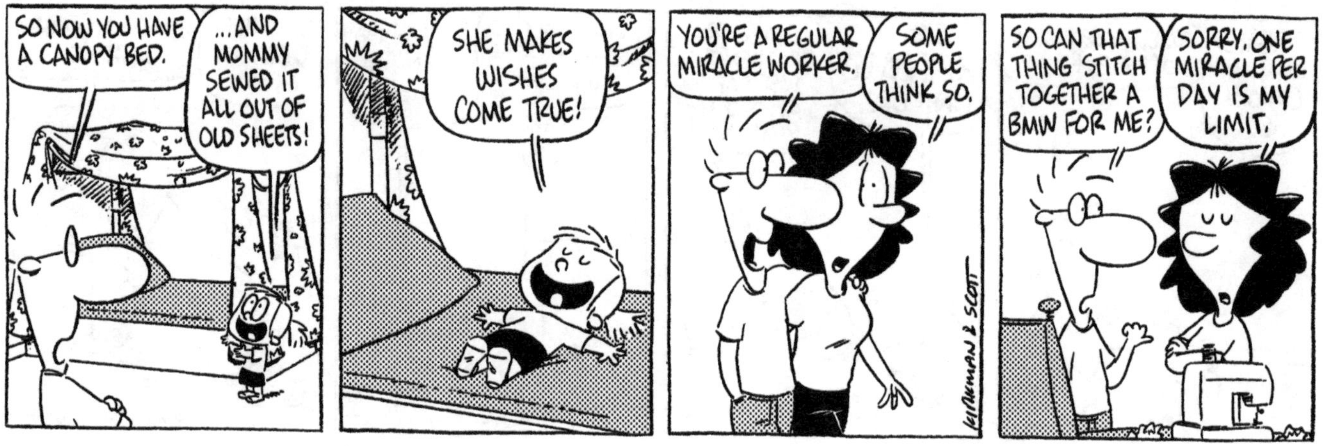
SO NOW YOU HAVE A CANOPY BED.
...AND MOMMY SEWED IT ALL OUT OF OLD SHEETS!
SHE MAKES WISHES COME TRUE!
YOU'RE A REGULAR MIRACLE WORKER.
SOME PEOPLE THINK SO.
KIRKMAN & SCOTT
SO CAN THAT THING STITCH TOGETHER A BMW FOR ME?
SORRY. ONE MIRACLE PER DAY IS MY LIMIT.

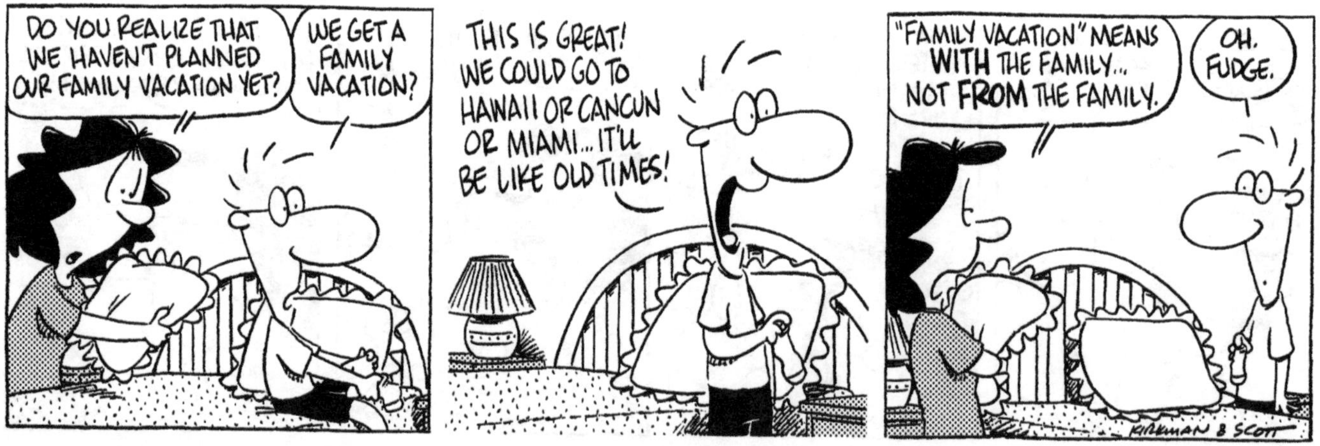
DO YOU REALIZE THAT WE HAVEN'T PLANNED OUR FAMILY VACATION YET?
WE GET A FAMILY VACATION?
THIS IS GREAT! WE COULD GO TO HAWAII OR CANCUN OR MIAMI... IT'LL BE LIKE OLD TIMES!
"FAMILY VACATION" MEANS WITH THE FAMILY... NOT FROM THE FAMILY.
OH. FUDGE.
KIRKMAN & SCOTT

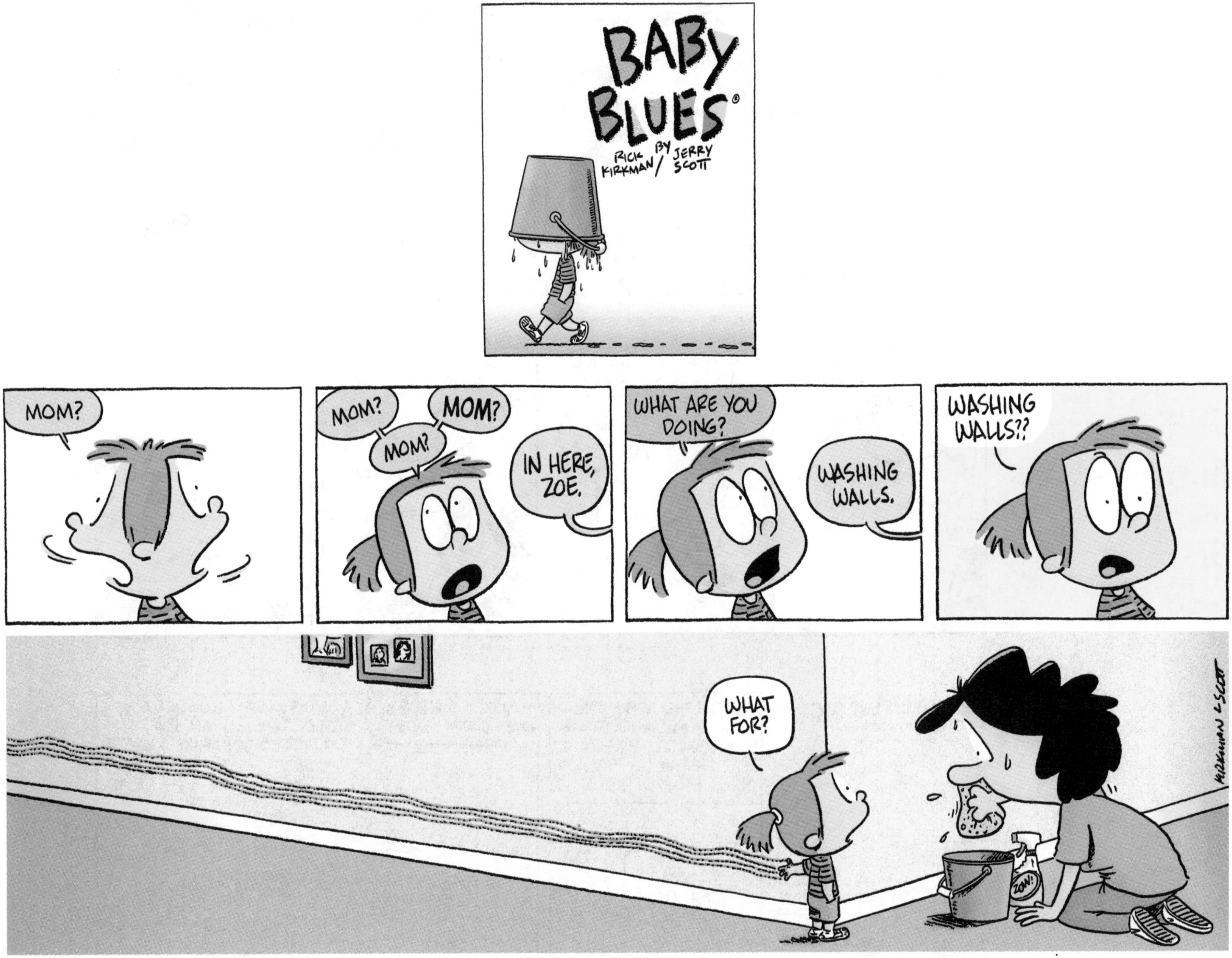
BABY BLUES®
BY RICK KIRKMAN / JERRY SCOTT
MOM?
MOM?
MOM?
MOM?
IN HERE, ZOE.
WHAT ARE YOU DOING?
WASHING WALLS.
WASHING WALLS??
WHAT FOR?
ZON!
KIRKMAN & SCOTT

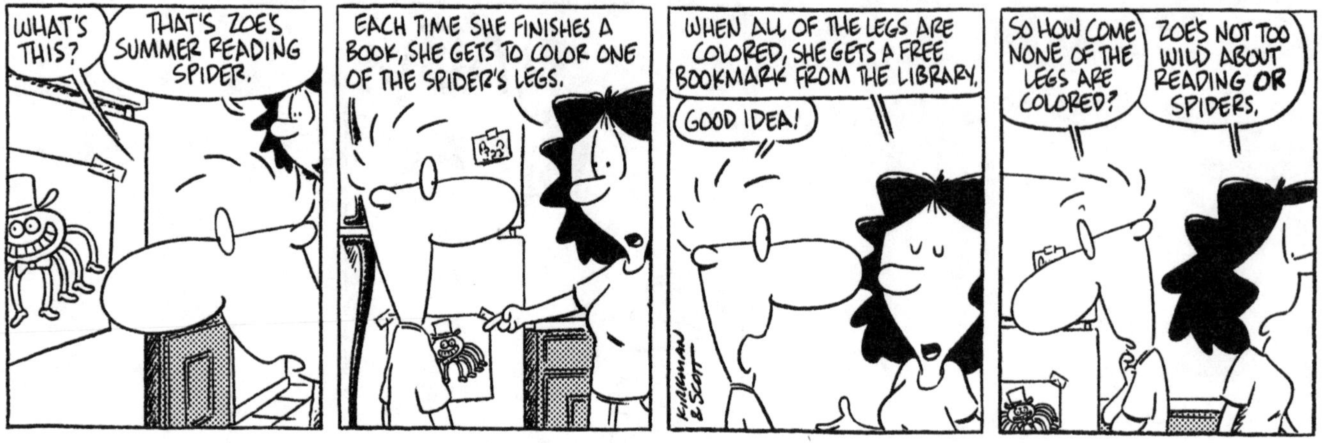
WHAT'S THIS?
THAT'S ZOE'S SUMMER READING SPIDER.
EACH TIME SHE FINISHES A BOOK, SHE GETS TO COLOR ONE OF THE SPIDER'S LEGS.
WHEN ALL OF THE LEGS ARE COLORED, SHE GETS A FREE BOOKMARK FROM THE LIBRARY.
GOOD IDEA!
SO HOW COME NONE OF THE LEGS ARE COLORED?
ZOE'S NOT TOO WILD ABOUT READING **OR** SPIDERS.
KIRKMAN & SCOTT

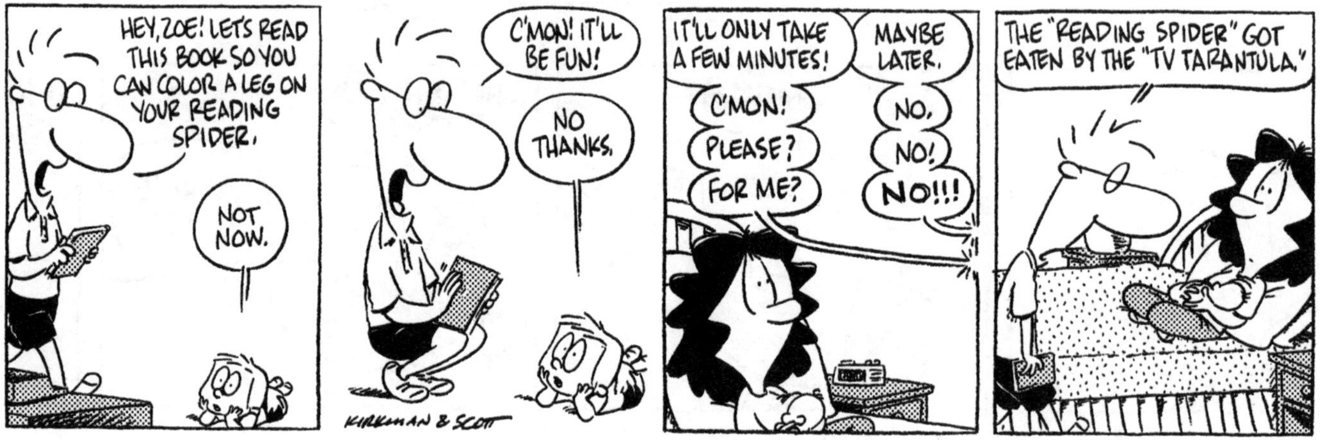
HEY, ZOE! LET'S READ THIS BOOK SO YOU CAN COLOR A LEG ON YOUR READING SPIDER.
NOT NOW.
C'MON! IT'LL BE FUN!
NO THANKS.
IT'LL ONLY TAKE A FEW MINUTES!
MAYBE LATER.
C'MON!
NO.
PLEASE?
NO!
FOR ME?
NO!!!
THE "READING SPIDER" GOT EATEN BY THE "TV TARANTULA."
KIRKMAN & SCOTT

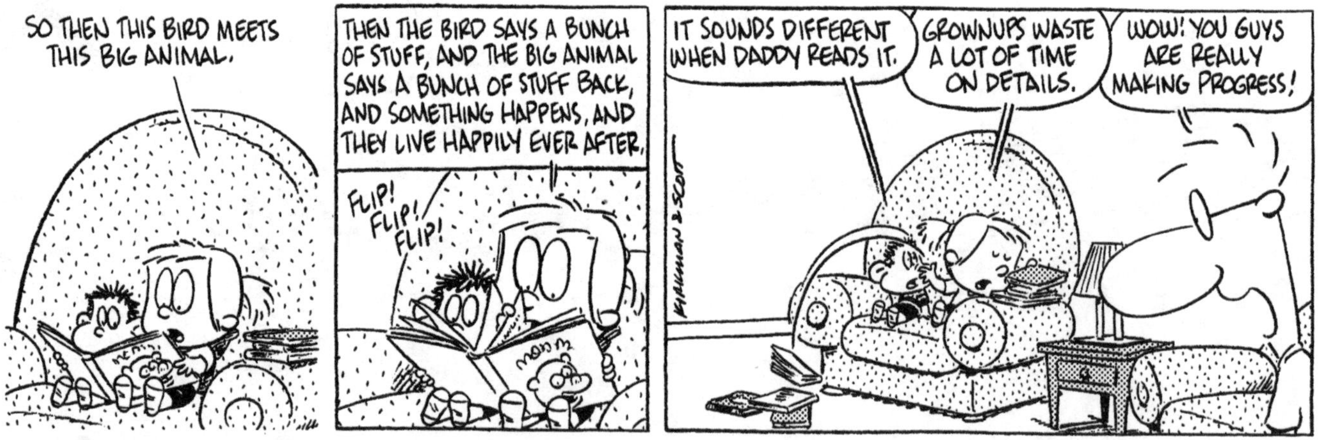
SO THEN THIS BIRD MEETS THIS BIG ANIMAL.
THEN THE BIRD SAYS A BUNCH OF STUFF, AND THE BIG ANIMAL SAYS A BUNCH OF STUFF BACK, AND SOMETHING HAPPENS, AND THEY LIVE HAPPILY EVER AFTER.
FLIP! FLIP! FLIP!
IT SOUNDS DIFFERENT WHEN DADDY READS IT.
GROWNUPS WASTE A LOT OF TIME ON DETAILS.
WOW! YOU GUYS ARE REALLY MAKING PROGRESS!
KIRKMAN & SCOTT

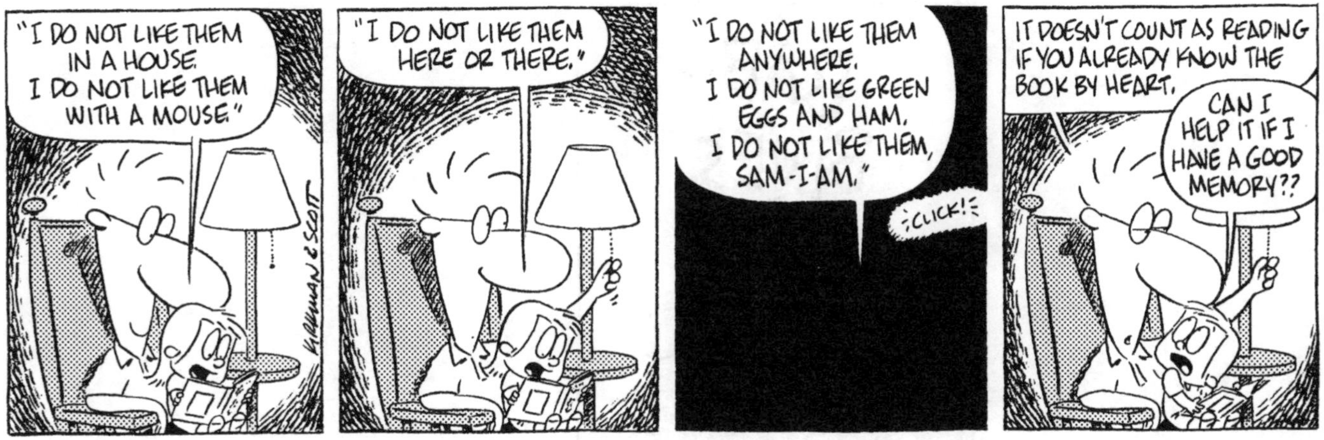
"I DO NOT LIKE THEM IN A HOUSE. I DO NOT LIKE THEM WITH A MOUSE."
KIRKMAN & SCOTT
"I DO NOT LIKE THEM HERE OR THERE."
"I DO NOT LIKE THEM ANYWHERE. I DO NOT LIKE GREEN EGGS AND HAM. I DO NOT LIKE THEM, SAM-I-AM."
CLICK!
IT DOESN'T COUNT AS READING IF YOU ALREADY KNOW THE BOOK BY HEART.
CAN I HELP IT IF I HAVE A GOOD MEMORY??

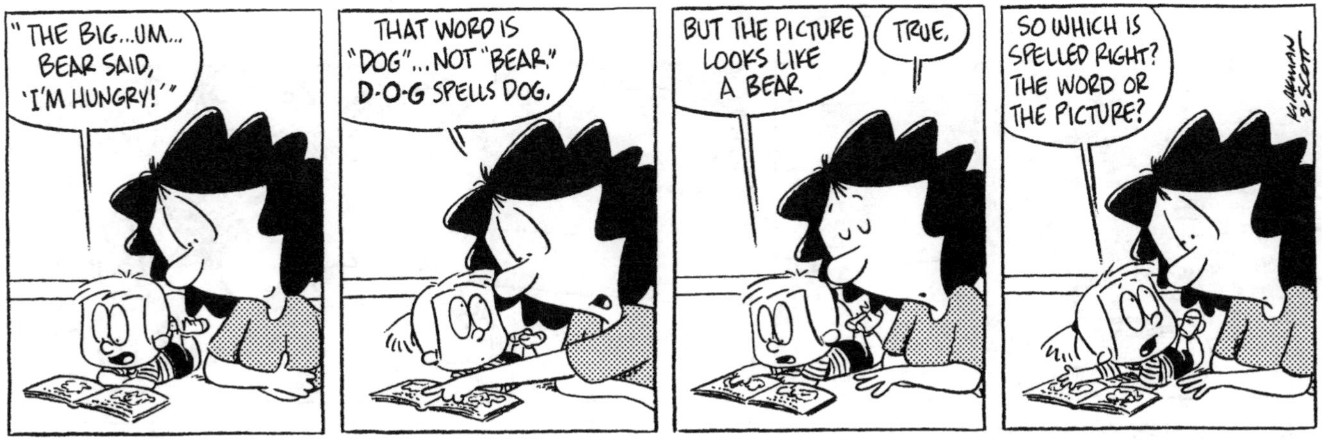
"THE BIG...UM... BEAR SAID, 'I'M HUNGRY!'"
THAT WORD IS "DOG"... NOT "BEAR." D-O-G SPELLS DOG.
BUT THE PICTURE LOOKS LIKE A BEAR.
TRUE.
SO WHICH IS SPELLED RIGHT? THE WORD OR THE PICTURE?
KIRKMAN & SCOTT

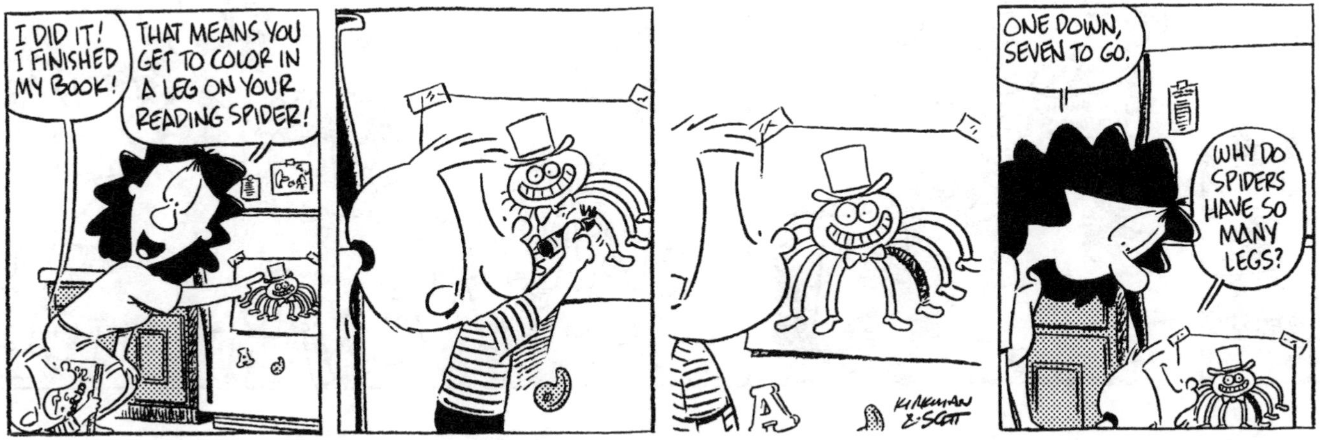
I DID IT! I FINISHED MY BOOK!
THAT MEANS YOU GET TO COLOR IN A LEG ON YOUR READING SPIDER!
KIRKMAN & SCOTT
ONE DOWN, SEVEN TO GO.
WHY DO SPIDERS HAVE SO MANY LEGS?

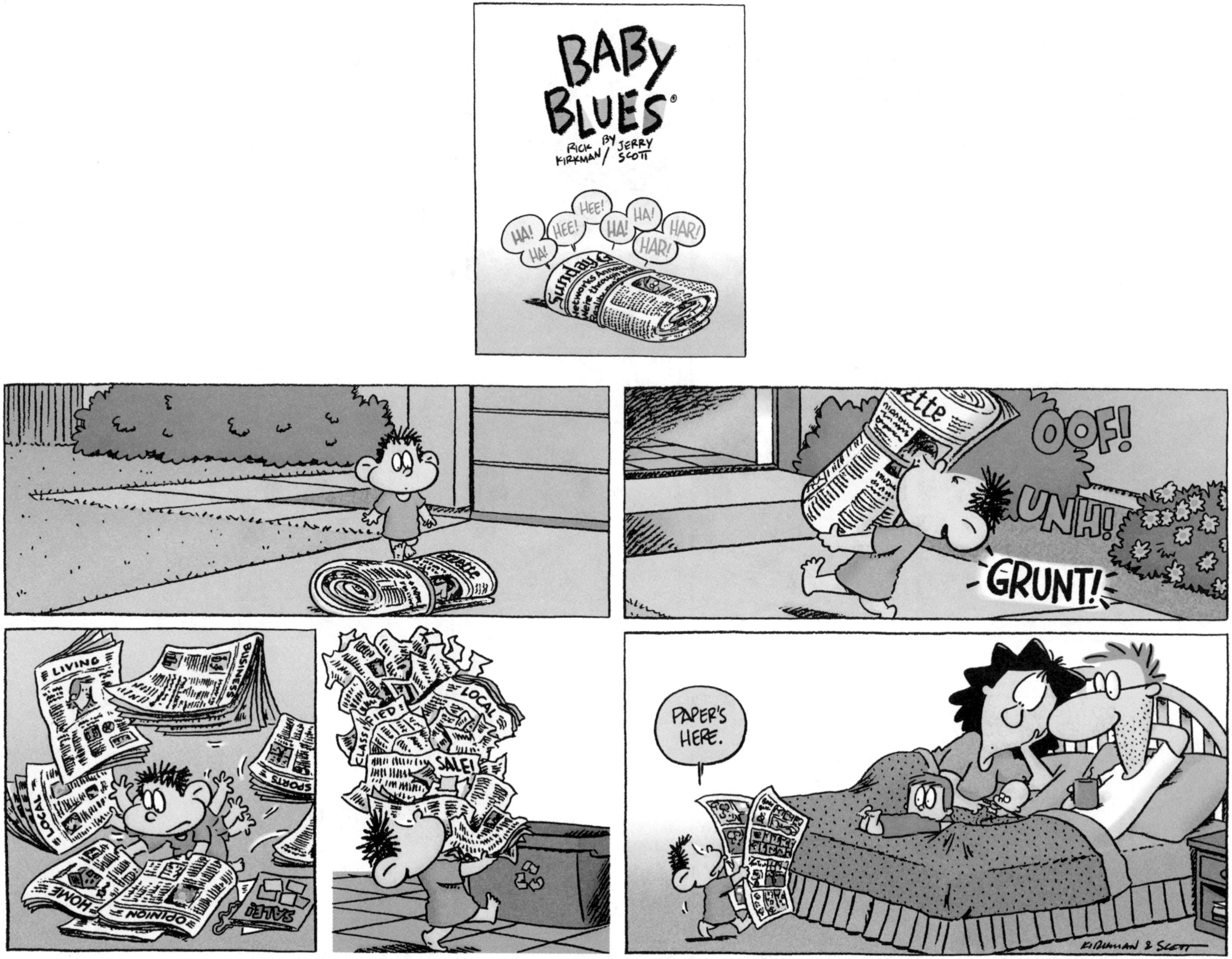
BABY BLUES®
BY RICK KIRKMAN / JERRY SCOTT
HA!
HA!
HEE!
HEE!
HA!
HA!
HAR!
HAR!
OOF!
UNH!
GRUNT!
LIVING
BUSINESS
LOCAL
SPORTS
HOME
OPINION
SALE!
LOCAL
SALE!
PAPER'S HERE.
KIRKMAN & SCOTT

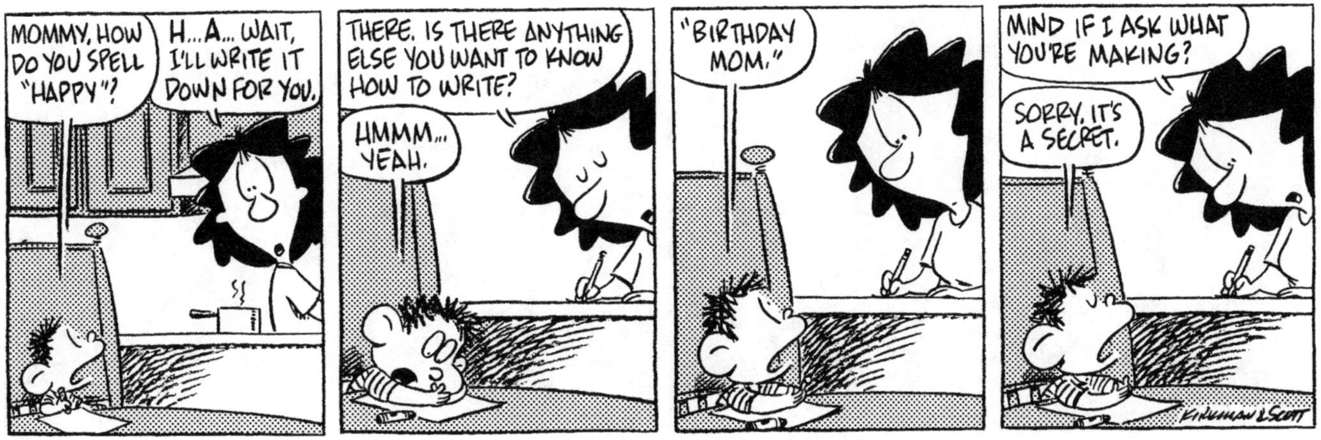
MOMMY, HOW DO YOU SPELL "HAPPY"?
H...A... WAIT, I'LL WRITE IT DOWN FOR YOU.
THERE. IS THERE ANYTHING ELSE YOU WANT TO KNOW HOW TO WRITE?
HMMM... YEAH.
"BIRTHDAY MOM."
MIND IF I ASK WHAT YOU'RE MAKING?
SORRY, IT'S A SECRET.
KIRKMAN & SCOTT

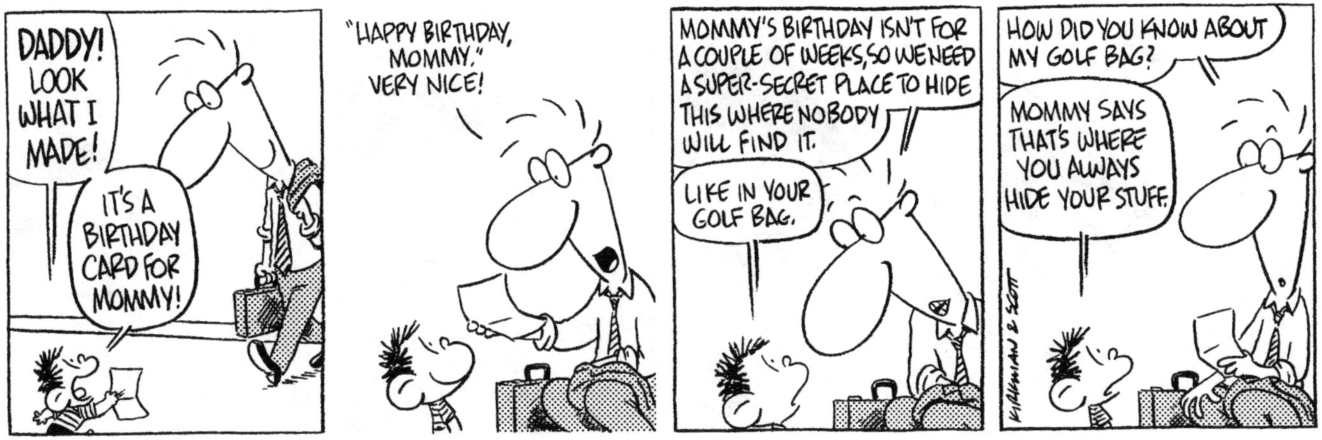
DADDY! LOOK WHAT I MADE!
IT'S A BIRTHDAY CARD FOR MOMMY!
"HAPPY BIRTHDAY, MOMMY." VERY NICE!
MOMMY'S BIRTHDAY ISN'T FOR A COUPLE OF WEEKS, SO WE NEED A SUPER-SECRET PLACE TO HIDE THIS WHERE NOBODY WILL FIND IT.
LIKE IN YOUR GOLF BAG.
KIRKMAN & SCOTT
HOW DID YOU KNOW ABOUT MY GOLF BAG?
MOMMY SAYS THAT'S WHERE YOU ALWAYS HIDE YOUR STUFF.

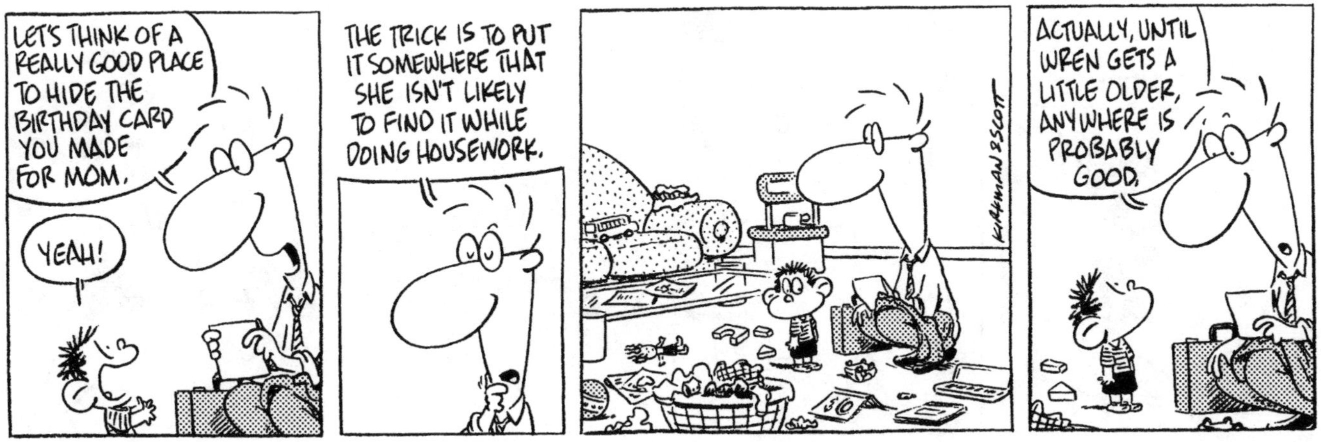
LET'S THINK OF A REALLY GOOD PLACE TO HIDE THE BIRTHDAY CARD YOU MADE FOR MOM.
YEAH!
THE TRICK IS TO PUT IT SOMEWHERE THAT SHE ISN'T LIKELY TO FIND IT WHILE DOING HOUSEWORK.
KIRKMAN & SCOTT
ACTUALLY, UNTIL WREN GETS A LITTLE OLDER, ANYWHERE IS PROBABLY GOOD.

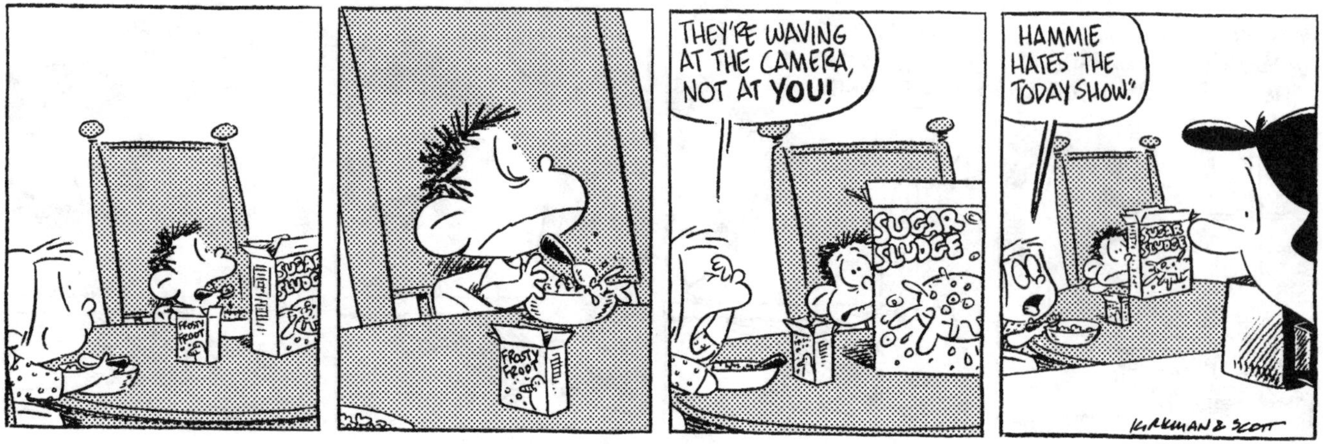
FROSTY FROOT
SUGAR SLUDGE
THEY'RE WAVING AT THE CAMERA, NOT AT **YOU!**
HAMMIE HATES "THE TODAY SHOW."
KIRKMAN & SCOTT

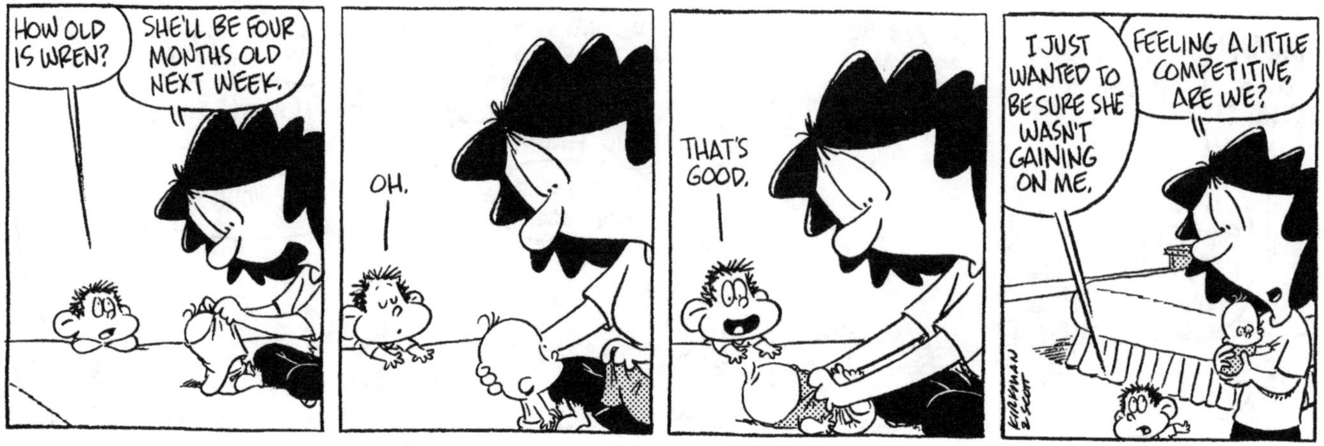
HOW OLD IS WREN?
SHE'LL BE FOUR MONTHS OLD NEXT WEEK.
OH.
THAT'S GOOD.
I JUST WANTED TO BE SURE SHE WASN'T GAINING ON ME.
FEELING A LITTLE COMPETITIVE, ARE WE?
KIRKMAN & SCOTT

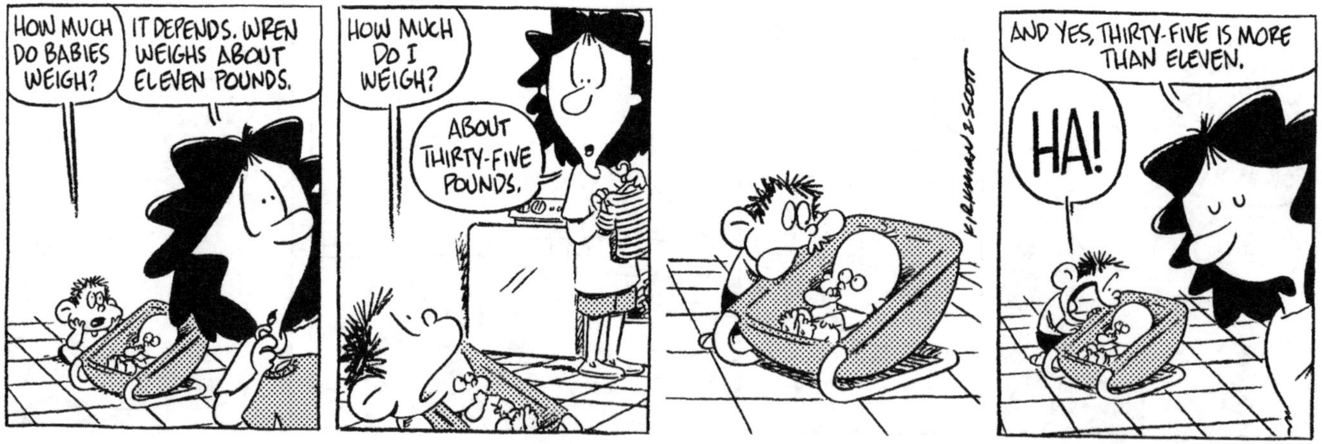
HOW MUCH DO BABIES WEIGH?
IT DEPENDS. WREN WEIGHS ABOUT ELEVEN POUNDS.
HOW MUCH DO I WEIGH?
ABOUT THIRTY-FIVE POUNDS.
KIRKMAN & SCOTT
AND YES, THIRTY-FIVE IS MORE THAN ELEVEN.
HA!

BAY-BEE BLOOZ

BY RIK KURK-MAN / JER-EE SKOT

T-T-T-T
h-u-u-h-h
e-e-e-e-e
KIRKMAN & SCOTT
IT'S "THE."
OH.
HOW'S THE READING LESSON GOING?

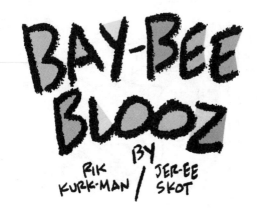

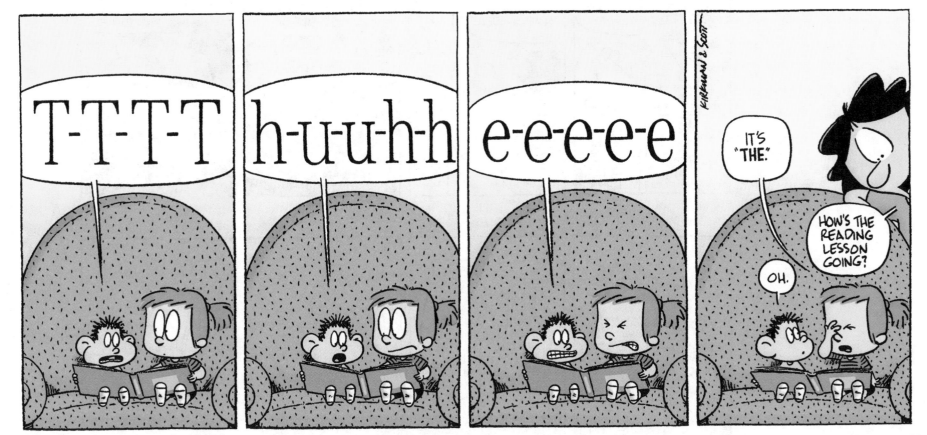

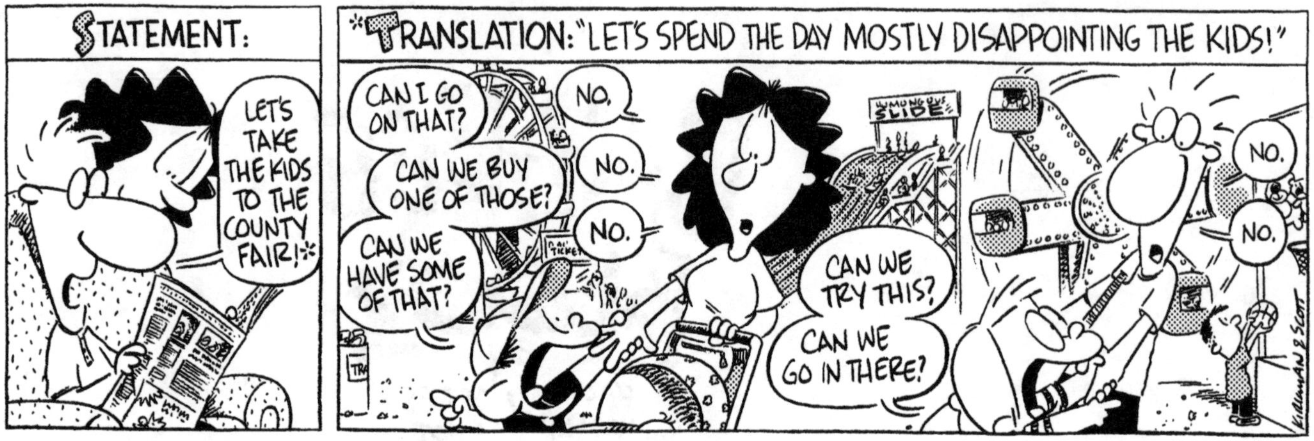
STATEMENT:
LET'S TAKE THE KIDS TO THE COUNTY FAIR!*
*TRANSLATION: "LET'S SPEND THE DAY MOSTLY DISAPPOINTING THE KIDS!"
CAN I GO ON THAT?
NO.
CAN WE BUY ONE OF THOSE?
NO.
CAN WE HAVE SOME OF THAT?
NO.
CAN WE TRY THIS?
NO.
CAN WE GO IN THERE?
NO.

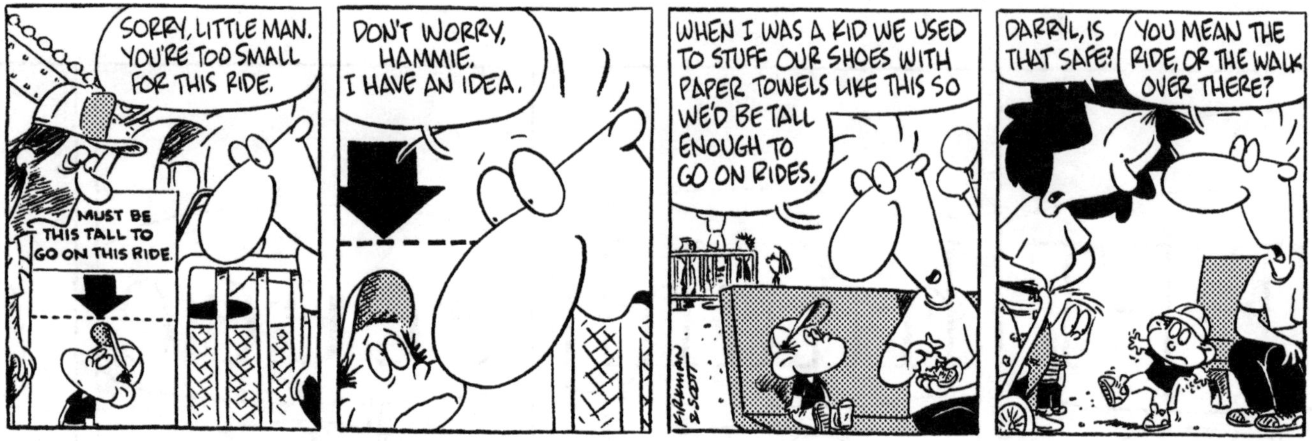
SORRY, LITTLE MAN. YOU'RE TOO SMALL FOR THIS RIDE.
MUST BE THIS TALL TO GO ON THIS RIDE.
DON'T WORRY, HAMMIE. I HAVE AN IDEA.
WHEN I WAS A KID WE USED TO STUFF OUR SHOES WITH PAPER TOWELS LIKE THIS SO WE'D BE TALL ENOUGH TO GO ON RIDES.
DARRYL, IS THAT SAFE?
YOU MEAN THE RIDE, OR THE WALK OVER THERE?

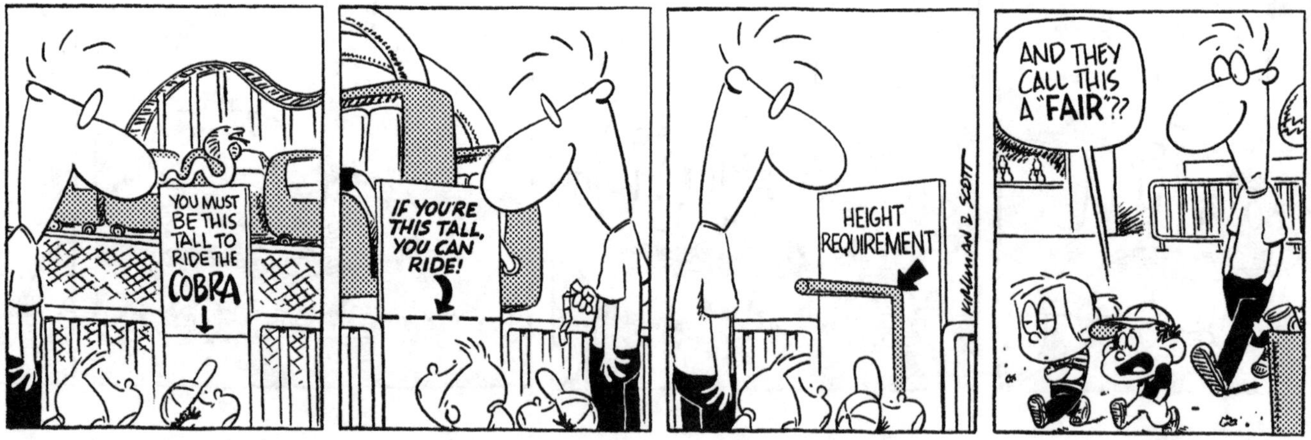
YOU MUST BE THIS TALL TO RIDE THE COBRA
IF YOU'RE THIS TALL, YOU CAN RIDE!
HEIGHT REQUIREMENT
AND THEY CALL THIS A "FAIR"??

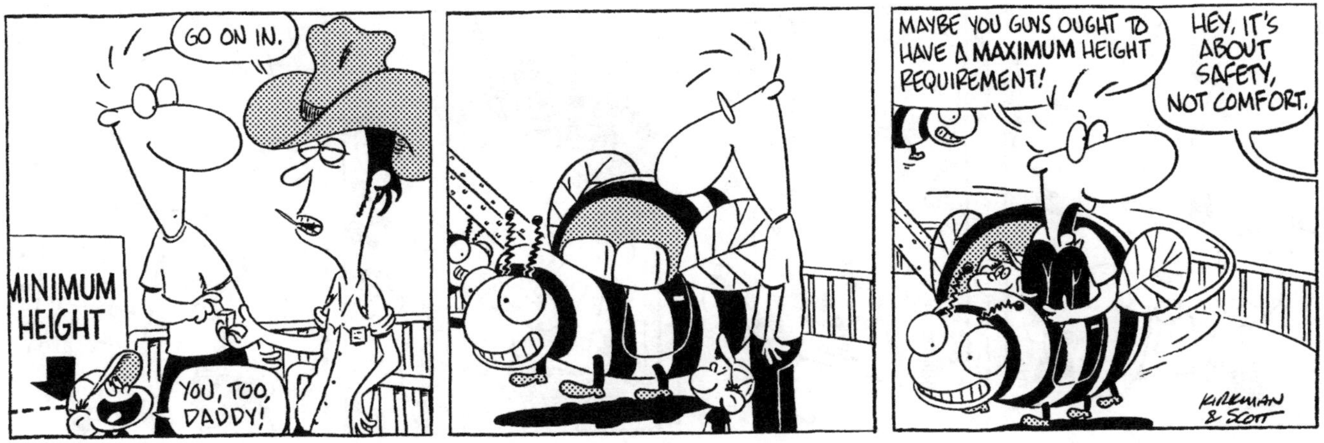
MINIMUM HEIGHT
GO ON IN.
YOU, TOO, DADDY!
MAYBE YOU GUYS OUGHT TO HAVE A **MAXIMUM** HEIGHT REQUIREMENT!
HEY, IT'S ABOUT SAFETY, NOT COMFORT.
KIRKMAN & SCOTT

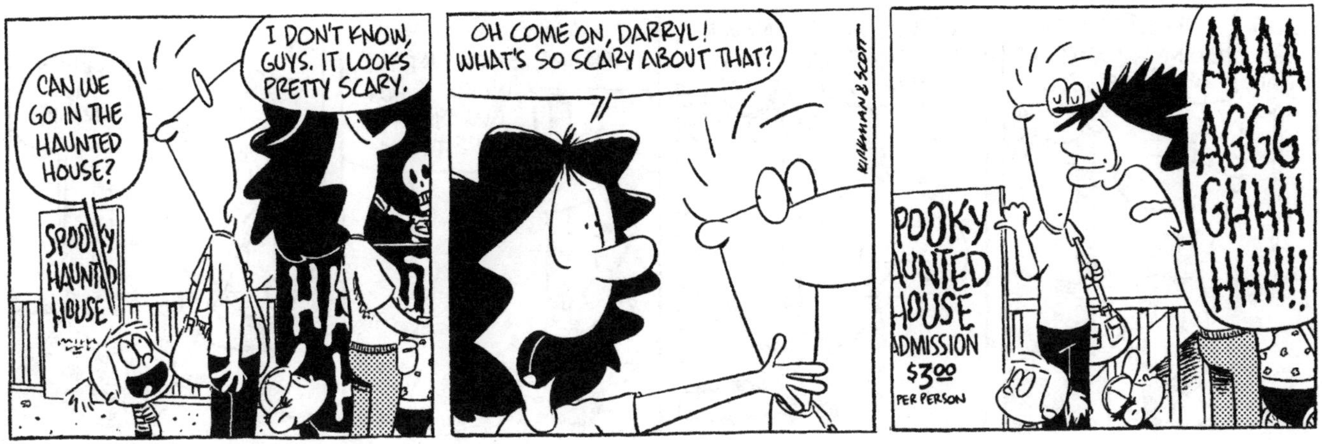
CAN WE GO IN THE HAUNTED HOUSE?
I DON'T KNOW, GUYS. IT LOOKS PRETTY SCARY.
SPOOKY HAUNTED HOUSE
OH COME ON, DARRYL! WHAT'S SO SCARY ABOUT THAT?
KIRKMAN & SCOTT
POOKY AUNTED HOUSE ADMISSION $3.00 PER PERSON
AAAA AGGG GHHH HHH!!

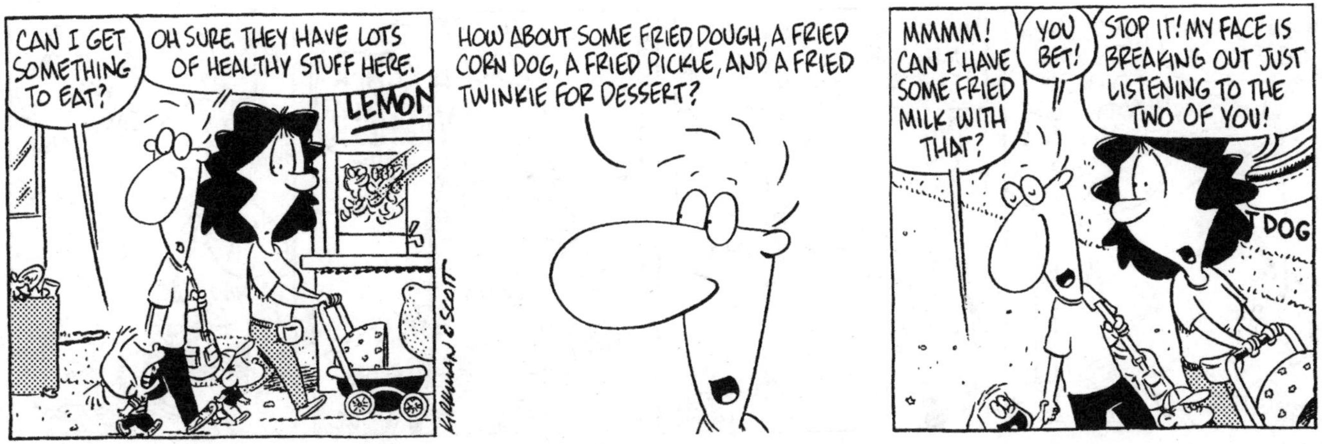
CAN I GET SOMETHING TO EAT?
OH SURE. THEY HAVE LOTS OF HEALTHY STUFF HERE.
LEMON
KIRKMAN & SCOTT
HOW ABOUT SOME FRIED DOUGH, A FRIED CORN DOG, A FRIED PICKLE, AND A FRIED TWINKIE FOR DESSERT?
MMMM! CAN I HAVE SOME FRIED MILK WITH THAT?
YOU BET!
STOP IT! MY FACE IS BREAKING OUT JUST LISTENING TO THE TWO OF YOU!
DOG

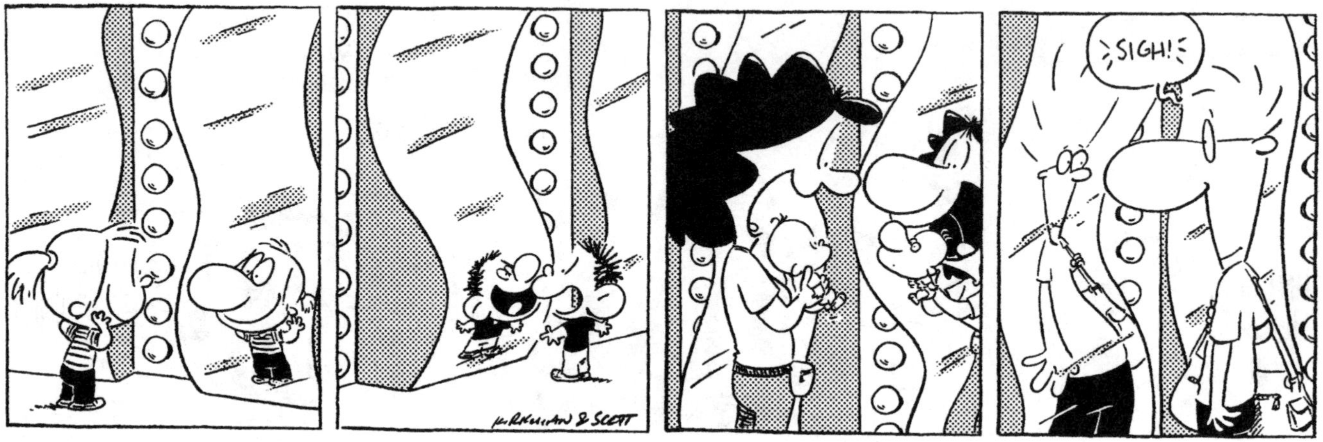
KIRKMAN & SCOTT
SIGH!

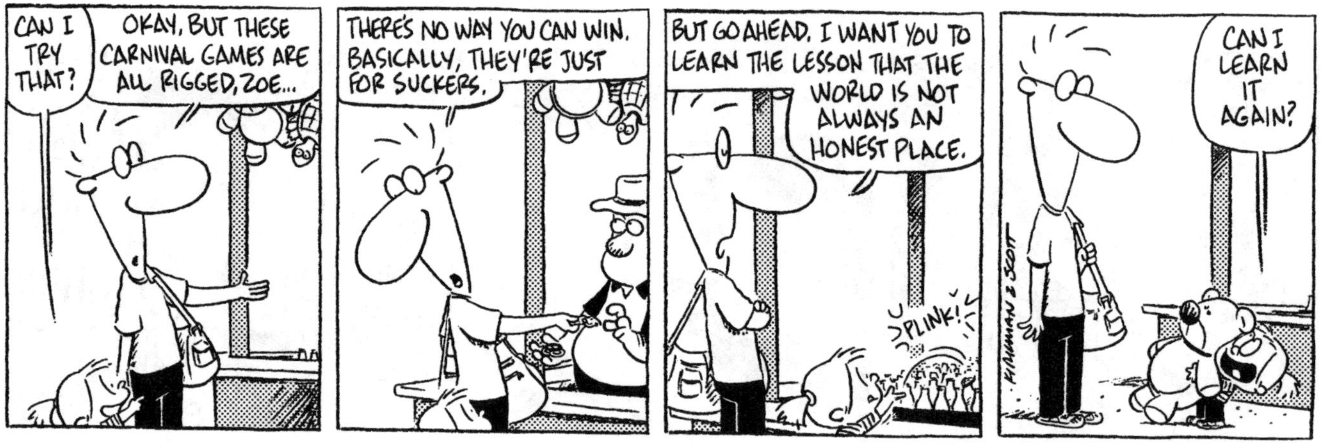
CAN I TRY THAT?
OKAY, BUT THESE CARNIVAL GAMES ARE ALL RIGGED, ZOE...
THERE'S NO WAY YOU CAN WIN. BASICALLY, THEY'RE JUST FOR SUCKERS.
BUT GO AHEAD. I WANT YOU TO LEARN THE LESSON THAT THE WORLD IS NOT ALWAYS AN HONEST PLACE.
PLINK!
KIRKMAN & SCOTT
CAN I LEARN IT AGAIN?

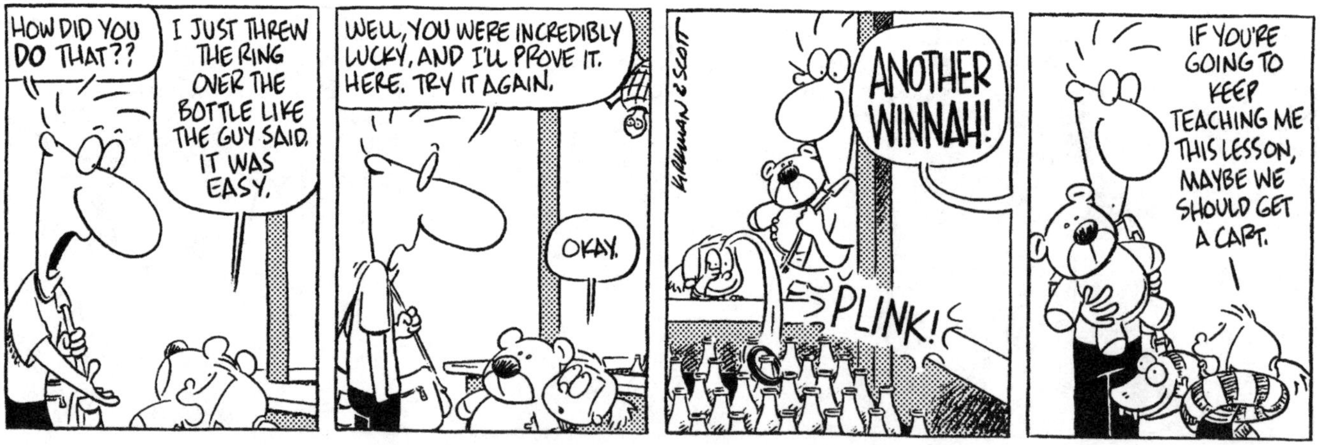
HOW DID YOU DO THAT??
I JUST THREW THE RING OVER THE BOTTLE LIKE THE GUY SAID. IT WAS EASY.
WELL, YOU WERE INCREDIBLY LUCKY, AND I'LL PROVE IT. HERE. TRY IT AGAIN.
OKAY.
KIRKMAN & SCOTT
ANOTHER WINNAH!
PLINK!
IF YOU'RE GOING TO KEEP TEACHING ME THIS LESSON, MAYBE WE SHOULD GET A CART.

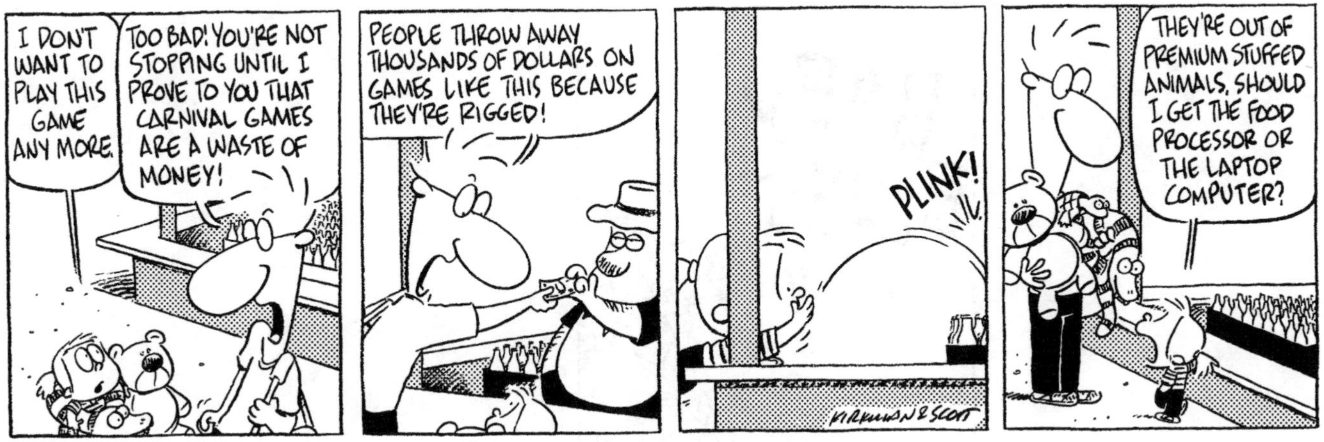
I DON'T WANT TO PLAY THIS GAME ANY MORE.
TOO BAD! YOU'RE NOT STOPPING UNTIL I PROVE TO YOU THAT CARNIVAL GAMES ARE A WASTE OF MONEY!
PEOPLE THROW AWAY THOUSANDS OF DOLLARS ON GAMES LIKE THIS BECAUSE THEY'RE RIGGED!
PLINK!
KIRKMAN & SCOTT
THEY'RE OUT OF PREMIUM STUFFED ANIMALS. SHOULD I GET THE FOOD PROCESSOR OR THE LAPTOP COMPUTER?

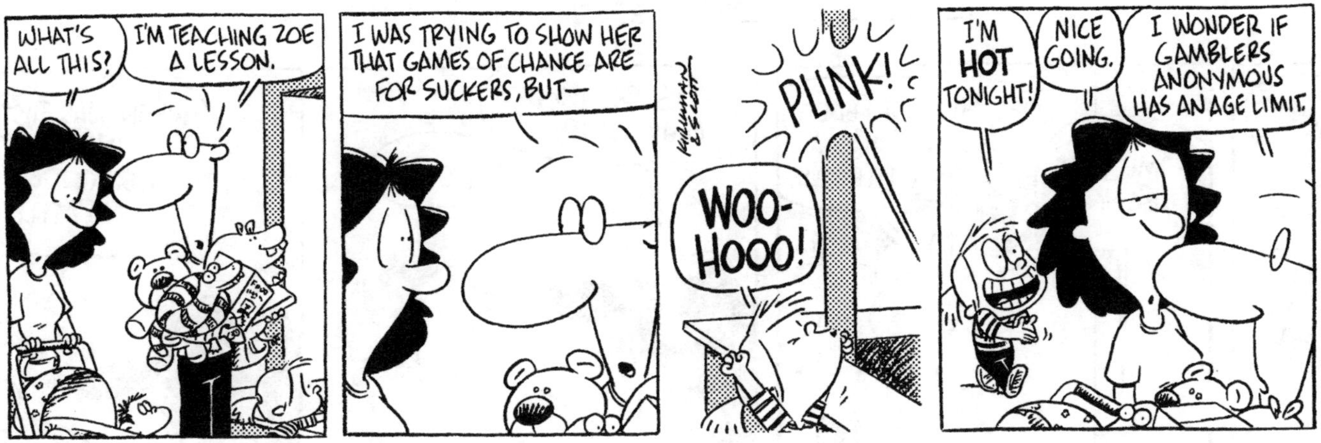
WHAT'S ALL THIS?
I'M TEACHING ZOE A LESSON.
I WAS TRYING TO SHOW HER THAT GAMES OF CHANCE ARE FOR SUCKERS, BUT—
PLINK!
WOO-HOOO!
I'M HOT TONIGHT!
NICE GOING.
I WONDER IF GAMBLERS ANONYMOUS HAS AN AGE LIMIT.

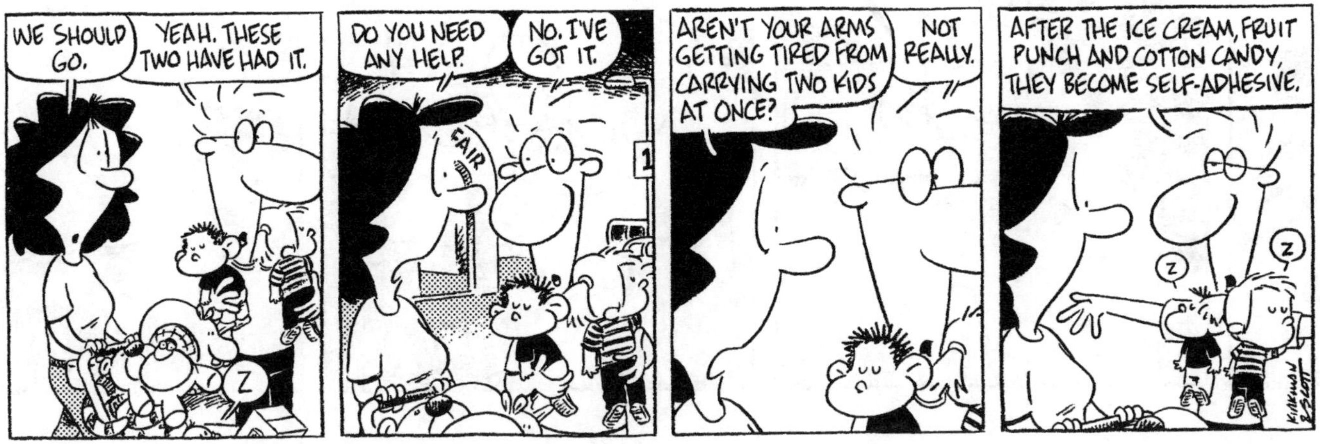
WE SHOULD GO.
YEAH. THESE TWO HAVE HAD IT.
Z
DO YOU NEED ANY HELP?
NO. I'VE GOT IT.
FAIR
AREN'T YOUR ARMS GETTING TIRED FROM CARRYING TWO KIDS AT ONCE?
NOT REALLY.
AFTER THE ICE CREAM, FRUIT PUNCH AND COTTON CANDY, THEY BECOME SELF-ADHESIVE.
Z
Z

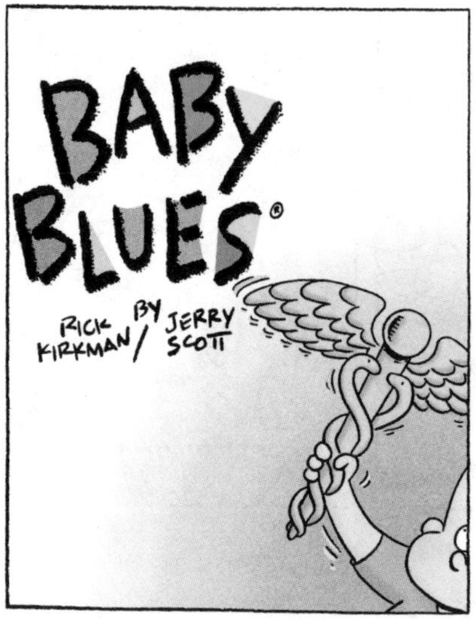
BABY BLUES®
BY RICK KIRKMAN / JERRY SCOTT

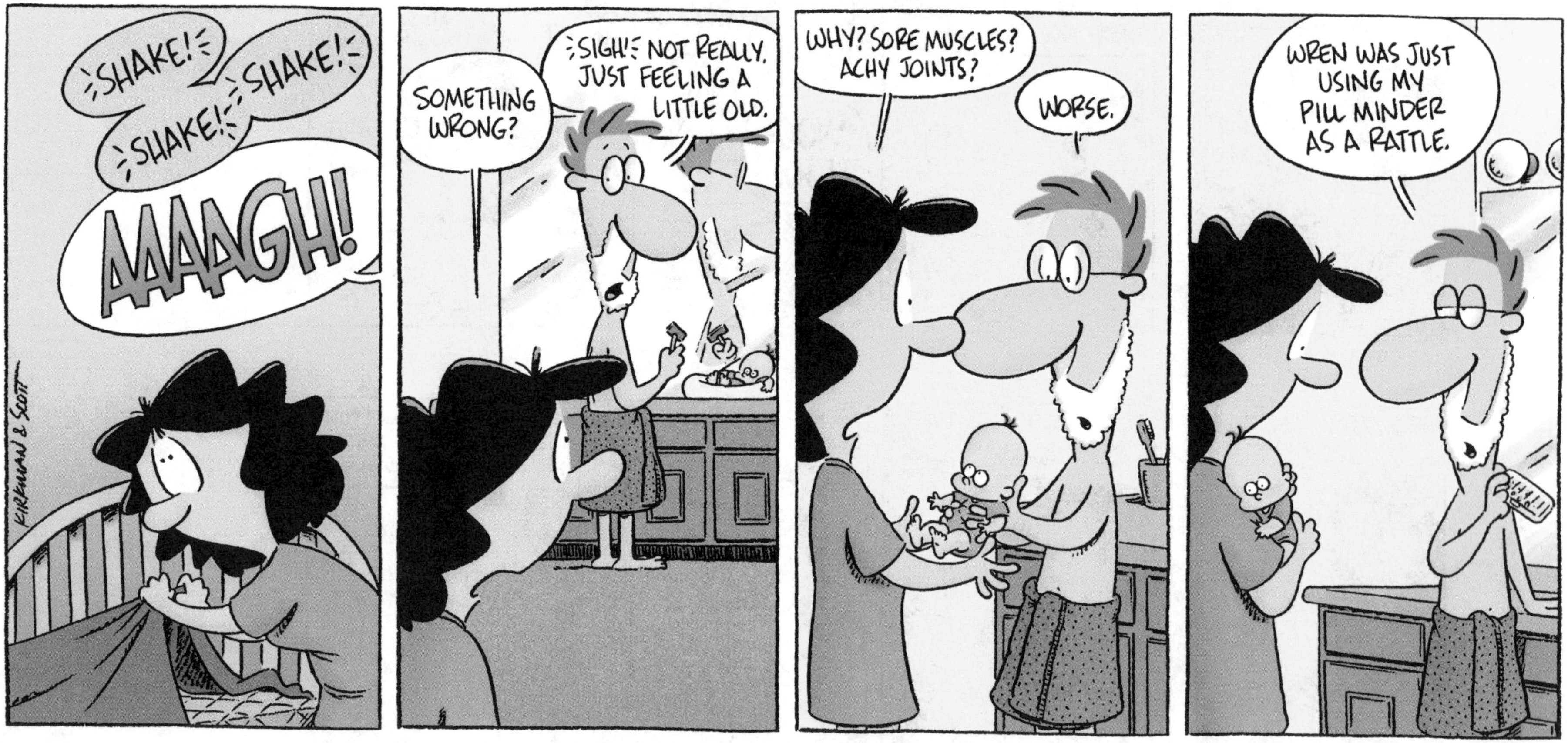
SHAKE!
SHAKE!
SHAKE!
AAAAGH!
KIRKMAN & SCOTT
SOMETHING WRONG?
SIGH! NOT REALLY. JUST FEELING A LITTLE OLD.
WHY? SORE MUSCLES? ACHY JOINTS?
WORSE.
WREN WAS JUST USING MY PILL MINDER AS A RATTLE.

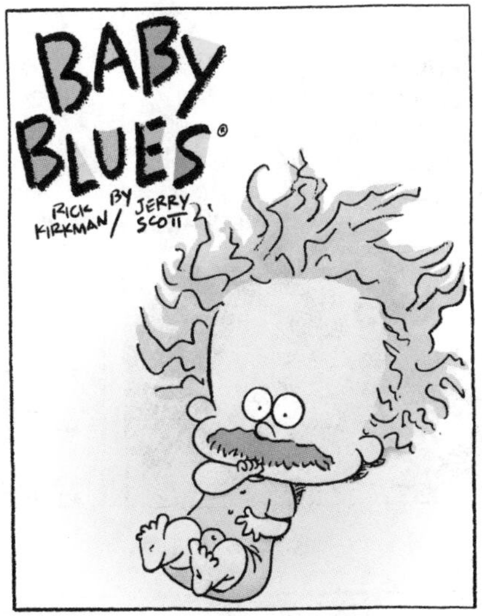
BABY BLUES®
BY RICK KIRKMAN / JERRY SCOTT

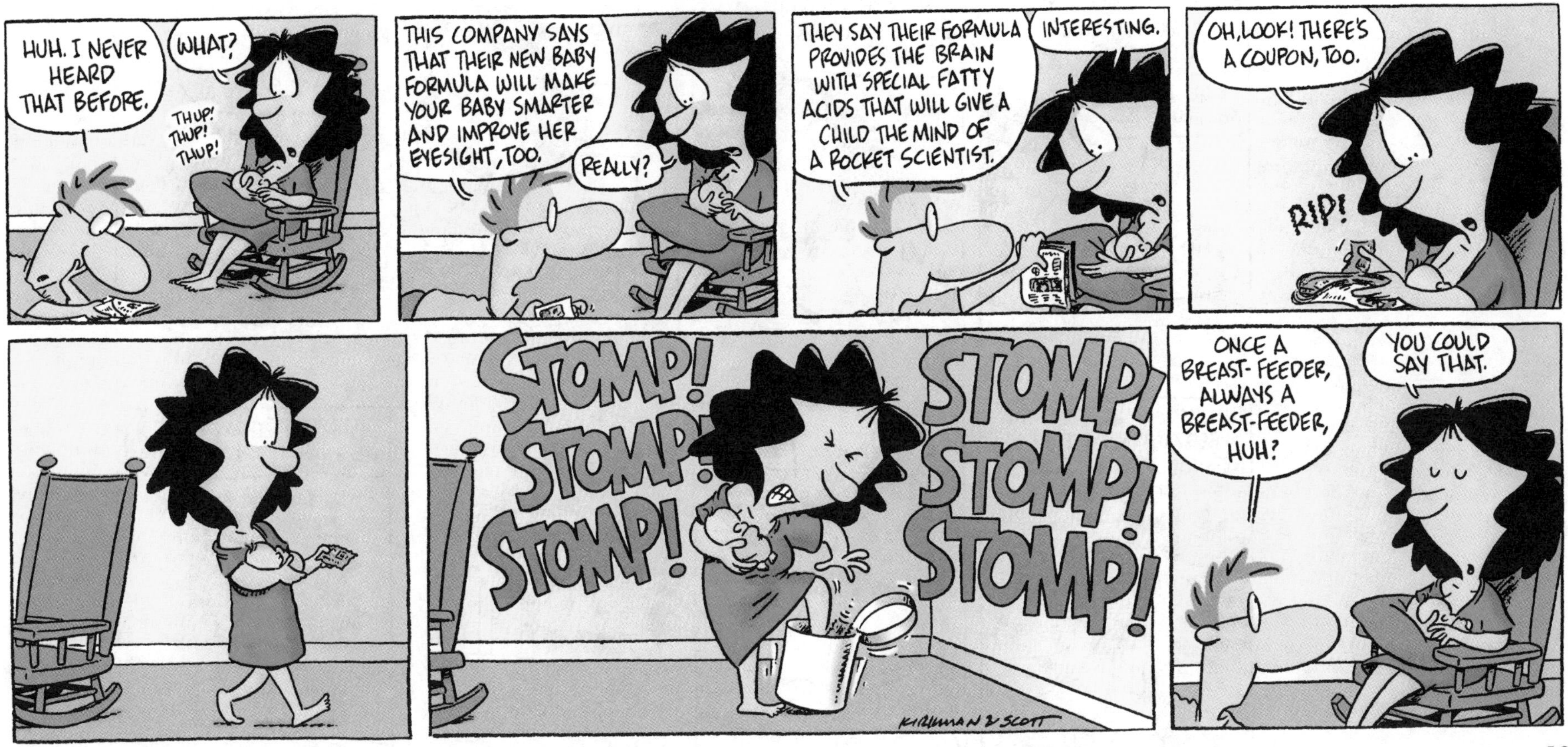
HUH. I NEVER HEARD THAT BEFORE.
WHAT?
THUP! THUP! THUP!
THIS COMPANY SAYS THAT THEIR NEW BABY FORMULA WILL MAKE YOUR BABY SMARTER AND IMPROVE HER EYESIGHT, TOO.
REALLY?
THEY SAY THEIR FORMULA PROVIDES THE BRAIN WITH SPECIAL FATTY ACIDS THAT WILL GIVE A CHILD THE MIND OF A ROCKET SCIENTIST.
INTERESTING.
OH, LOOK! THERE'S A COUPON, TOO.
RIP!
STOMP! STOMP! STOMP!
STOMP! STOMP! STOMP!
KIRKMAN & SCOTT
ONCE A BREAST-FEEDER, ALWAYS A BREAST-FEEDER, HUH?
YOU COULD SAY THAT.

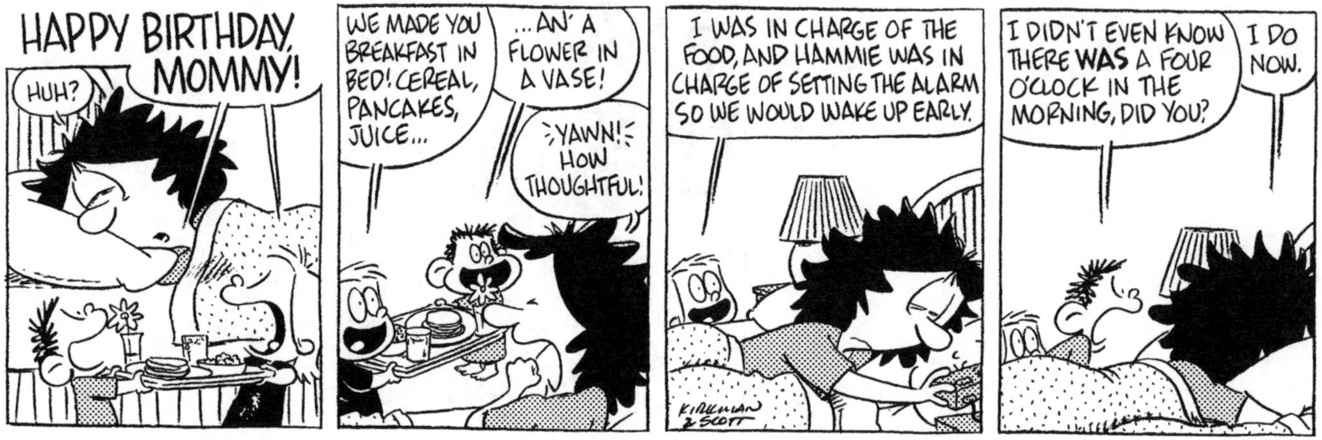
HAPPY BIRTHDAY, MOMMY!
HUH?
WE MADE YOU BREAKFAST IN BED! CEREAL, PANCAKES, JUICE...
...AN' A FLOWER IN A VASE!
YAWN! HOW THOUGHTFUL!
I WAS IN CHARGE OF THE FOOD, AND HAMMIE WAS IN CHARGE OF SETTING THE ALARM SO WE WOULD WAKE UP EARLY.
I DIDN'T EVEN KNOW THERE WAS A FOUR O'CLOCK IN THE MORNING, DID YOU?
I DO NOW.

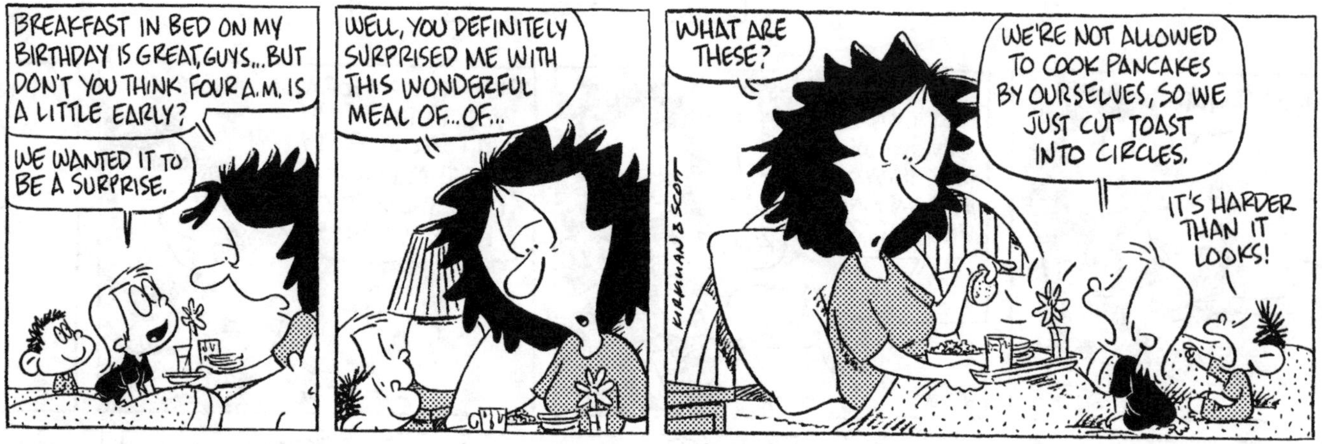
BREAKFAST IN BED ON MY BIRTHDAY IS GREAT, GUYS... BUT DON'T YOU THINK FOUR A.M. IS A LITTLE EARLY?
WE WANTED IT TO BE A SURPRISE.
WELL, YOU DEFINITELY SURPRISED ME WITH THIS WONDERFUL MEAL OF...OF...
WHAT ARE THESE?
WE'RE NOT ALLOWED TO COOK PANCAKES BY OURSELVES, SO WE JUST CUT TOAST INTO CIRCLES.
IT'S HARDER THAN IT LOOKS!

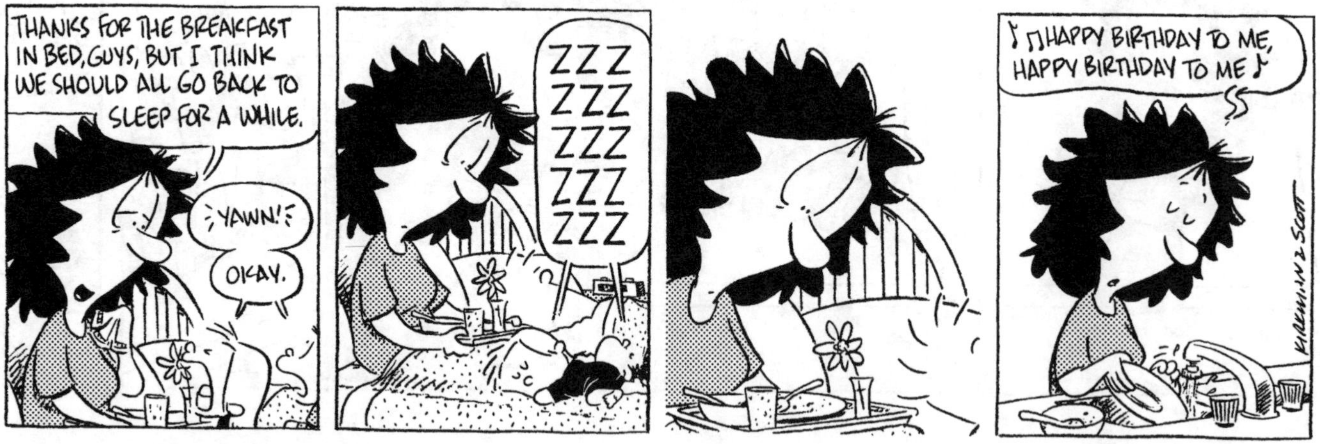
THANKS FOR THE BREAKFAST IN BED, GUYS, BUT I THINK WE SHOULD ALL GO BACK TO SLEEP FOR A WHILE.
YAWN!
OKAY.
ZZZ ZZZ ZZZ ZZZ ZZZ
♪ ♫ HAPPY BIRTHDAY TO ME, HAPPY BIRTHDAY TO ME ♪

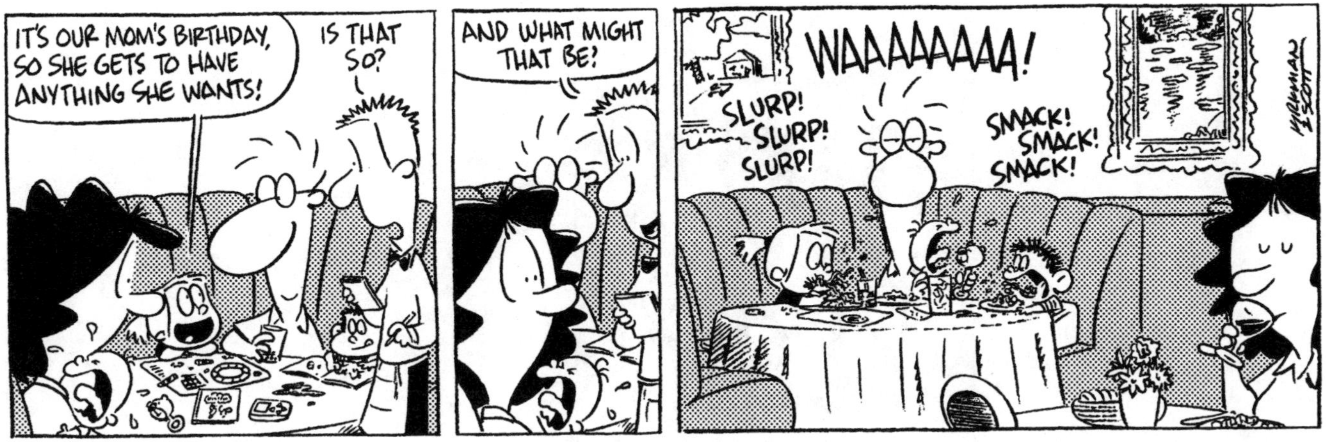
IT'S OUR MOM'S BIRTHDAY, SO SHE GETS TO HAVE ANYTHING SHE WANTS!
IS THAT SO?
AND WHAT MIGHT THAT BE?
WAAAAAAAA!
SLURP! SLURP! SLURP!
SMACK! SMACK! SMACK!
KIRKMAN & SCOTT

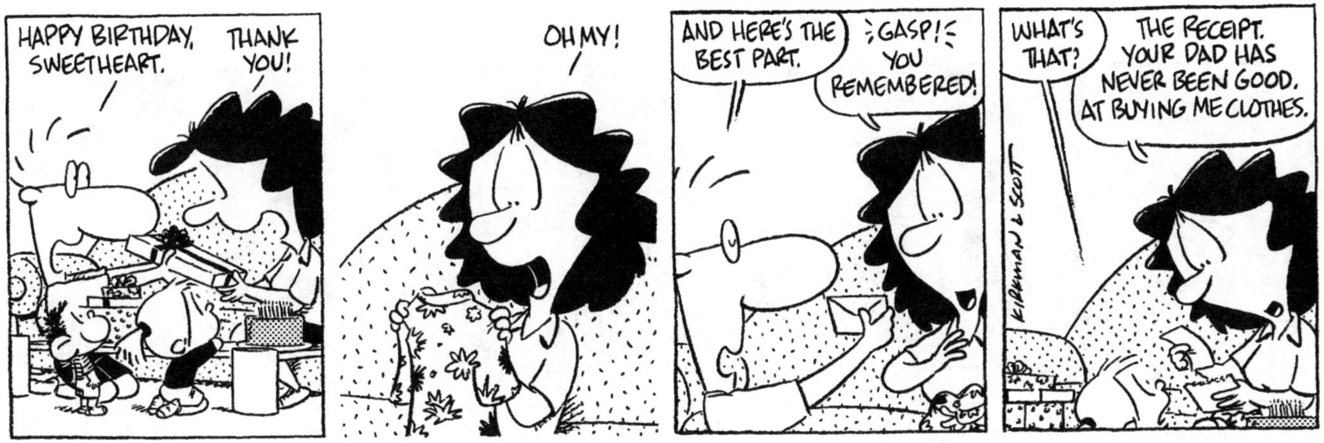
HAPPY BIRTHDAY, SWEETHEART.
THANK YOU!
OH MY!
AND HERE'S THE BEST PART.
GASP! YOU REMEMBERED!
KIRKMAN & SCOTT
WHAT'S THAT?
THE RECEIPT. YOUR DAD HAS NEVER BEEN GOOD AT BUYING ME CLOTHES.

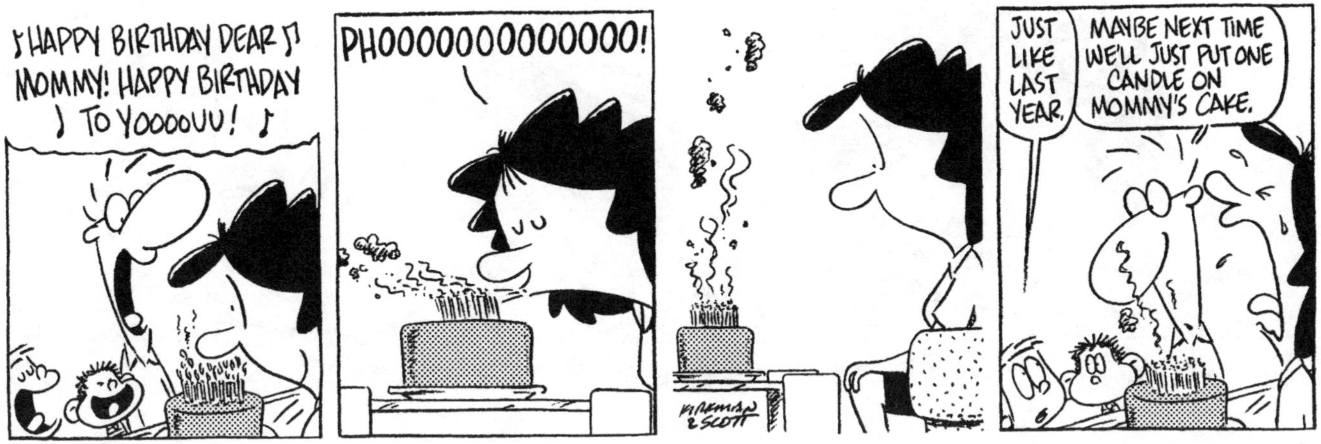
♪ HAPPY BIRTHDAY DEAR ♫ MOMMY! HAPPY BIRTHDAY ♪ TO YOOOOUU! ♪
PHOOOOOOOOOOOOO!
KIRKMAN & SCOTT
JUST LIKE LAST YEAR.
MAYBE NEXT TIME WE'LL JUST PUT ONE CANDLE ON MOMMY'S CAKE.

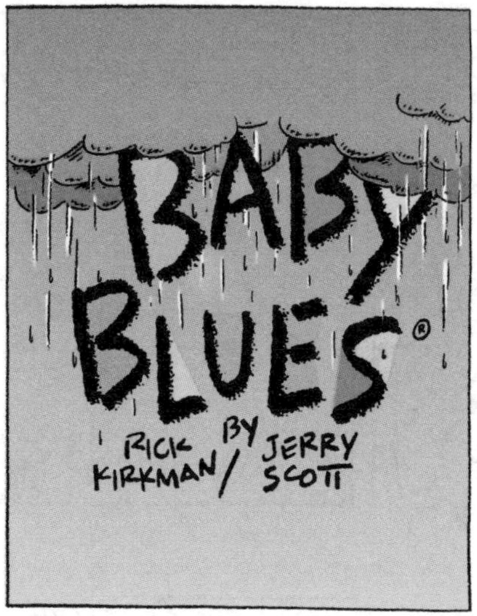

BABY BLUES®
BY RICK KIRKMAN / JERRY SCOTT

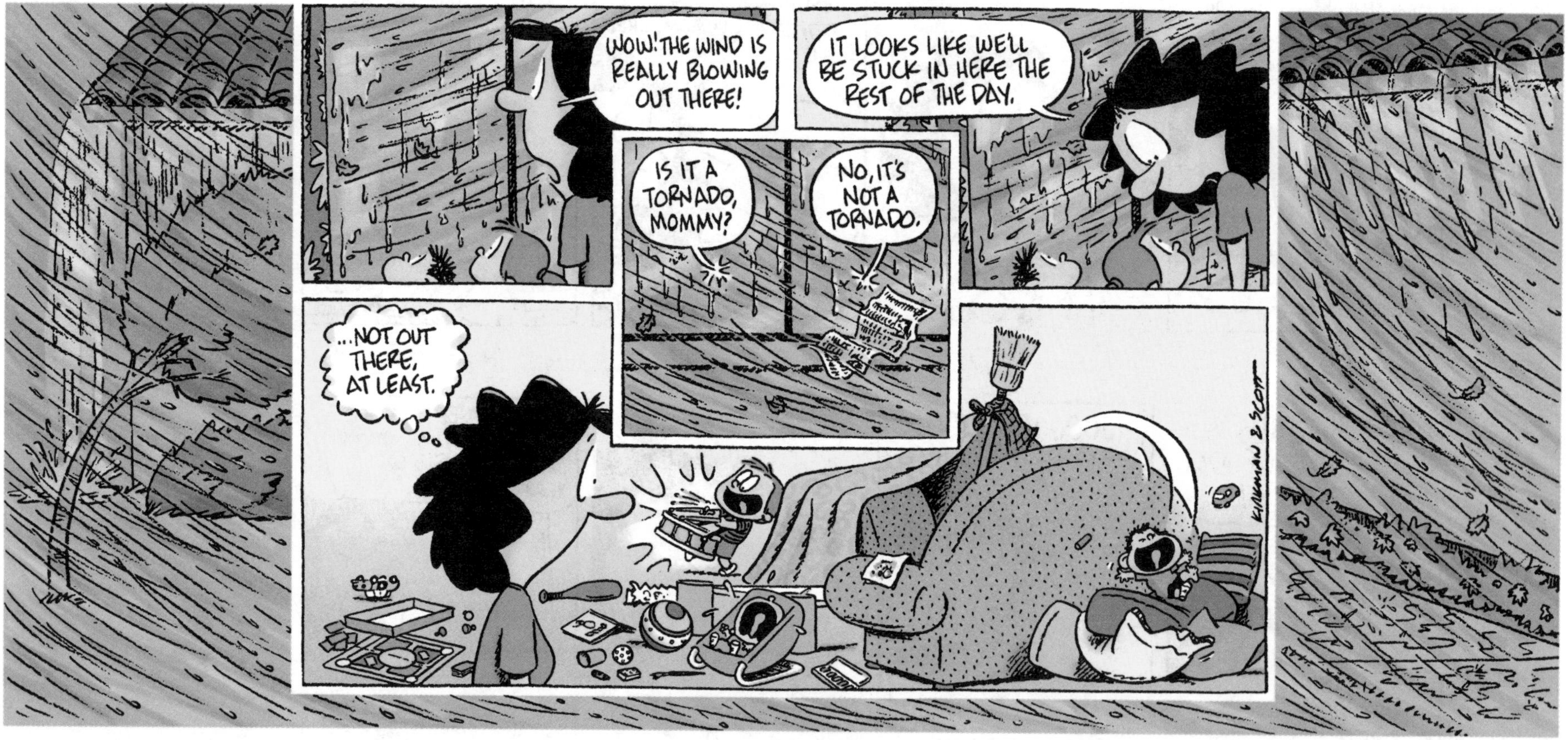

WOW! THE WIND IS REALLY BLOWING OUT THERE!
IT LOOKS LIKE WE'LL BE STUCK IN HERE THE REST OF THE DAY.
IS IT A TORNADO, MOMMY?
NO, IT'S NOT A TORNADO.
...NOT OUT THERE, AT LEAST.
KIRKMAN & SCOTT

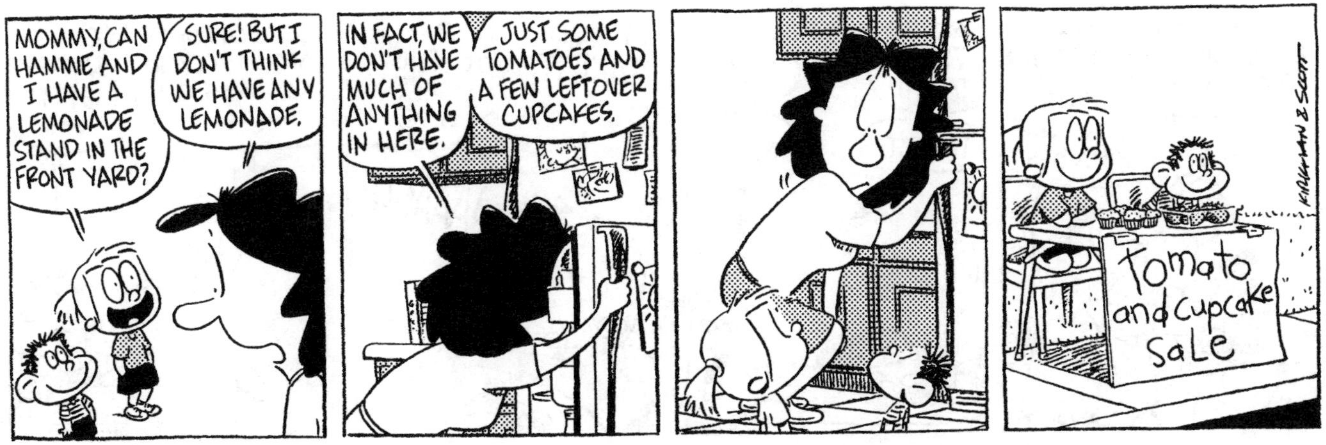
MOMMY, CAN HAMMIE AND I HAVE A LEMONADE STAND IN THE FRONT YARD?
SURE! BUT I DON'T THINK WE HAVE ANY LEMONADE.
IN FACT, WE DON'T HAVE MUCH OF ANYTHING IN HERE.
JUST SOME TOMATOES AND A FEW LEFTOVER CUPCAKES.
Tomato and Cupcake Sale
KIRKMAN & SCOTT

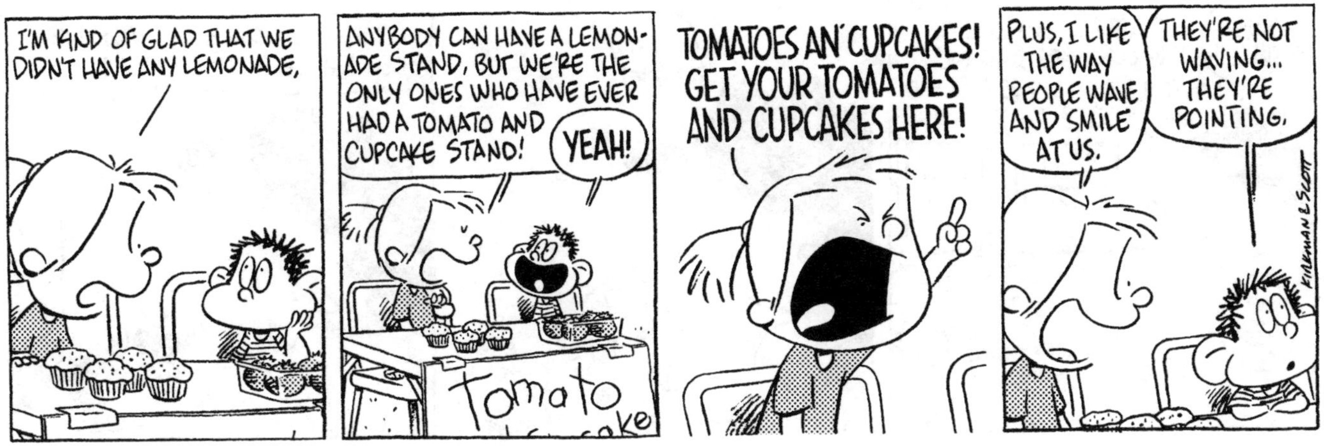
I'M KIND OF GLAD THAT WE DIDN'T HAVE ANY LEMONADE,
ANYBODY CAN HAVE A LEMONADE STAND, BUT WE'RE THE ONLY ONES WHO HAVE EVER HAD A TOMATO AND CUPCAKE STAND!
YEAH!
Tomato
TOMATOES AN' CUPCAKES! GET YOUR TOMATOES AND CUPCAKES HERE!
PLUS, I LIKE THE WAY PEOPLE WAVE AND SMILE AT US.
THEY'RE NOT WAVING... THEY'RE POINTING.
KIRKMAN & SCOTT

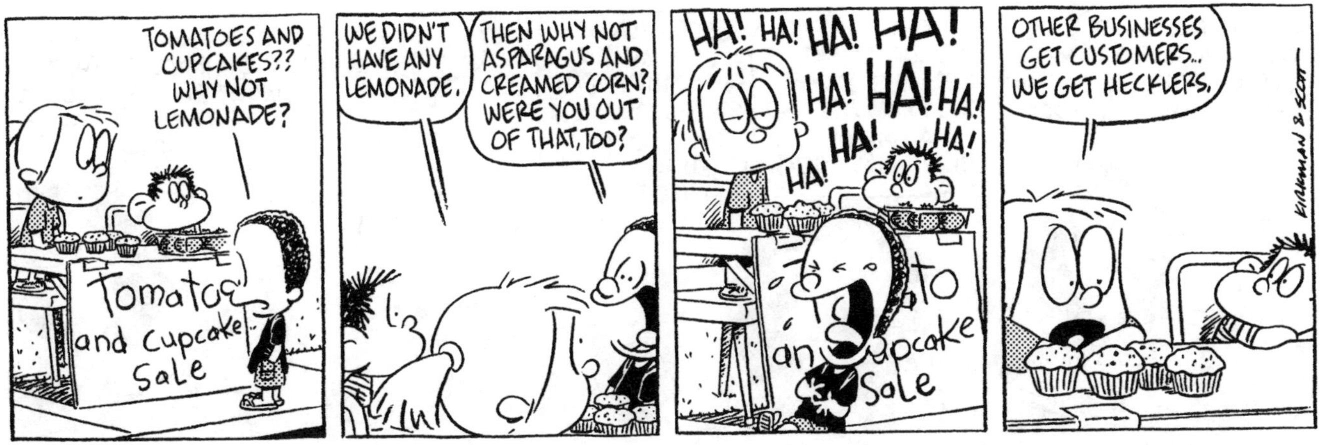
TOMATOES AND CUPCAKES?? WHY NOT LEMONADE?
Tomato and cupcake Sale
WE DIDN'T HAVE ANY LEMONADE.
THEN WHY NOT ASPARAGUS AND CREAMED CORN? WERE YOU OUT OF THAT, TOO?
HA! HA! HA! HA! HA! HA! HA! HA! HA! HA!
OTHER BUSINESSES GET CUSTOMERS... WE GET HECKLERS.
KIRKMAN & SCOTT

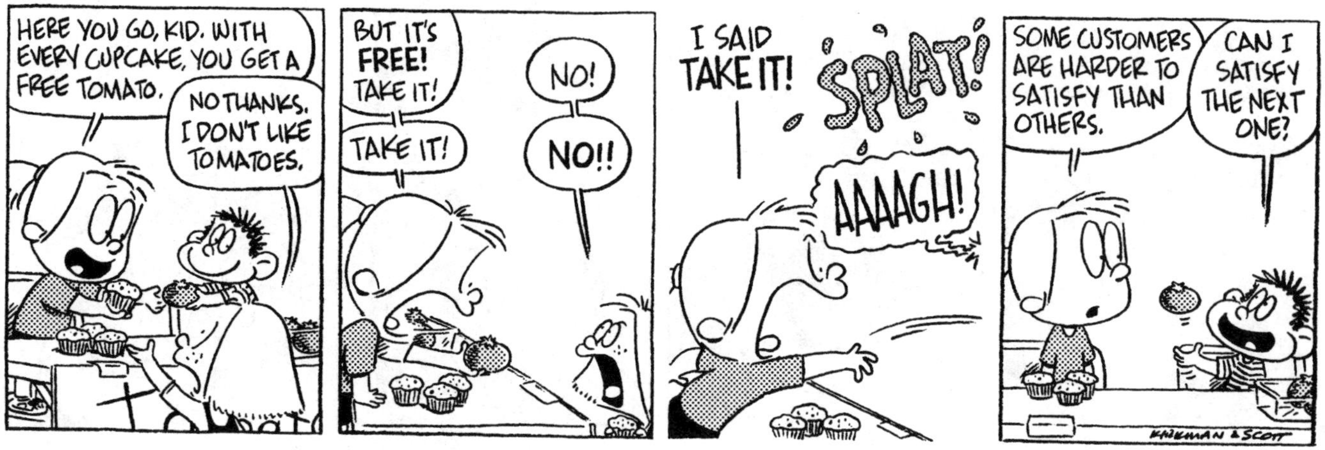
HERE YOU GO, KID. WITH EVERY CUPCAKE, YOU GET A FREE TOMATO.
NO THANKS. I DON'T LIKE TOMATOES.
BUT IT'S FREE! TAKE IT!
TAKE IT!
NO!
NO!!
I SAID TAKE IT!
SPLAT!
AAAAGH!
SOME CUSTOMERS ARE HARDER TO SATISFY THAN OTHERS.
CAN I SATISFY THE NEXT ONE?
KIRKMAN & SCOTT

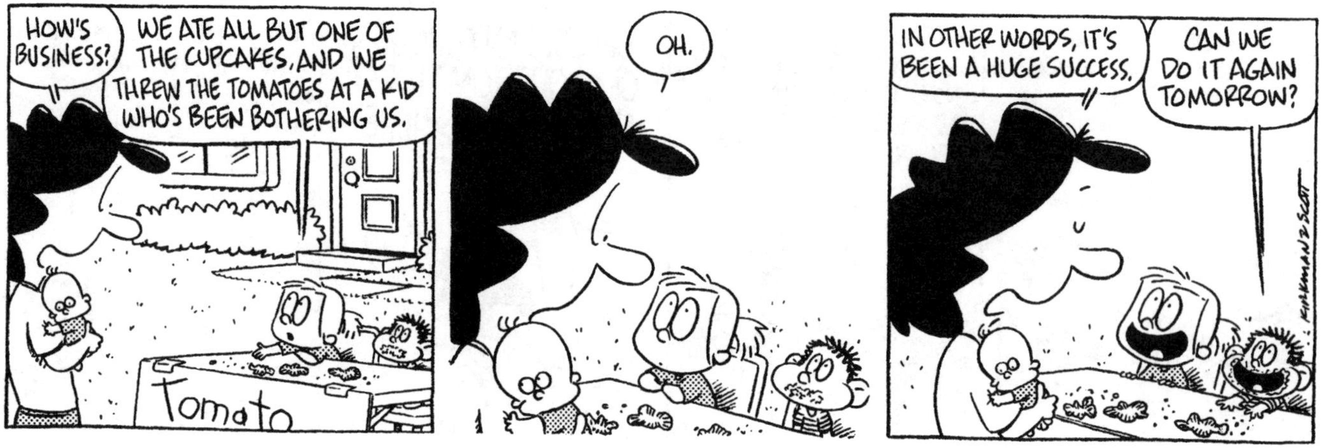
HOW'S BUSINESS?
WE ATE ALL BUT ONE OF THE CUPCAKES, AND WE THREW THE TOMATOES AT A KID WHO'S BEEN BOTHERING US.
Tomato
OH.
IN OTHER WORDS, IT'S BEEN A HUGE SUCCESS.
CAN WE DO IT AGAIN TOMORROW?
KIRKMAN & SCOTT

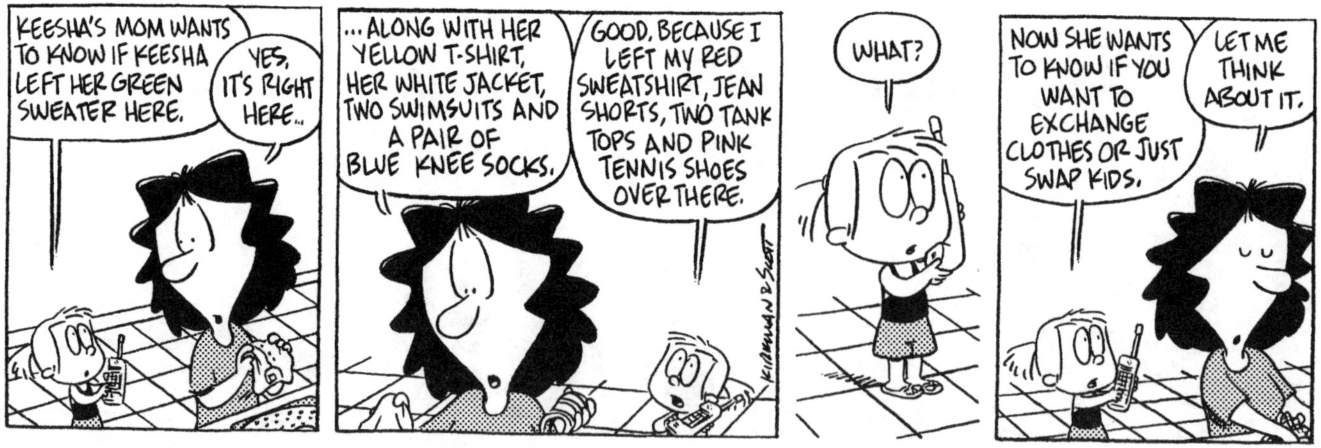
KEESHA'S MOM WANTS TO KNOW IF KEESHA LEFT HER GREEN SWEATER HERE.
YES, IT'S RIGHT HERE...
...ALONG WITH HER YELLOW T-SHIRT, HER WHITE JACKET, TWO SWIMSUITS AND A PAIR OF BLUE KNEE SOCKS.
GOOD, BECAUSE I LEFT MY RED SWEATSHIRT, JEAN SHORTS, TWO TANK TOPS AND PINK TENNIS SHOES OVER THERE.
KIRKMAN & SCOTT
WHAT?
NOW SHE WANTS TO KNOW IF YOU WANT TO EXCHANGE CLOTHES OR JUST SWAP KIDS.
LET ME THINK ABOUT IT.

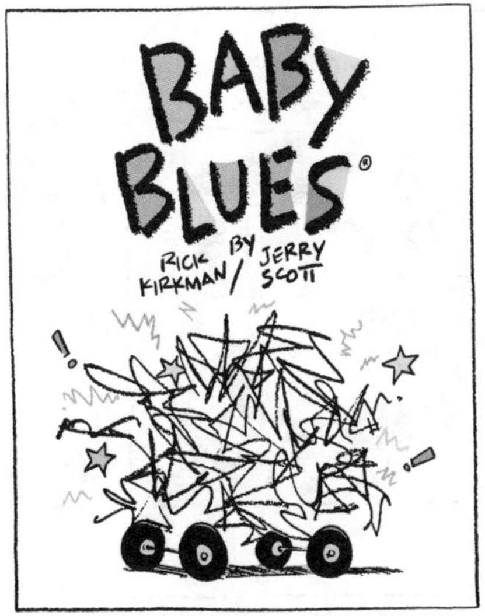
BABY BLUES®
BY RICK KIRKMAN / JERRY SCOTT

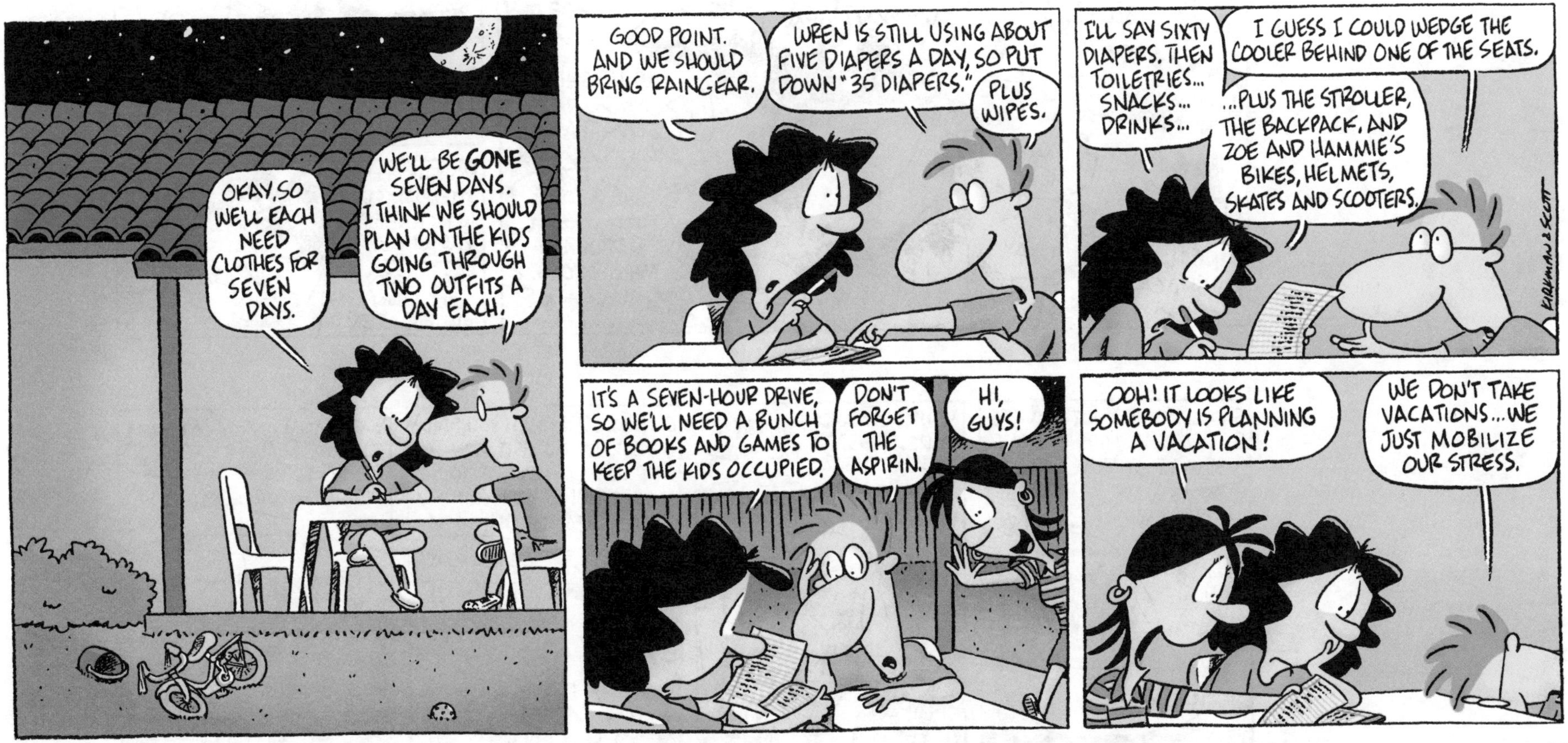
OKAY, SO WE'LL EACH NEED CLOTHES FOR SEVEN DAYS.
WE'LL BE GONE SEVEN DAYS. I THINK WE SHOULD PLAN ON THE KIDS GOING THROUGH TWO OUTFITS A DAY EACH.
GOOD POINT. AND WE SHOULD BRING RAINGEAR.
WREN IS STILL USING ABOUT FIVE DIAPERS A DAY, SO PUT DOWN "35 DIAPERS."
PLUS WIPES.
I'LL SAY SIXTY DIAPERS. THEN TOILETRIES... SNACKS... DRINKS...
I GUESS I COULD WEDGE THE COOLER BEHIND ONE OF THE SEATS.
...PLUS THE STROLLER, THE BACKPACK, AND ZOE AND HAMMIE'S BIKES, HELMETS, SKATES AND SCOOTERS.
KIRKMAN & SCOTT
IT'S A SEVEN-HOUR DRIVE, SO WE'LL NEED A BUNCH OF BOOKS AND GAMES TO KEEP THE KIDS OCCUPIED.
DON'T FORGET THE ASPIRIN.
HI, GUYS!
OOH! IT LOOKS LIKE SOMEBODY IS PLANNING A VACATION!
WE DON'T TAKE VACATIONS... WE JUST MOBILIZE OUR STRESS.

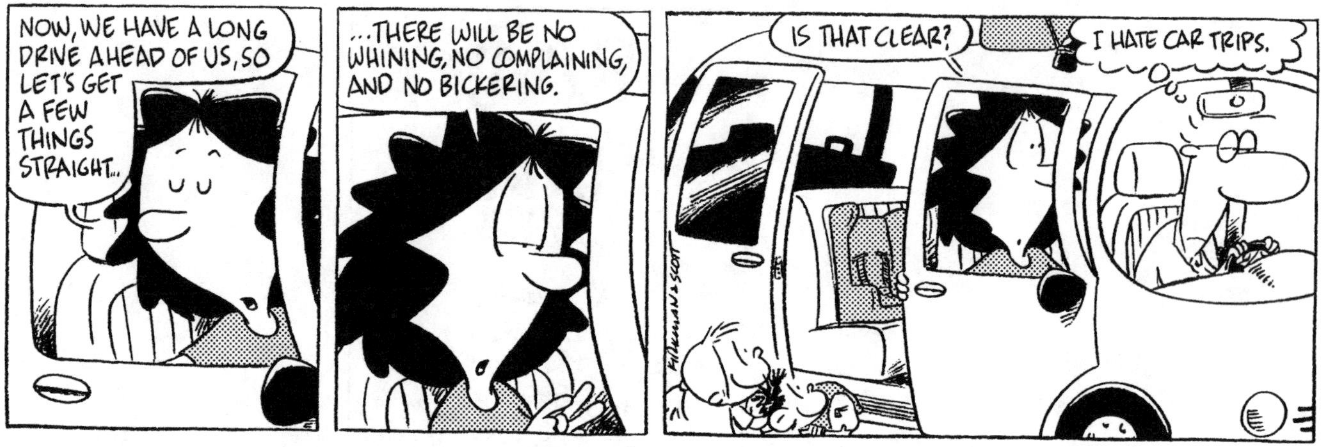
NOW, WE HAVE A LONG DRIVE AHEAD OF US, SO LET'S GET A FEW THINGS STRAIGHT...
...THERE WILL BE NO WHINING, NO COMPLAINING, AND NO BICKERING.
IS THAT CLEAR?
I HATE CAR TRIPS.
KIRKMAN & SCOTT

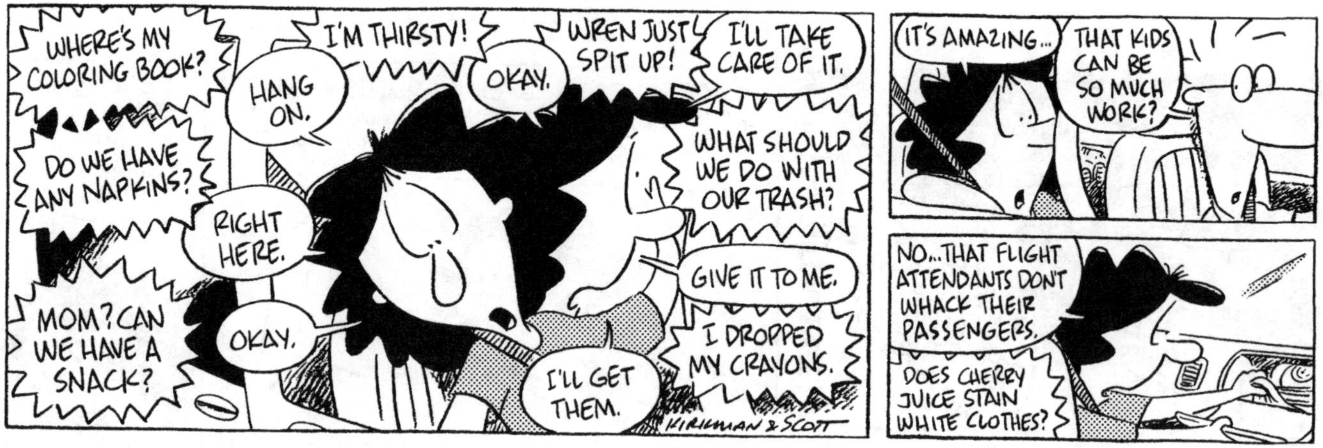
WHERE'S MY COLORING BOOK?
HANG ON.
I'M THIRSTY!
OKAY.
WREN JUST SPIT UP!
I'LL TAKE CARE OF IT.
DO WE HAVE ANY NAPKINS?
RIGHT HERE.
WHAT SHOULD WE DO WITH OUR TRASH?
GIVE IT TO ME.
MOM? CAN WE HAVE A SNACK?
OKAY.
I DROPPED MY CRAYONS.
I'LL GET THEM.
KIRKMAN & SCOTT
IT'S AMAZING...
THAT KIDS CAN BE SO MUCH WORK?
NO...THAT FLIGHT ATTENDANTS DON'T WHACK THEIR PASSENGERS.
DOES CHERRY JUICE STAIN WHITE CLOTHES?

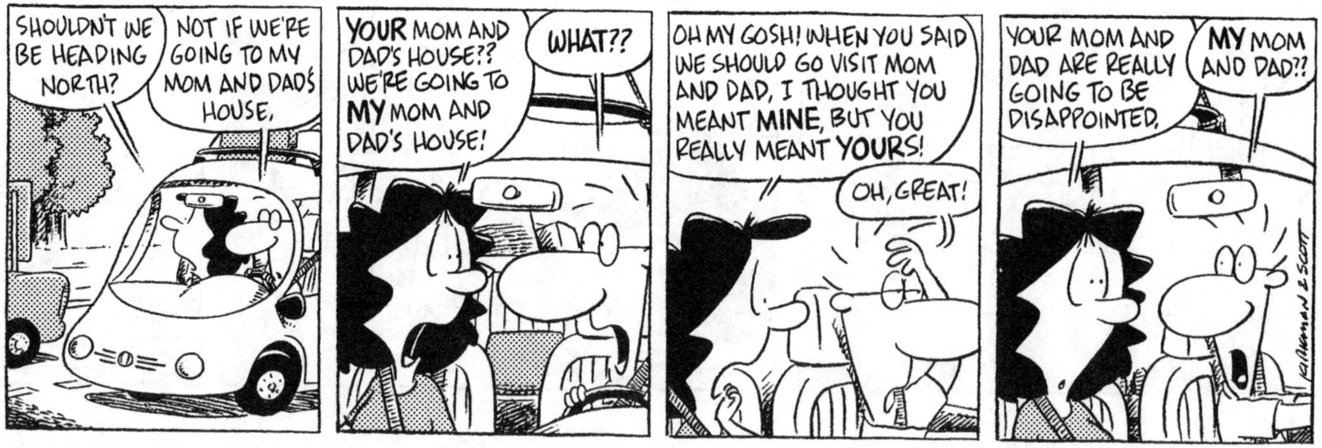
SHOULDN'T WE BE HEADING NORTH?
NOT IF WE'RE GOING TO MY MOM AND DAD'S HOUSE.
YOUR MOM AND DAD'S HOUSE?? WE'RE GOING TO MY MOM AND DAD'S HOUSE!
WHAT??
OH MY GOSH! WHEN YOU SAID WE SHOULD GO VISIT MOM AND DAD, I THOUGHT YOU MEANT MINE, BUT YOU REALLY MEANT YOURS!
OH, GREAT!
YOUR MOM AND DAD ARE REALLY GOING TO BE DISAPPOINTED.
MY MOM AND DAD??
KIRKMAN & SCOTT

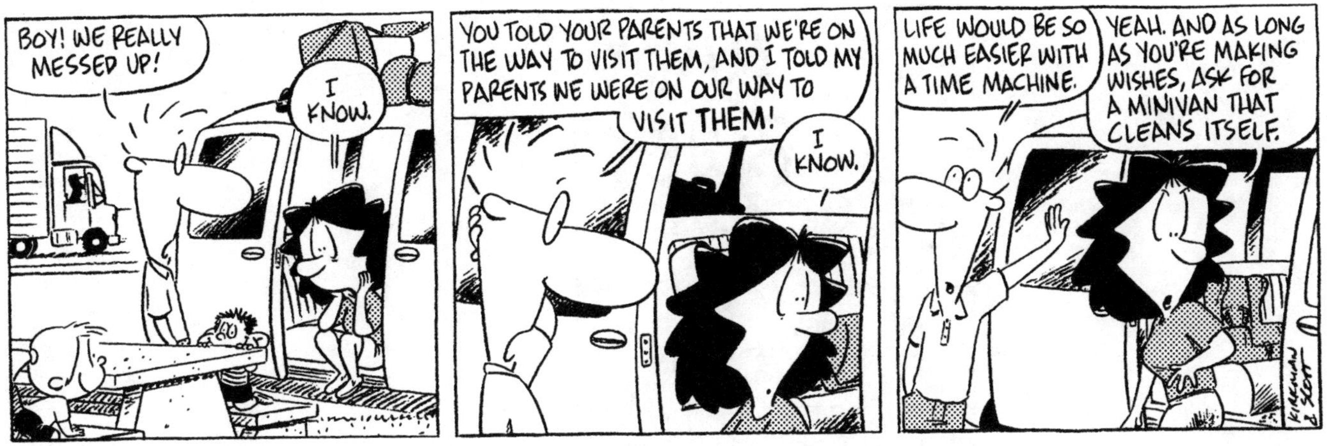
BOY! WE REALLY MESSED UP!
I KNOW.
YOU TOLD YOUR PARENTS THAT WE'RE ON THE WAY TO VISIT THEM, AND I TOLD MY PARENTS WE WERE ON OUR WAY TO VISIT **THEM**!
I KNOW.
LIFE WOULD BE SO MUCH EASIER WITH A TIME MACHINE.
YEAH. AND AS LONG AS YOU'RE MAKING WISHES, ASK FOR A MINIVAN THAT CLEANS ITSELF.
KIRKMAN & SCOTT

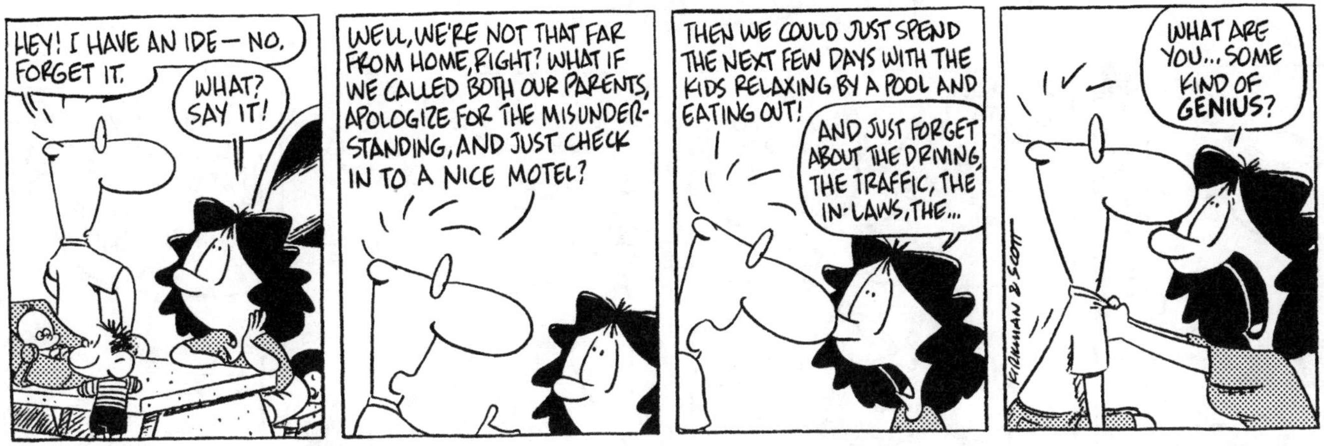
HEY! I HAVE AN IDE— NO. FORGET IT.
WHAT? SAY IT!
WELL, WE'RE NOT THAT FAR FROM HOME, RIGHT? WHAT IF WE CALLED BOTH OUR PARENTS, APOLOGIZE FOR THE MISUNDERSTANDING, AND JUST CHECK IN TO A NICE MOTEL?
THEN WE COULD JUST SPEND THE NEXT FEW DAYS WITH THE KIDS RELAXING BY A POOL AND EATING OUT!
AND JUST FORGET ABOUT THE DRIVING, THE TRAFFIC, THE IN-LAWS, THE...
KIRKMAN & SCOTT
WHAT ARE YOU... SOME KIND OF **GENIUS**?

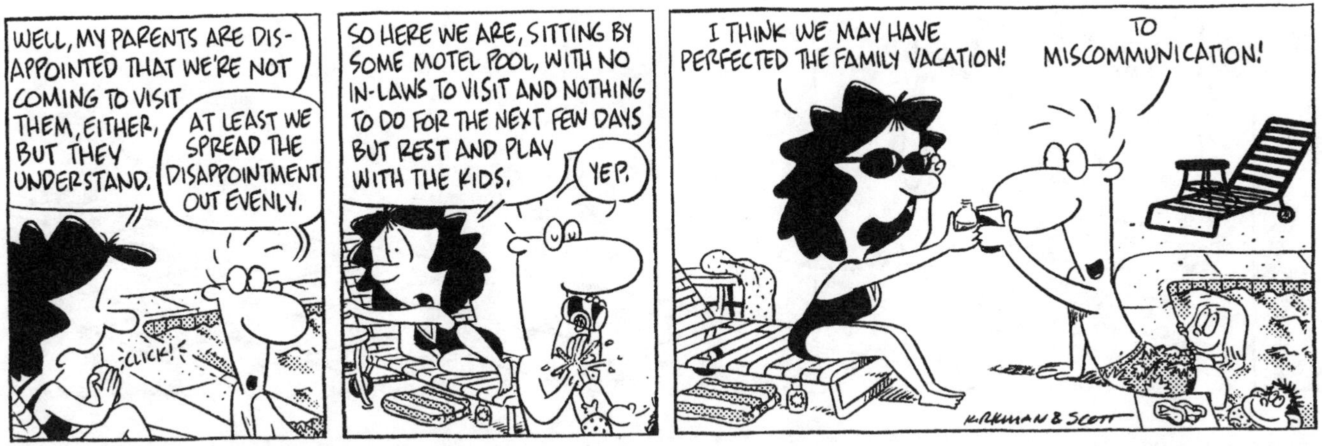
WELL, MY PARENTS ARE DISAPPOINTED THAT WE'RE NOT COMING TO VISIT THEM, EITHER, BUT THEY UNDERSTAND.
AT LEAST WE SPREAD THE DISAPPOINTMENT OUT EVENLY.
CLICK!
SO HERE WE ARE, SITTING BY SOME MOTEL POOL, WITH NO IN-LAWS TO VISIT AND NOTHING TO DO FOR THE NEXT FEW DAYS BUT REST AND PLAY WITH THE KIDS.
YEP.
I THINK WE MAY HAVE PERFECTED THE FAMILY VACATION!
TO MISCOMMUNICATION!
KIRKMAN & SCOTT

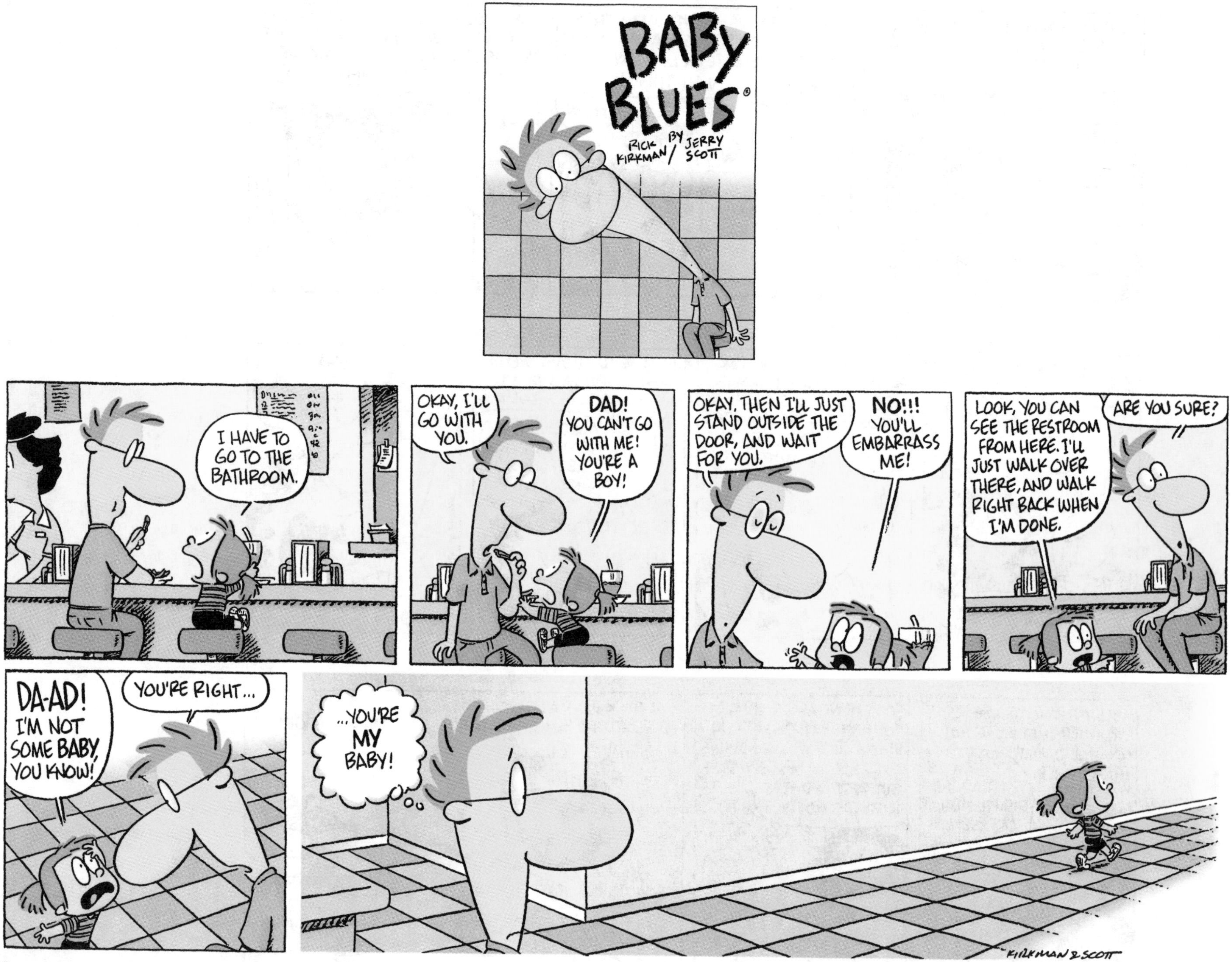
BABY BLUES®
BY RICK KIRKMAN / JERRY SCOTT
I HAVE TO GO TO THE BATHROOM.
OKAY, I'LL GO WITH YOU.
DAD! YOU CAN'T GO WITH ME! YOU'RE A BOY!
OKAY, THEN I'LL JUST STAND OUTSIDE THE DOOR, AND WAIT FOR YOU.
NO!!! YOU'LL EMBARRASS ME!
LOOK, YOU CAN SEE THE RESTROOM FROM HERE. I'LL JUST WALK OVER THERE, AND WALK RIGHT BACK WHEN I'M DONE.
ARE YOU SURE?
DA-AD! I'M NOT SOME BABY, YOU KNOW!
YOU'RE RIGHT...
...YOU'RE MY BABY!
KIRKMAN & SCOTT

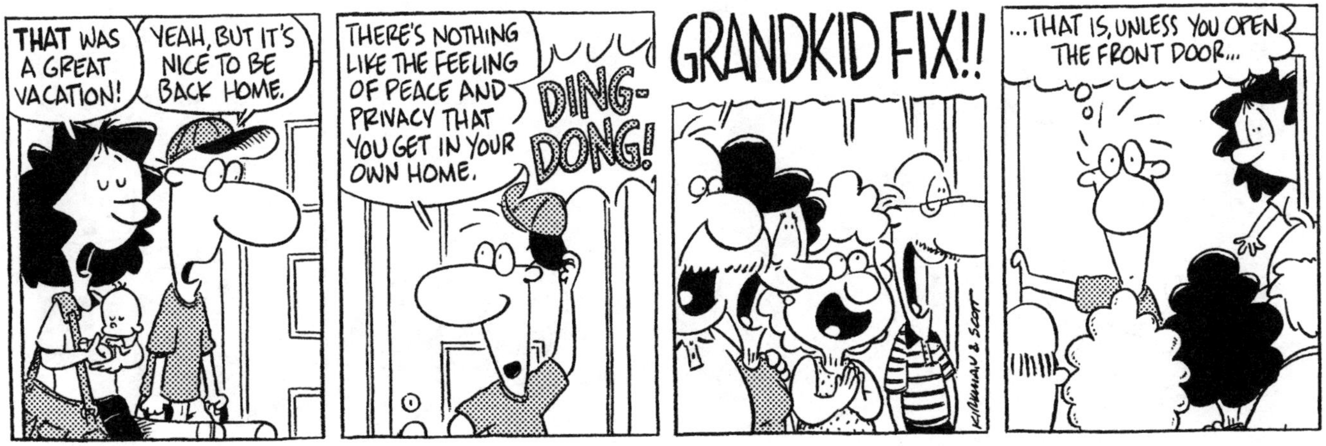
THAT WAS A GREAT VACATION!
YEAH, BUT IT'S NICE TO BE BACK HOME.
THERE'S NOTHING LIKE THE FEELING OF PEACE AND PRIVACY THAT YOU GET IN YOUR OWN HOME.
DING-DONG!
GRANDKID FIX!!
KIRKMAN & SCOTT
...THAT IS, UNLESS YOU OPEN THE FRONT DOOR...

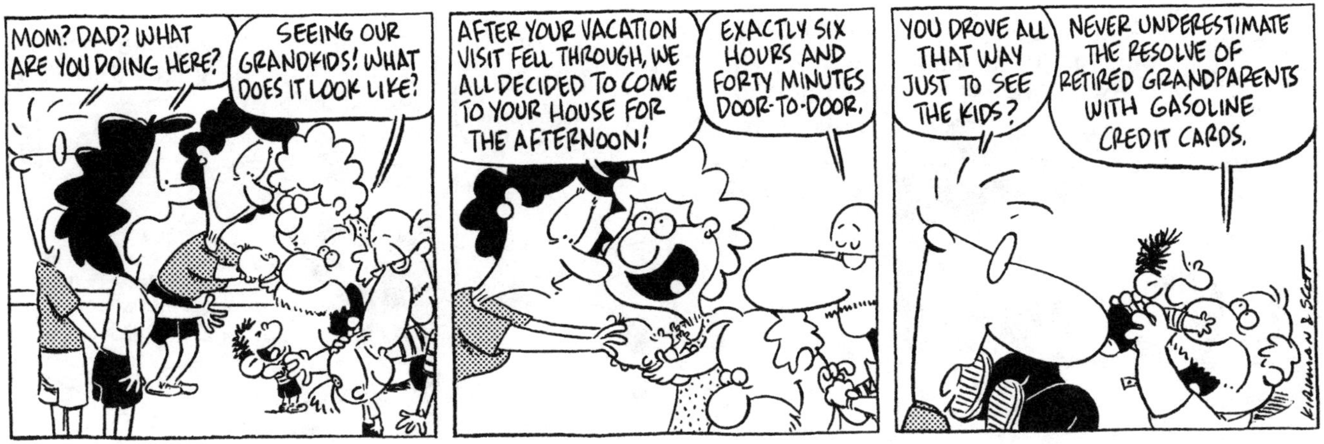
MOM? DAD? WHAT ARE YOU DOING HERE?
SEEING OUR GRANDKIDS! WHAT DOES IT LOOK LIKE?
AFTER YOUR VACATION VISIT FELL THROUGH, WE ALL DECIDED TO COME TO YOUR HOUSE FOR THE AFTERNOON!
EXACTLY SIX HOURS AND FORTY MINUTES DOOR-TO-DOOR.
YOU DROVE ALL THAT WAY JUST TO SEE THE KIDS?
NEVER UNDERESTIMATE THE RESOLVE OF RETIRED GRANDPARENTS WITH GASOLINE CREDIT CARDS.
KIRKMAN & SCOTT

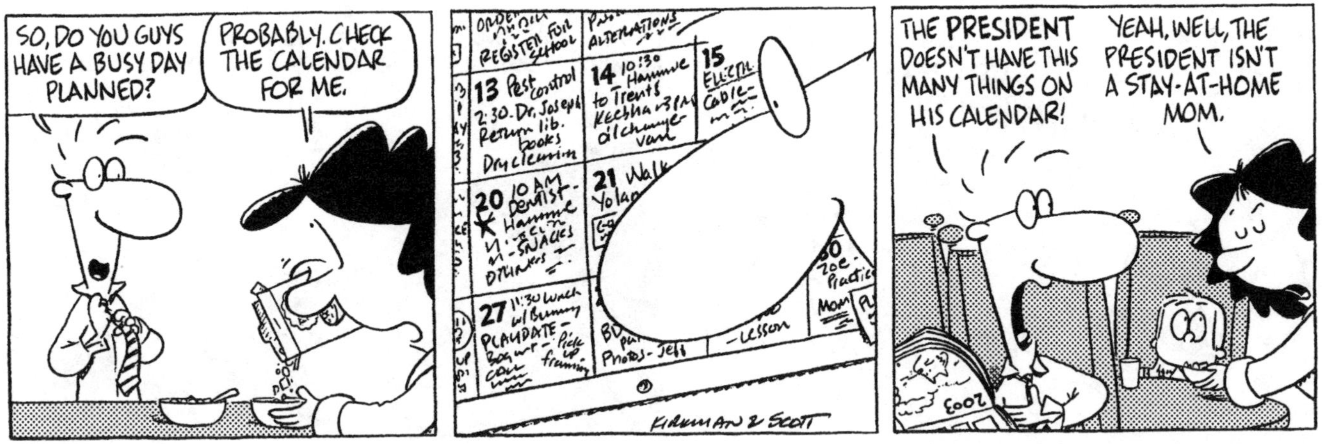
SO, DO YOU GUYS HAVE A BUSY DAY PLANNED?
PROBABLY. CHECK THE CALENDAR FOR ME.
REGISTER FOR SCHOOL
ALTERATIONS
13 Pest control
14
15
20 10 AM DENTIST
21
27 11:30 Lunch
PLAYDATE
KIRKMAN & SCOTT
THE PRESIDENT DOESN'T HAVE THIS MANY THINGS ON HIS CALENDAR!
YEAH, WELL, THE PRESIDENT ISN'T A STAY-AT-HOME MOM.

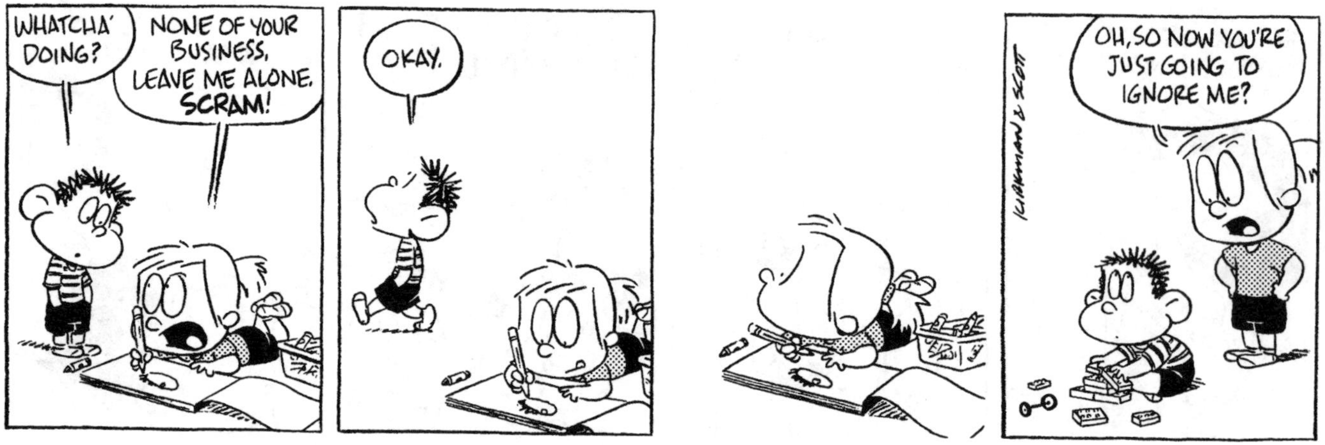

WHATCHA' DOING?
NONE OF YOUR BUSINESS. LEAVE ME ALONE. SCRAM!
OKAY.
KIRKMAN & SCOTT
OH, SO NOW YOU'RE JUST GOING TO IGNORE ME?

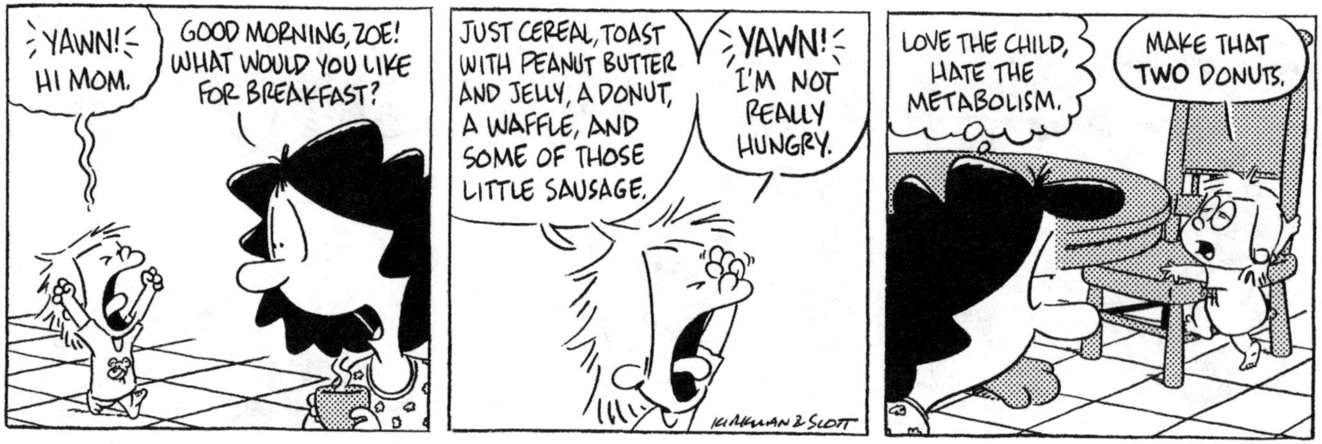

YAWN! HI MOM.
GOOD MORNING, ZOE! WHAT WOULD YOU LIKE FOR BREAKFAST?
JUST CEREAL, TOAST WITH PEANUT BUTTER AND JELLY, A DONUT, A WAFFLE, AND SOME OF THOSE LITTLE SAUSAGE.
YAWN! I'M NOT REALLY HUNGRY.
KIRKMAN & SCOTT
LOVE THE CHILD, HATE THE METABOLISM.
MAKE THAT TWO DONUTS.

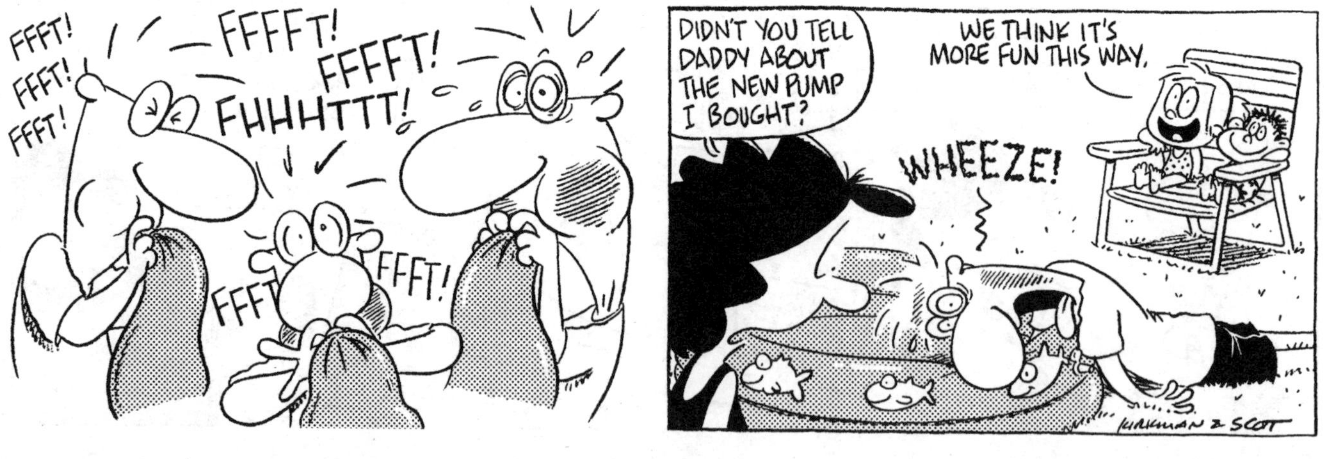

FFFT! FFFT! FFFT!
FFFFT!
FFFFT!
FHHHTTT!
FFFT
FFFT!
DIDN'T YOU TELL DADDY ABOUT THE NEW PUMP I BOUGHT?
WE THINK IT'S MORE FUN THIS WAY.
WHEEZE!
KIRKMAN & SCOTT

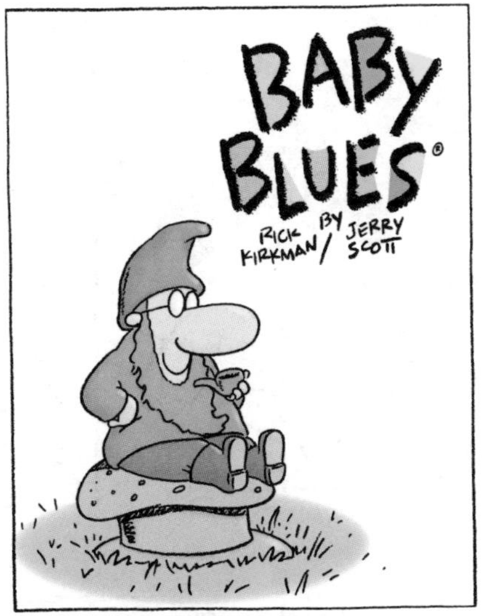
BABY BLUES®
BY RICK KIRKMAN / JERRY SCOTT

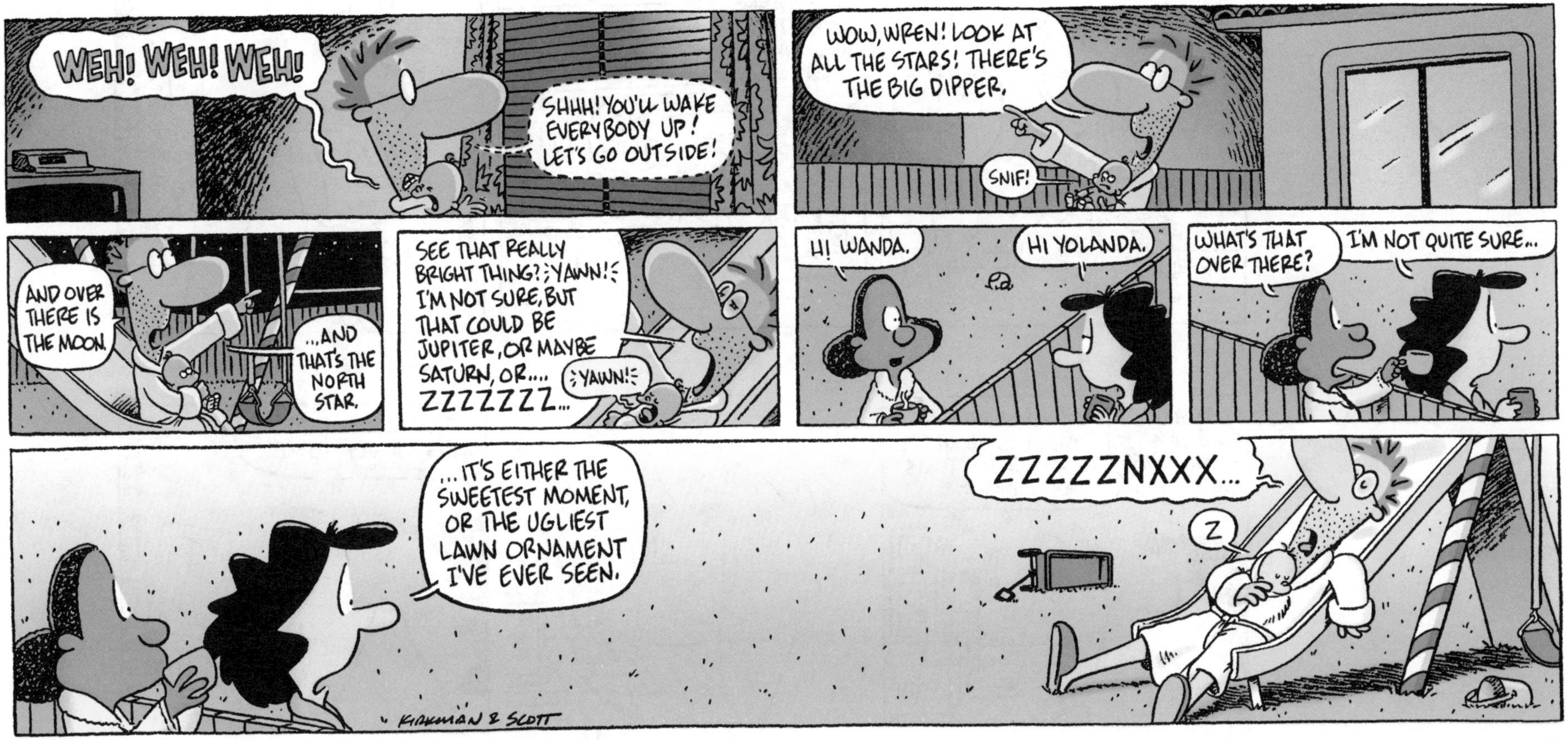
WEH! WEH! WEH!
SHHH! YOU'LL WAKE EVERYBODY UP! LET'S GO OUTSIDE!
WOW, WREN! LOOK AT ALL THE STARS! THERE'S THE BIG DIPPER.
SNIF!
AND OVER THERE IS THE MOON.
...AND THAT'S THE NORTH STAR.
SEE THAT REALLY BRIGHT THING? YAWN! I'M NOT SURE, BUT THAT COULD BE JUPITER, OR MAYBE SATURN, OR.... ZZZZZZZ...
YAWN!
HI WANDA.
HI YOLANDA.
WHAT'S THAT OVER THERE?
I'M NOT QUITE SURE...
...IT'S EITHER THE SWEETEST MOMENT, OR THE UGLIEST LAWN ORNAMENT I'VE EVER SEEN.
ZZZZZNXXX...
Z
KIRKMAN & SCOTT

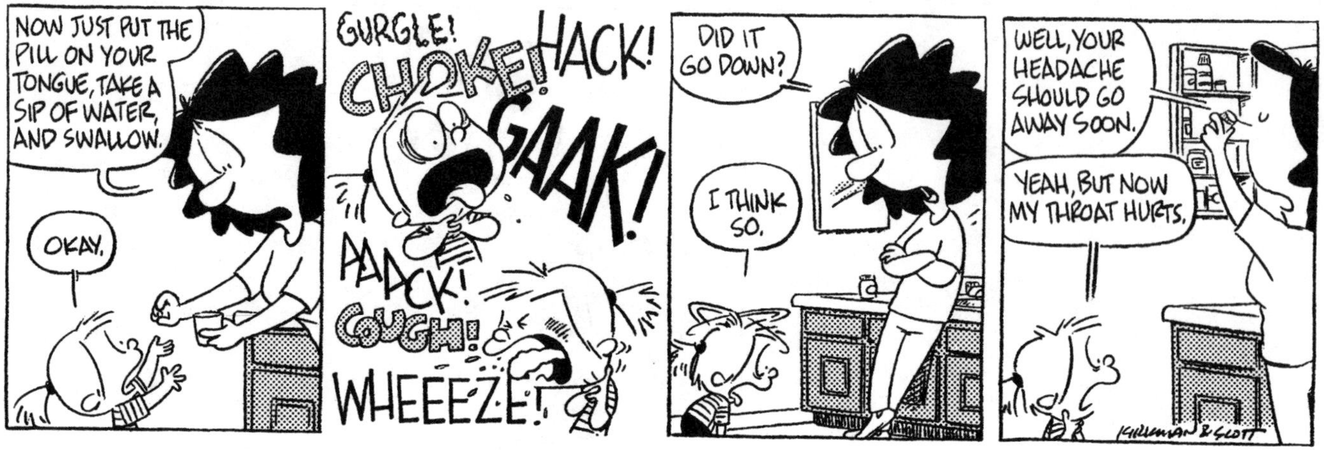
NOW JUST PUT THE PILL ON YOUR TONGUE, TAKE A SIP OF WATER, AND SWALLOW.
OKAY.
GURGLE!
CHOKE!
HACK!
GAAK!
PAACK!
COUGH!
WHEEEZE!
DID IT GO DOWN?
I THINK SO.
WELL, YOUR HEADACHE SHOULD GO AWAY SOON.
YEAH, BUT NOW MY THROAT HURTS.
KIRKMAN & SCOTT

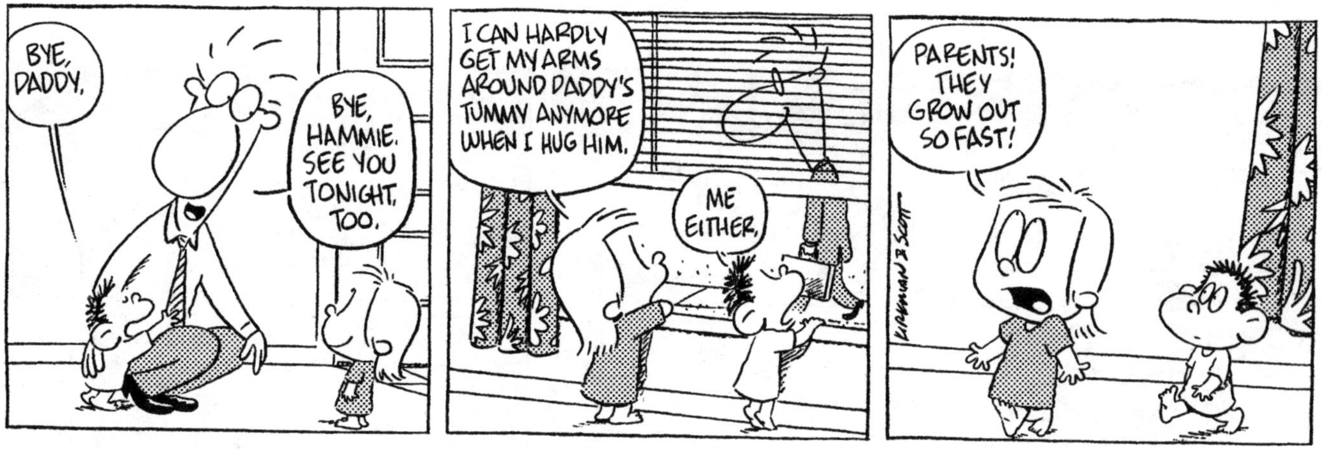
BYE, DADDY.
BYE, HAMMIE. SEE YOU TONIGHT, TOO.
I CAN HARDLY GET MY ARMS AROUND DADDY'S TUMMY ANYMORE WHEN I HUG HIM.
ME EITHER.
KIRKMAN & SCOTT
PARENTS! THEY GROW OUT SO FAST!

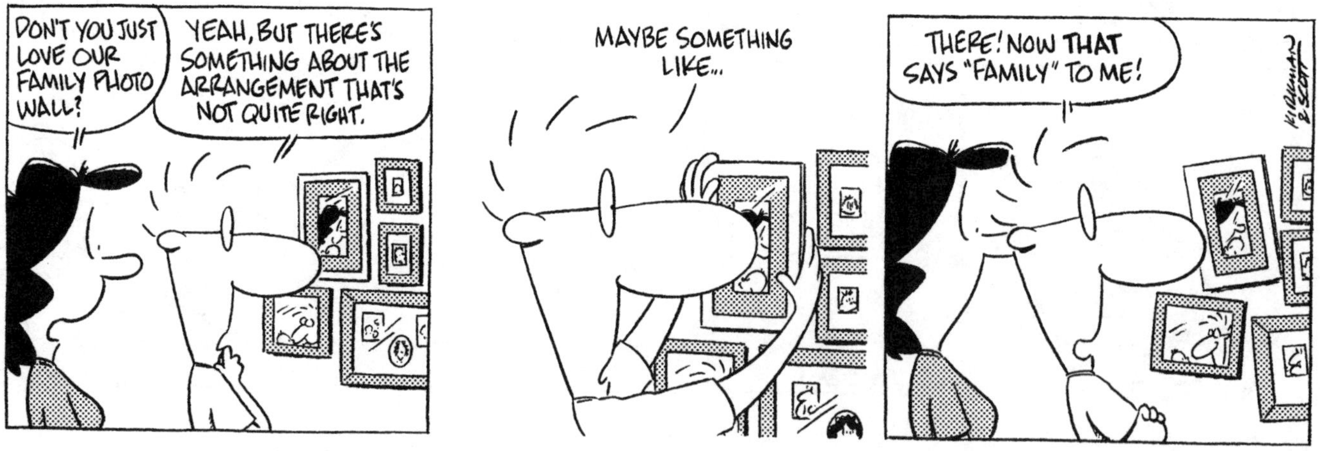
DON'T YOU JUST LOVE OUR FAMILY PHOTO WALL?
YEAH, BUT THERE'S SOMETHING ABOUT THE ARRANGEMENT THAT'S NOT QUITE RIGHT.
MAYBE SOMETHING LIKE...
THERE! NOW **THAT** SAYS "FAMILY" TO ME!
KIRKMAN & SCOTT

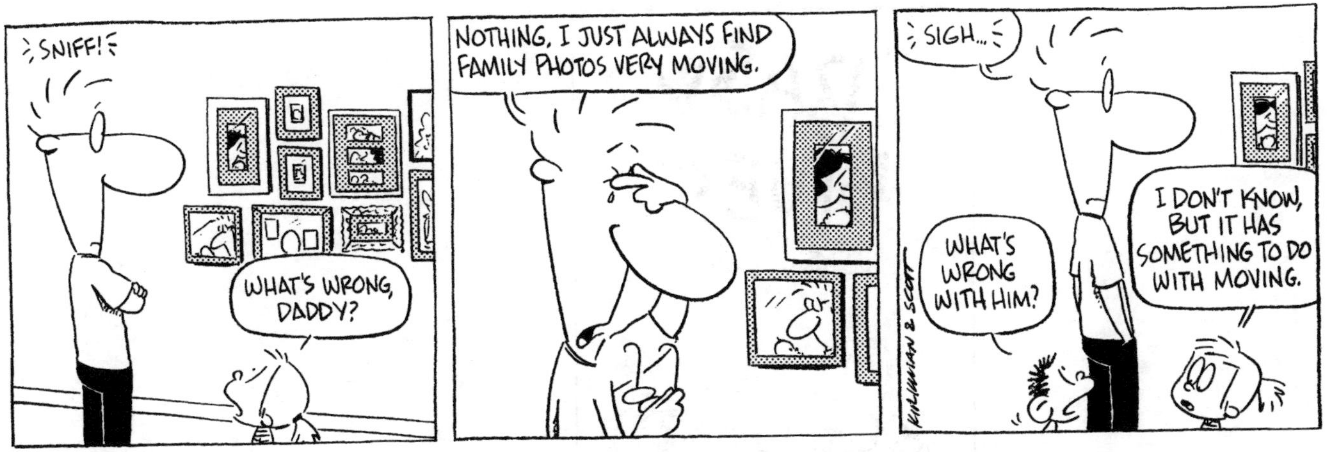
SNIFF!
WHAT'S WRONG, DADDY?
NOTHING. I JUST ALWAYS FIND FAMILY PHOTOS VERY MOVING.
SIGH...
KIRKMAN & SCOTT
WHAT'S WRONG WITH HIM?
I DON'T KNOW, BUT IT HAS SOMETHING TO DO WITH MOVING.

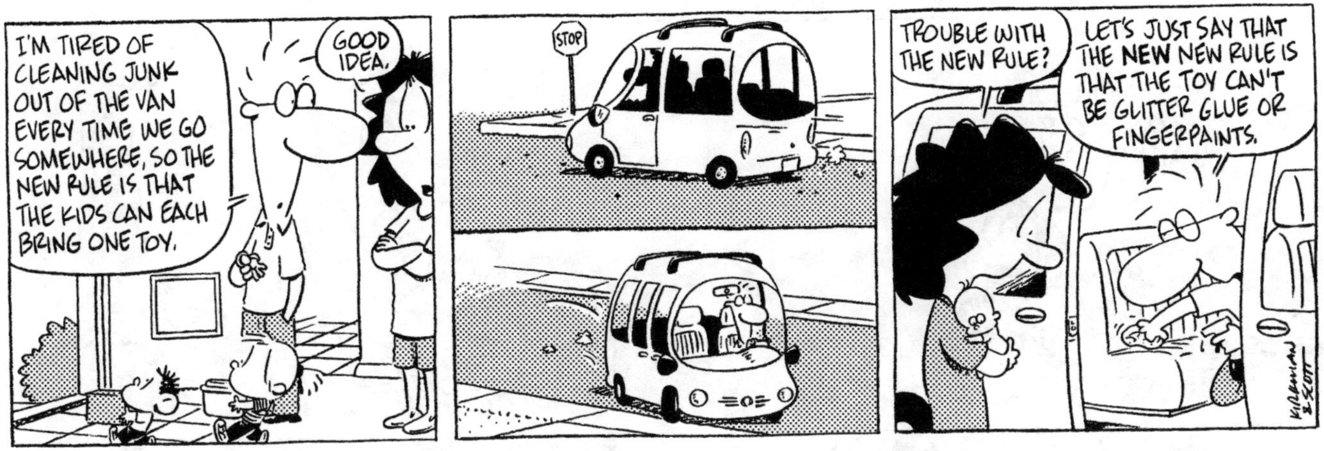
I'M TIRED OF CLEANING JUNK OUT OF THE VAN EVERY TIME WE GO SOMEWHERE, SO THE NEW RULE IS THAT THE KIDS CAN EACH BRING ONE TOY.
GOOD IDEA.
STOP
TROUBLE WITH THE NEW RULE?
LET'S JUST SAY THAT THE **NEW** NEW RULE IS THAT THE TOY CAN'T BE GLITTER GLUE OR FINGERPAINTS.
KIRKMAN & SCOTT

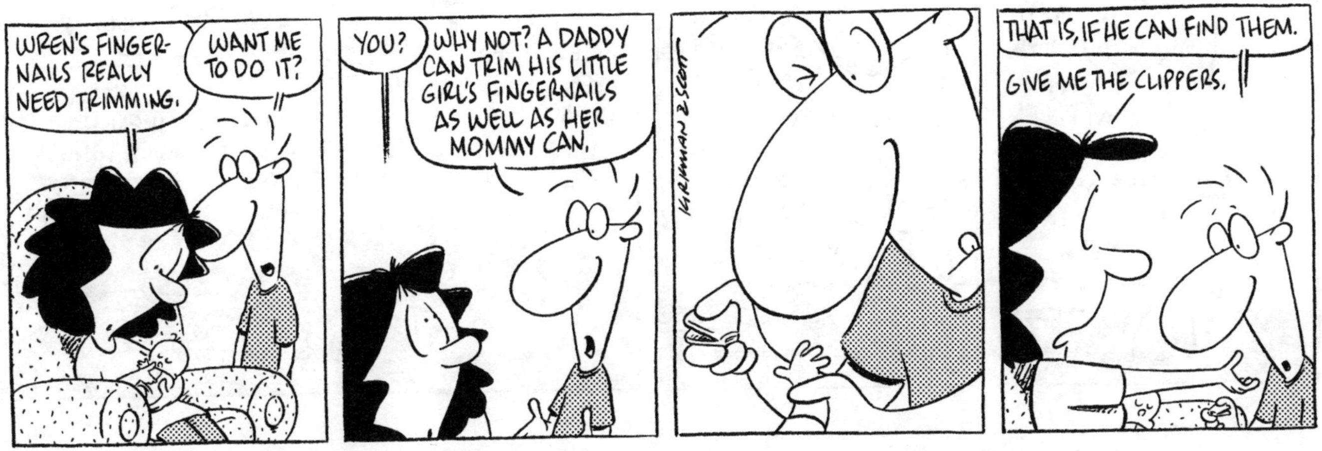
WREN'S FINGER-NAILS REALLY NEED TRIMMING.
WANT ME TO DO IT?
YOU?
WHY NOT? A DADDY CAN TRIM HIS LITTLE GIRL'S FINGERNAILS AS WELL AS HER MOMMY CAN.
KIRKMAN & SCOTT
THAT IS, IF HE CAN FIND THEM.
GIVE ME THE CLIPPERS.

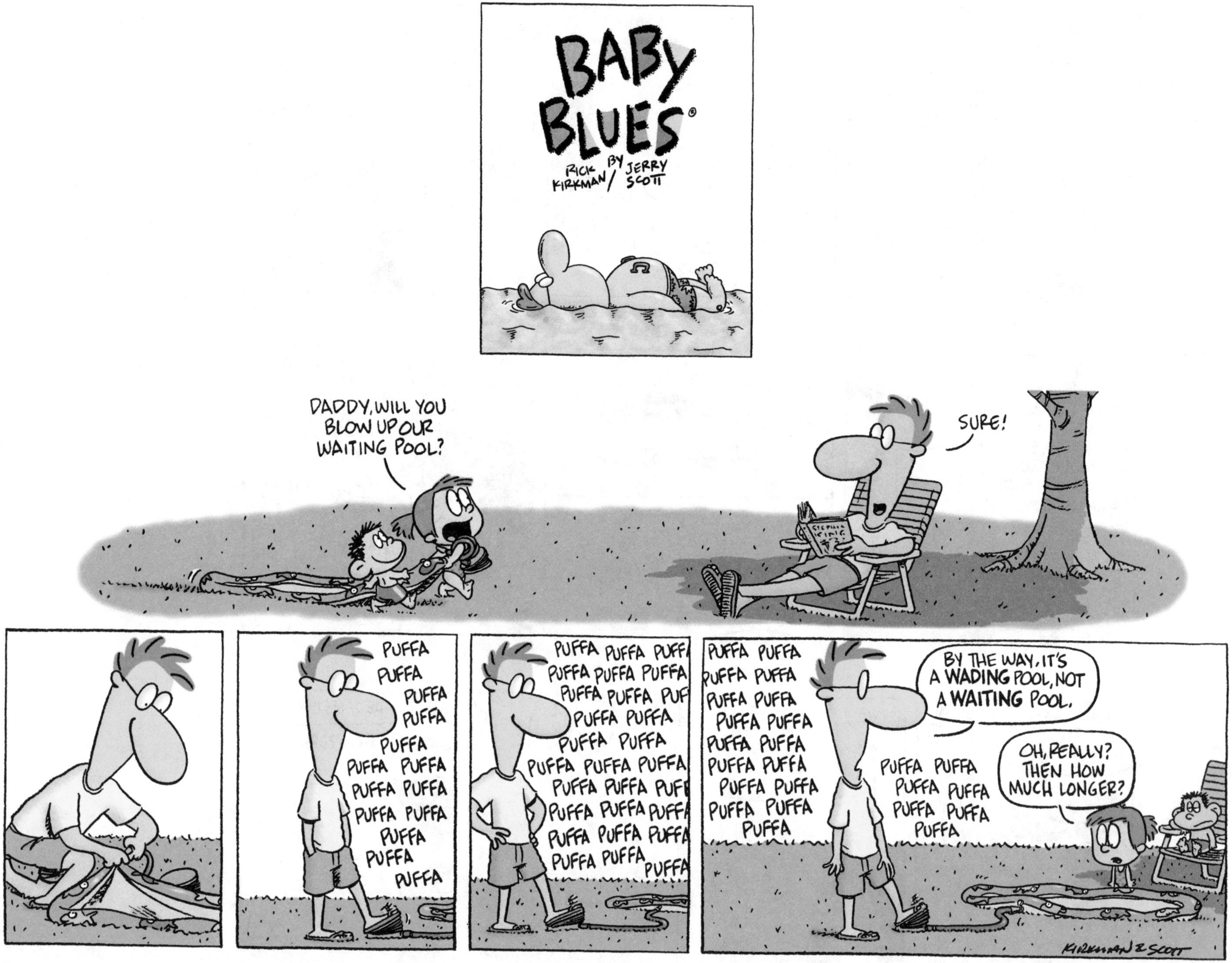
BABY BLUES®
BY RICK KIRKMAN / JERRY SCOTT
DADDY, WILL YOU BLOW UP OUR WAITING POOL?
SURE!
PUFFA PUFFA PUFFA PUFFA PUFFA PUFFA PUFFA PUFFA PUFFA PUFFA PUFFA PUFFA PUFFA PUFFA
PUFFA PUFFA
PUFFA PUFFA PUFFA PUFFA PUFFA PUFFA PUFFA PUFFA PUFFA PUFFA PUFFA PUFFA PUFFA PUFFA PUFFA PUFFA PUFFA
BY THE WAY, IT'S A **WADING** POOL, NOT A **WAITING** POOL.
PUFFA PUFFA PUFFA PUFFA PUFFA PUFFA PUFFA
OH, REALLY? THEN HOW MUCH LONGER?
KIRKMAN & SCOTT

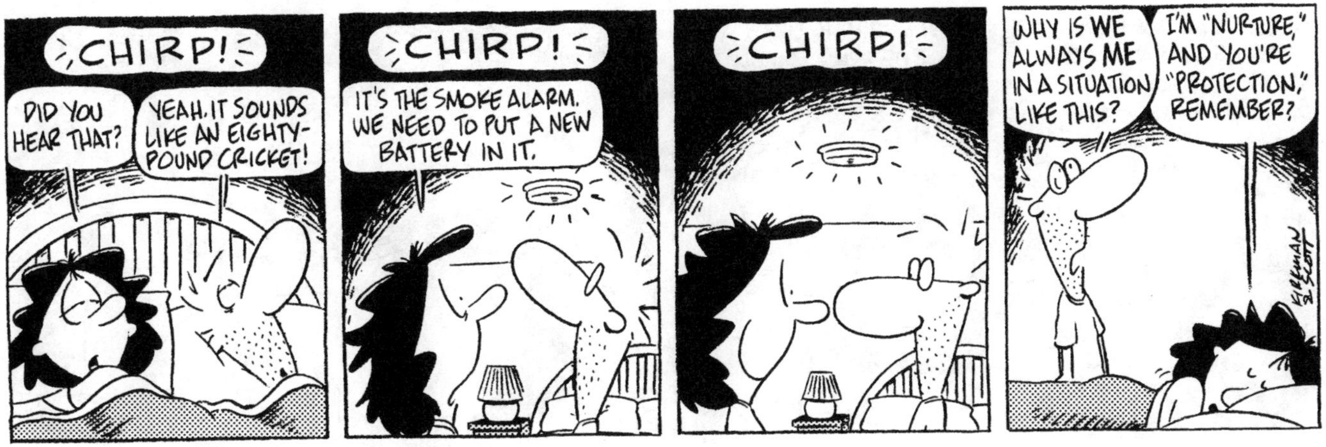
CHIRP!
DID YOU HEAR THAT?
YEAH. IT SOUNDS LIKE AN EIGHTY-POUND CRICKET!
CHIRP!
IT'S THE SMOKE ALARM. WE NEED TO PUT A NEW BATTERY IN IT.
CHIRP!
WHY IS WE ALWAYS ME IN A SITUATION LIKE THIS?
I'M "NURTURE," AND YOU'RE "PROTECTION," REMEMBER?
KIRKMAN & SCOTT

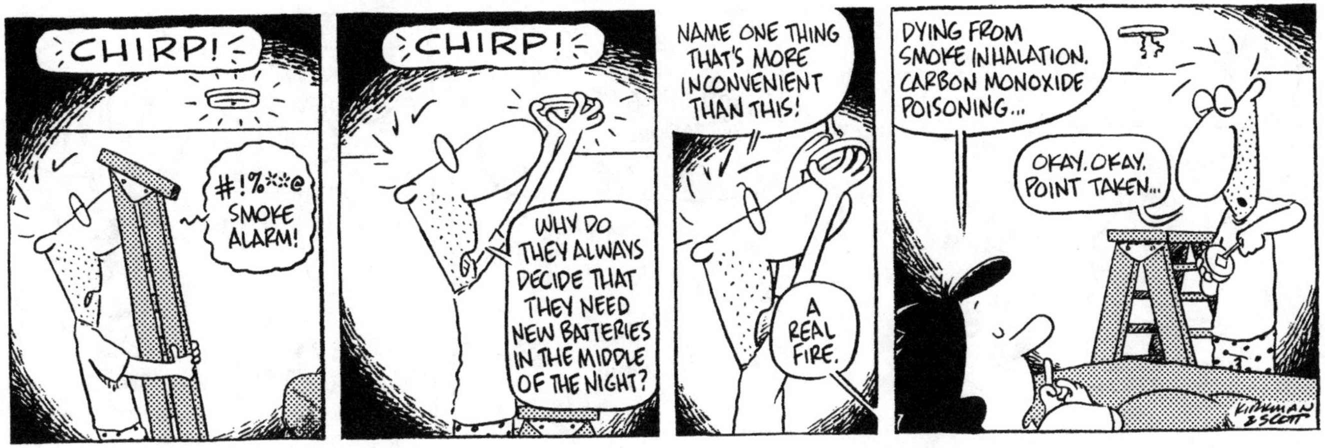
CHIRP!
#!%*@ SMOKE ALARM!
CHIRP!
WHY DO THEY ALWAYS DECIDE THAT THEY NEED NEW BATTERIES IN THE MIDDLE OF THE NIGHT?
NAME ONE THING THAT'S MORE INCONVENIENT THAN THIS!
A REAL FIRE.
DYING FROM SMOKE INHALATION. CARBON MONOXIDE POISONING...
OKAY. OKAY. POINT TAKEN...
KIRKMAN & SCOTT

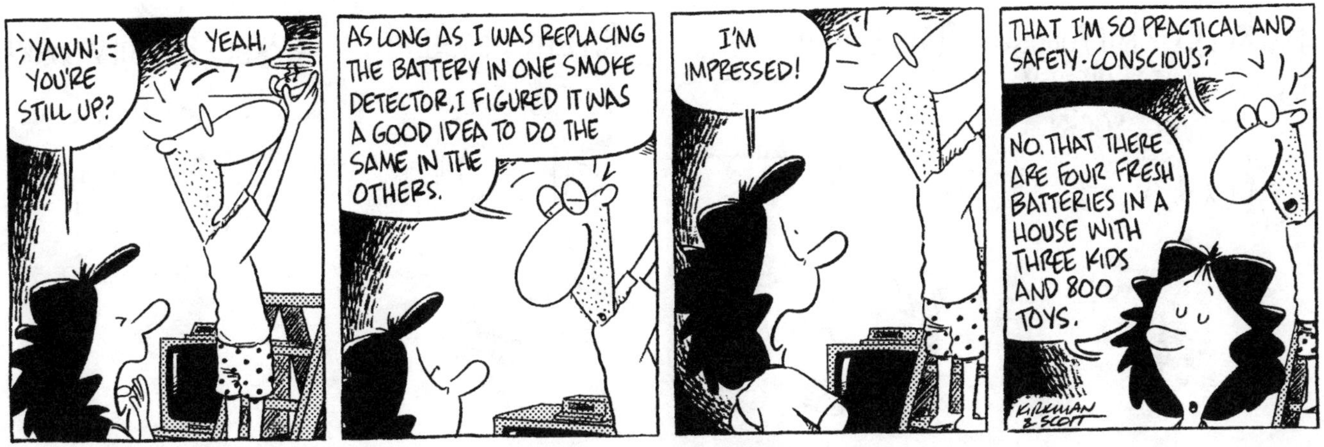
YAWN! YOU'RE STILL UP?
YEAH.
AS LONG AS I WAS REPLACING THE BATTERY IN ONE SMOKE DETECTOR, I FIGURED IT WAS A GOOD IDEA TO DO THE SAME IN THE OTHERS.
I'M IMPRESSED!
THAT I'M SO PRACTICAL AND SAFETY-CONSCIOUS?
NO. THAT THERE ARE FOUR FRESH BATTERIES IN A HOUSE WITH THREE KIDS AND 800 TOYS.
KIRKMAN & SCOTT

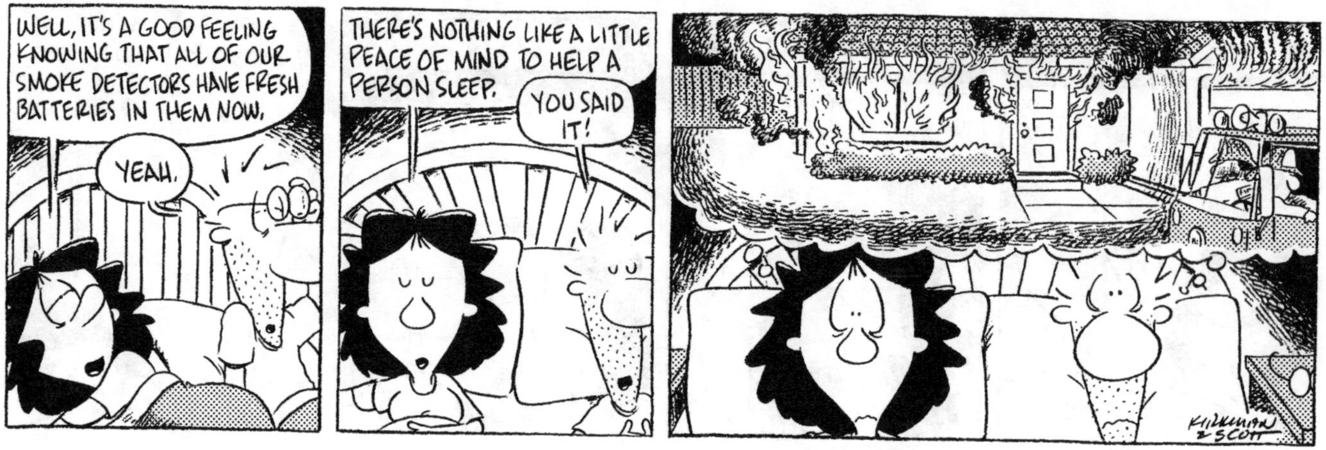
WELL, IT'S A GOOD FEELING KNOWING THAT ALL OF OUR SMOKE DETECTORS HAVE FRESH BATTERIES IN THEM NOW.
YEAH.
THERE'S NOTHING LIKE A LITTLE PEACE OF MIND TO HELP A PERSON SLEEP.
YOU SAID IT!
KIRKMAN & SCOTT

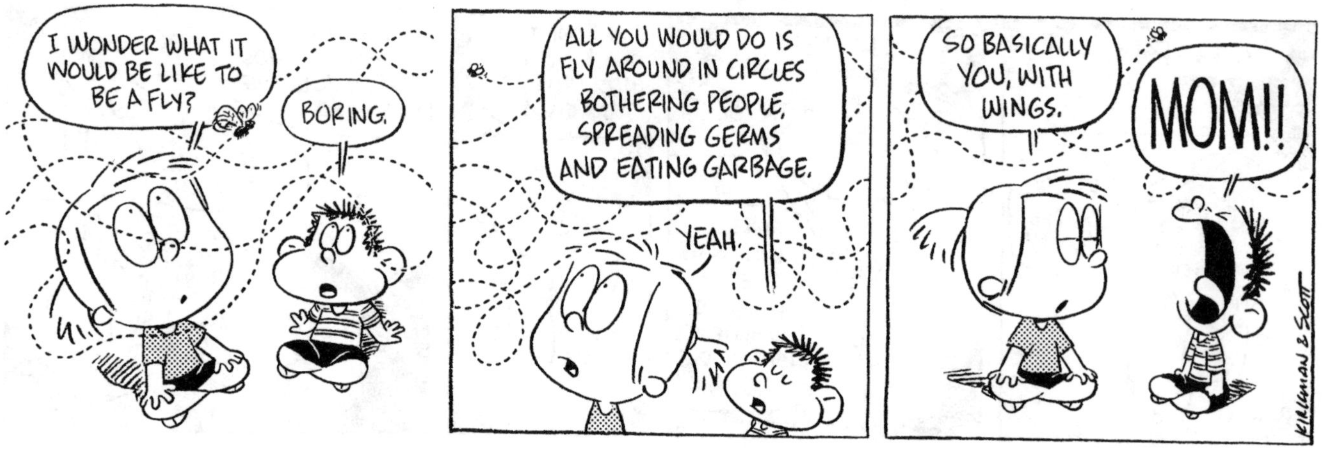
I WONDER WHAT IT WOULD BE LIKE TO BE A FLY?
BORING.
ALL YOU WOULD DO IS FLY AROUND IN CIRCLES BOTHERING PEOPLE, SPREADING GERMS AND EATING GARBAGE.
YEAH.
SO BASICALLY YOU, WITH WINGS.
MOM!!
KIRKMAN & SCOTT

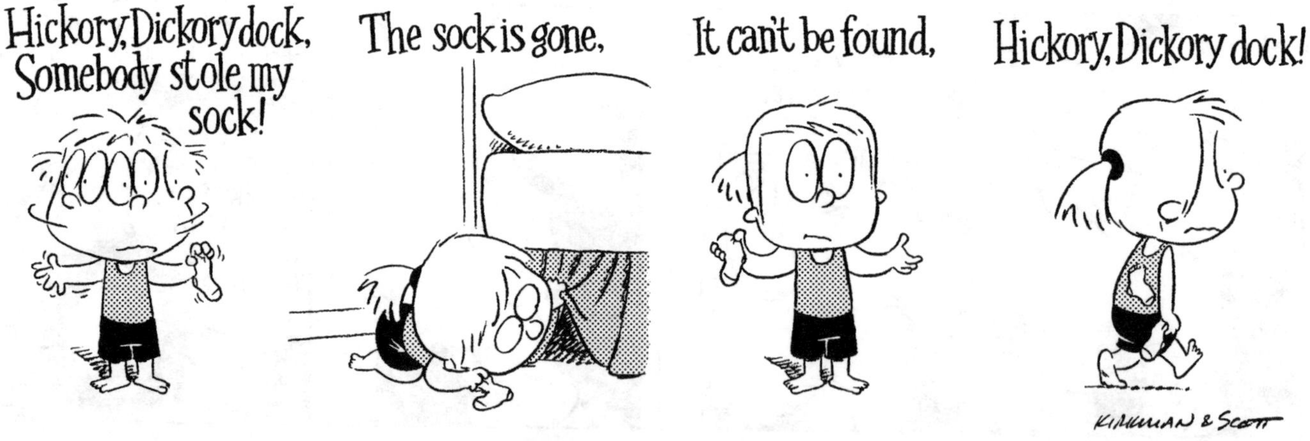
Hickory, Dickory dock, Somebody stole my sock!
The sock is gone,
It can't be found,
Hickory, Dickory dock!
KIRKMAN & SCOTT

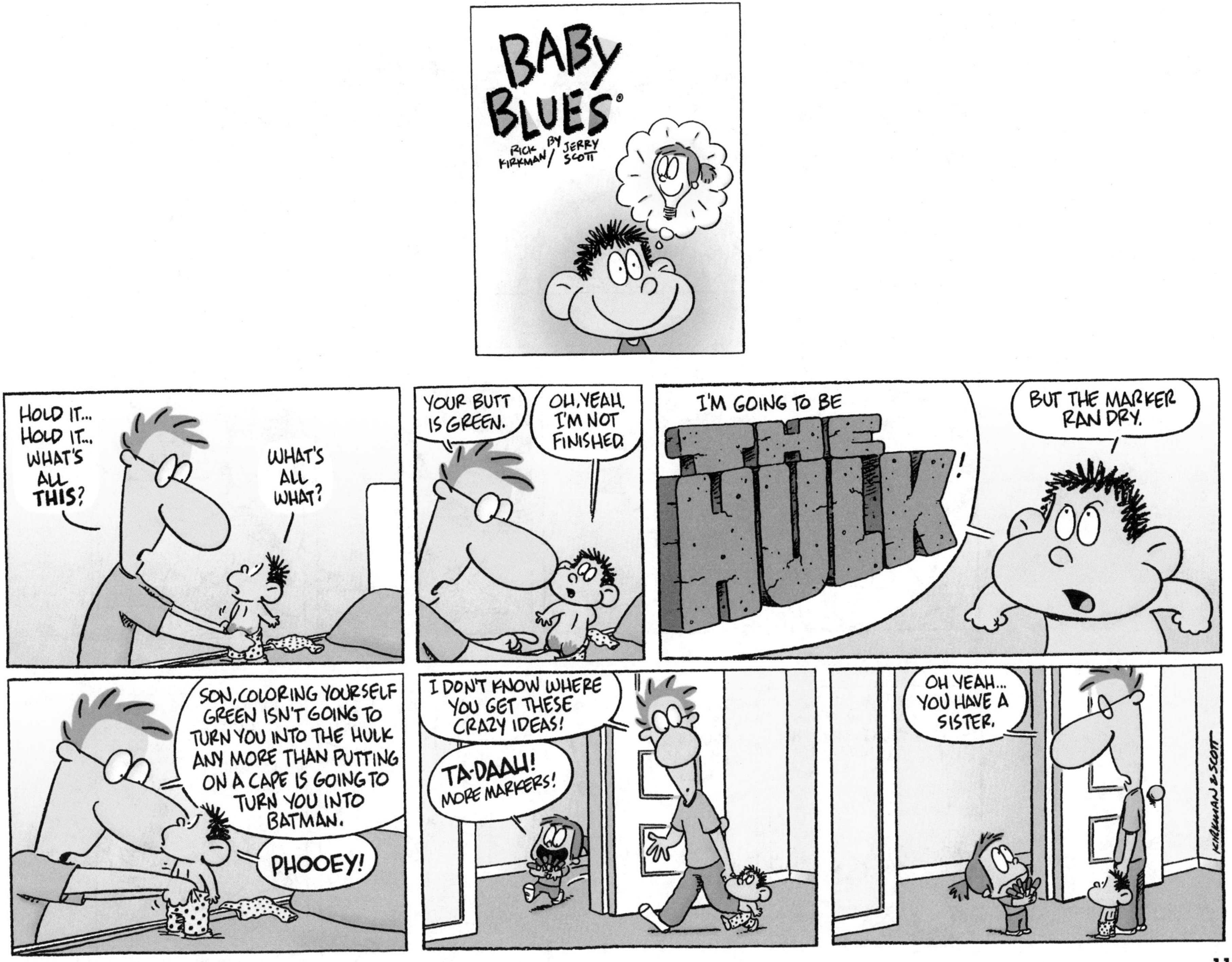
BABY BLUES®
BY RICK KIRKMAN / JERRY SCOTT
HOLD IT... HOLD IT... WHAT'S ALL THIS?
WHAT'S ALL WHAT?
YOUR BUTT IS GREEN.
OH, YEAH. I'M NOT FINISHED.
I'M GOING TO BE THE HULK!
BUT THE MARKER RAN DRY.
SON, COLORING YOURSELF GREEN ISN'T GOING TO TURN YOU INTO THE HULK ANY MORE THAN PUTTING ON A CAPE IS GOING TO TURN YOU INTO BATMAN.
PHOOEY!
I DON'T KNOW WHERE YOU GET THESE CRAZY IDEAS!
TA-DAAH! MORE MARKERS!
OH YEAH... YOU HAVE A SISTER.
KIRKMAN & SCOTT

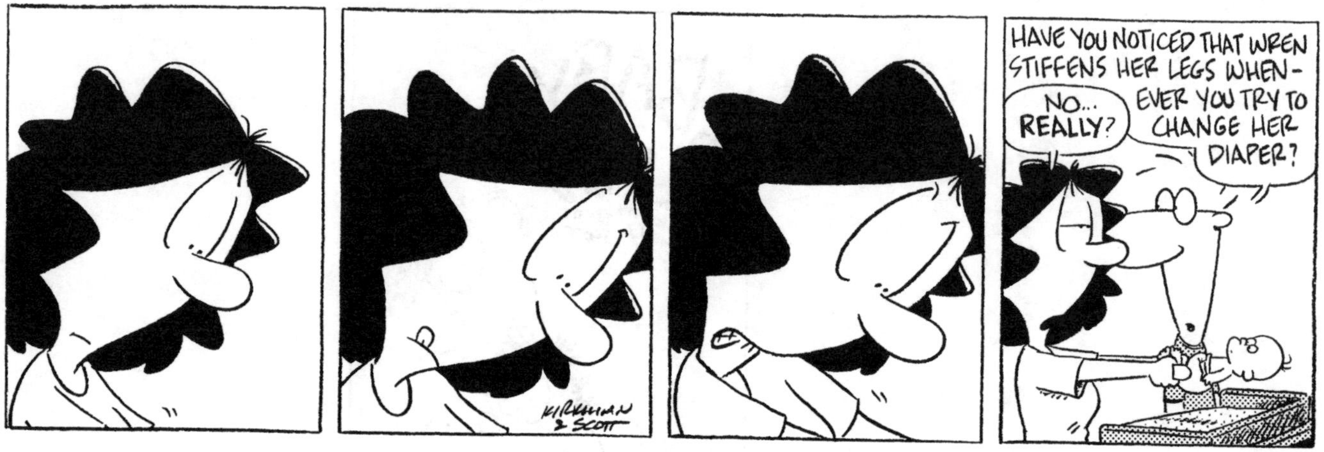
KIRKMAN & SCOTT
HAVE YOU NOTICED THAT WREN STIFFENS HER LEGS WHEN-
NO... REALLY?
EVER YOU TRY TO CHANGE HER DIAPER?

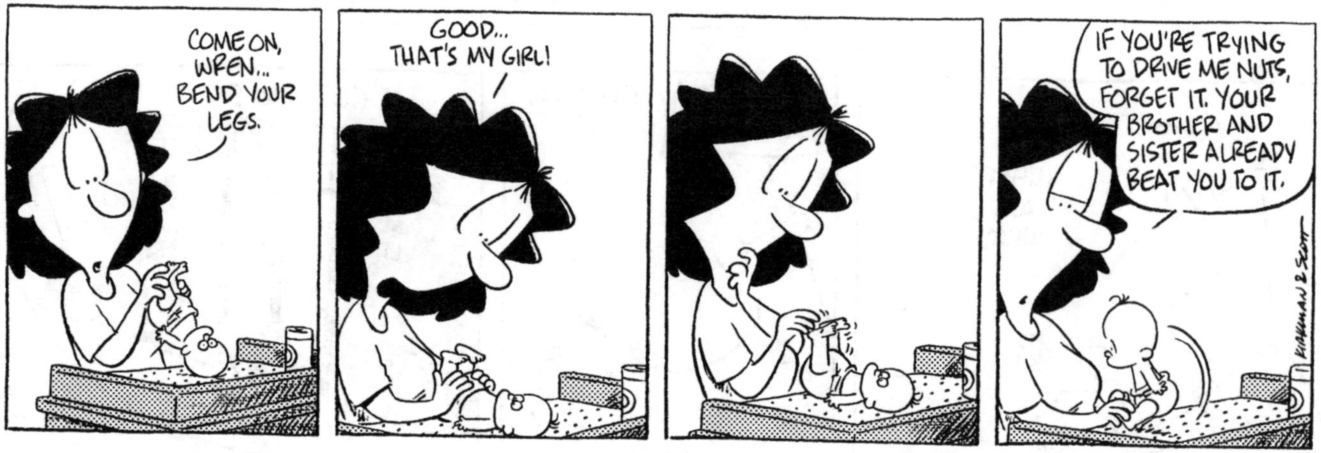
COME ON, WREN... BEND YOUR LEGS.
GOOD... THAT'S MY GIRL!
IF YOU'RE TRYING TO DRIVE ME NUTS, FORGET IT. YOUR BROTHER AND SISTER ALREADY BEAT YOU TO IT.
KIRKMAN & SCOTT

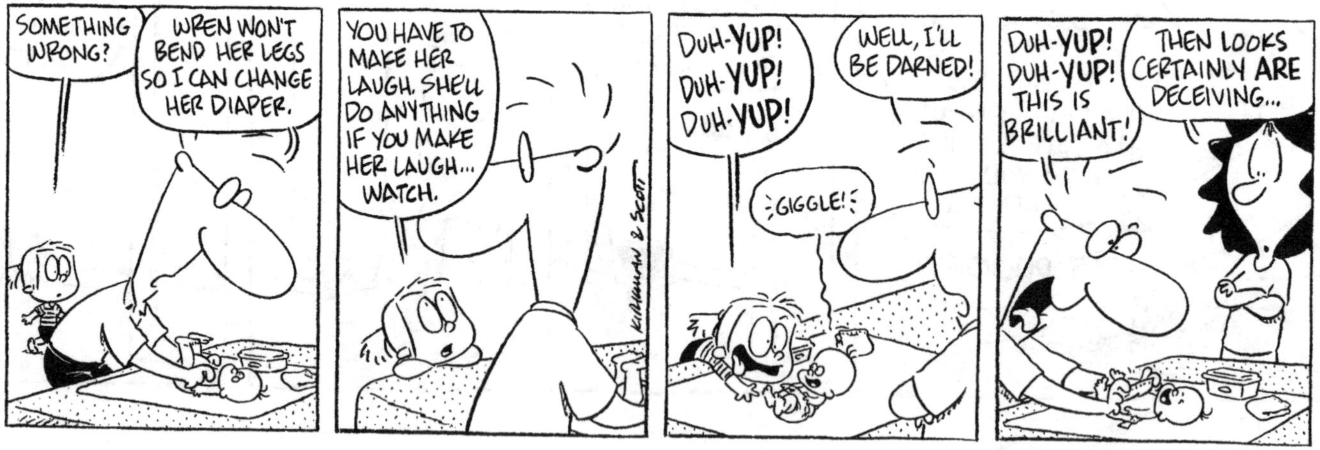
SOMETHING WRONG?
WREN WON'T BEND HER LEGS SO I CAN CHANGE HER DIAPER.
YOU HAVE TO MAKE HER LAUGH. SHE'LL DO ANYTHING IF YOU MAKE HER LAUGH... WATCH.
KIRKMAN & SCOTT
DUH-YUP! DUH-YUP! DUH-YUP!
WELL, I'LL BE DARNED!
GIGGLE!
DUH-YUP! DUH-YUP! THIS IS BRILLIANT!
THEN LOOKS CERTAINLY ARE DECEIVING...

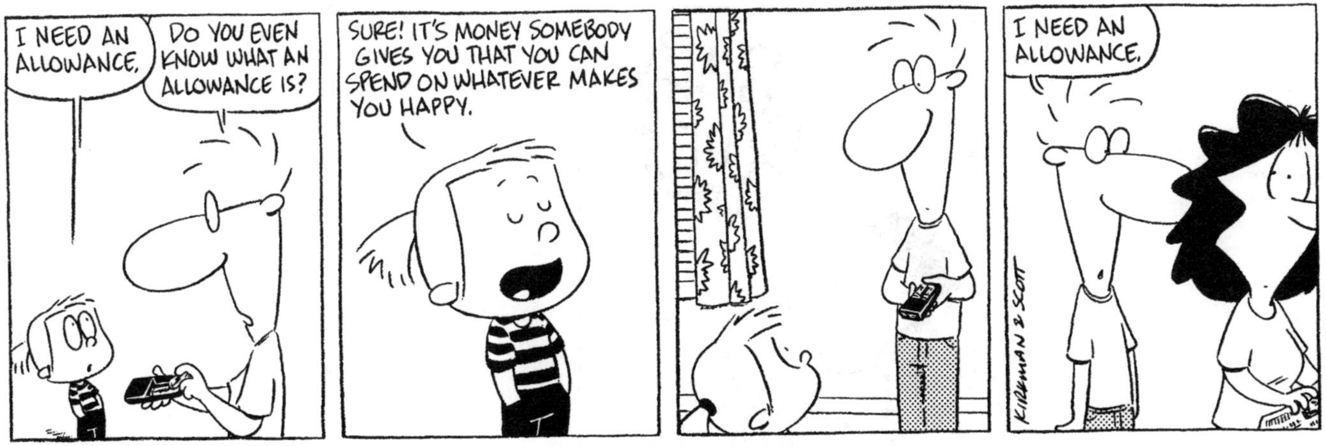
I NEED AN ALLOWANCE.
DO YOU EVEN KNOW WHAT AN ALLOWANCE IS?
SURE! IT'S MONEY SOMEBODY GIVES YOU THAT YOU CAN SPEND ON WHATEVER MAKES YOU HAPPY.
I NEED AN ALLOWANCE.
KIRKMAN & SCOTT

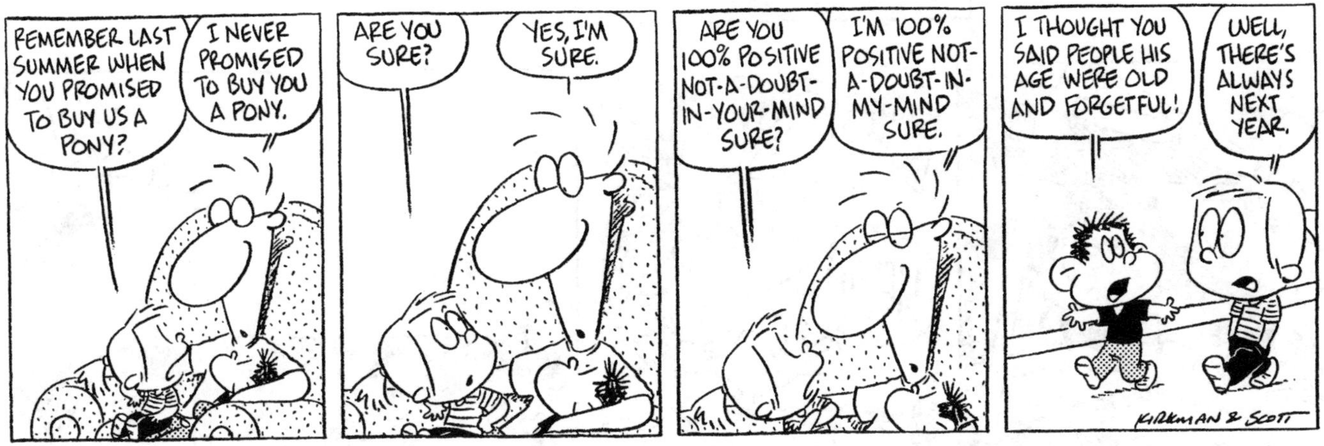
REMEMBER LAST SUMMER WHEN YOU PROMISED TO BUY US A PONY?
I NEVER PROMISED TO BUY YOU A PONY.
ARE YOU SURE?
YES, I'M SURE.
ARE YOU 100% POSITIVE NOT-A-DOUBT-IN-YOUR-MIND SURE?
I'M 100% POSITIVE NOT-A-DOUBT-IN-MY-MIND SURE.
I THOUGHT YOU SAID PEOPLE HIS AGE WERE OLD AND FORGETFUL!
WELL, THERE'S ALWAYS NEXT YEAR.
KIRKMAN & SCOTT

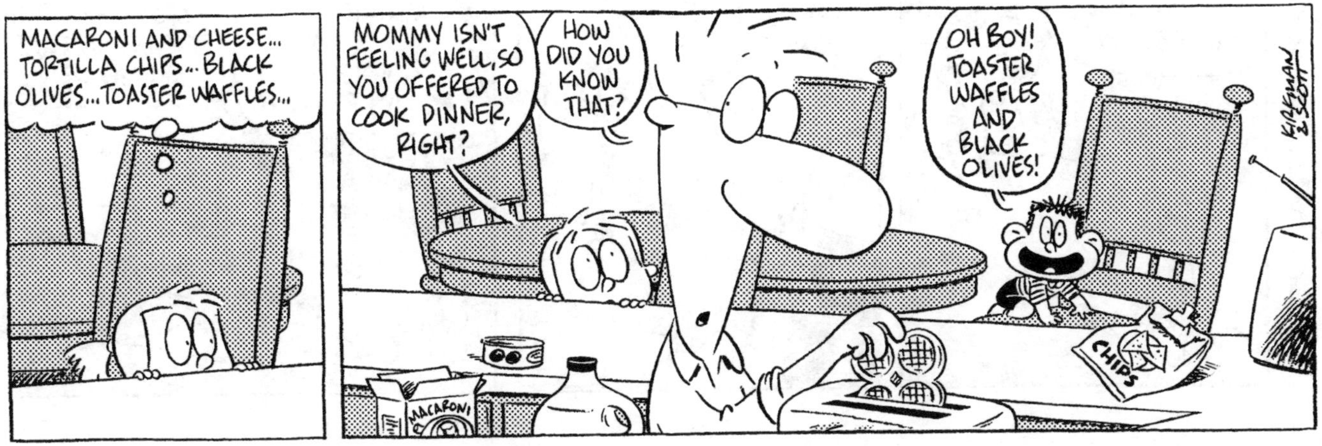
MACARONI AND CHEESE... TORTILLA CHIPS... BLACK OLIVES... TOASTER WAFFLES...
MOMMY ISN'T FEELING WELL, SO YOU OFFERED TO COOK DINNER, RIGHT?
HOW DID YOU KNOW THAT?
OH BOY! TOASTER WAFFLES AND BLACK OLIVES!
MACARONI
CHIPS
KIRKMAN & SCOTT

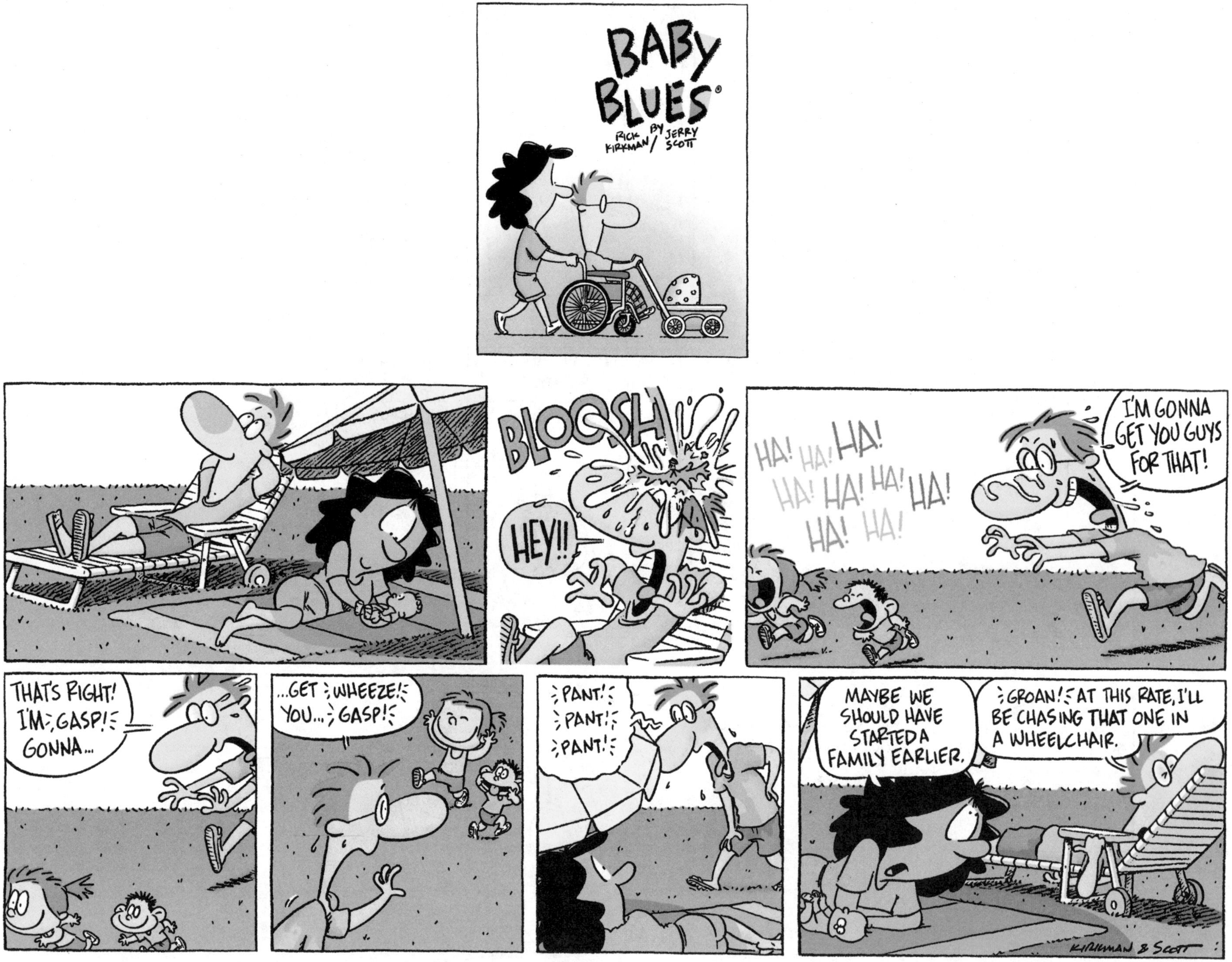
BABY BLUES®
BY RICK KIRKMAN / JERRY SCOTT
BLOOSH
HEY!!
HA! HA! HA! HA! HA! HA! HA! HA! HA!
I'M GONNA GET YOU GUYS FOR THAT!
THAT'S RIGHT! I'M ;GASP!; GONNA...
...GET ;WHEEZE!; YOU... ;GASP!;
;PANT!; ;PANT!; ;PANT!;
MAYBE WE SHOULD HAVE STARTED A FAMILY EARLIER.
;GROAN!; AT THIS RATE, I'LL BE CHASING THAT ONE IN A WHEELCHAIR.
KIRKMAN & SCOTT

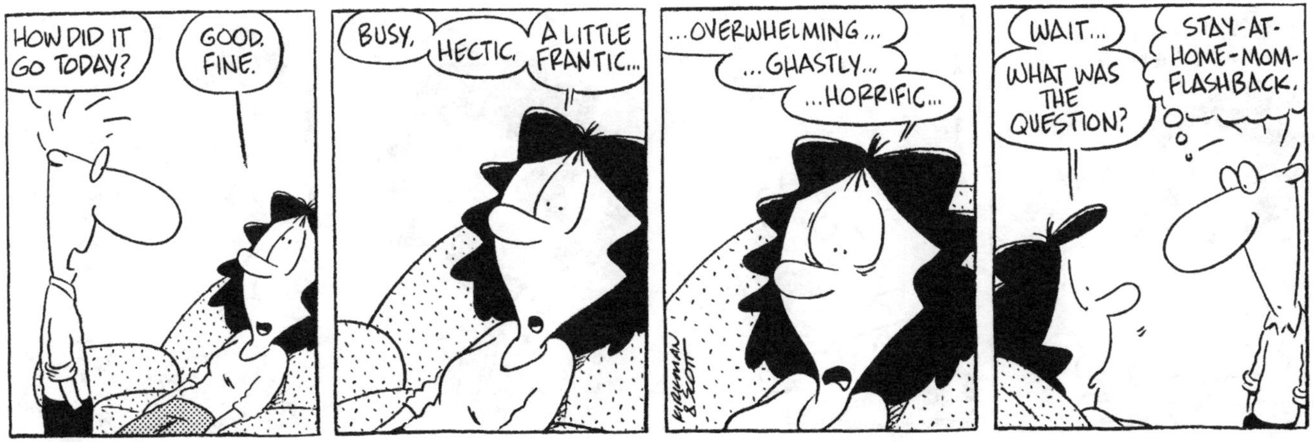
HOW DID IT GO TODAY?
GOOD. FINE.
BUSY,
HECTIC,
A LITTLE FRANTIC...
...OVERWHELMING...
...GHASTLY...
...HORRIFIC...
KIRKMAN & SCOTT
WAIT...
WHAT WAS THE QUESTION?
STAY-AT-HOME-MOM-FLASHBACK.

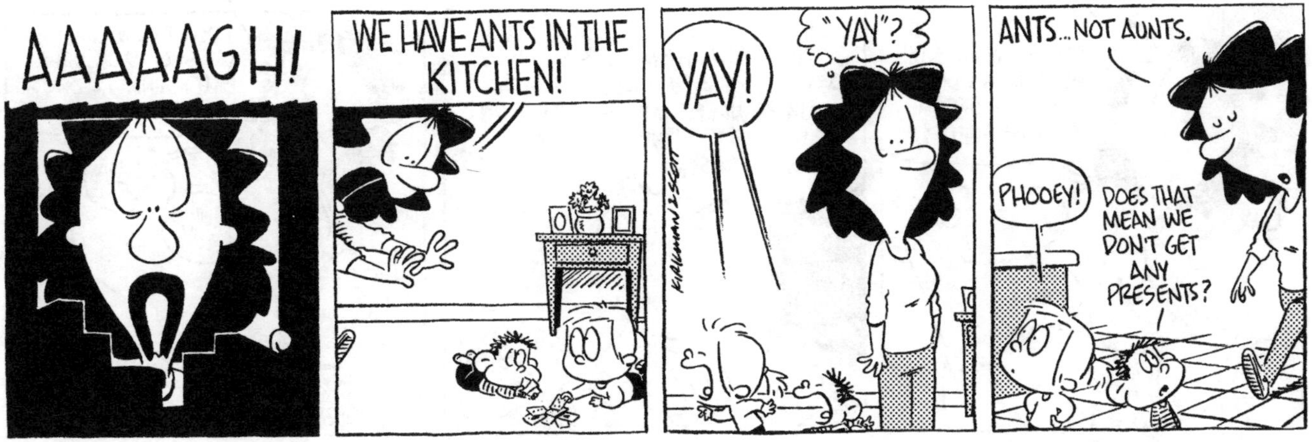
AAAAAGH!
WE HAVE ANTS IN THE KITCHEN!
KIRKMAN & SCOTT
YAY!
"YAY"?
ANTS...NOT AUNTS.
PHOOEY!
DOES THAT MEAN WE DON'T GET ANY PRESENTS?

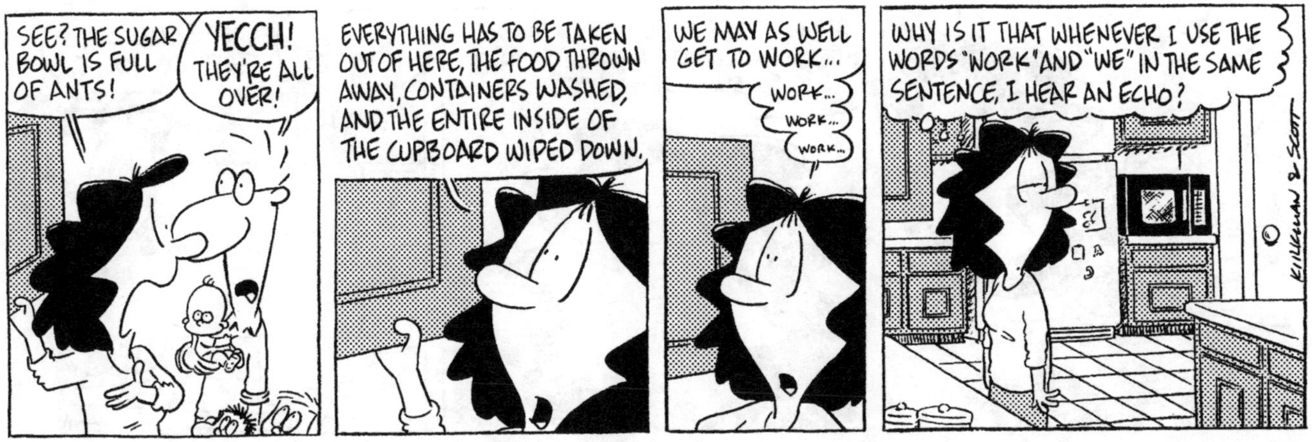
SEE? THE SUGAR BOWL IS FULL OF ANTS!
YECCH! THEY'RE ALL OVER!
EVERYTHING HAS TO BE TAKEN OUT OF HERE, THE FOOD THROWN AWAY, CONTAINERS WASHED, AND THE ENTIRE INSIDE OF THE CUPBOARD WIPED DOWN.
WE MAY AS WELL GET TO WORK...
WORK...
WORK...
WORK...
WHY IS IT THAT WHENEVER I USE THE WORDS "WORK" AND "WE" IN THE SAME SENTENCE, I HEAR AN ECHO?
KIRKMAN & SCOTT

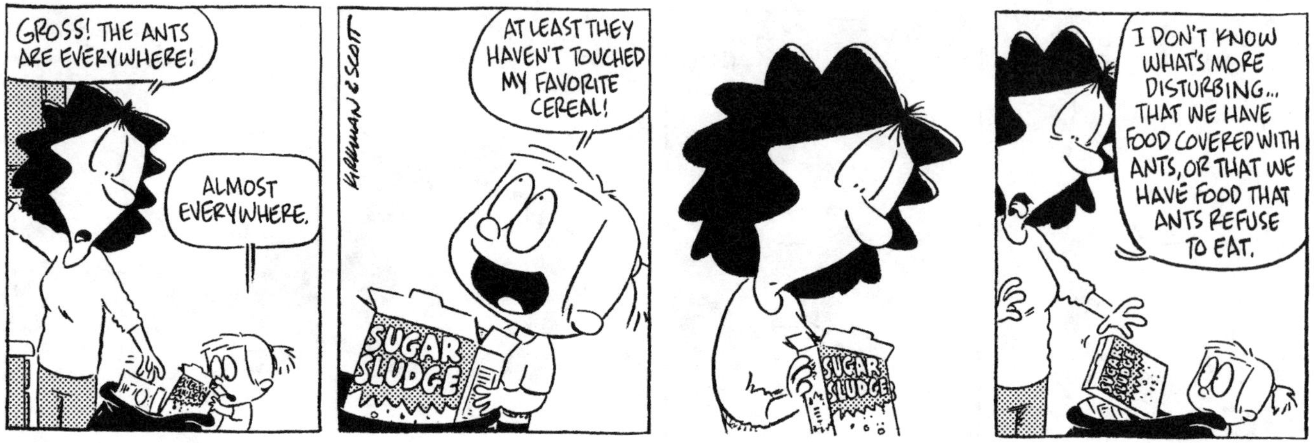
GROSS! THE ANTS ARE EVERYWHERE!
ALMOST EVERYWHERE.
KIRKMAN & SCOTT
AT LEAST THEY HAVEN'T TOUCHED MY FAVORITE CEREAL!
SUGAR SLUDGE
I DON'T KNOW WHAT'S MORE DISTURBING... THAT WE HAVE FOOD COVERED WITH ANTS, OR THAT WE HAVE FOOD THAT ANTS REFUSE TO EAT.

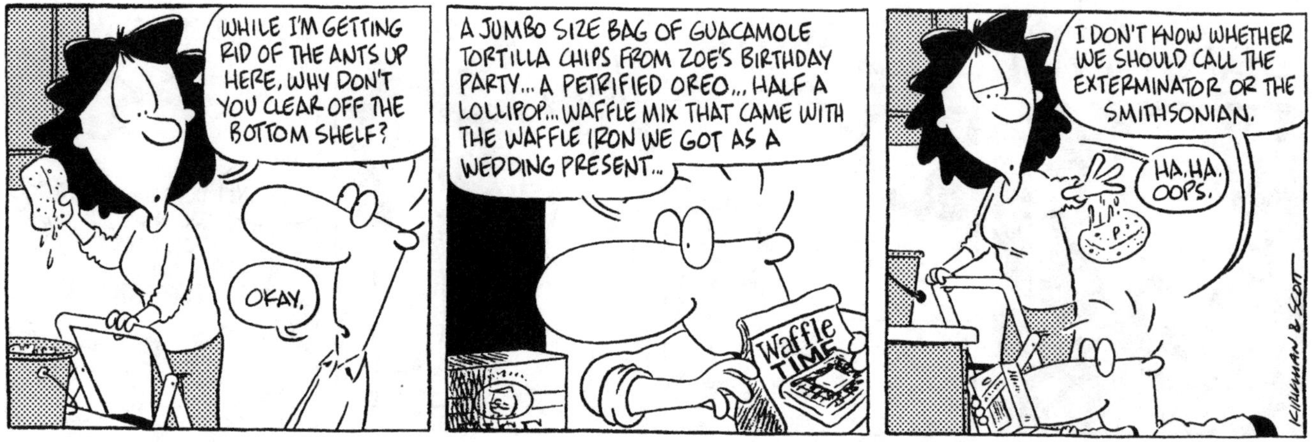
WHILE I'M GETTING RID OF THE ANTS UP HERE, WHY DON'T YOU CLEAR OFF THE BOTTOM SHELF?
OKAY.
A JUMBO SIZE BAG OF GUACAMOLE TORTILLA CHIPS FROM ZOE'S BIRTHDAY PARTY... A PETRIFIED OREO... HALF A LOLLIPOP... WAFFLE MIX THAT CAME WITH THE WAFFLE IRON WE GOT AS A WEDDING PRESENT...
Waffle TIME
I DON'T KNOW WHETHER WE SHOULD CALL THE EXTERMINATOR OR THE SMITHSONIAN.
HA.HA. OOPS.
KIRKMAN & SCOTT

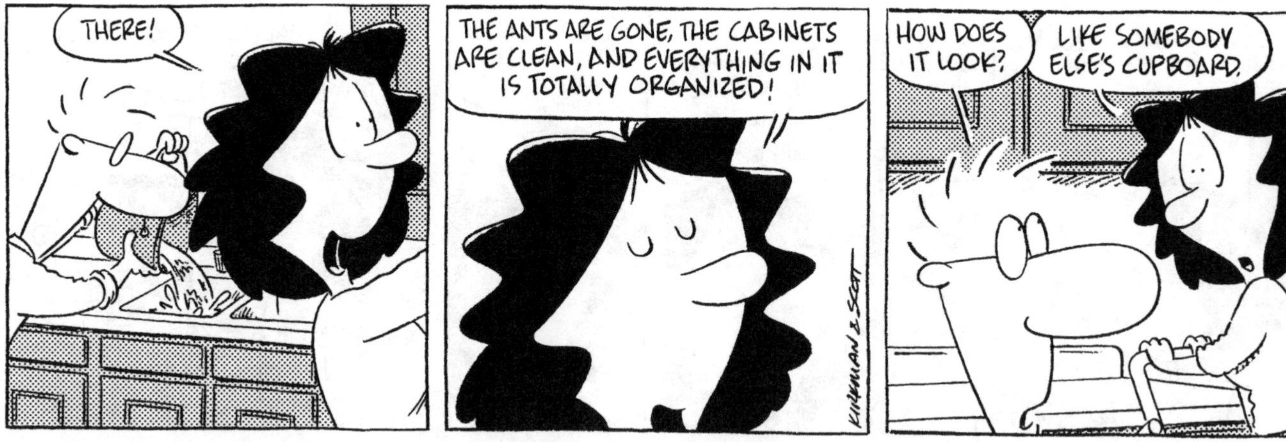
THERE!
THE ANTS ARE GONE, THE CABINETS ARE CLEAN, AND EVERYTHING IN IT IS TOTALLY ORGANIZED!
KIRKMAN & SCOTT
HOW DOES IT LOOK?
LIKE SOMEBODY ELSE'S CUPBOARD.

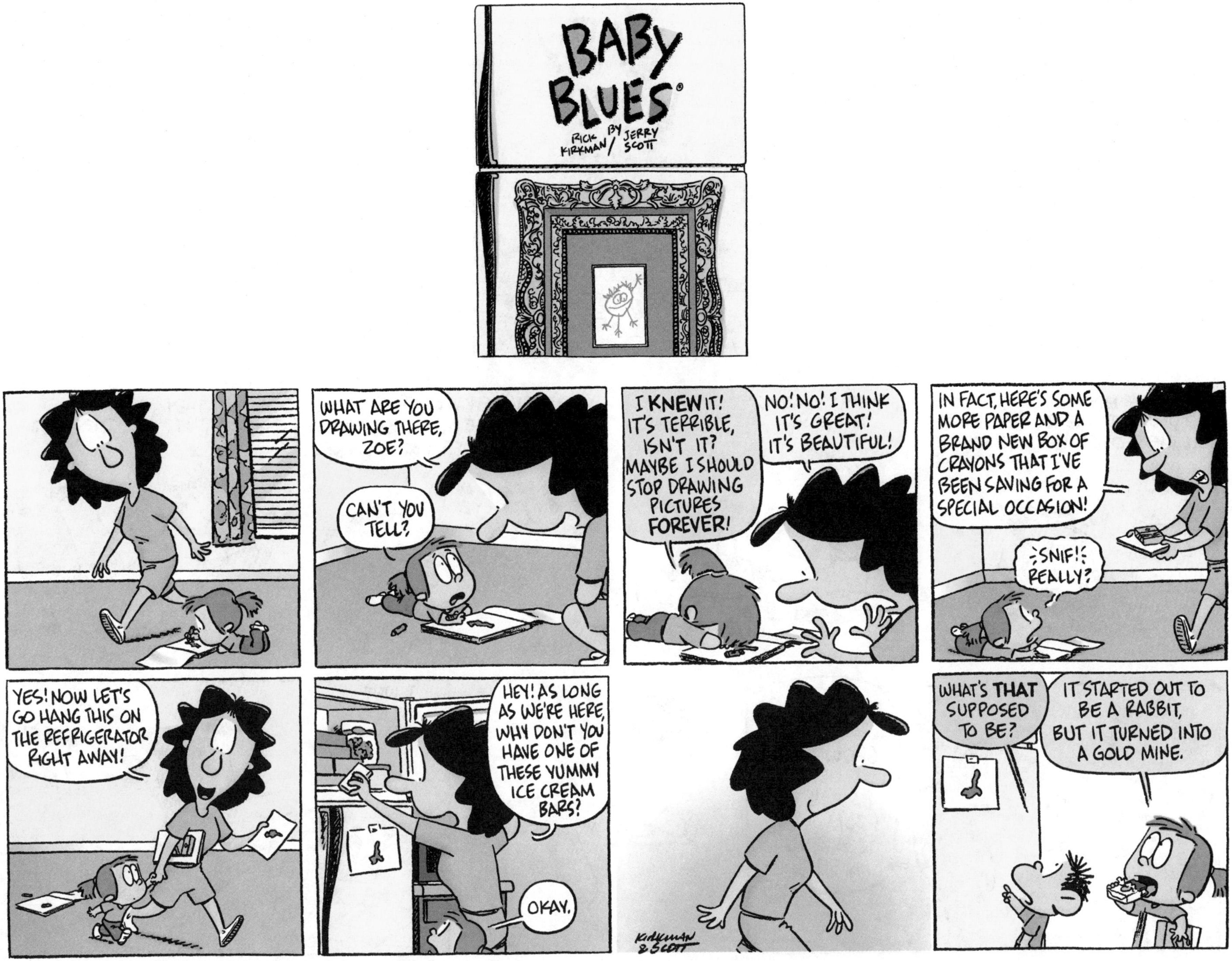
BABY BLUES®
RICK KIRKMAN / BY JERRY SCOTT
WHAT ARE YOU DRAWING THERE, ZOE?
CAN'T YOU TELL?
I **KNEW** IT! IT'S TERRIBLE, ISN'T IT? MAYBE I SHOULD STOP DRAWING PICTURES **FOREVER**!
NO! NO! I THINK IT'S GREAT! IT'S BEAUTIFUL!
IN FACT, HERE'S SOME MORE PAPER AND A BRAND NEW BOX OF CRAYONS THAT I'VE BEEN SAVING FOR A SPECIAL OCCASION!
SNIF! REALLY?
YES! NOW LET'S GO HANG THIS ON THE REFRIGERATOR RIGHT AWAY!
HEY! AS LONG AS WE'RE HERE, WHY DON'T YOU HAVE ONE OF THESE YUMMY ICE CREAM BARS?
OKAY.
KIRKMAN & SCOTT
WHAT'S **THAT** SUPPOSED TO BE?
IT STARTED OUT TO BE A RABBIT, BUT IT TURNED INTO A GOLD MINE.

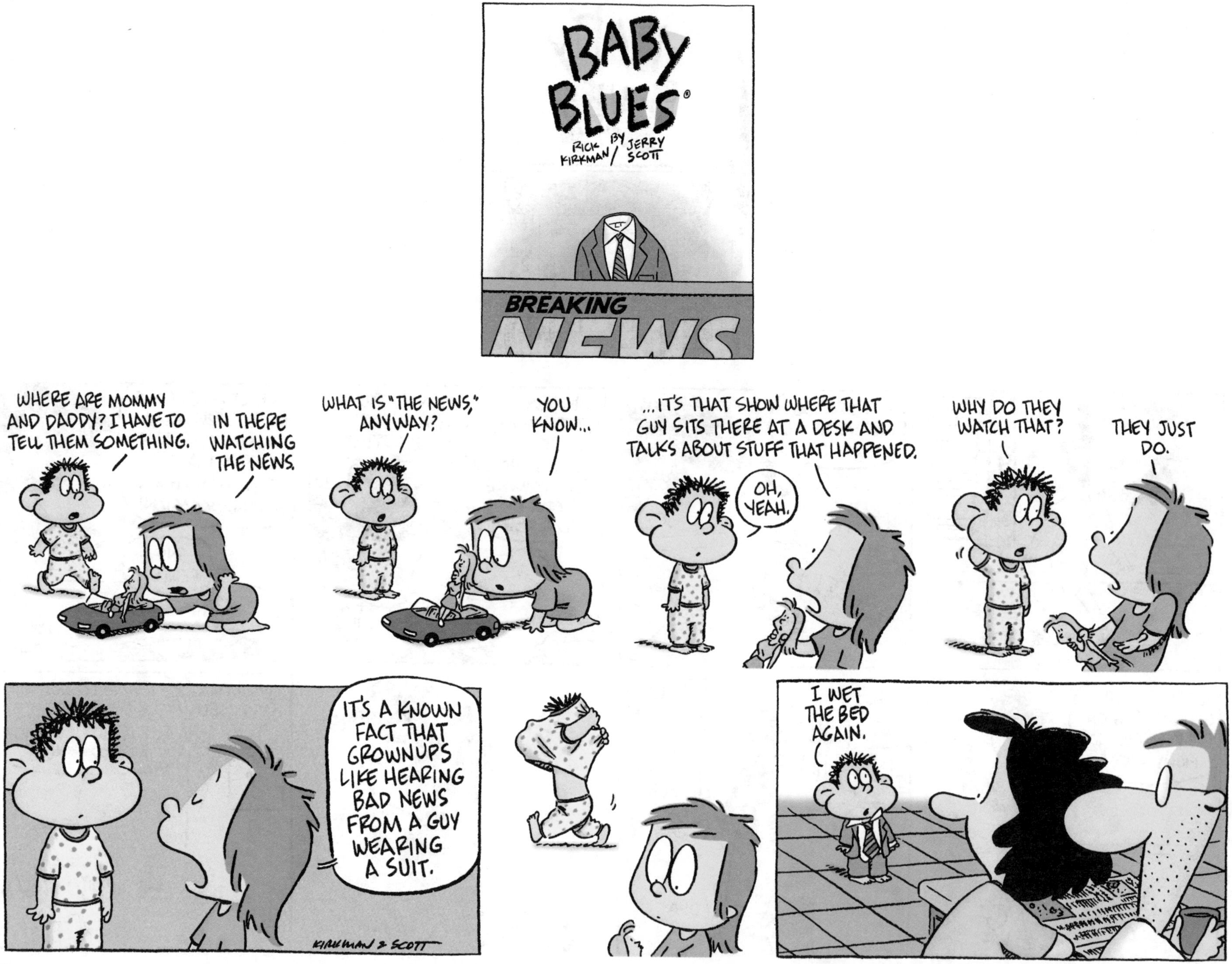
BABY BLUES®
BY RICK KIRKMAN / JERRY SCOTT
BREAKING NEWS
WHERE ARE MOMMY AND DADDY? I HAVE TO TELL THEM SOMETHING.
IN THERE WATCHING THE NEWS.
WHAT IS "THE NEWS," ANYWAY?
YOU KNOW...
...IT'S THAT SHOW WHERE THAT GUY SITS THERE AT A DESK AND TALKS ABOUT STUFF THAT HAPPENED.
OH, YEAH.
WHY DO THEY WATCH THAT?
THEY JUST DO.
IT'S A KNOWN FACT THAT GROWNUPS LIKE HEARING BAD NEWS FROM A GUY WEARING A SUIT.
KIRKMAN & SCOTT
I WET THE BED AGAIN.

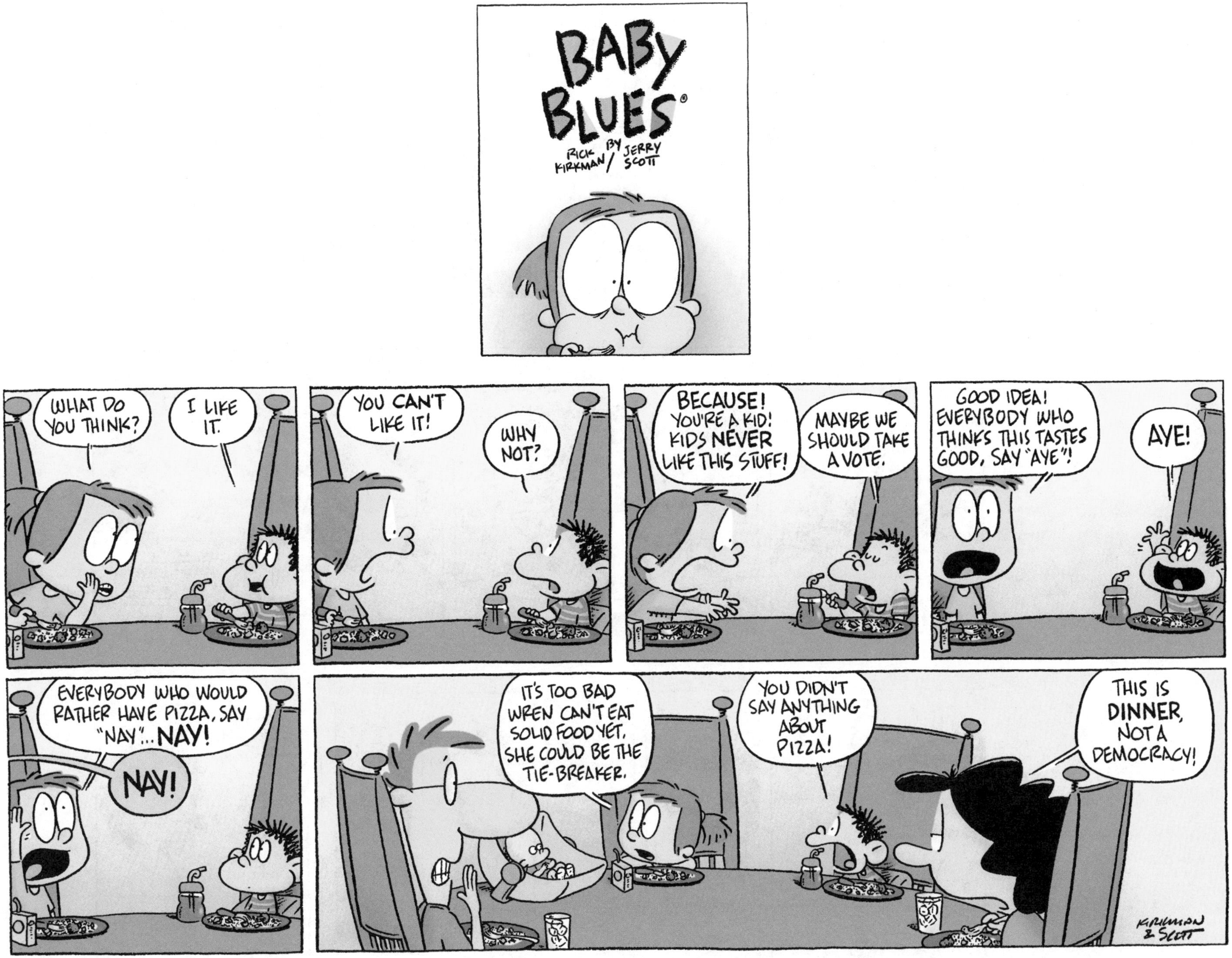
BABY BLUES®
BY RICK KIRKMAN / JERRY SCOTT
WHAT DO YOU THINK?
I LIKE IT.
YOU CAN'T LIKE IT!
WHY NOT?
BECAUSE! YOU'RE A KID! KIDS NEVER LIKE THIS STUFF!
MAYBE WE SHOULD TAKE A VOTE.
GOOD IDEA! EVERYBODY WHO THINKS THIS TASTES GOOD, SAY "AYE"!
AYE!
EVERYBODY WHO WOULD RATHER HAVE PIZZA, SAY "NAY"... NAY!
NAY!
IT'S TOO BAD WREN CAN'T EAT SOLID FOOD YET. SHE COULD BE THE TIE-BREAKER.
YOU DIDN'T SAY ANYTHING ABOUT PIZZA!
THIS IS DINNER, NOT A DEMOCRACY!
KIRKMAN & SCOTT

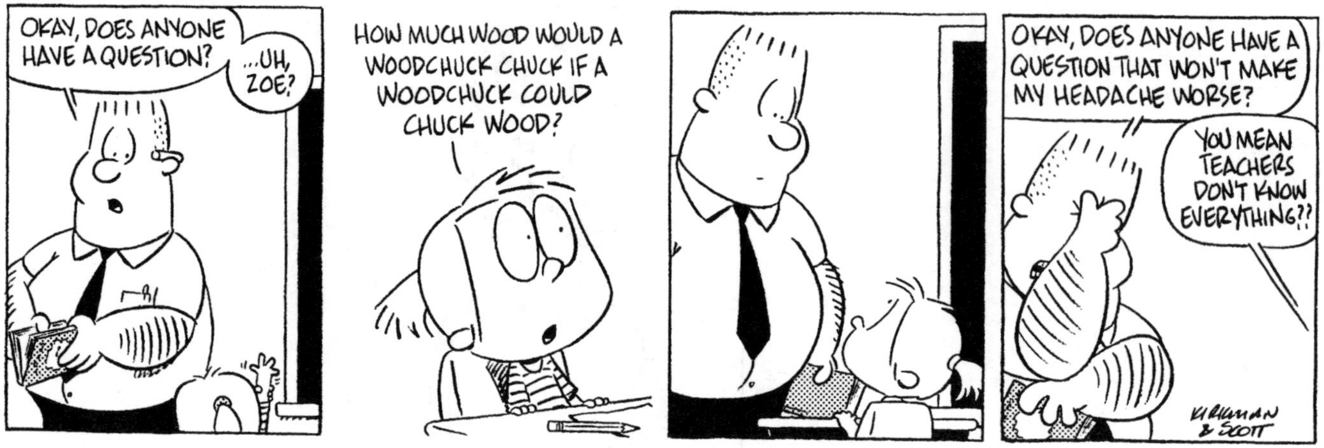
OKAY, DOES ANYONE HAVE A QUESTION?
...UH, ZOE?
HOW MUCH WOOD WOULD A WOODCHUCK CHUCK IF A WOODCHUCK COULD CHUCK WOOD?
OKAY, DOES ANYONE HAVE A QUESTION THAT WON'T MAKE MY HEADACHE WORSE?
YOU MEAN TEACHERS DON'T KNOW EVERYTHING??
KIRKMAN & SCOTT

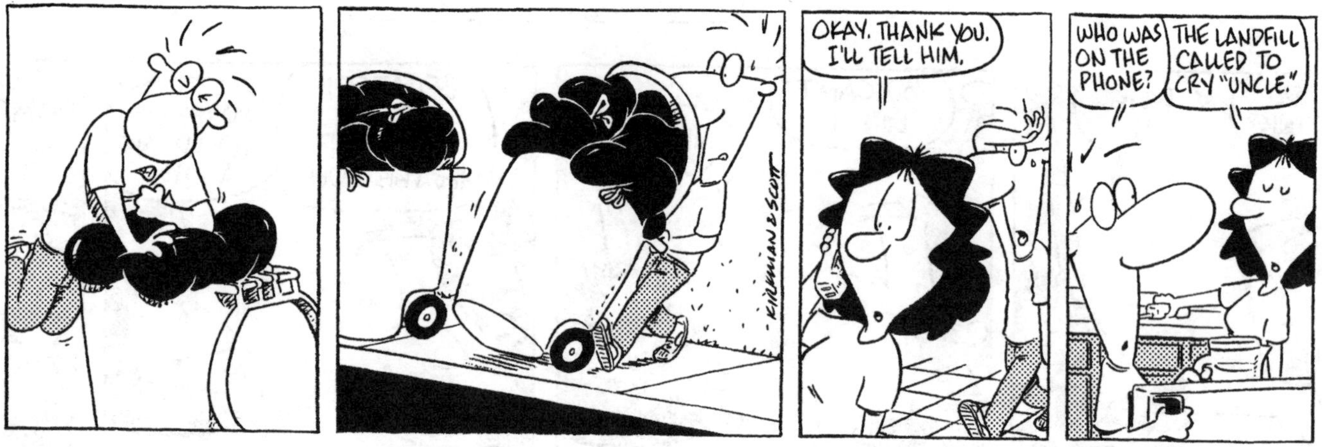
KIRKMAN & SCOTT
OKAY. THANK YOU. I'LL TELL HIM.
WHO WAS ON THE PHONE?
THE LANDFILL CALLED TO CRY "UNCLE."

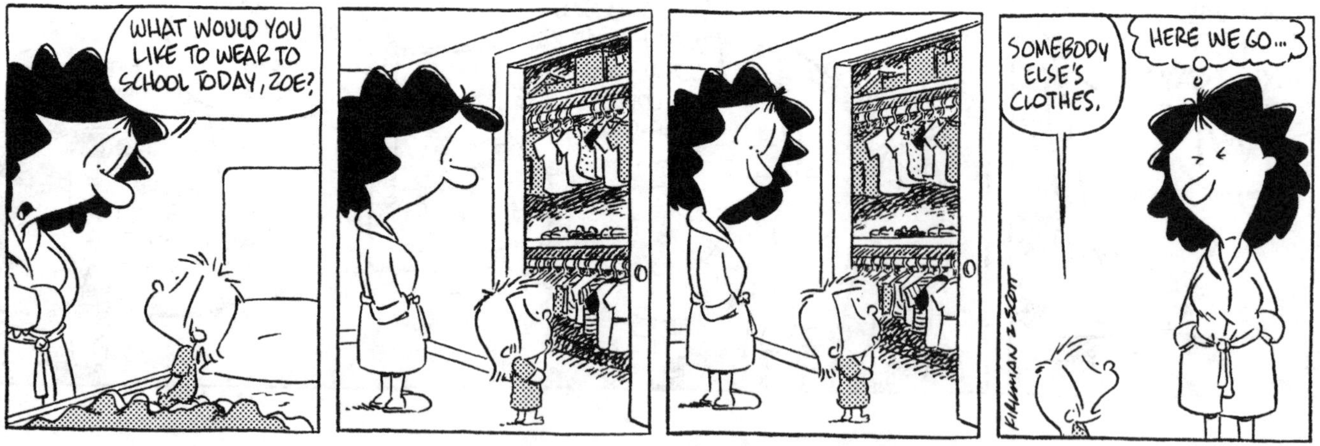
WHAT WOULD YOU LIKE TO WEAR TO SCHOOL TODAY, ZOE?
KIRKMAN & SCOTT
SOMEBODY ELSE'S CLOTHES.
HERE WE GO...

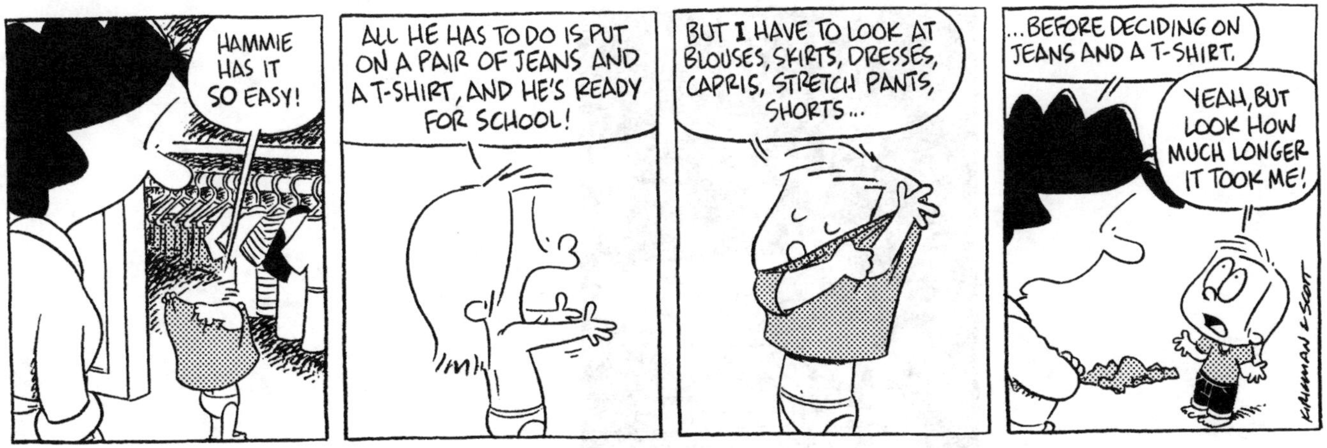
HAMMIE HAS IT SO EASY!
ALL HE HAS TO DO IS PUT ON A PAIR OF JEANS AND A T-SHIRT, AND HE'S READY FOR SCHOOL!
BUT I HAVE TO LOOK AT BLOUSES, SKIRTS, DRESSES, CAPRIS, STRETCH PANTS, SHORTS...
...BEFORE DECIDING ON JEANS AND A T-SHIRT.
YEAH, BUT LOOK HOW MUCH LONGER IT TOOK ME!
KIRKMAN & SCOTT

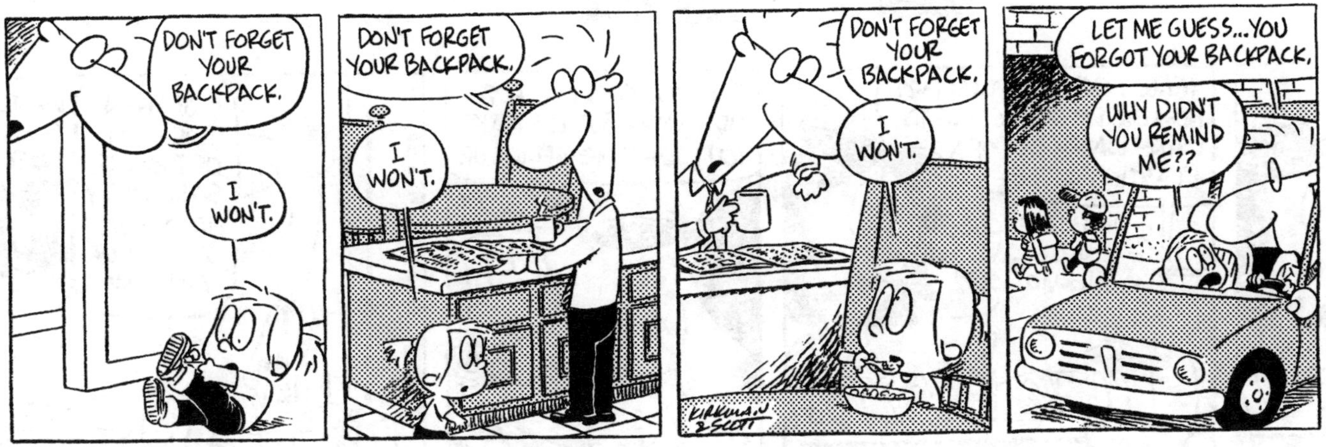
DON'T FORGET YOUR BACKPACK.
I WON'T.
DON'T FORGET YOUR BACKPACK.
I WON'T.
DON'T FORGET YOUR BACKPACK.
I WON'T.
KIRKMAN & SCOTT
LET ME GUESS...YOU FORGOT YOUR BACKPACK.
WHY DIDN'T YOU REMIND ME??

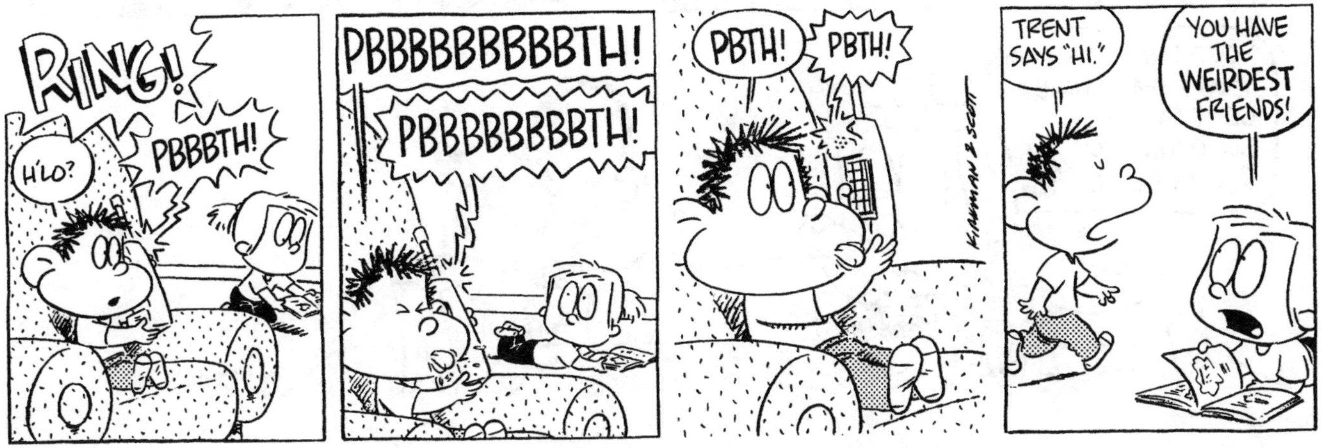
RING!
H'LO?
PBBBTH!
PBBBBBBBBBTH!
PBBBBBBBBTH!
PBTH!
PBTH!
KIRKMAN & SCOTT
TRENT SAYS "HI."
YOU HAVE THE WEIRDEST FRIENDS!

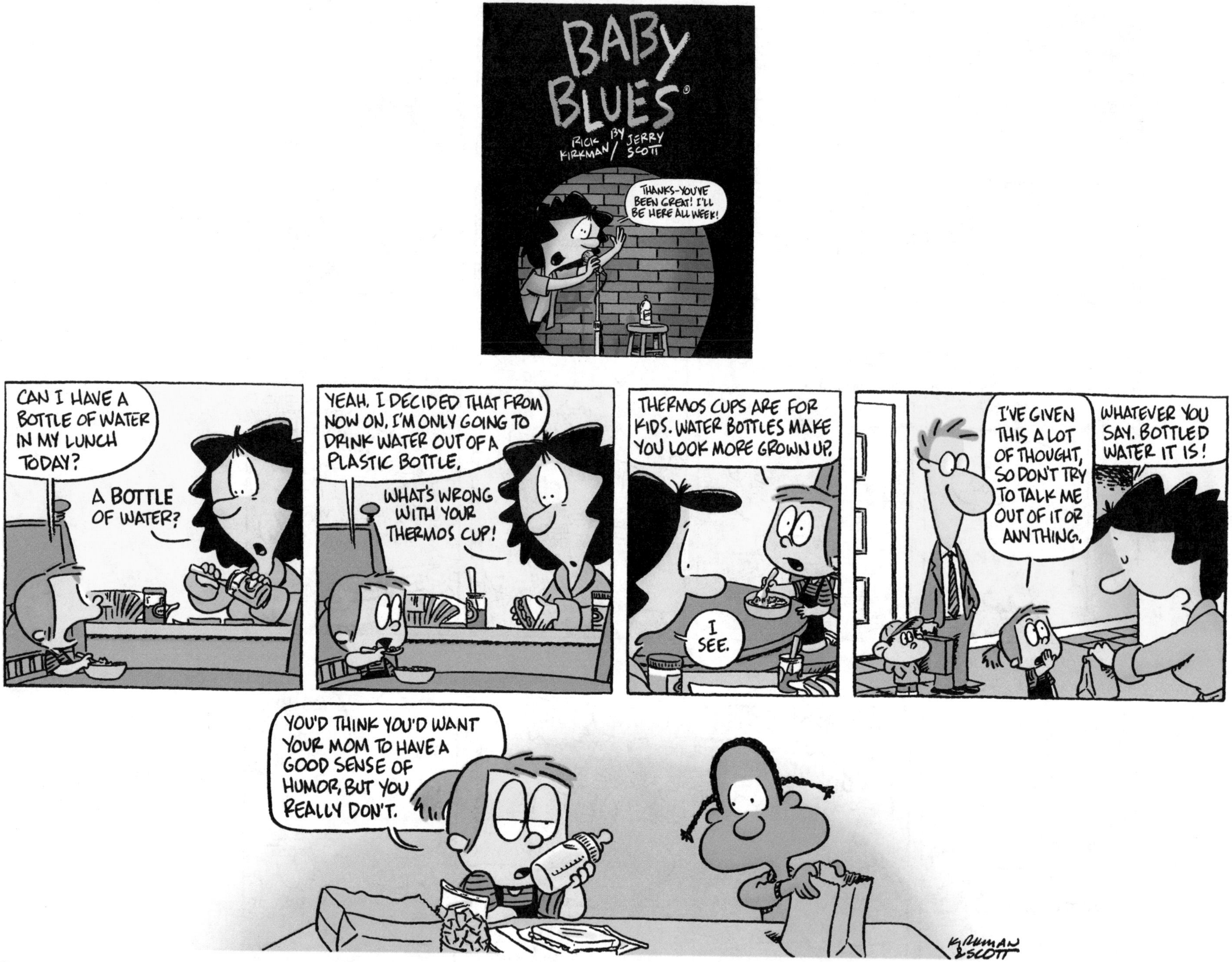
BABY BLUES
BY RICK KIRKMAN / JERRY SCOTT
THANKS–YOU'VE BEEN GREAT! I'LL BE HERE ALL WEEK!
CAN I HAVE A BOTTLE OF WATER IN MY LUNCH TODAY?
A BOTTLE OF WATER?
YEAH. I DECIDED THAT FROM NOW ON, I'M ONLY GOING TO DRINK WATER OUT OF A PLASTIC BOTTLE.
WHAT'S WRONG WITH YOUR THERMOS CUP?
THERMOS CUPS ARE FOR KIDS. WATER BOTTLES MAKE YOU LOOK MORE GROWN UP.
I SEE.
I'VE GIVEN THIS A LOT OF THOUGHT, SO DON'T TRY TO TALK ME OUT OF IT OR ANYTHING.
WHATEVER YOU SAY. BOTTLED WATER IT IS!
YOU'D THINK YOU'D WANT YOUR MOM TO HAVE A GOOD SENSE OF HUMOR, BUT YOU REALLY DON'T.
KIRKMAN & SCOTT

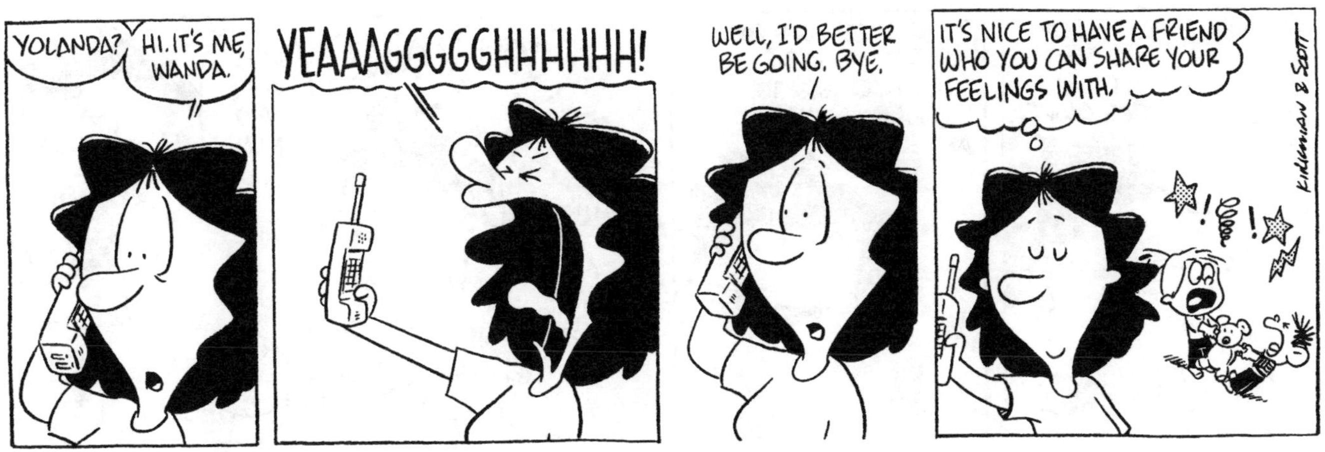

YOLANDA?
HI. IT'S ME, WANDA.
YEAAAGGGGGHHHHHH!
WELL, I'D BETTER BE GOING. BYE.
IT'S NICE TO HAVE A FRIEND WHO YOU CAN SHARE YOUR FEELINGS WITH.
KIRKMAN & SCOTT

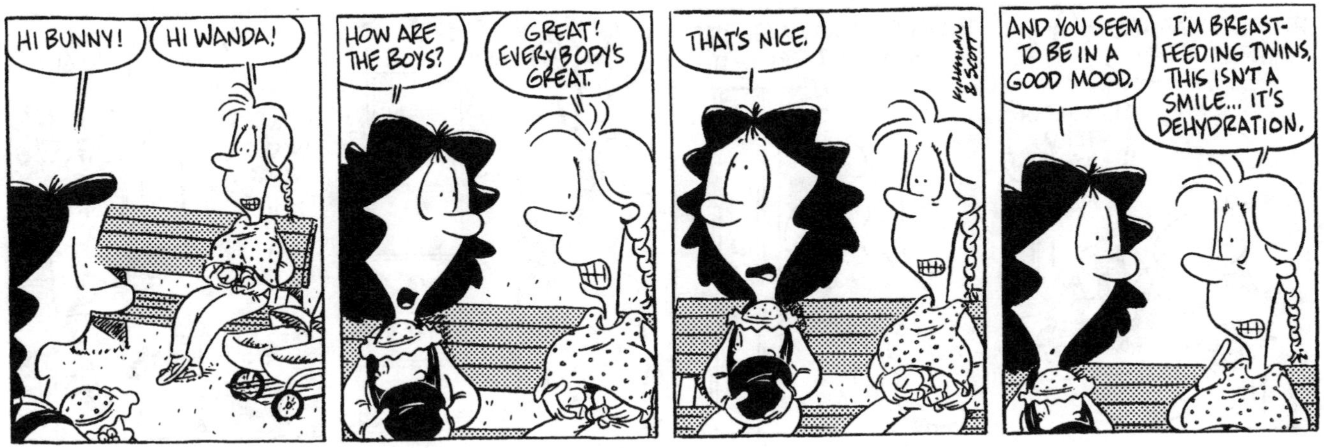

HI BUNNY!
HI WANDA!
HOW ARE THE BOYS?
GREAT! EVERYBODY'S GREAT.
THAT'S NICE.
KIRKMAN & SCOTT
AND YOU SEEM TO BE IN A GOOD MOOD.
I'M BREAST-FEEDING TWINS. THIS ISN'T A SMILE... IT'S DEHYDRATION.

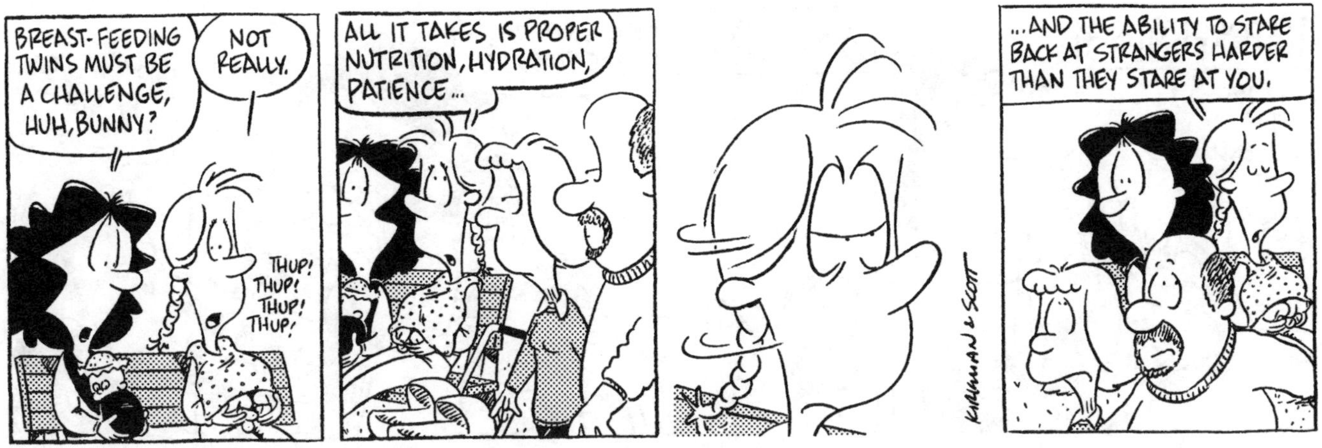

BREAST-FEEDING TWINS MUST BE A CHALLENGE, HUH, BUNNY?
NOT REALLY.
THUP! THUP! THUP! THUP!
ALL IT TAKES IS PROPER NUTRITION, HYDRATION, PATIENCE...
KIRKMAN & SCOTT
...AND THE ABILITY TO STARE BACK AT STRANGERS HARDER THAN THEY STARE AT YOU.

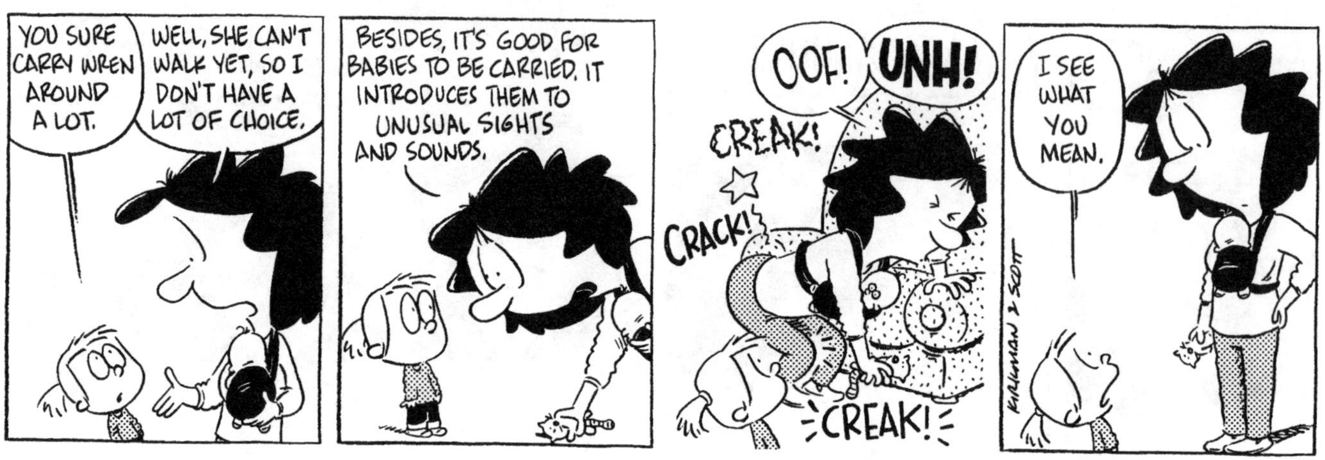
YOU SURE CARRY WREN AROUND A LOT.
WELL, SHE CAN'T WALK YET, SO I DON'T HAVE A LOT OF CHOICE.
BESIDES, IT'S GOOD FOR BABIES TO BE CARRIED. IT INTRODUCES THEM TO UNUSUAL SIGHTS AND SOUNDS.
OOF!
UNH!
CREAK!
CRACK!
CREAK!
I SEE WHAT YOU MEAN.
KIRKMAN & SCOTT

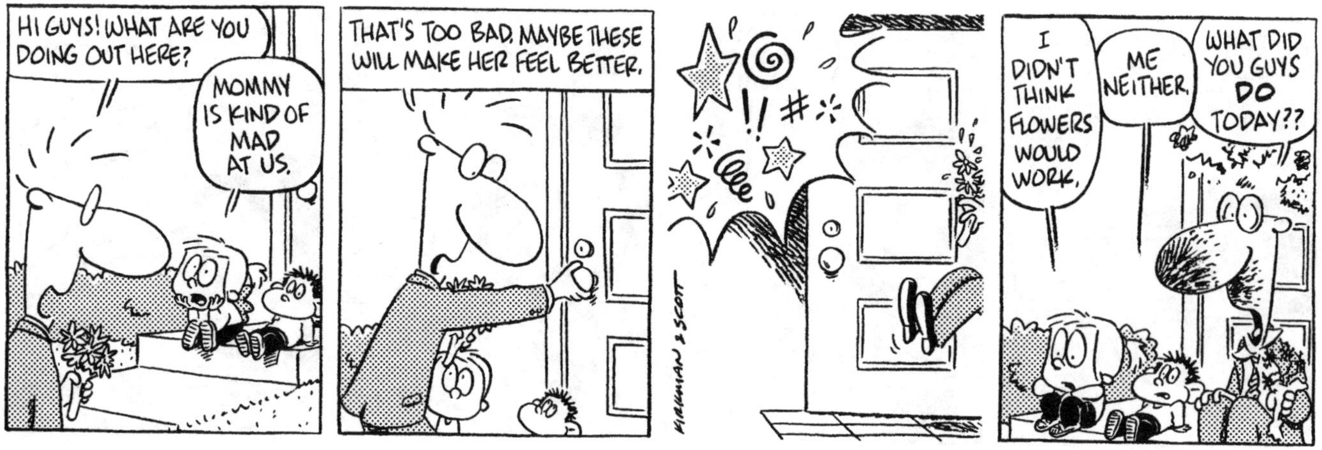
HI GUYS! WHAT ARE YOU DOING OUT HERE?
MOMMY IS KIND OF MAD AT US.
THAT'S TOO BAD. MAYBE THESE WILL MAKE HER FEEL BETTER.
KIRKMAN & SCOTT
I DIDN'T THINK FLOWERS WOULD WORK.
ME NEITHER.
WHAT DID YOU GUYS DO TODAY??

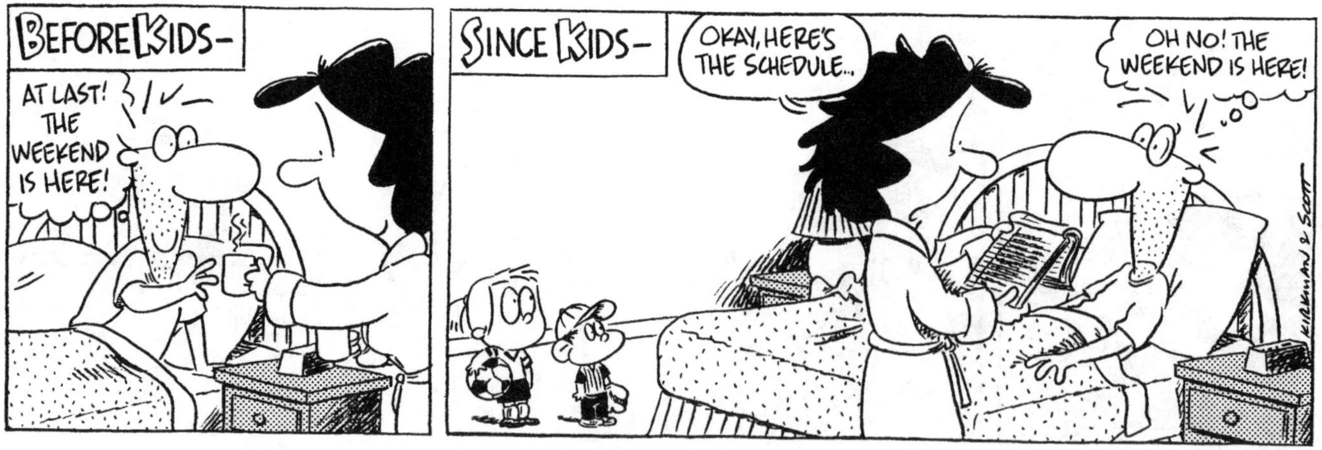
BEFORE KIDS-
AT LAST! THE WEEKEND IS HERE!
SINCE KIDS-
OKAY, HERE'S THE SCHEDULE...
OH NO! THE WEEKEND IS HERE!
KIRKMAN & SCOTT

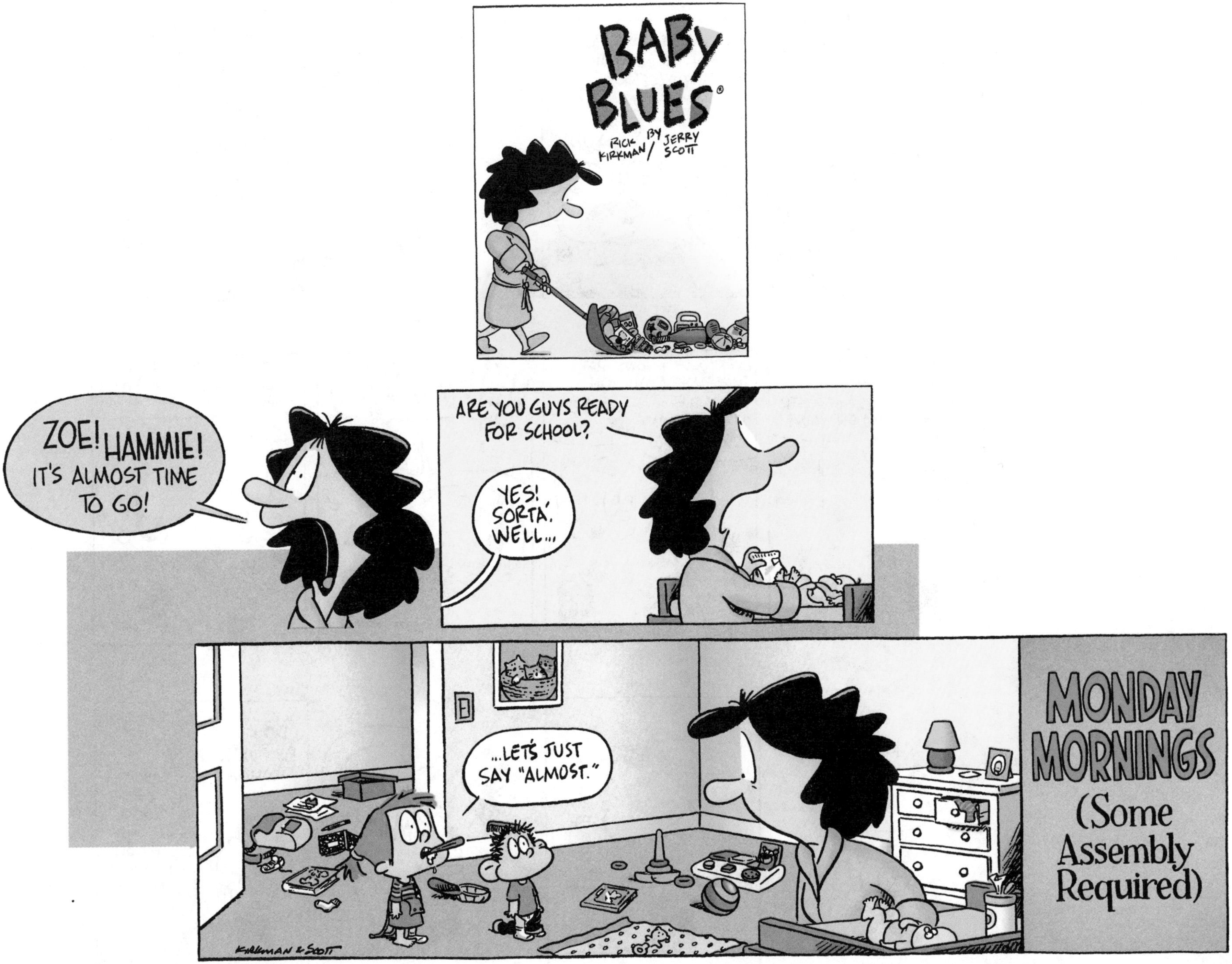
BABY BLUES®
BY RICK KIRKMAN / JERRY SCOTT
ZOE! HAMMIE! IT'S ALMOST TIME TO GO!
ARE YOU GUYS READY FOR SCHOOL?
YES! SORTA. WELL...
...LET'S JUST SAY "ALMOST."
KIRKMAN & SCOTT
MONDAY MORNINGS
(Some Assembly Required)

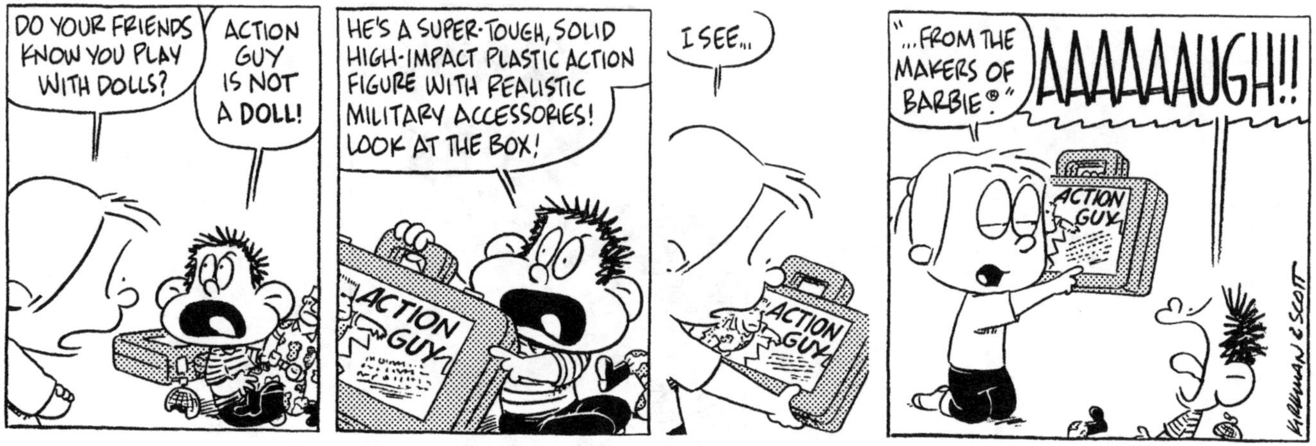
DO YOUR FRIENDS KNOW YOU PLAY WITH DOLLS?
ACTION GUY IS NOT A **DOLL**!
HE'S A SUPER-TOUGH, SOLID HIGH-IMPACT PLASTIC ACTION FIGURE WITH REALISTIC MILITARY ACCESSORIES! LOOK AT THE BOX!
ACTION GUY
I SEE...
"...FROM THE MAKERS OF BARBIE®"
AAAAAAUGH!!
ACTION GUY
KIRKMAN & SCOTT

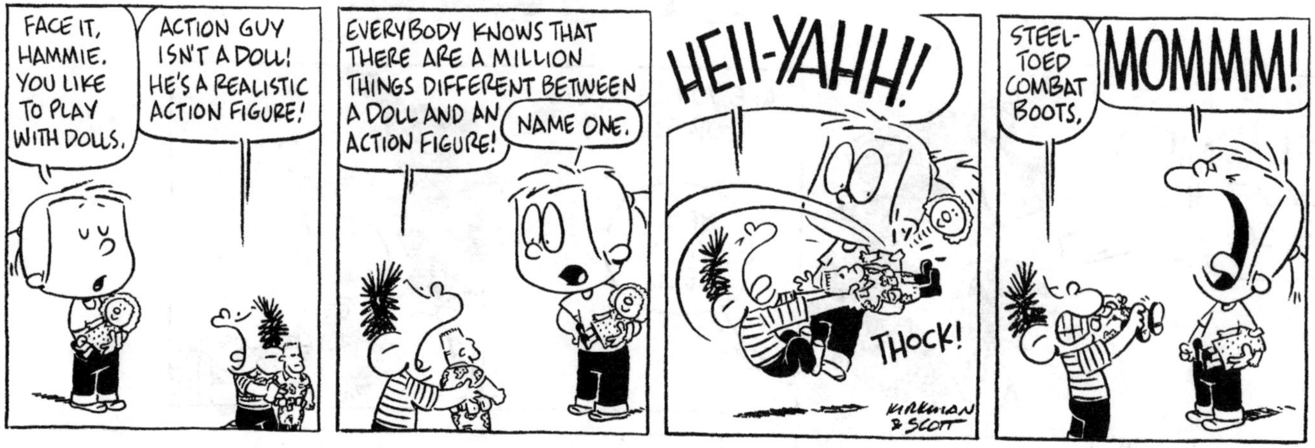
FACE IT, HAMMIE. YOU LIKE TO PLAY WITH DOLLS.
ACTION GUY ISN'T A DOLL! HE'S A REALISTIC ACTION FIGURE!
EVERYBODY KNOWS THAT THERE ARE A MILLION THINGS DIFFERENT BETWEEN A DOLL AND AN ACTION FIGURE!
NAME ONE.
HEII-YAHH!
THOCK!
KIRKMAN & SCOTT
STEEL-TOED COMBAT BOOTS.
MOMMM!

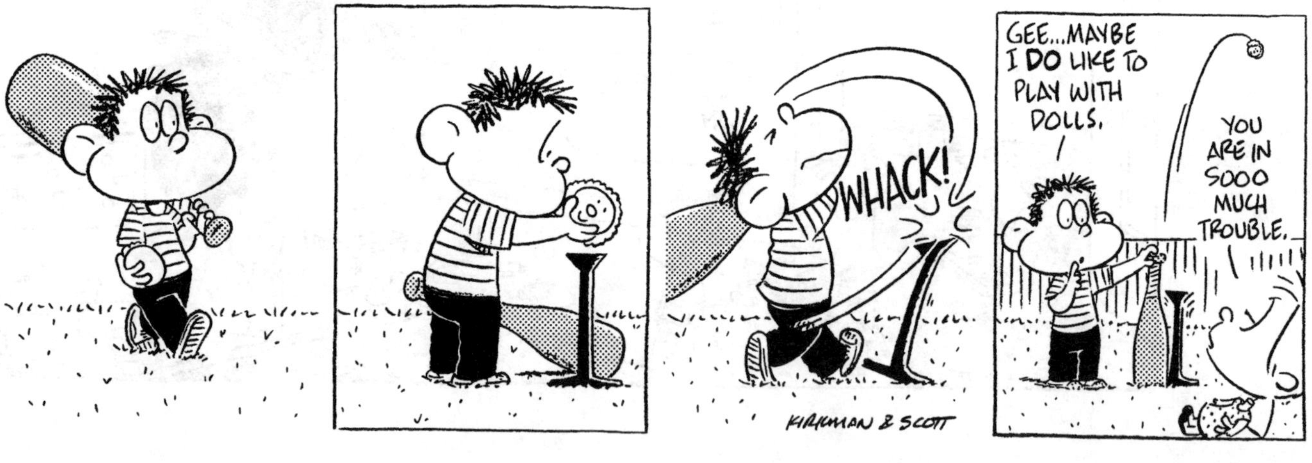
WHACK!
KIRKMAN & SCOTT
GEE...MAYBE I **DO** LIKE TO PLAY WITH DOLLS.
YOU ARE IN SOOO MUCH TROUBLE.

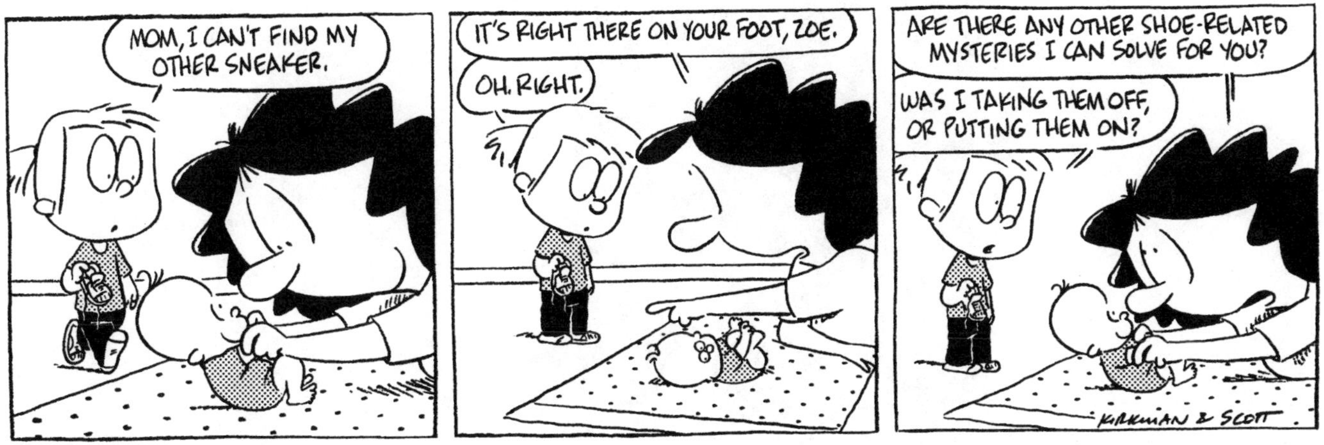
MOM, I CAN'T FIND MY OTHER SNEAKER.
IT'S RIGHT THERE ON YOUR FOOT, ZOE.
OH, RIGHT.
ARE THERE ANY OTHER SHOE-RELATED MYSTERIES I CAN SOLVE FOR YOU?
WAS I TAKING THEM OFF, OR PUTTING THEM ON?
KIRKMAN & SCOTT

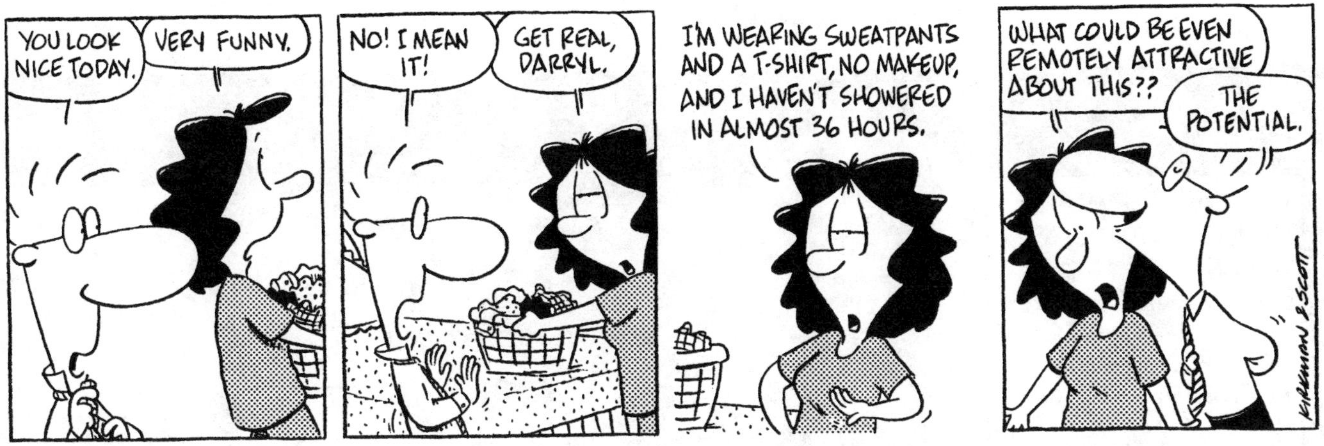
YOU LOOK NICE TODAY.
VERY FUNNY.
NO! I MEAN IT!
GET REAL, DARRYL.
I'M WEARING SWEATPANTS AND A T-SHIRT, NO MAKEUP, AND I HAVEN'T SHOWERED IN ALMOST 36 HOURS.
WHAT COULD BE EVEN REMOTELY ATTRACTIVE ABOUT THIS??
THE POTENTIAL.
KIRKMAN & SCOTT

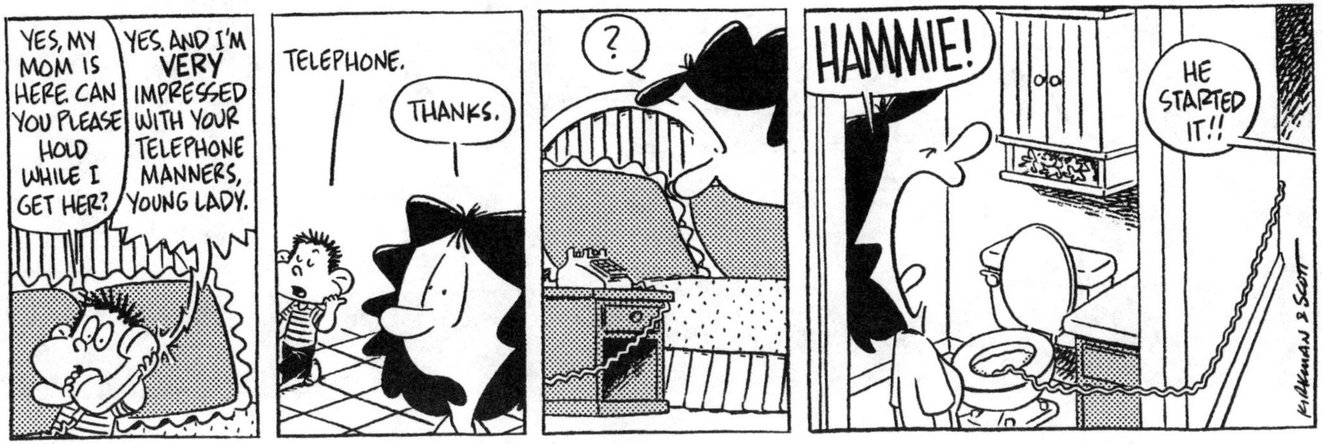
YES, MY MOM IS HERE. CAN YOU PLEASE HOLD WHILE I GET HER?
YES. AND I'M VERY IMPRESSED WITH YOUR TELEPHONE MANNERS, YOUNG LADY.
TELEPHONE.
THANKS.
?
HAMMIE!
HE STARTED IT!!
KIRKMAN & SCOTT

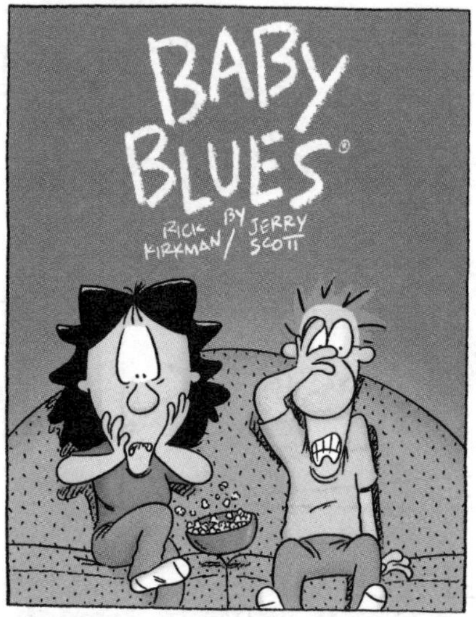
BABY BLUES®
BY RICK KIRKMAN / JERRY SCOTT

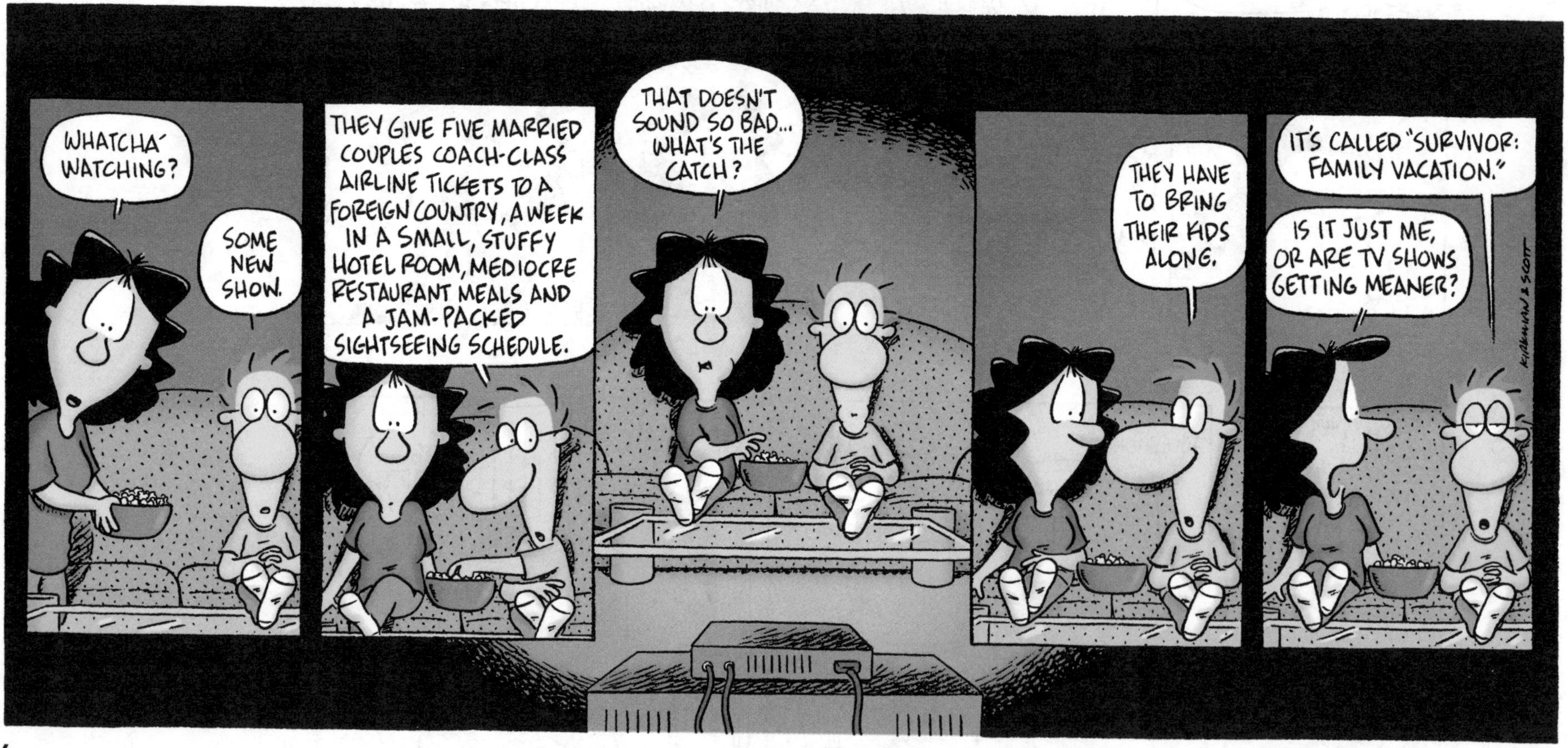
WHATCHA' WATCHING?
SOME NEW SHOW.
THEY GIVE FIVE MARRIED COUPLES COACH-CLASS AIRLINE TICKETS TO A FOREIGN COUNTRY, A WEEK IN A SMALL, STUFFY HOTEL ROOM, MEDIOCRE RESTAURANT MEALS AND A JAM-PACKED SIGHTSEEING SCHEDULE.
THAT DOESN'T SOUND SO BAD... WHAT'S THE CATCH?
THEY HAVE TO BRING THEIR KIDS ALONG.
IT'S CALLED "SURVIVOR: FAMILY VACATION."
IS IT JUST ME, OR ARE TV SHOWS GETTING MEANER?
KIRKMAN & SCOTT

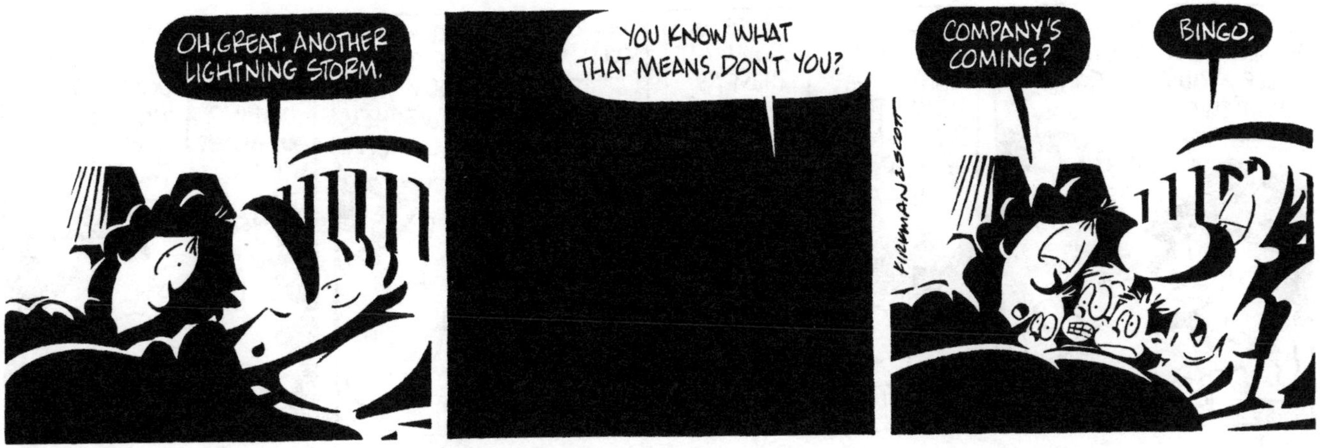

OH, GREAT. ANOTHER LIGHTNING STORM.
YOU KNOW WHAT THAT MEANS, DON'T YOU?
COMPANY'S COMING?
BINGO.
KIRKMAN & SCOTT

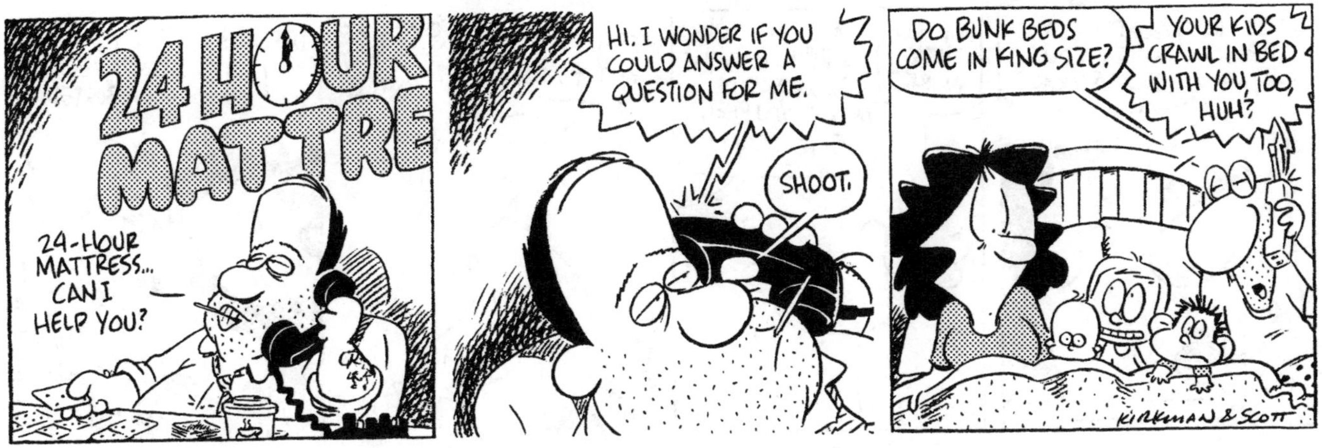

24 HOUR MATTRE
24-HOUR MATTRESS... CAN I HELP YOU?
HI. I WONDER IF YOU COULD ANSWER A QUESTION FOR ME.
SHOOT.
DO BUNK BEDS COME IN KING SIZE?
YOUR KIDS CRAWL IN BED WITH YOU, TOO, HUH?
KIRKMAN & SCOTT

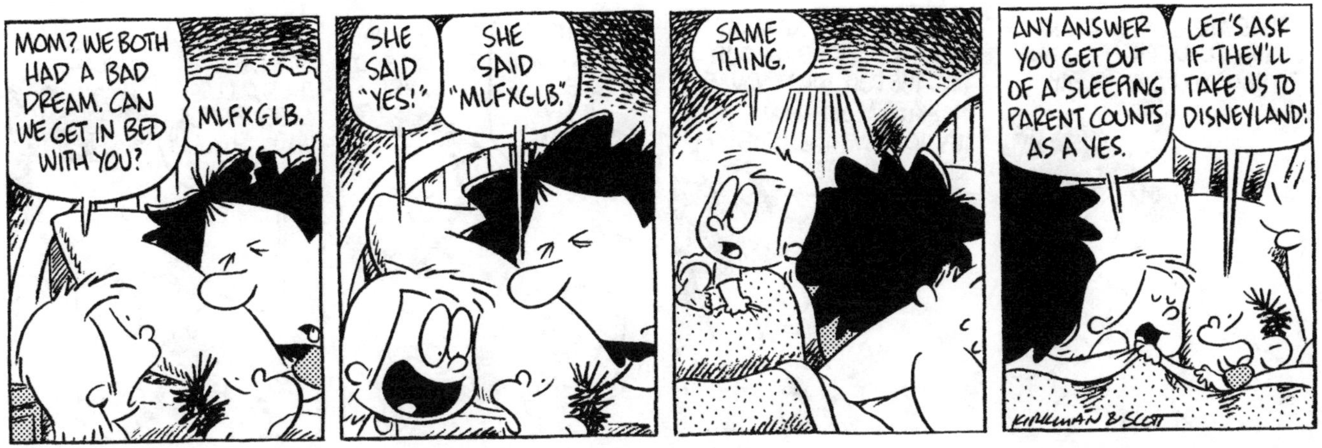

MOM? WE BOTH HAD A BAD DREAM. CAN WE GET IN BED WITH YOU?
MLFXGLB.
SHE SAID "YES!"
SHE SAID "MLFXGLB."
SAME THING.
ANY ANSWER YOU GET OUT OF A SLEEPING PARENT COUNTS AS A YES.
LET'S ASK IF THEY'LL TAKE US TO DISNEYLAND!
KIRKMAN & SCOTT

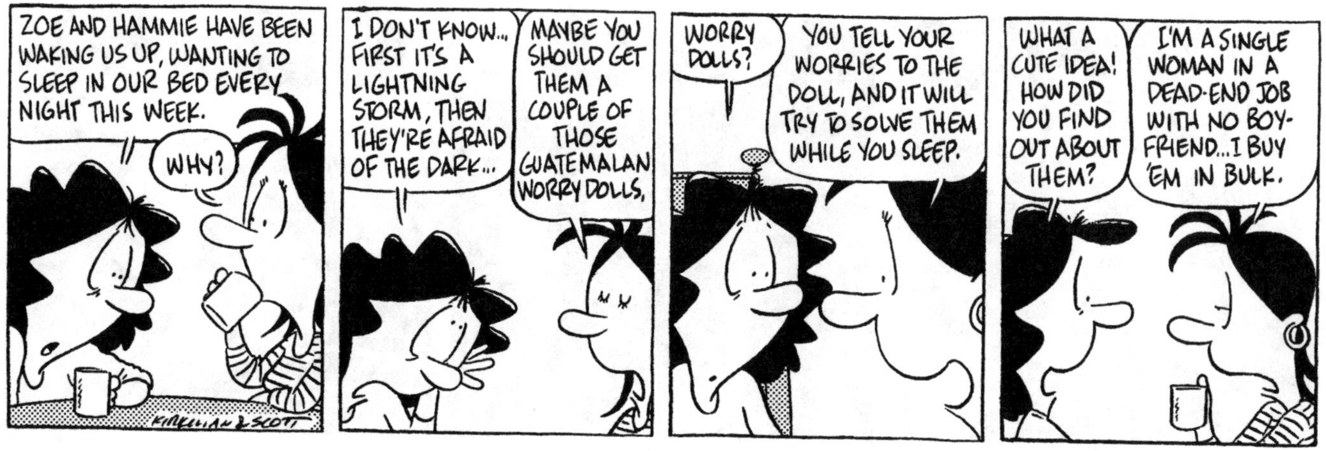
ZOE AND HAMMIE HAVE BEEN WAKING US UP, WANTING TO SLEEP IN OUR BED EVERY NIGHT THIS WEEK.
WHY?
I DON'T KNOW... FIRST IT'S A LIGHTNING STORM, THEN THEY'RE AFRAID OF THE DARK...
MAYBE YOU SHOULD GET THEM A COUPLE OF THOSE GUATEMALAN WORRY DOLLS.
WORRY DOLLS?
YOU TELL YOUR WORRIES TO THE DOLL, AND IT WILL TRY TO SOLVE THEM WHILE YOU SLEEP.
WHAT A CUTE IDEA! HOW DID YOU FIND OUT ABOUT THEM?
I'M A SINGLE WOMAN IN A DEAD-END JOB WITH NO BOY-FRIEND... I BUY 'EM IN BULK.
KIRKMAN & SCOTT

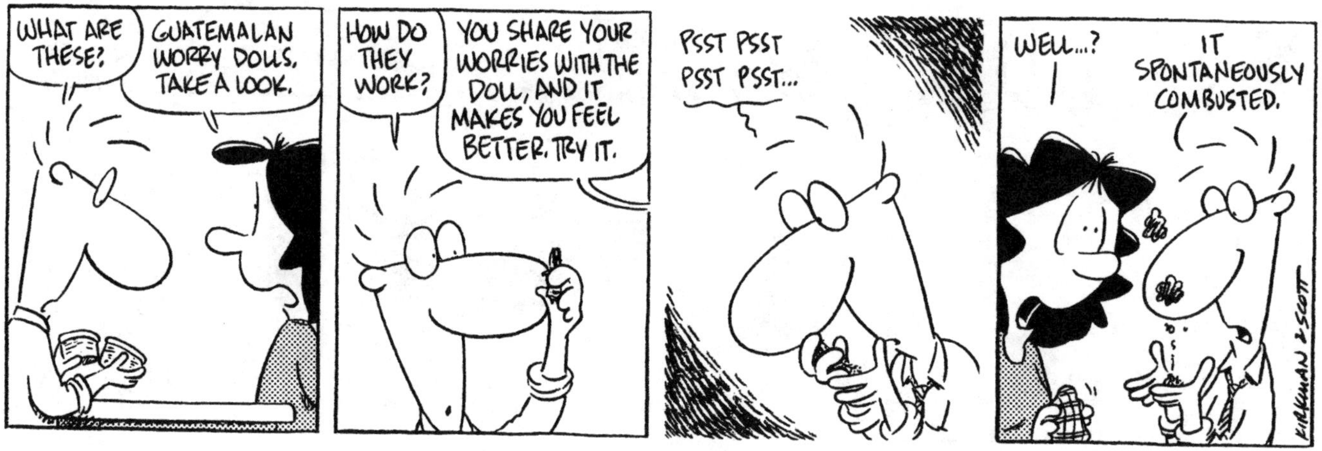
WHAT ARE THESE?
GUATEMALAN WORRY DOLLS. TAKE A LOOK.
HOW DO THEY WORK?
YOU SHARE YOUR WORRIES WITH THE DOLL, AND IT MAKES YOU FEEL BETTER. TRY IT.
PSST PSST PSST PSST...
WELL...?
IT SPONTANEOUSLY COMBUSTED.
KIRKMAN & SCOTT

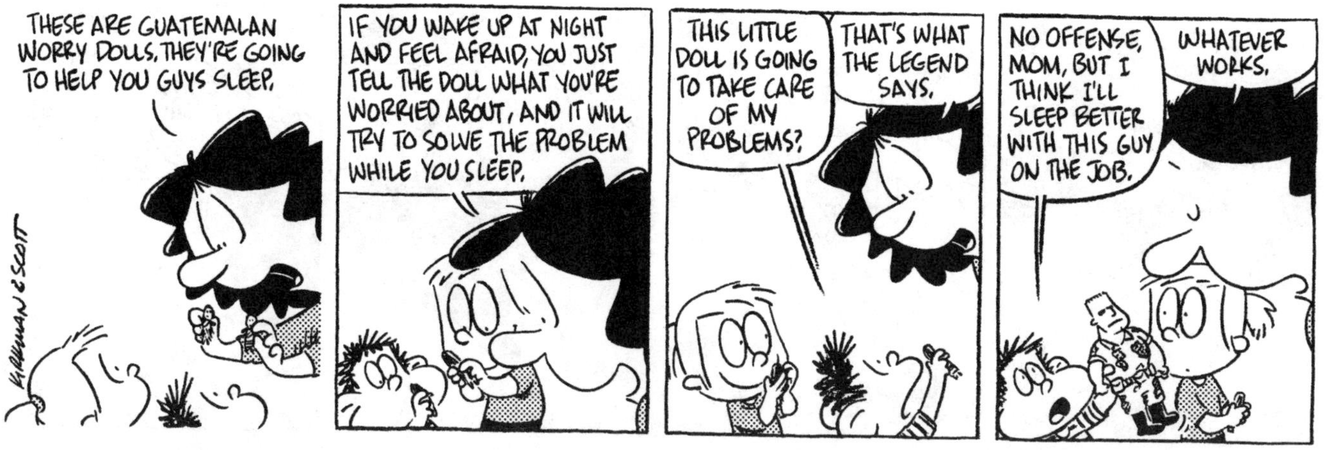
THESE ARE GUATEMALAN WORRY DOLLS. THEY'RE GOING TO HELP YOU GUYS SLEEP.
KIRKMAN & SCOTT
IF YOU WAKE UP AT NIGHT AND FEEL AFRAID, YOU JUST TELL THE DOLL WHAT YOU'RE WORRIED ABOUT, AND IT WILL TRY TO SOLVE THE PROBLEM WHILE YOU SLEEP.
THIS LITTLE DOLL IS GOING TO TAKE CARE OF MY PROBLEMS?
THAT'S WHAT THE LEGEND SAYS.
NO OFFENSE, MOM, BUT I THINK I'LL SLEEP BETTER WITH THIS GUY ON THE JOB.
WHATEVER WORKS.

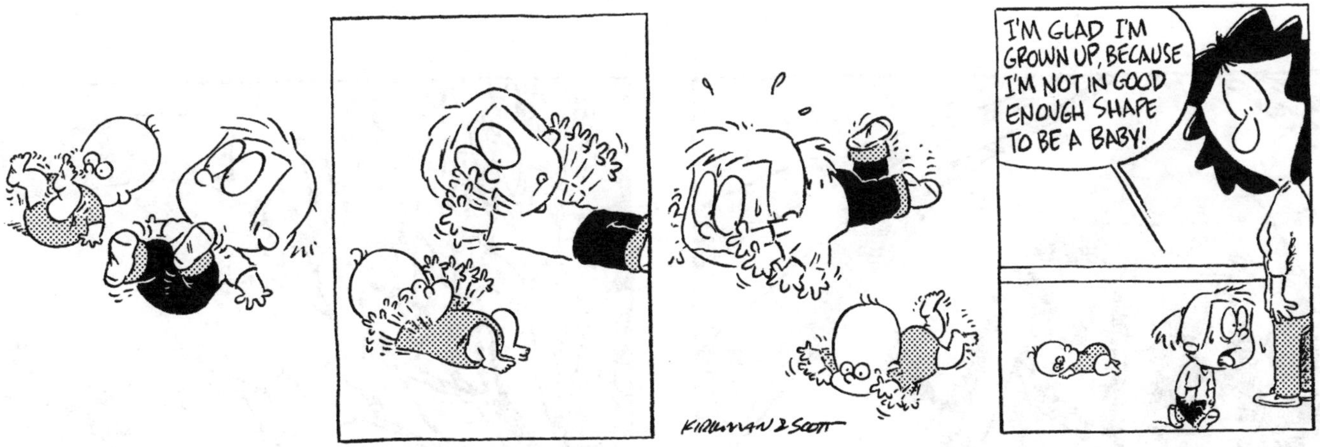
KIRKMAN & SCOTT
I'M GLAD I'M GROWN UP, BECAUSE I'M NOT IN GOOD ENOUGH SHAPE TO BE A BABY!

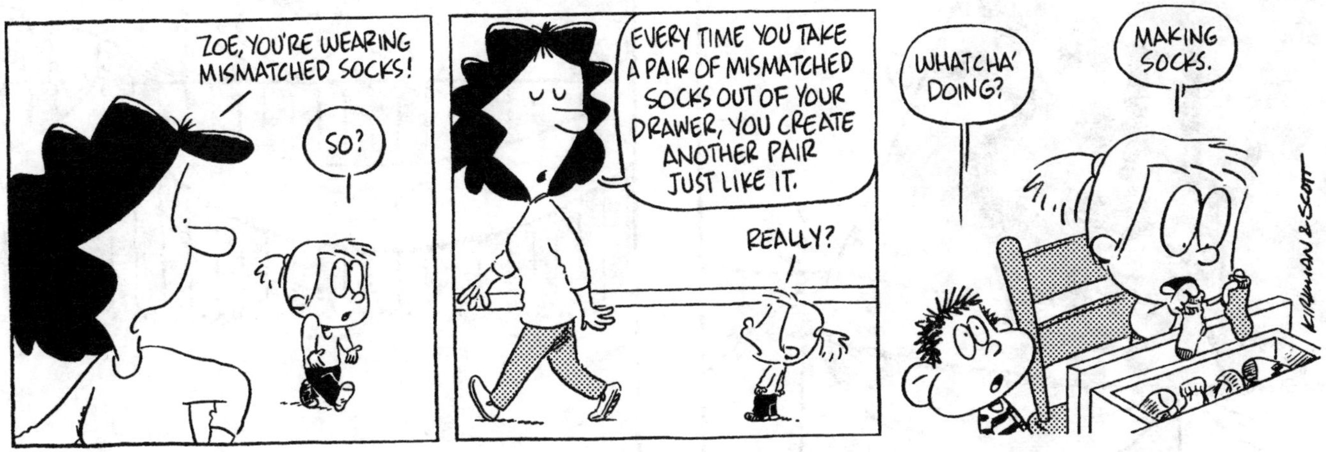
ZOE, YOU'RE WEARING MISMATCHED SOCKS!
SO?
EVERY TIME YOU TAKE A PAIR OF MISMATCHED SOCKS OUT OF YOUR DRAWER, YOU CREATE ANOTHER PAIR JUST LIKE IT.
REALLY?
WHATCHA' DOING?
MAKING SOCKS.
KIRKMAN & SCOTT

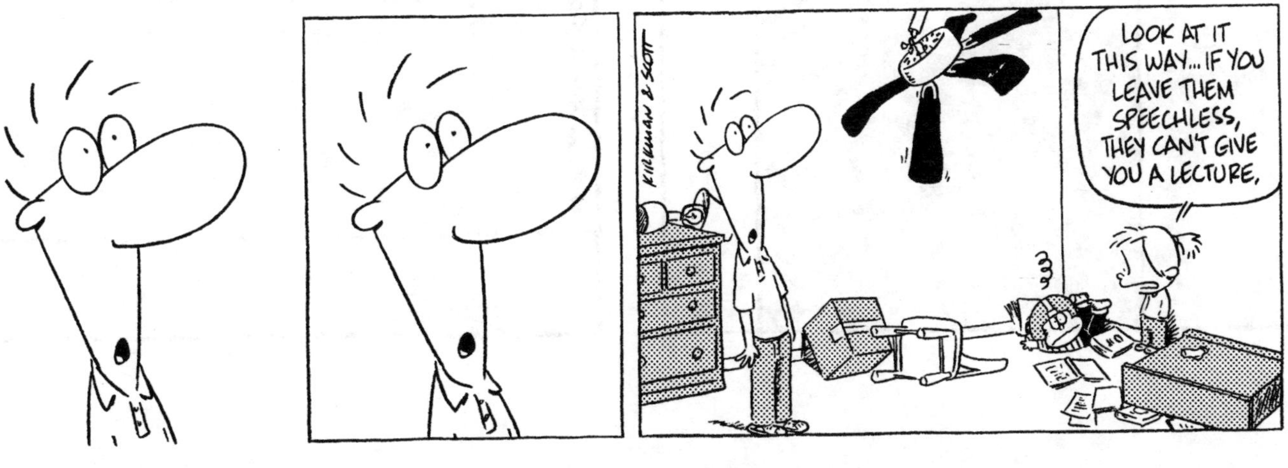
KIRKMAN & SCOTT
LOOK AT IT THIS WAY... IF YOU LEAVE THEM SPEECHLESS, THEY CAN'T GIVE YOU A LECTURE.

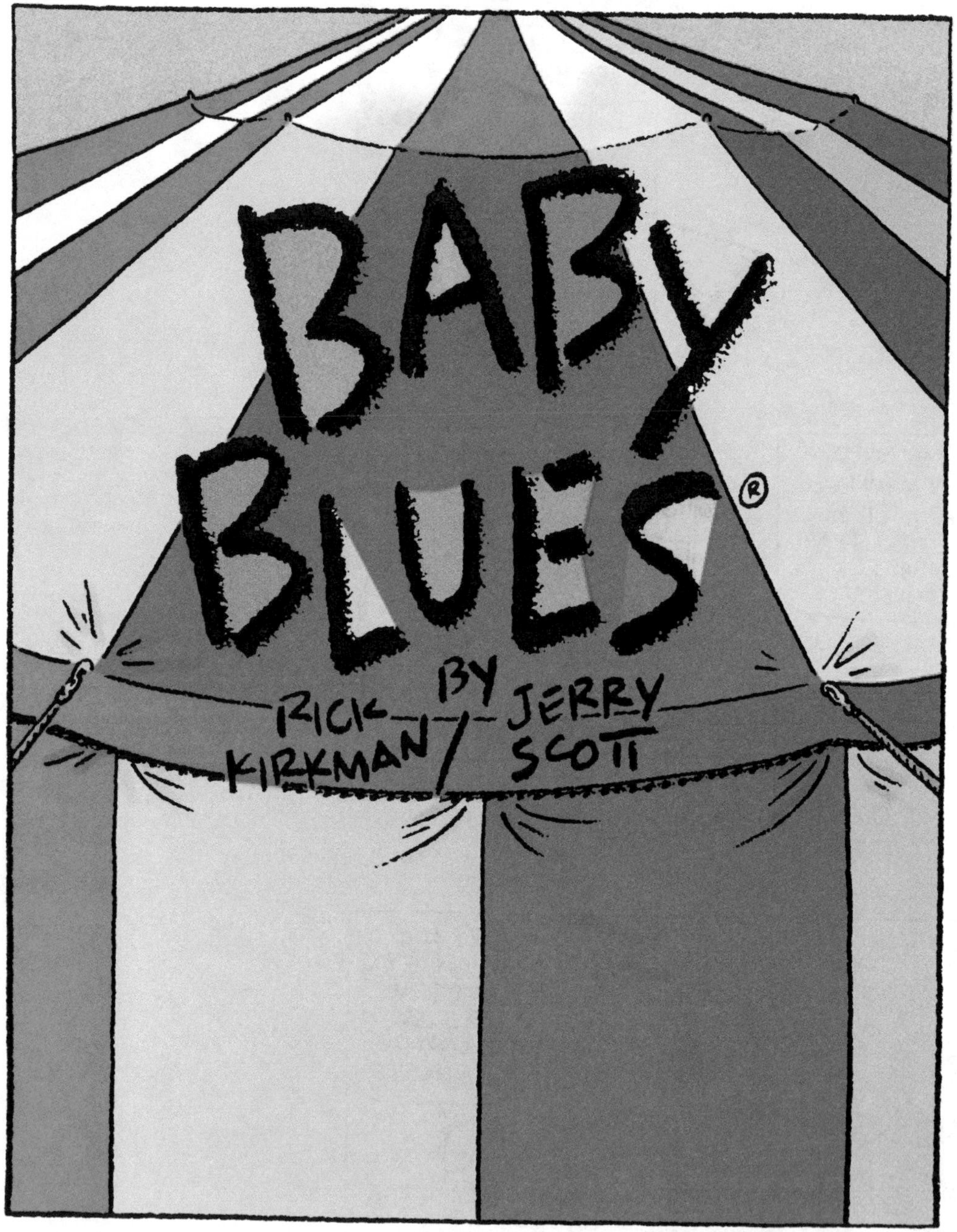
BABY BLUES®
BY
RICK KIRKMAN / JERRY SCOTT

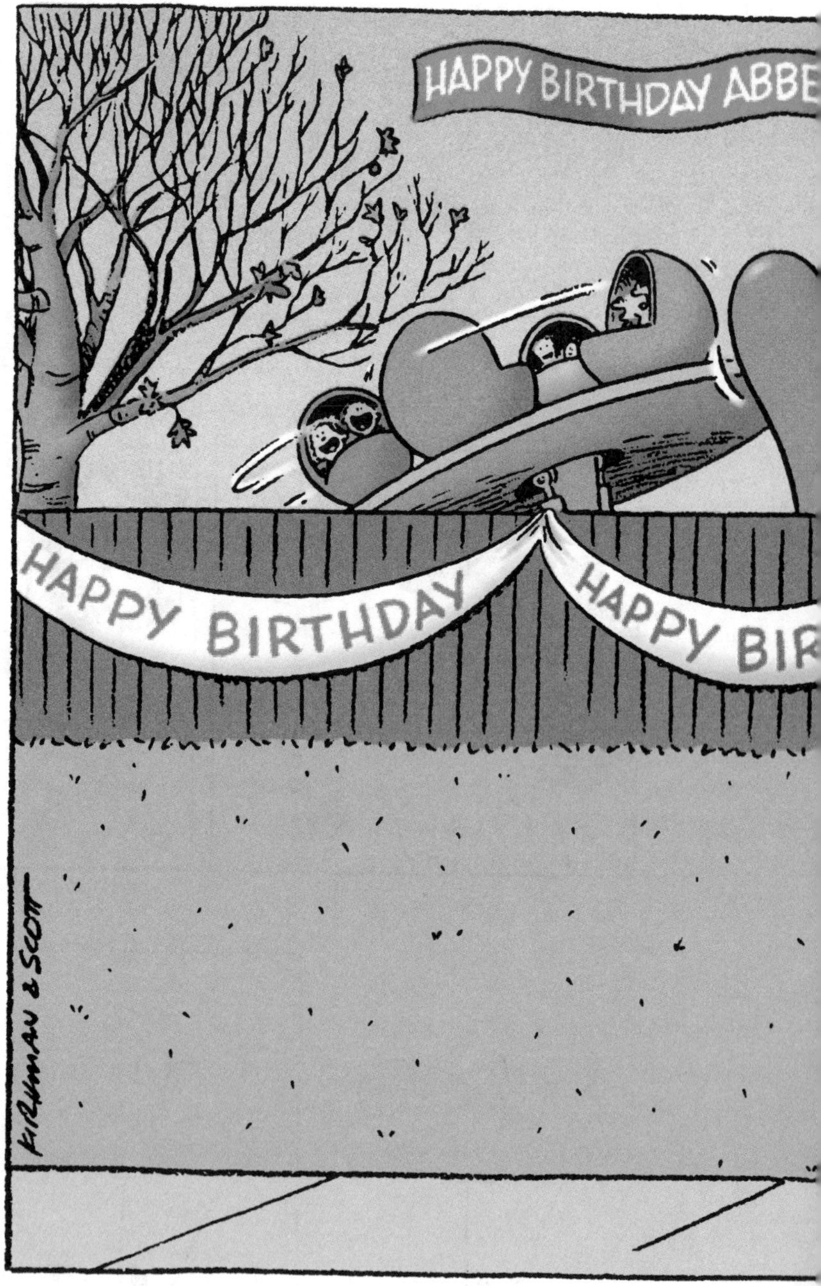
HAPPY BIRTHDAY ABBE
HAPPY BIRTHDAY
HAPPY BIR
KIRKMAN & SCOTT

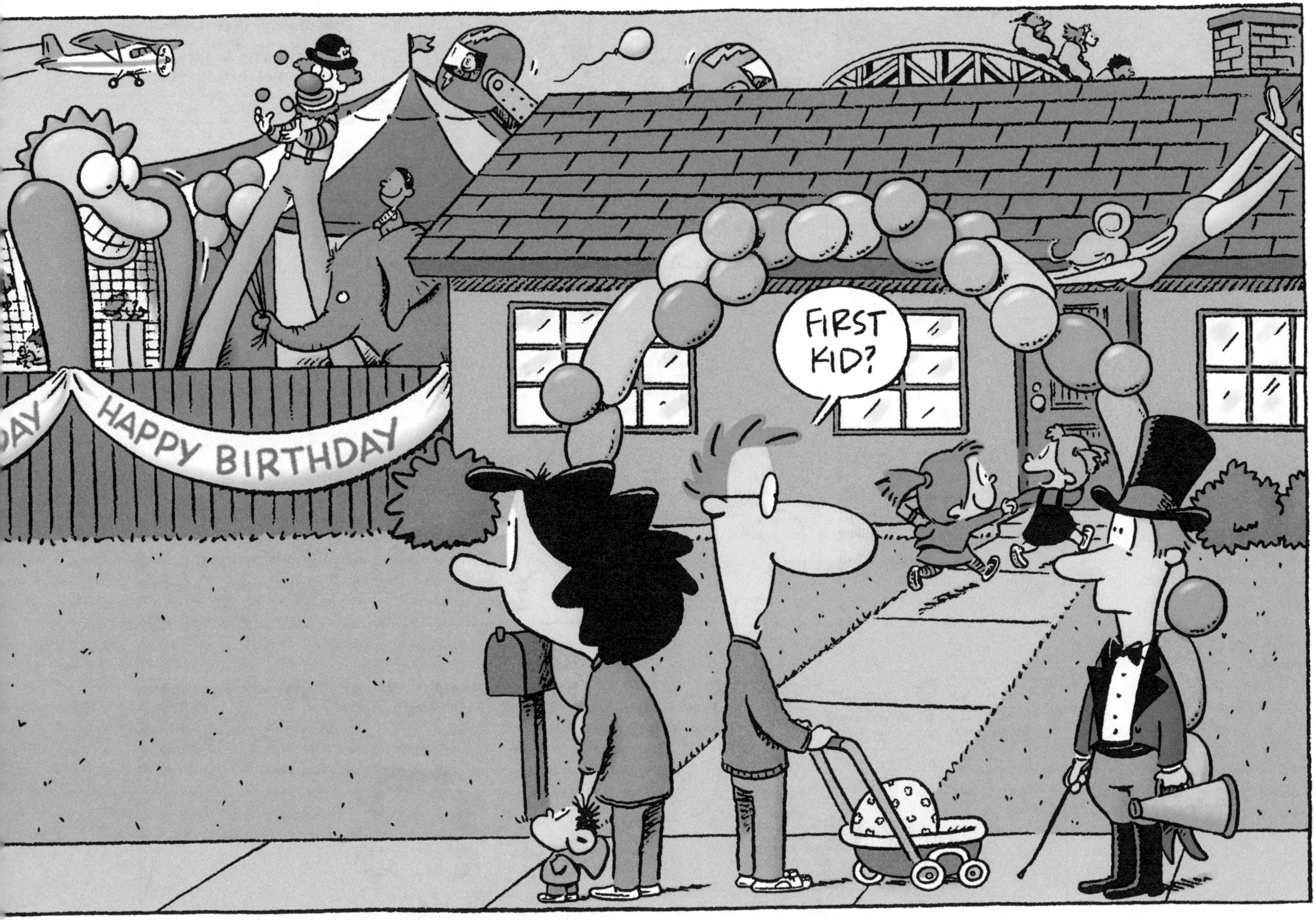
DAY HAPPY BIRTHDAY
FIRST KID?

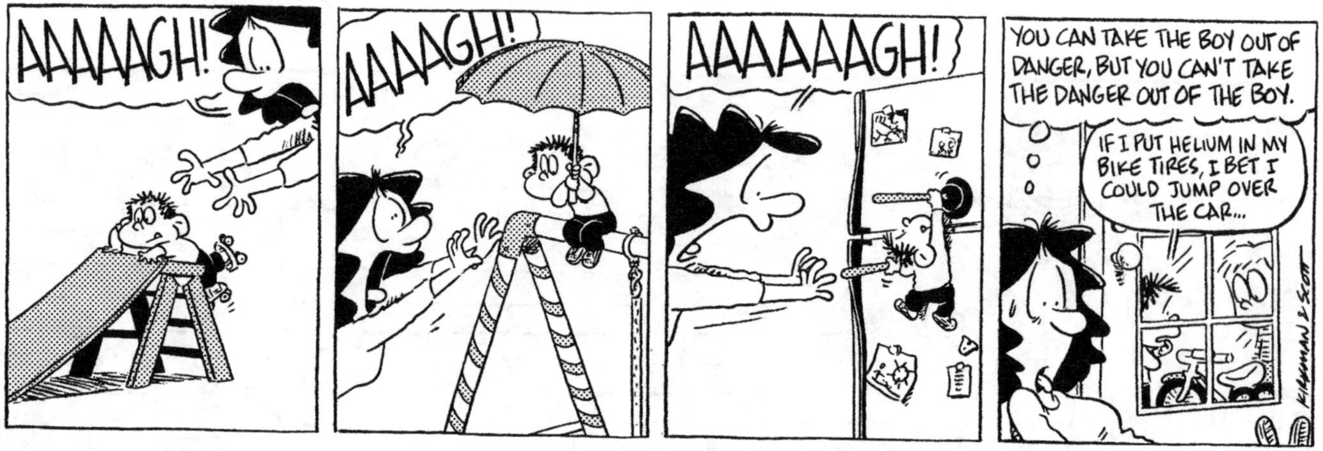
AAAAAGH!
AAAAGH!
AAAAAAAGH!
YOU CAN TAKE THE BOY OUT OF DANGER, BUT YOU CAN'T TAKE THE DANGER OUT OF THE BOY.
IF I PUT HELIUM IN MY BIKE TIRES, I BET I COULD JUMP OVER THE CAR...
KIRKMAN & SCOTT

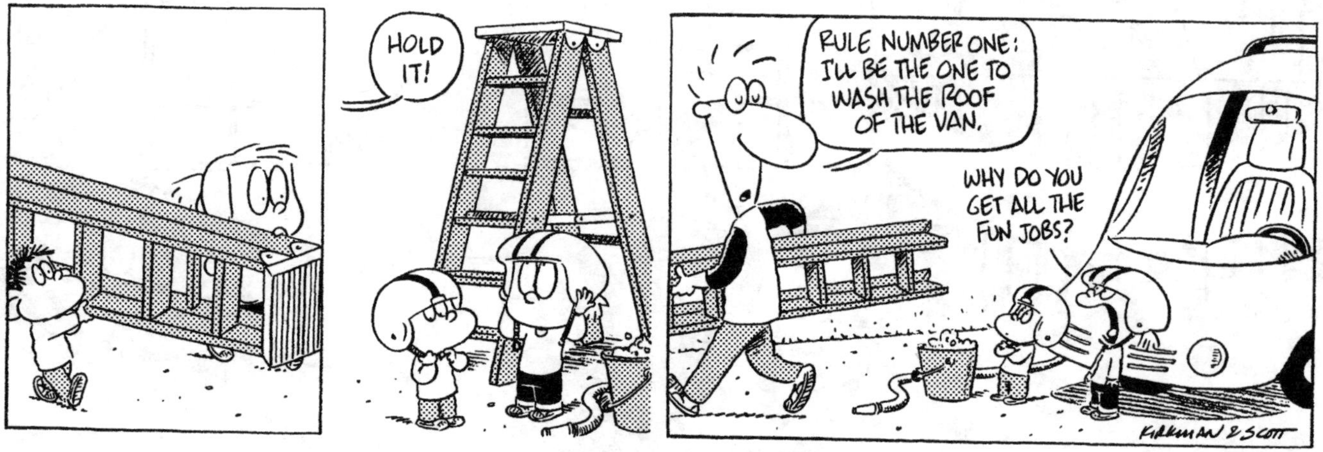
HOLD IT!
RULE NUMBER ONE: I'LL BE THE ONE TO WASH THE ROOF OF THE VAN.
WHY DO YOU GET ALL THE FUN JOBS?
KIRKMAN & SCOTT

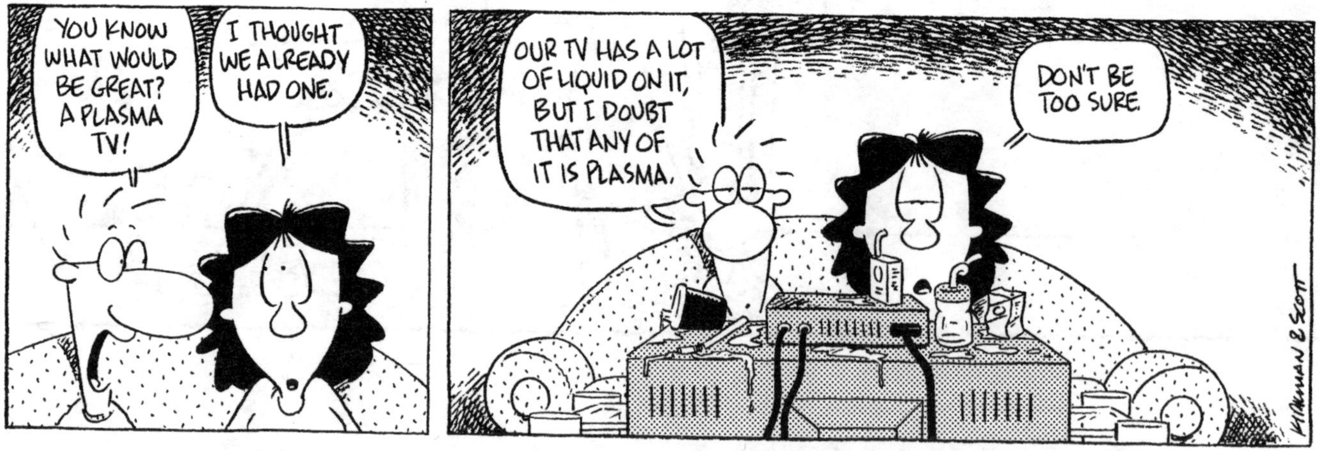
YOU KNOW WHAT WOULD BE GREAT? A PLASMA TV!
I THOUGHT WE ALREADY HAD ONE.
OUR TV HAS A LOT OF LIQUID ON IT, BUT I DOUBT THAT ANY OF IT IS PLASMA.
DON'T BE TOO SURE.
KIRKMAN & SCOTT

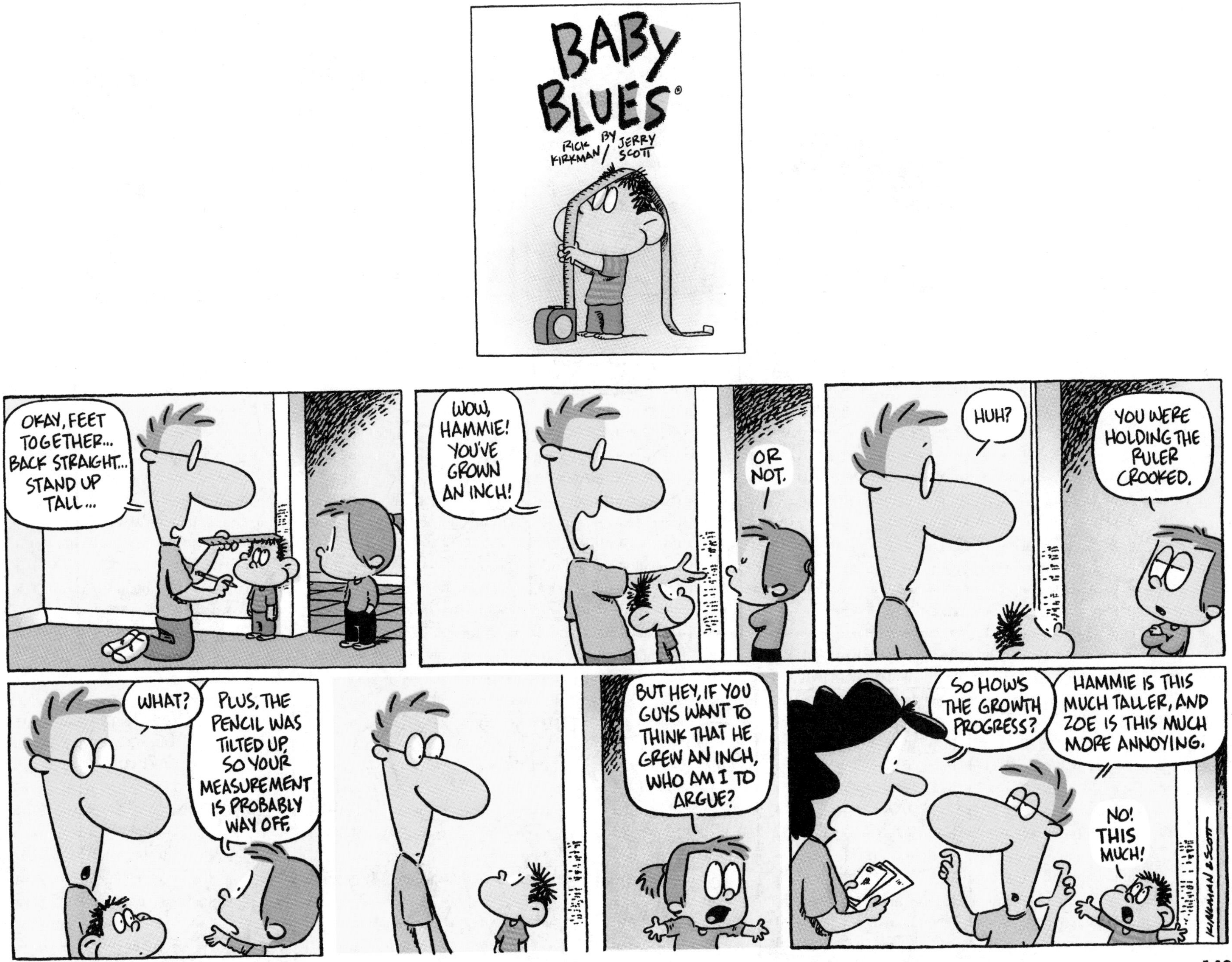
BABY BLUES®
BY RICK KIRKMAN / JERRY SCOTT
OKAY, FEET TOGETHER... BACK STRAIGHT... STAND UP TALL...
WOW, HAMMIE! YOU'VE GROWN AN INCH!
OR NOT.
HUH?
YOU WERE HOLDING THE RULER CROOKED.
WHAT?
PLUS, THE PENCIL WAS TILTED UP, SO YOUR MEASUREMENT IS PROBABLY WAY OFF.
BUT HEY, IF YOU GUYS WANT TO THINK THAT HE GREW AN INCH, WHO AM I TO ARGUE?
SO HOW'S THE GROWTH PROGRESS?
HAMMIE IS THIS MUCH TALLER, AND ZOE IS THIS MUCH MORE ANNOYING.
NO! THIS MUCH!
KIRKMAN & SCOTT

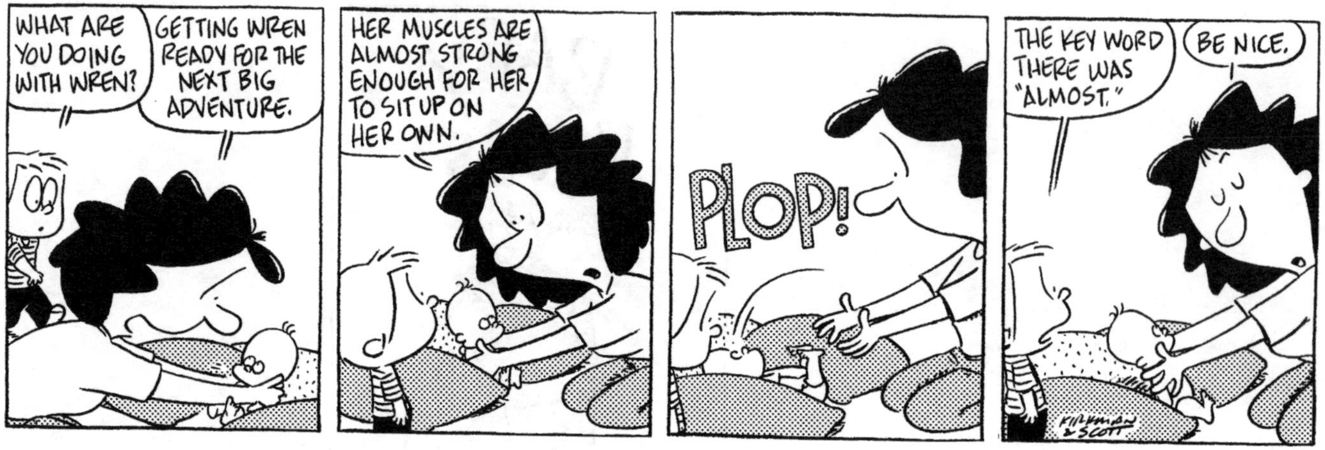
WHAT ARE YOU DOING WITH WREN?
GETTING WREN READY FOR THE NEXT BIG ADVENTURE.
HER MUSCLES ARE ALMOST STRONG ENOUGH FOR HER TO SIT UP ON HER OWN.
PLOP!
THE KEY WORD THERE WAS "ALMOST."
BE NICE.
KIRKMAN & SCOTT

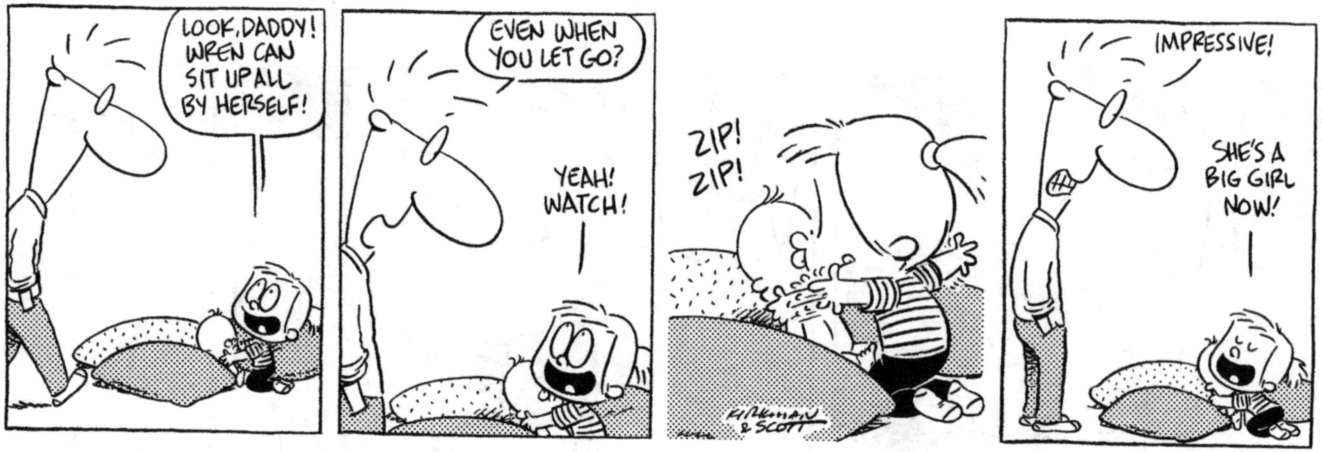
LOOK, DADDY! WREN CAN SIT UP ALL BY HERSELF!
EVEN WHEN YOU LET GO?
YEAH! WATCH!
ZIP! ZIP!
KIRKMAN & SCOTT
IMPRESSIVE!
SHE'S A BIG GIRL NOW!

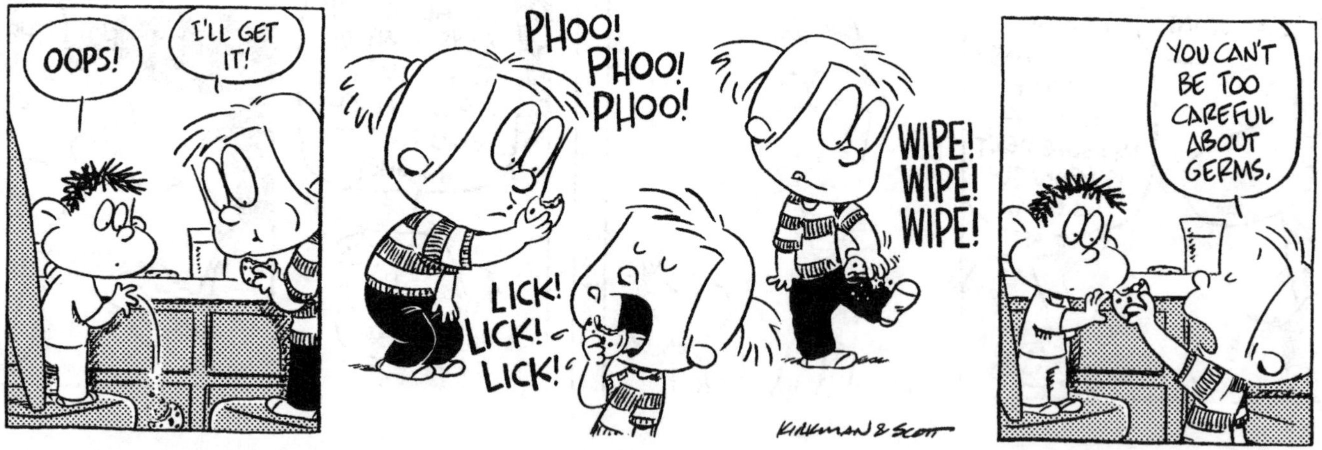
OOPS!
I'LL GET IT!
PHOO! PHOO! PHOO!
LICK! LICK! LICK!
WIPE! WIPE! WIPE!
KIRKMAN & SCOTT
YOU CAN'T BE TOO CAREFUL ABOUT GERMS.

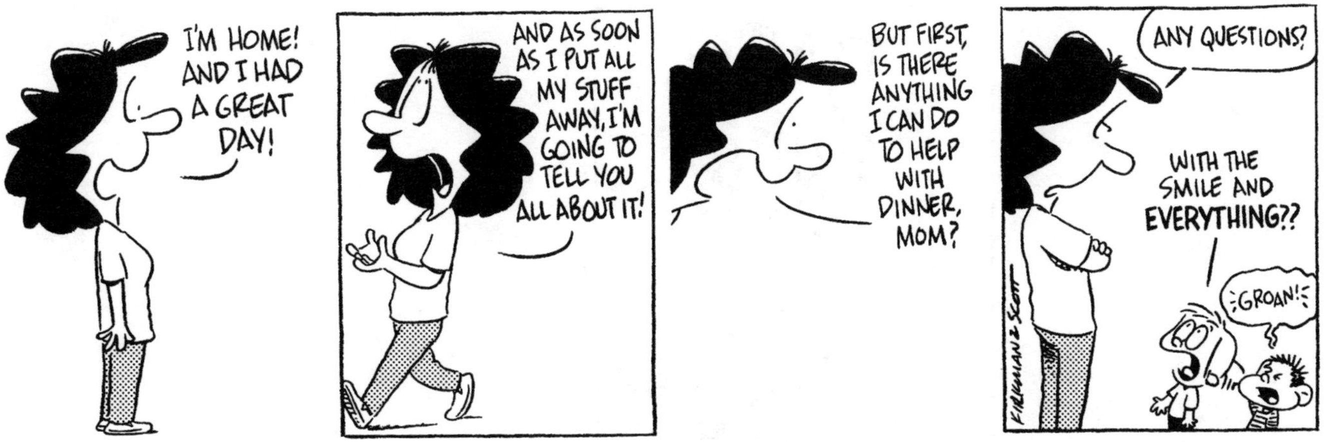
I'M HOME! AND I HAD A GREAT DAY!
AND AS SOON AS I PUT ALL MY STUFF AWAY, I'M GOING TO TELL YOU ALL ABOUT IT!
BUT FIRST, IS THERE ANYTHING I CAN DO TO HELP WITH DINNER, MOM?
ANY QUESTIONS?
WITH THE SMILE AND EVERYTHING??
GROAN!
KIRKMAN & SCOTT

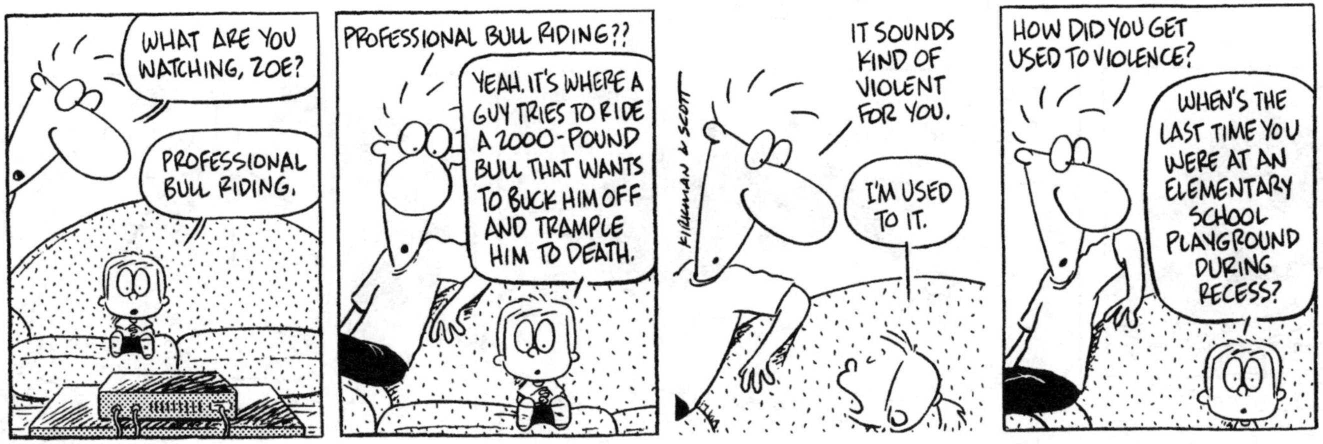
WHAT ARE YOU WATCHING, ZOE?
PROFESSIONAL BULL RIDING.
PROFESSIONAL BULL RIDING??
YEAH. IT'S WHERE A GUY TRIES TO RIDE A 2000-POUND BULL THAT WANTS TO BUCK HIM OFF AND TRAMPLE HIM TO DEATH.
KIRKMAN & SCOTT
IT SOUNDS KIND OF VIOLENT FOR YOU.
I'M USED TO IT.
HOW DID YOU GET USED TO VIOLENCE?
WHEN'S THE LAST TIME YOU WERE AT AN ELEMENTARY SCHOOL PLAYGROUND DURING RECESS?

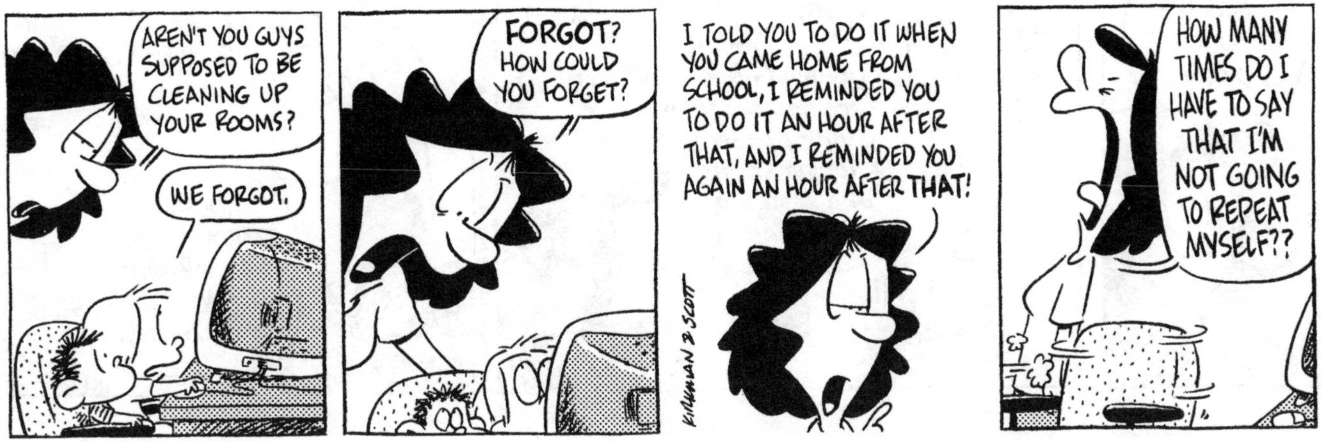
AREN'T YOU GUYS SUPPOSED TO BE CLEANING UP YOUR ROOMS?
WE FORGOT.
FORGOT? HOW COULD YOU FORGET?
KIRKMAN & SCOTT
I TOLD YOU TO DO IT WHEN YOU CAME HOME FROM SCHOOL, I REMINDED YOU TO DO IT AN HOUR AFTER THAT, AND I REMINDED YOU AGAIN AN HOUR AFTER THAT!
HOW MANY TIMES DO I HAVE TO SAY THAT I'M NOT GOING TO REPEAT MYSELF??

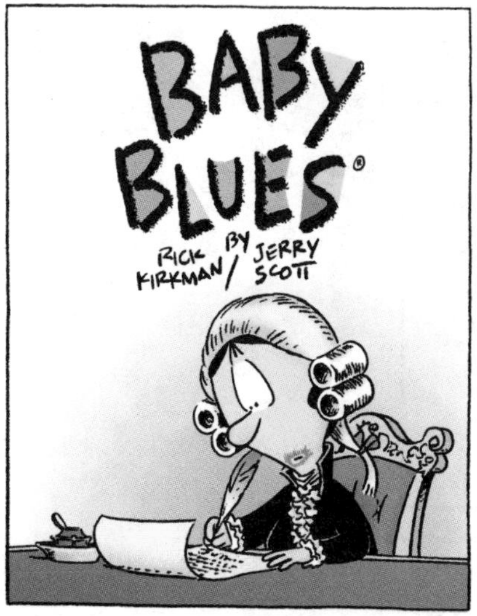
BABY BLUES®
RICK KIRKMAN / BY JERRY SCOTT

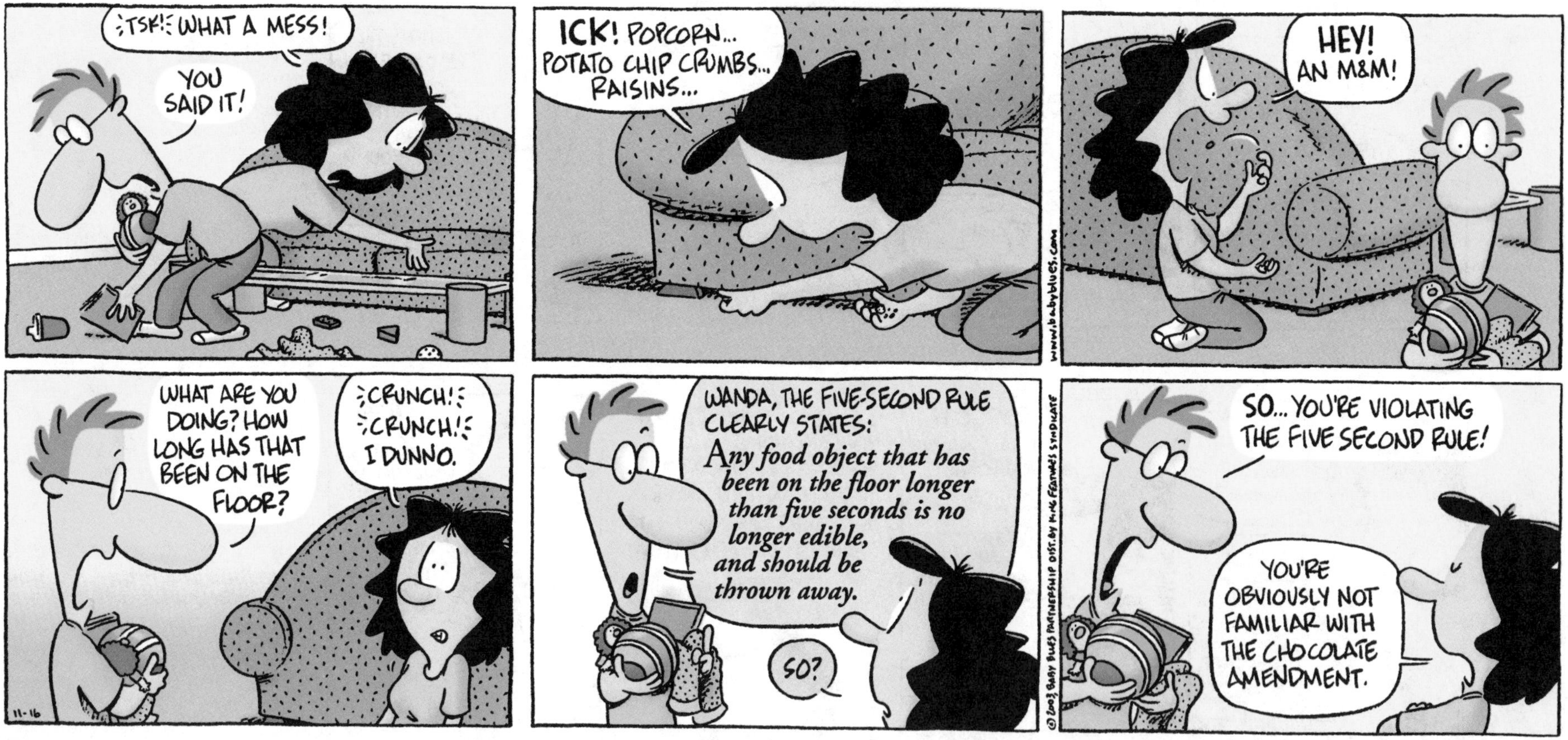
TSK! WHAT A MESS!
YOU SAID IT!
ICK! POPCORN... POTATO CHIP CRUMBS... RAISINS...
HEY! AN M&M!
www.babyblues.com
11-16
WHAT ARE YOU DOING? HOW LONG HAS THAT BEEN ON THE FLOOR?
CRUNCH! CRUNCH! I DUNNO.
WANDA, THE FIVE-SECOND RULE CLEARLY STATES:
Any food object that has been on the floor longer than five seconds is no longer edible, and should be thrown away.
SO?
©2003 BABY BLUES PARTNERSHIP DIST. BY KING FEATURES SYNDICATE
SO... YOU'RE VIOLATING THE FIVE SECOND RULE!
YOU'RE OBVIOUSLY NOT FAMILIAR WITH THE CHOCOLATE AMENDMENT.

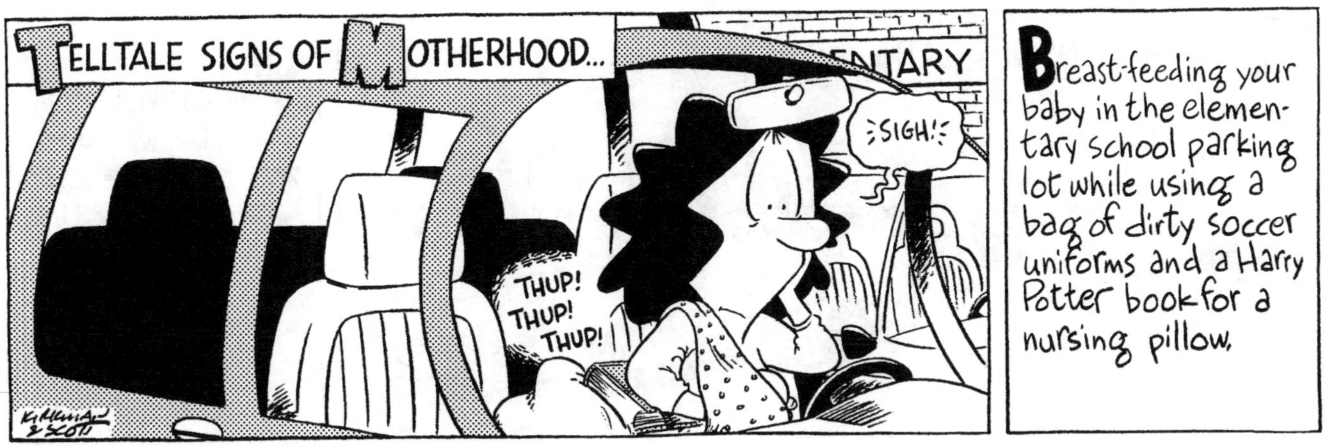
TELLTALE SIGNS OF MOTHERHOOD...
ENTARY
SIGH!
THUP! THUP! THUP!
KIRKMAN & SCOTT

Breast-feeding your baby in the elementary school parking lot while using a bag of dirty soccer uniforms and a Harry Potter book for a nursing pillow.

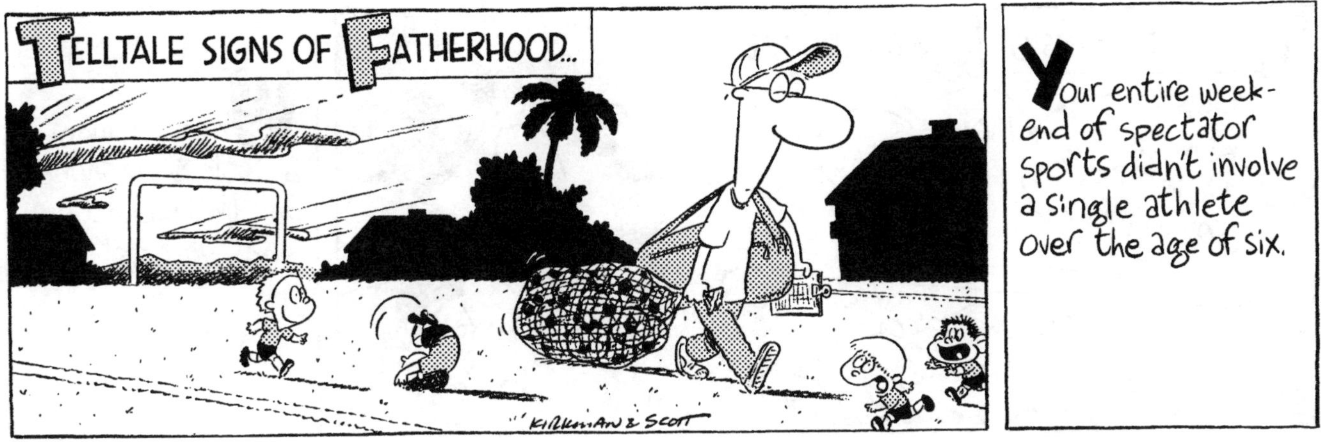
TELLTALE SIGNS OF FATHERHOOD...
KIRKMAN & SCOTT

Your entire weekend of spectator sports didn't involve a single athlete over the age of six.

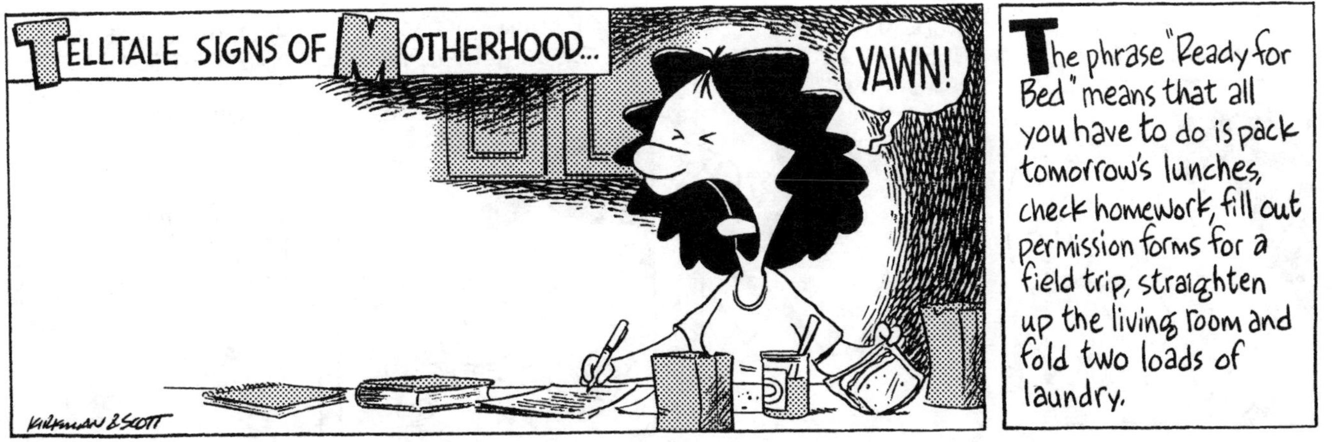
TELLTALE SIGNS OF MOTHERHOOD...
YAWN!
KIRKMAN & SCOTT

The phrase "Ready for Bed" means that all you have to do is pack tomorrow's lunches, check homework, fill out permission forms for a field trip, straighten up the living room and fold two loads of laundry.

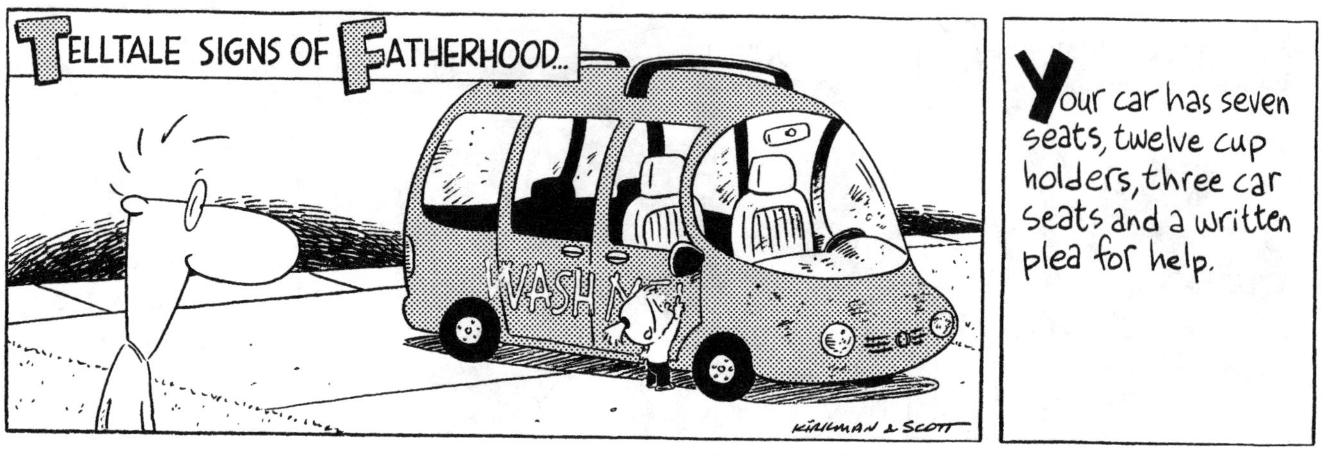
TELLTALE SIGNS OF FATHERHOOD...
WASH ME!
KIRKMAN & SCOTT

Your car has seven seats, twelve cup holders, three car seats and a written plea for help.

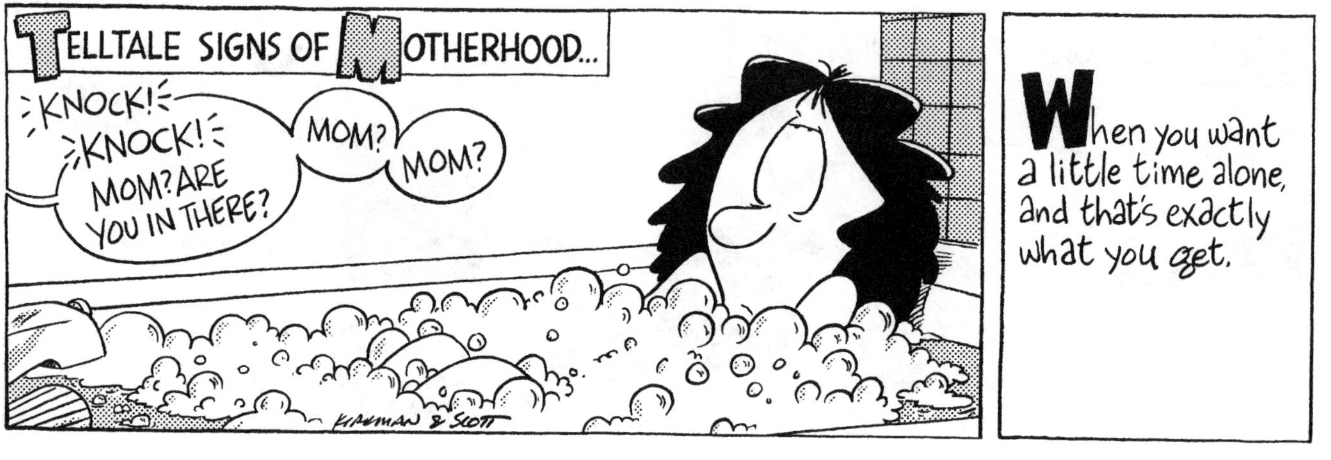
TELLTALE SIGNS OF MOTHERHOOD...
KNOCK! KNOCK! MOM? ARE YOU IN THERE?
MOM?
MOM?
KIRKMAN & SCOTT

When you want a little time alone, and that's exactly what you get.

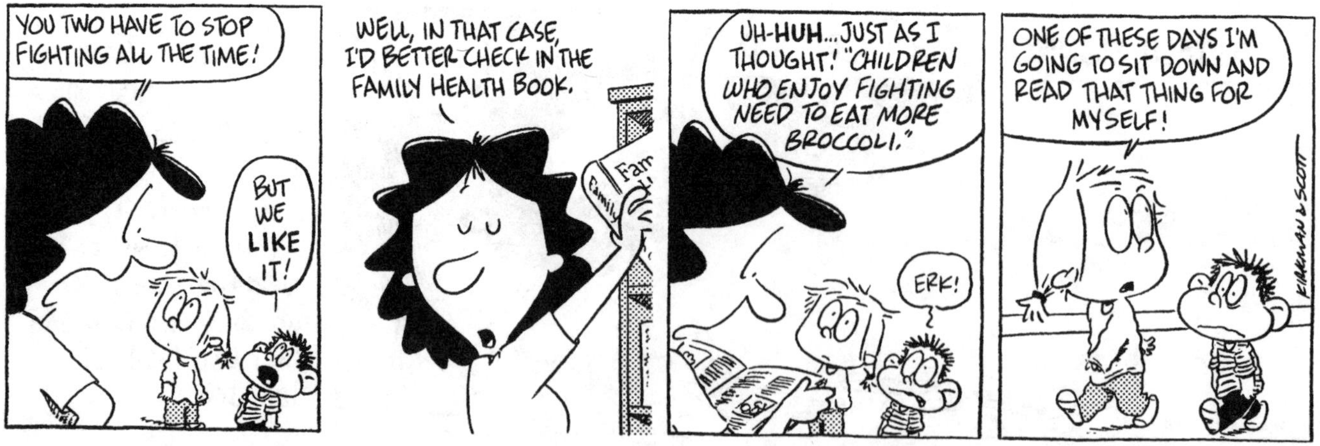
YOU TWO HAVE TO STOP FIGHTING ALL THE TIME!
BUT WE LIKE IT!
WELL, IN THAT CASE, I'D BETTER CHECK IN THE FAMILY HEALTH BOOK.
UH-HUH... JUST AS I THOUGHT! "CHILDREN WHO ENJOY FIGHTING NEED TO EAT MORE BROCCOLI."
ERK!
ONE OF THESE DAYS I'M GOING TO SIT DOWN AND READ THAT THING FOR MYSELF!
KIRKMAN & SCOTT

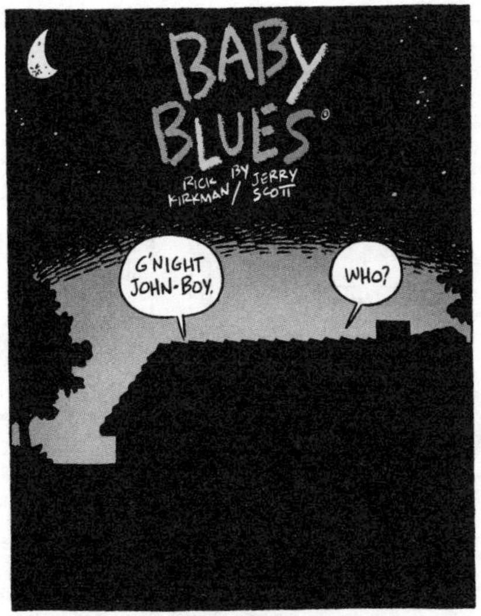
BABY BLUES
RICK KIRKMAN / BY JERRY SCOTT
G'NIGHT JOHN-BOY.
WHO?

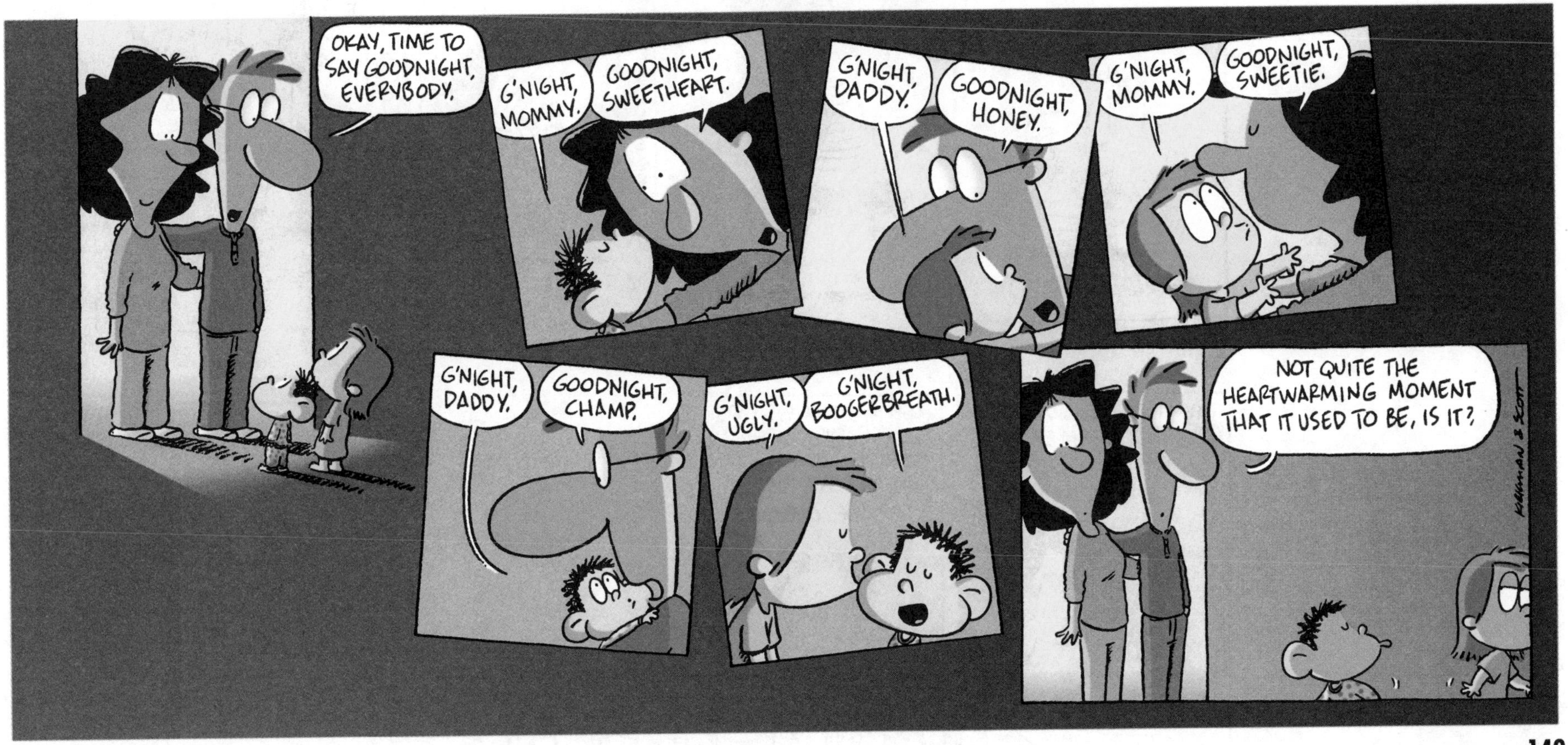
OKAY, TIME TO SAY GOODNIGHT, EVERYBODY.
G'NIGHT, MOMMY.
GOODNIGHT, SWEETHEART.
G'NIGHT, DADDY.
GOODNIGHT, HONEY.
G'NIGHT, MOMMY.
GOODNIGHT, SWEETIE.
G'NIGHT, DADDY.
GOODNIGHT, CHAMP.
G'NIGHT, UGLY.
G'NIGHT, BOOGERBREATH.
NOT QUITE THE HEARTWARMING MOMENT THAT IT USED TO BE, IS IT?
KIRKMAN & SCOTT

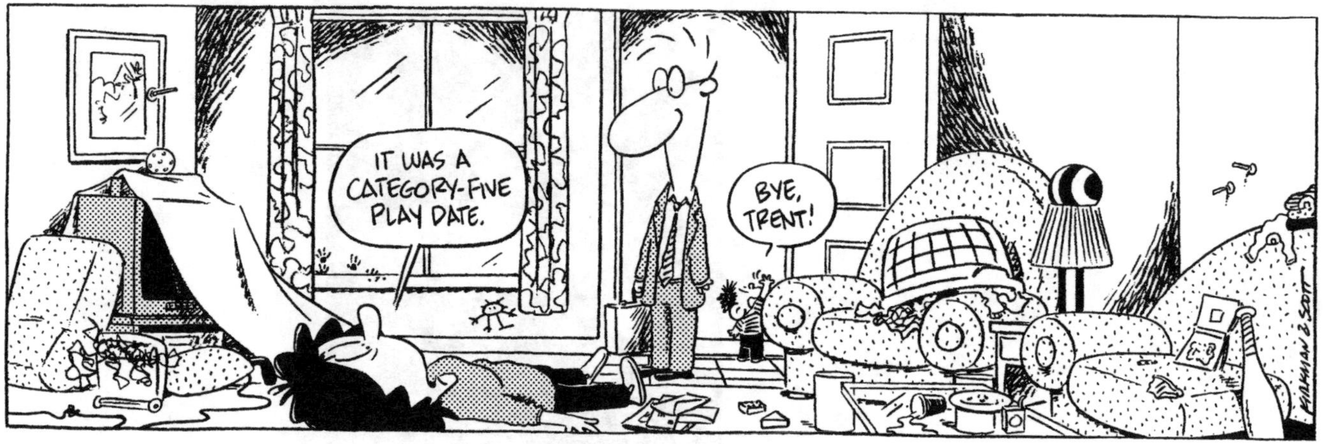
IT WAS A CATEGORY-FIVE PLAY DATE.
BYE, TRENT!
KIRKMAN & SCOTT

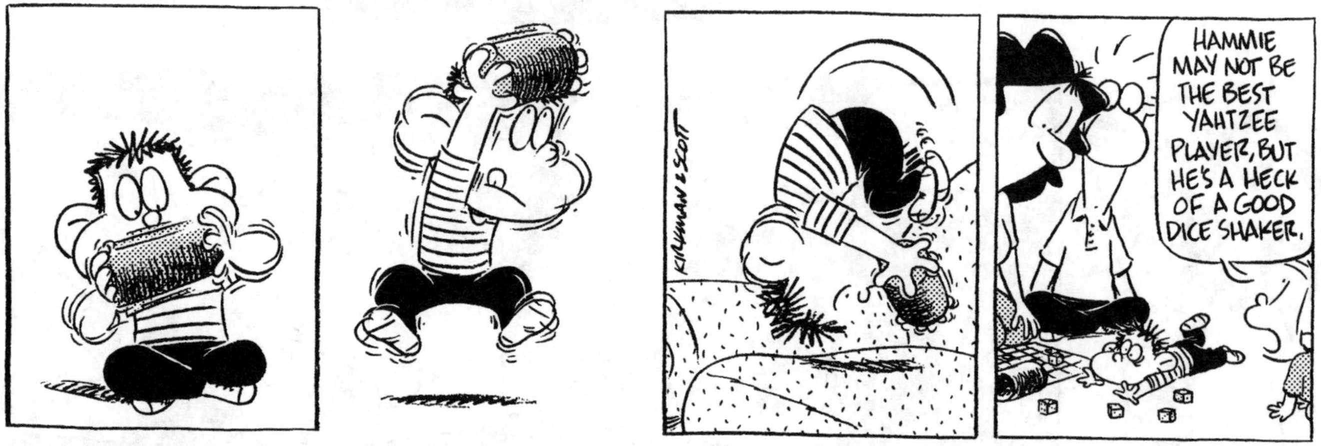
KIRKMAN & SCOTT
HAMMIE MAY NOT BE THE BEST YAHTZEE PLAYER, BUT HE'S A HECK OF A GOOD DICE SHAKER.

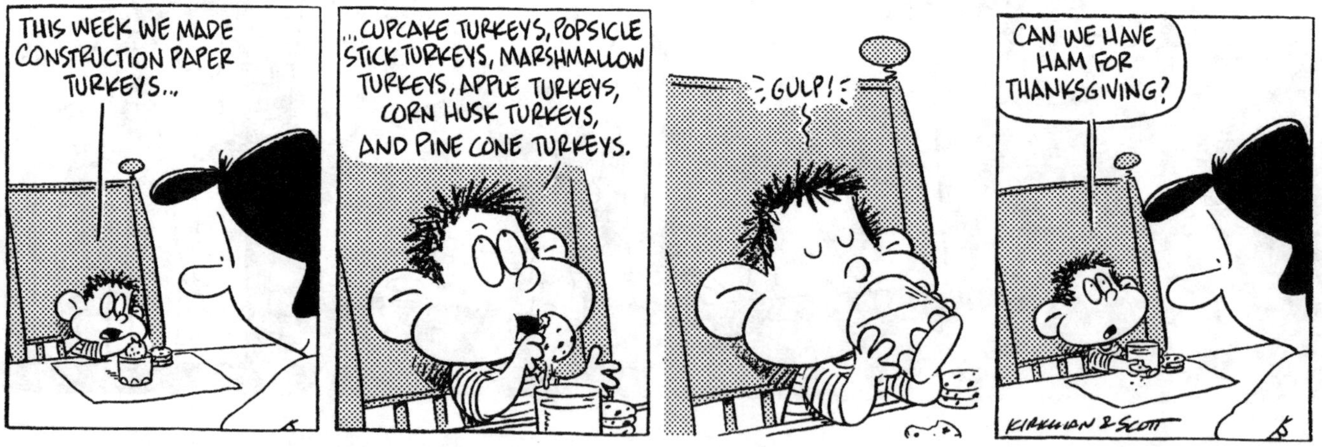
THIS WEEK WE MADE CONSTRUCTION PAPER TURKEYS...
...CUPCAKE TURKEYS, POPSICLE STICK TURKEYS, MARSHMALLOW TURKEYS, APPLE TURKEYS, CORN HUSK TURKEYS, AND PINE CONE TURKEYS.
GULP!
CAN WE HAVE HAM FOR THANKSGIVING?
KIRKMAN & SCOTT

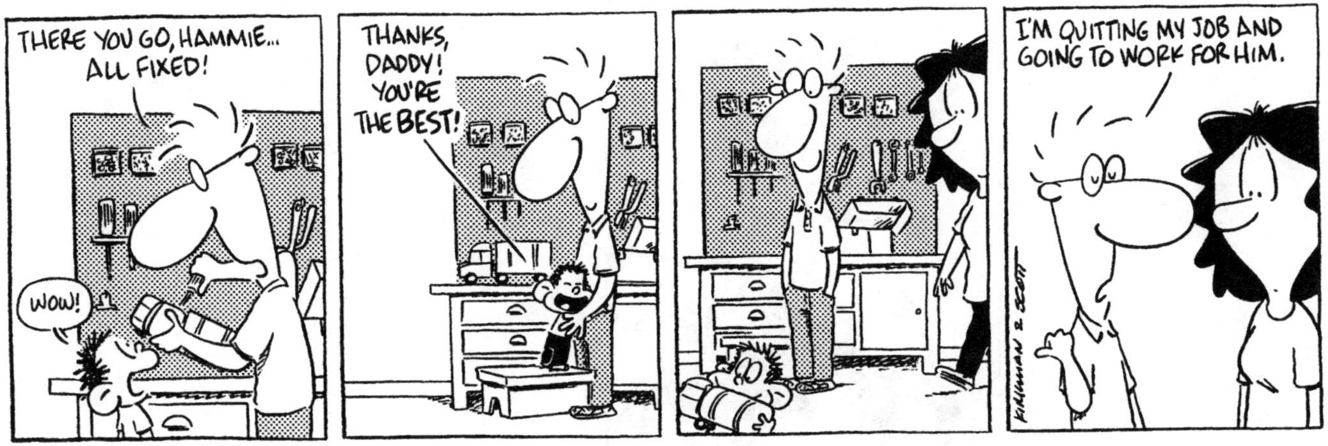
THERE YOU GO, HAMMIE... ALL FIXED!
WOW!
THANKS, DADDY! YOU'RE THE BEST!
I'M QUITTING MY JOB AND GOING TO WORK FOR HIM.
KIRKMAN & SCOTT

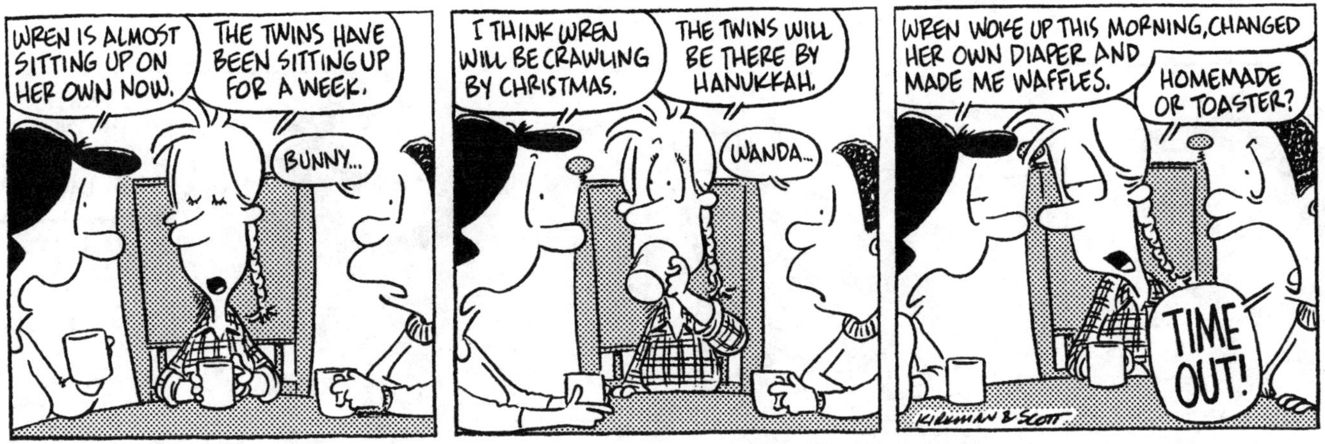
WREN IS ALMOST SITTING UP ON HER OWN NOW.
THE TWINS HAVE BEEN SITTING UP FOR A WEEK.
BUNNY...
I THINK WREN WILL BE CRAWLING BY CHRISTMAS.
THE TWINS WILL BE THERE BY HANUKKAH.
WANDA...
WREN WOKE UP THIS MORNING, CHANGED HER OWN DIAPER AND MADE ME WAFFLES.
HOMEMADE OR TOASTER?
TIME OUT!
KIRKMAN & SCOTT

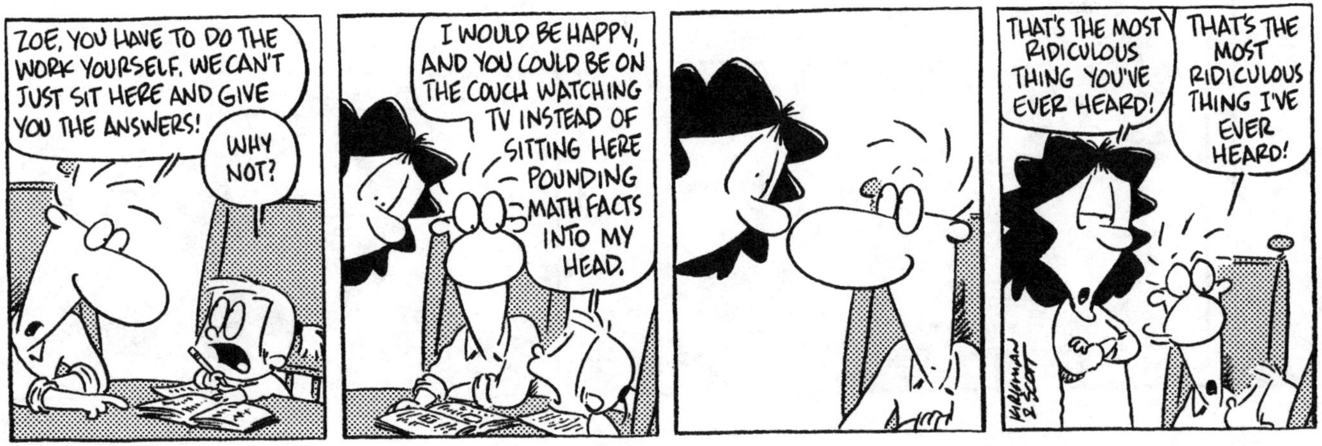
ZOE, YOU HAVE TO DO THE WORK YOURSELF. WE CAN'T JUST SIT HERE AND GIVE YOU THE ANSWERS!
WHY NOT?
I WOULD BE HAPPY, AND YOU COULD BE ON THE COUCH WATCHING TV INSTEAD OF SITTING HERE POUNDING MATH FACTS INTO MY HEAD.
THAT'S THE MOST RIDICULOUS THING YOU'VE EVER HEARD!
THAT'S THE MOST RIDICULOUS THING I'VE EVER HEARD!
KIRKMAN & SCOTT

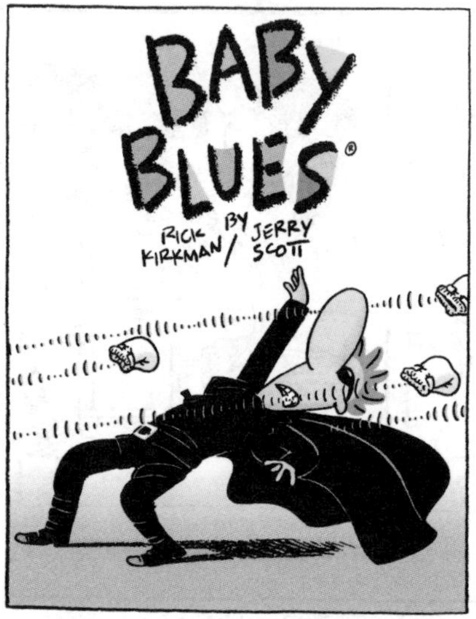
BABY BLUES®
BY RICK KIRKMAN / JERRY SCOTT

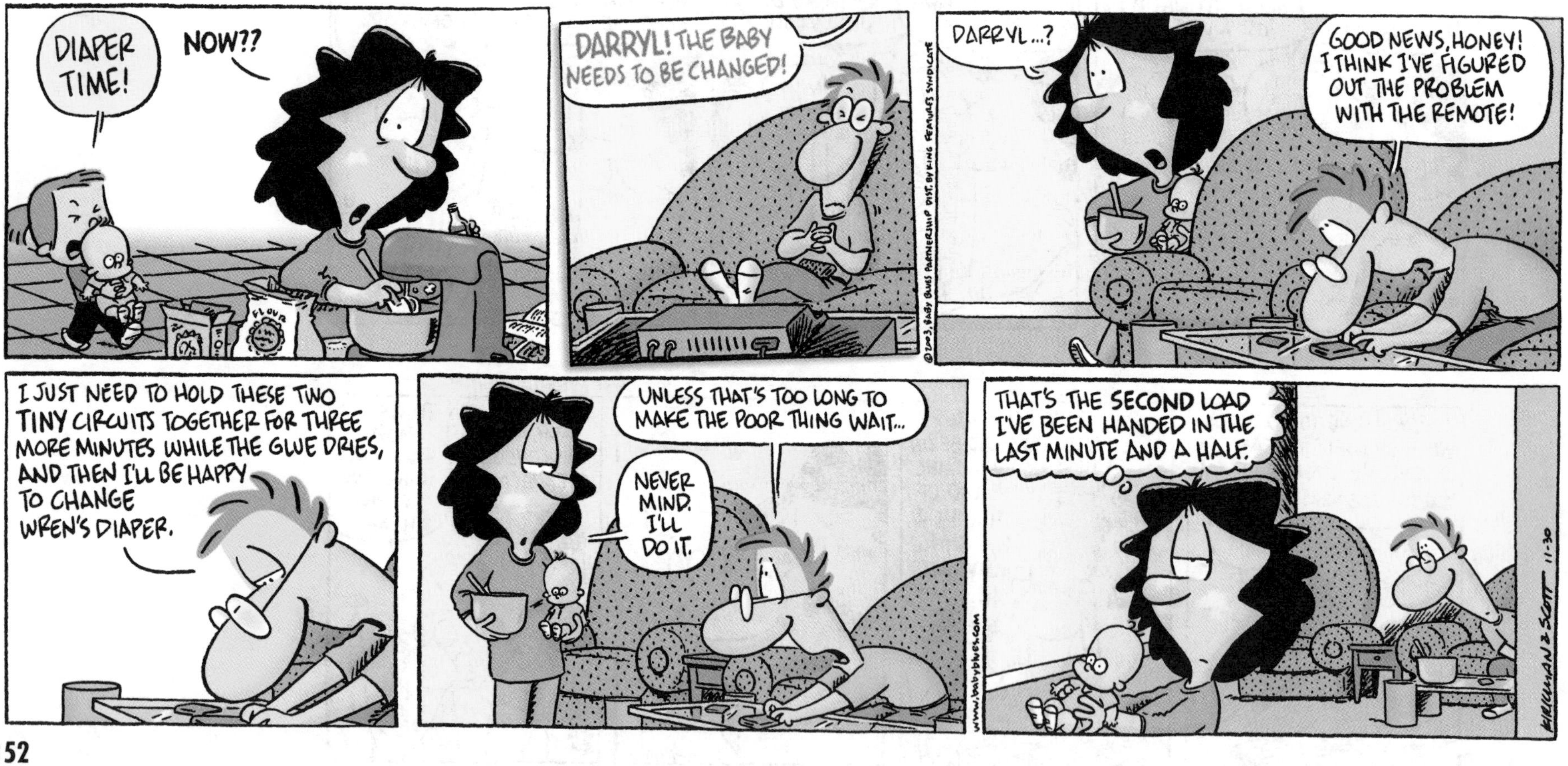
DIAPER TIME!
NOW??
DARRYL! THE BABY NEEDS TO BE CHANGED!
©2003, BABY BLUES PARTNERSHIP DIST. BY KING FEATURES SYNDICATE
DARRYL...?
GOOD NEWS, HONEY! I THINK I'VE FIGURED OUT THE PROBLEM WITH THE REMOTE!
I JUST NEED TO HOLD THESE TWO TINY CIRCUITS TOGETHER FOR THREE MORE MINUTES WHILE THE GLUE DRIES, AND THEN I'LL BE HAPPY TO CHANGE WREN'S DIAPER.
UNLESS THAT'S TOO LONG TO MAKE THE POOR THING WAIT...
NEVER MIND. I'LL DO IT.
www.babyblues.com
THAT'S THE SECOND LOAD I'VE BEEN HANDED IN THE LAST MINUTE AND A HALF.
KIRKMAN & SCOTT 11-30

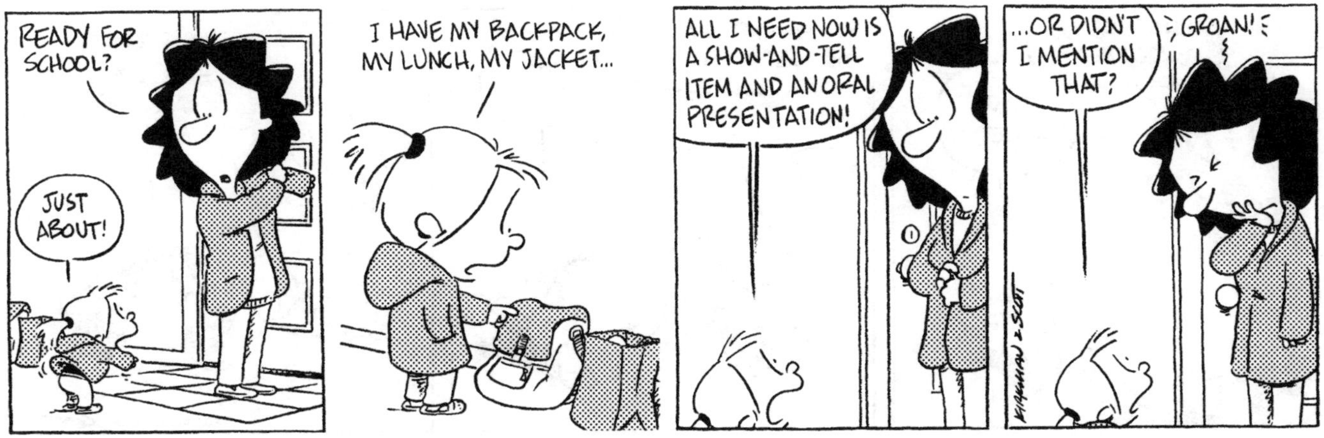
READY FOR SCHOOL?
JUST ABOUT!
I HAVE MY BACKPACK, MY LUNCH, MY JACKET...
ALL I NEED NOW IS A SHOW-AND-TELL ITEM AND AN ORAL PRESENTATION!
...OR DIDN'T I MENTION THAT?
GROAN!

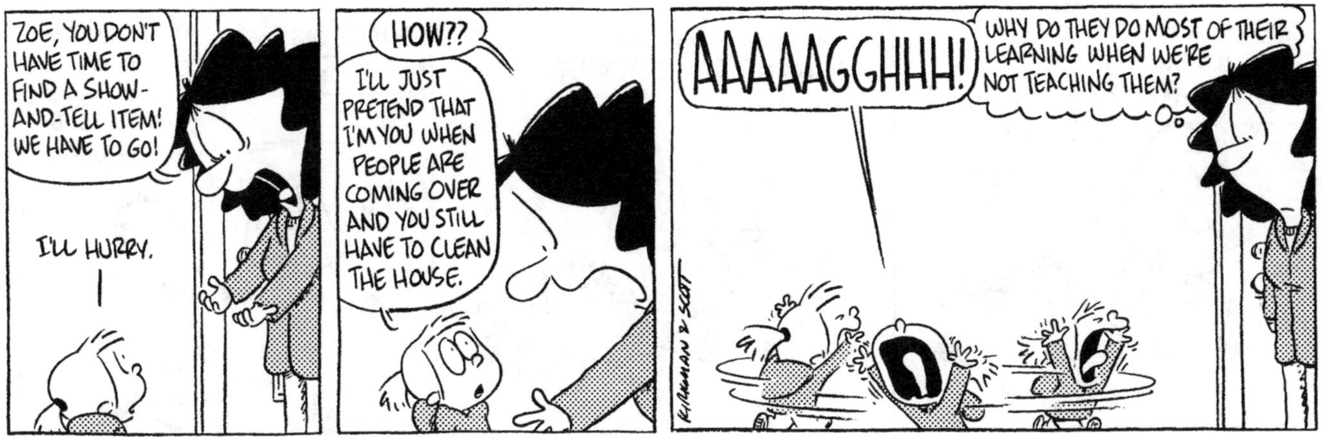
ZOE, YOU DON'T HAVE TIME TO FIND A SHOW-AND-TELL ITEM! WE HAVE TO GO!
I'LL HURRY.
HOW??
I'LL JUST PRETEND THAT I'M YOU WHEN PEOPLE ARE COMING OVER AND YOU STILL HAVE TO CLEAN THE HOUSE.
AAAAAGGHHH!
WHY DO THEY DO MOST OF THEIR LEARNING WHEN WE'RE NOT TEACHING THEM?

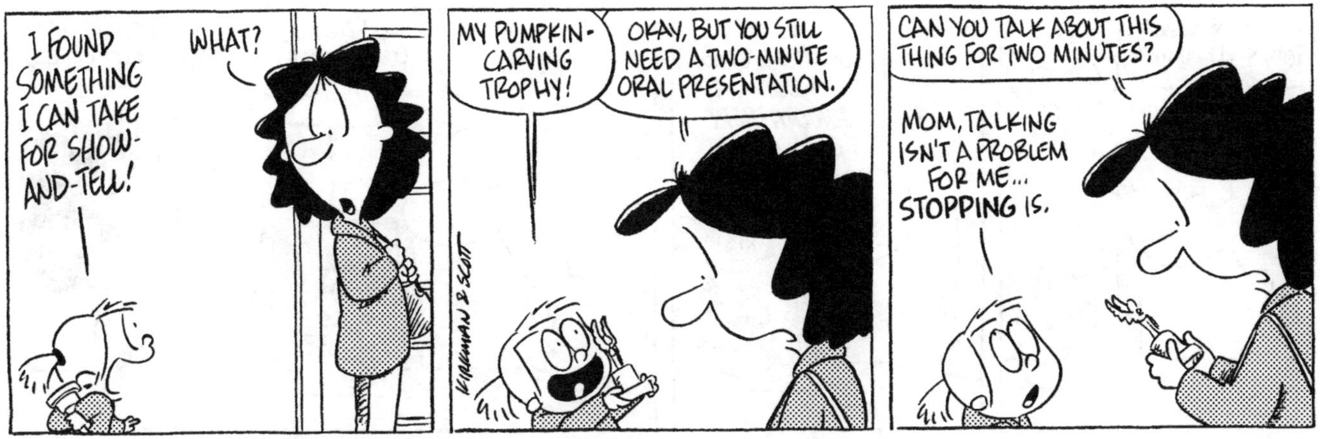
I FOUND SOMETHING I CAN TAKE FOR SHOW-AND-TELL!
WHAT?
MY PUMPKIN-CARVING TROPHY!
OKAY, BUT YOU STILL NEED A TWO-MINUTE ORAL PRESENTATION.
CAN YOU TALK ABOUT THIS THING FOR TWO MINUTES?
MOM, TALKING ISN'T A PROBLEM FOR ME... STOPPING IS.

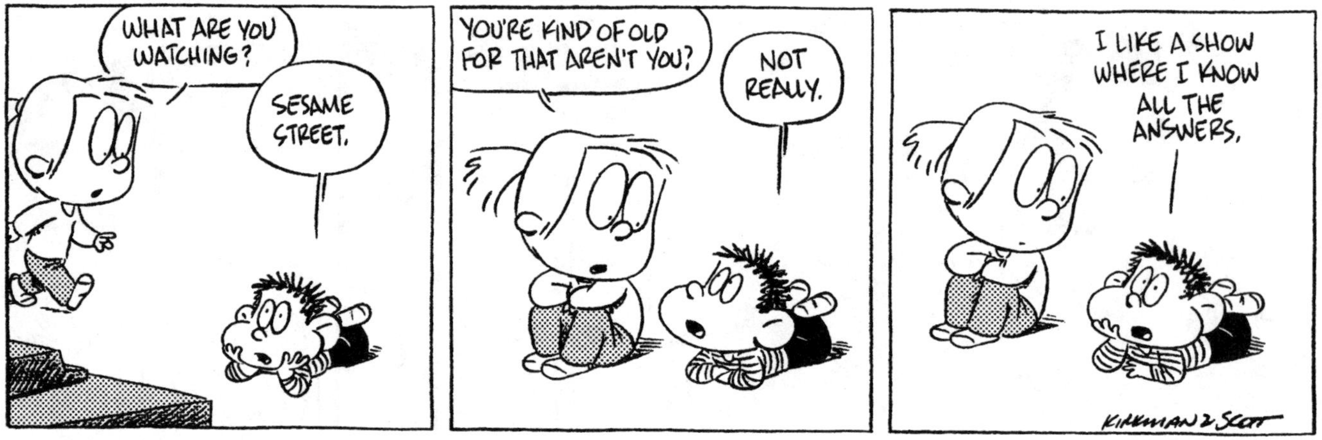
WHAT ARE YOU WATCHING?
SESAME STREET.
YOU'RE KIND OF OLD FOR THAT AREN'T YOU?
NOT REALLY.
I LIKE A SHOW WHERE I KNOW ALL THE ANSWERS.
KIRKMAN & SCOTT

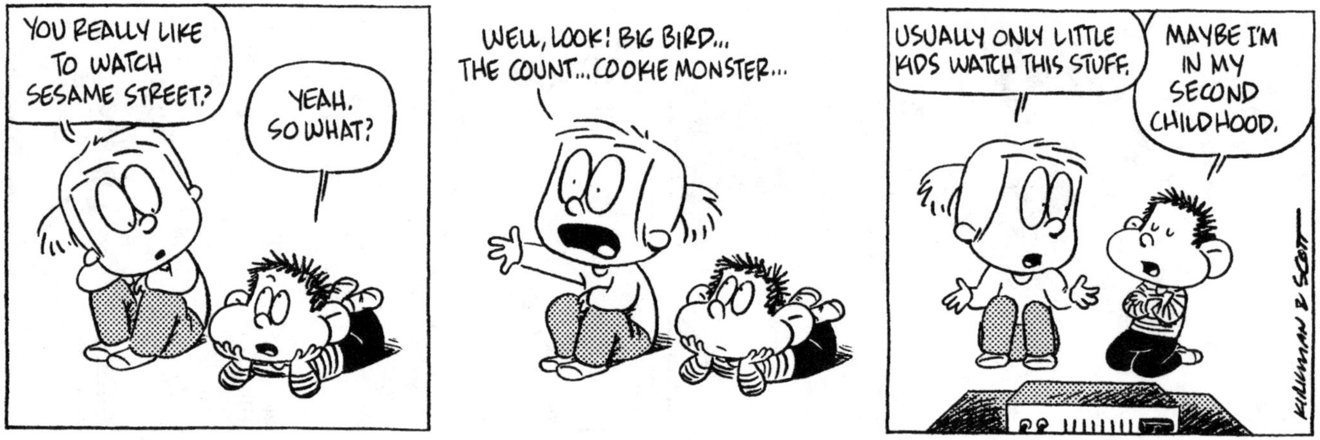
YOU REALLY LIKE TO WATCH SESAME STREET?
YEAH. SO WHAT?
WELL, LOOK! BIG BIRD... THE COUNT... COOKIE MONSTER...
USUALLY ONLY LITTLE KIDS WATCH THIS STUFF.
MAYBE I'M IN MY SECOND CHILDHOOD.
KIRKMAN & SCOTT

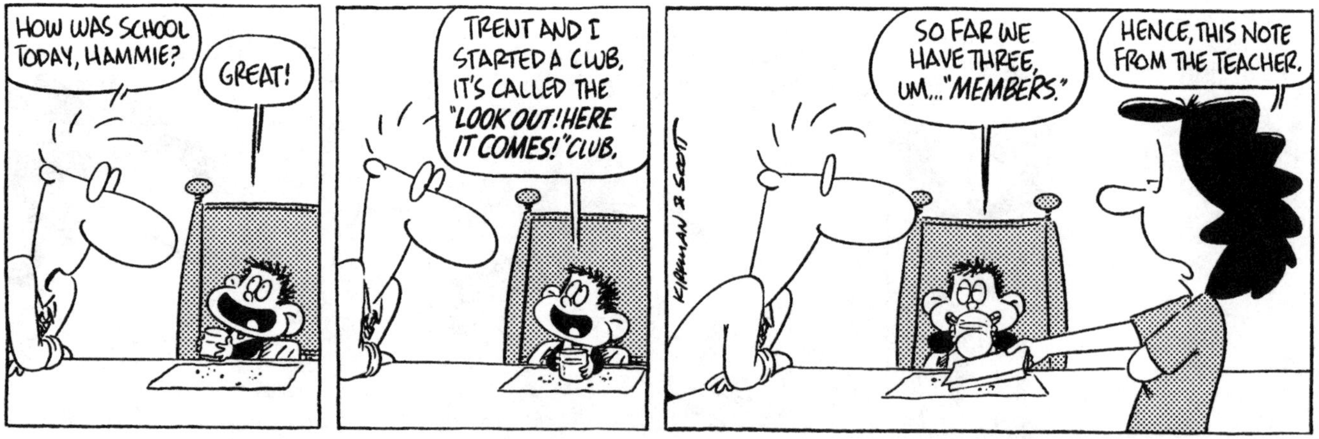
HOW WAS SCHOOL TODAY, HAMMIE?
GREAT!
TRENT AND I STARTED A CLUB. IT'S CALLED THE "LOOK OUT! HERE IT COMES!" CLUB.
KIRKMAN & SCOTT
SO FAR WE HAVE THREE, UM... "MEMBERS."
HENCE, THIS NOTE FROM THE TEACHER.

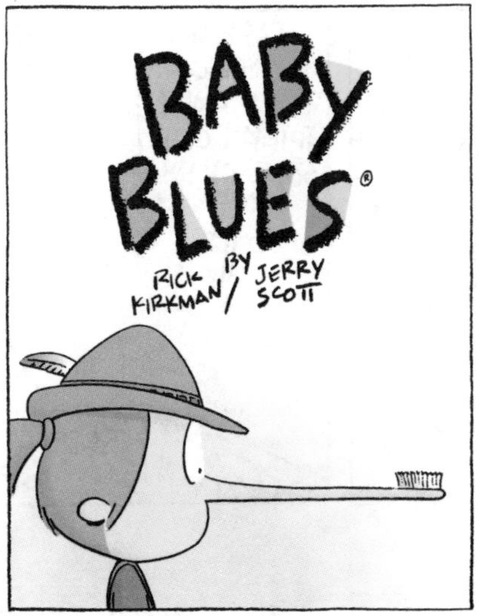
BABY BLUES®
BY RICK KIRKMAN / JERRY SCOTT

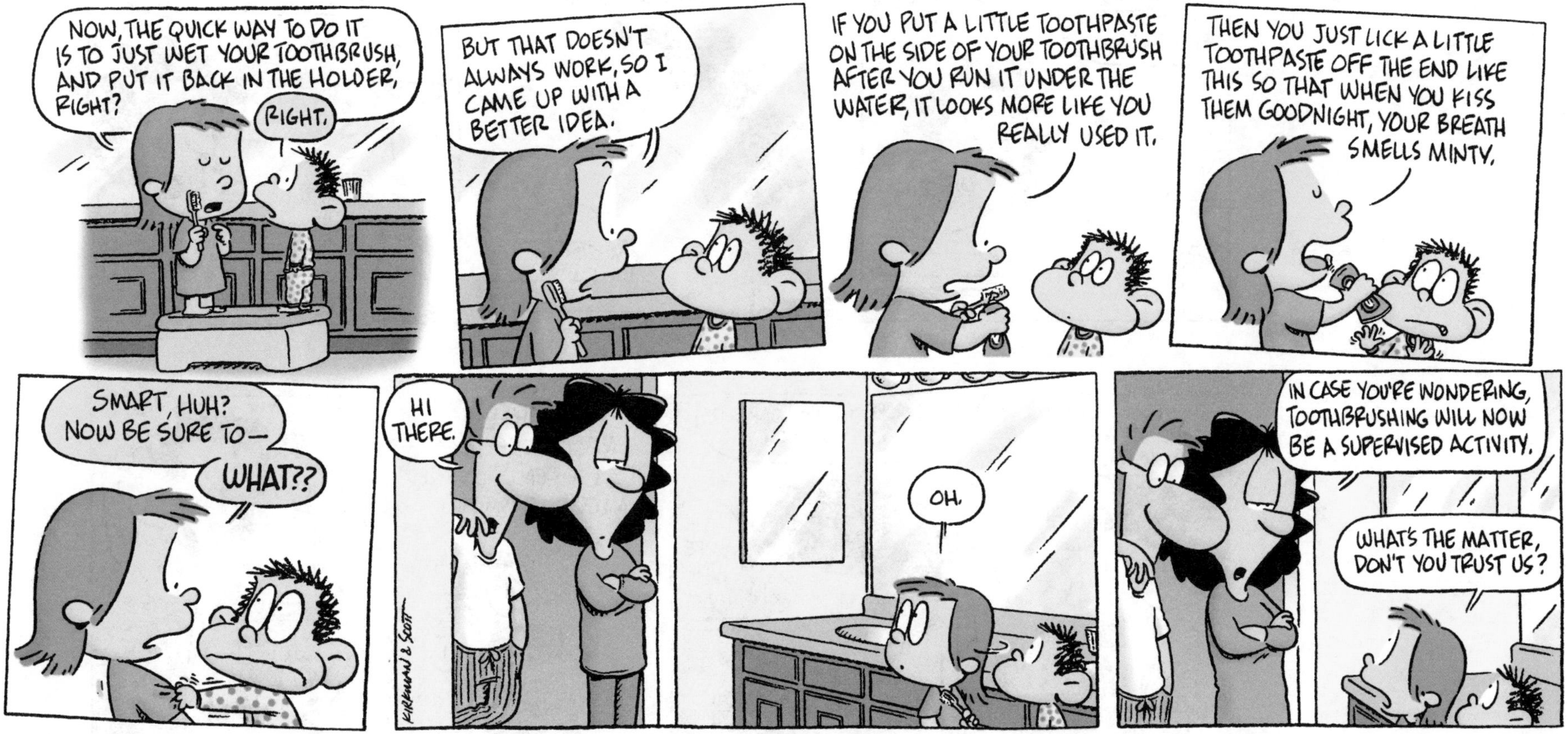
NOW, THE QUICK WAY TO DO IT IS TO JUST WET YOUR TOOTHBRUSH, AND PUT IT BACK IN THE HOLDER, RIGHT?
RIGHT.
BUT THAT DOESN'T ALWAYS WORK, SO I CAME UP WITH A BETTER IDEA.
IF YOU PUT A LITTLE TOOTHPASTE ON THE SIDE OF YOUR TOOTHBRUSH AFTER YOU RUN IT UNDER THE WATER, IT LOOKS MORE LIKE YOU REALLY USED IT.
THEN YOU JUST LICK A LITTLE TOOTHPASTE OFF THE END LIKE THIS SO THAT WHEN YOU KISS THEM GOODNIGHT, YOUR BREATH SMELLS MINTY.
SMART, HUH? NOW BE SURE TO—
WHAT??
KIRKMAN & SCOTT
HI THERE.
OH.
IN CASE YOU'RE WONDERING, TOOTHBRUSHING WILL NOW BE A SUPERVISED ACTIVITY.
WHAT'S THE MATTER, DON'T YOU TRUST US?

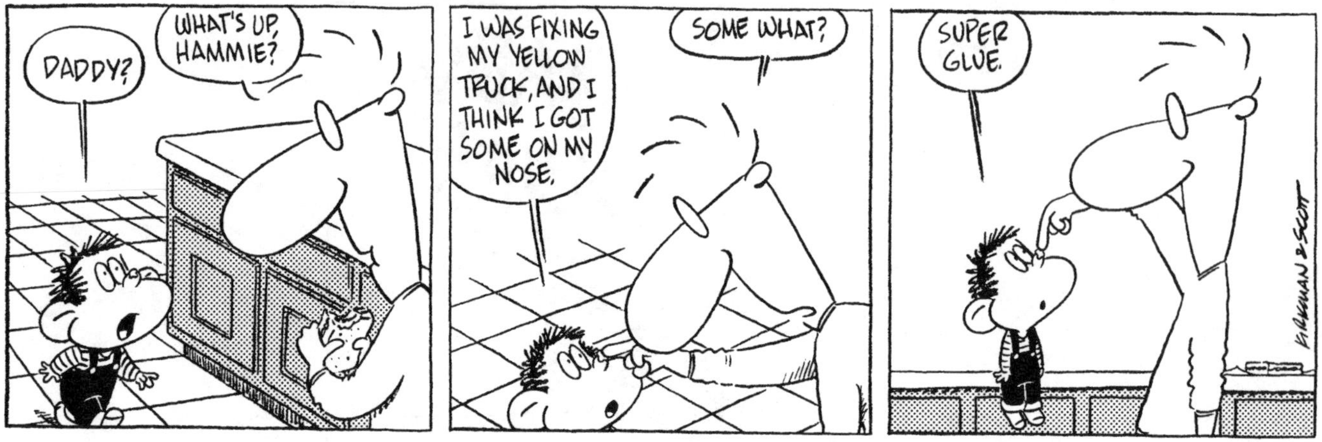
DADDY?
WHAT'S UP, HAMMIE?
I WAS FIXING MY YELLOW TRUCK, AND I THINK I GOT SOME ON MY NOSE.
SOME WHAT?
SUPER GLUE.
KIRKMAN & SCOTT

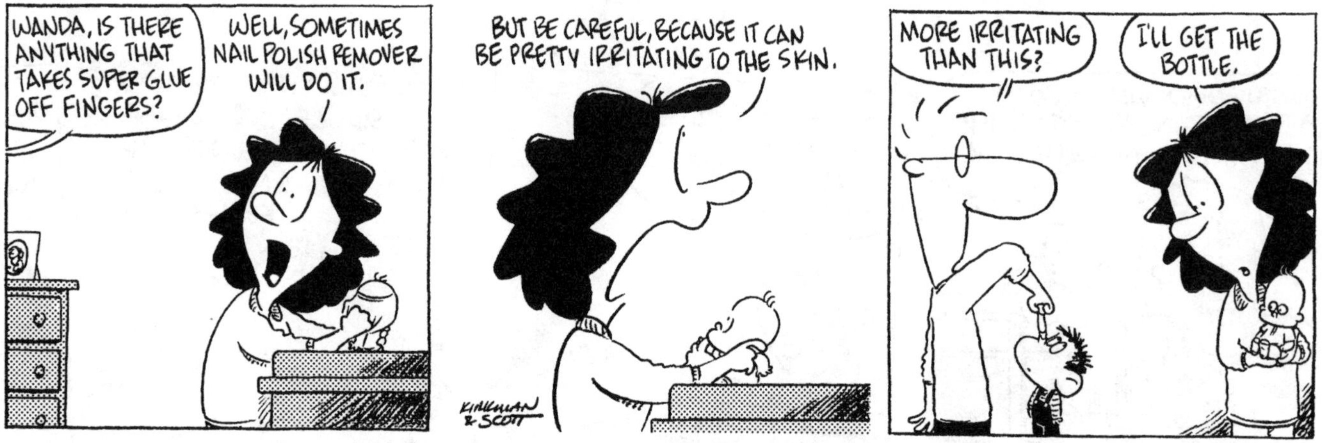
WANDA, IS THERE ANYTHING THAT TAKES SUPER GLUE OFF FINGERS?
WELL, SOMETIMES NAIL POLISH REMOVER WILL DO IT.
BUT BE CAREFUL, BECAUSE IT CAN BE PRETTY IRRITATING TO THE SKIN.
KIRKMAN & SCOTT
MORE IRRITATING THAN THIS?
I'LL GET THE BOTTLE.

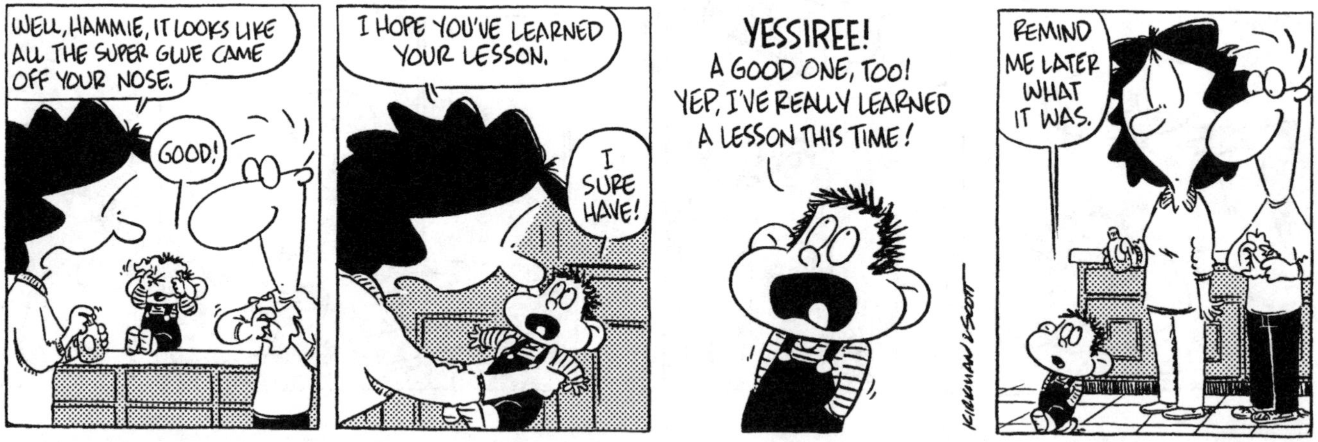
WELL, HAMMIE, IT LOOKS LIKE ALL THE SUPER GLUE CAME OFF YOUR NOSE.
GOOD!
I HOPE YOU'VE LEARNED YOUR LESSON.
I SURE HAVE!
YESSIREE!
A GOOD ONE, TOO!
YEP, I'VE REALLY LEARNED A LESSON THIS TIME!
KIRKMAN & SCOTT
REMIND ME LATER WHAT IT WAS.

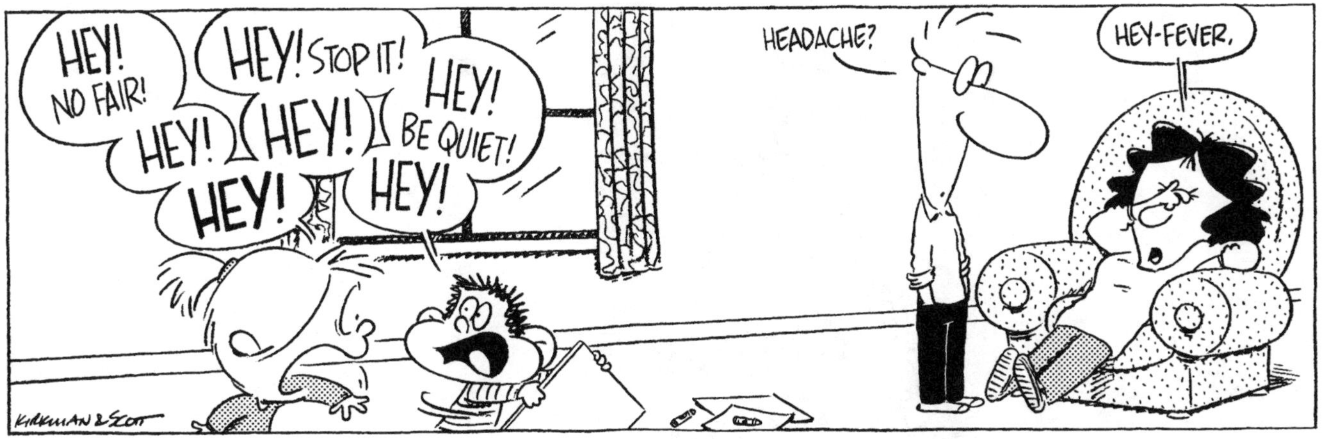
HEY! NO FAIR!
HEY! STOP IT!
HEY! BE QUIET!
HEY!
HEY!
HEY!
HEY!
KIRKMAN & SCOTT
HEADACHE?
HEY-FEVER.

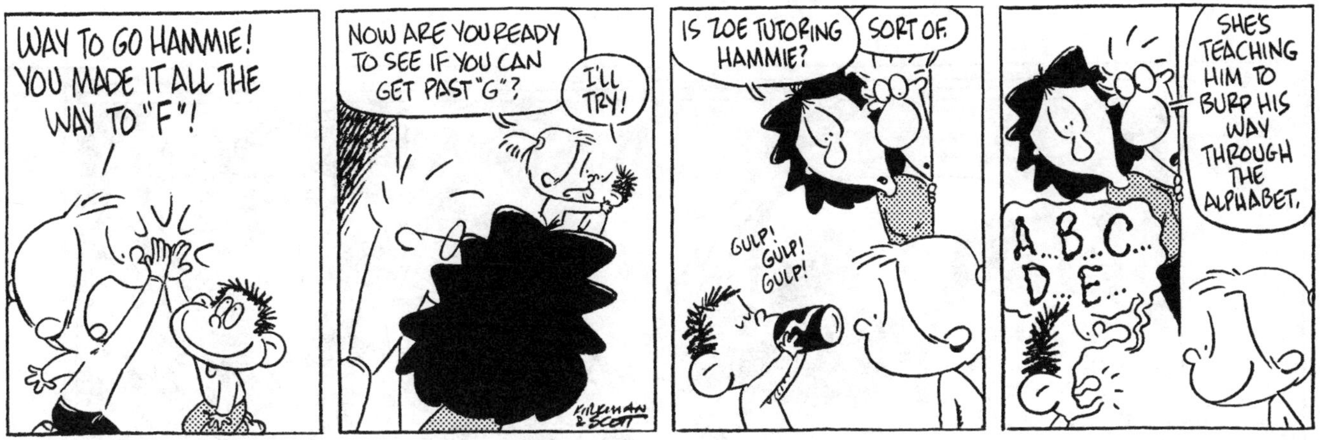
WAY TO GO HAMMIE! YOU MADE IT ALL THE WAY TO "F"!
NOW ARE YOU READY TO SEE IF YOU CAN GET PAST "G"?
I'LL TRY!
KIRKMAN & SCOTT
IS ZOE TUTORING HAMMIE?
SORT OF.
GULP! GULP! GULP!
SHE'S TEACHING HIM TO BURP HIS WAY THROUGH THE ALPHABET.
A..B..C..
D..E..

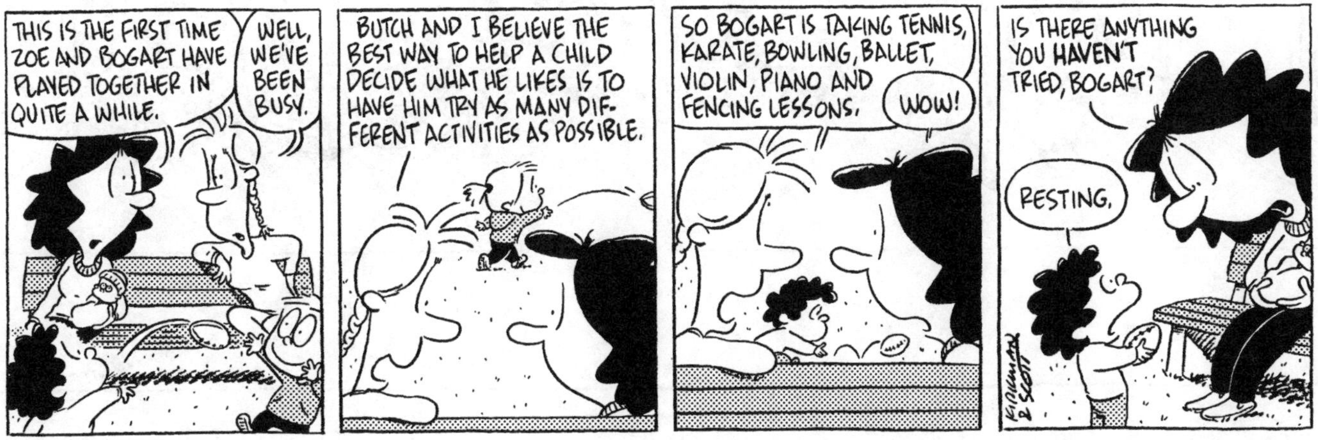
THIS IS THE FIRST TIME ZOE AND BOGART HAVE PLAYED TOGETHER IN QUITE A WHILE.
WELL, WE'VE BEEN BUSY.
BUTCH AND I BELIEVE THE BEST WAY TO HELP A CHILD DECIDE WHAT HE LIKES IS TO HAVE HIM TRY AS MANY DIFFERENT ACTIVITIES AS POSSIBLE.
SO BOGART IS TAKING TENNIS, KARATE, BOWLING, BALLET, VIOLIN, PIANO AND FENCING LESSONS.
WOW!
IS THERE ANYTHING YOU HAVEN'T TRIED, BOGART?
RESTING.
KIRKMAN & SCOTT

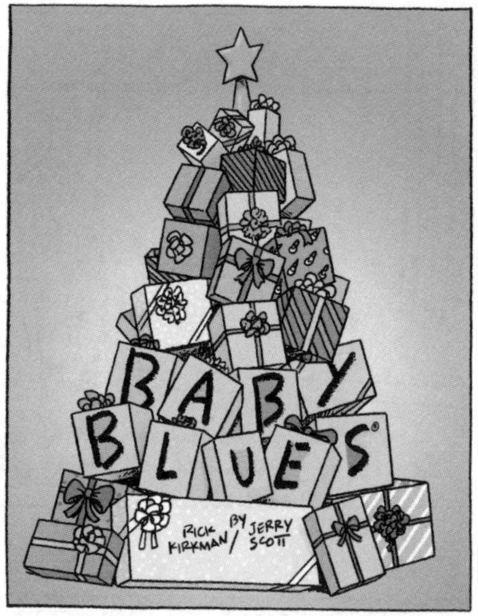
BABY BLUES®
RICK KIRKMAN / BY JERRY SCOTT

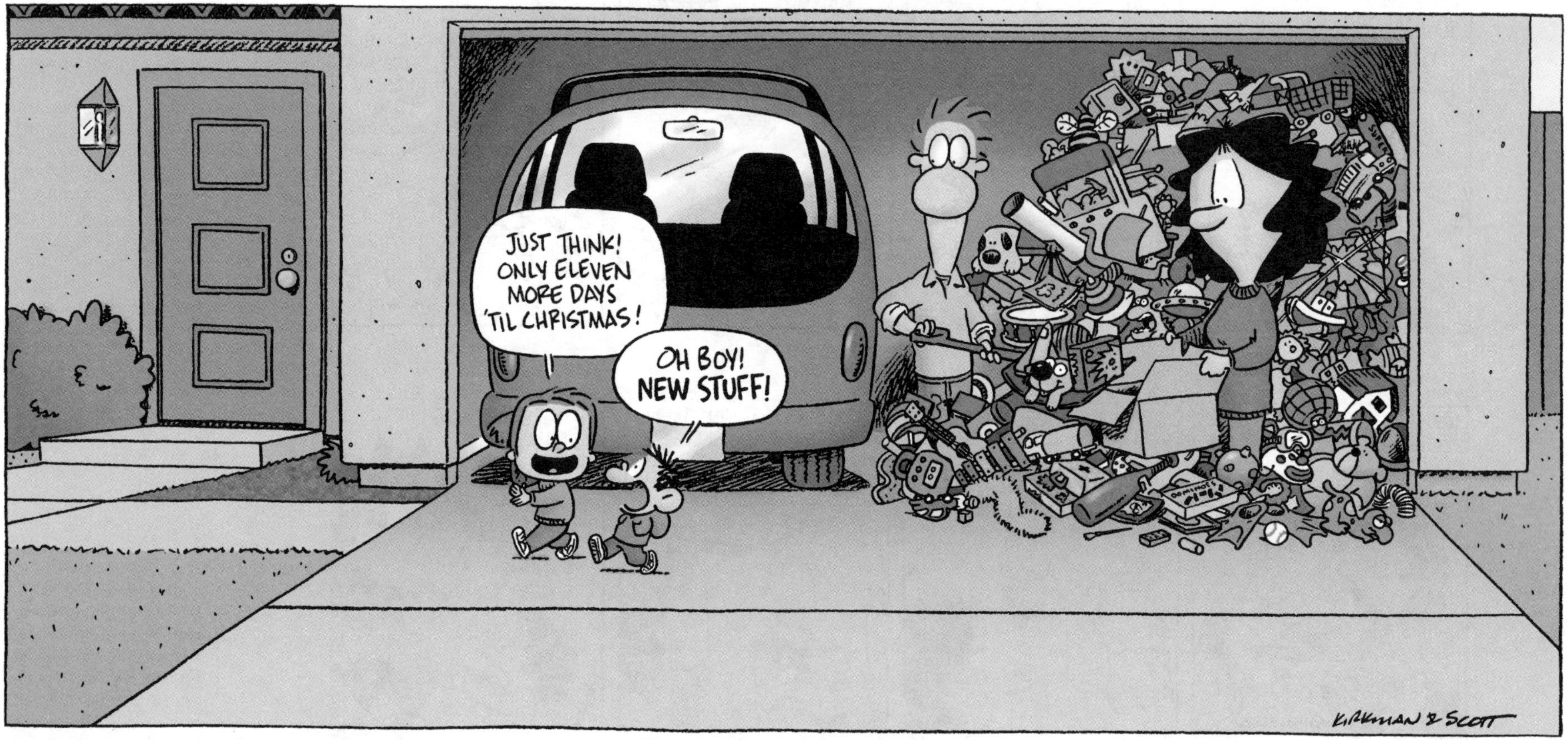
JUST THINK! ONLY ELEVEN MORE DAYS 'TIL CHRISTMAS!
OH BOY! NEW STUFF!
KIRKMAN & SCOTT

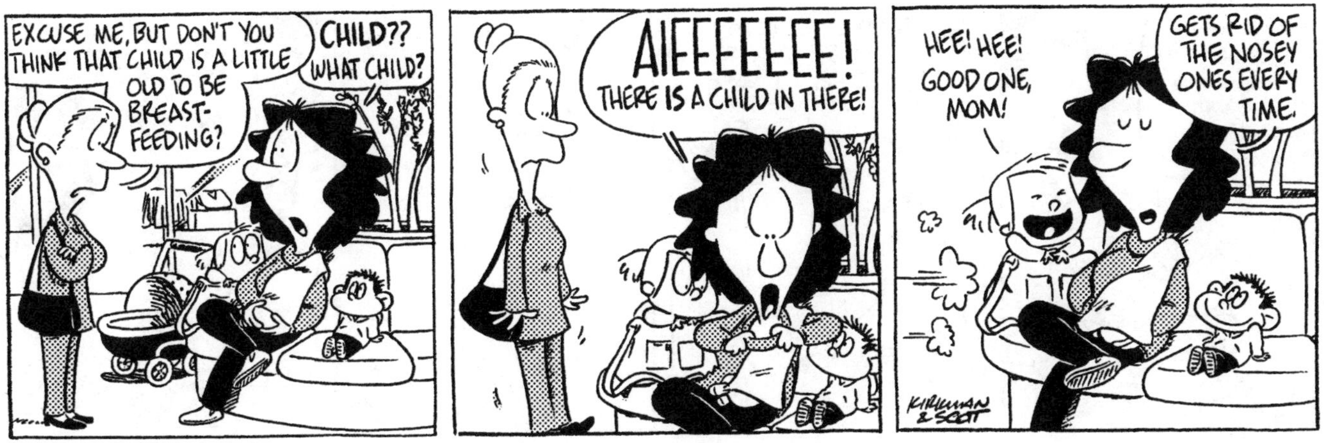
EXCUSE ME, BUT DON'T YOU THINK THAT CHILD IS A LITTLE OLD TO BE BREAST-FEEDING?
CHILD?? WHAT CHILD?
AIEEEEEEE! THERE IS A CHILD IN THERE!
HEE! HEE! GOOD ONE, MOM!
GETS RID OF THE NOSEY ONES EVERY TIME.
KIRKMAN & SCOTT

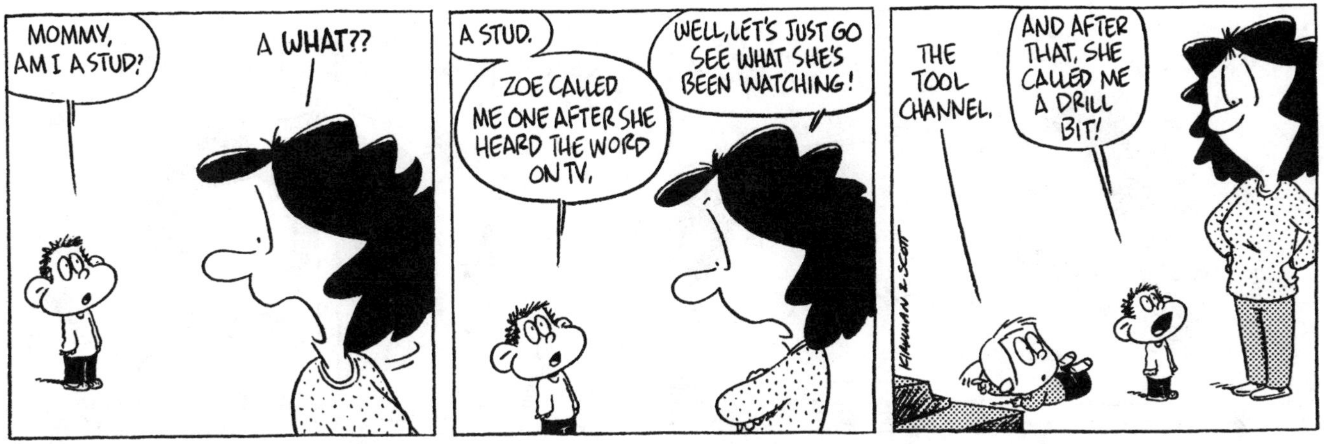
MOMMY, AM I A STUD?
A WHAT??
A STUD.
ZOE CALLED ME ONE AFTER SHE HEARD THE WORD ON TV.
WELL, LET'S JUST GO SEE WHAT SHE'S BEEN WATCHING!
THE TOOL CHANNEL.
AND AFTER THAT, SHE CALLED ME A DRILL BIT!
KIRKMAN & SCOTT

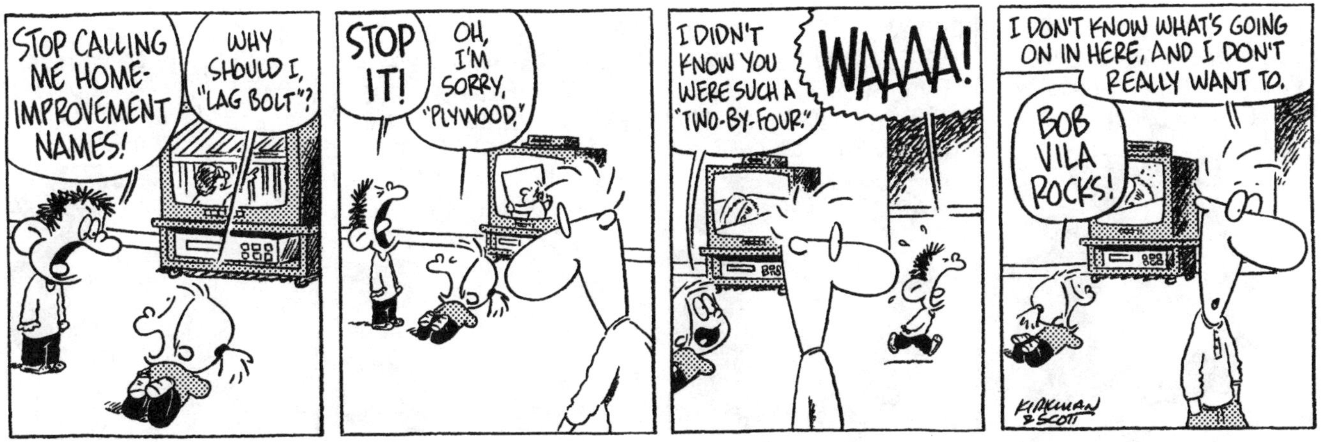
STOP CALLING ME HOME-IMPROVEMENT NAMES!
WHY SHOULD I, "LAG BOLT"?
STOP IT!
OH, I'M SORRY, "PLYWOOD."
I DIDN'T KNOW YOU WERE SUCH A "TWO-BY-FOUR."
WAAAA!
I DON'T KNOW WHAT'S GOING ON IN HERE, AND I DON'T REALLY WANT TO.
BOB VILA ROCKS!
KIRKMAN & SCOTT

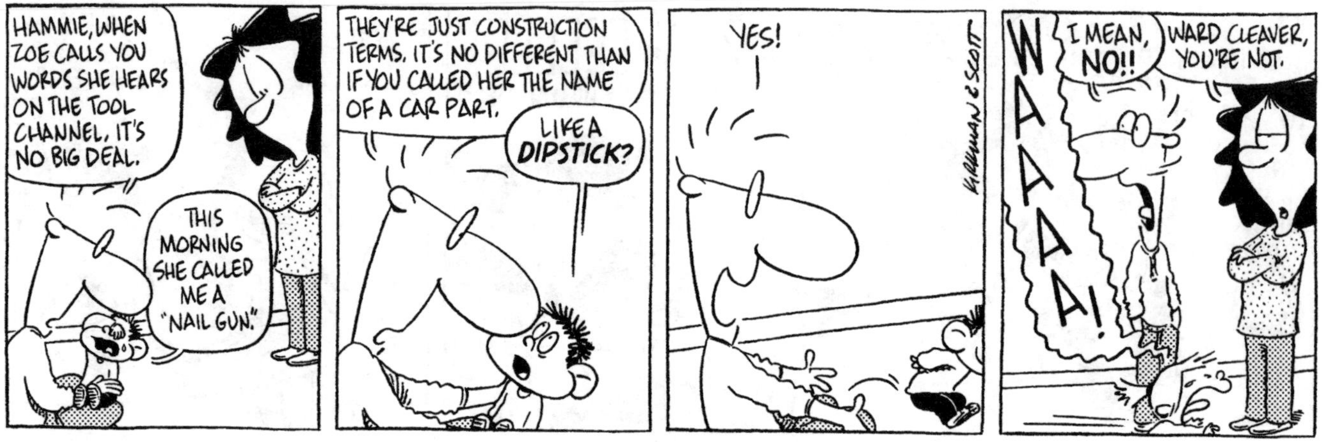
HAMMIE, WHEN ZOE CALLS YOU WORDS SHE HEARS ON THE TOOL CHANNEL, IT'S NO BIG DEAL.
THIS MORNING SHE CALLED ME A "NAIL GUN."
THEY'RE JUST CONSTRUCTION TERMS. IT'S NO DIFFERENT THAN IF YOU CALLED HER THE NAME OF A CAR PART.
LIKE A DIPSTICK?
YES!
KIRKMAN & SCOTT
WAAAAA!
I MEAN, NO!!
WARD CLEAVER, YOU'RE NOT.

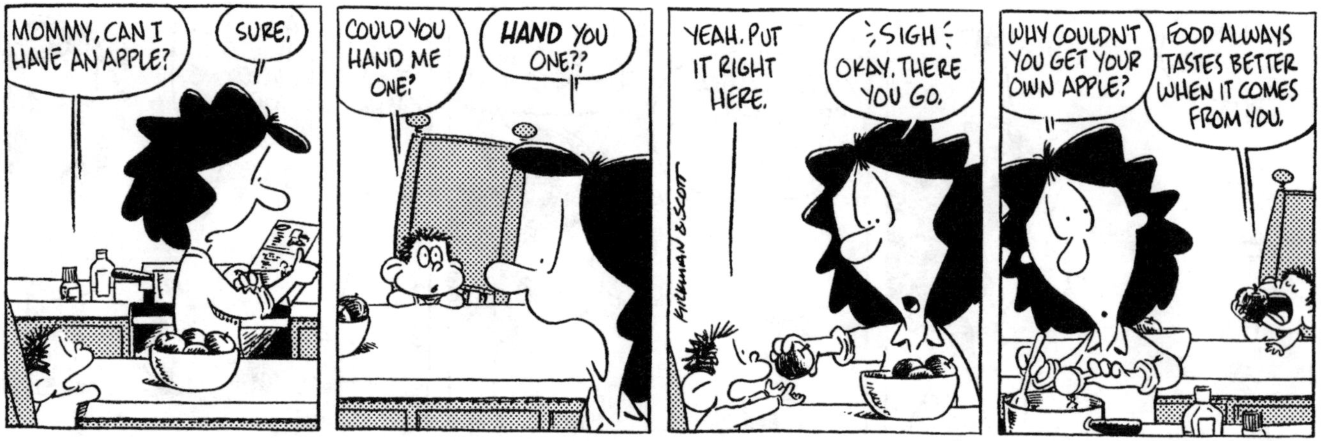
MOMMY, CAN I HAVE AN APPLE?
SURE.
COULD YOU HAND ME ONE?
HAND YOU ONE??
YEAH. PUT IT RIGHT HERE.
KIRKMAN & SCOTT
SIGH
OKAY. THERE YOU GO.
WHY COULDN'T YOU GET YOUR OWN APPLE?
FOOD ALWAYS TASTES BETTER WHEN IT COMES FROM YOU.

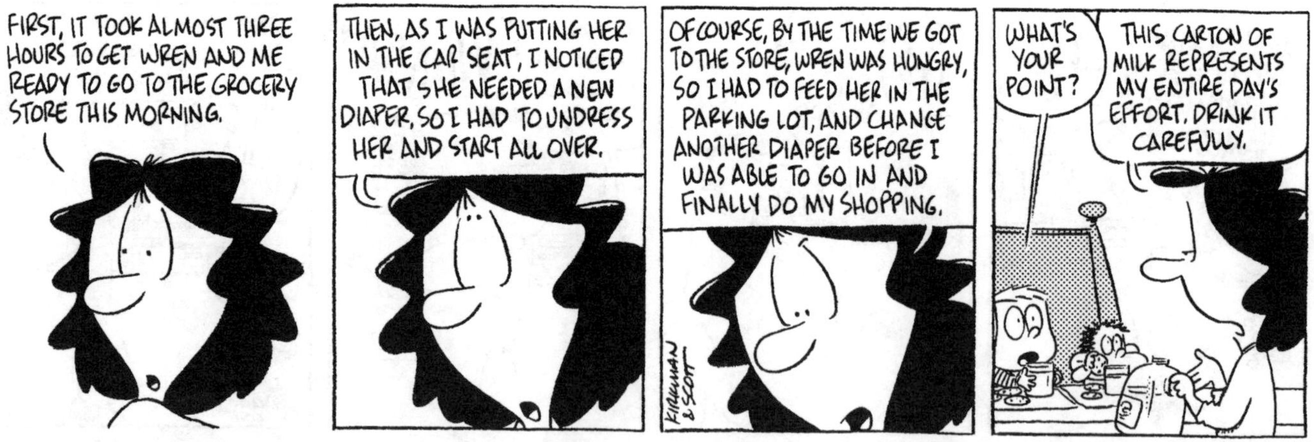
FIRST, IT TOOK ALMOST THREE HOURS TO GET WREN AND ME READY TO GO TO THE GROCERY STORE THIS MORNING.
THEN, AS I WAS PUTTING HER IN THE CAR SEAT, I NOTICED THAT SHE NEEDED A NEW DIAPER, SO I HAD TO UNDRESS HER AND START ALL OVER.
OF COURSE, BY THE TIME WE GOT TO THE STORE, WREN WAS HUNGRY, SO I HAD TO FEED HER IN THE PARKING LOT, AND CHANGE ANOTHER DIAPER BEFORE I WAS ABLE TO GO IN AND FINALLY DO MY SHOPPING.
KIRKMAN & SCOTT
WHAT'S YOUR POINT?
THIS CARTON OF MILK REPRESENTS MY ENTIRE DAY'S EFFORT. DRINK IT CAREFULLY.

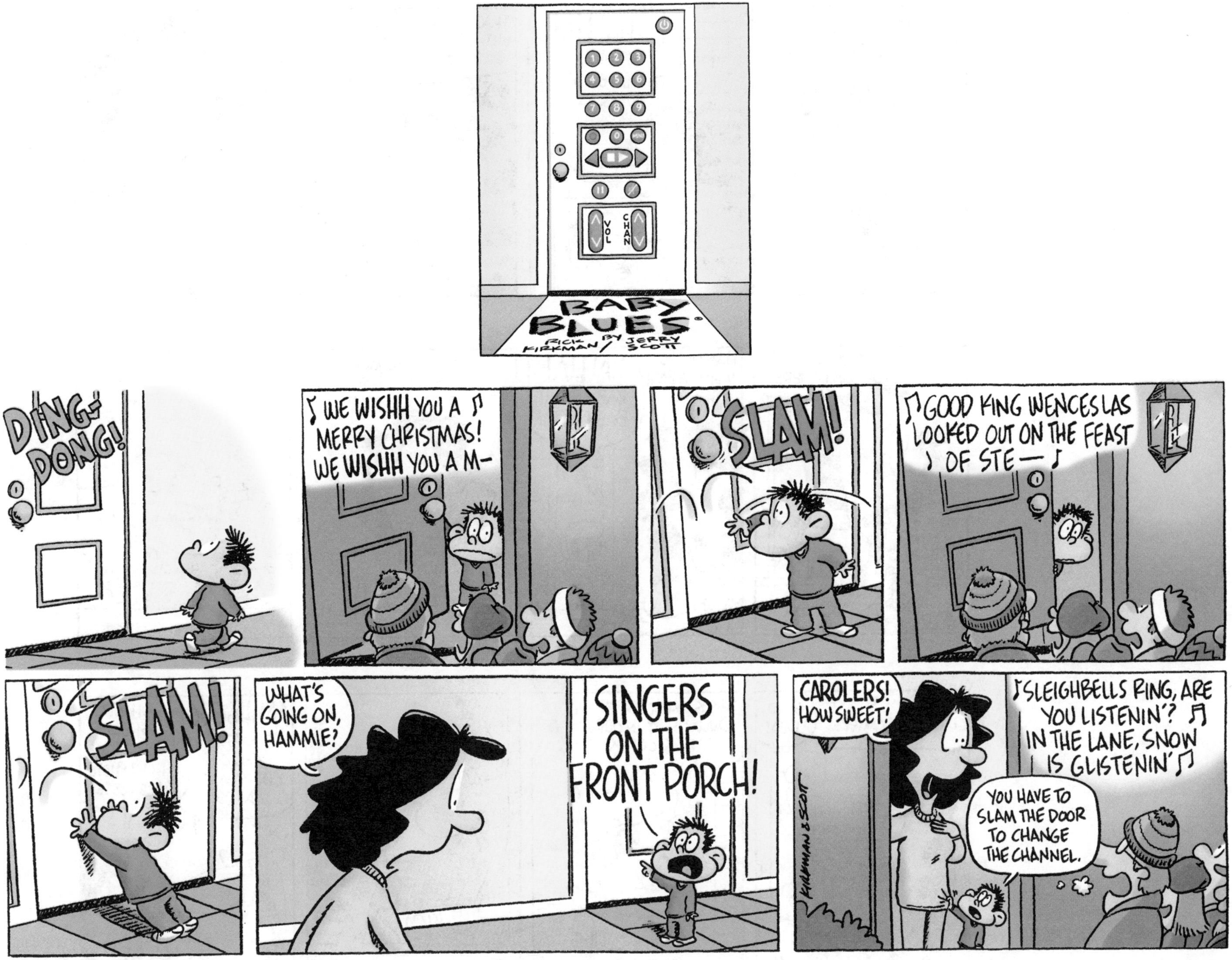
VOL
CHAN
BABY BLUES®
BY RICK KIRKMAN / JERRY SCOTT
DING-DONG!
♪ WE WISHH YOU A ♪ MERRY CHRISTMAS! WE WISHH YOU A M-
SLAM!
♪ GOOD KING WENCESLAS LOOKED OUT ON THE FEAST OF STE— ♪
SLAM!
WHAT'S GOING ON, HAMMIE?
SINGERS ON THE FRONT PORCH!
CAROLERS! HOW SWEET!
♪ SLEIGHBELLS RING, ARE YOU LISTENIN'? ♪ IN THE LANE, SNOW IS GLISTENIN' ♪
YOU HAVE TO SLAM THE DOOR TO CHANGE THE CHANNEL.
KIRKMAN & SCOTT

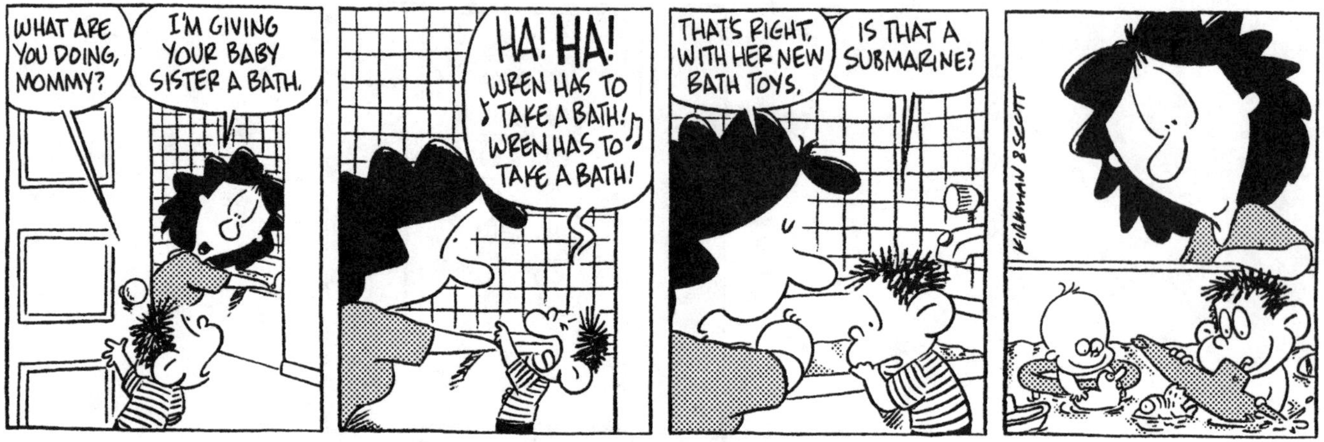
WHAT ARE YOU DOING, MOMMY?
I'M GIVING YOUR BABY SISTER A BATH.
HA! HA! WREN HAS TO TAKE A BATH! WREN HAS TO TAKE A BATH!
THAT'S RIGHT, WITH HER NEW BATH TOYS.
IS THAT A SUBMARINE?
KIRKMAN & SCOTT

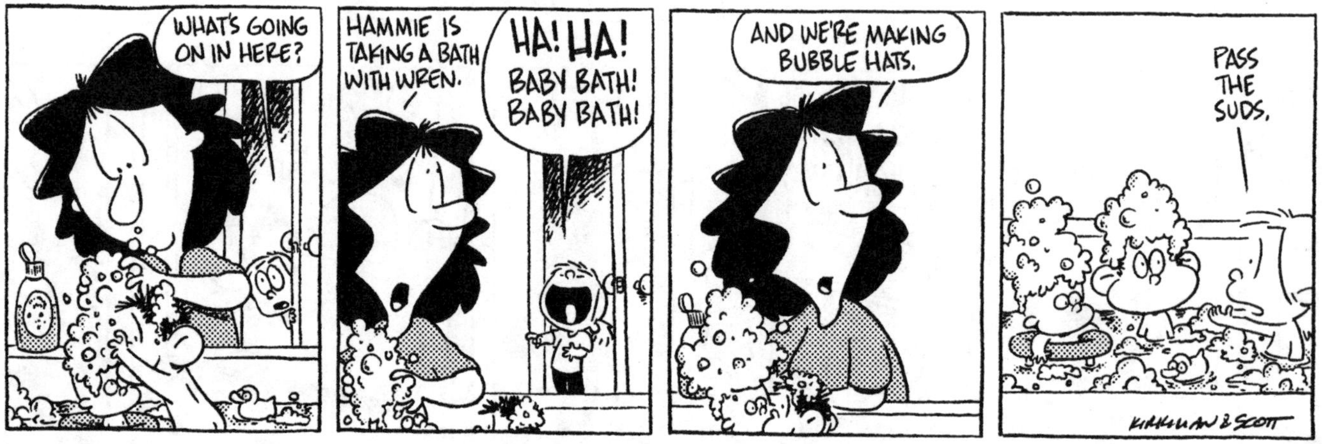
WHAT'S GOING ON IN HERE?
HAMMIE IS TAKING A BATH WITH WREN.
HA! HA! BABY BATH! BABY BATH!
AND WE'RE MAKING BUBBLE HATS.
PASS THE SUDS.
KIRKMAN & SCOTT

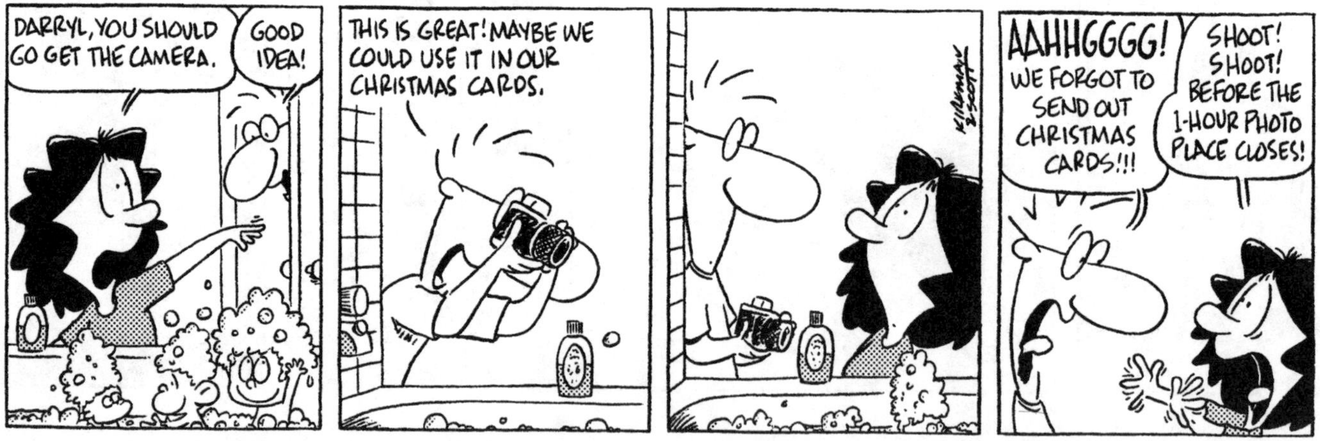
DARRYL, YOU SHOULD GO GET THE CAMERA.
GOOD IDEA!
THIS IS GREAT! MAYBE WE COULD USE IT IN OUR CHRISTMAS CARDS.
KIRKMAN & SCOTT
AAHHGGGG! WE FORGOT TO SEND OUT CHRISTMAS CARDS!!!
SHOOT! SHOOT! BEFORE THE 1-HOUR PHOTO PLACE CLOSES!

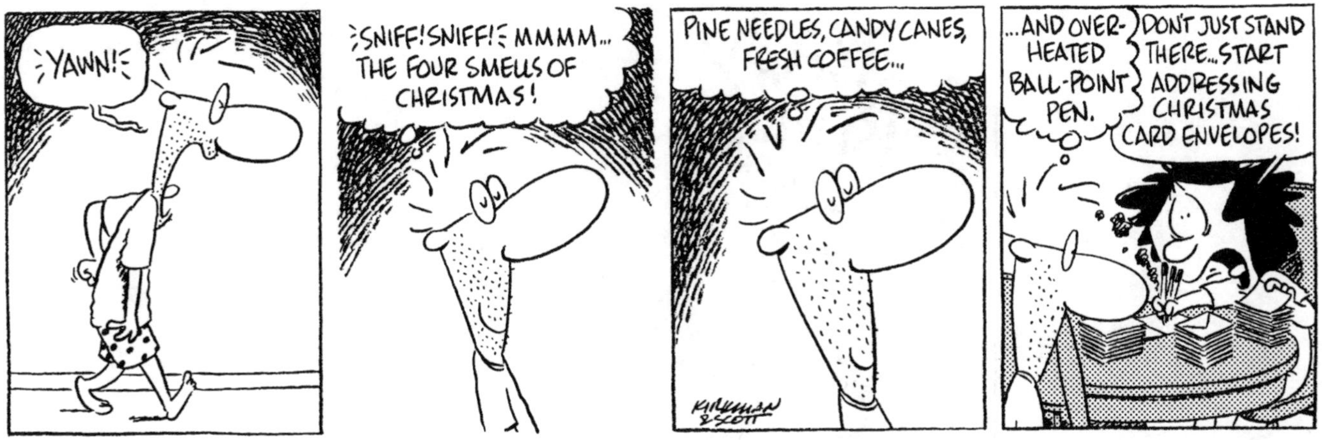
YAWN!
SNIFF! SNIFF! MMMM... THE FOUR SMELLS OF CHRISTMAS!
PINE NEEDLES, CANDY CANES, FRESH COFFEE...
...AND OVER-HEATED BALL-POINT PEN.
DON'T JUST STAND THERE... START ADDRESSING CHRISTMAS CARD ENVELOPES!
KIRKMAN & SCOTT

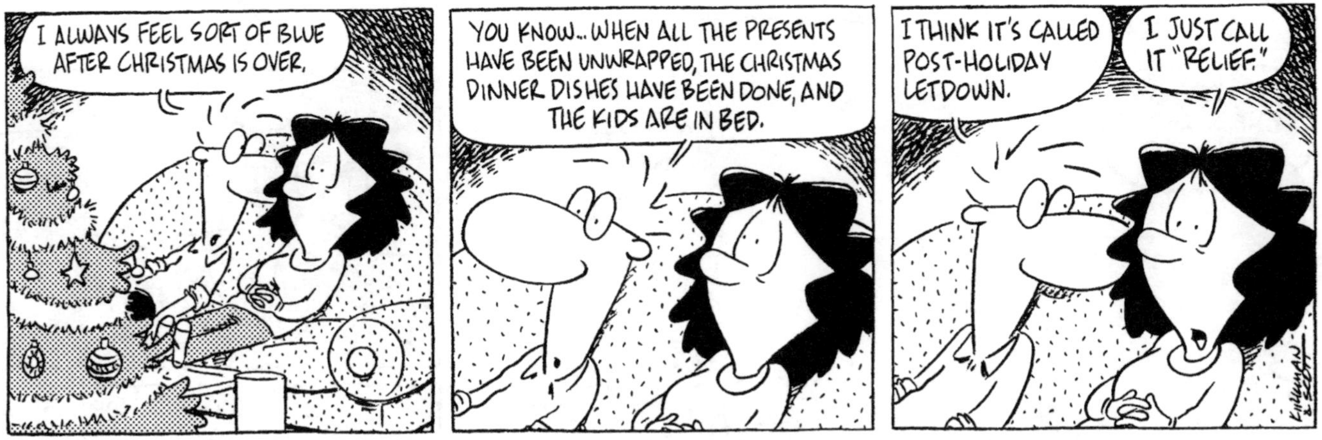
I ALWAYS FEEL SORT OF BLUE AFTER CHRISTMAS IS OVER.
YOU KNOW... WHEN ALL THE PRESENTS HAVE BEEN UNWRAPPED, THE CHRISTMAS DINNER DISHES HAVE BEEN DONE, AND THE KIDS ARE IN BED.
I THINK IT'S CALLED POST-HOLIDAY LETDOWN.
I JUST CALL IT "RELIEF."

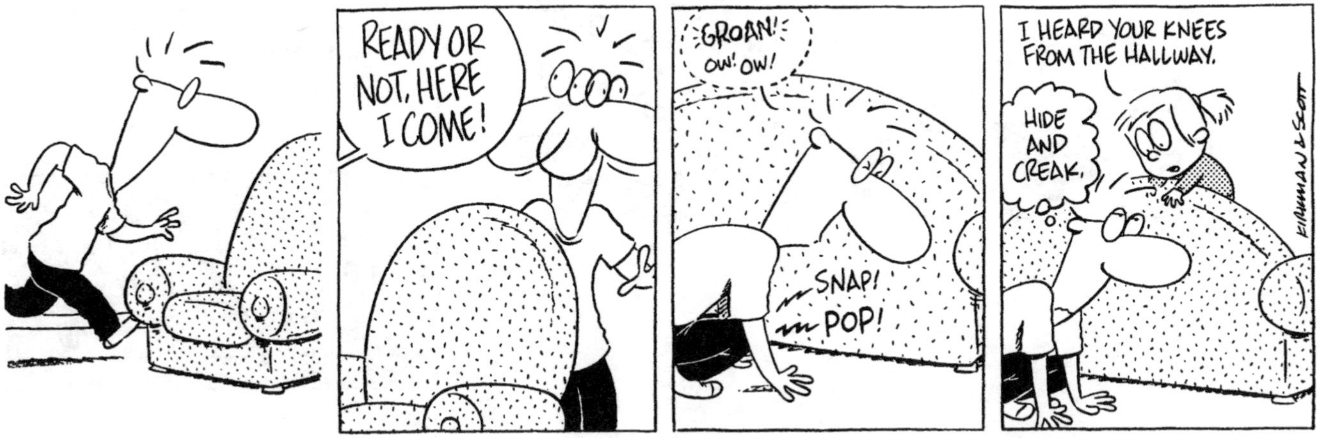
READY OR NOT, HERE I COME!
GROAN! OW! OW!
SNAP!
POP!
I HEARD YOUR KNEES FROM THE HALLWAY.
HIDE AND CREAK.
KIRKMAN & SCOTT

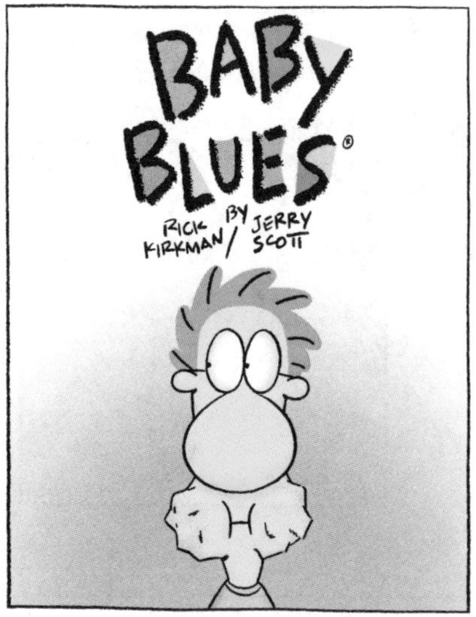
BABY BLUES®
BY RICK KIRKMAN / JERRY SCOTT

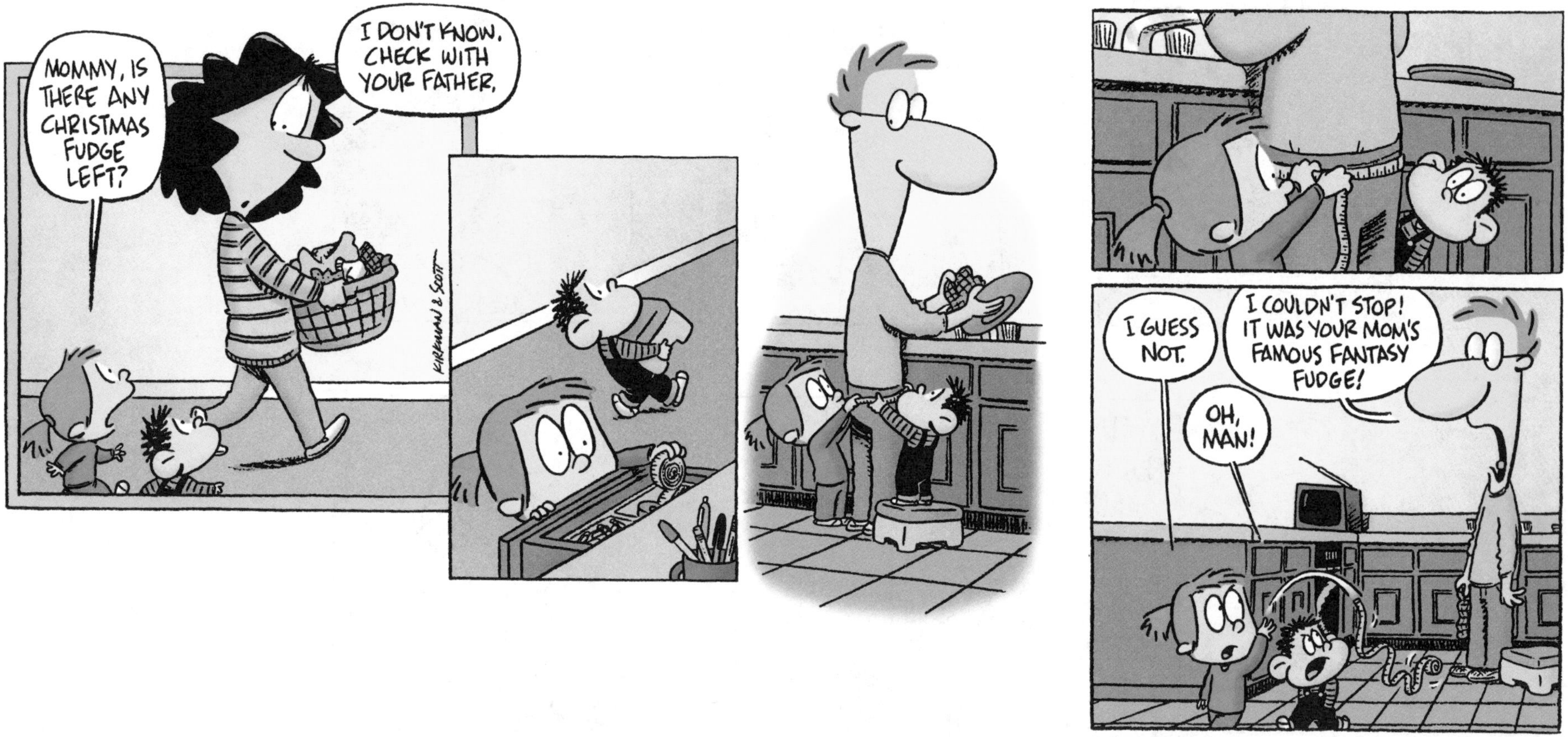
MOMMY, IS THERE ANY CHRISTMAS FUDGE LEFT?
I DON'T KNOW. CHECK WITH YOUR FATHER.
KIRKMAN & SCOTT
I GUESS NOT.
I COULDN'T STOP! IT WAS YOUR MOM'S FAMOUS FANTASY FUDGE!
OH, MAN!

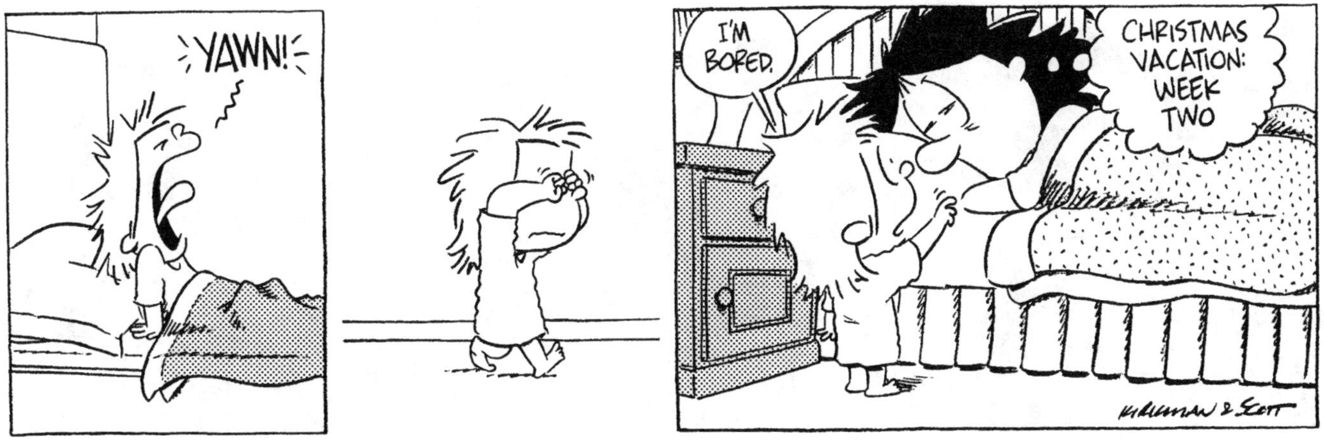
YAWN!
I'M BORED.
CHRISTMAS VACATION: WEEK TWO

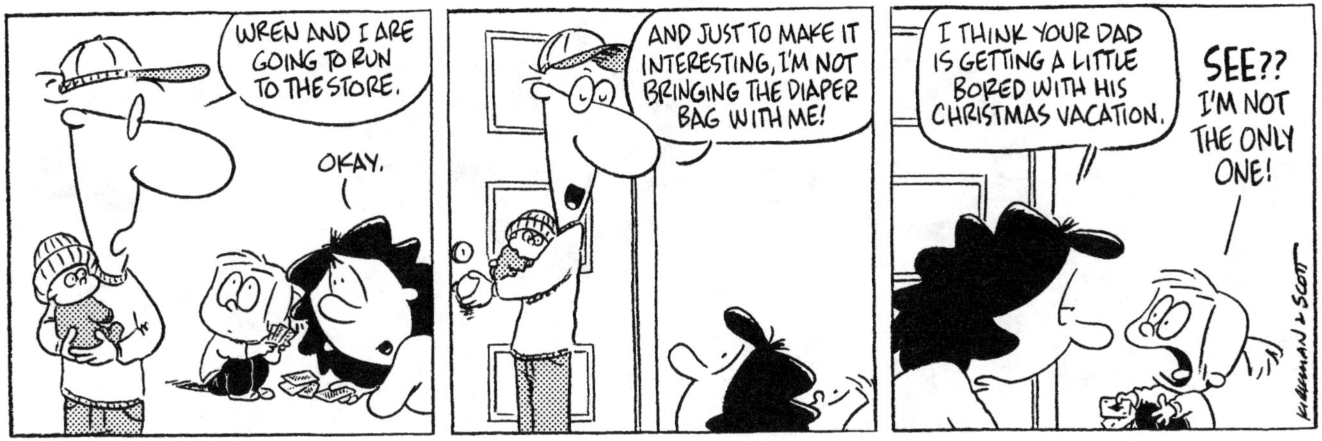
WREN AND I ARE GOING TO RUN TO THE STORE.
OKAY.
AND JUST TO MAKE IT INTERESTING, I'M NOT BRINGING THE DIAPER BAG WITH ME!
I THINK YOUR DAD IS GETTING A LITTLE BORED WITH HIS CHRISTMAS VACATION.
SEE?? I'M NOT THE ONLY ONE!

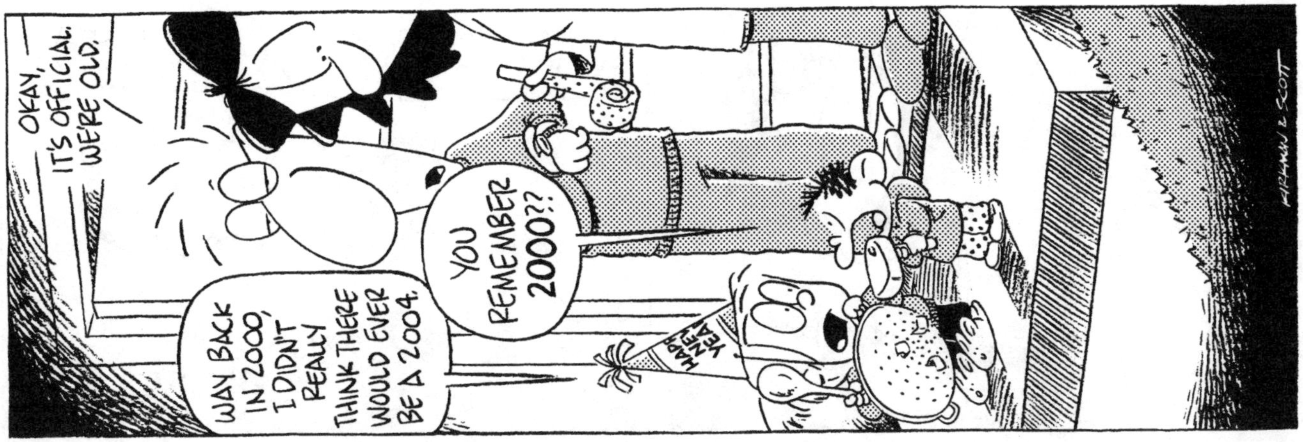
WAY BACK IN 2000, I DIDN'T REALLY THINK THERE WOULD EVER BE A 2004.
YOU REMEMBER 2000??
OKAY, IT'S OFFICIAL. WE'RE OLD.

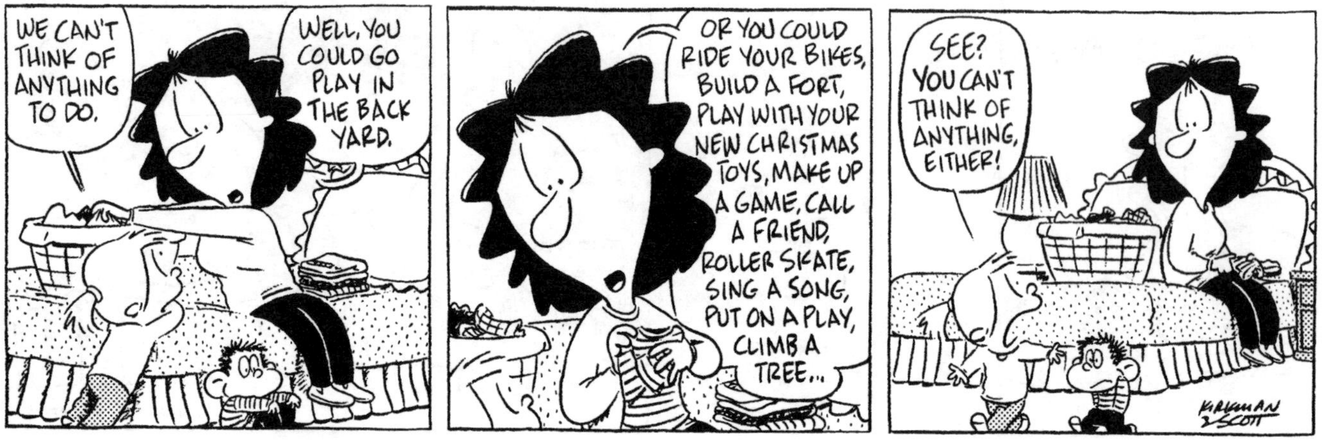
WE CAN'T THINK OF ANYTHING TO DO.
WELL, YOU COULD GO PLAY IN THE BACK YARD.
OR YOU COULD RIDE YOUR BIKES, BUILD A FORT, PLAY WITH YOUR NEW CHRISTMAS TOYS, MAKE UP A GAME, CALL A FRIEND, ROLLER SKATE, SING A SONG, PUT ON A PLAY, CLIMB A TREE...
SEE? YOU CAN'T THINK OF ANYTHING, EITHER!
KIRKMAN & SCOTT

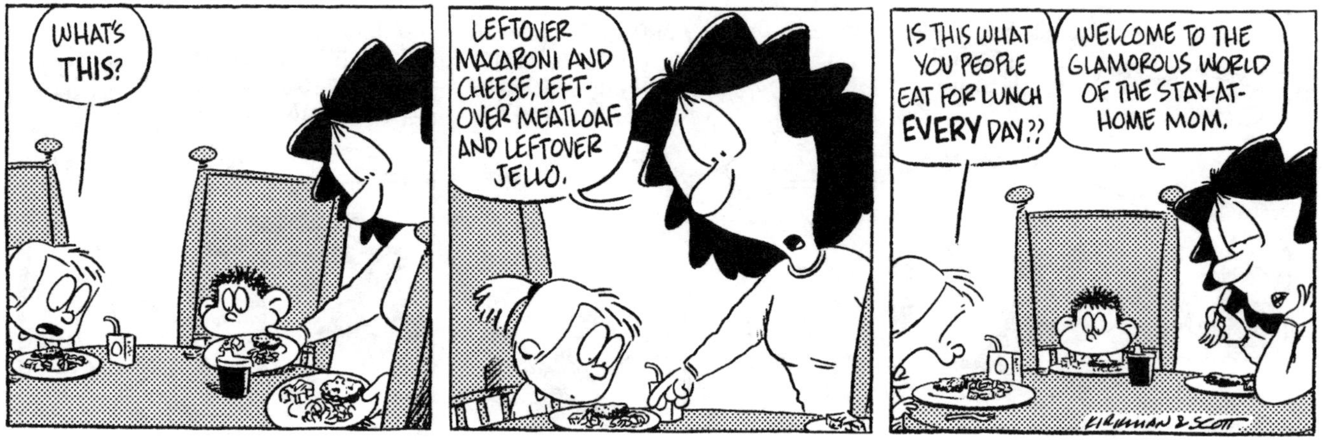
WHAT'S THIS?
LEFTOVER MACARONI AND CHEESE, LEFT-OVER MEATLOAF AND LEFTOVER JELLO.
IS THIS WHAT YOU PEOPLE EAT FOR LUNCH EVERY DAY??
WELCOME TO THE GLAMOROUS WORLD OF THE STAY-AT-HOME MOM.
KIRKMAN & SCOTT

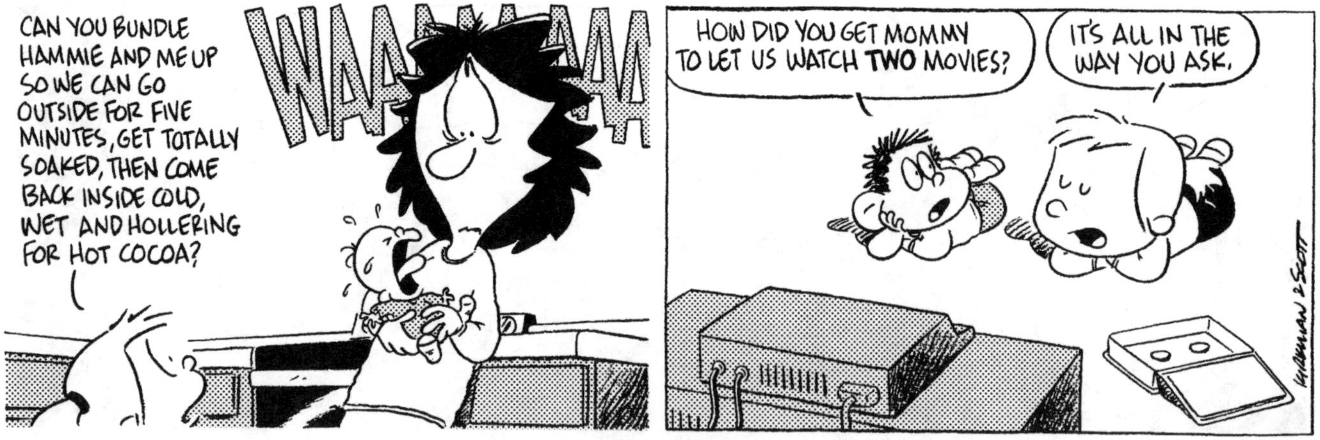
CAN YOU BUNDLE HAMMIE AND ME UP SO WE CAN GO OUTSIDE FOR FIVE MINUTES, GET TOTALLY SOAKED, THEN COME BACK INSIDE COLD, WET AND HOLLERING FOR HOT COCOA?
WAAAAAAA
HOW DID YOU GET MOMMY TO LET US WATCH TWO MOVIES?
IT'S ALL IN THE WAY YOU ASK.
KIRKMAN & SCOTT

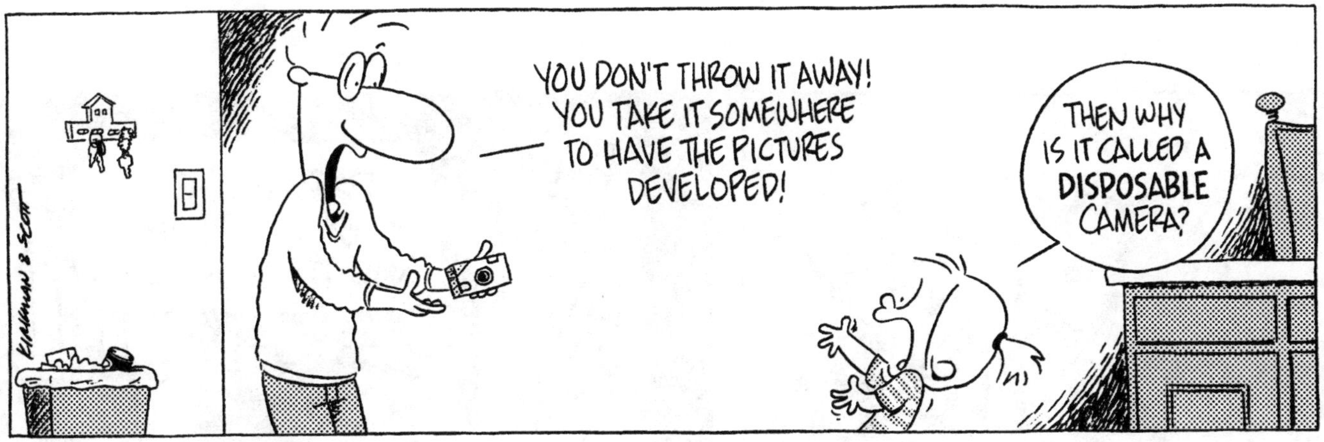
YOU DON'T THROW IT AWAY! YOU TAKE IT SOMEWHERE TO HAVE THE PICTURES DEVELOPED!
THEN WHY IS IT CALLED A **DISPOSABLE** CAMERA?

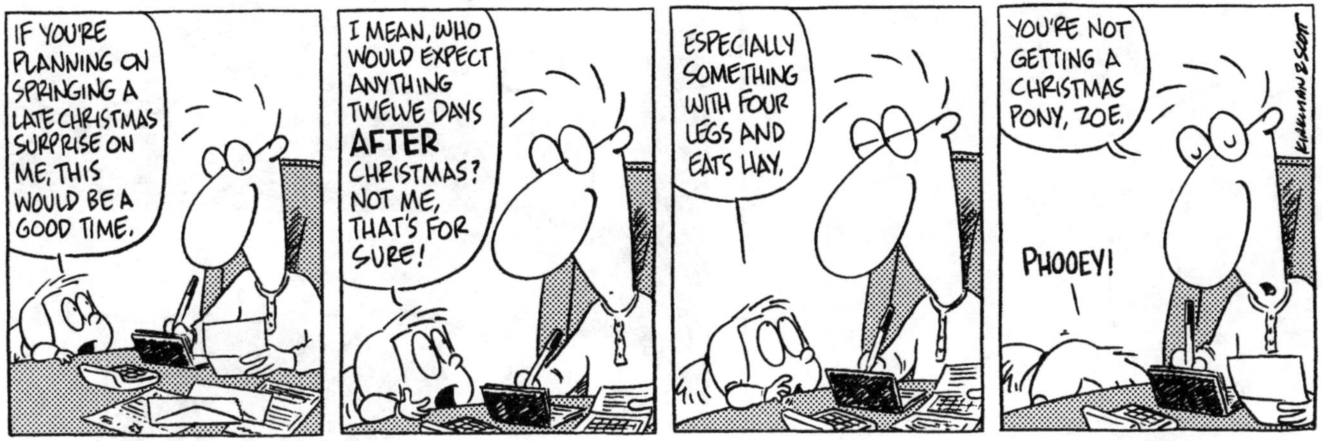
IF YOU'RE PLANNING ON SPRINGING A LATE CHRISTMAS SURPRISE ON ME, THIS WOULD BE A GOOD TIME.
I MEAN, WHO WOULD EXPECT ANYTHING TWELVE DAYS **AFTER** CHRISTMAS? NOT ME, THAT'S FOR SURE!
ESPECIALLY SOMETHING WITH FOUR LEGS AND EATS HAY.
YOU'RE NOT GETTING A CHRISTMAS PONY, ZOE.
PHOOEY!

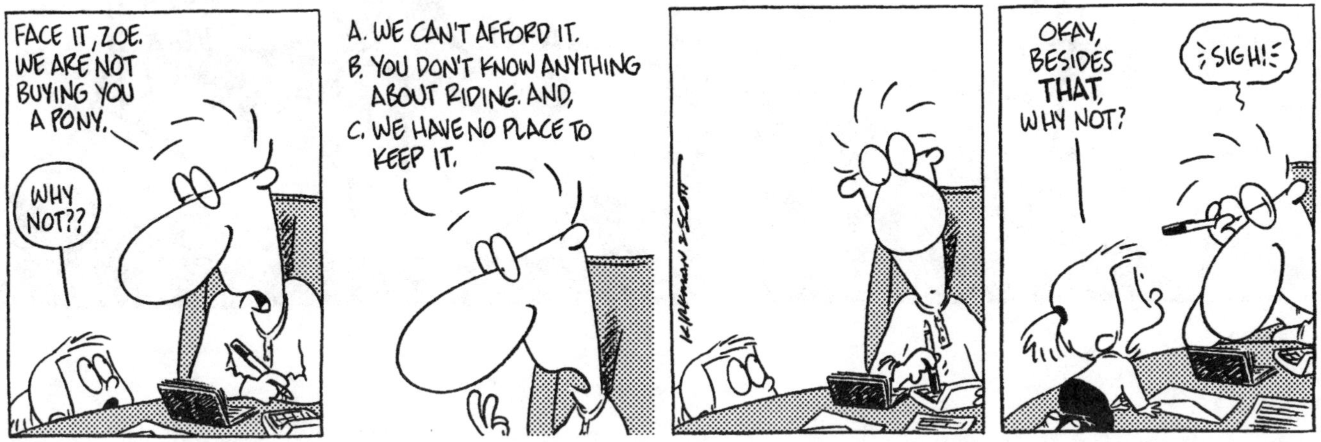
FACE IT, ZOE. WE ARE NOT BUYING YOU A PONY.
WHY NOT??
A. WE CAN'T AFFORD IT.
B. YOU DON'T KNOW ANYTHING ABOUT RIDING. AND,
C. WE HAVE NO PLACE TO KEEP IT.
OKAY, BESIDES **THAT**, WHY NOT?
SIGH!

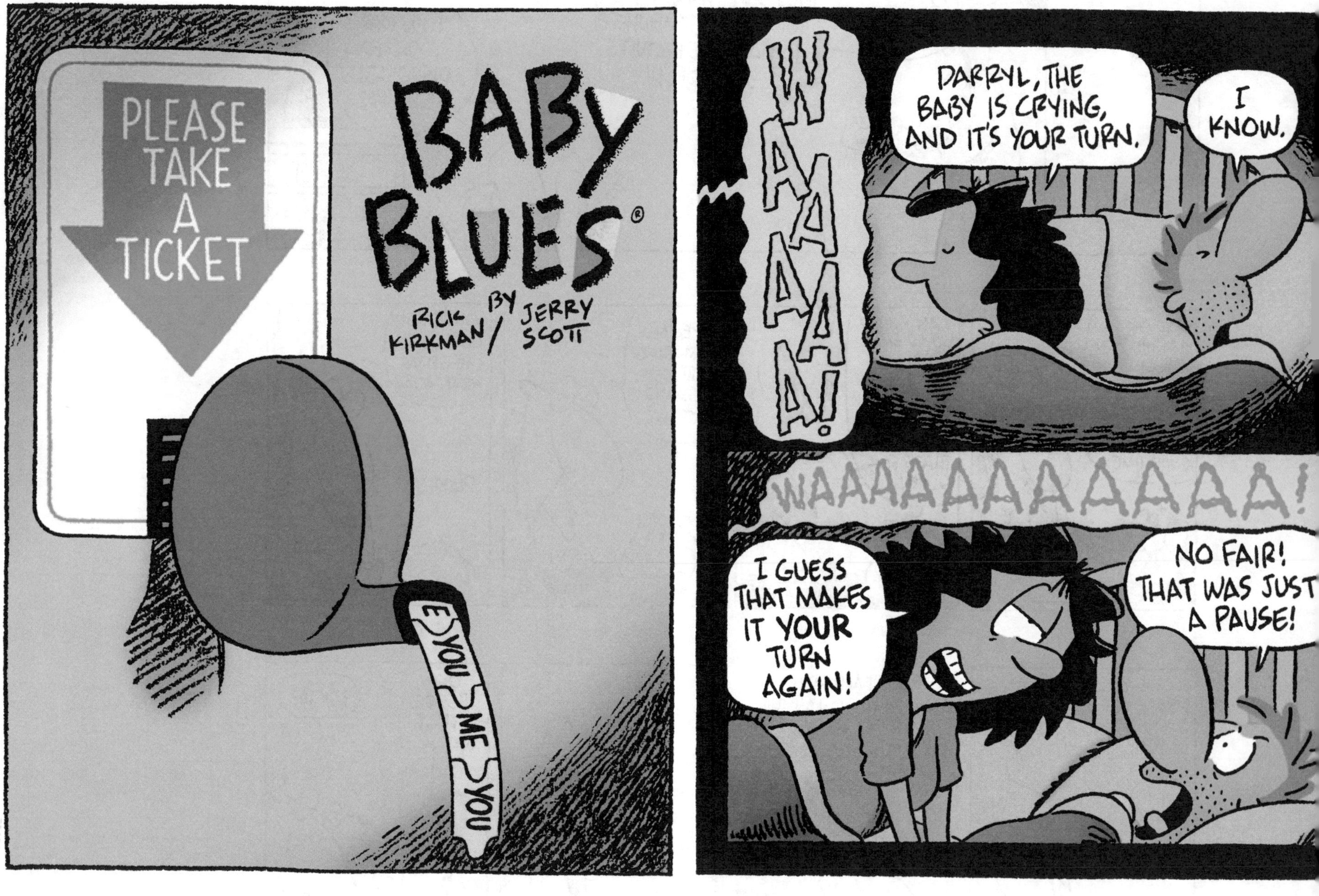
PLEASE TAKE A TICKET
BABY BLUES®
BY RICK KIRKMAN / JERRY SCOTT
E YOU ME YOU
WAAAAA!
DARRYL, THE BABY IS CRYING, AND IT'S YOUR TURN.
I KNOW.
WAAAAAAAAAAA!
I GUESS THAT MAKES IT YOUR TURN AGAIN!
NO FAIR! THAT WAS JUST A PAUSE!

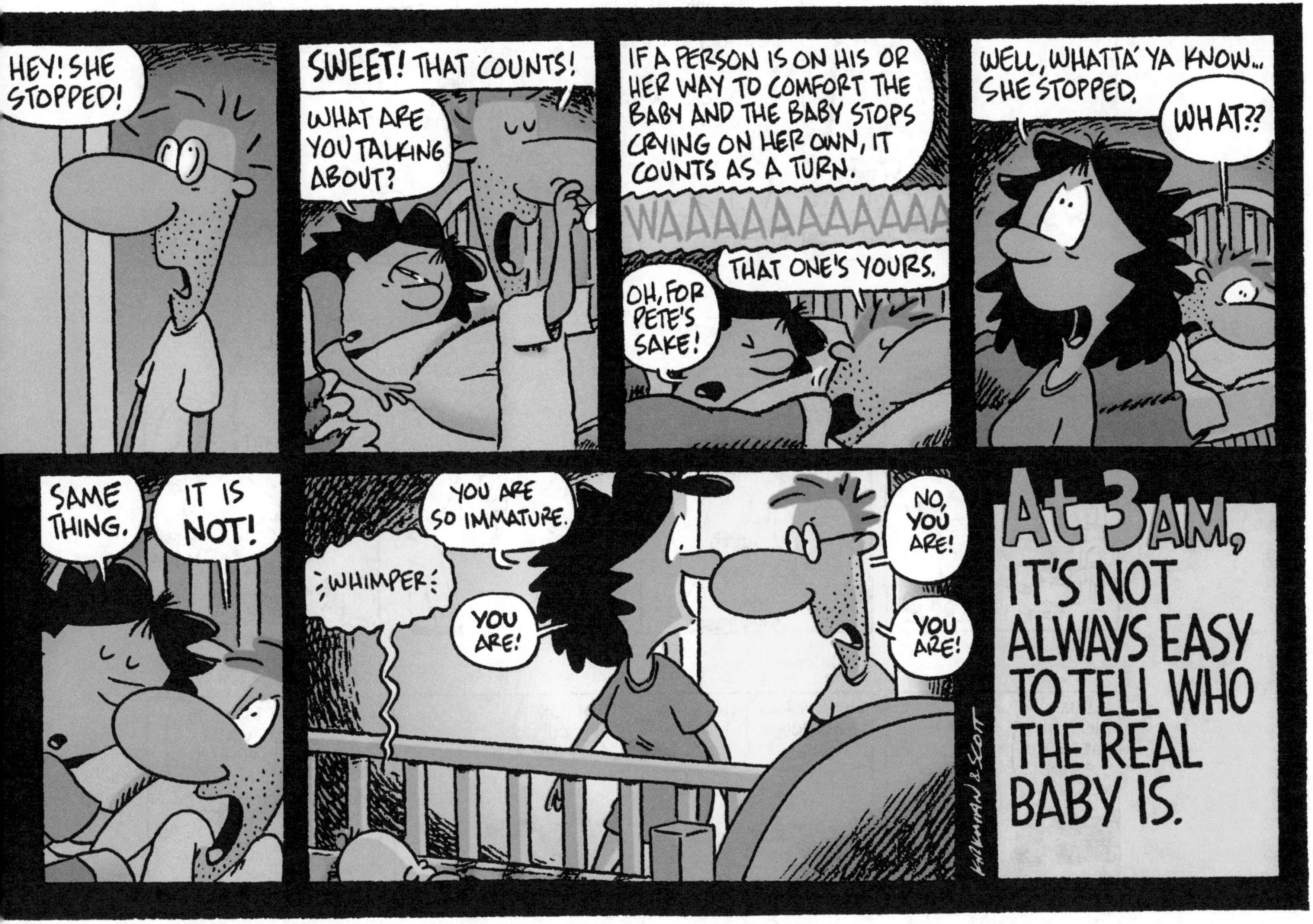
HEY! SHE STOPPED!
SWEET! THAT COUNTS!
WHAT ARE YOU TALKING ABOUT?
IF A PERSON IS ON HIS OR HER WAY TO COMFORT THE BABY AND THE BABY STOPS CRYING ON HER OWN, IT COUNTS AS A TURN.
WAAAAAAAAAAA
THAT ONE'S YOURS.
OH, FOR PETE'S SAKE!
WELL, WHATTA' YA KNOW... SHE STOPPED.
WHAT??
SAME THING.
IT IS NOT!
YOU ARE SO IMMATURE.
NO, YOU ARE!
WHIMPER
YOU ARE!
YOU ARE!
KIRKMAN & SCOTT
At 3AM, IT'S NOT ALWAYS EASY TO TELL WHO THE REAL BABY IS.

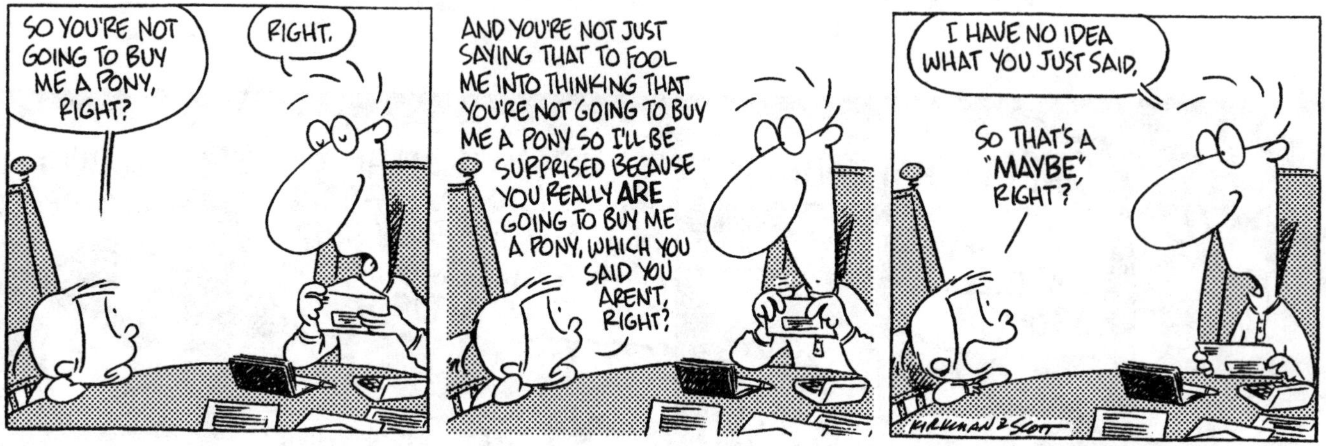
SO YOU'RE NOT GOING TO BUY ME A PONY, RIGHT?
RIGHT.
AND YOU'RE NOT JUST SAYING THAT TO FOOL ME INTO THINKING THAT YOU'RE NOT GOING TO BUY ME A PONY SO I'LL BE SURPRISED BECAUSE YOU REALLY **ARE** GOING TO BUY ME A PONY, WHICH YOU SAID YOU AREN'T, RIGHT?
I HAVE NO IDEA WHAT YOU JUST SAID.
SO THAT'S A "**MAYBE**," RIGHT?
KIRKMAN & SCOTT

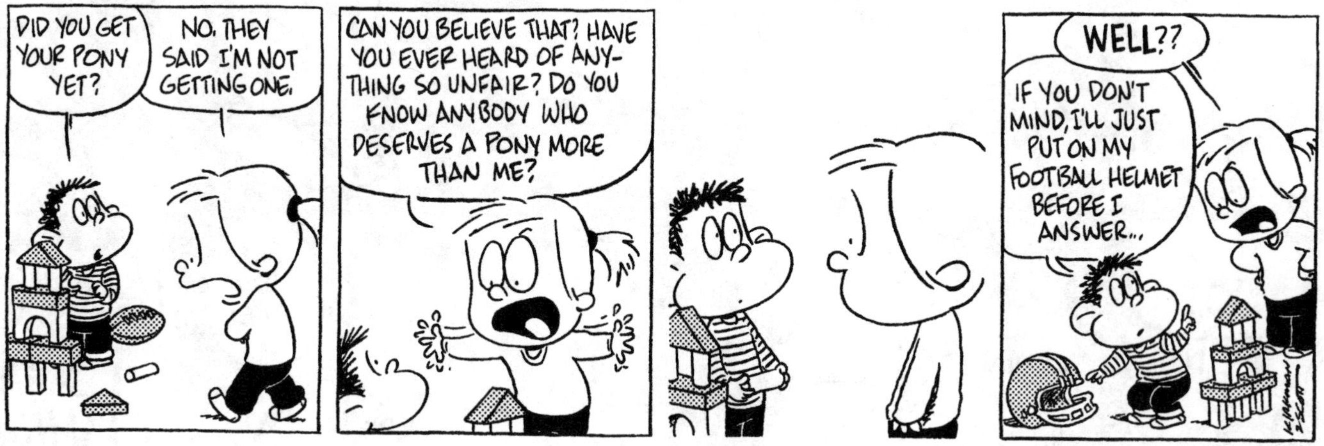
DID YOU GET YOUR PONY YET?
NO. THEY SAID I'M NOT GETTING ONE.
CAN YOU BELIEVE THAT? HAVE YOU EVER HEARD OF ANYTHING SO UNFAIR? DO YOU KNOW ANYBODY WHO DESERVES A PONY MORE THAN ME?
WELL??
IF YOU DON'T MIND, I'LL JUST PUT ON MY FOOTBALL HELMET BEFORE I ANSWER...
KIRKMAN & SCOTT

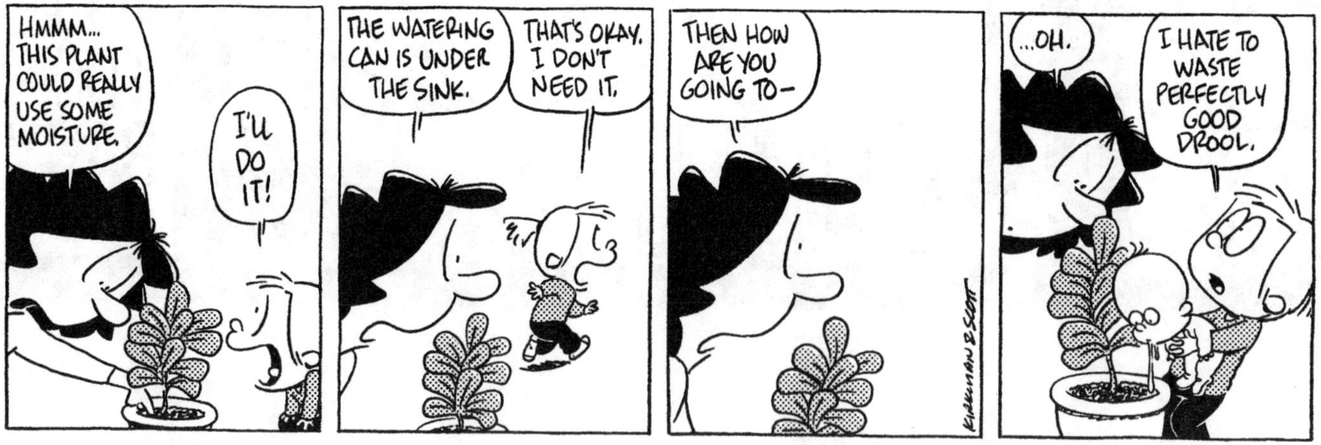
HMMM... THIS PLANT COULD REALLY USE SOME MOISTURE.
I'LL DO IT!
THE WATERING CAN IS UNDER THE SINK.
THAT'S OKAY. I DON'T NEED IT.
THEN HOW ARE YOU GOING TO—
KIRKMAN & SCOTT
...OH.
I HATE TO WASTE PERFECTLY GOOD DROOL.

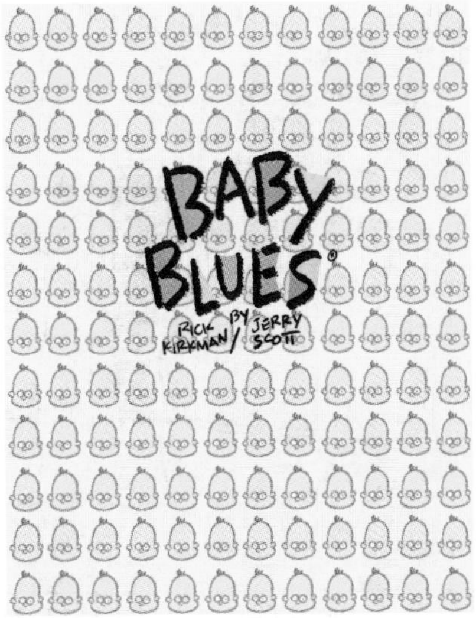
BABY BLUES®
RICK KIRKMAN / BY / JERRY SCOTT

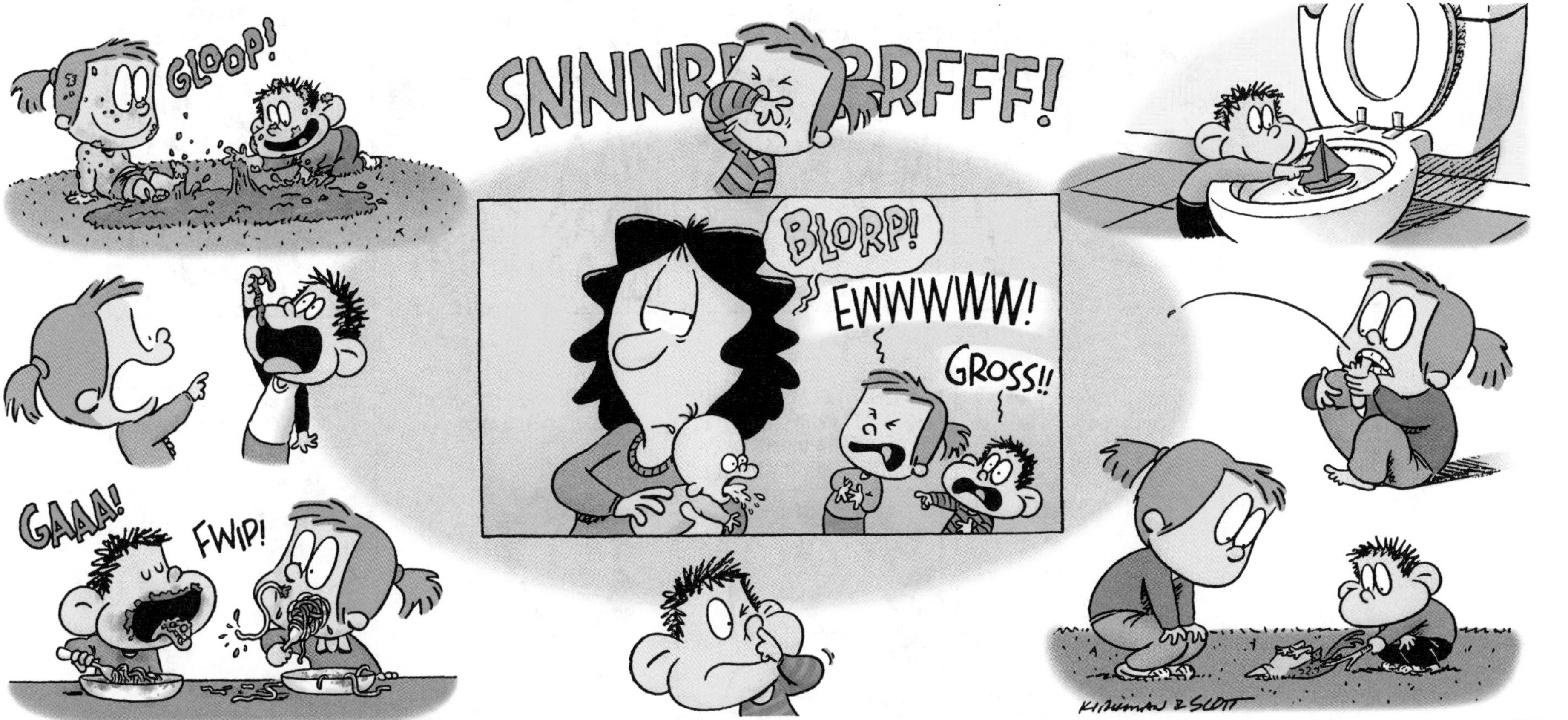
GLOOP!
SNNR
RFFF!
BLORP!
EWWWWW!
GROSS!!
GAAA!
FWIP!
KIRKMAN & SCOTT

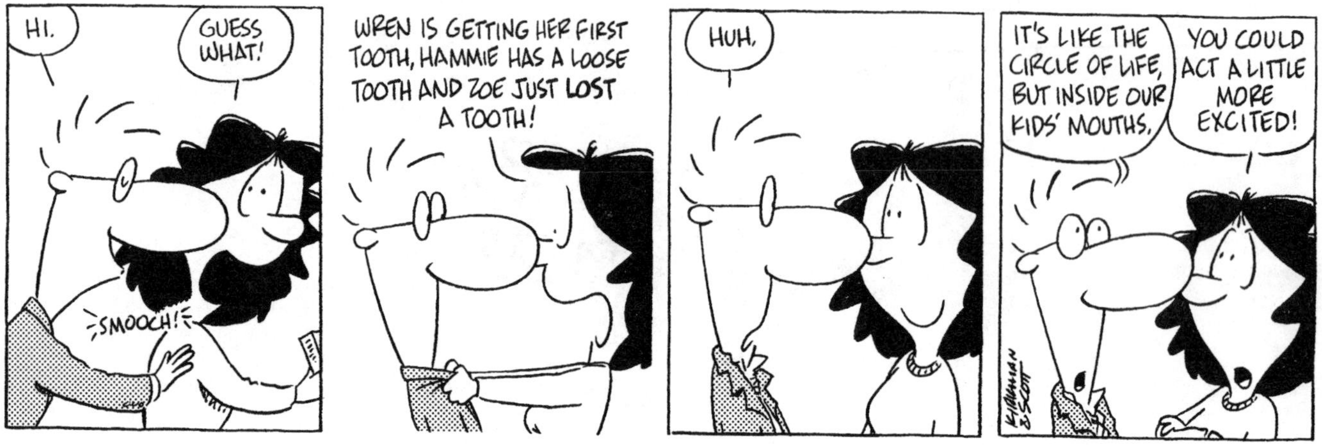
HI.
GUESS WHAT!
SMOOCH!
WREN IS GETTING HER FIRST TOOTH, HAMMIE HAS A LOOSE TOOTH AND ZOE JUST **LOST** A TOOTH!
HUH.
IT'S LIKE THE CIRCLE OF LIFE, BUT INSIDE OUR KIDS' MOUTHS.
YOU COULD ACT A LITTLE MORE EXCITED!

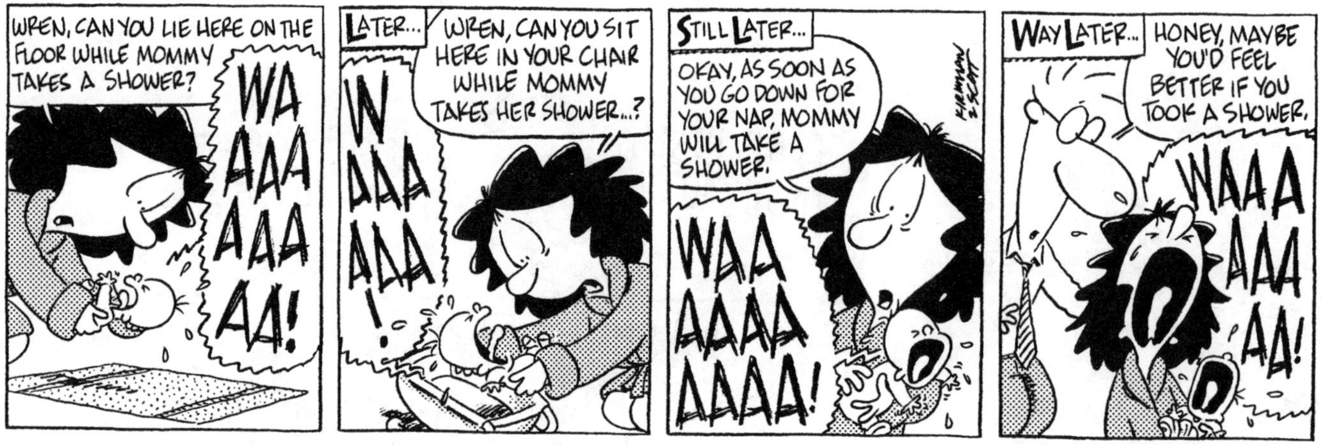
WREN, CAN YOU LIE HERE ON THE FLOOR WHILE MOMMY TAKES A SHOWER?
WAAAAAAAAA!
LATER...
WREN, CAN YOU SIT HERE IN YOUR CHAIR WHILE MOMMY TAKES HER SHOWER...?
WAAAAAA!
STILL LATER...
OKAY, AS SOON AS YOU GO DOWN FOR YOUR NAP, MOMMY WILL TAKE A SHOWER.
WAAAAAAAAAA!
WAY LATER...
HONEY, MAYBE YOU'D FEEL BETTER IF YOU TOOK A SHOWER.
WAAAAAAAA!

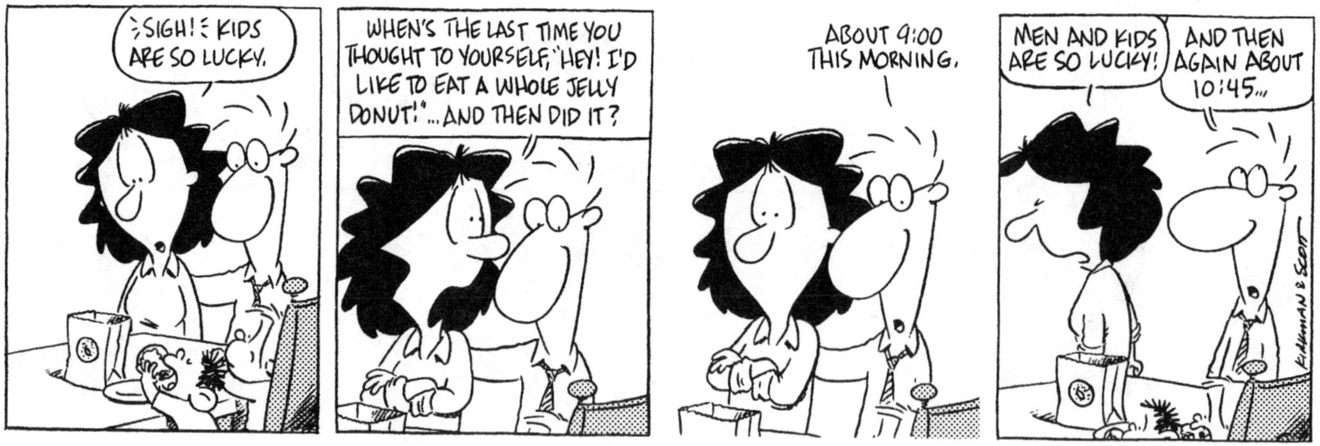
SIGH! KIDS ARE SO LUCKY.
WHEN'S THE LAST TIME YOU THOUGHT TO YOURSELF, "HEY! I'D LIKE TO EAT A WHOLE JELLY DONUT!"... AND THEN DID IT?
ABOUT 9:00 THIS MORNING.
MEN AND KIDS ARE SO LUCKY!
AND THEN AGAIN ABOUT 10:45...

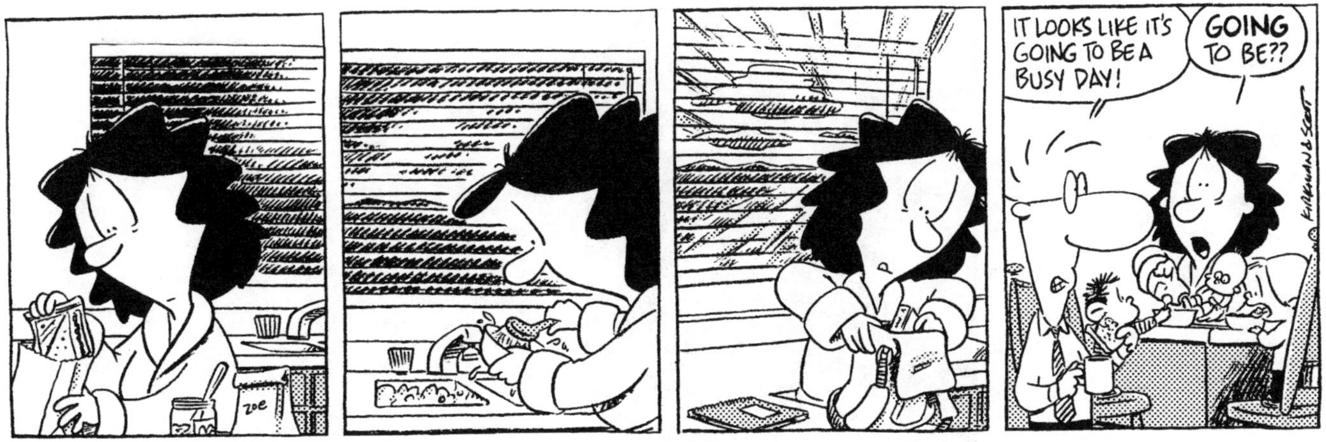
ZOE
IT LOOKS LIKE IT'S GOING TO BE A BUSY DAY!
GOING TO BE??
KIRKMAN & SCOTT

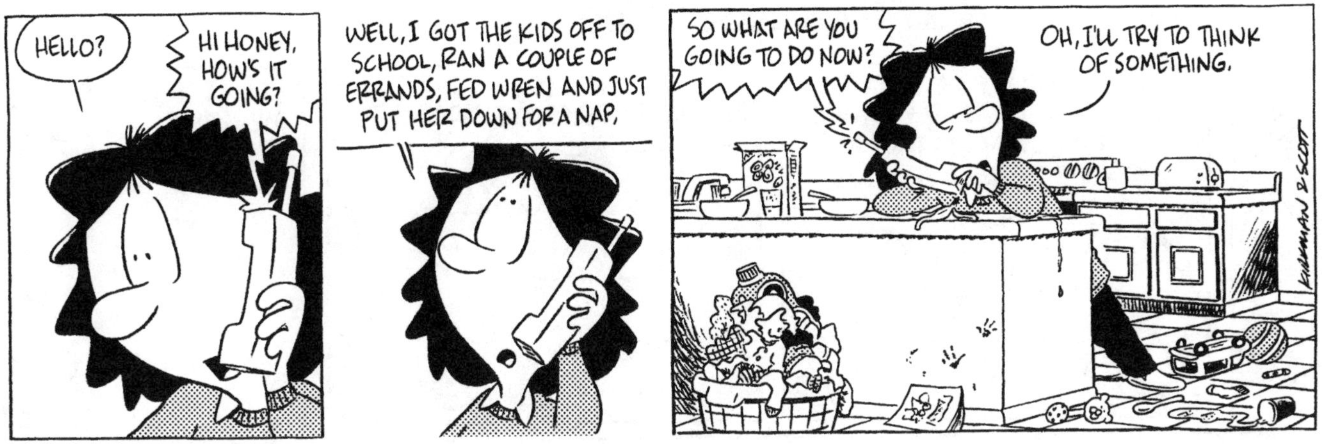
HELLO?
HI HONEY. HOW'S IT GOING?
WELL, I GOT THE KIDS OFF TO SCHOOL, RAN A COUPLE OF ERRANDS, FED WREN AND JUST PUT HER DOWN FOR A NAP.
SO WHAT ARE YOU GOING TO DO NOW?
OH, I'LL TRY TO THINK OF SOMETHING.
KIRKMAN & SCOTT

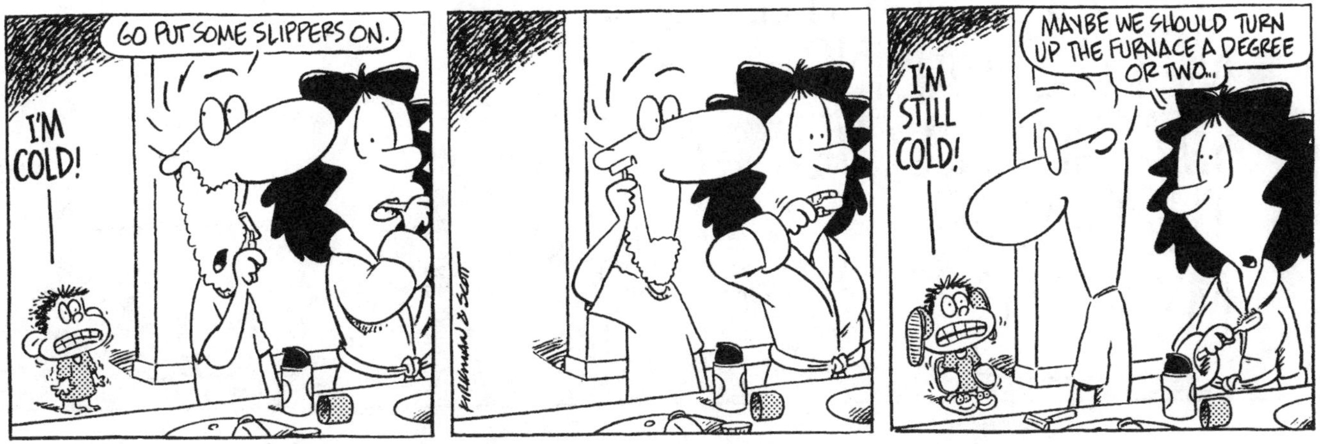
I'M COLD!
GO PUT SOME SLIPPERS ON.
KIRKMAN & SCOTT
I'M STILL COLD!
MAYBE WE SHOULD TURN UP THE FURNACE A DEGREE OR TWO...

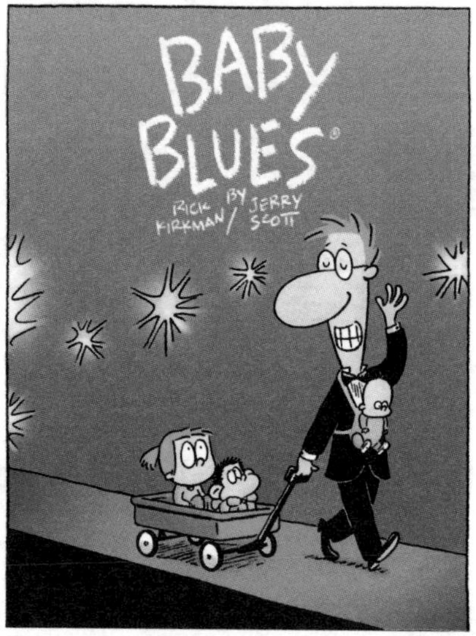
BABY BLUES®
BY RICK KIRKMAN / JERRY SCOTT

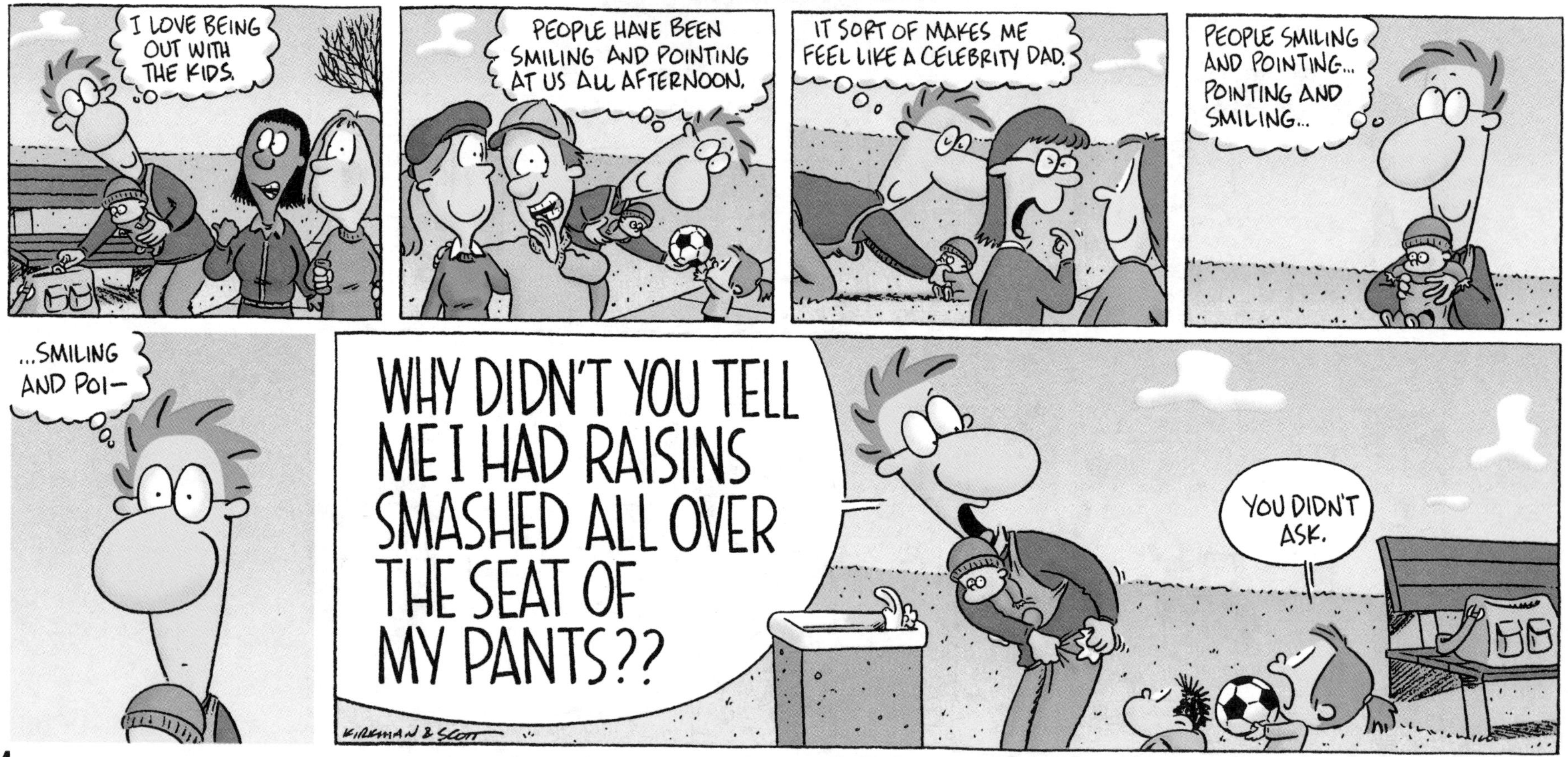
I LOVE BEING OUT WITH THE KIDS.
PEOPLE HAVE BEEN SMILING AND POINTING AT US ALL AFTERNOON.
IT SORT OF MAKES ME FEEL LIKE A CELEBRITY DAD.
PEOPLE SMILING AND POINTING... POINTING AND SMILING...
...SMILING AND POI—
WHY DIDN'T YOU TELL ME I HAD RAISINS SMASHED ALL OVER THE SEAT OF MY PANTS??
YOU DIDN'T ASK.
KIRKMAN & SCOTT

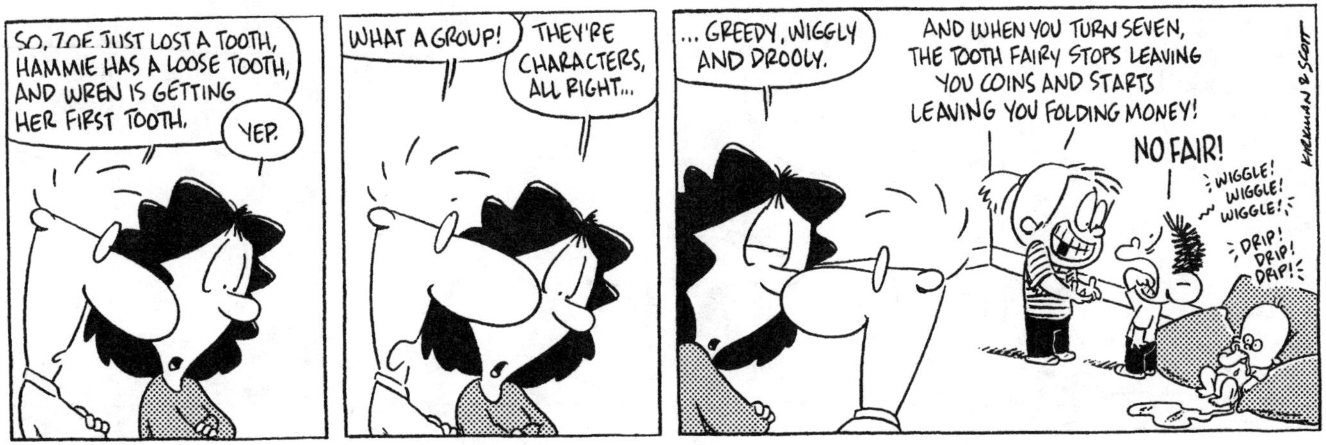
SO, ZOE JUST LOST A TOOTH, HAMMIE HAS A LOOSE TOOTH, AND WREN IS GETTING HER FIRST TOOTH.
YEP.
WHAT A GROUP!
THEY'RE CHARACTERS, ALL RIGHT...
... GREEDY, WIGGLY AND DROOLY.
AND WHEN YOU TURN SEVEN, THE TOOTH FAIRY STOPS LEAVING YOU COINS AND STARTS LEAVING YOU FOLDING MONEY!
NO FAIR!
WIGGLE! WIGGLE! WIGGLE!
DRIP! DRIP! DRIP!
KIRKMAN & SCOTT

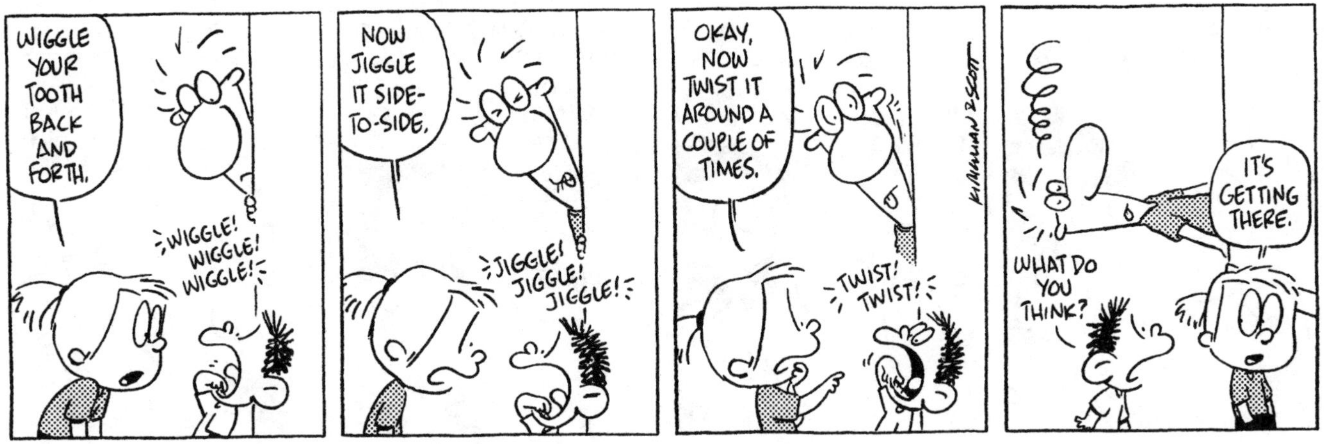
WIGGLE YOUR TOOTH BACK AND FORTH.
WIGGLE! WIGGLE! WIGGLE!
NOW JIGGLE IT SIDE-TO-SIDE.
JIGGLE! JIGGLE! JIGGLE!
OKAY, NOW TWIST IT AROUND A COUPLE OF TIMES.
TWIST! TWIST!
KIRKMAN & SCOTT
WHAT DO YOU THINK?
IT'S GETTING THERE.

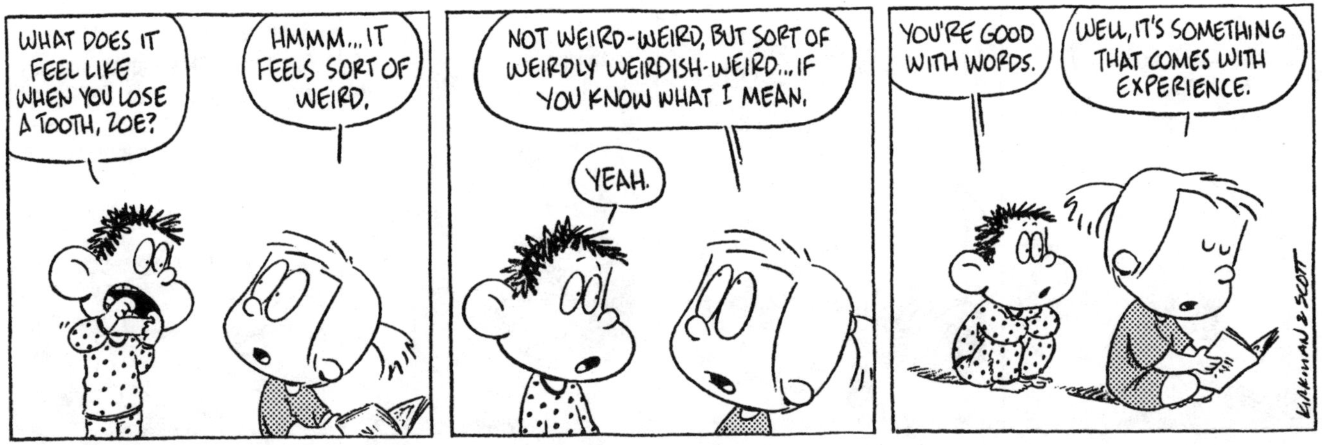
WHAT DOES IT FEEL LIKE WHEN YOU LOSE A TOOTH, ZOE?
HMMM... IT FEELS SORT OF WEIRD.
NOT WEIRD-WEIRD, BUT SORT OF WEIRDLY WEIRDISH-WEIRD... IF YOU KNOW WHAT I MEAN.
YEAH.
YOU'RE GOOD WITH WORDS.
WELL, IT'S SOMETHING THAT COMES WITH EXPERIENCE.
KIRKMAN & SCOTT

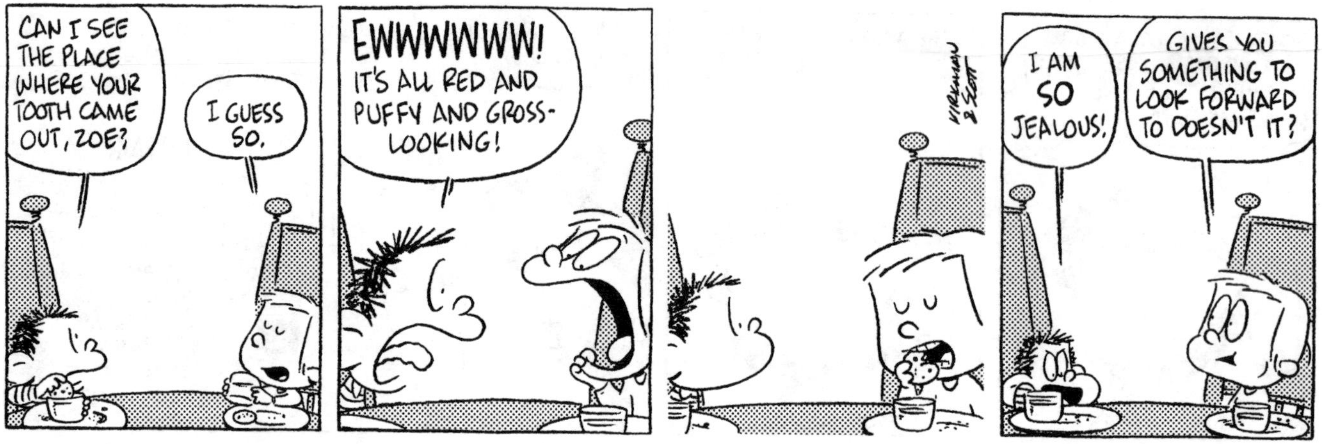
CAN I SEE THE PLACE WHERE YOUR TOOTH CAME OUT, ZOE?
I GUESS SO.
EWWWWWW! IT'S ALL RED AND PUFFY AND GROSS-LOOKING!
KIRKMAN & SCOTT
I AM SO JEALOUS!
GIVES YOU SOMETHING TO LOOK FORWARD TO DOESN'T IT?

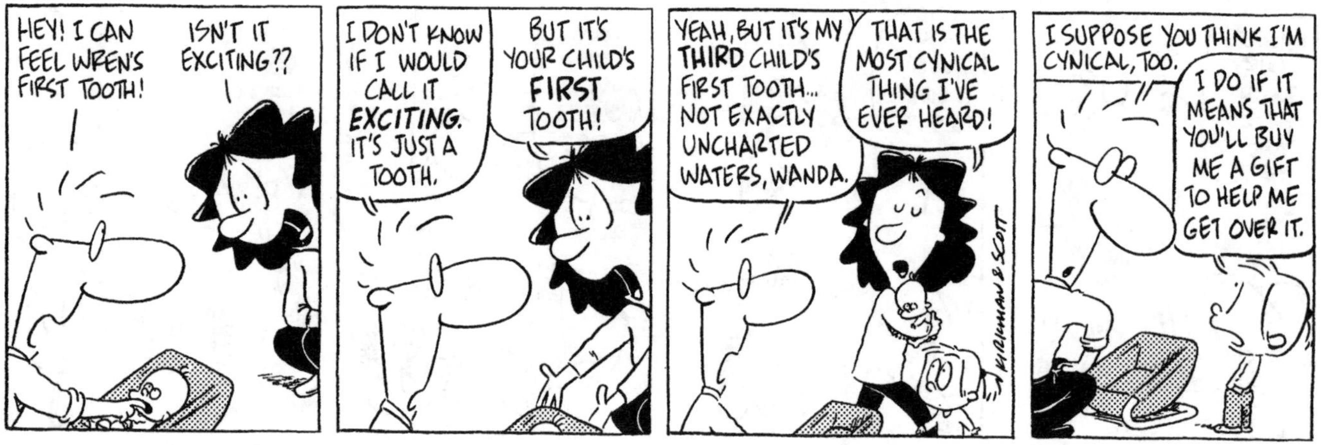
HEY! I CAN FEEL WREN'S FIRST TOOTH!
ISN'T IT EXCITING??
I DON'T KNOW IF I WOULD CALL IT EXCITING. IT'S JUST A TOOTH.
BUT IT'S YOUR CHILD'S FIRST TOOTH!
YEAH, BUT IT'S MY THIRD CHILD'S FIRST TOOTH... NOT EXACTLY UNCHARTED WATERS, WANDA.
THAT IS THE MOST CYNICAL THING I'VE EVER HEARD!
KIRKMAN & SCOTT
I SUPPOSE YOU THINK I'M CYNICAL, TOO.
I DO IF IT MEANS THAT YOU'LL BUY ME A GIFT TO HELP ME GET OVER IT.

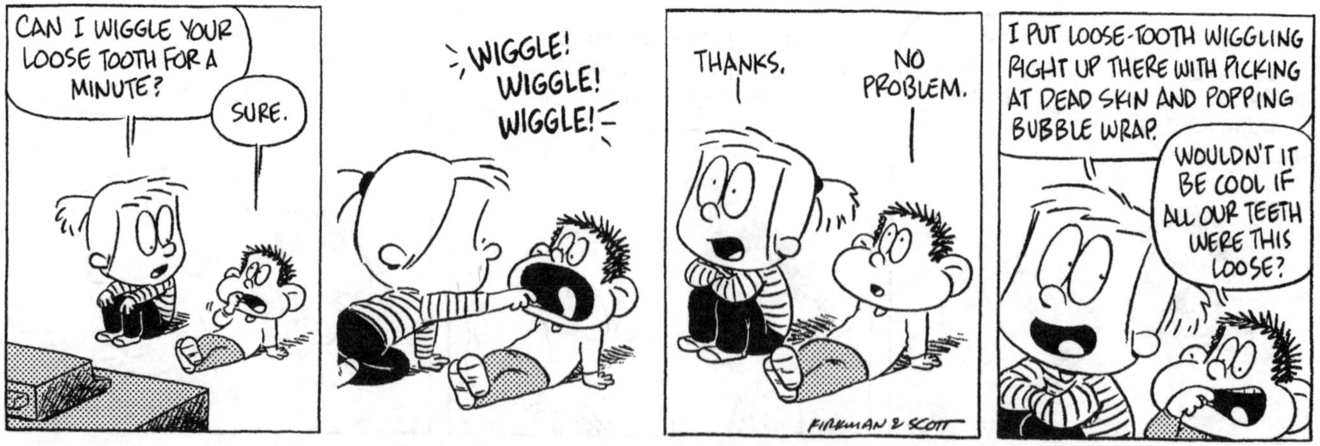
CAN I WIGGLE YOUR LOOSE TOOTH FOR A MINUTE?
SURE.
WIGGLE! WIGGLE! WIGGLE!
THANKS.
NO PROBLEM.
KIRKMAN & SCOTT
I PUT LOOSE-TOOTH WIGGLING RIGHT UP THERE WITH PICKING AT DEAD SKIN AND POPPING BUBBLE WRAP.
WOULDN'T IT BE COOL IF ALL OUR TEETH WERE THIS LOOSE?

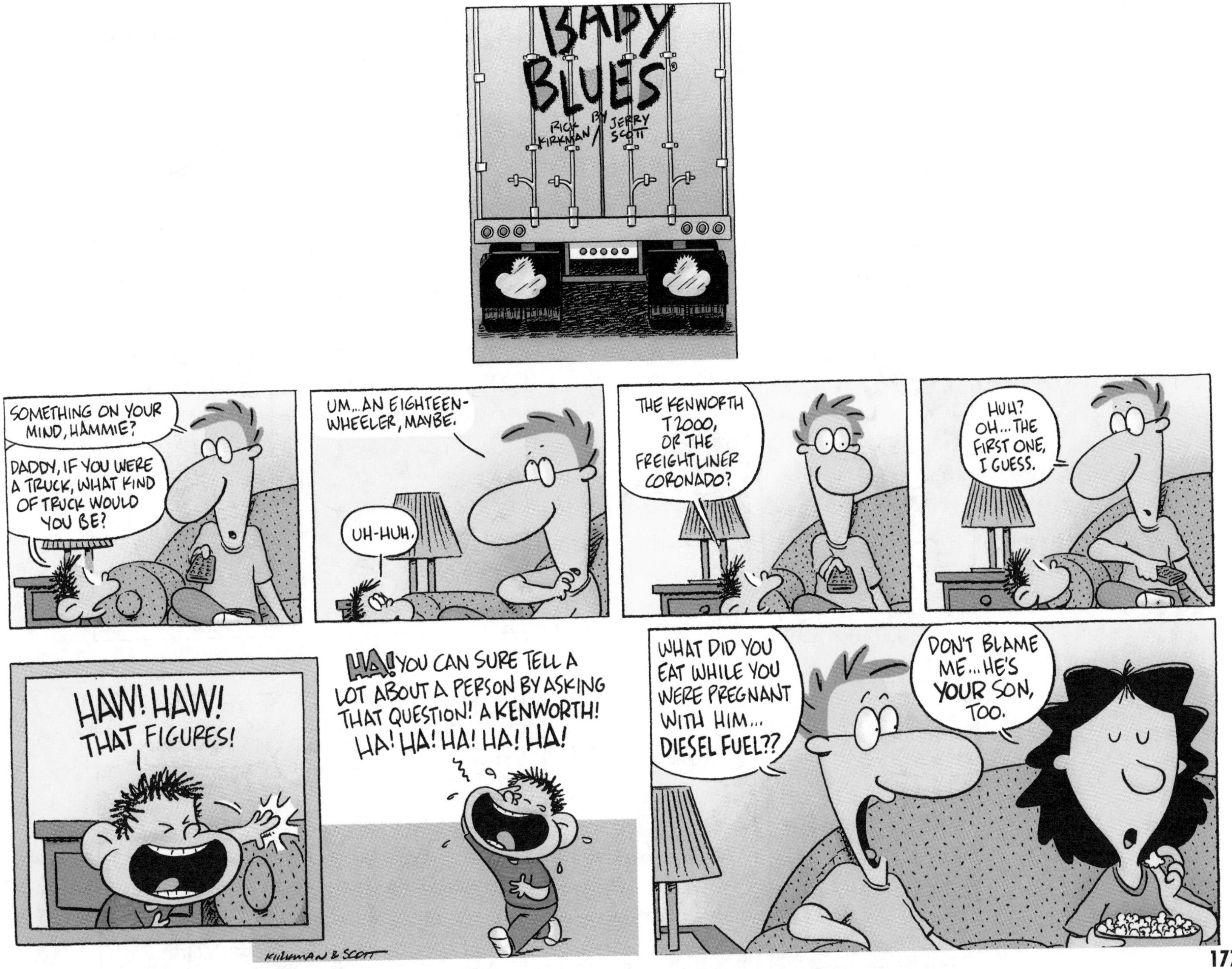
BABY BLUES®
BY RICK KIRKMAN / JERRY SCOTT
SOMETHING ON YOUR MIND, HAMMIE?
DADDY, IF YOU WERE A TRUCK, WHAT KIND OF TRUCK WOULD YOU BE?
UM... AN EIGHTEEN-WHEELER, MAYBE.
UH-HUH.
THE KENWORTH T2000, OR THE FREIGHTLINER CORONADO?
HUH? OH... THE FIRST ONE, I GUESS.
HAW! HAW! THAT FIGURES!
HA! YOU CAN SURE TELL A LOT ABOUT A PERSON BY ASKING THAT QUESTION! A KENWORTH! HA! HA! HA! HA! HA!
KIRKMAN & SCOTT
WHAT DID YOU EAT WHILE YOU WERE PREGNANT WITH HIM... DIESEL FUEL??
DON'T BLAME ME... HE'S YOUR SON, TOO.

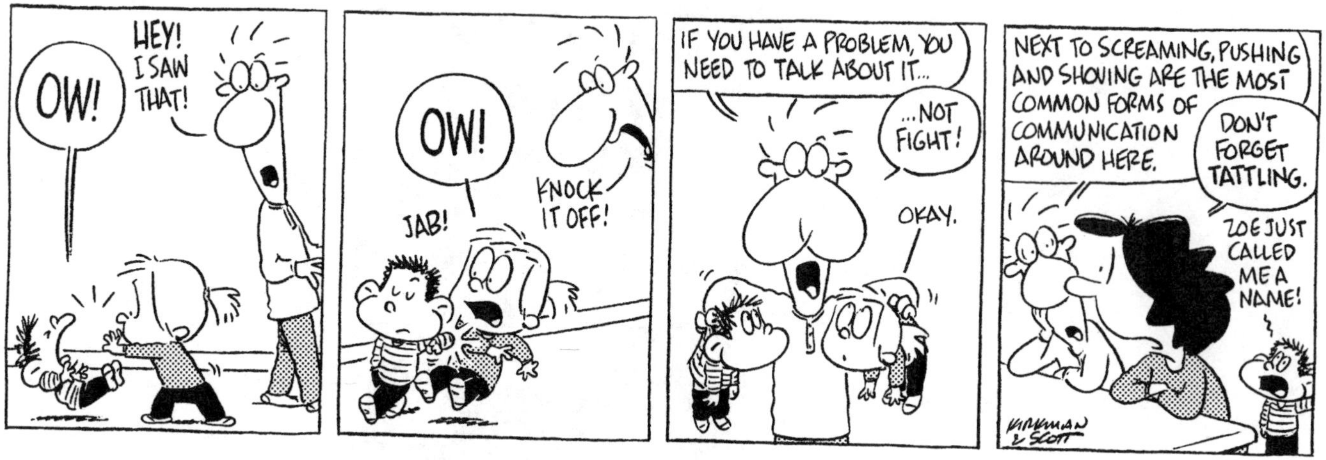
OW!
HEY! I SAW THAT!
OW!
JAB!
KNOCK IT OFF!
IF YOU HAVE A PROBLEM, YOU NEED TO TALK ABOUT IT...
...NOT FIGHT!
OKAY.
NEXT TO SCREAMING, PUSHING AND SHOVING ARE THE MOST COMMON FORMS OF COMMUNICATION AROUND HERE.
DON'T FORGET TATTLING.
ZOE JUST CALLED ME A NAME!
KIRKMAN & SCOTT

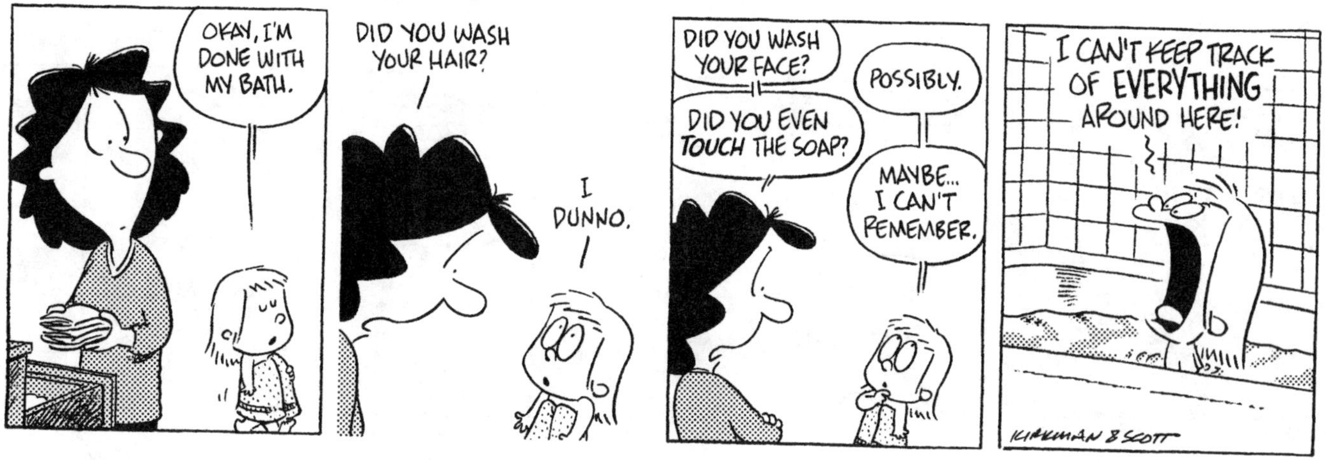
OKAY, I'M DONE WITH MY BATH.
DID YOU WASH YOUR HAIR?
I DUNNO.
DID YOU WASH YOUR FACE?
POSSIBLY.
DID YOU EVEN TOUCH THE SOAP?
MAYBE... I CAN'T REMEMBER.
I CAN'T KEEP TRACK OF EVERYTHING AROUND HERE!
KIRKMAN & SCOTT

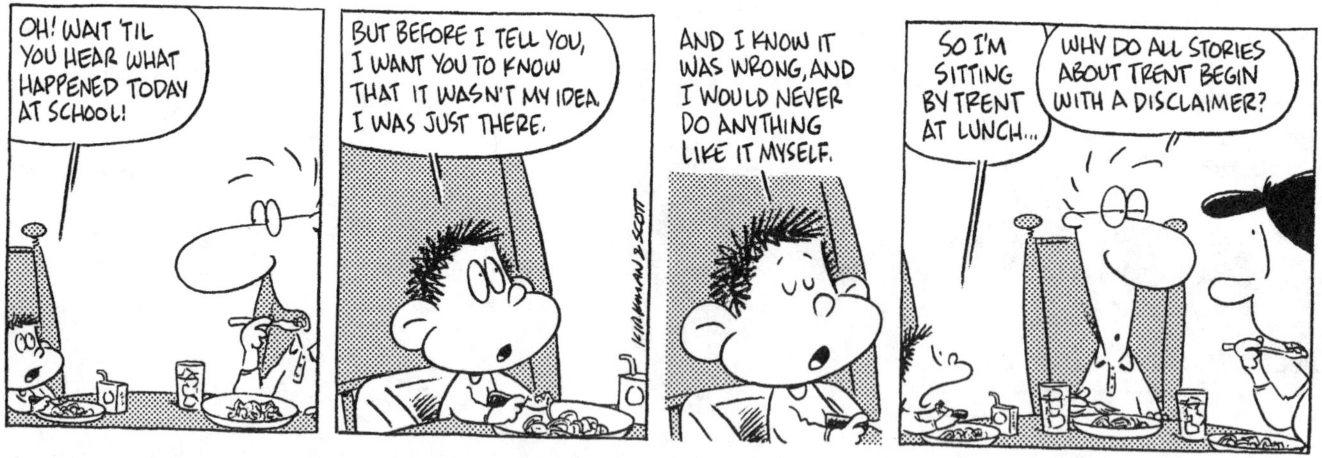
OH! WAIT 'TIL YOU HEAR WHAT HAPPENED TODAY AT SCHOOL!
BUT BEFORE I TELL YOU, I WANT YOU TO KNOW THAT IT WASN'T MY IDEA. I WAS JUST THERE.
KIRKMAN & SCOTT
AND I KNOW IT WAS WRONG, AND I WOULD NEVER DO ANYTHING LIKE IT MYSELF.
SO I'M SITTING BY TRENT AT LUNCH...
WHY DO ALL STORIES ABOUT TRENT BEGIN WITH A DISCLAIMER?

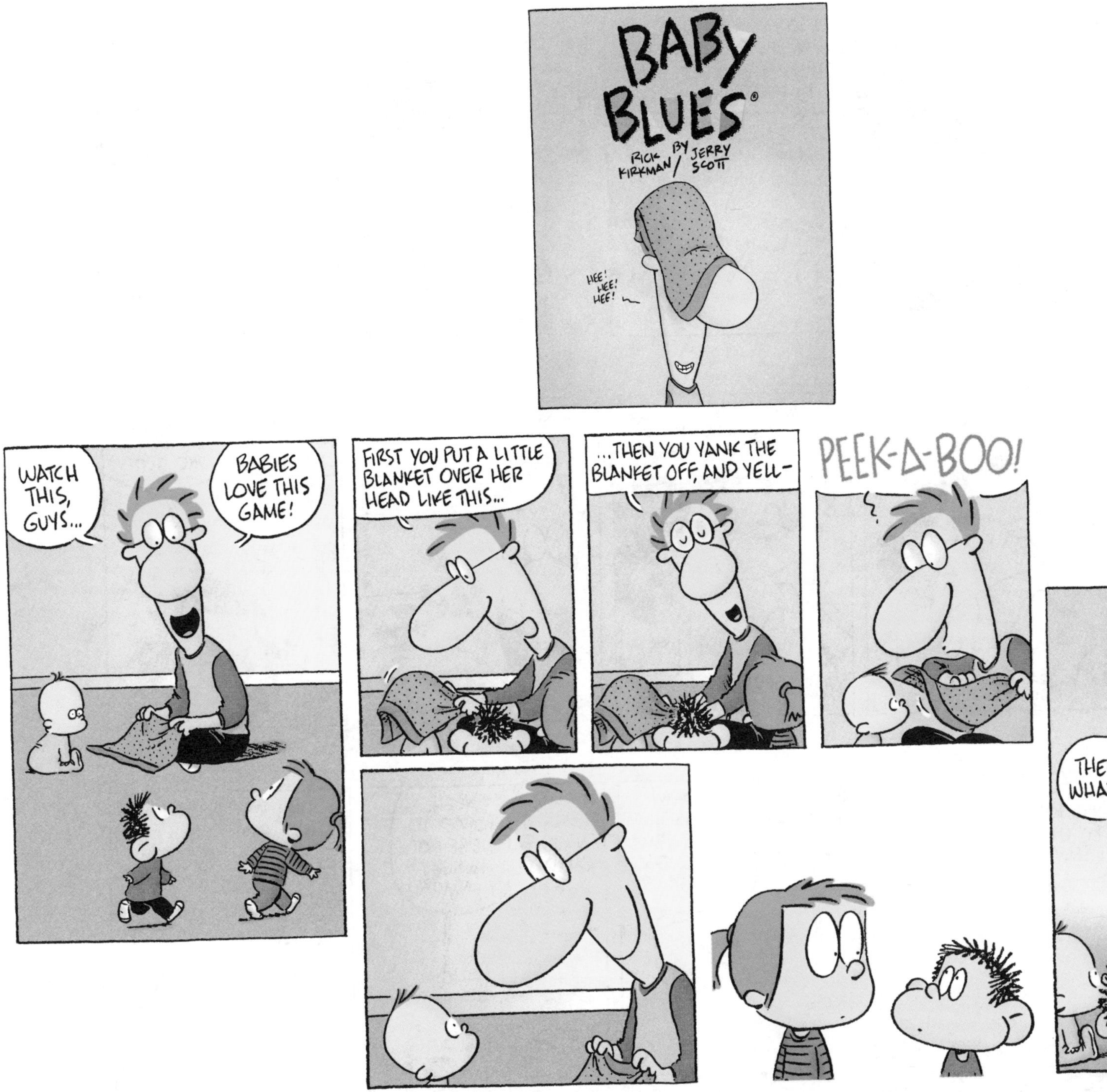
BABY BLUES®
BY RICK KIRKMAN / JERRY SCOTT
HEE! HEE! HEE!
WATCH THIS, GUYS...
BABIES LOVE THIS GAME!
FIRST YOU PUT A LITTLE BLANKET OVER HER HEAD LIKE THIS...
...THEN YOU YANK THE BLANKET OFF, AND YELL-
PEEK-A-BOO!
THEN NOTHING! THAT'S THE WHOLE GAME!
THEN WHAT?
SURE, DAD.
KIRKMAN & SCOTT

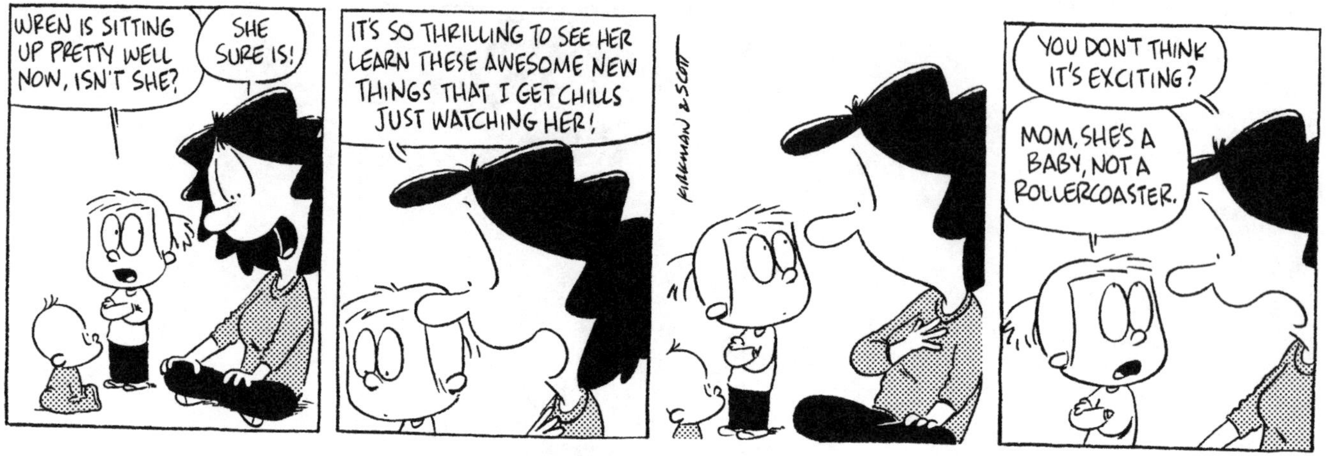
WREN IS SITTING UP PRETTY WELL NOW, ISN'T SHE?
SHE SURE IS!
IT'S SO THRILLING TO SEE HER LEARN THESE AWESOME NEW THINGS THAT I GET CHILLS JUST WATCHING HER!
KIRKMAN & SCOTT
YOU DON'T THINK IT'S EXCITING?
MOM, SHE'S A BABY, NOT A ROLLERCOASTER.

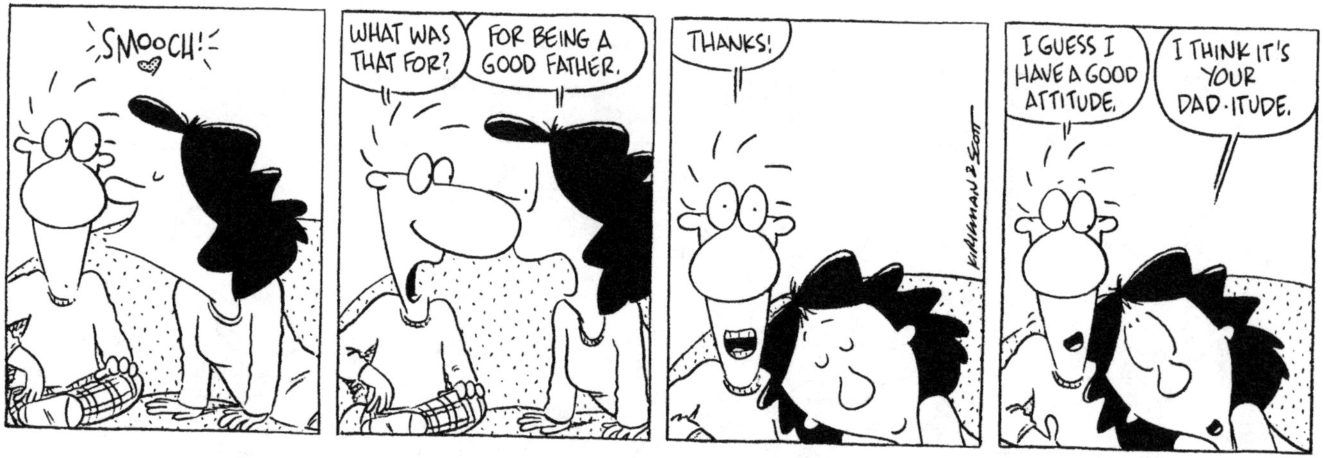
SMOOCH!
WHAT WAS THAT FOR?
FOR BEING A GOOD FATHER.
THANKS!
KIRKMAN & SCOTT
I GUESS I HAVE A GOOD ATTITUDE.
I THINK IT'S YOUR DAD-ITUDE.

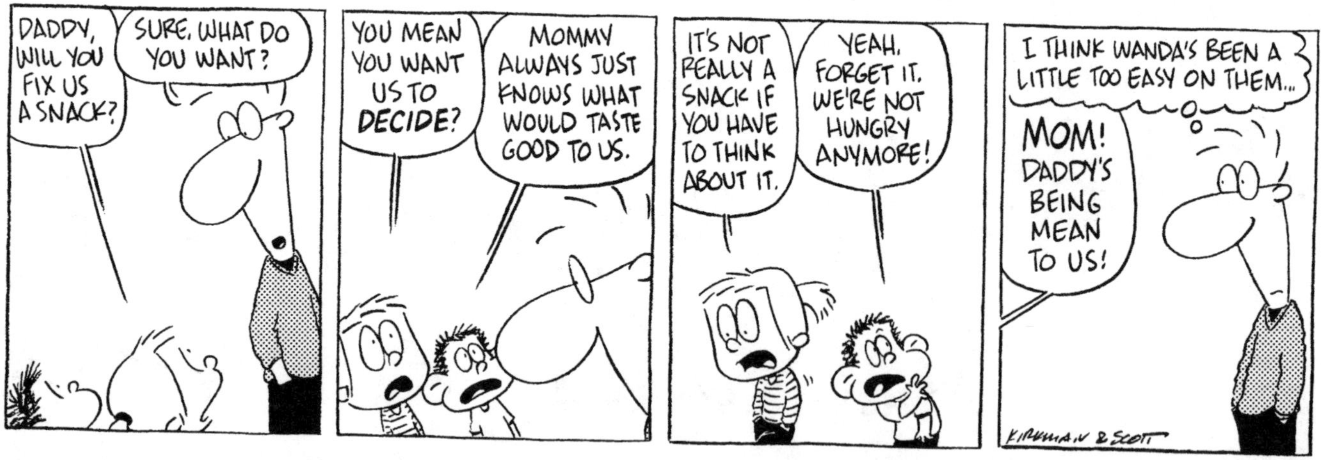
DADDY, WILL YOU FIX US A SNACK?
SURE. WHAT DO YOU WANT?
YOU MEAN YOU WANT US TO **DECIDE**?
MOMMY ALWAYS JUST KNOWS WHAT WOULD TASTE GOOD TO US.
IT'S NOT REALLY A SNACK IF YOU HAVE TO THINK ABOUT IT.
YEAH. FORGET IT. WE'RE NOT HUNGRY ANYMORE!
I THINK WANDA'S BEEN A LITTLE TOO EASY ON THEM...
MOM! DADDY'S BEING MEAN TO US!
KIRKMAN & SCOTT

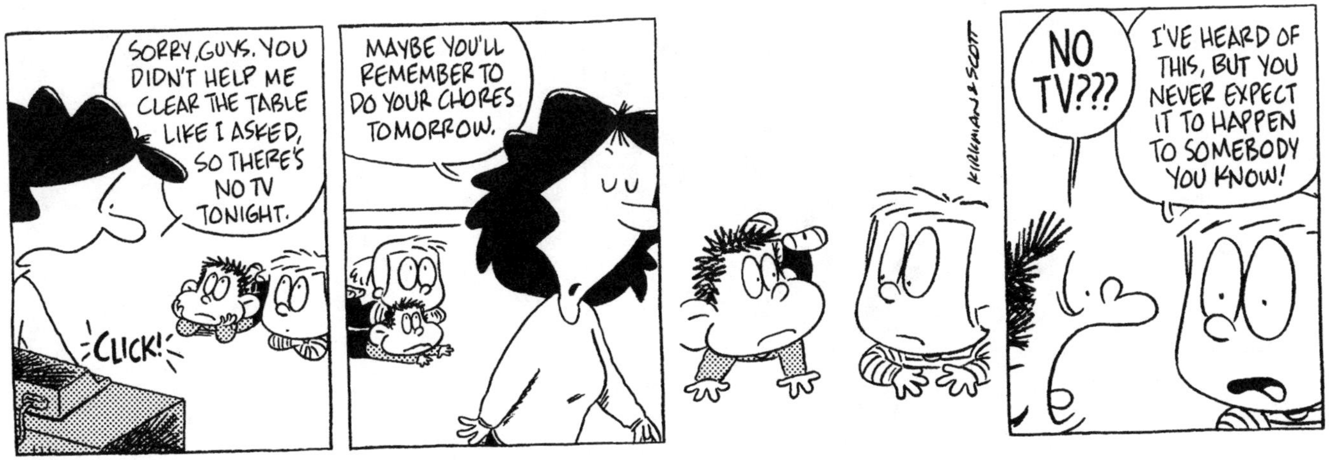
SORRY, GUYS. YOU DIDN'T HELP ME CLEAR THE TABLE LIKE I ASKED, SO THERE'S NO TV TONIGHT.
CLICK!
MAYBE YOU'LL REMEMBER TO DO YOUR CHORES TOMORROW.
KIRKMAN & SCOTT
NO TV???
I'VE HEARD OF THIS, BUT YOU NEVER EXPECT IT TO HAPPEN TO SOMEBODY YOU KNOW!

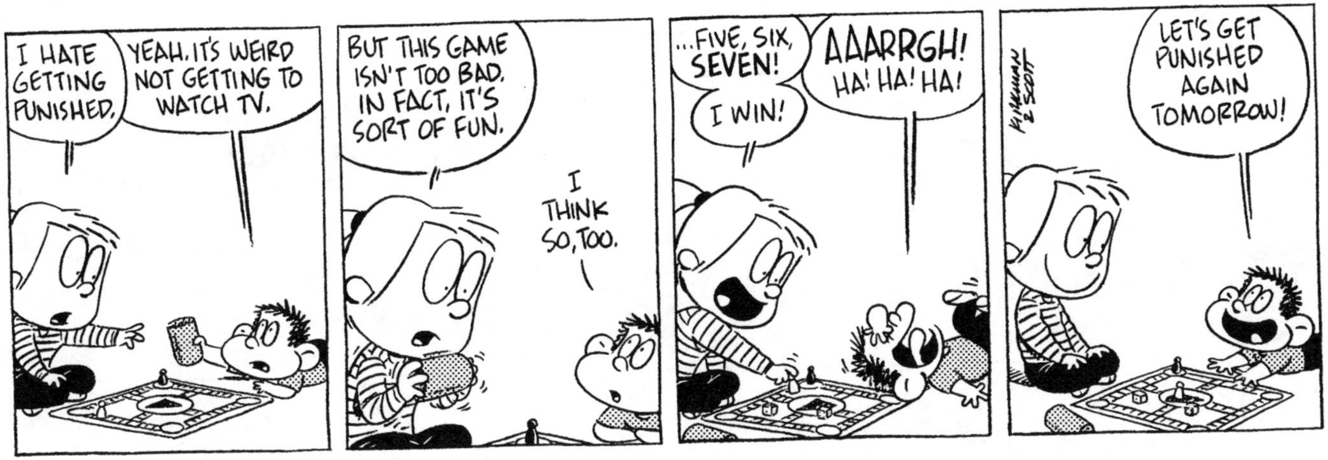
I HATE GETTING PUNISHED.
YEAH. IT'S WEIRD NOT GETTING TO WATCH TV.
BUT THIS GAME ISN'T TOO BAD. IN FACT, IT'S SORT OF FUN.
I THINK SO, TOO.
...FIVE, SIX, SEVEN!
I WIN!
AAARRGH! HA! HA! HA!
KIRKMAN & SCOTT
LET'S GET PUNISHED AGAIN TOMORROW!

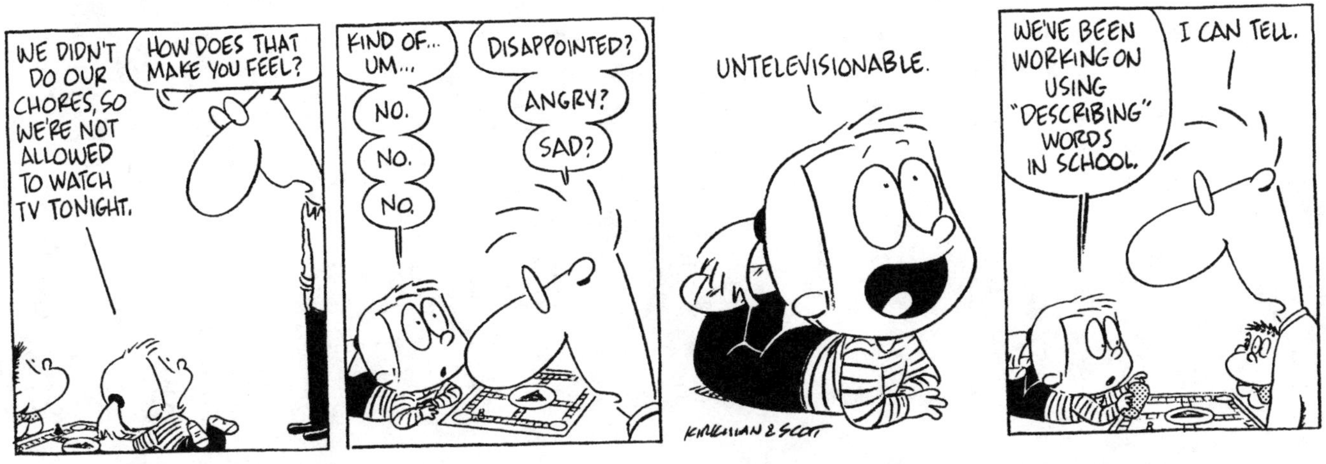
WE DIDN'T DO OUR CHORES, SO WE'RE NOT ALLOWED TO WATCH TV TONIGHT.
HOW DOES THAT MAKE YOU FEEL?
KIND OF... UM...
DISAPPOINTED?
NO.
ANGRY?
NO.
SAD?
NO.
UNTELEVISIONABLE.
KIRKMAN & SCOTT
WE'VE BEEN WORKING ON USING "DESCRIBING" WORDS IN SCHOOL.
I CAN TELL.

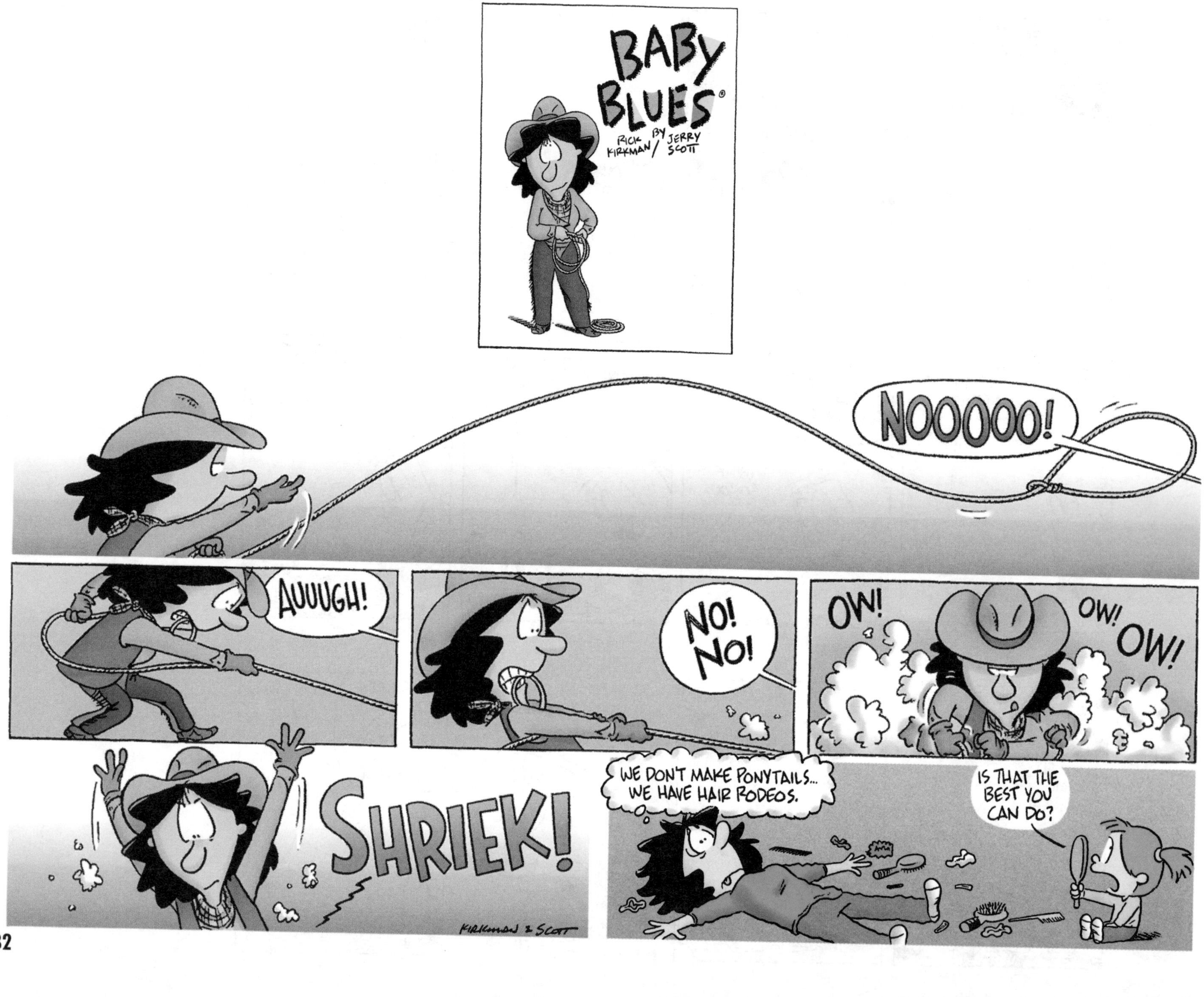
BABY BLUES®
BY RICK KIRKMAN / JERRY SCOTT
NOOOOO!
AUUUGH!
NO! NO!
OW!
OW!
OW!
SHRIEK!
KIRKMAN & SCOTT
WE DON'T MAKE PONYTAILS... WE HAVE HAIR RODEOS.
IS THAT THE BEST YOU CAN DO?

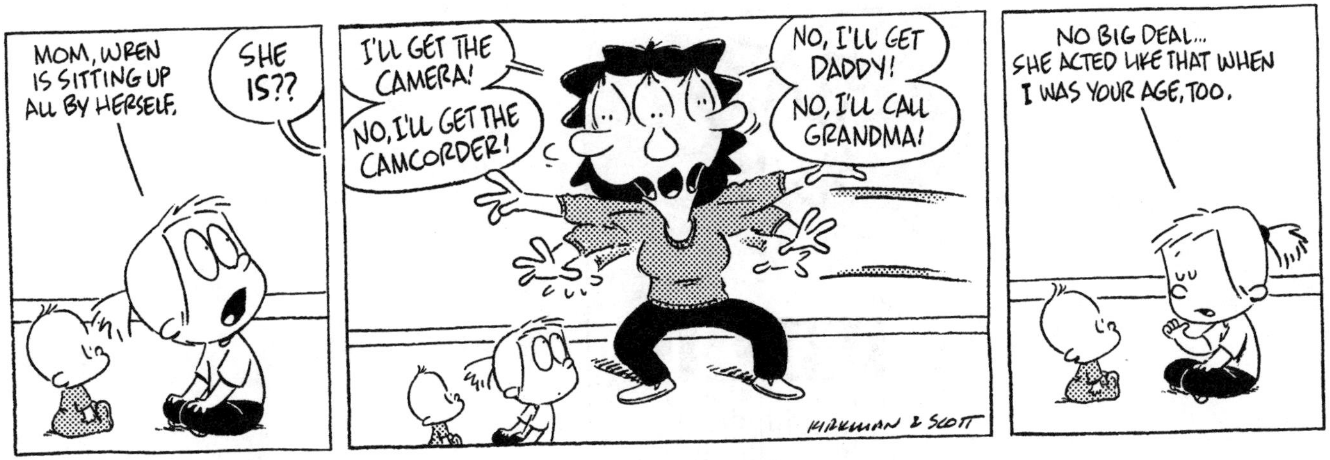
MOM, WREN IS SITTING UP ALL BY HERSELF.
SHE IS??
I'LL GET THE CAMERA!
NO, I'LL GET THE CAMCORDER!
NO, I'LL GET DADDY!
NO, I'LL CALL GRANDMA!
KIRKMAN & SCOTT
NO BIG DEAL... SHE ACTED LIKE THAT WHEN I WAS YOUR AGE, TOO.

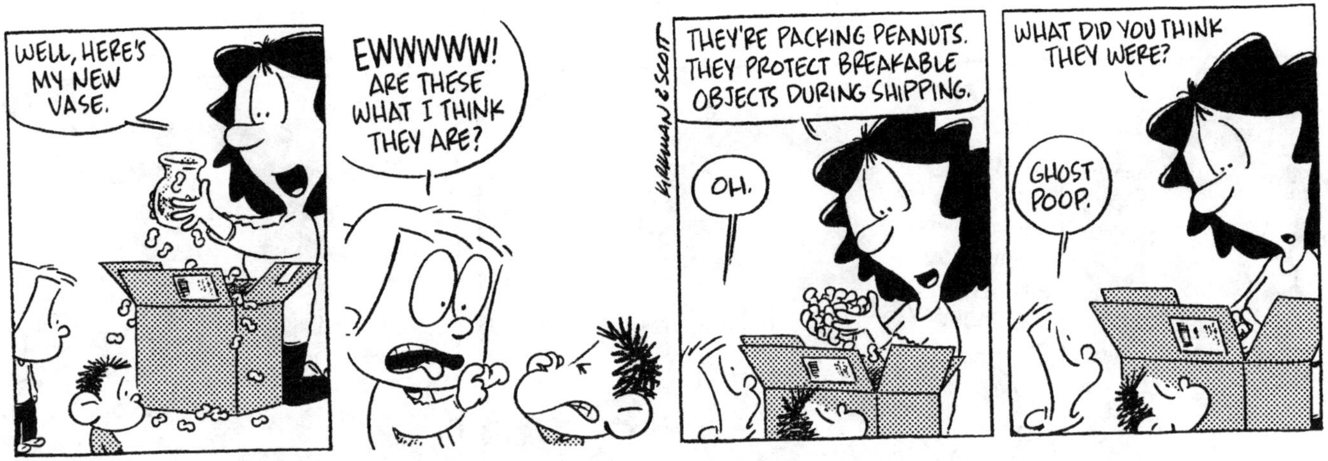
WELL, HERE'S MY NEW VASE.
EWWWWW! ARE THESE WHAT I THINK THEY ARE?
KIRKMAN & SCOTT
THEY'RE PACKING PEANUTS. THEY PROTECT BREAKABLE OBJECTS DURING SHIPPING.
OH.
WHAT DID YOU THINK THEY WERE?
GHOST POOP.

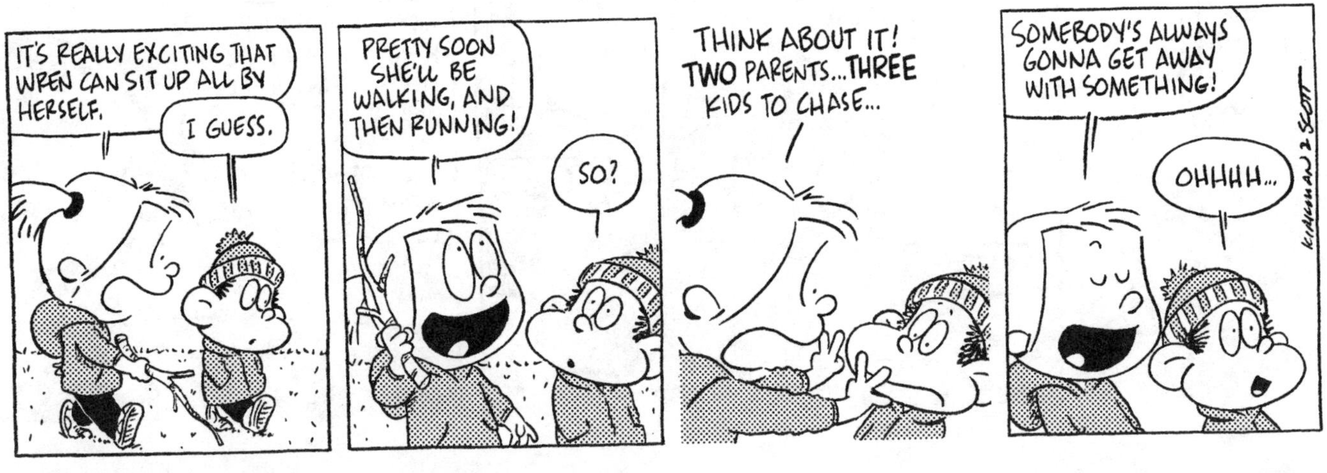
IT'S REALLY EXCITING THAT WREN CAN SIT UP ALL BY HERSELF.
I GUESS.
PRETTY SOON SHE'LL BE WALKING, AND THEN RUNNING!
SO?
THINK ABOUT IT! TWO PARENTS...THREE KIDS TO CHASE...
SOMEBODY'S ALWAYS GONNA GET AWAY WITH SOMETHING!
OHHHH...
KIRKMAN & SCOTT

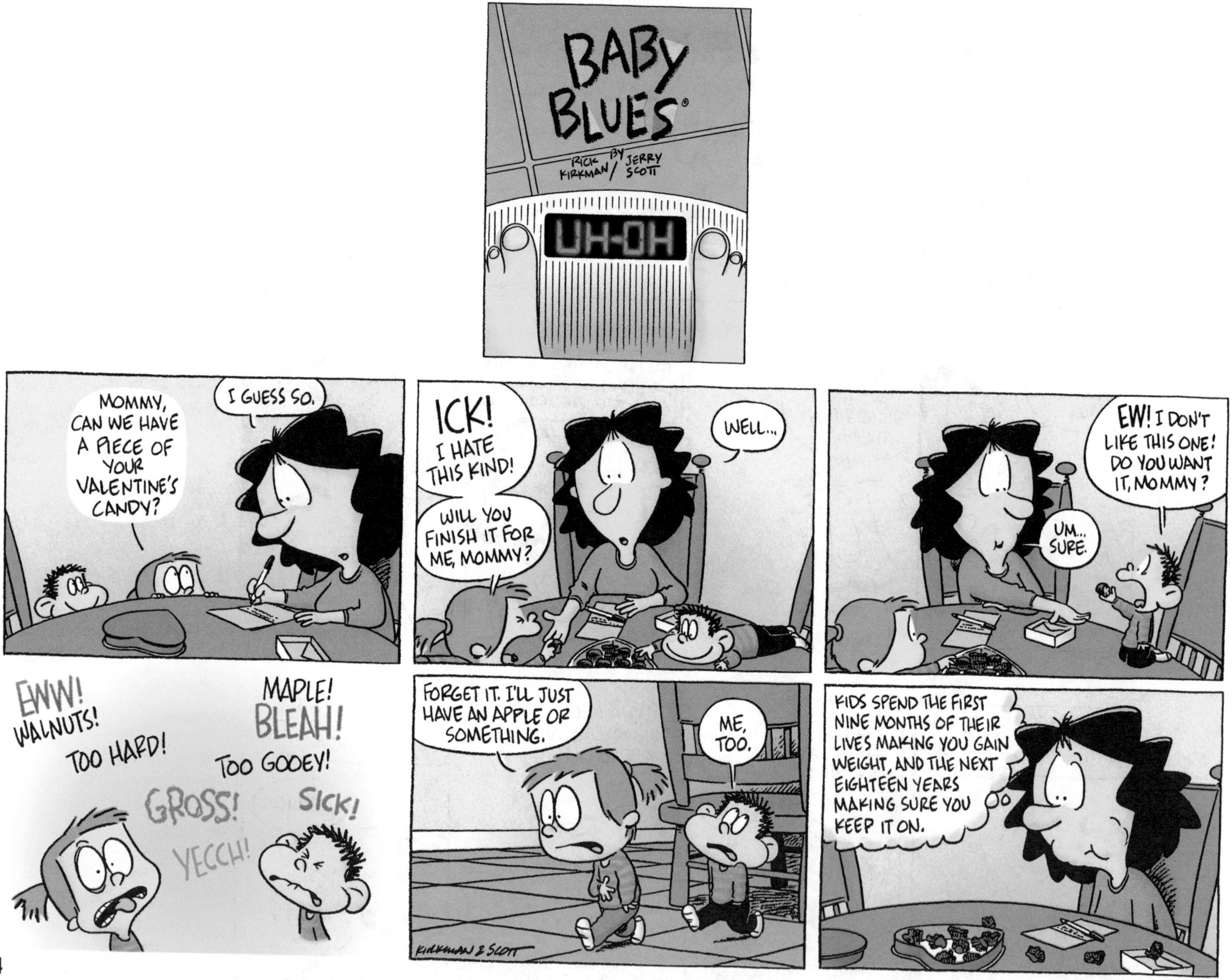
BABY BLUES®
BY RICK KIRKMAN / JERRY SCOTT
UH-OH
MOMMY, CAN WE HAVE A PIECE OF YOUR VALENTINE'S CANDY?
I GUESS SO.
ICK! I HATE THIS KIND!
WILL YOU FINISH IT FOR ME, MOMMY?
WELL...
EW! I DON'T LIKE THIS ONE! DO YOU WANT IT, MOMMY?
UM... SURE.
EWW! WALNUTS!
MAPLE! BLEAH!
TOO HARD!
TOO GOOEY!
GROSS!
SICK!
YECCH!
FORGET IT. I'LL JUST HAVE AN APPLE OR SOMETHING.
ME, TOO.
KIRKMAN & SCOTT
KIDS SPEND THE FIRST NINE MONTHS OF THEIR LIVES MAKING YOU GAIN WEIGHT, AND THE NEXT EIGHTEEN YEARS MAKING SURE YOU KEEP IT ON.

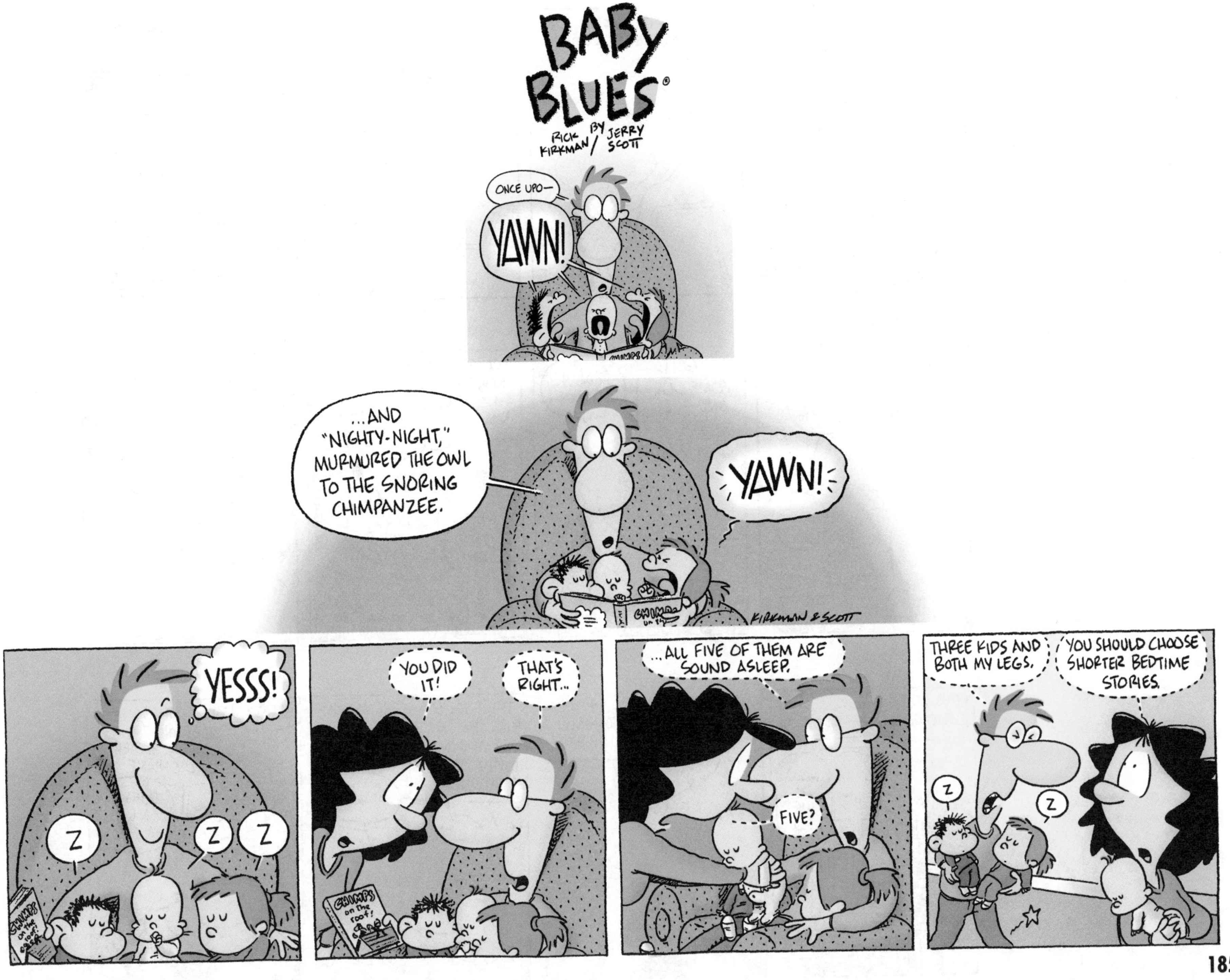
BABY BLUES®
BY RICK KIRKMAN / JERRY SCOTT
ONCE UPO—
YAWN!
...AND "NIGHTY-NIGHT," MURMURED THE OWL TO THE SNORING CHIMPANZEE.
YAWN!
KIRKMAN & SCOTT
YESSS!
Z
Z
Z
YOU DID IT!
THAT'S RIGHT...
CHIMPS on the roof!
...ALL FIVE OF THEM ARE SOUND ASLEEP.
FIVE?
THREE KIDS AND BOTH MY LEGS.
YOU SHOULD CHOOSE SHORTER BEDTIME STORIES.
Z
Z

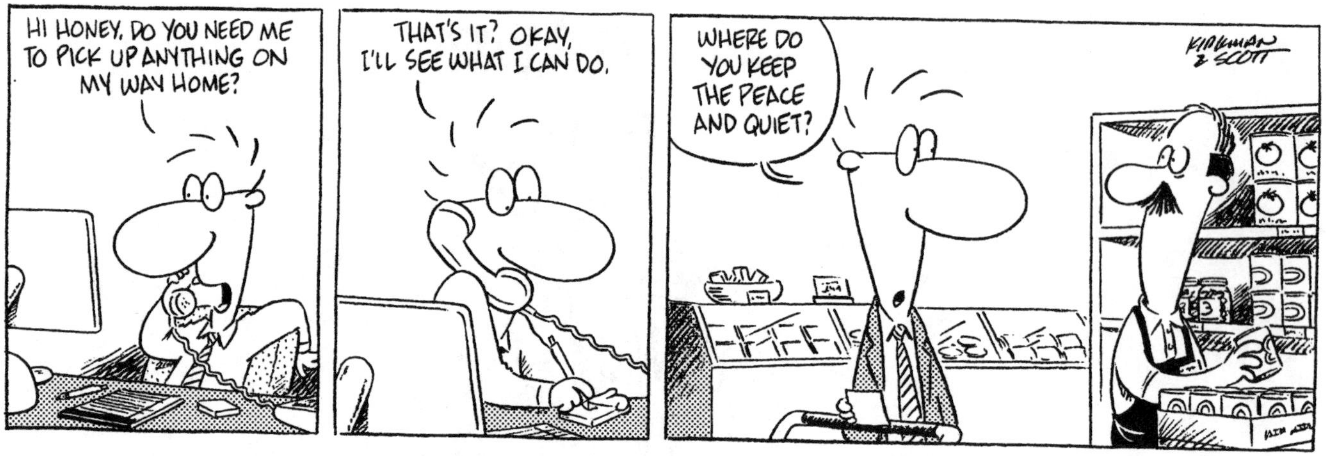
HI HONEY, DO YOU NEED ME TO PICK UP ANYTHING ON MY WAY HOME?
THAT'S IT? OKAY, I'LL SEE WHAT I CAN DO.
WHERE DO YOU KEEP THE PEACE AND QUIET?
KIRKMAN & SCOTT

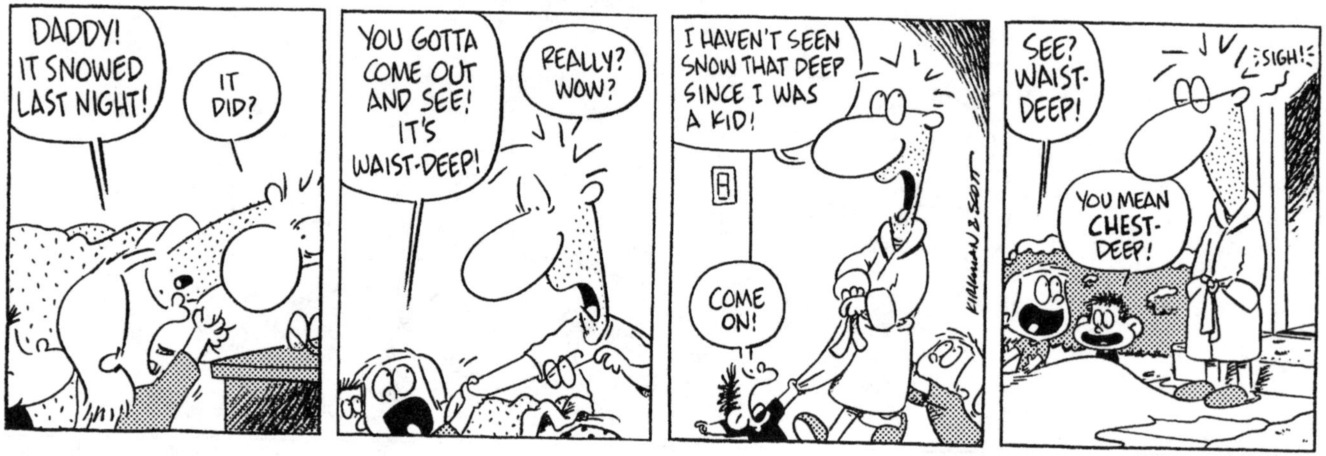
DADDY! IT SNOWED LAST NIGHT!
IT DID?
YOU GOTTA COME OUT AND SEE! IT'S WAIST-DEEP!
REALLY? WOW?
I HAVEN'T SEEN SNOW THAT DEEP SINCE I WAS A KID!
COME ON!
KIRKMAN & SCOTT
SEE? WAIST-DEEP!
SIGH!
YOU MEAN CHEST-DEEP!

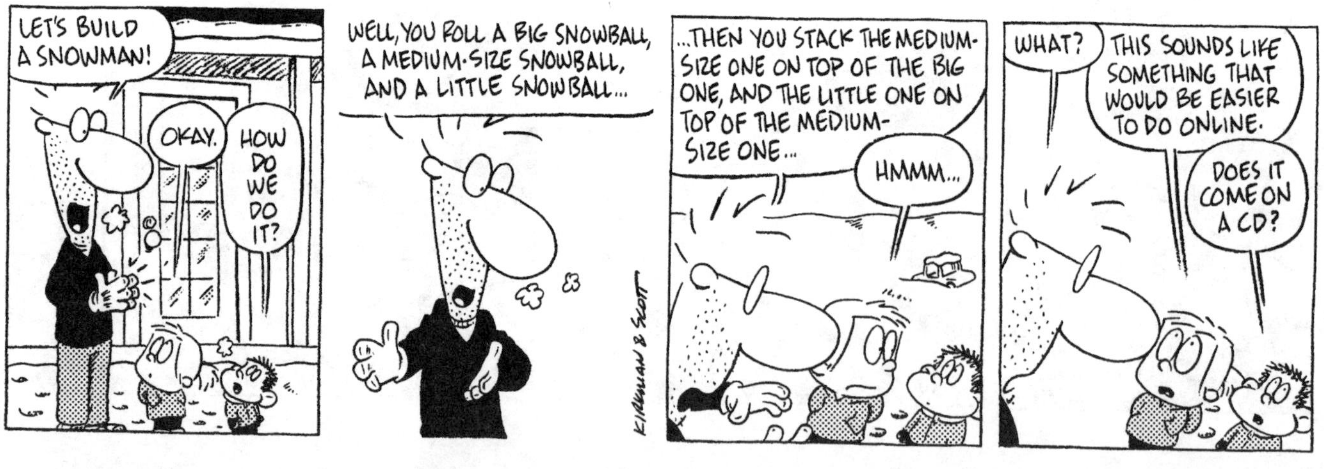
LET'S BUILD A SNOWMAN!
OKAY.
HOW DO WE DO IT?
WELL, YOU ROLL A BIG SNOWBALL, A MEDIUM-SIZE SNOWBALL, AND A LITTLE SNOWBALL...
KIRKMAN & SCOTT
...THEN YOU STACK THE MEDIUM-SIZE ONE ON TOP OF THE BIG ONE, AND THE LITTLE ONE ON TOP OF THE MEDIUM-SIZE ONE...
HMMM...
WHAT?
THIS SOUNDS LIKE SOMETHING THAT WOULD BE EASIER TO DO ONLINE.
DOES IT COME ON A CD?

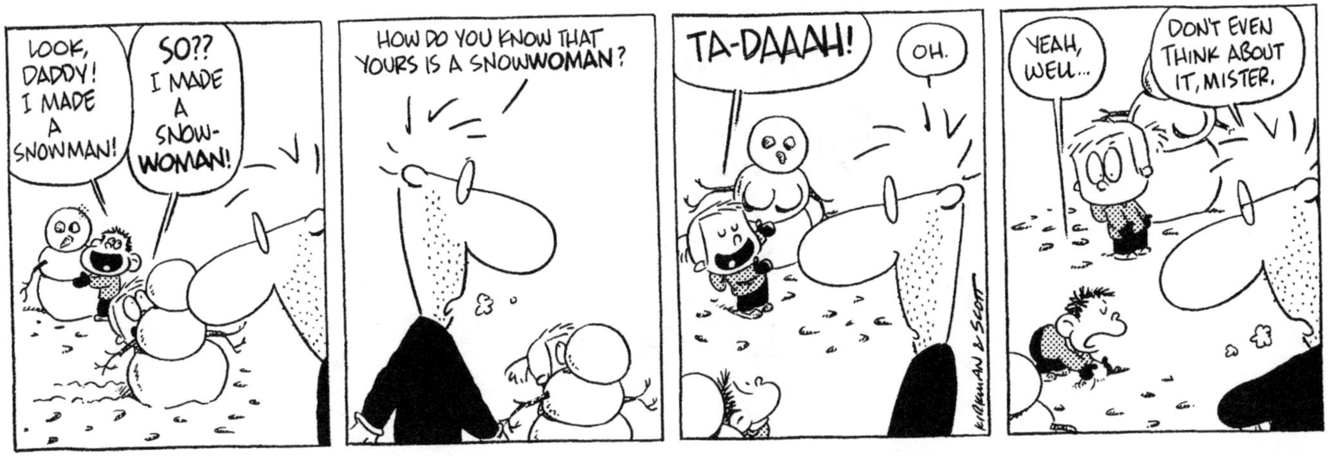
LOOK, DADDY! I MADE A SNOWMAN!
SO?? I MADE A SNOW-WOMAN!
HOW DO YOU KNOW THAT YOURS IS A SNOWWOMAN?
TA-DAAAH!
OH.
YEAH, WELL...
DON'T EVEN THINK ABOUT IT, MISTER.

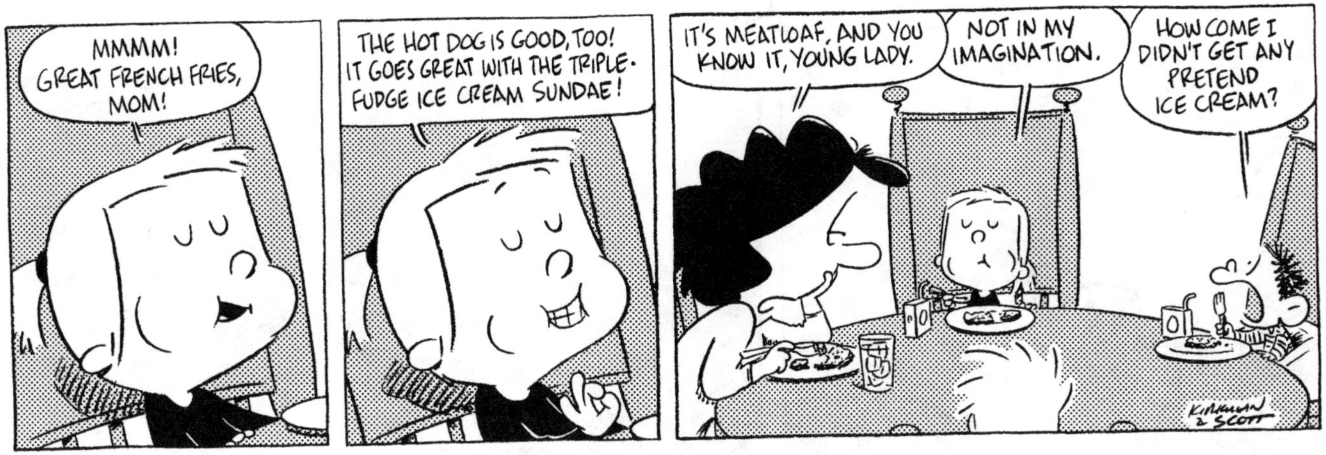
MMMM! GREAT FRENCH FRIES, MOM!
THE HOT DOG IS GOOD, TOO! IT GOES GREAT WITH THE TRIPLE-FUDGE ICE CREAM SUNDAE!
IT'S MEATLOAF, AND YOU KNOW IT, YOUNG LADY.
NOT IN MY IMAGINATION.
HOW COME I DIDN'T GET ANY PRETEND ICE CREAM?

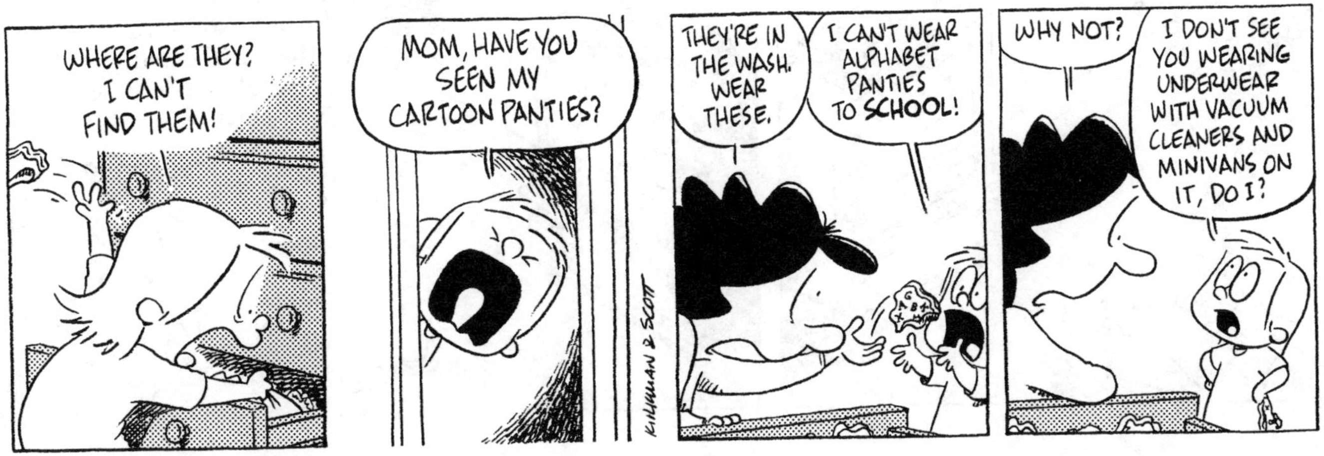
WHERE ARE THEY? I CAN'T FIND THEM!
MOM, HAVE YOU SEEN MY CARTOON PANTIES?
THEY'RE IN THE WASH. WEAR THESE.
I CAN'T WEAR ALPHABET PANTIES TO SCHOOL!
WHY NOT?
I DON'T SEE YOU WEARING UNDERWEAR WITH VACUUM CLEANERS AND MINIVANS ON IT, DO I?

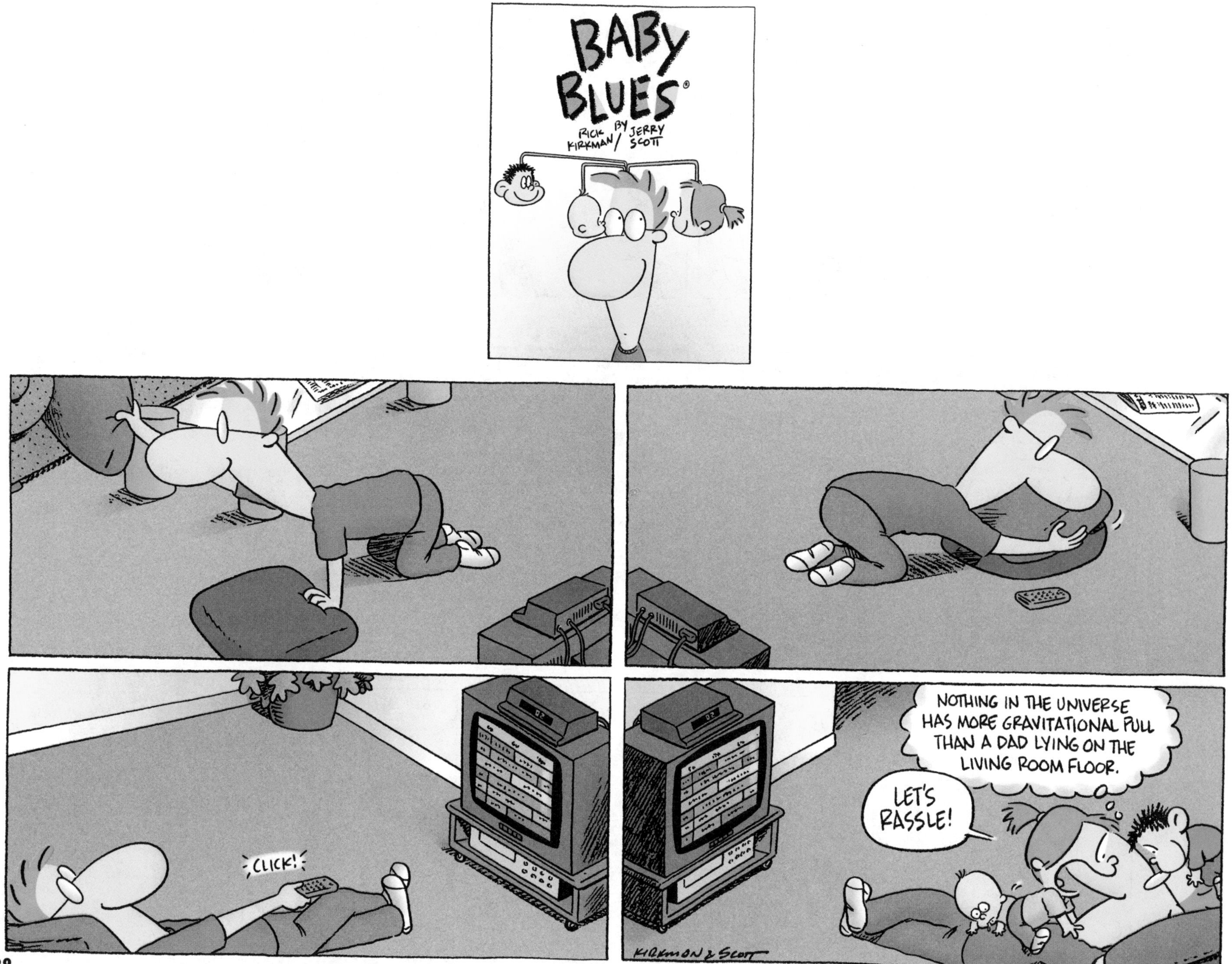
BABY BLUES®
BY RICK KIRKMAN / JERRY SCOTT
CLICK!
NOTHING IN THE UNIVERSE HAS MORE GRAVITATIONAL PULL THAN A DAD LYING ON THE LIVING ROOM FLOOR.
LET'S RASSLE!
KIRKMAN & SCOTT

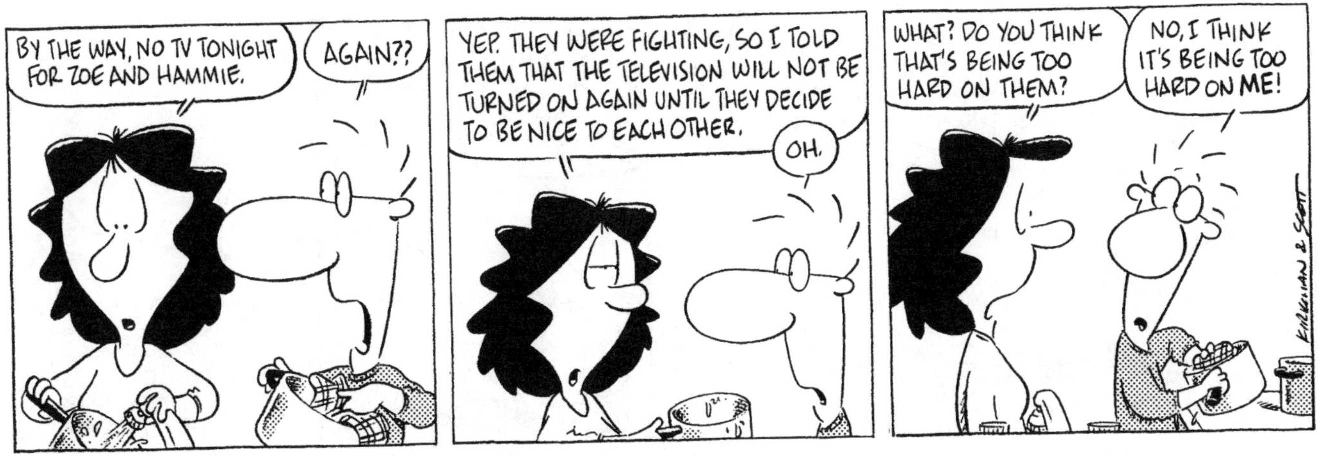
BY THE WAY, NO TV TONIGHT FOR ZOE AND HAMMIE.
AGAIN??
YEP. THEY WERE FIGHTING, SO I TOLD THEM THAT THE TELEVISION WILL NOT BE TURNED ON AGAIN UNTIL THEY DECIDE TO BE NICE TO EACH OTHER.
OH.
WHAT? DO YOU THINK THAT'S BEING TOO HARD ON THEM?
NO, I THINK IT'S BEING TOO HARD ON ME!
KIRKMAN & SCOTT

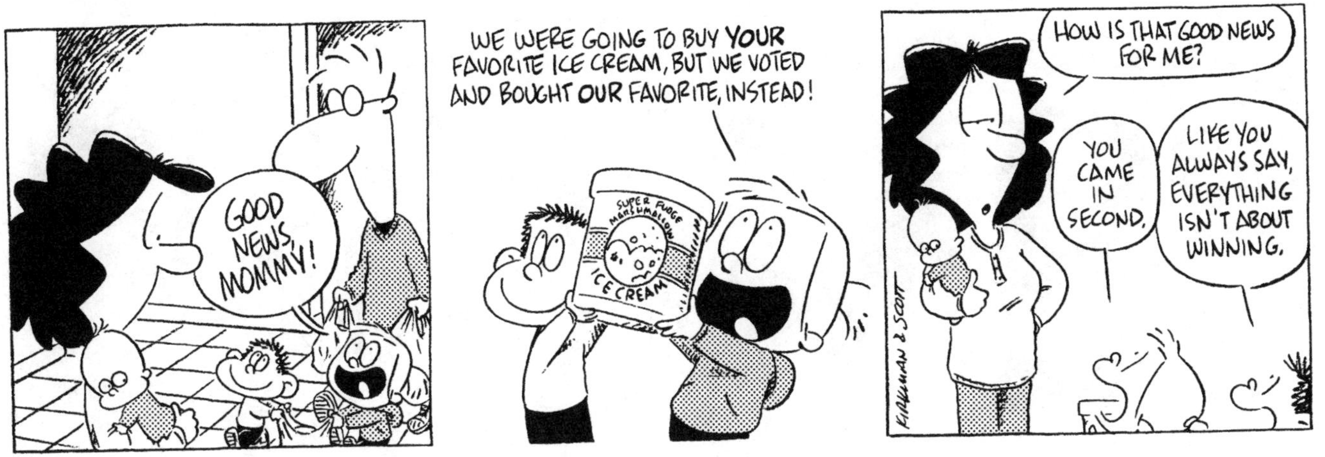
GOOD NEWS, MOMMY!
WE WERE GOING TO BUY YOUR FAVORITE ICE CREAM, BUT WE VOTED AND BOUGHT OUR FAVORITE, INSTEAD!
SUPER FUDGE MARSHMALLOW
ICE CREAM
KIRKMAN & SCOTT
HOW IS THAT GOOD NEWS FOR ME?
YOU CAME IN SECOND.
LIKE YOU ALWAYS SAY, EVERYTHING ISN'T ABOUT WINNING.

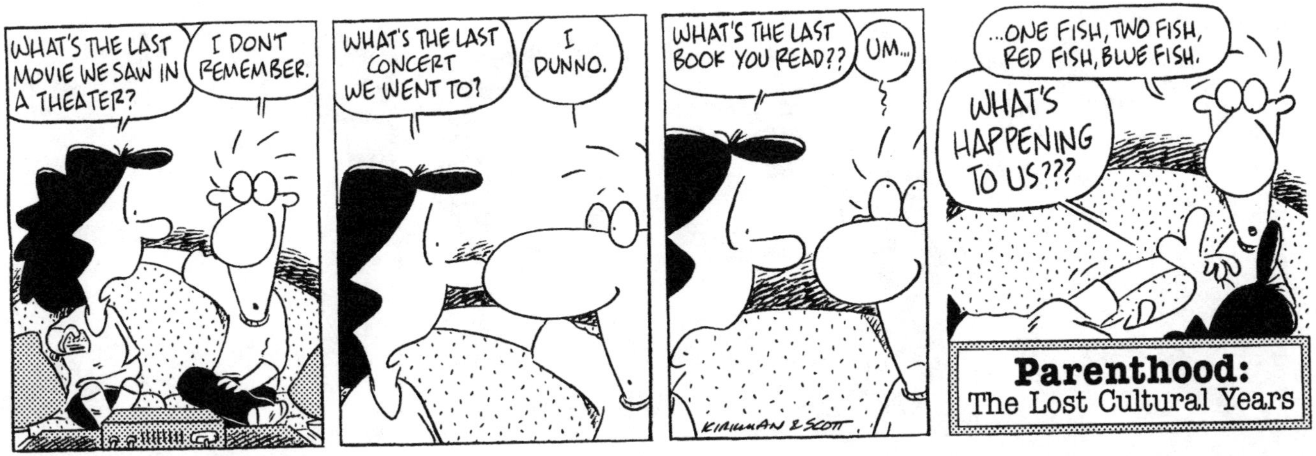
WHAT'S THE LAST MOVIE WE SAW IN A THEATER?
I DON'T REMEMBER.
WHAT'S THE LAST CONCERT WE WENT TO?
I DUNNO.
WHAT'S THE LAST BOOK YOU READ??
UM...
KIRKMAN & SCOTT
...ONE FISH, TWO FISH, RED FISH, BLUE FISH.
WHAT'S HAPPENING TO US???
Parenthood:
The Lost Cultural Years

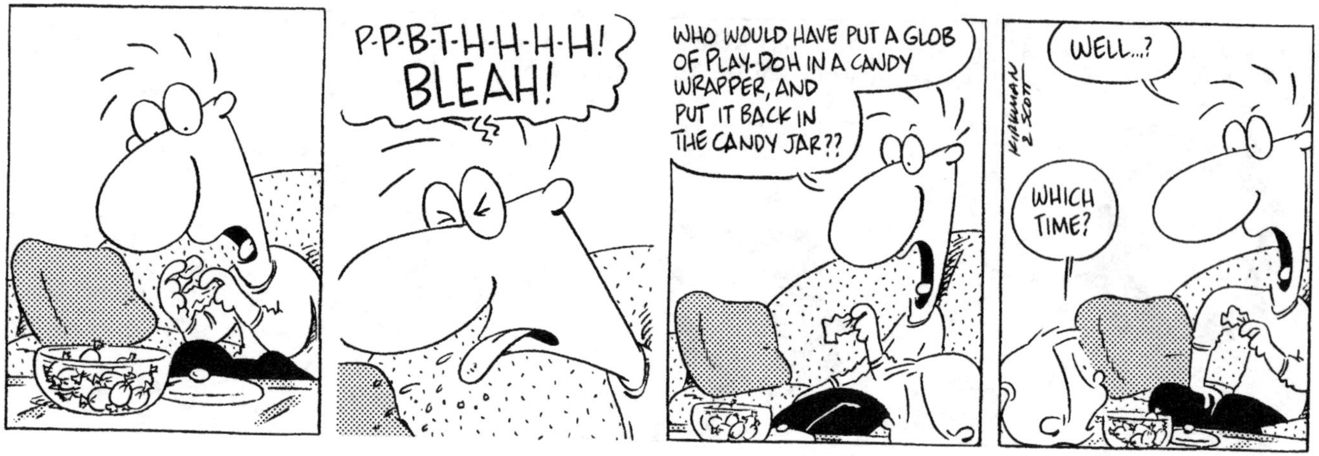
P-P-B-T-H-H-H-H! BLEAH!
WHO WOULD HAVE PUT A GLOB OF PLAY-DOH IN A CANDY WRAPPER, AND PUT IT BACK IN THE CANDY JAR??
WELL...?
WHICH TIME?
KIRKMAN & SCOTT

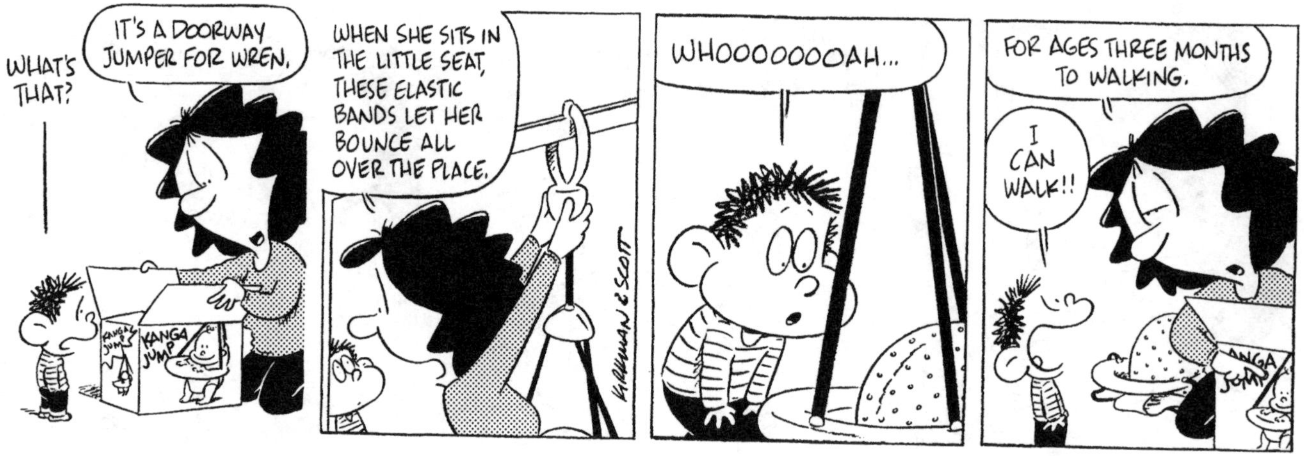
WHAT'S THAT?
IT'S A DOORWAY JUMPER FOR WREN.
KANGA JUMP
WHEN SHE SITS IN THE LITTLE SEAT, THESE ELASTIC BANDS LET HER BOUNCE ALL OVER THE PLACE.
KIRKMAN & SCOTT
WHOOOOOOOOAH...
FOR AGES THREE MONTHS TO WALKING.
I CAN WALK!!

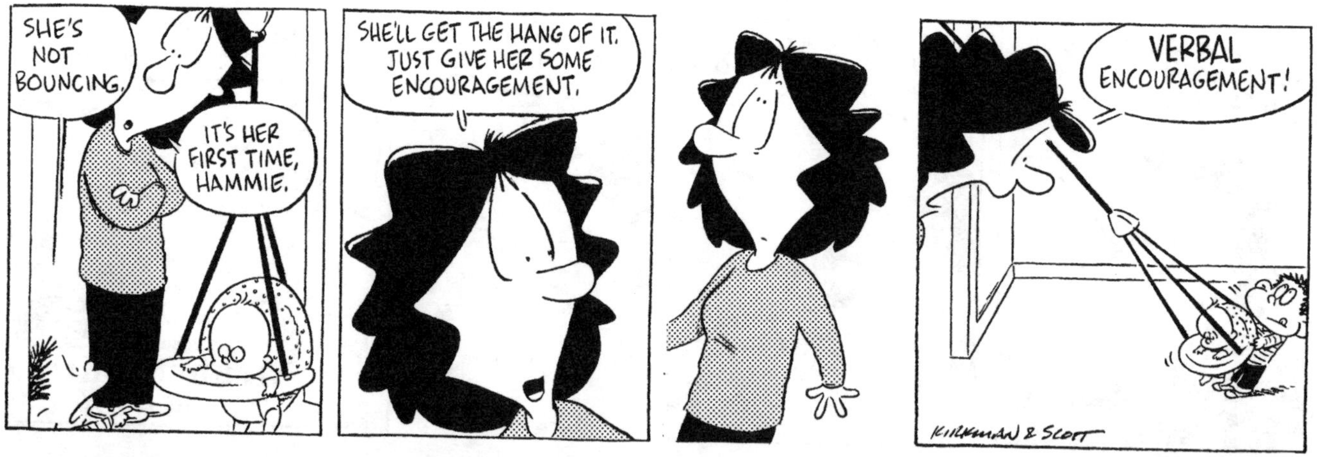
SHE'S NOT BOUNCING.
IT'S HER FIRST TIME, HAMMIE.
SHE'LL GET THE HANG OF IT. JUST GIVE HER SOME ENCOURAGEMENT.
VERBAL ENCOURAGEMENT!
KIRKMAN & SCOTT

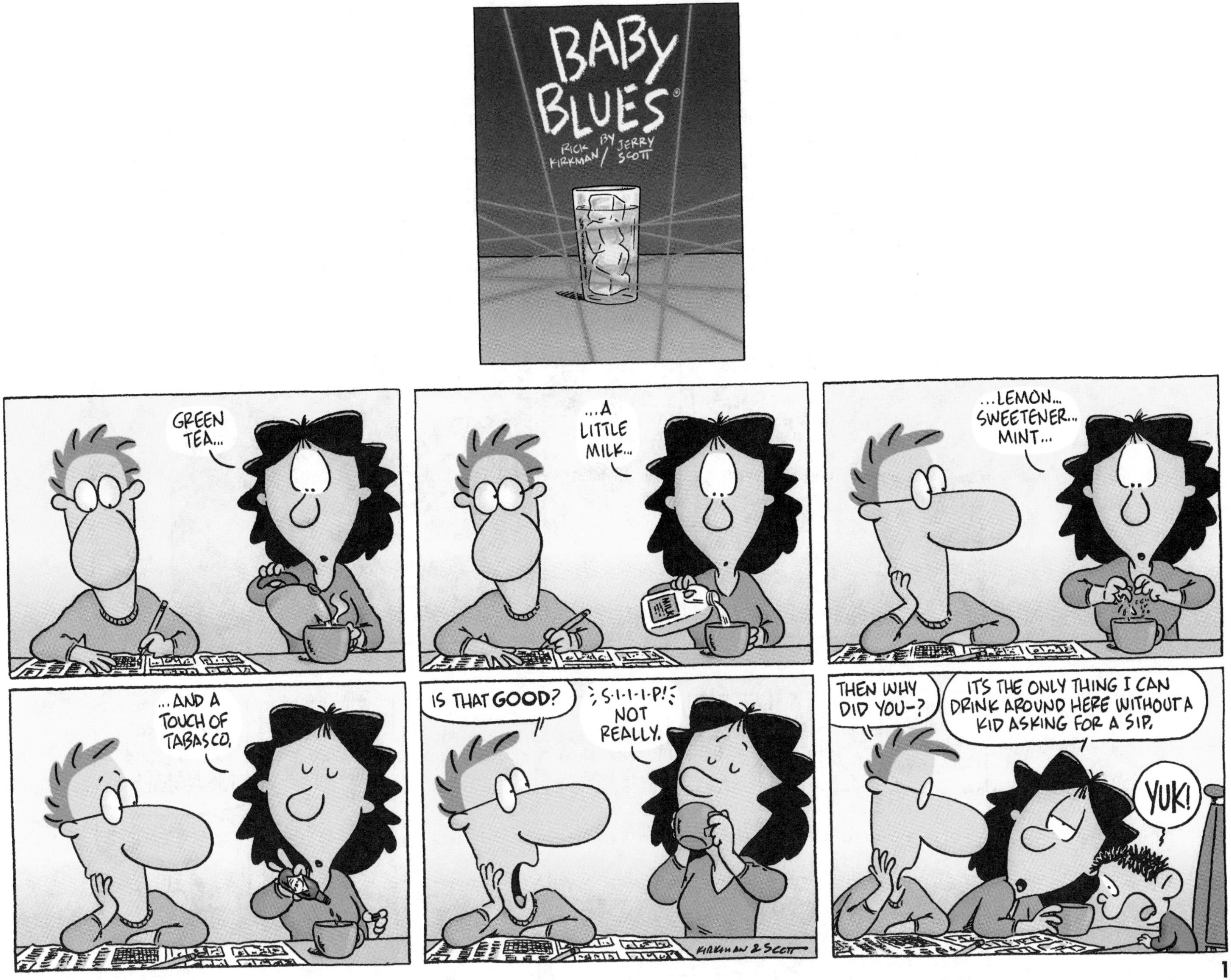
BABY BLUES®
BY RICK KIRKMAN / JERRY SCOTT
GREEN TEA...
...A LITTLE MILK...
MILK
...LEMON... SWEETENER... MINT...
...AND A TOUCH OF TABASCO.
IS THAT GOOD?
S-I-I-I-P! NOT REALLY.
KIRKMAN & SCOTT
THEN WHY DID YOU-?
IT'S THE ONLY THING I CAN DRINK AROUND HERE WITHOUT A KID ASKING FOR A SIP.
YUK!

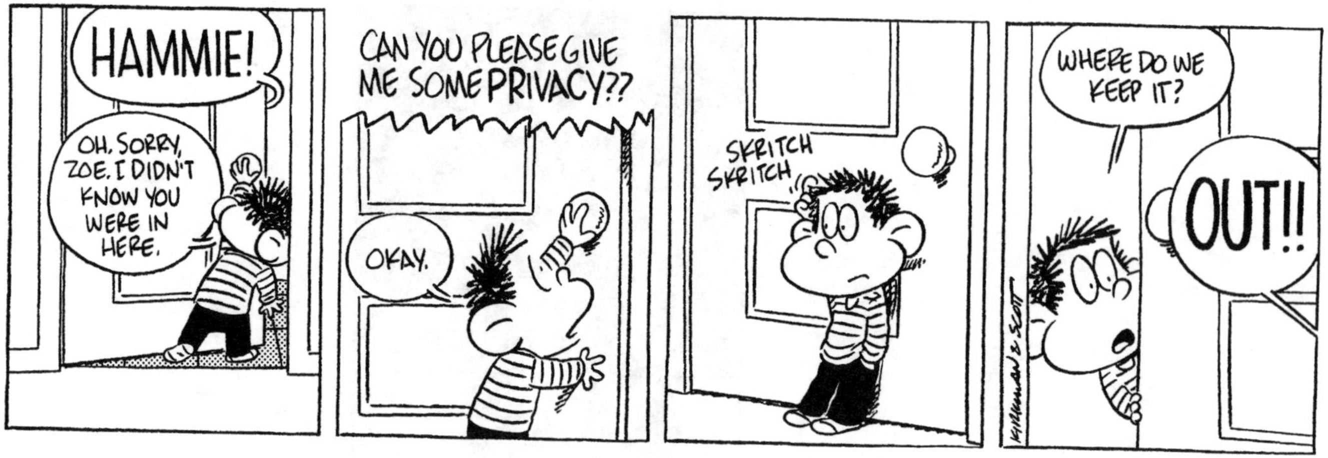
HAMMIE!
OH, SORRY, ZOE. I DIDN'T KNOW YOU WERE IN HERE.
CAN YOU PLEASE GIVE ME SOME PRIVACY??
OKAY.
SKRITCH SKRITCH
WHERE DO WE KEEP IT?
OUT!!
KIRKMAN & SCOTT

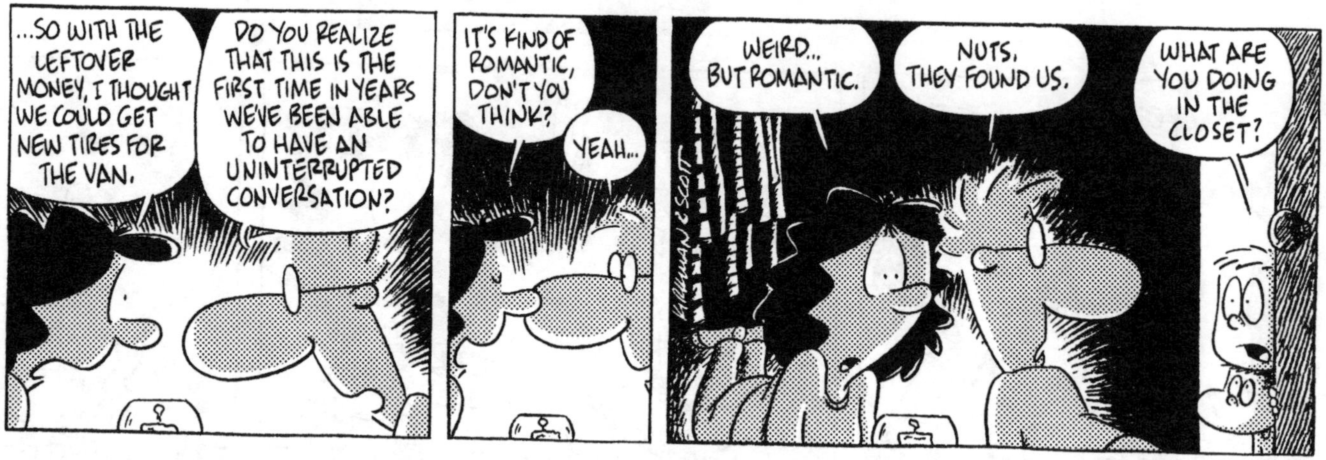
...SO WITH THE LEFTOVER MONEY, I THOUGHT WE COULD GET NEW TIRES FOR THE VAN.
DO YOU REALIZE THAT THIS IS THE FIRST TIME IN YEARS WE'VE BEEN ABLE TO HAVE AN UNINTERRUPTED CONVERSATION?
IT'S KIND OF ROMANTIC, DON'T YOU THINK?
YEAH...
KIRKMAN & SCOTT
WEIRD... BUT ROMANTIC.
NUTS. THEY FOUND US.
WHAT ARE YOU DOING IN THE CLOSET?

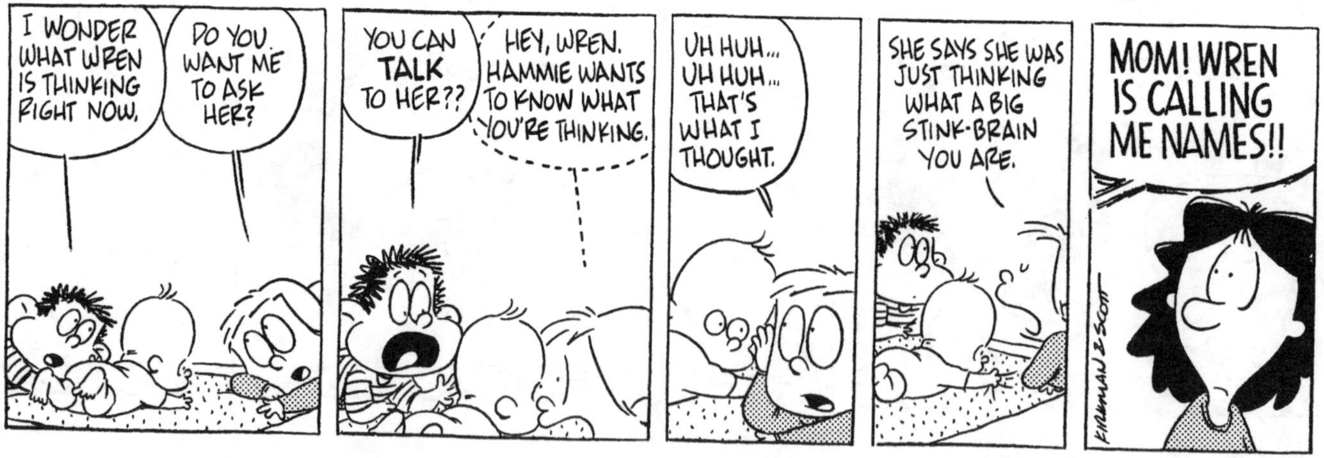
I WONDER WHAT WREN IS THINKING RIGHT NOW.
DO YOU WANT ME TO ASK HER?
YOU CAN TALK TO HER??
HEY, WREN. HAMMIE WANTS TO KNOW WHAT YOU'RE THINKING.
UH HUH... UH HUH... THAT'S WHAT I THOUGHT.
SHE SAYS SHE WAS JUST THINKING WHAT A BIG STINK-BRAIN YOU ARE.
KIRKMAN & SCOTT
MOM! WREN IS CALLING ME NAMES!!

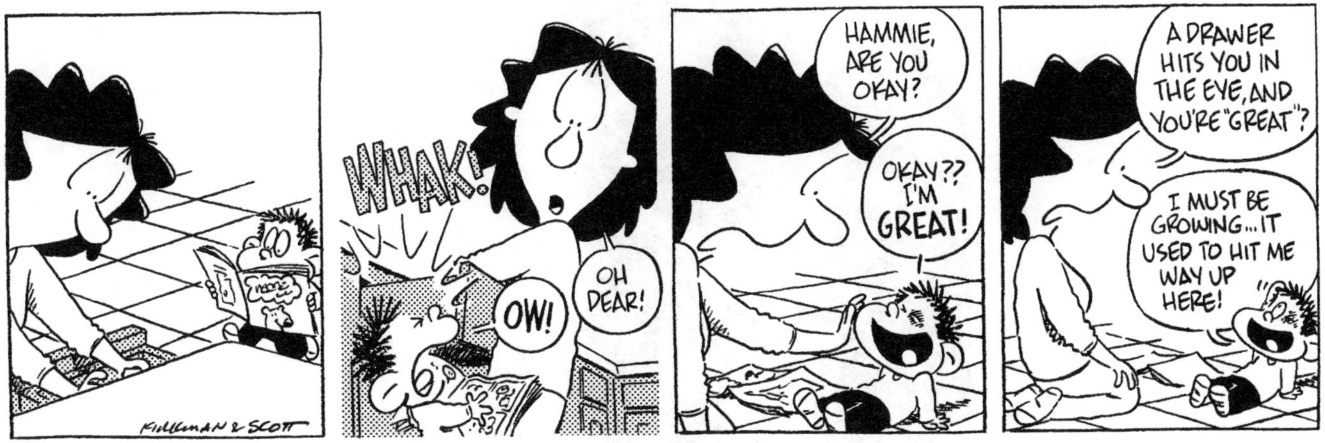
KIRKMAN & SCOTT
WHAK!
OW!
OH DEAR!
HAMMIE, ARE YOU OKAY?
OKAY?? I'M GREAT!
A DRAWER HITS YOU IN THE EYE, AND YOU'RE "GREAT"?
I MUST BE GROWING... IT USED TO HIT ME WAY UP HERE!

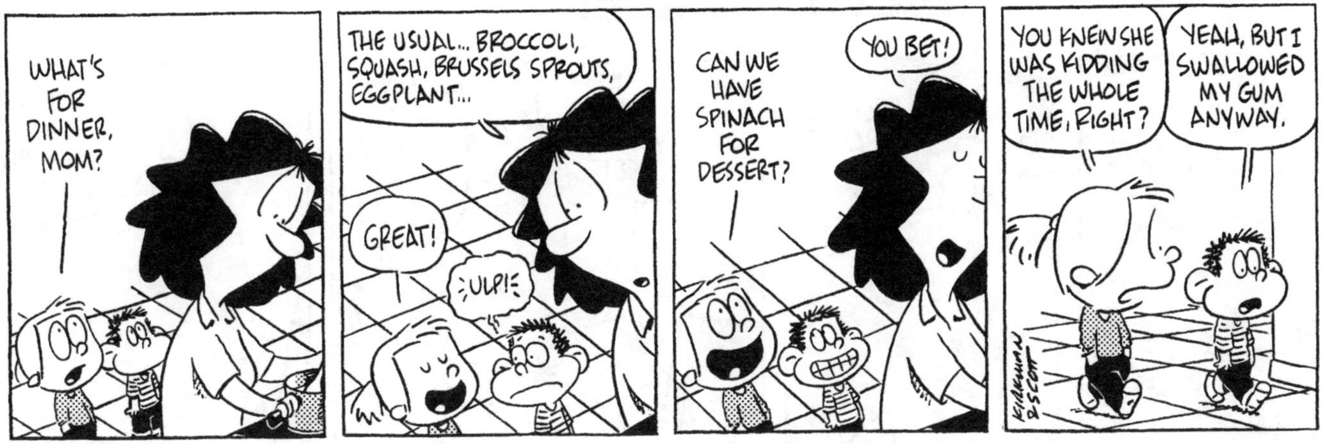
WHAT'S FOR DINNER, MOM?
THE USUAL... BROCCOLI, SQUASH, BRUSSELS SPROUTS, EGGPLANT...
GREAT!
ULP!
CAN WE HAVE SPINACH FOR DESSERT?
YOU BET!
YOU KNEW SHE WAS KIDDING THE WHOLE TIME, RIGHT?
YEAH, BUT I SWALLOWED MY GUM ANYWAY.
KIRKMAN & SCOTT

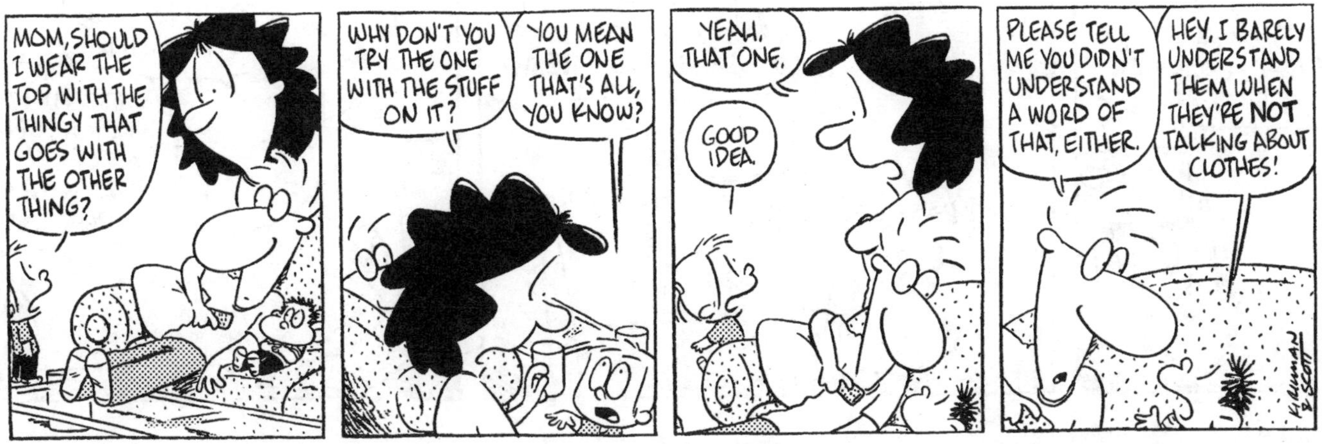
MOM, SHOULD I WEAR THE TOP WITH THE THINGY THAT GOES WITH THE OTHER THING?
WHY DON'T YOU TRY THE ONE WITH THE STUFF ON IT?
YOU MEAN THE ONE THAT'S ALL, YOU KNOW?
YEAH, THAT ONE.
GOOD IDEA.
PLEASE TELL ME YOU DIDN'T UNDERSTAND A WORD OF THAT, EITHER.
HEY, I BARELY UNDERSTAND THEM WHEN THEY'RE NOT TALKING ABOUT CLOTHES!
KIRKMAN & SCOTT

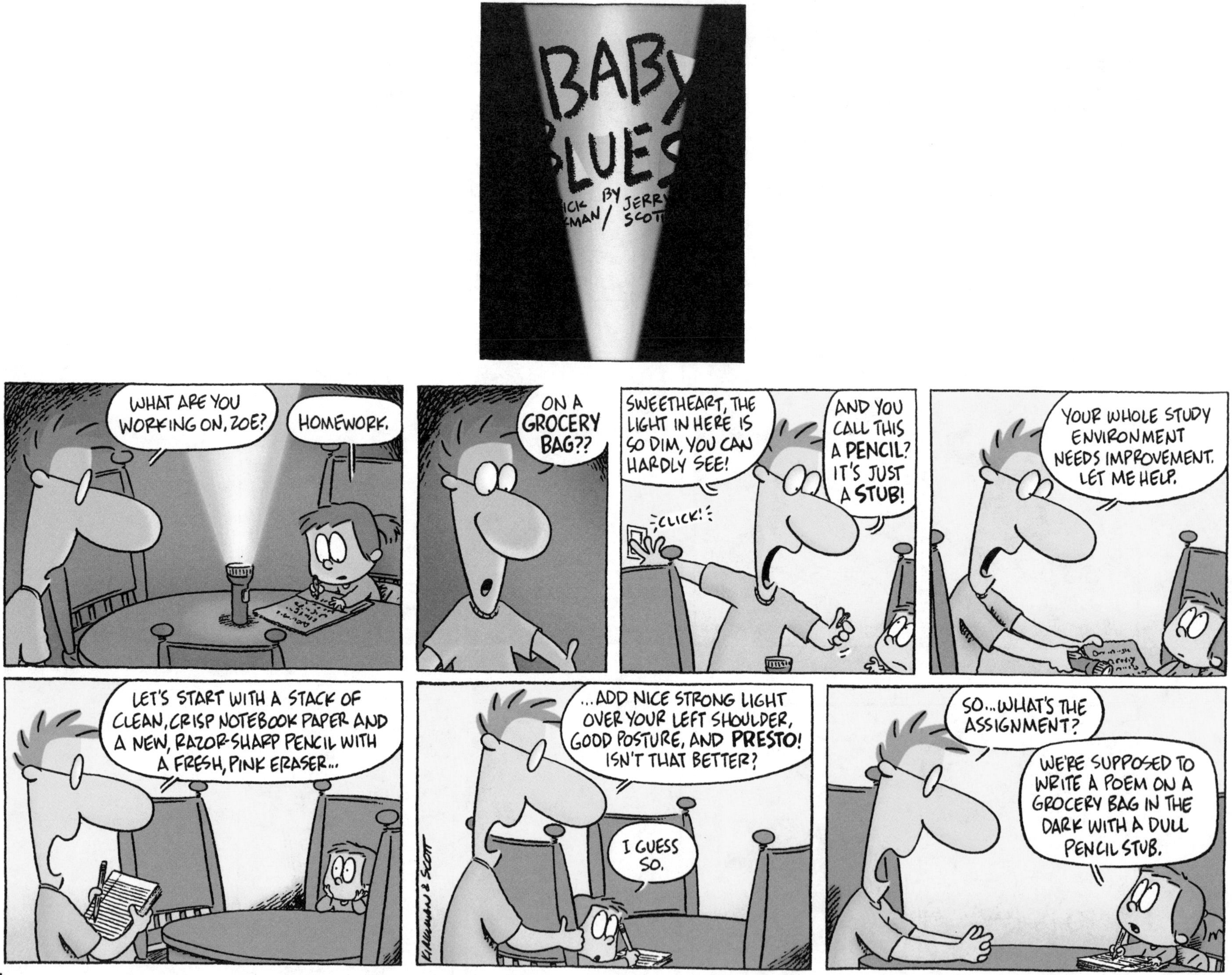
BABY BLUES
BY RICK KIRKMAN / JERRY SCOTT
WHAT ARE YOU WORKING ON, ZOE?
HOMEWORK.
ON A GROCERY BAG??
SWEETHEART, THE LIGHT IN HERE IS SO DIM, YOU CAN HARDLY SEE!
CLICK!
AND YOU CALL THIS A PENCIL? IT'S JUST A STUB!
YOUR WHOLE STUDY ENVIRONMENT NEEDS IMPROVEMENT. LET ME HELP.
LET'S START WITH A STACK OF CLEAN, CRISP NOTEBOOK PAPER AND A NEW, RAZOR-SHARP PENCIL WITH A FRESH, PINK ERASER...
...ADD NICE STRONG LIGHT OVER YOUR LEFT SHOULDER, GOOD POSTURE, AND PRESTO! ISN'T THAT BETTER?
I GUESS SO.
KIRKMAN & SCOTT
SO...WHAT'S THE ASSIGNMENT?
WE'RE SUPPOSED TO WRITE A POEM ON A GROCERY BAG IN THE DARK WITH A DULL PENCIL STUB.

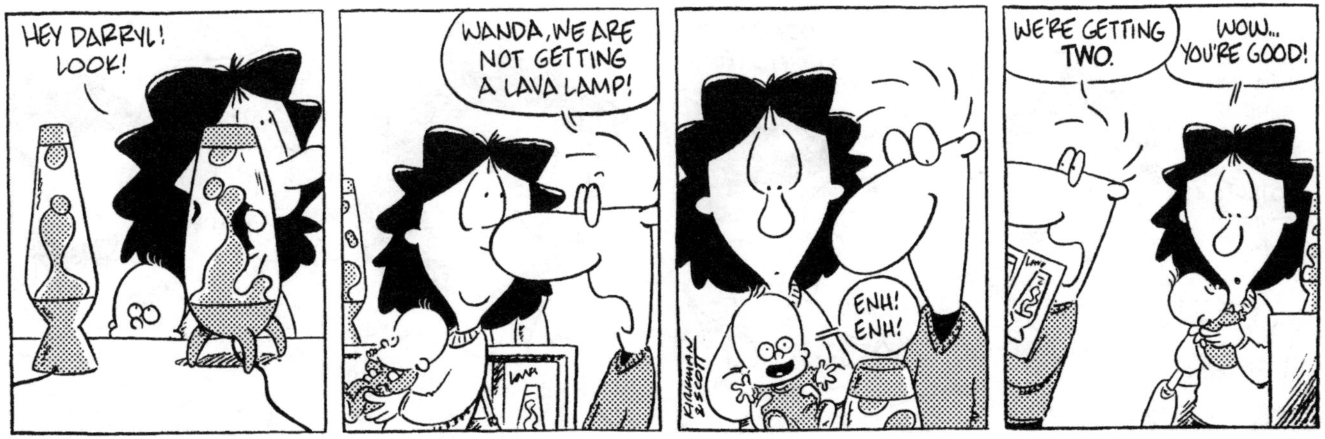
HEY DARRYL! LOOK!
WANDA, WE ARE NOT GETTING A LAVA LAMP!
ENH! ENH!
WE'RE GETTING **TWO**.
WOW... YOU'RE GOOD!

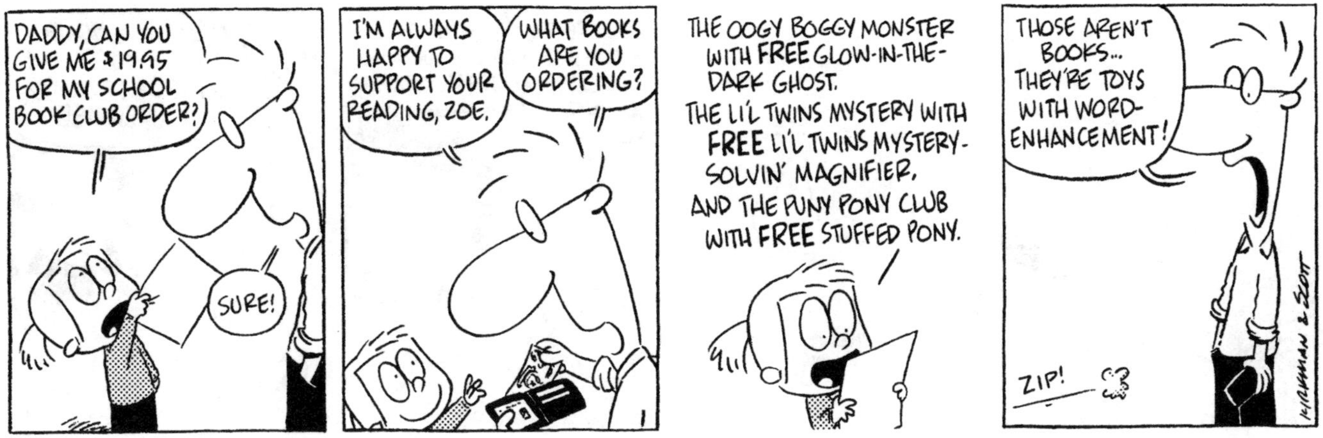
DADDY, CAN YOU GIVE ME $19.95 FOR MY SCHOOL BOOK CLUB ORDER?
SURE!
I'M ALWAYS HAPPY TO SUPPORT YOUR READING, ZOE.
WHAT BOOKS ARE YOU ORDERING?
THE OOGY BOGGY MONSTER WITH **FREE** GLOW-IN-THE-DARK GHOST. THE LI'L TWINS MYSTERY WITH **FREE** LI'L TWINS MYSTERY-SOLVIN' MAGNIFIER, AND THE PUNY PONY CLUB WITH **FREE** STUFFED PONY.
THOSE AREN'T BOOKS... THEY'RE TOYS WITH WORD-ENHANCEMENT!
ZIP!

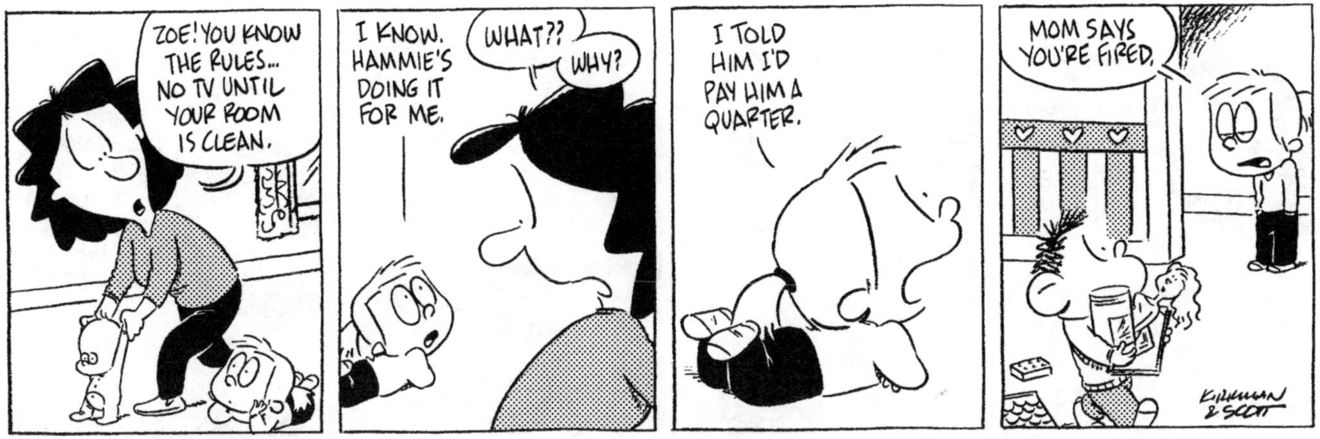
ZOE! YOU KNOW THE RULES... NO TV UNTIL YOUR ROOM IS CLEAN.
I KNOW. HAMMIE'S DOING IT FOR ME.
WHAT??
WHY?
I TOLD HIM I'D PAY HIM A QUARTER.
MOM SAYS YOU'RE FIRED.

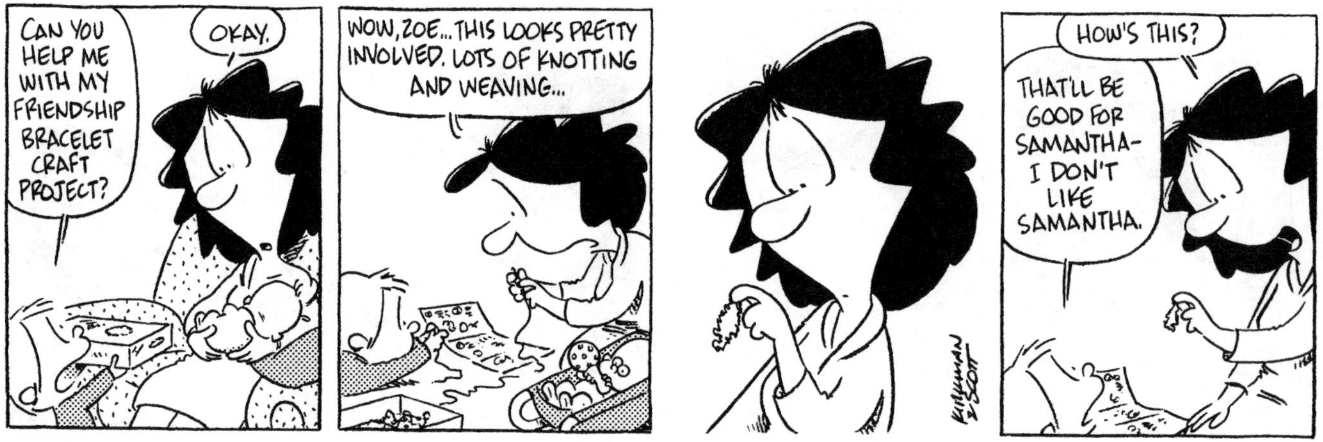
CAN YOU HELP ME WITH MY FRIENDSHIP BRACELET CRAFT PROJECT?
OKAY.
WOW, ZOE... THIS LOOKS PRETTY INVOLVED. LOTS OF KNOTTING AND WEAVING...
HOW'S THIS?
THAT'LL BE GOOD FOR SAMANTHA- I DON'T LIKE SAMANTHA.
KIRKMAN & SCOTT

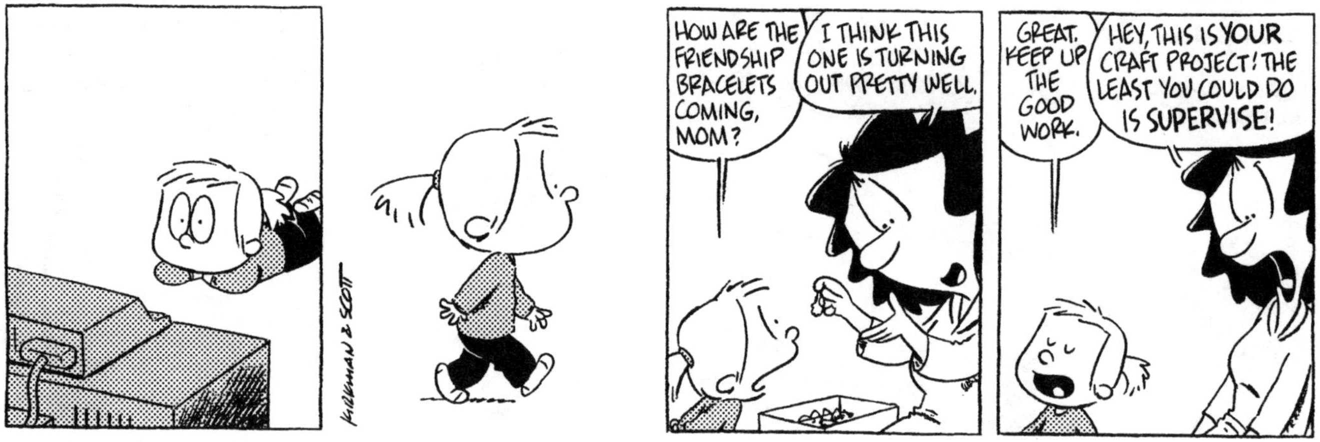
KIRKMAN & SCOTT
HOW ARE THE FRIENDSHIP BRACELETS COMING, MOM?
I THINK THIS ONE IS TURNING OUT PRETTY WELL.
GREAT. KEEP UP THE GOOD WORK.
HEY, THIS IS YOUR CRAFT PROJECT! THE LEAST YOU COULD DO IS SUPERVISE!

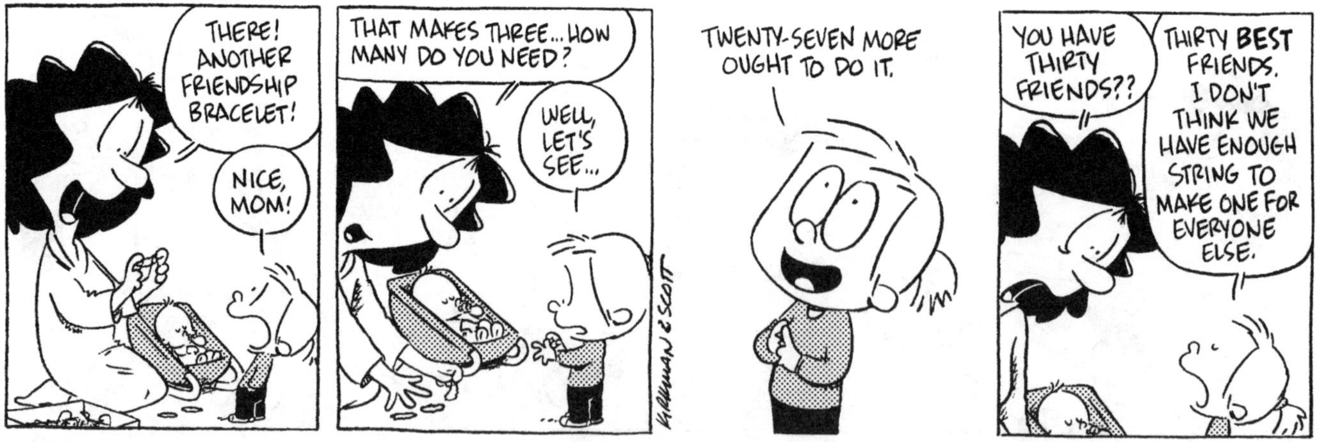
THERE! ANOTHER FRIENDSHIP BRACELET!
NICE, MOM!
THAT MAKES THREE... HOW MANY DO YOU NEED?
WELL, LET'S SEE...
KIRKMAN & SCOTT
TWENTY-SEVEN MORE OUGHT TO DO IT.
YOU HAVE THIRTY FRIENDS??
THIRTY BEST FRIENDS. I DON'T THINK WE HAVE ENOUGH STRING TO MAKE ONE FOR EVERYONE ELSE.

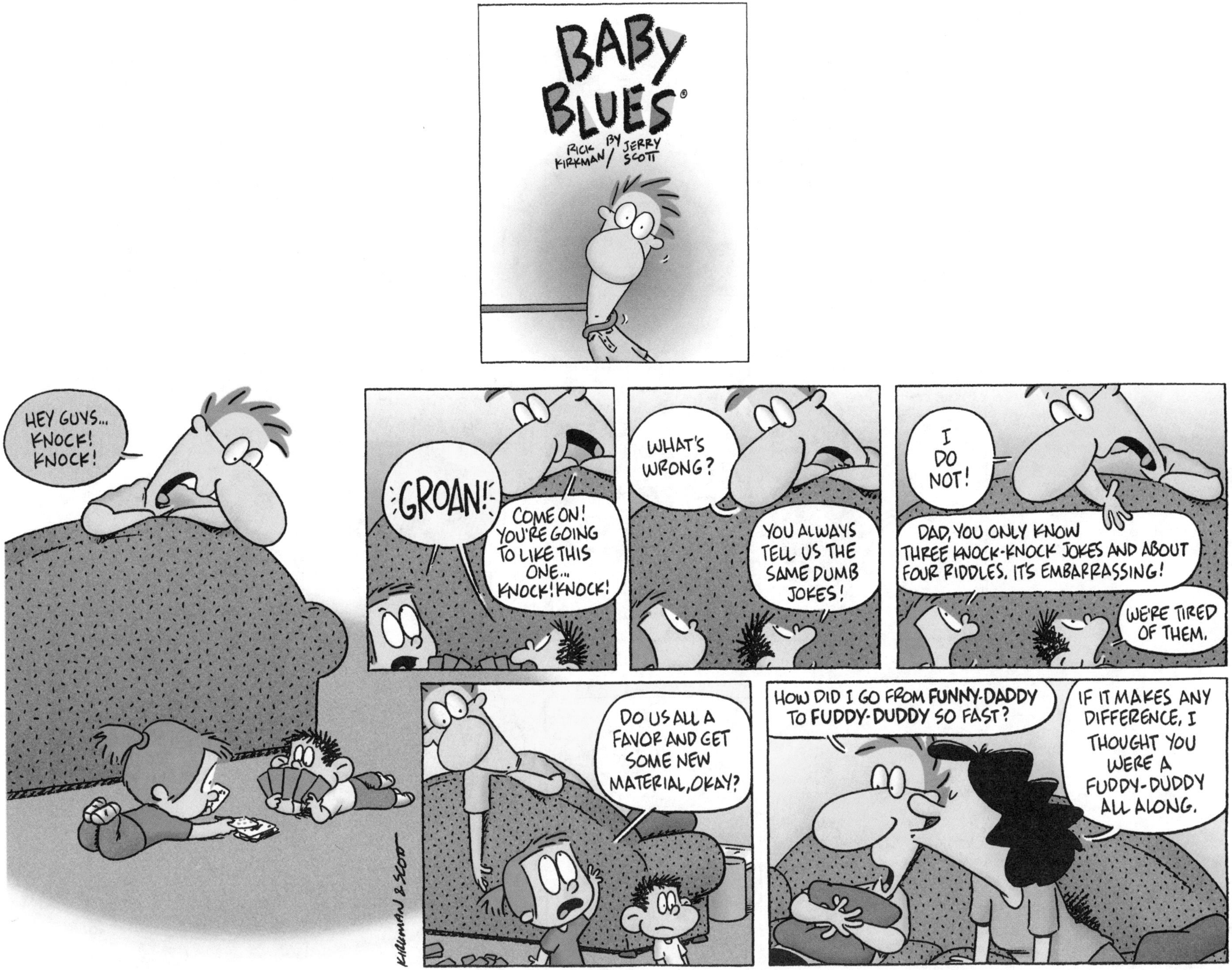
BABY BLUES®
BY RICK KIRKMAN / JERRY SCOTT
HEY GUYS... KNOCK! KNOCK!
GROAN!
COME ON! YOU'RE GOING TO LIKE THIS ONE... KNOCK! KNOCK!
WHAT'S WRONG?
YOU ALWAYS TELL US THE SAME DUMB JOKES!
I DO NOT!
DAD, YOU ONLY KNOW THREE KNOCK-KNOCK JOKES AND ABOUT FOUR RIDDLES. IT'S EMBARRASSING!
WE'RE TIRED OF THEM.
DO US ALL A FAVOR AND GET SOME NEW MATERIAL, OKAY?
HOW DID I GO FROM **FUNNY-DADDY** TO **FUDDY-DUDDY** SO FAST?
IF IT MAKES ANY DIFFERENCE, I THOUGHT YOU WERE A FUDDY-DUDDY ALL ALONG.
KIRKMAN & SCOTT

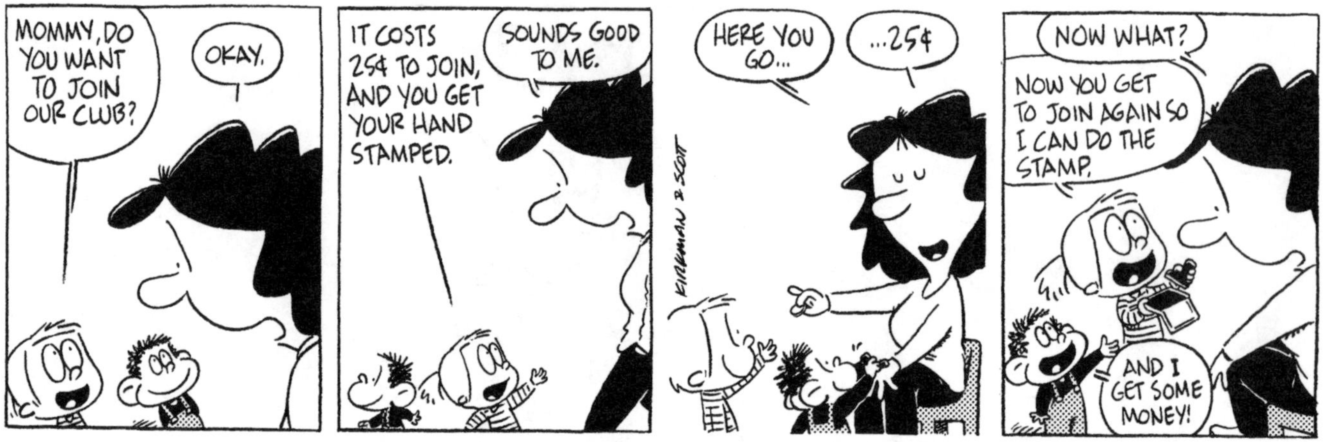
MOMMY, DO YOU WANT TO JOIN OUR CLUB?
OKAY.
IT COSTS 25¢ TO JOIN, AND YOU GET YOUR HAND STAMPED.
SOUNDS GOOD TO ME.
HERE YOU GO...
...25¢
NOW WHAT?
NOW YOU GET TO JOIN AGAIN SO I CAN DO THE STAMP.
AND I GET SOME MONEY!
KIRKMAN & SCOTT

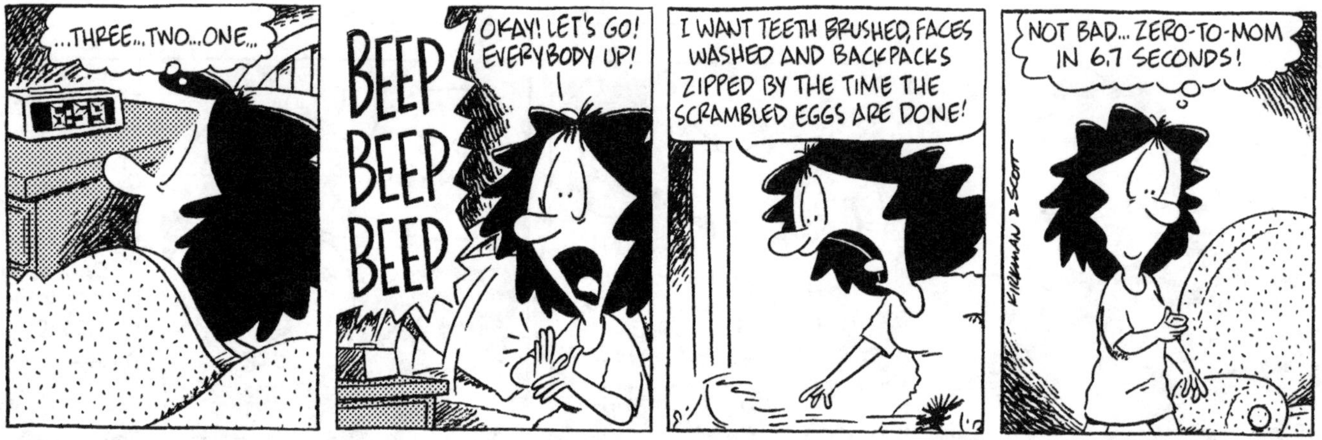
...THREE...TWO...ONE...
BEEP BEEP BEEP
OKAY! LET'S GO! EVERYBODY UP!
I WANT TEETH BRUSHED, FACES WASHED AND BACKPACKS ZIPPED BY THE TIME THE SCRAMBLED EGGS ARE DONE!
NOT BAD... ZERO-TO-MOM IN 6.7 SECONDS!
KIRKMAN & SCOTT

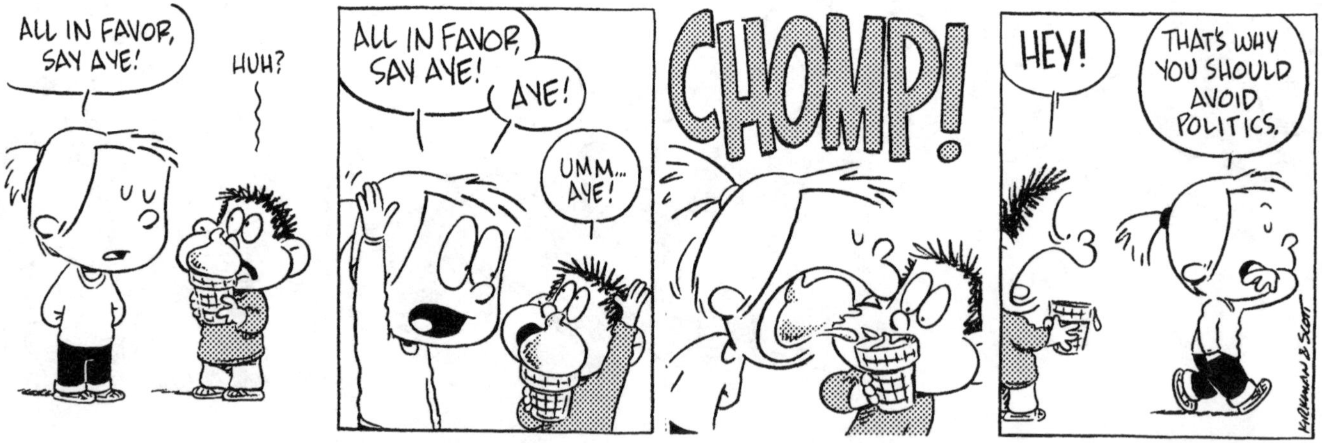
ALL IN FAVOR, SAY AYE!
HUH?
ALL IN FAVOR, SAY AYE!
AYE!
UMM... AYE!
CHOMP!
HEY!
THAT'S WHY YOU SHOULD AVOID POLITICS.
KIRKMAN & SCOTT

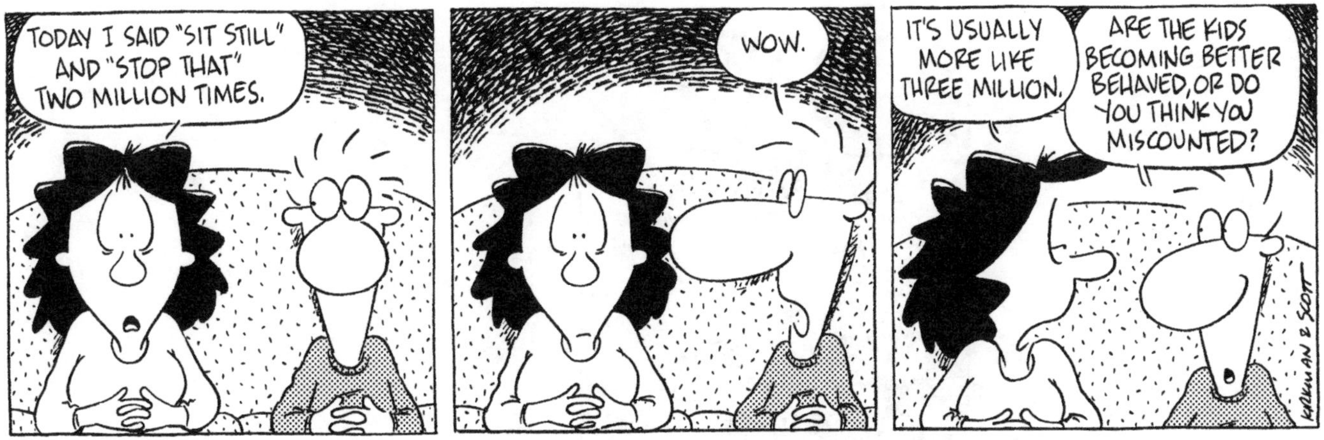
TODAY I SAID "SIT STILL" AND "STOP THAT" TWO MILLION TIMES.
WOW.
IT'S USUALLY MORE LIKE THREE MILLION.
ARE THE KIDS BECOMING BETTER BEHAVED, OR DO YOU THINK YOU MISCOUNTED?
KIRKMAN & SCOTT

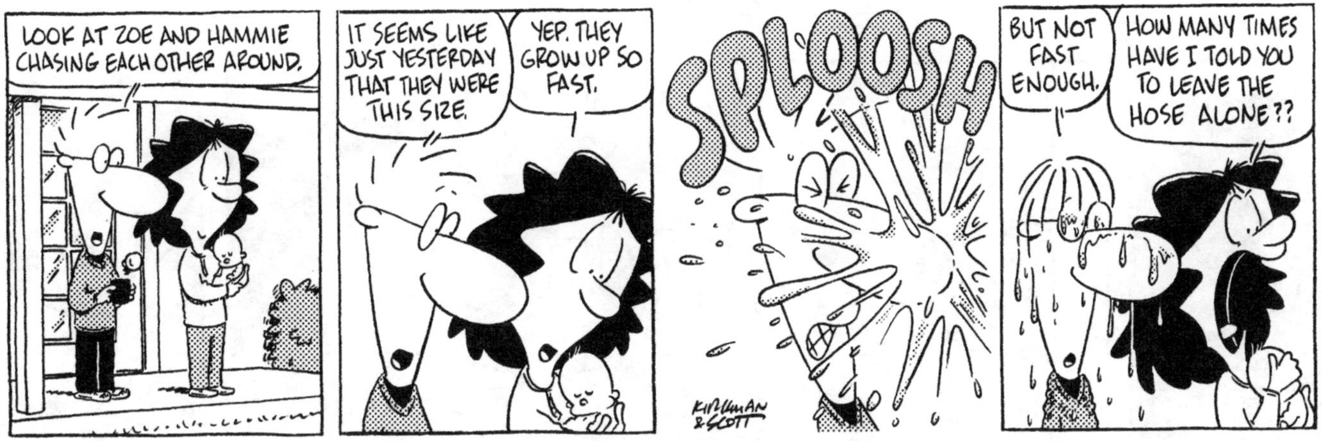
LOOK AT ZOE AND HAMMIE CHASING EACH OTHER AROUND.
IT SEEMS LIKE JUST YESTERDAY THAT THEY WERE THIS SIZE.
YEP. THEY GROW UP SO FAST.
SPLOOSH
KIRKMAN & SCOTT
BUT NOT FAST ENOUGH.
HOW MANY TIMES HAVE I TOLD YOU TO LEAVE THE HOSE ALONE??

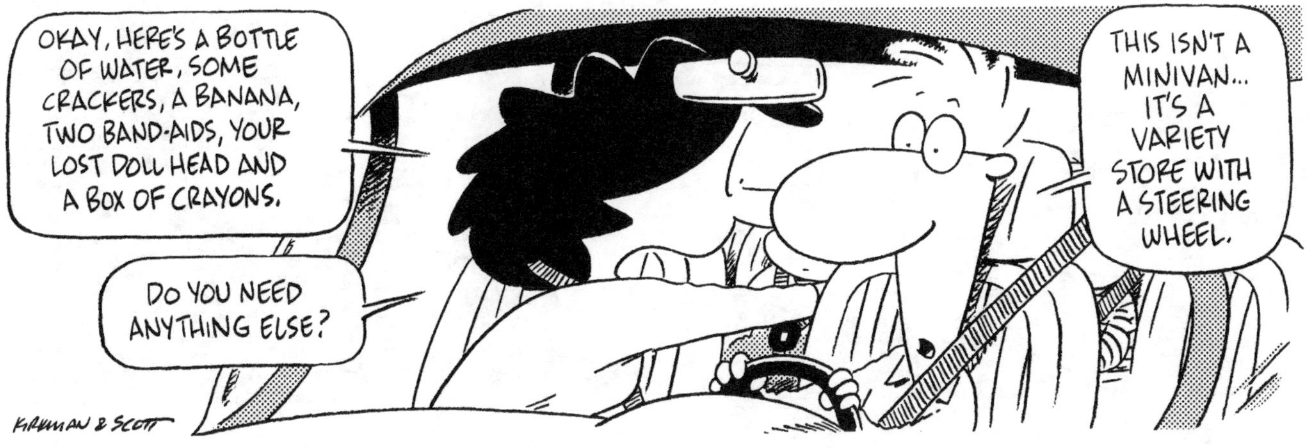
OKAY, HERE'S A BOTTLE OF WATER, SOME CRACKERS, A BANANA, TWO BAND-AIDS, YOUR LOST DOLL HEAD AND A BOX OF CRAYONS.
DO YOU NEED ANYTHING ELSE?
THIS ISN'T A MINIVAN... IT'S A VARIETY STORE WITH A STEERING WHEEL.
KIRKMAN & SCOTT

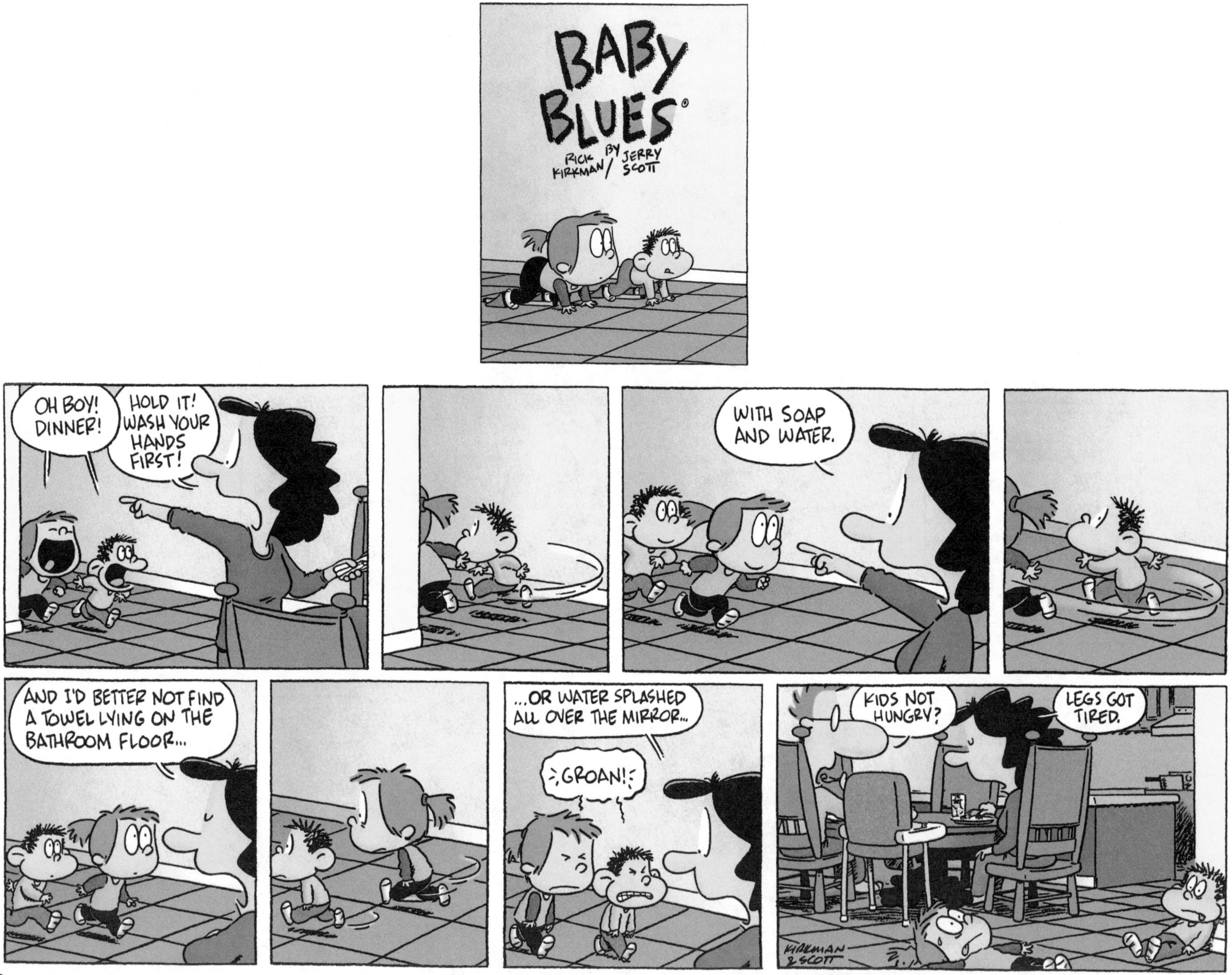
BABY BLUES®
BY RICK KIRKMAN / JERRY SCOTT
OH BOY! DINNER!
HOLD IT! WASH YOUR HANDS FIRST!
WITH SOAP AND WATER.
AND I'D BETTER NOT FIND A TOWEL LYING ON THE BATHROOM FLOOR...
...OR WATER SPLASHED ALL OVER THE MIRROR...
GROAN!
KIDS NOT HUNGRY?
LEGS GOT TIRED.
KIRKMAN & SCOTT

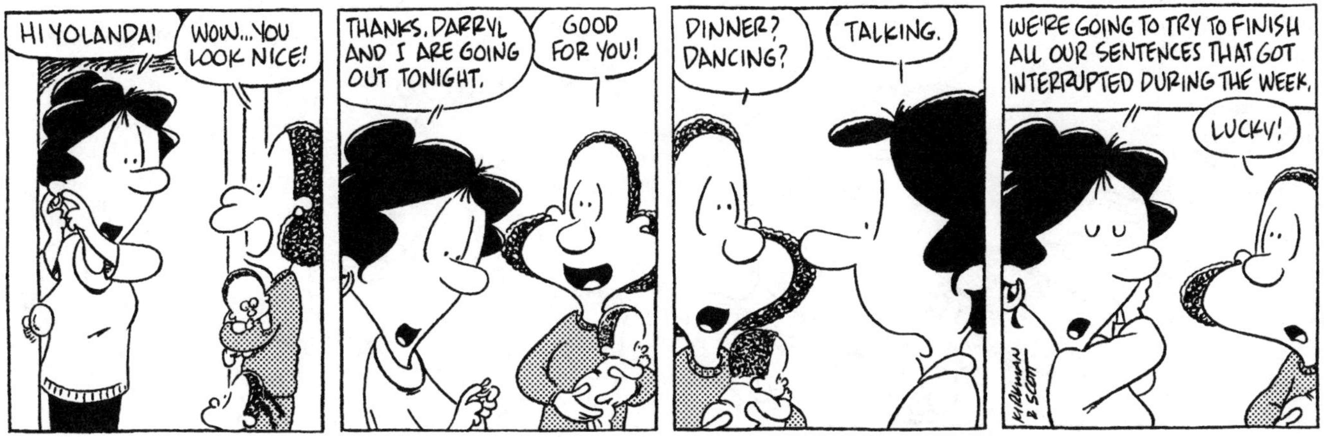
HI YOLANDA!
WOW...YOU LOOK NICE!
THANKS, DARRYL AND I ARE GOING OUT TONIGHT.
GOOD FOR YOU!
DINNER? DANCING?
TALKING.
WE'RE GOING TO TRY TO FINISH ALL OUR SENTENCES THAT GOT INTERRUPTED DURING THE WEEK.
LUCKY!
KIRKMAN & SCOTT

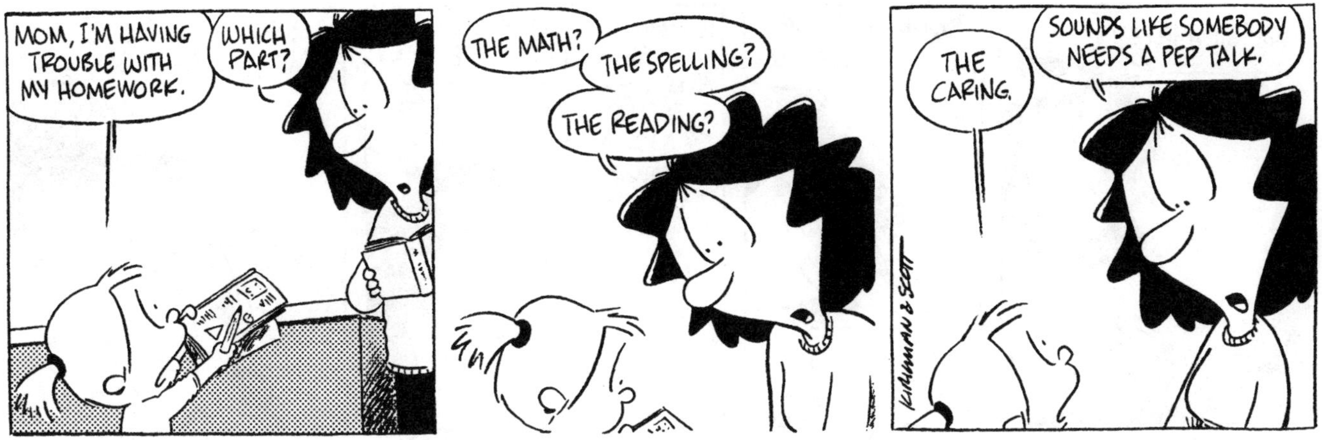
MOM, I'M HAVING TROUBLE WITH MY HOMEWORK.
WHICH PART?
THE MATH?
THE SPELLING?
THE READING?
THE CARING.
SOUNDS LIKE SOMEBODY NEEDS A PEP TALK.
KIRKMAN & SCOTT

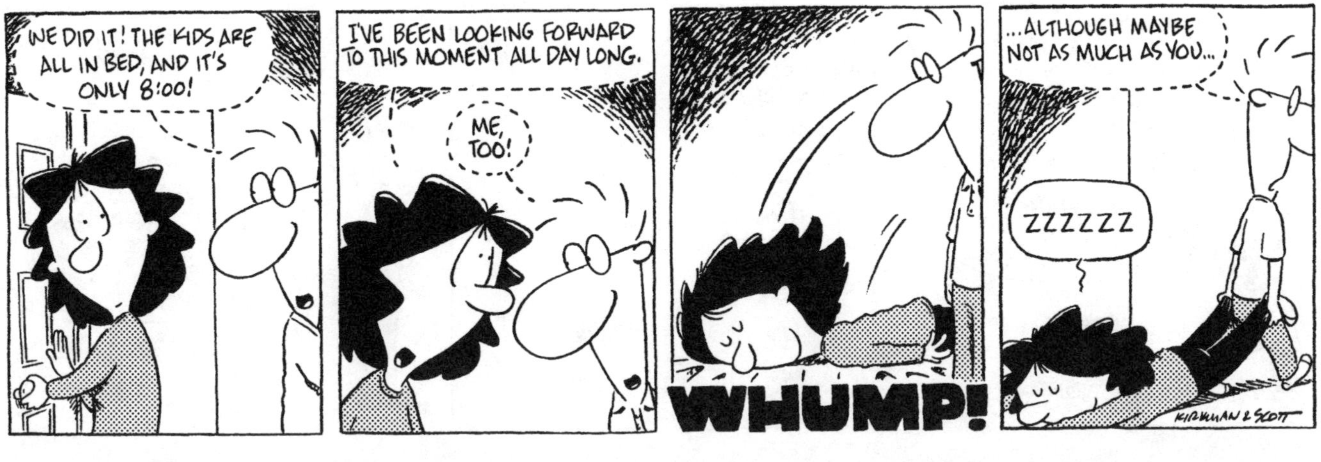
WE DID IT! THE KIDS ARE ALL IN BED, AND IT'S ONLY 8:00!
I'VE BEEN LOOKING FORWARD TO THIS MOMENT ALL DAY LONG.
ME, TOO!
WHUMP!
...ALTHOUGH MAYBE NOT AS MUCH AS YOU...
ZZZZZZ
KIRKMAN & SCOTT

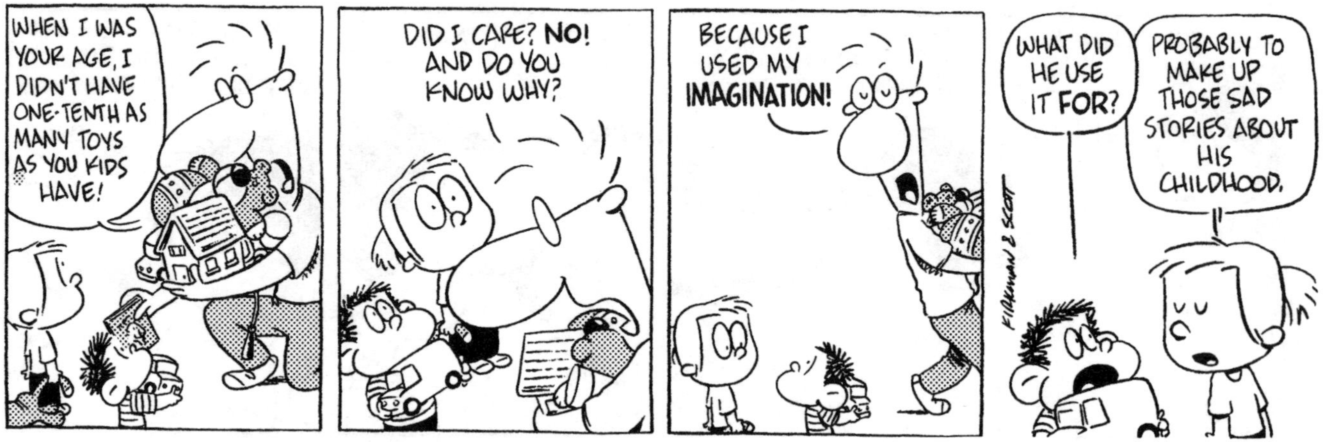
WHEN I WAS YOUR AGE, I DIDN'T HAVE ONE-TENTH AS MANY TOYS AS YOU KIDS HAVE!
DID I CARE? NO! AND DO YOU KNOW WHY?
BECAUSE I USED MY IMAGINATION!
WHAT DID HE USE IT FOR?
PROBABLY TO MAKE UP THOSE SAD STORIES ABOUT HIS CHILDHOOD.
KIRKMAN & SCOTT

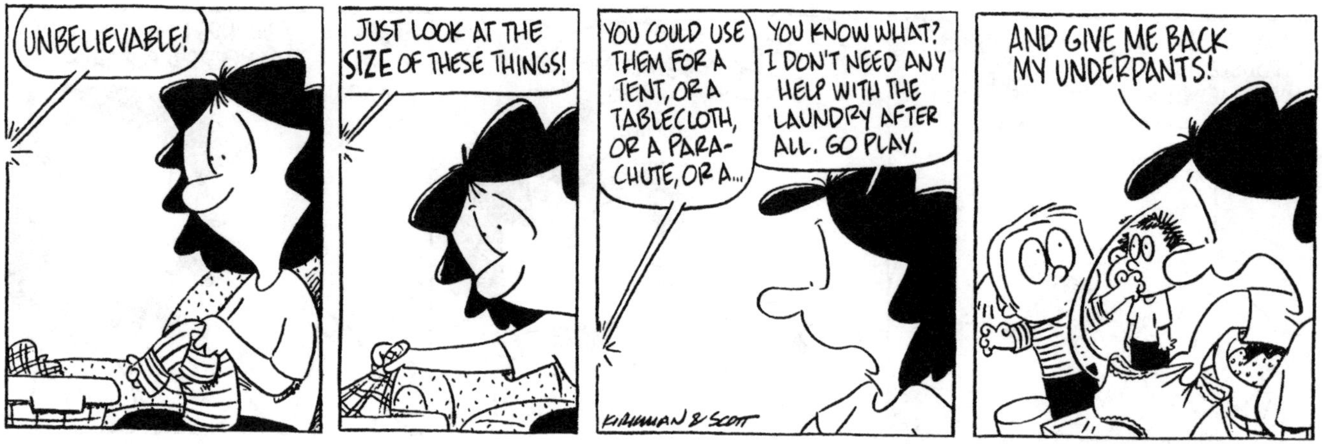
UNBELIEVABLE!
JUST LOOK AT THE SIZE OF THESE THINGS!
YOU COULD USE THEM FOR A TENT, OR A TABLECLOTH, OR A PARA-CHUTE, OR A...
YOU KNOW WHAT? I DON'T NEED ANY HELP WITH THE LAUNDRY AFTER ALL. GO PLAY.
KIRKMAN & SCOTT
AND GIVE ME BACK MY UNDERPANTS!

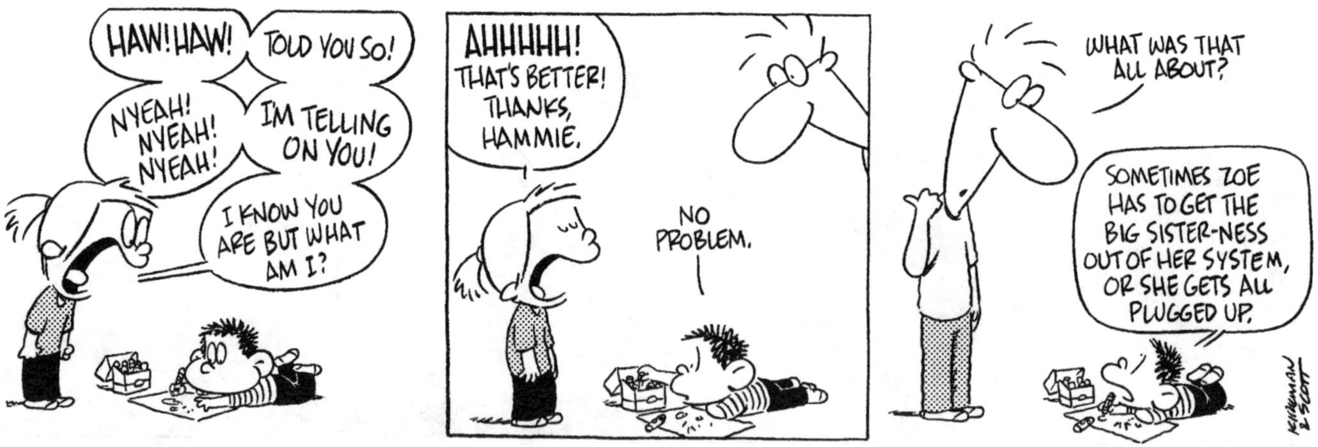
HAW! HAW!
TOLD YOU SO!
NYEAH! NYEAH! NYEAH!
I'M TELLING ON YOU!
I KNOW YOU ARE BUT WHAT AM I?
AHHHHH! THAT'S BETTER! THANKS, HAMMIE.
NO PROBLEM.
WHAT WAS THAT ALL ABOUT?
SOMETIMES ZOE HAS TO GET THE BIG SISTER-NESS OUT OF HER SYSTEM, OR SHE GETS ALL PLUGGED UP.
KIRKMAN & SCOTT

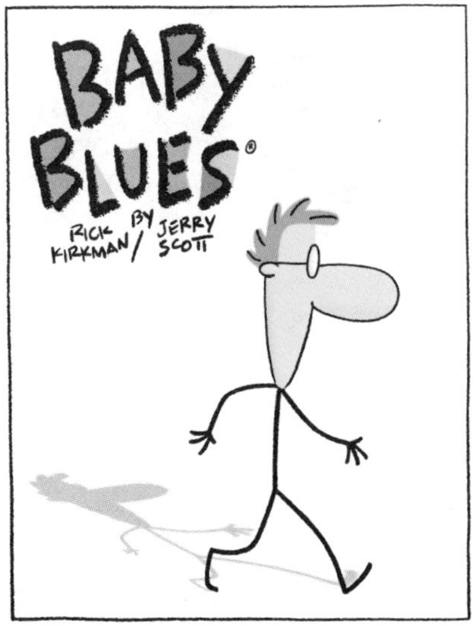
BABY BLUES®
BY RICK KIRKMAN / JERRY SCOTT

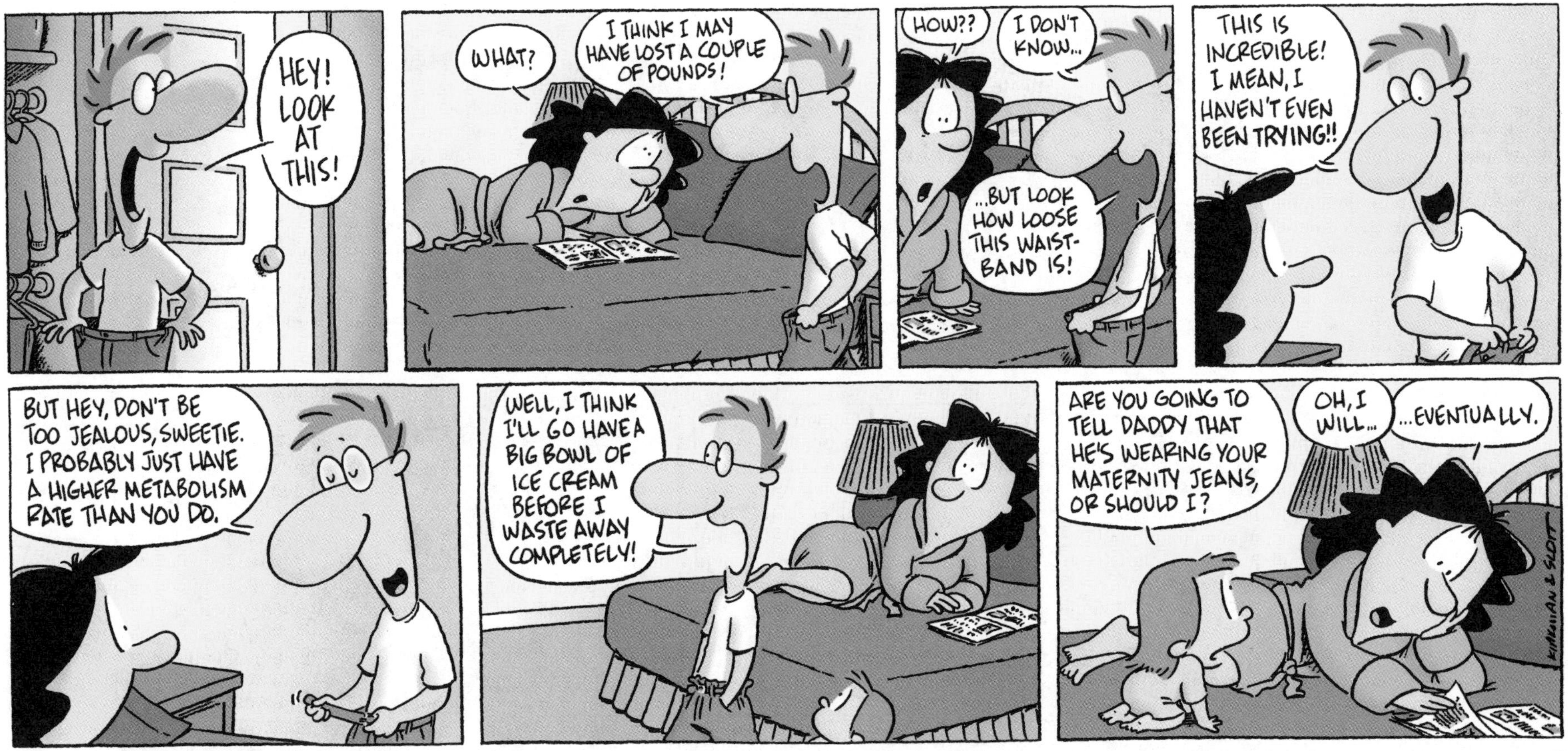
HEY! LOOK AT THIS!
WHAT?
I THINK I MAY HAVE LOST A COUPLE OF POUNDS!
HOW??
I DON'T KNOW...
...BUT LOOK HOW LOOSE THIS WAIST-BAND IS!
THIS IS INCREDIBLE! I MEAN, I HAVEN'T EVEN BEEN TRYING!!
BUT HEY, DON'T BE TOO JEALOUS, SWEETIE. I PROBABLY JUST HAVE A HIGHER METABOLISM RATE THAN YOU DO.
WELL, I THINK I'LL GO HAVE A BIG BOWL OF ICE CREAM BEFORE I WASTE AWAY COMPLETELY!
ARE YOU GOING TO TELL DADDY THAT HE'S WEARING YOUR MATERNITY JEANS, OR SHOULD I?
OH, I WILL...
...EVENTUALLY.
KIRKMAN & SCOTT

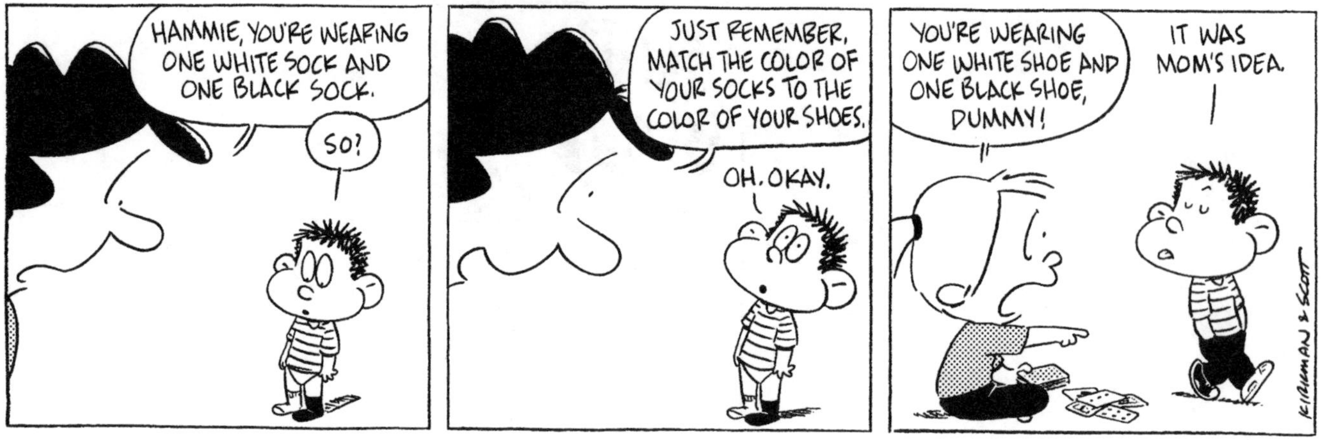
HAMMIE, YOU'RE WEARING ONE WHITE SOCK AND ONE BLACK SOCK.
SO?
JUST REMEMBER, MATCH THE COLOR OF YOUR SOCKS TO THE COLOR OF YOUR SHOES.
OH. OKAY.
YOU'RE WEARING ONE WHITE SHOE AND ONE BLACK SHOE, DUMMY!
IT WAS MOM'S IDEA.
KIRKMAN & SCOTT

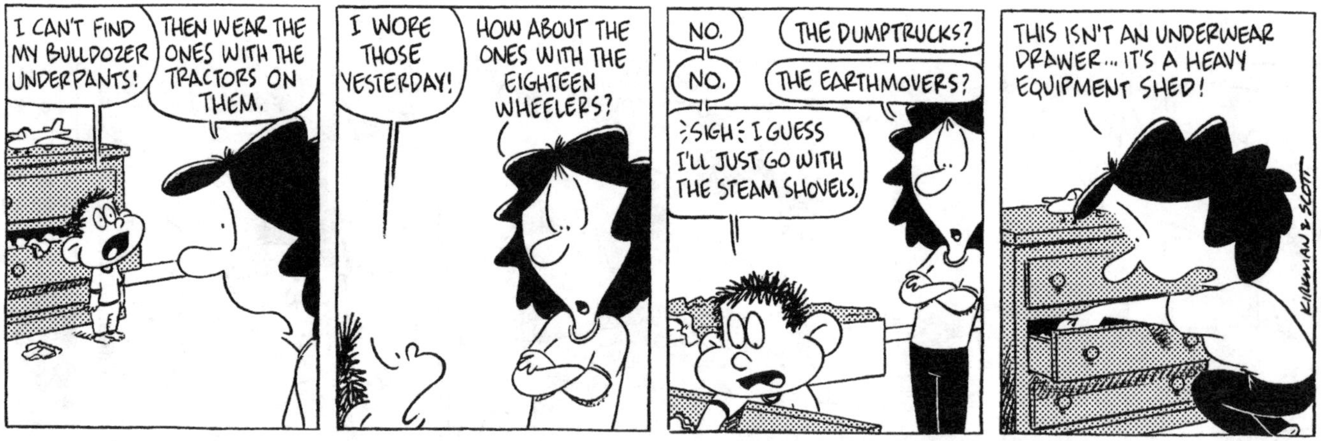
I CAN'T FIND MY BULLDOZER UNDERPANTS!
THEN WEAR THE ONES WITH THE TRACTORS ON THEM.
I WORE THOSE YESTERDAY!
HOW ABOUT THE ONES WITH THE EIGHTEEN WHEELERS?
NO.
THE DUMPTRUCKS?
NO.
THE EARTHMOVERS?
:SIGH: I GUESS I'LL JUST GO WITH THE STEAM SHOVELS.
THIS ISN'T AN UNDERWEAR DRAWER... IT'S A HEAVY EQUIPMENT SHED!
KIRKMAN & SCOTT

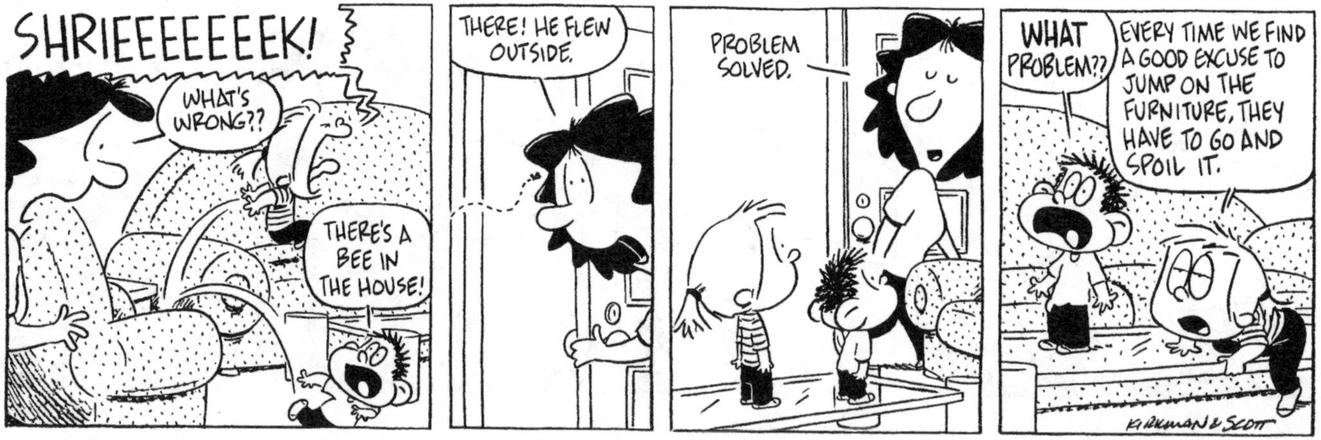
SHRIEEEEEEEEK!
WHAT'S WRONG??
THERE'S A BEE IN THE HOUSE!
THERE! HE FLEW OUTSIDE.
PROBLEM SOLVED.
WHAT PROBLEM??
EVERY TIME WE FIND A GOOD EXCUSE TO JUMP ON THE FURNITURE, THEY HAVE TO GO AND SPOIL IT.
KIRKMAN & SCOTT

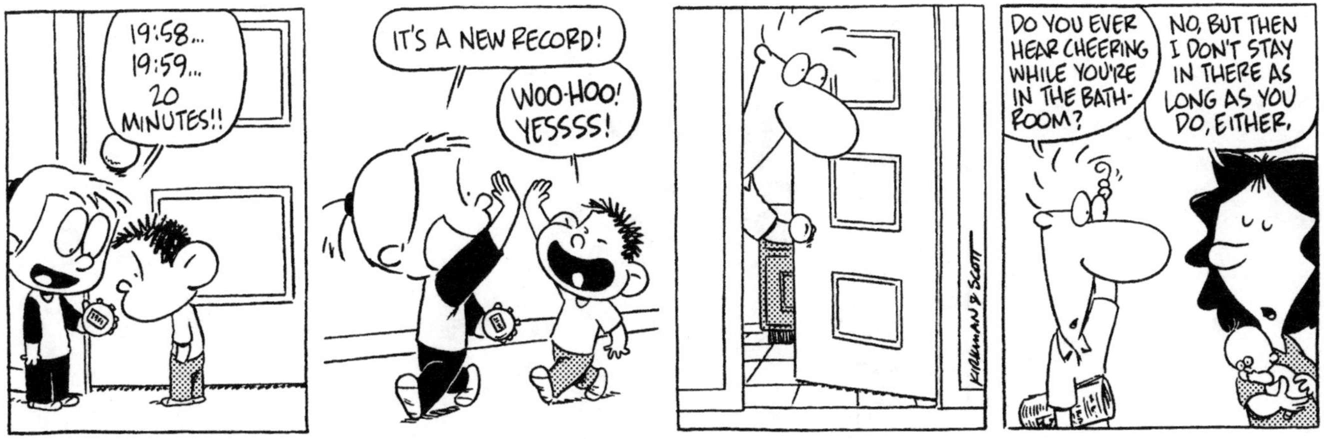
19:58...
19:59...
20 MINUTES!!
IT'S A NEW RECORD!
WOO-HOO! YESSSS!
DO YOU EVER HEAR CHEERING WHILE YOU'RE IN THE BATHROOM?
NO, BUT THEN I DON'T STAY IN THERE AS LONG AS YOU DO, EITHER.
KIRKMAN & SCOTT

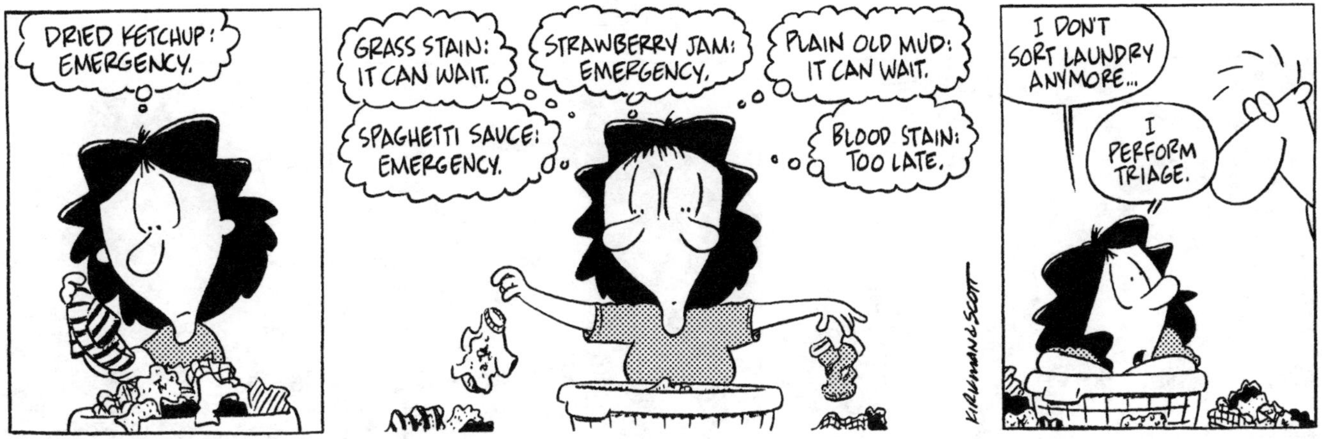
DRIED KETCHUP: EMERGENCY.
GRASS STAIN: IT CAN WAIT.
STRAWBERRY JAM: EMERGENCY.
PLAIN OLD MUD: IT CAN WAIT.
SPAGHETTI SAUCE: EMERGENCY.
BLOOD STAIN: TOO LATE.
I DON'T SORT LAUNDRY ANYMORE...
I PERFORM TRIAGE.
KIRKMAN & SCOTT

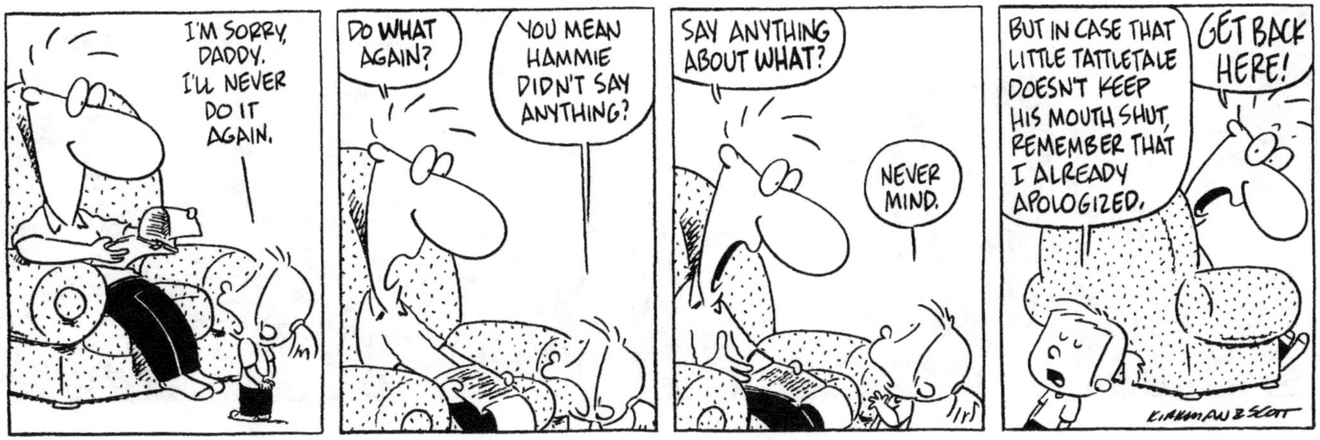
I'M SORRY, DADDY. I'LL NEVER DO IT AGAIN.
DO WHAT AGAIN?
YOU MEAN HAMMIE DIDN'T SAY ANYTHING?
SAY ANYTHING ABOUT WHAT?
NEVER MIND.
BUT IN CASE THAT LITTLE TATTLETALE DOESN'T KEEP HIS MOUTH SHUT, REMEMBER THAT I ALREADY APOLOGIZED.
GET BACK HERE!
KIRKMAN & SCOTT

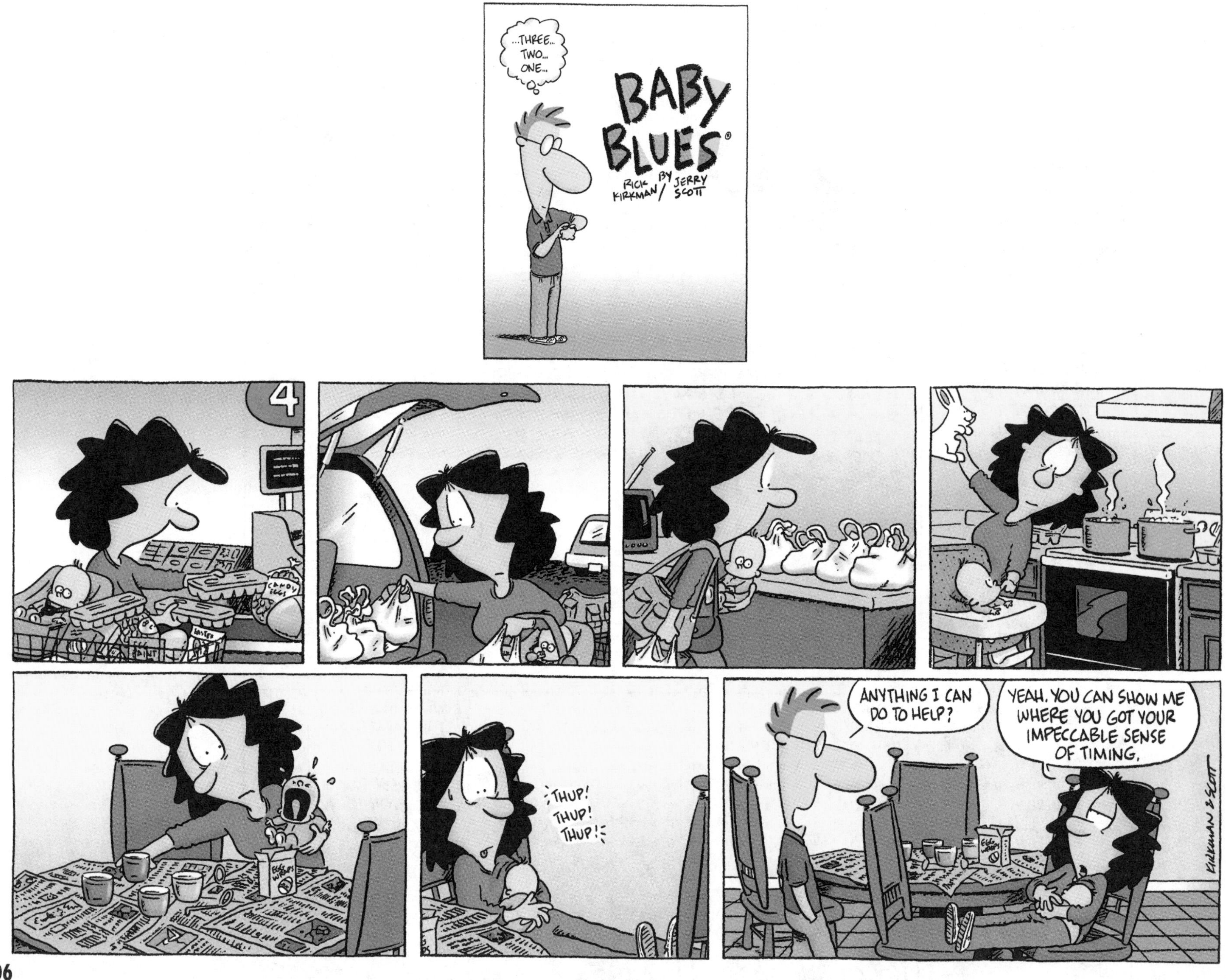
...THREE... TWO... ONE...
BABY BLUES®
BY RICK KIRKMAN / JERRY SCOTT
4
CANDY EGGS
THUP! THUP! THUP!
ANYTHING I CAN DO TO HELP?
YEAH. YOU CAN SHOW ME WHERE YOU GOT YOUR IMPECCABLE SENSE OF TIMING.
KIRKMAN & SCOTT

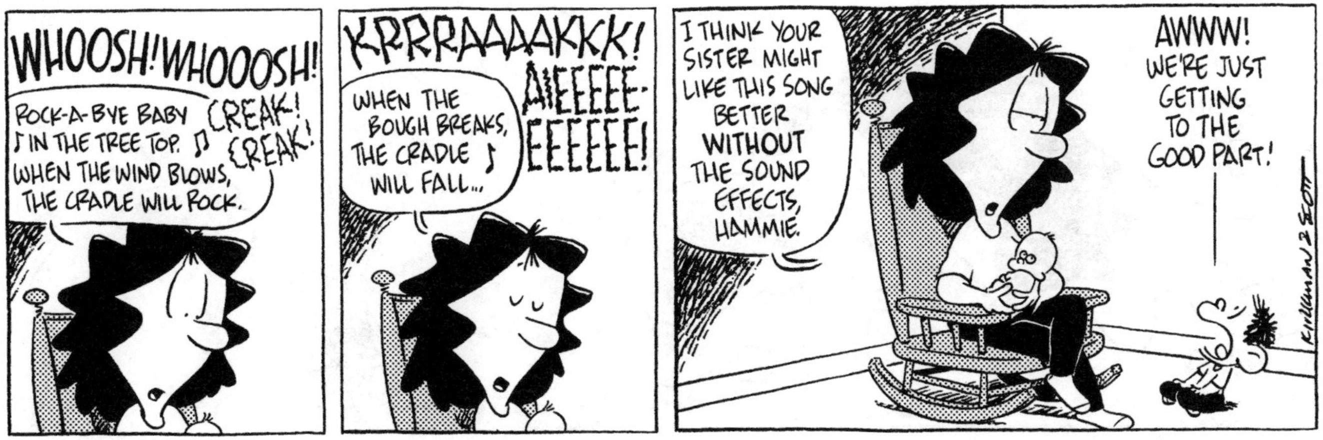
WHOOSH! WHOOOSH!
ROCK-A-BYE BABY ♪ IN THE TREE TOP. ♫ WHEN THE WIND BLOWS, THE CRADLE WILL ROCK.
CREAK! CREAK!
KRRRAAAAKKK!
WHEN THE BOUGH BREAKS, THE CRADLE ♪ WILL FALL...
AIEEEEE-EEEEEE!
I THINK YOUR SISTER MIGHT LIKE THIS SONG BETTER WITHOUT THE SOUND EFFECTS, HAMMIE.
AWWW! WE'RE JUST GETTING TO THE GOOD PART!
KIRKMAN & SCOTT

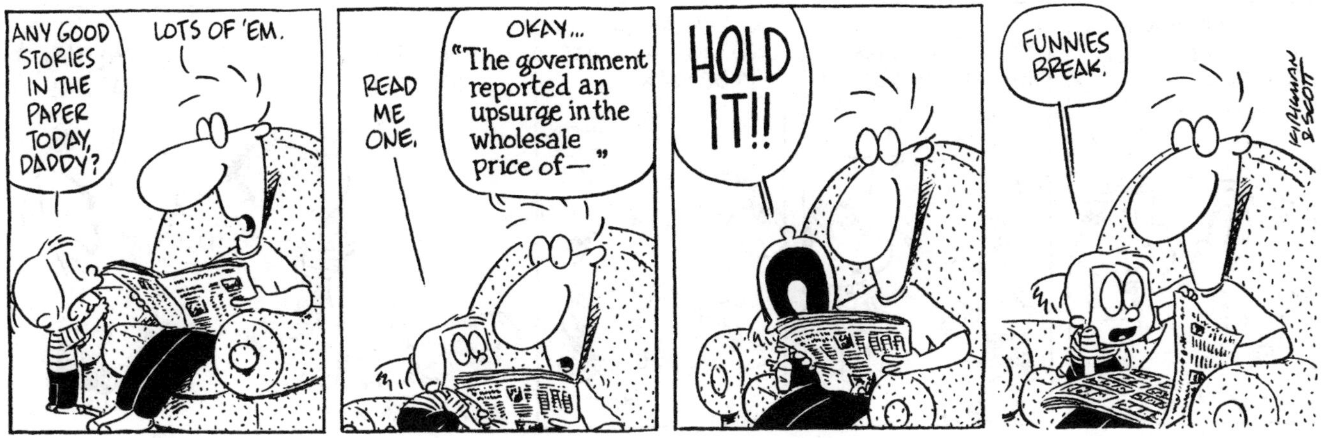
ANY GOOD STORIES IN THE PAPER TODAY, DADDY?
LOTS OF 'EM.
READ ME ONE.
OKAY... "The government reported an upsurge in the wholesale price of—"
HOLD IT!!
FUNNIES BREAK.
KIRKMAN & SCOTT

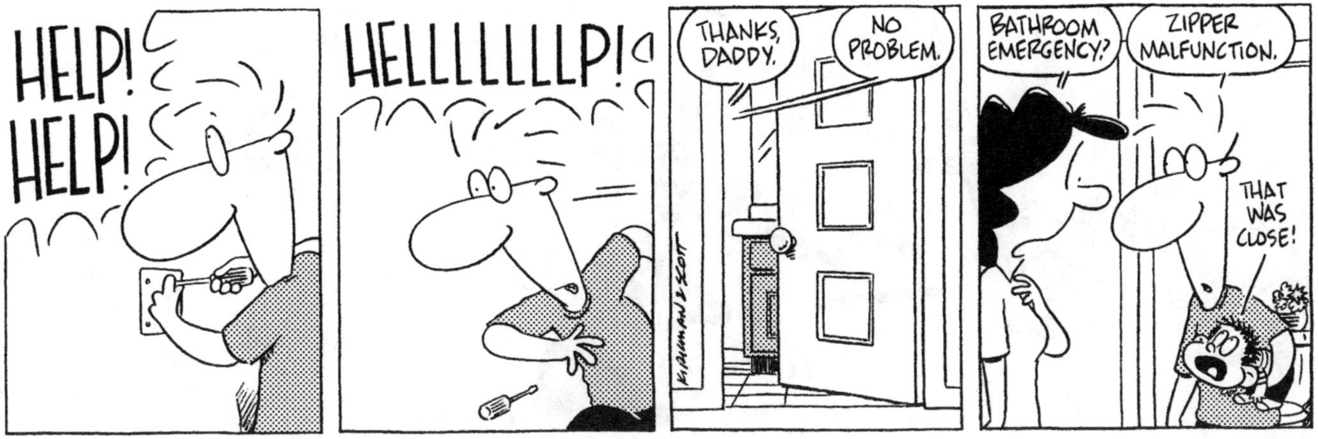
HELP! HELP!
HELLLLLLLP!
THANKS, DADDY.
NO PROBLEM.
KIRKMAN & SCOTT
BATHROOM EMERGENCY?
ZIPPER MALFUNCTION.
THAT WAS CLOSE!

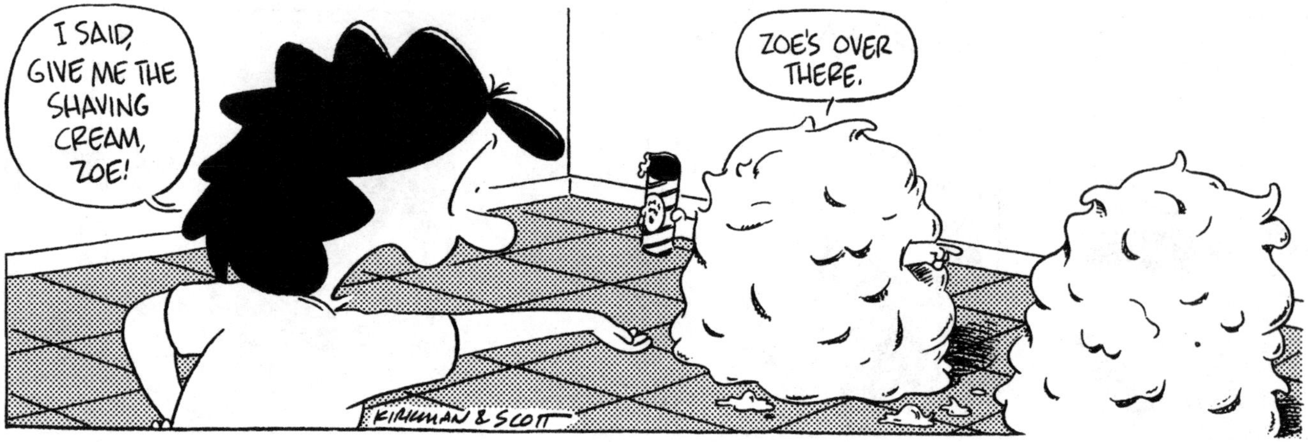
I SAID, GIVE ME THE SHAVING CREAM, ZOE!
ZOE'S OVER THERE.
KIRKMAN & SCOTT

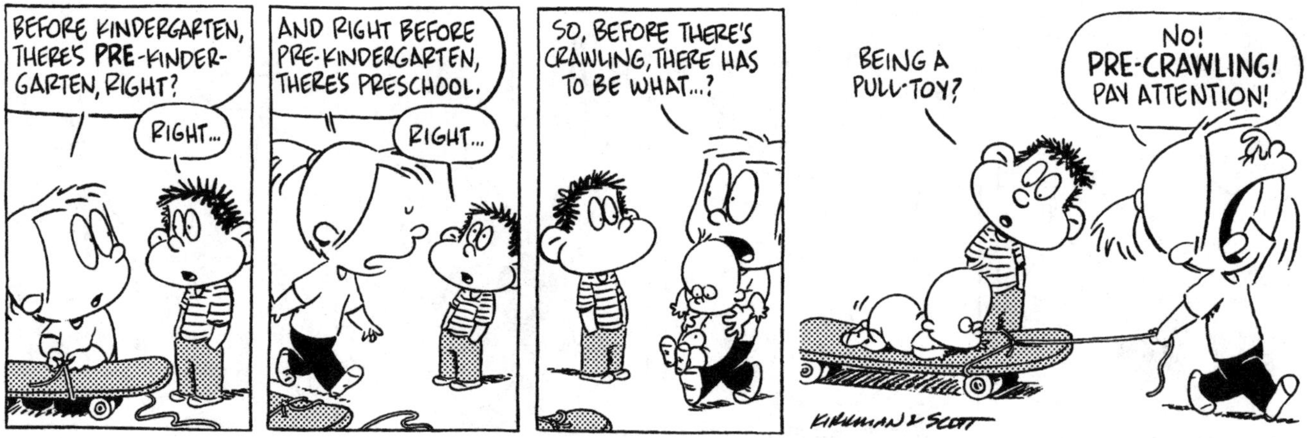
BEFORE KINDERGARTEN, THERE'S PRE-KINDER-GARTEN, RIGHT?
RIGHT...
AND RIGHT BEFORE PRE-KINDERGARTEN, THERE'S PRESCHOOL.
RIGHT...
SO, BEFORE THERE'S CRAWLING, THERE HAS TO BE WHAT...?
BEING A PULL-TOY?
NO! PRE-CRAWLING! PAY ATTENTION!
KIRKMAN & SCOTT

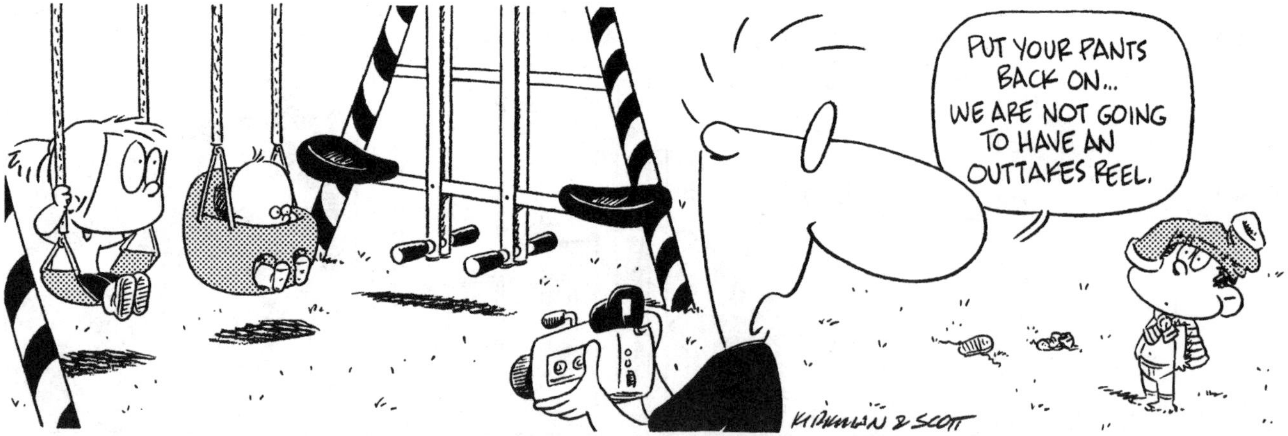
PUT YOUR PANTS BACK ON... WE ARE NOT GOING TO HAVE AN OUTTAKES REEL.
KIRKMAN & SCOTT

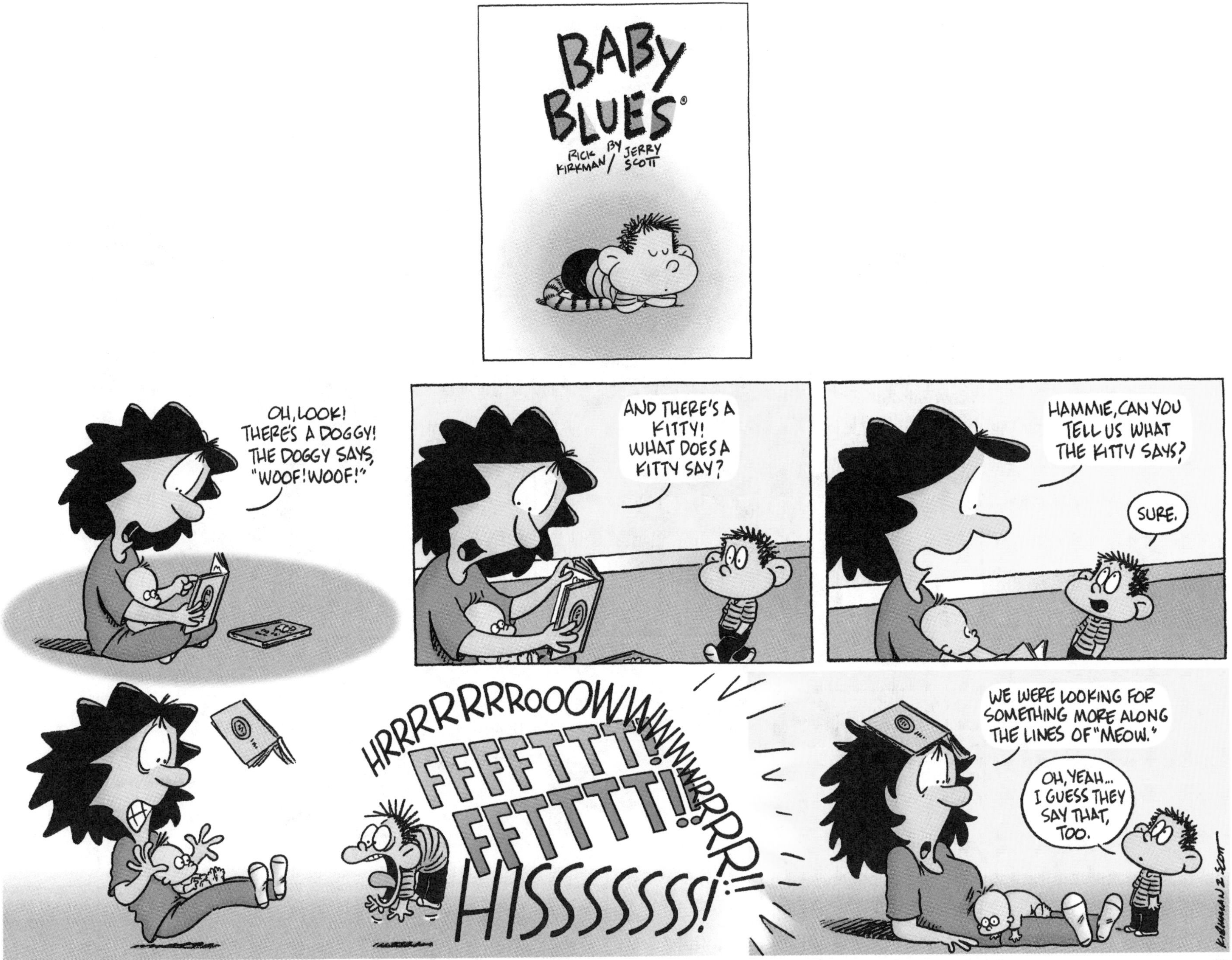
BABY BLUES®
BY RICK KIRKMAN / JERRY SCOTT
OH, LOOK! THERE'S A DOGGY! THE DOGGY SAYS, "WOOF! WOOF!"
AND THERE'S A KITTY! WHAT DOES A KITTY SAY?
HAMMIE, CAN YOU TELL US WHAT THE KITTY SAYS?
SURE.
HRRRRRRROOOWWWWWRRRR!!!
FFFFTTTT!
FFTTTTT!!
HISSSSSSSS!
WE WERE LOOKING FOR SOMETHING MORE ALONG THE LINES OF "MEOW."
OH, YEAH... I GUESS THEY SAY THAT, TOO.

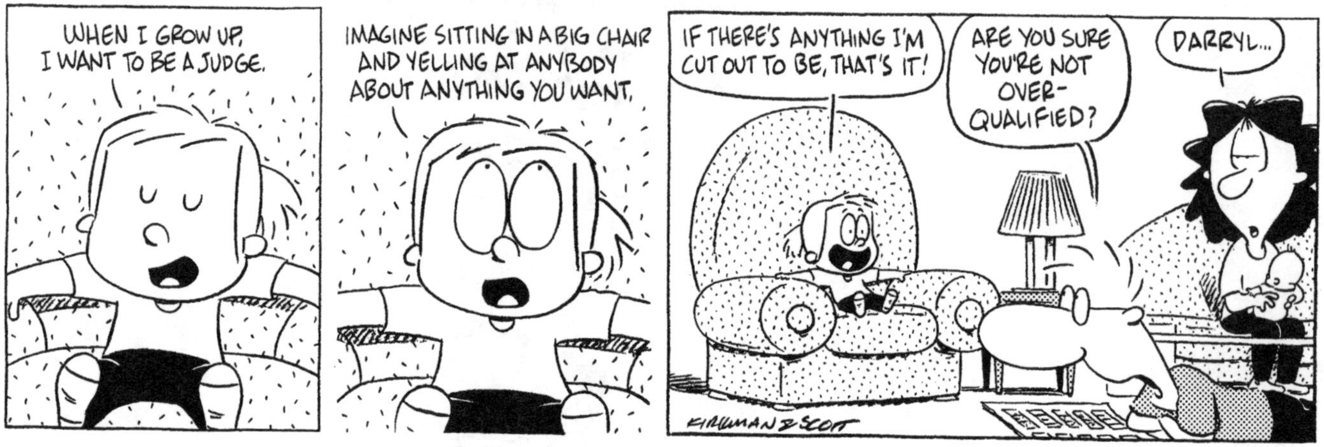
WHEN I GROW UP, I WANT TO BE A JUDGE.
IMAGINE SITTING IN A BIG CHAIR AND YELLING AT ANYBODY ABOUT ANYTHING YOU WANT.
IF THERE'S ANYTHING I'M CUT OUT TO BE, THAT'S IT!
ARE YOU SURE YOU'RE NOT OVER-QUALIFIED?
DARRYL...
KIRKMAN & SCOTT

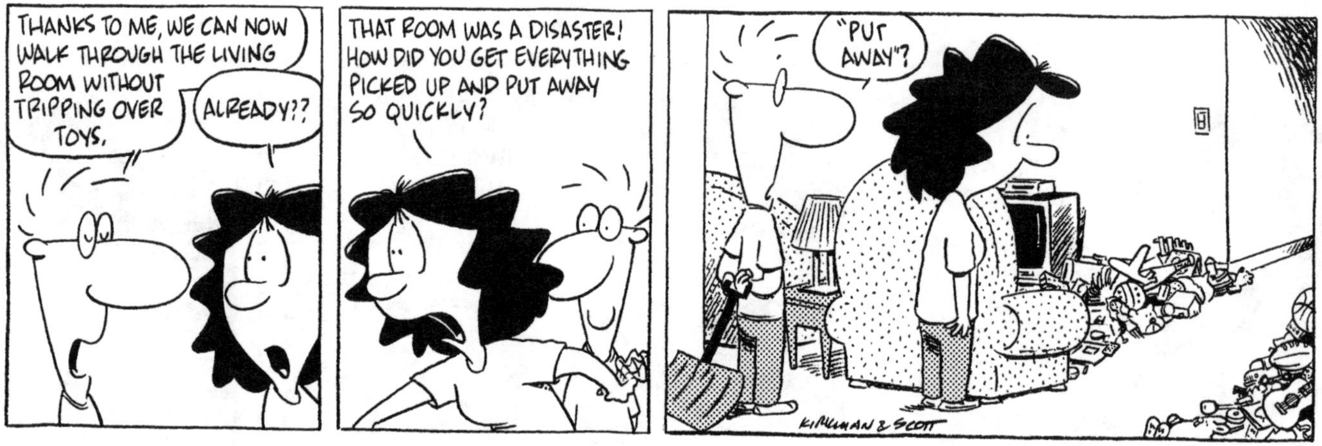
THANKS TO ME, WE CAN NOW WALK THROUGH THE LIVING ROOM WITHOUT TRIPPING OVER TOYS.
ALREADY??
THAT ROOM WAS A DISASTER! HOW DID YOU GET EVERYTHING PICKED UP AND PUT AWAY SO QUICKLY?
"PUT AWAY"?
KIRKMAN & SCOTT

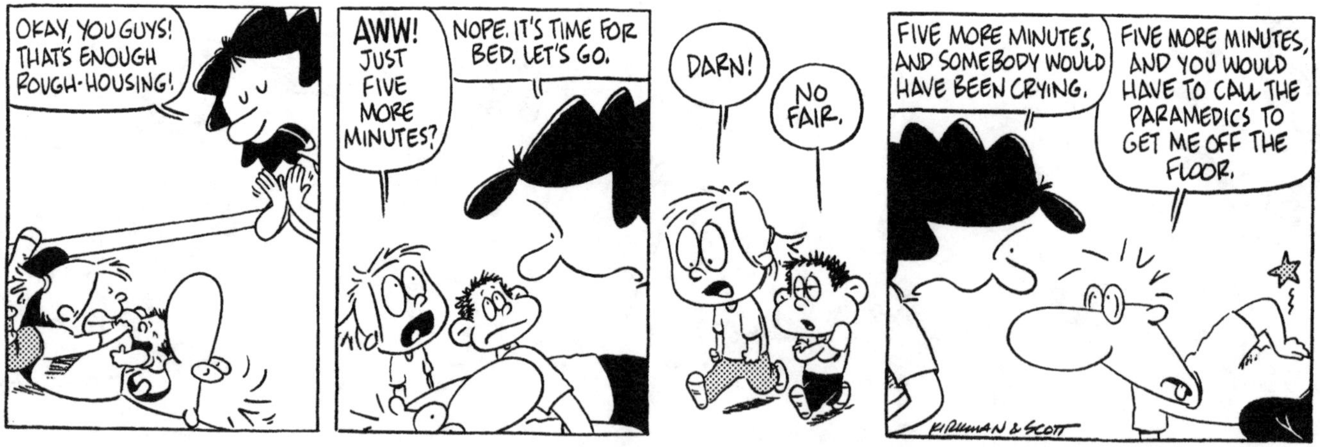
OKAY, YOU GUYS! THAT'S ENOUGH ROUGH-HOUSING!
AWW! JUST FIVE MORE MINUTES?
NOPE. IT'S TIME FOR BED. LET'S GO.
DARN!
NO FAIR.
FIVE MORE MINUTES, AND SOMEBODY WOULD HAVE BEEN CRYING.
FIVE MORE MINUTES, AND YOU WOULD HAVE TO CALL THE PARAMEDICS TO GET ME OFF THE FLOOR.
KIRKMAN & SCOTT

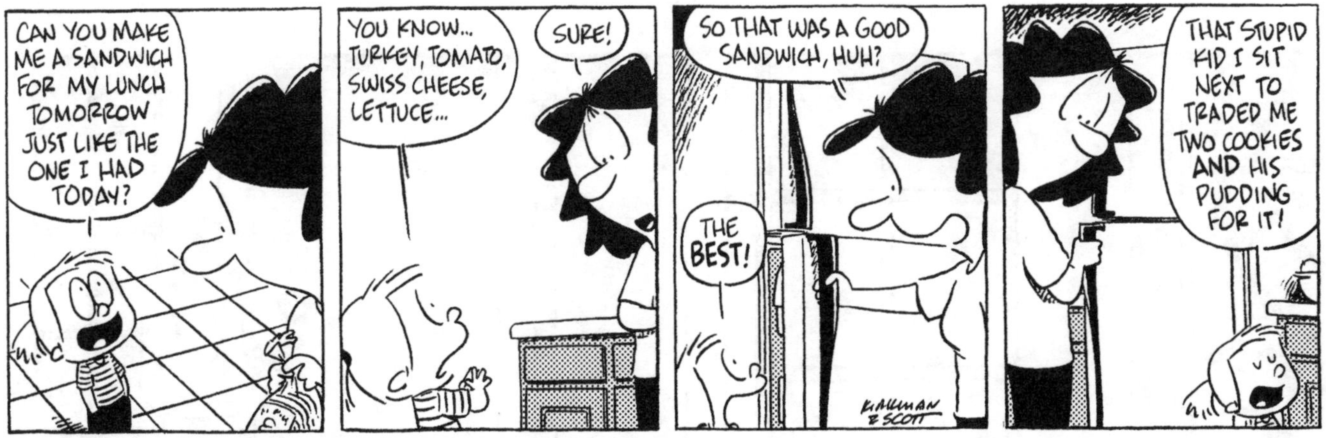
CAN YOU MAKE ME A SANDWICH FOR MY LUNCH TOMORROW JUST LIKE THE ONE I HAD TODAY?
YOU KNOW... TURKEY, TOMATO, SWISS CHEESE, LETTUCE...
SURE!
SO THAT WAS A GOOD SANDWICH, HUH?
THE BEST!
KIRKMAN & SCOTT
THAT STUPID KID I SIT NEXT TO TRADED ME TWO COOKIES AND HIS PUDDING FOR IT!

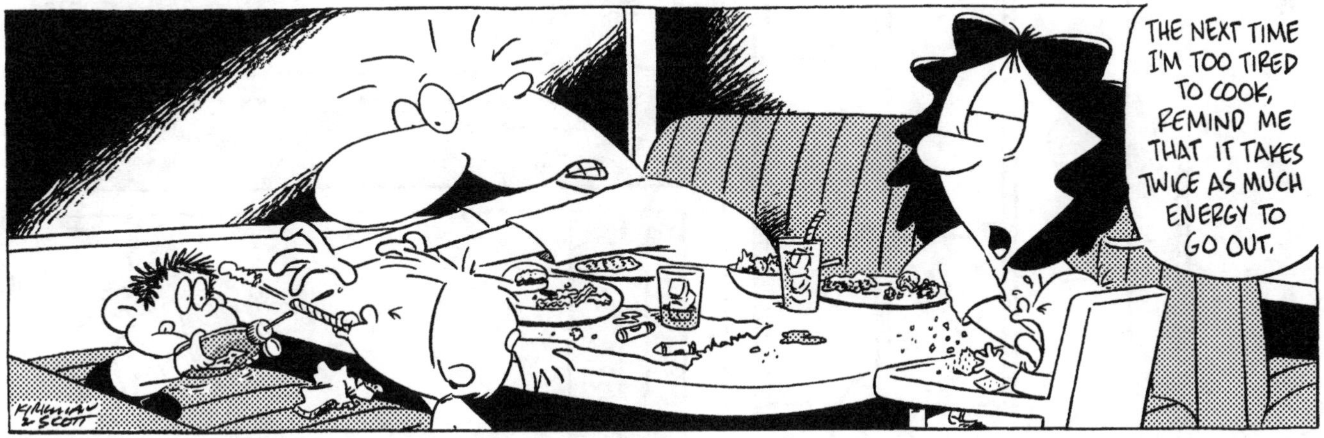
THE NEXT TIME I'M TOO TIRED TO COOK, REMIND ME THAT IT TAKES TWICE AS MUCH ENERGY TO GO OUT.
KIRKMAN & SCOTT

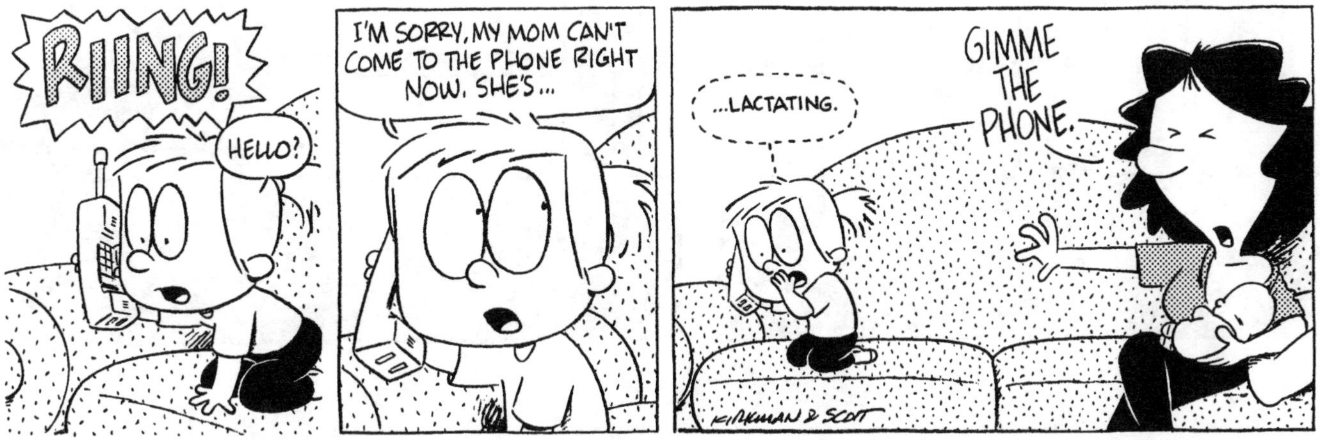
RIING!
HELLO?
I'M SORRY, MY MOM CAN'T COME TO THE PHONE RIGHT NOW. SHE'S...
...LACTATING.
GIMME THE PHONE.
KIRKMAN & SCOTT

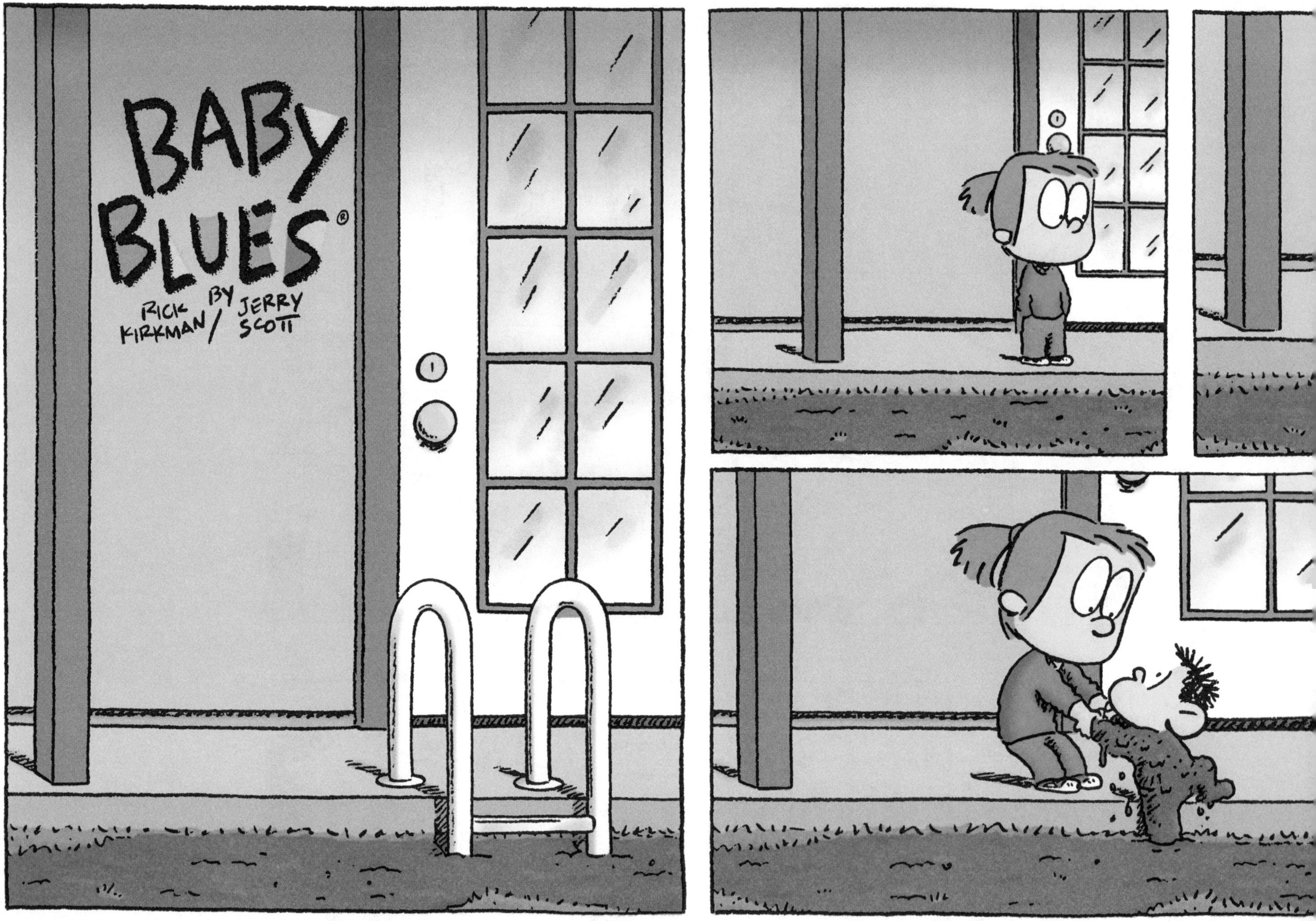
BABY BLUES®
BY RICK KIRKMAN / JERRY SCOTT

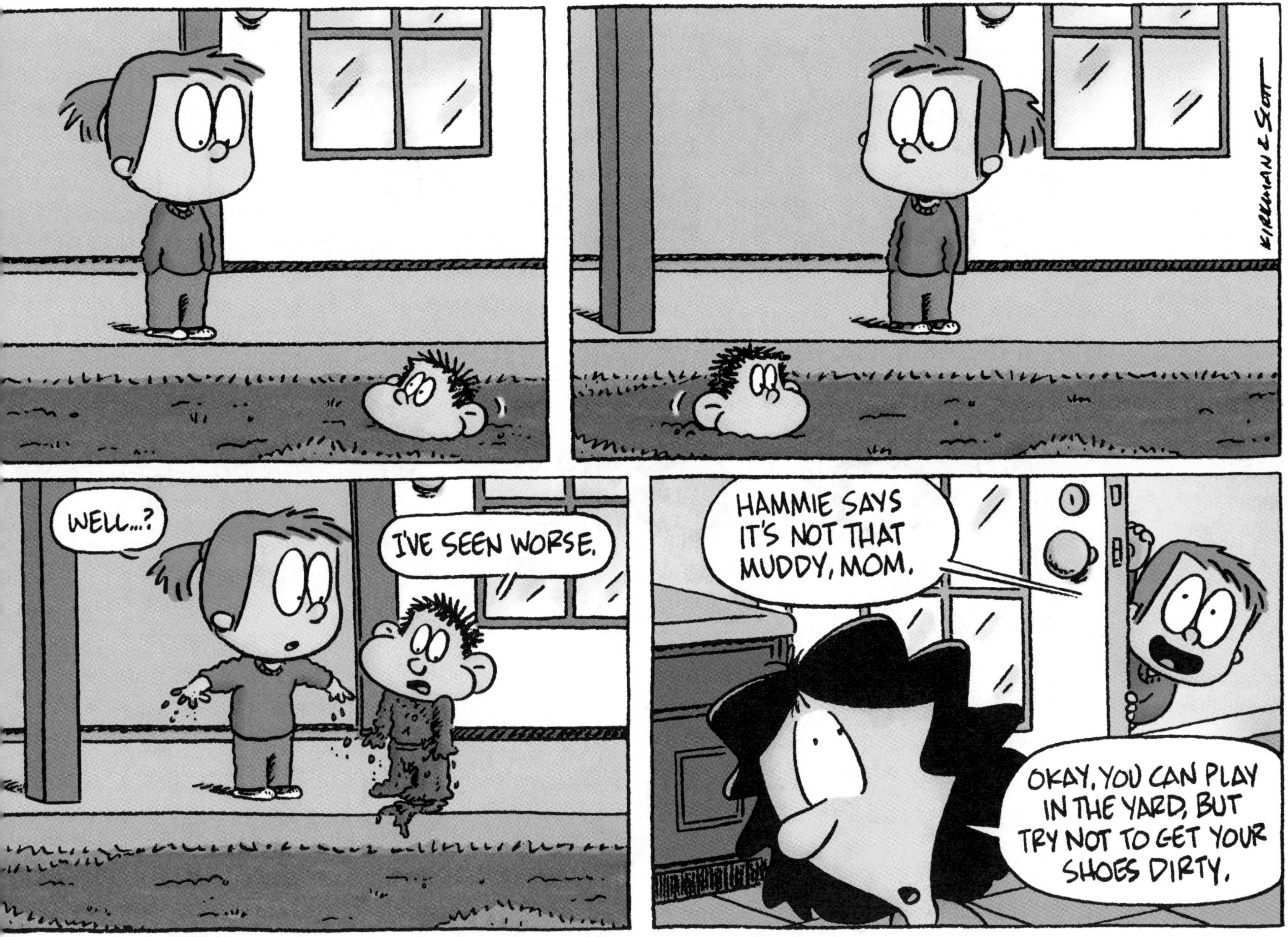
KIRKMAN & SCOTT
WELL...?
I'VE SEEN WORSE.
HAMMIE SAYS IT'S NOT THAT MUDDY, MOM.
OKAY, YOU CAN PLAY IN THE YARD, BUT TRY NOT TO GET YOUR SHOES DIRTY.

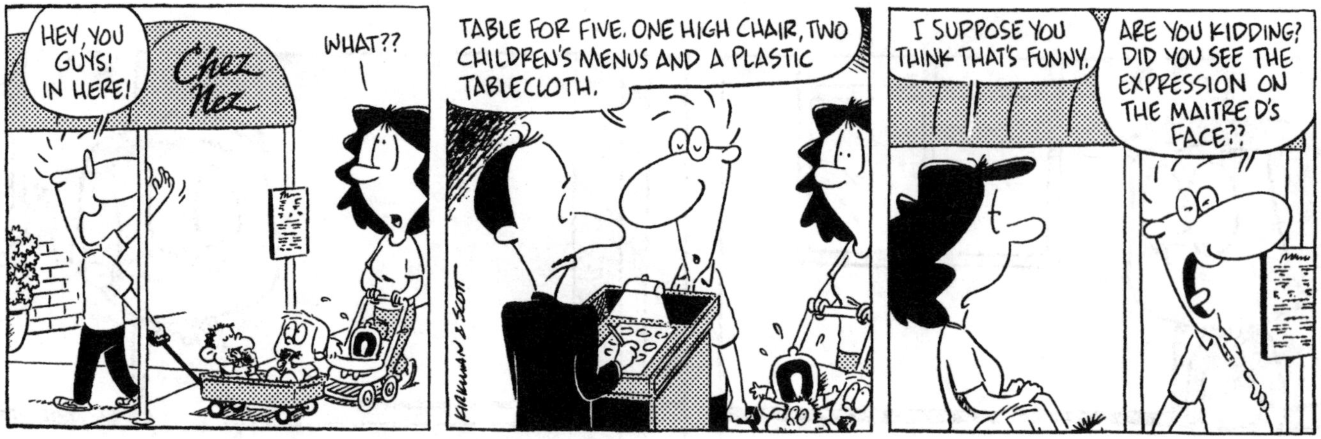
HEY, YOU GUYS! IN HERE!
Chez Nez
WHAT??
TABLE FOR FIVE. ONE HIGH CHAIR, TWO CHILDREN'S MENUS AND A PLASTIC TABLECLOTH.
I SUPPOSE YOU THINK THAT'S FUNNY.
ARE YOU KIDDING? DID YOU SEE THE EXPRESSION ON THE MAITRE D'S FACE??
KIRKMAN & SCOTT

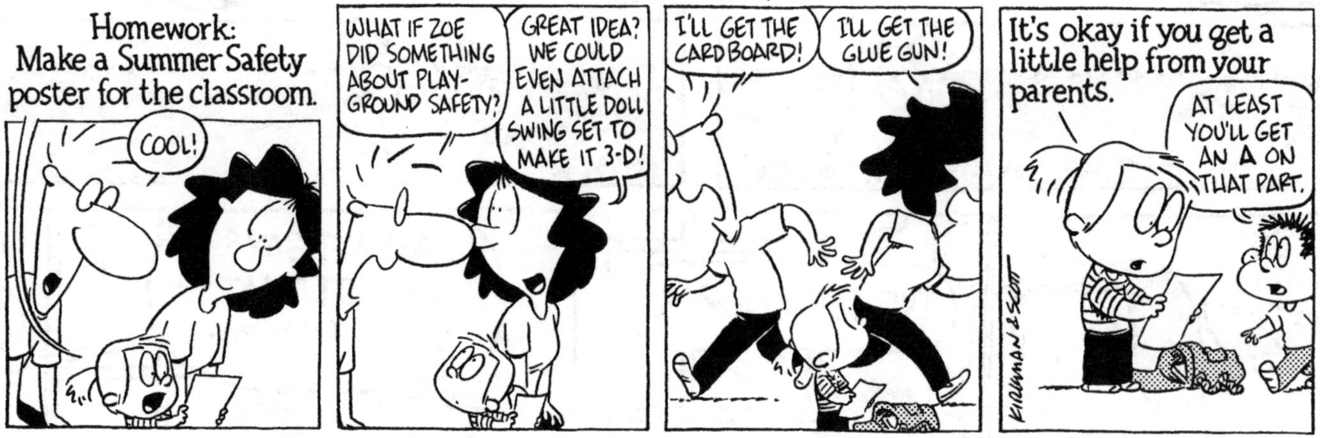
Homework: Make a Summer Safety poster for the classroom.
COOL!
WHAT IF ZOE DID SOMETHING ABOUT PLAY-GROUND SAFETY?
GREAT IDEA? WE COULD EVEN ATTACH A LITTLE DOLL SWING SET TO MAKE IT 3-D!
I'LL GET THE CARDBOARD!
I'LL GET THE GLUE GUN!
It's okay if you get a little help from your parents.
AT LEAST YOU'LL GET AN A ON THAT PART.
KIRKMAN & SCOTT

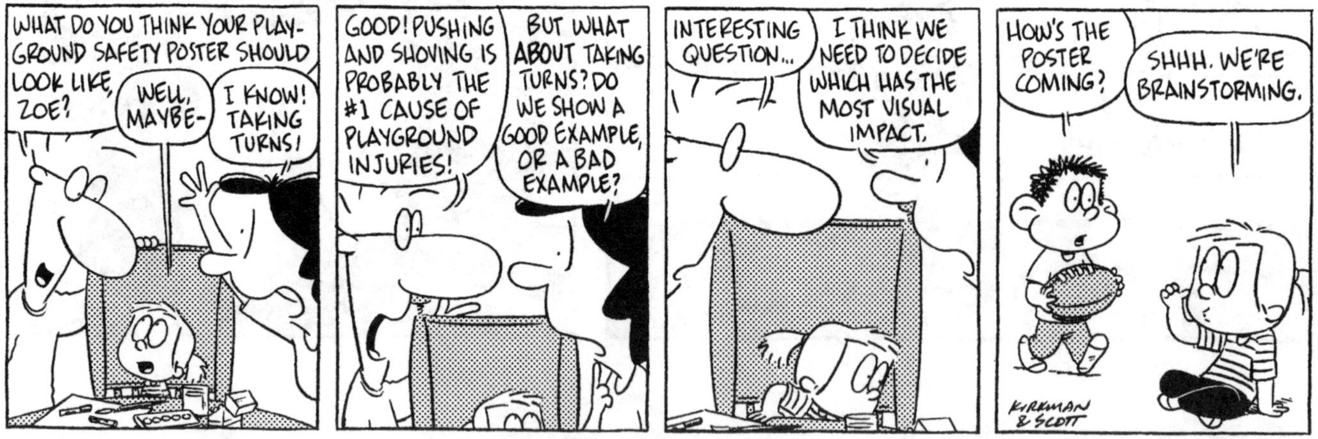
WHAT DO YOU THINK YOUR PLAY-GROUND SAFETY POSTER SHOULD LOOK LIKE, ZOE?
WELL, MAYBE-
I KNOW! TAKING TURNS!
GOOD! PUSHING AND SHOVING IS PROBABLY THE #1 CAUSE OF PLAYGROUND INJURIES!
BUT WHAT ABOUT TAKING TURNS? DO WE SHOW A GOOD EXAMPLE, OR A BAD EXAMPLE?
INTERESTING QUESTION...
I THINK WE NEED TO DECIDE WHICH HAS THE MOST VISUAL IMPACT.
HOW'S THE POSTER COMING?
SHHH. WE'RE BRAINSTORMING.
KIRKMAN & SCOTT

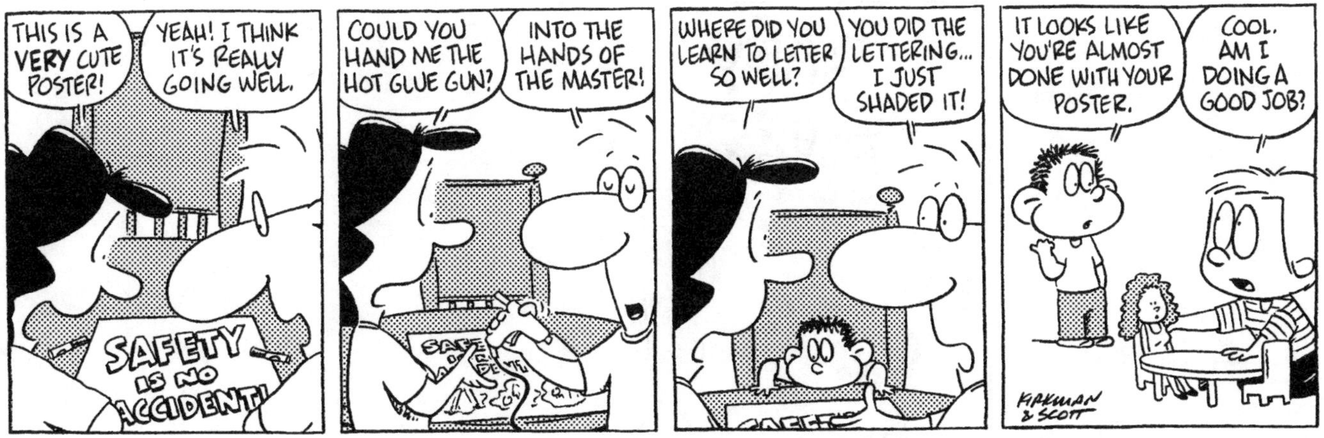
THIS IS A VERY CUTE POSTER!
YEAH! I THINK IT'S REALLY GOING WELL.
SAFETY IS NO ACCIDENT!
COULD YOU HAND ME THE HOT GLUE GUN?
INTO THE HANDS OF THE MASTER!
WHERE DID YOU LEARN TO LETTER SO WELL?
YOU DID THE LETTERING... I JUST SHADED IT!
IT LOOKS LIKE YOU'RE ALMOST DONE WITH YOUR POSTER.
COOL. AM I DOING A GOOD JOB?
KIRKMAN & SCOTT

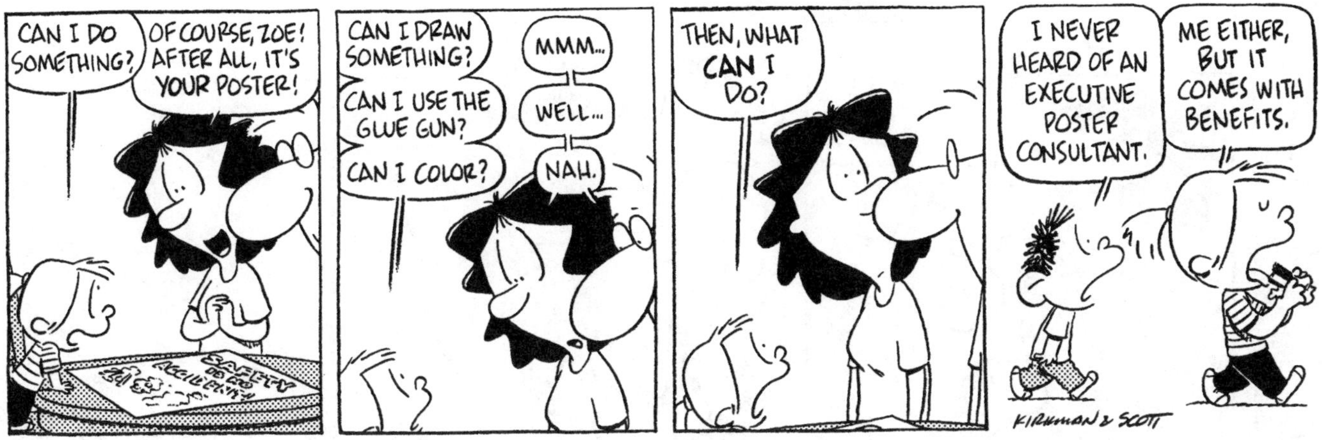
CAN I DO SOMETHING?
OF COURSE, ZOE! AFTER ALL, IT'S YOUR POSTER!
CAN I DRAW SOMETHING?
MMM...
CAN I USE THE GLUE GUN?
WELL...
CAN I COLOR?
NAH.
THEN, WHAT CAN I DO?
I NEVER HEARD OF AN EXECUTIVE POSTER CONSULTANT.
ME EITHER, BUT IT COMES WITH BENEFITS.
KIRKMAN & SCOTT

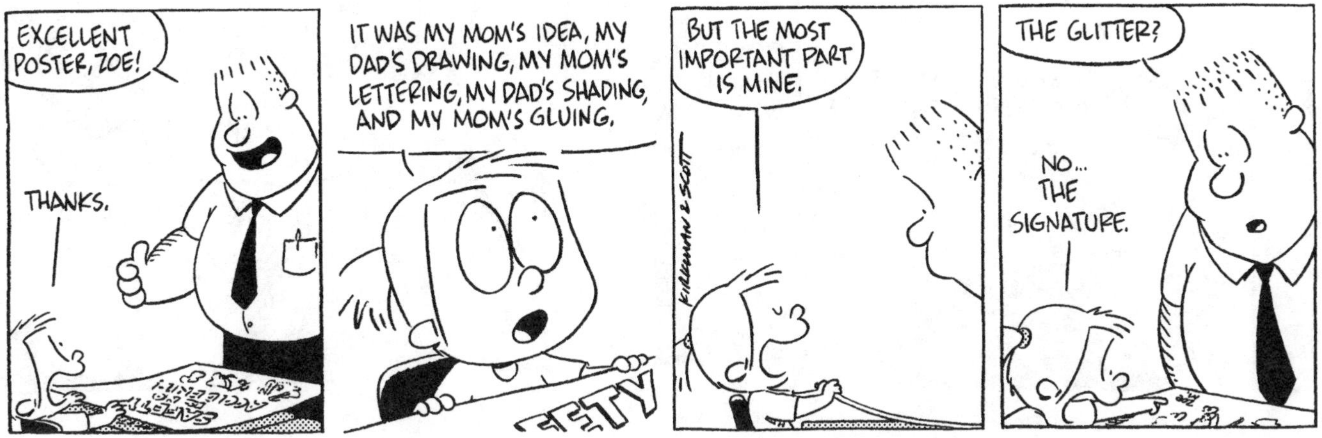
EXCELLENT POSTER, ZOE!
THANKS.
IT WAS MY MOM'S IDEA, MY DAD'S DRAWING, MY MOM'S LETTERING, MY DAD'S SHADING, AND MY MOM'S GLUING.
KIRKMAN & SCOTT
BUT THE MOST IMPORTANT PART IS MINE.
THE GLITTER?
NO... THE SIGNATURE.

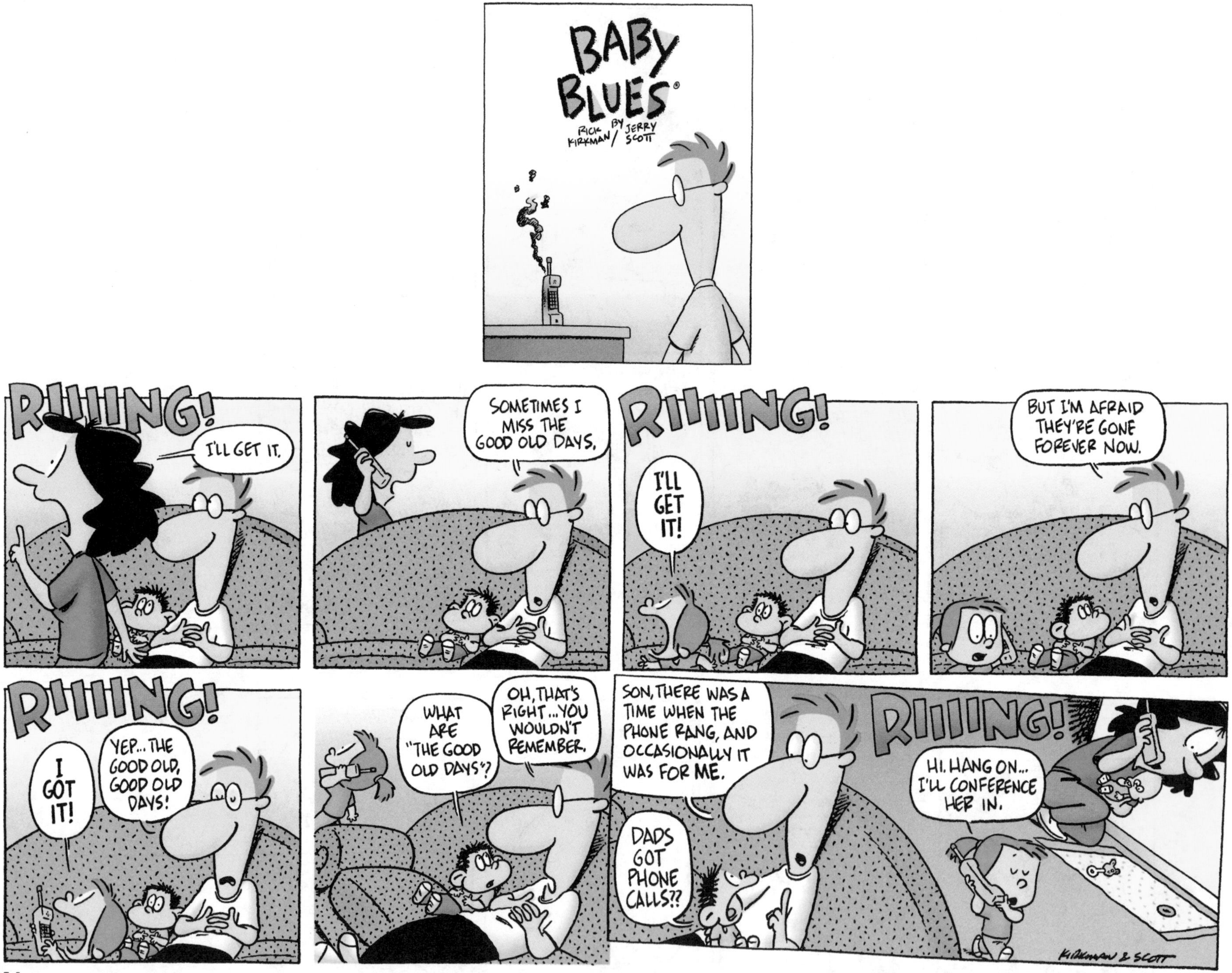

BABY BLUES®
BY RICK KIRKMAN / JERRY SCOTT
RIIIING!
I'LL GET IT.
SOMETIMES I MISS THE GOOD OLD DAYS.
RIIIING!
I'LL GET IT!
BUT I'M AFRAID THEY'RE GONE FOREVER NOW.
RIIIING!
I GOT IT!
YEP... THE GOOD OLD, GOOD OLD DAYS!
WHAT ARE "THE GOOD OLD DAYS"?
OH, THAT'S RIGHT... YOU WOULDN'T REMEMBER.
SON, THERE WAS A TIME WHEN THE PHONE RANG, AND OCCASIONALLY IT WAS FOR ME.
DADS GOT PHONE CALLS??
RIIIING!
HI. HANG ON... I'LL CONFERENCE HER IN.
KIRKMAN & SCOTT

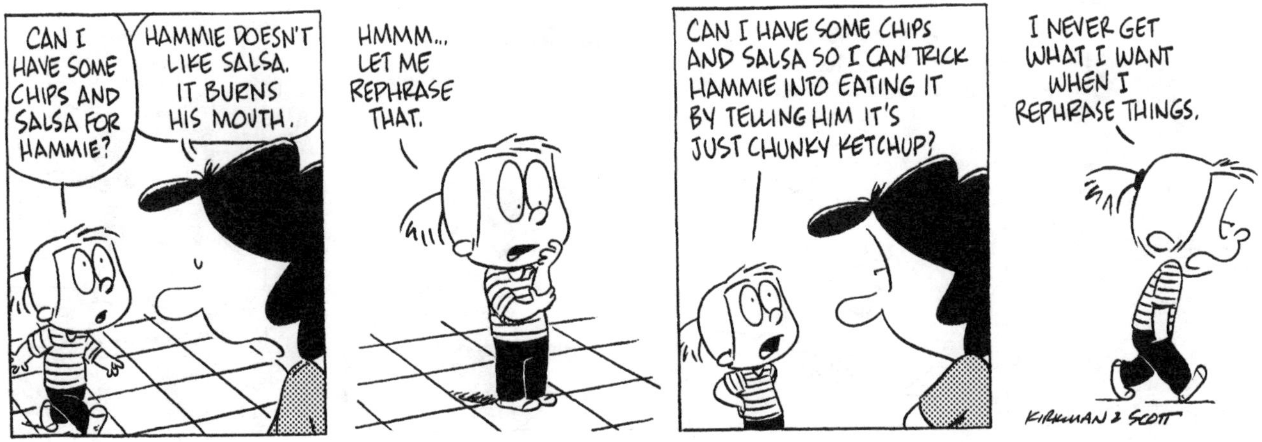
CAN I HAVE SOME CHIPS AND SALSA FOR HAMMIE?
HAMMIE DOESN'T LIKE SALSA. IT BURNS HIS MOUTH.
HMMM... LET ME REPHRASE THAT.
CAN I HAVE SOME CHIPS AND SALSA SO I CAN TRICK HAMMIE INTO EATING IT BY TELLING HIM IT'S JUST CHUNKY KETCHUP?
I NEVER GET WHAT I WANT WHEN I REPHRASE THINGS.
KIRKMAN & SCOTT

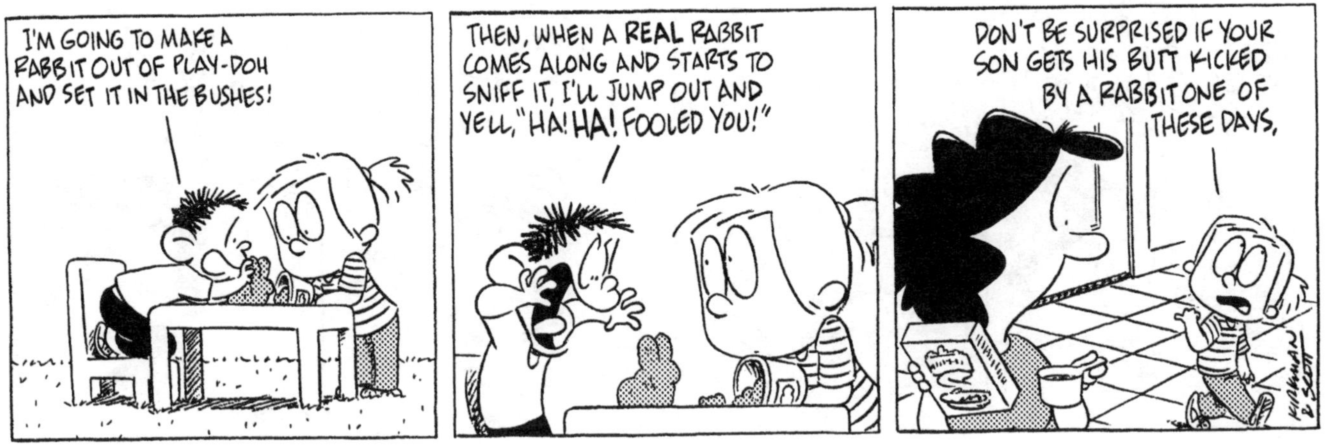
I'M GOING TO MAKE A RABBIT OUT OF PLAY-DOH AND SET IT IN THE BUSHES!
THEN, WHEN A REAL RABBIT COMES ALONG AND STARTS TO SNIFF IT, I'LL JUMP OUT AND YELL, "HA! HA! FOOLED YOU!"
DON'T BE SURPRISED IF YOUR SON GETS HIS BUTT KICKED BY A RABBIT ONE OF THESE DAYS.
KIRKMAN & SCOTT

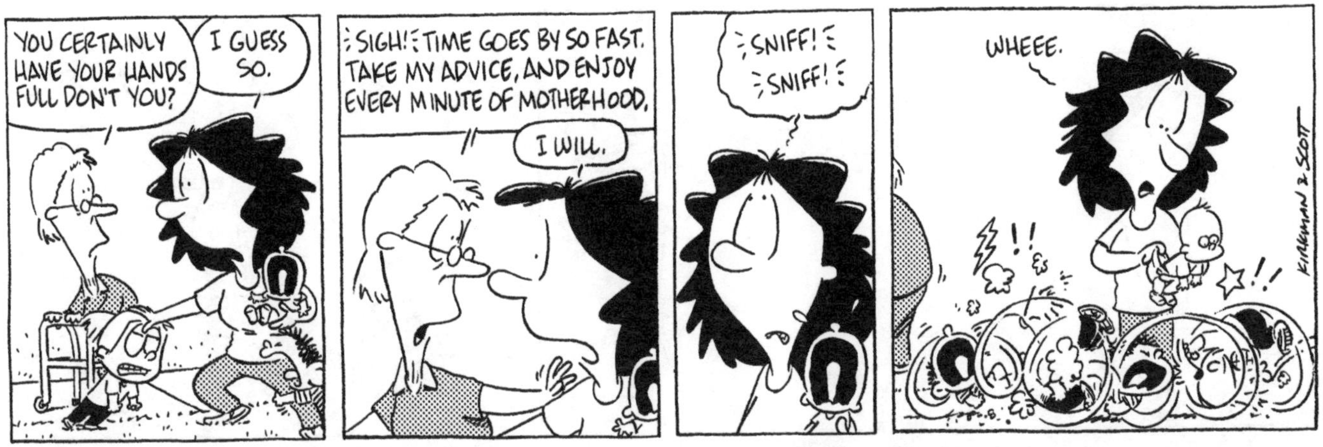
YOU CERTAINLY HAVE YOUR HANDS FULL DON'T YOU?
I GUESS SO.
SIGH! TIME GOES BY SO FAST. TAKE MY ADVICE, AND ENJOY EVERY MINUTE OF MOTHERHOOD.
I WILL.
SNIFF!
SNIFF!
WHEEE.
KIRKMAN & SCOTT

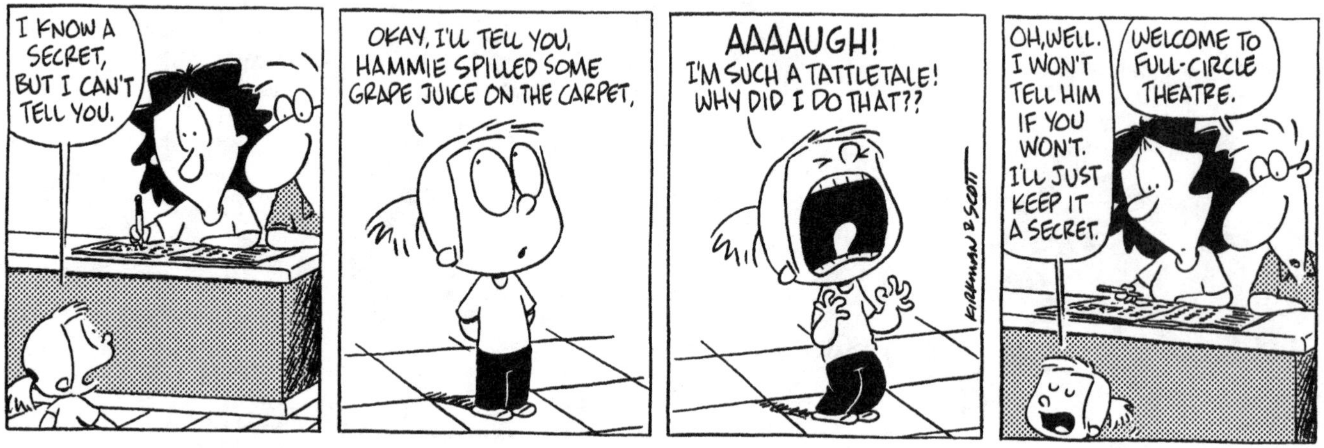
I KNOW A SECRET, BUT I CAN'T TELL YOU.
OKAY, I'LL TELL YOU. HAMMIE SPILLED SOME GRAPE JUICE ON THE CARPET.
AAAAUGH!
I'M SUCH A TATTLETALE! WHY DID I DO THAT??
KIRKMAN & SCOTT
OH, WELL. I WON'T TELL HIM IF YOU WON'T. I'LL JUST KEEP IT A SECRET.
WELCOME TO FULL-CIRCLE THEATRE.

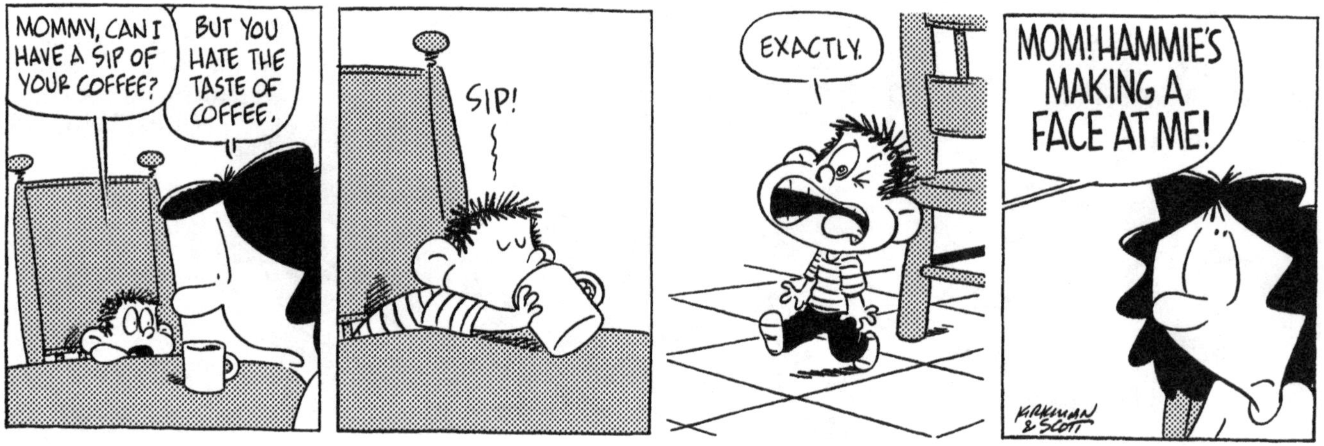
MOMMY, CAN I HAVE A SIP OF YOUR COFFEE?
BUT YOU HATE THE TASTE OF COFFEE.
SIP!
EXACTLY.
MOM! HAMMIE'S MAKING A FACE AT ME!
KIRKMAN & SCOTT

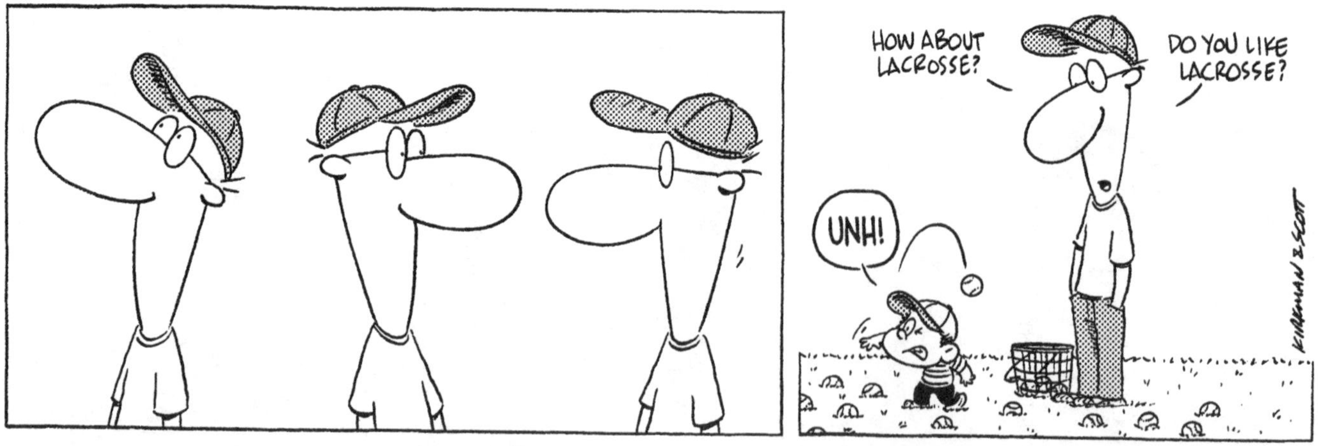
HOW ABOUT LACROSSE?
DO YOU LIKE LACROSSE?
UNH!
KIRKMAN & SCOTT

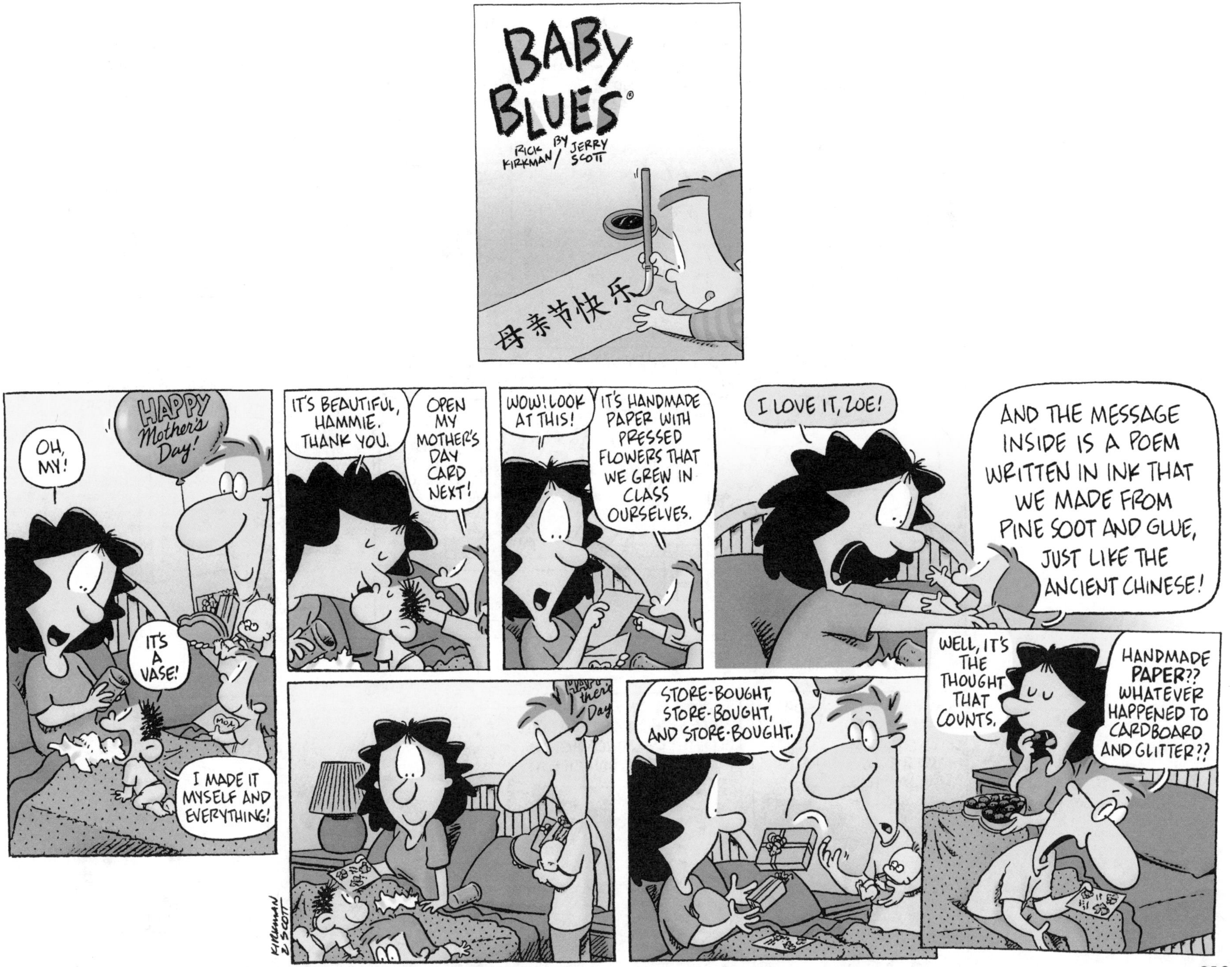
BABY BLUES®
BY RICK KIRKMAN / JERRY SCOTT
母亲节快乐
HAPPY Mother's Day!
OH, MY!
IT'S A VASE!
I MADE IT MYSELF AND EVERYTHING!
IT'S BEAUTIFUL, HAMMIE. THANK YOU.
OPEN MY MOTHER'S DAY CARD NEXT!
WOW! LOOK AT THIS!
IT'S HANDMADE PAPER WITH PRESSED FLOWERS THAT WE GREW IN CLASS OURSELVES.
I LOVE IT, ZOE!
AND THE MESSAGE INSIDE IS A POEM WRITTEN IN INK THAT WE MADE FROM PINE SOOT AND GLUE, JUST LIKE THE ANCIENT CHINESE!
KIRKMAN & SCOTT
STORE-BOUGHT, STORE-BOUGHT, AND STORE-BOUGHT.
WELL, IT'S THE THOUGHT THAT COUNTS.
HANDMADE PAPER?? WHATEVER HAPPENED TO CARDBOARD AND GLITTER??

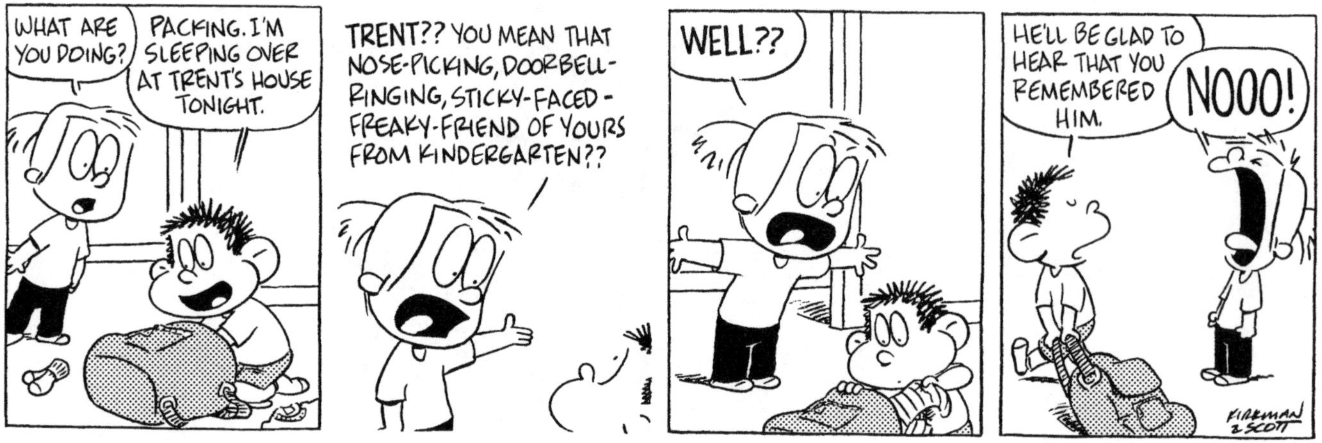

WHAT ARE YOU DOING?
PACKING. I'M SLEEPING OVER AT TRENT'S HOUSE TONIGHT.
TRENT?? YOU MEAN THAT NOSE-PICKING, DOORBELL-RINGING, STICKY-FACED-FREAKY-FRIEND OF YOURS FROM KINDERGARTEN??
WELL??
HE'LL BE GLAD TO HEAR THAT YOU REMEMBERED HIM.
NOOO!
KIRKMAN & SCOTT

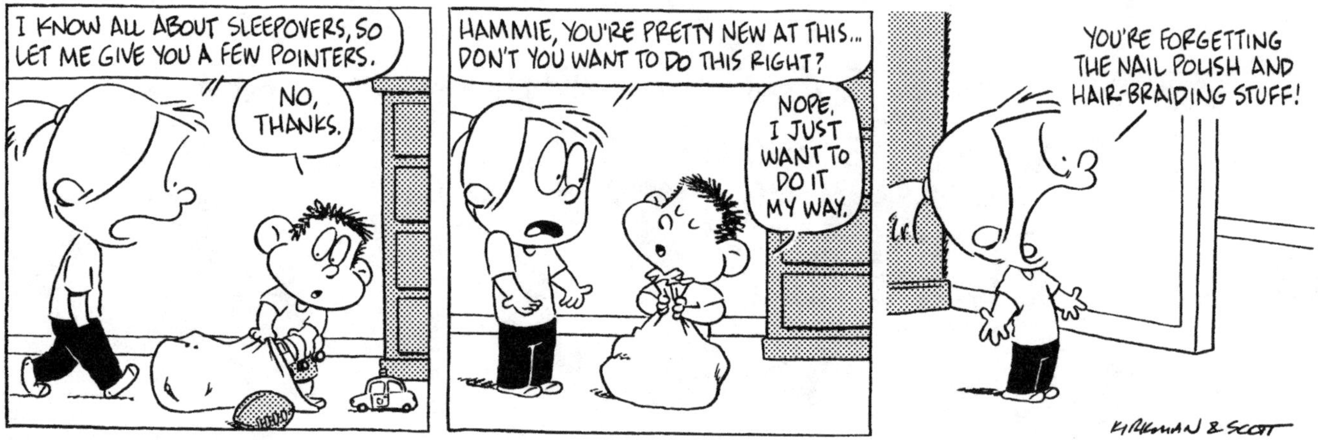

I KNOW ALL ABOUT SLEEPOVERS, SO LET ME GIVE YOU A FEW POINTERS.
NO, THANKS.
HAMMIE, YOU'RE PRETTY NEW AT THIS... DON'T YOU WANT TO DO THIS RIGHT?
NOPE, I JUST WANT TO DO IT MY WAY.
YOU'RE FORGETTING THE NAIL POLISH AND HAIR-BRAIDING STUFF!
KIRKMAN & SCOTT

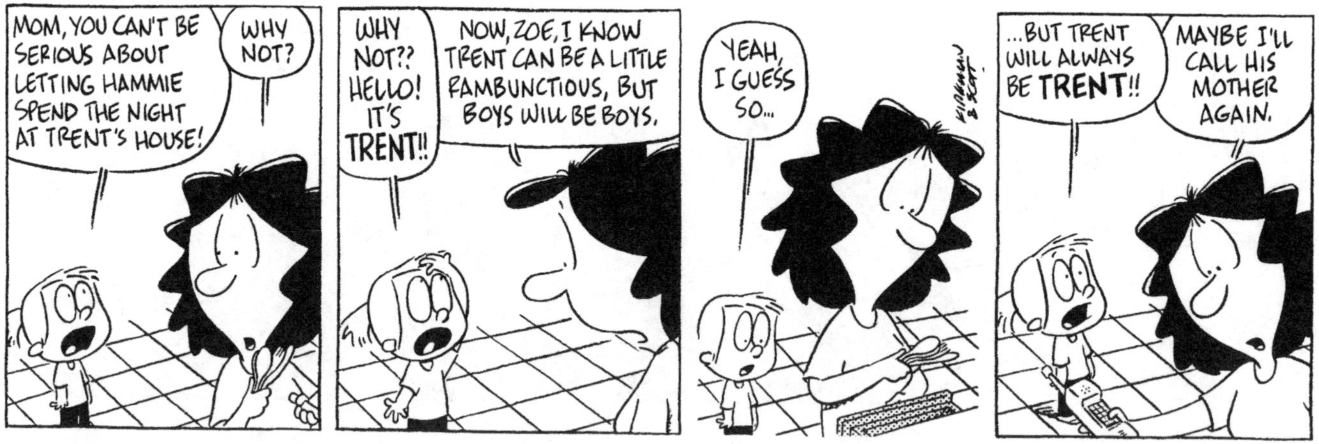

MOM, YOU CAN'T BE SERIOUS ABOUT LETTING HAMMIE SPEND THE NIGHT AT TRENT'S HOUSE!
WHY NOT?
WHY NOT?? HELLO! IT'S TRENT!!
NOW, ZOE, I KNOW TRENT CAN BE A LITTLE RAMBUNCTIOUS, BUT BOYS WILL BE BOYS.
YEAH, I GUESS SO...
...BUT TRENT WILL ALWAYS BE TRENT!!
MAYBE I'LL CALL HIS MOTHER AGAIN.

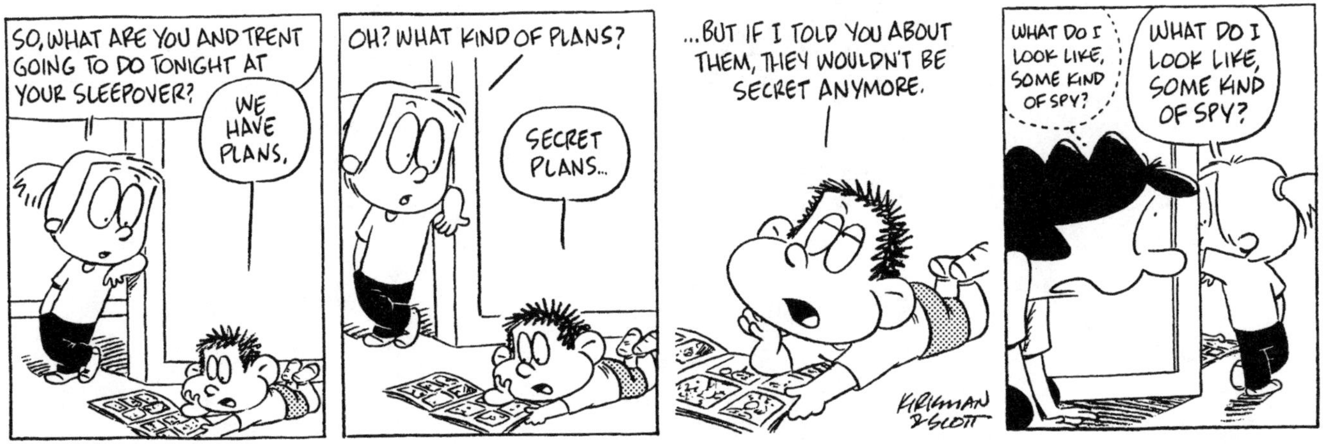
SO, WHAT ARE YOU AND TRENT GOING TO DO TONIGHT AT YOUR SLEEPOVER?
WE HAVE PLANS.
OH? WHAT KIND OF PLANS?
SECRET PLANS...
...BUT IF I TOLD YOU ABOUT THEM, THEY WOULDN'T BE SECRET ANYMORE.
WHAT DO I LOOK LIKE, SOME KIND OF SPY?
WHAT DO I LOOK LIKE, SOME KIND OF SPY?
KIRKMAN & SCOTT

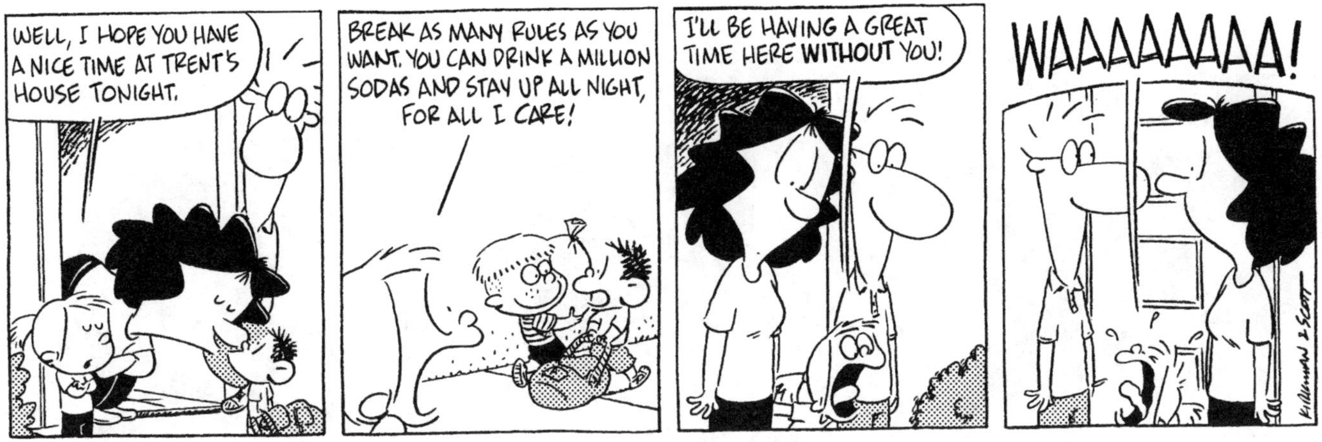
WELL, I HOPE YOU HAVE A NICE TIME AT TRENT'S HOUSE TONIGHT.
BREAK AS MANY RULES AS YOU WANT. YOU CAN DRINK A MILLION SODAS AND STAY UP ALL NIGHT, FOR ALL I CARE!
I'LL BE HAVING A GREAT TIME HERE **WITHOUT** YOU!
WAAAAAAAA!
KIRKMAN & SCOTT

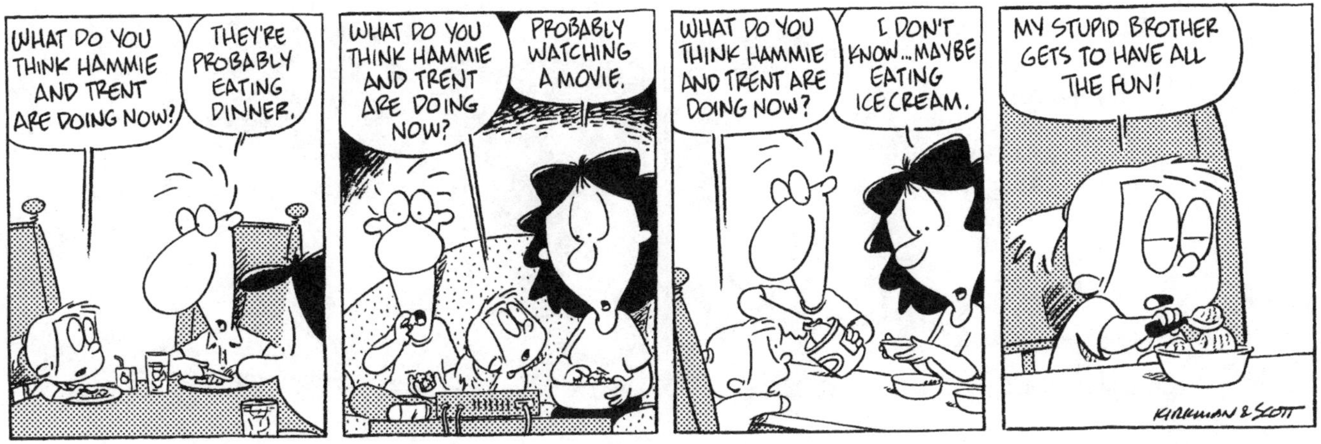
WHAT DO YOU THINK HAMMIE AND TRENT ARE DOING NOW?
THEY'RE PROBABLY EATING DINNER.
WHAT DO YOU THINK HAMMIE AND TRENT ARE DOING NOW?
PROBABLY WATCHING A MOVIE.
WHAT DO YOU THINK HAMMIE AND TRENT ARE DOING NOW?
I DON'T KNOW...MAYBE EATING ICE CREAM.
MY STUPID BROTHER GETS TO HAVE ALL THE FUN!
KIRKMAN & SCOTT

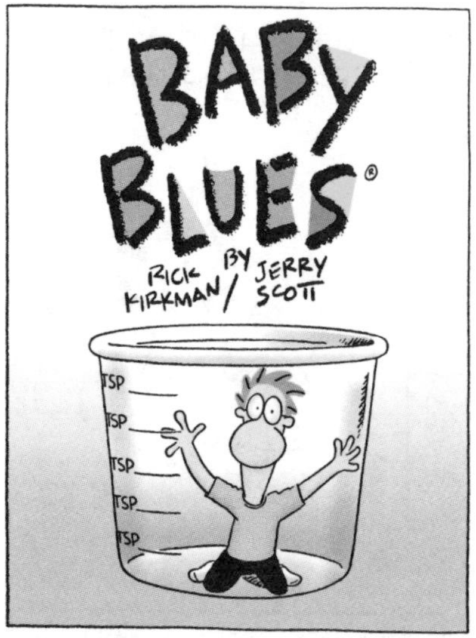
BABY BLUES®
BY RICK KIRKMAN / JERRY SCOTT
TSP
TSP
TSP
TSP
TSP

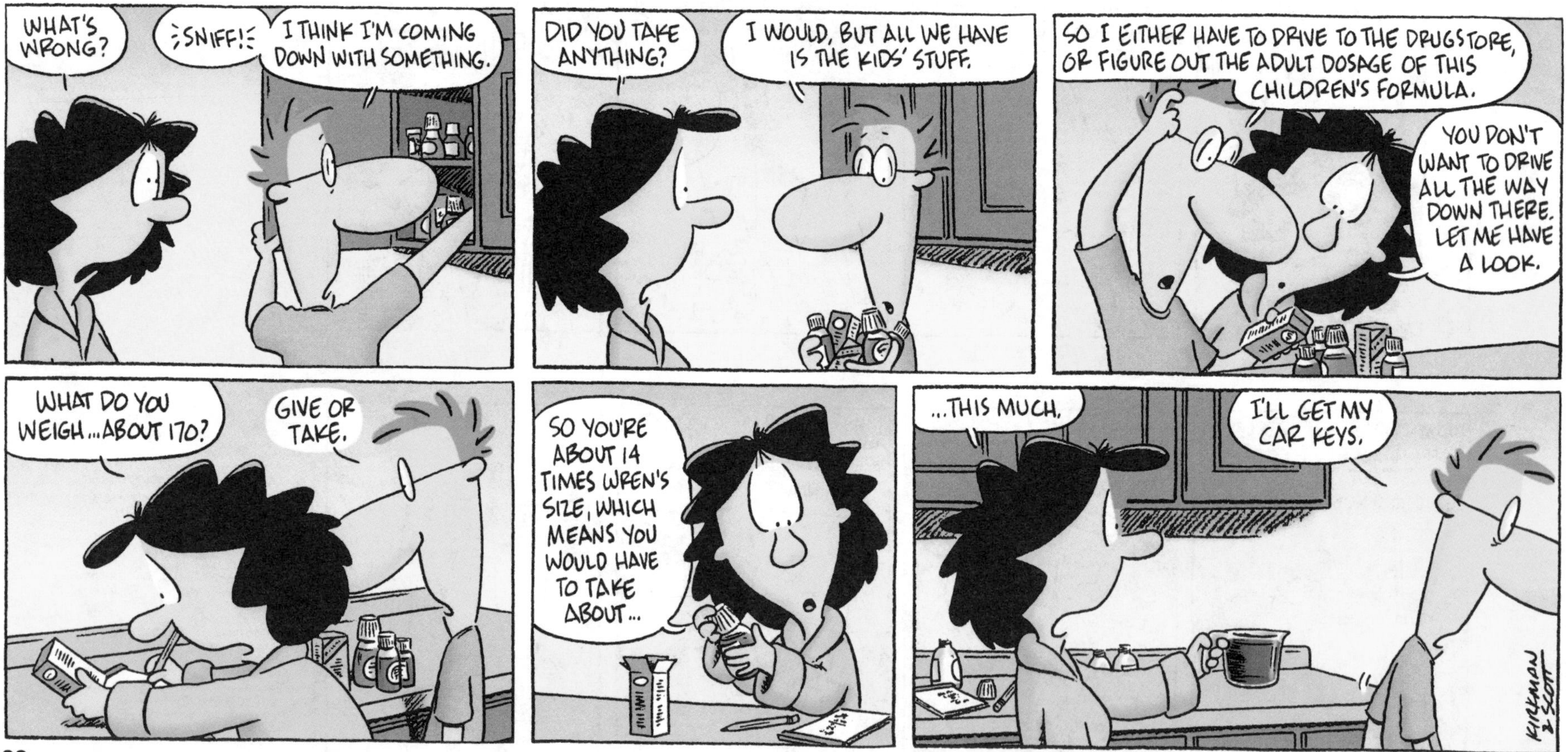
WHAT'S WRONG?
SNIFF!
I THINK I'M COMING DOWN WITH SOMETHING.
DID YOU TAKE ANYTHING?
I WOULD, BUT ALL WE HAVE IS THE KIDS' STUFF.
SO I EITHER HAVE TO DRIVE TO THE DRUGSTORE, OR FIGURE OUT THE ADULT DOSAGE OF THIS CHILDREN'S FORMULA.
YOU DON'T WANT TO DRIVE ALL THE WAY DOWN THERE. LET ME HAVE A LOOK.
WHAT DO YOU WEIGH...ABOUT 170?
GIVE OR TAKE.
SO YOU'RE ABOUT 14 TIMES WREN'S SIZE, WHICH MEANS YOU WOULD HAVE TO TAKE ABOUT...
...THIS MUCH.
I'LL GET MY CAR KEYS.
KIRKMAN & SCOTT

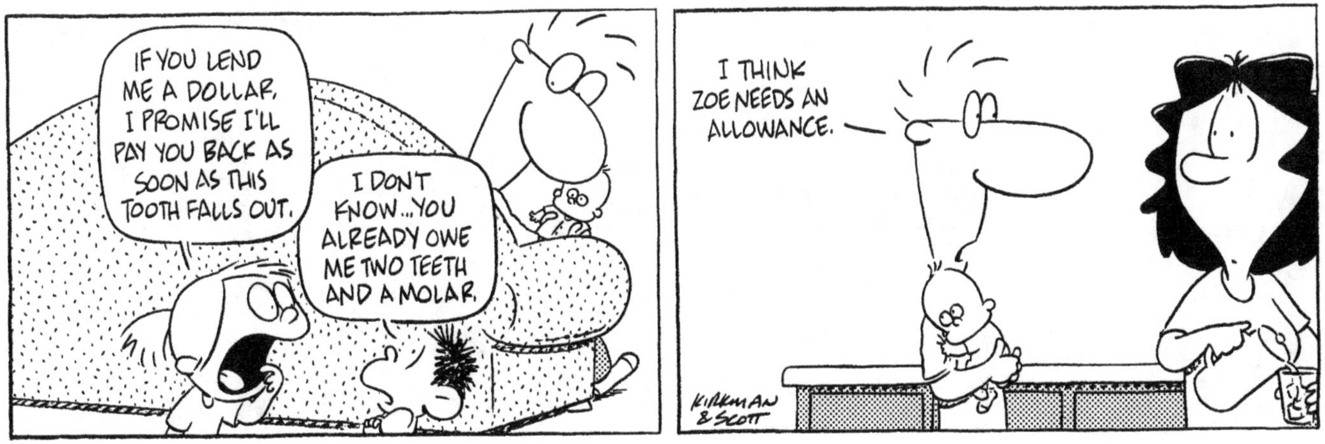
IF YOU LEND ME A DOLLAR, I PROMISE I'LL PAY YOU BACK AS SOON AS THIS TOOTH FALLS OUT.
I DON'T KNOW...YOU ALREADY OWE ME TWO TEETH AND A MOLAR.
I THINK ZOE NEEDS AN ALLOWANCE.
KIRKMAN & SCOTT

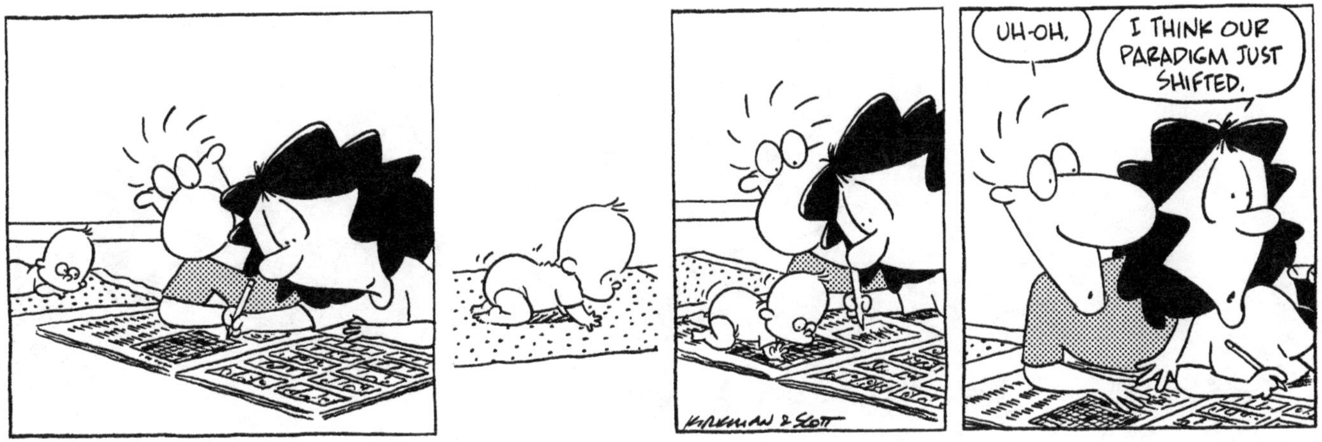
KIRKMAN & SCOTT
UH-OH.
I THINK OUR PARADIGM JUST SHIFTED.

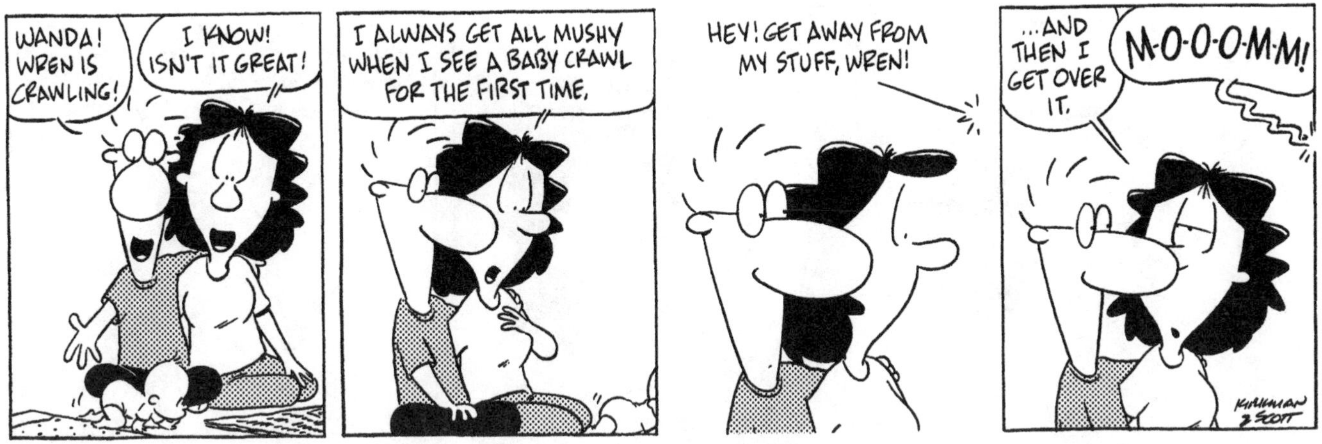
WANDA! WREN IS CRAWLING!
I KNOW! ISN'T IT GREAT!
I ALWAYS GET ALL MUSHY WHEN I SEE A BABY CRAWL FOR THE FIRST TIME.
HEY! GET AWAY FROM MY STUFF, WREN!
...AND THEN I GET OVER IT.
M-O-O-O-M-M!
KIRKMAN & SCOTT

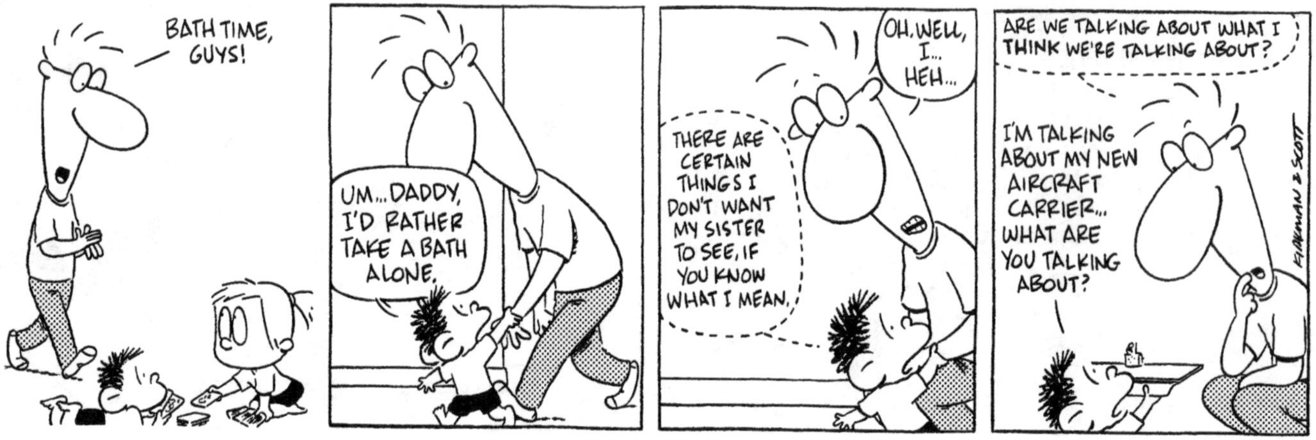
BATH TIME, GUYS!
UM... DADDY, I'D RATHER TAKE A BATH ALONE.
THERE ARE CERTAIN THINGS I DON'T WANT MY SISTER TO SEE, IF YOU KNOW WHAT I MEAN.
OH, WELL, I... HEH...
ARE WE TALKING ABOUT WHAT I THINK WE'RE TALKING ABOUT?
I'M TALKING ABOUT MY NEW AIRCRAFT CARRIER... WHAT ARE YOU TALKING ABOUT?
KIRKMAN & SCOTT

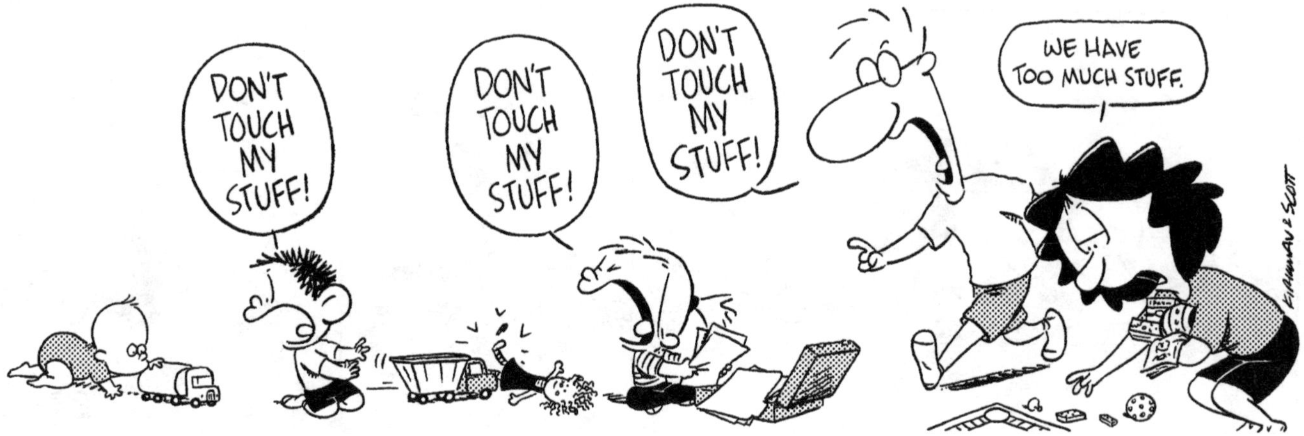
DON'T TOUCH MY STUFF!
DON'T TOUCH MY STUFF!
DON'T TOUCH MY STUFF!
WE HAVE TOO MUCH STUFF.
KIRKMAN & SCOTT

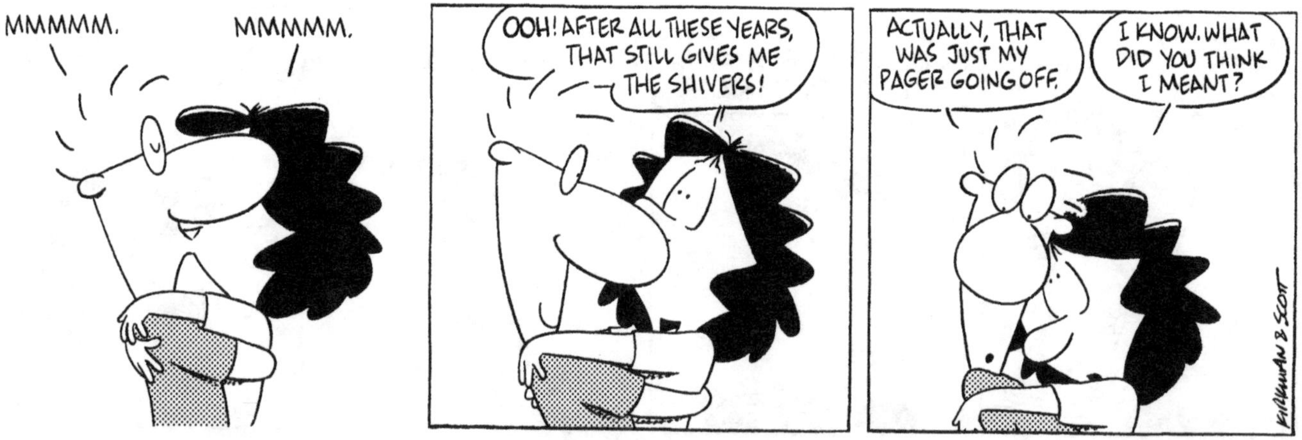
MMMMM.
MMMMM.
OOH! AFTER ALL THESE YEARS, THAT STILL GIVES ME THE SHIVERS!
ACTUALLY, THAT WAS JUST MY PAGER GOING OFF.
I KNOW. WHAT DID YOU THINK I MEANT?
KIRKMAN & SCOTT

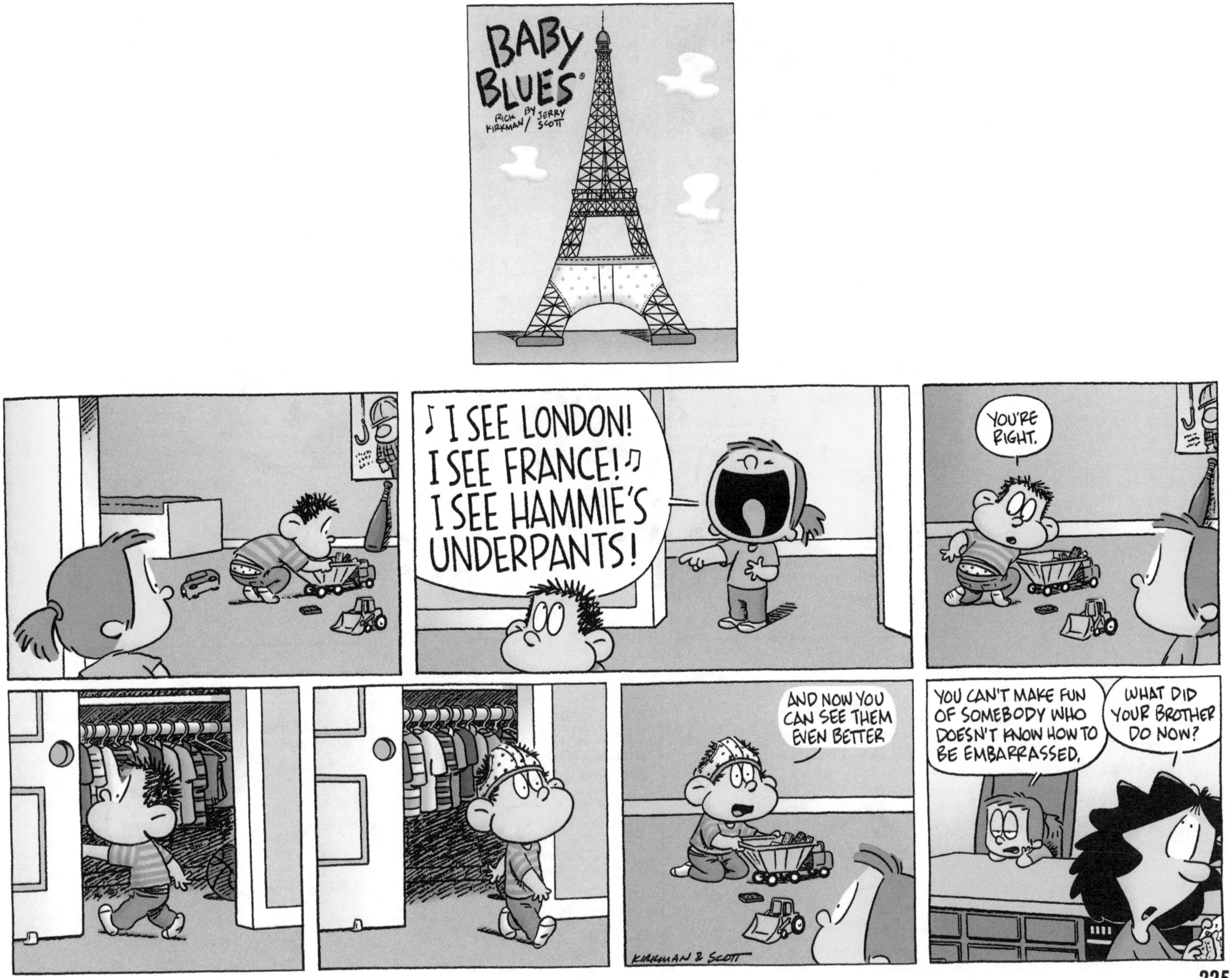

BABY BLUES®
BY RICK KIRKMAN / JERRY SCOTT
♪ I SEE LONDON! I SEE FRANCE! ♫ I SEE HAMMIE'S UNDERPANTS!
YOU'RE RIGHT.
AND NOW YOU CAN SEE THEM EVEN BETTER
KIRKMAN & SCOTT
YOU CAN'T MAKE FUN OF SOMEBODY WHO DOESN'T KNOW HOW TO BE EMBARRASSED.
WHAT DID YOUR BROTHER DO NOW?

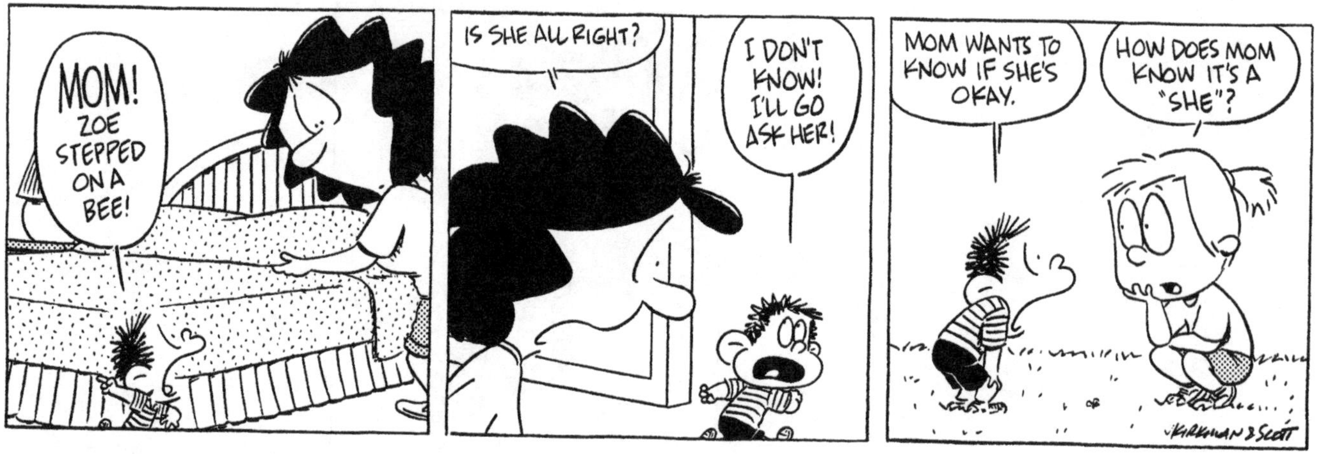
MOM! ZOE STEPPED ON A BEE!
IS SHE ALL RIGHT?
I DON'T KNOW! I'LL GO ASK HER!
MOM WANTS TO KNOW IF SHE'S OKAY.
HOW DOES MOM KNOW IT'S A "SHE"?
KIRKMAN & SCOTT

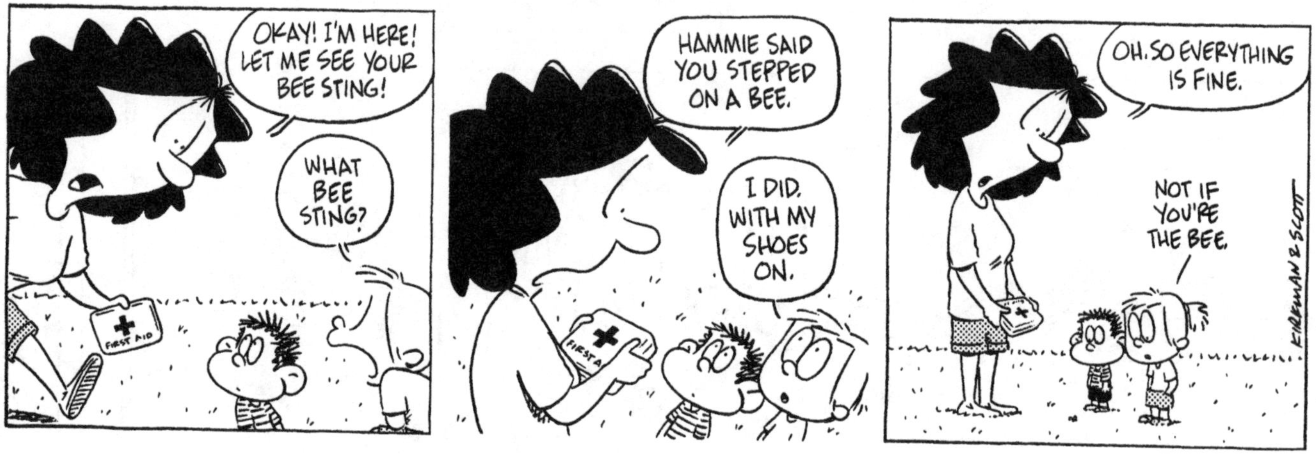
OKAY! I'M HERE! LET ME SEE YOUR BEE STING!
WHAT BEE STING?
FIRST AID
HAMMIE SAID YOU STEPPED ON A BEE.
I DID. WITH MY SHOES ON.
OH. SO EVERYTHING IS FINE.
NOT IF YOU'RE THE BEE.
KIRKMAN & SCOTT

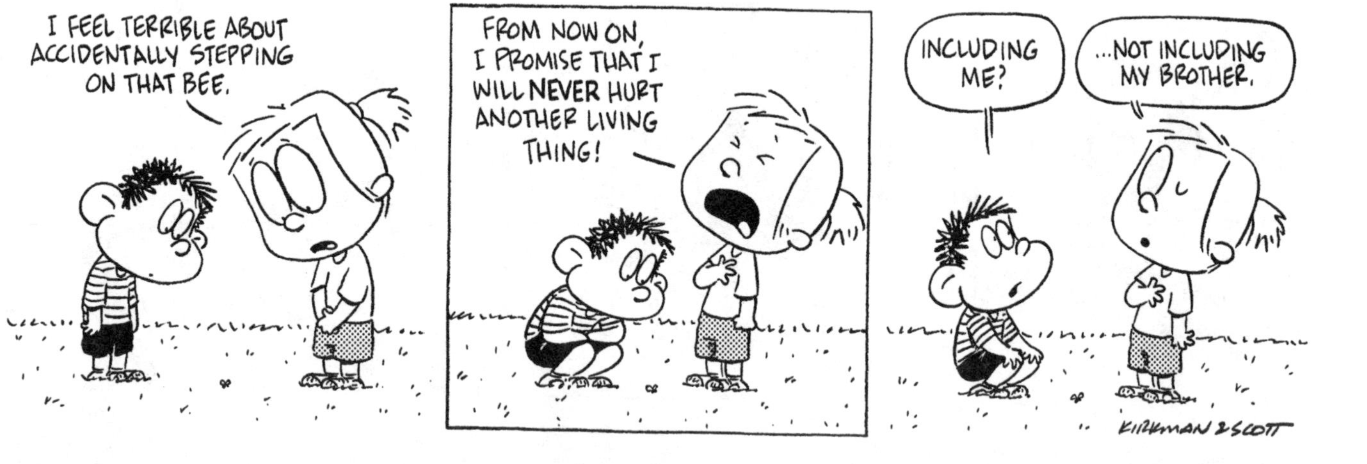
I FEEL TERRIBLE ABOUT ACCIDENTALLY STEPPING ON THAT BEE.
FROM NOW ON, I PROMISE THAT I WILL NEVER HURT ANOTHER LIVING THING!
INCLUDING ME?
...NOT INCLUDING MY BROTHER.
KIRKMAN & SCOTT

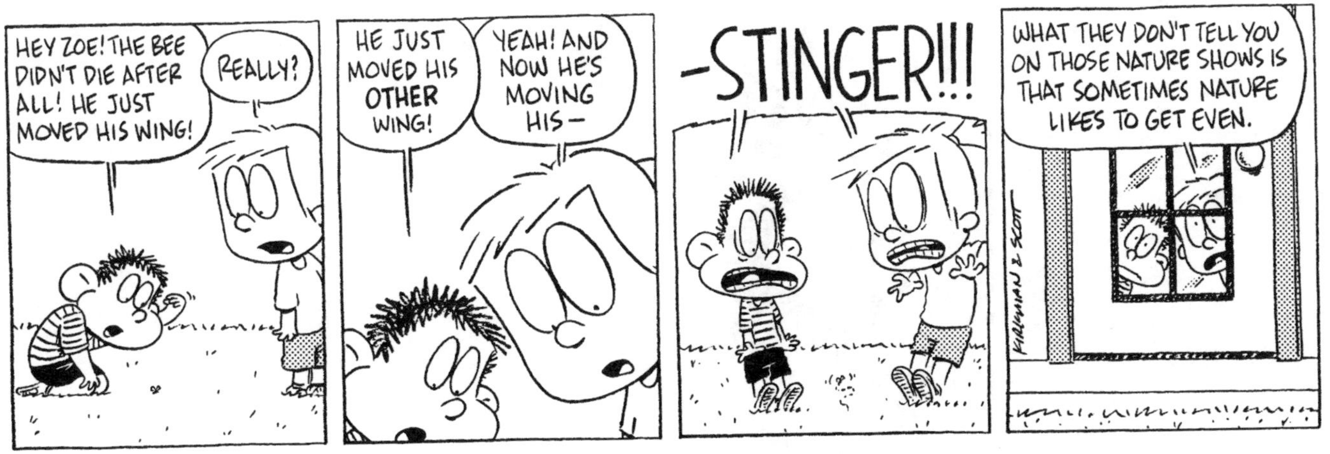
HEY ZOE! THE BEE DIDN'T DIE AFTER ALL! HE JUST MOVED HIS WING!
REALLY?
HE JUST MOVED HIS **OTHER** WING!
YEAH! AND NOW HE'S MOVING HIS—
-STINGER!!!
WHAT THEY DON'T TELL YOU ON THOSE NATURE SHOWS IS THAT SOMETIMES NATURE LIKES TO GET EVEN.
KIRKMAN & SCOTT

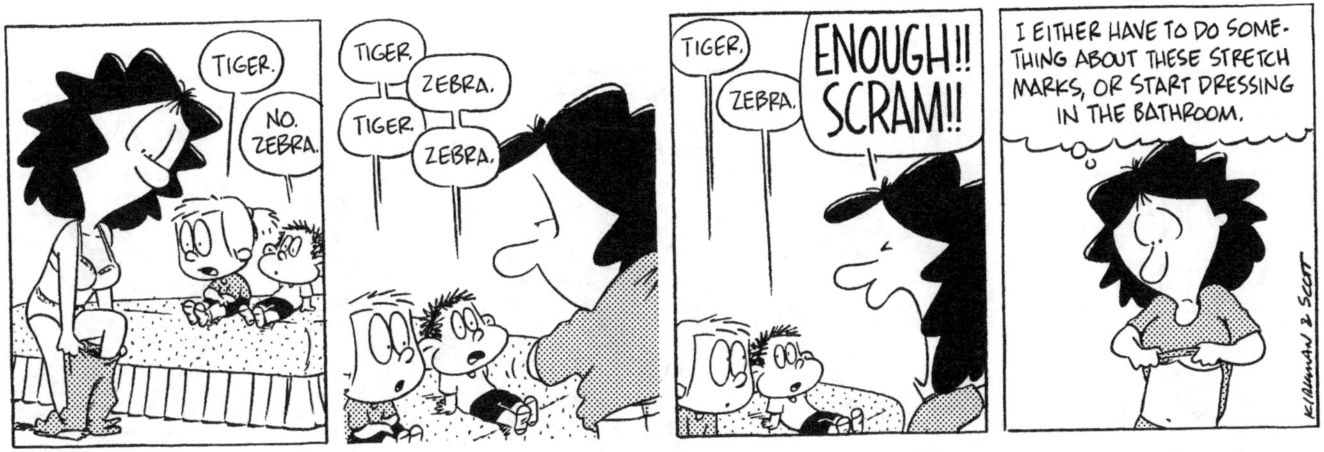
TIGER.
NO. ZEBRA.
TIGER.
ZEBRA.
TIGER.
ZEBRA.
TIGER.
ZEBRA.
ENOUGH!! SCRAM!!
I EITHER HAVE TO DO SOMETHING ABOUT THESE STRETCH MARKS, OR START DRESSING IN THE BATHROOM.
KIRKMAN & SCOTT

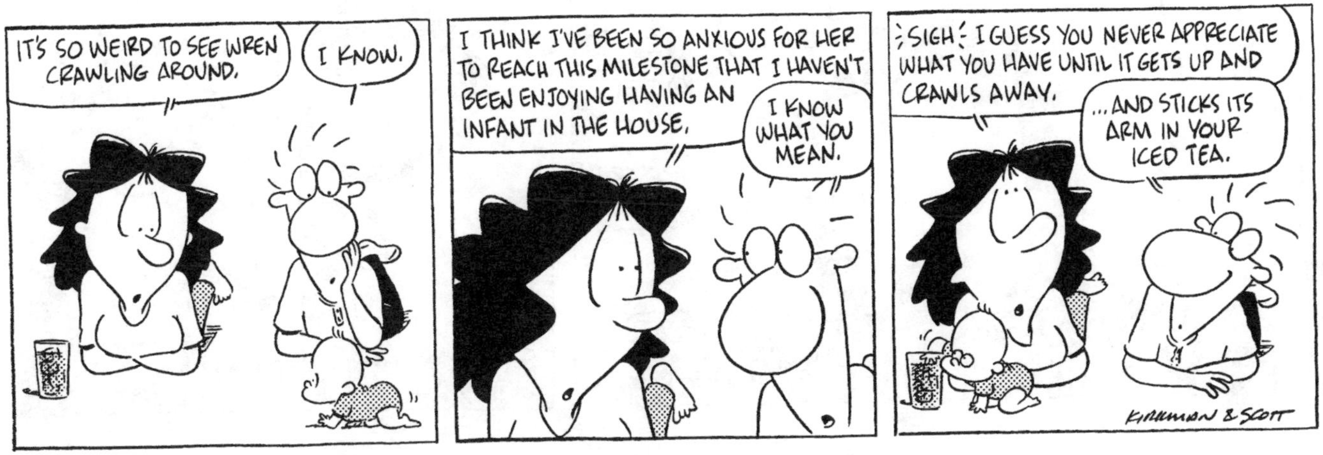
IT'S SO WEIRD TO SEE WREN CRAWLING AROUND.
I KNOW.
I THINK I'VE BEEN SO ANXIOUS FOR HER TO REACH THIS MILESTONE THAT I HAVEN'T BEEN ENJOYING HAVING AN INFANT IN THE HOUSE.
I KNOW WHAT YOU MEAN.
SIGH I GUESS YOU NEVER APPRECIATE WHAT YOU HAVE UNTIL IT GETS UP AND CRAWLS AWAY.
...AND STICKS ITS ARM IN YOUR ICED TEA.
KIRKMAN & SCOTT

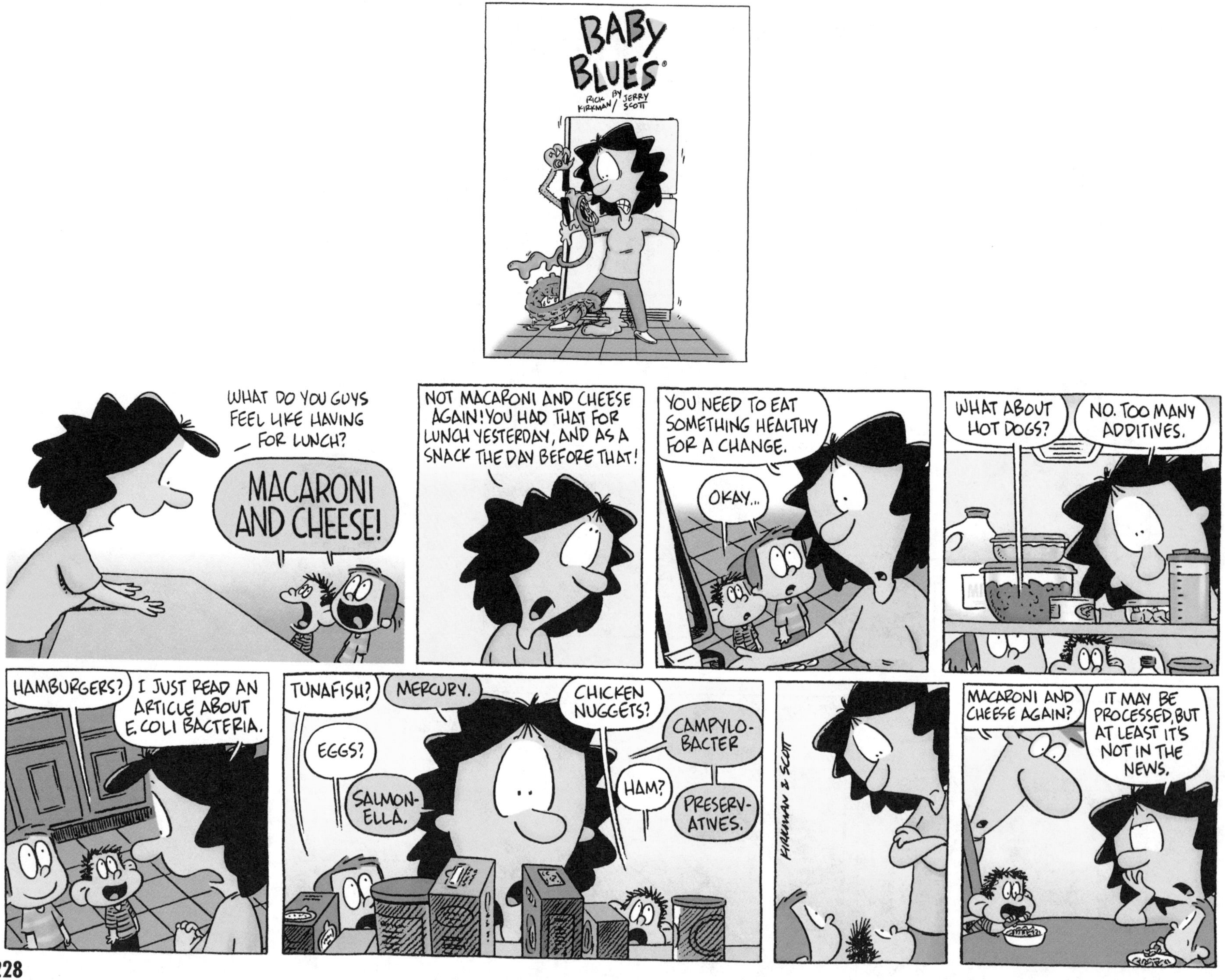
BABY BLUES®
BY RICK KIRKMAN / JERRY SCOTT
WHAT DO YOU GUYS FEEL LIKE HAVING FOR LUNCH?
MACARONI AND CHEESE!
NOT MACARONI AND CHEESE AGAIN! YOU HAD THAT FOR LUNCH YESTERDAY, AND AS A SNACK THE DAY BEFORE THAT!
YOU NEED TO EAT SOMETHING HEALTHY FOR A CHANGE.
OKAY...
WHAT ABOUT HOT DOGS?
NO. TOO MANY ADDITIVES.
HAMBURGERS?
I JUST READ AN ARTICLE ABOUT E. COLI BACTERIA.
TUNAFISH?
MERCURY.
EGGS?
SALMONELLA.
CHICKEN NUGGETS?
CAMPYLOBACTER
HAM?
PRESERVATIVES.
KIRKMAN & SCOTT
MACARONI AND CHEESE AGAIN?
IT MAY BE PROCESSED, BUT AT LEAST IT'S NOT IN THE NEWS.

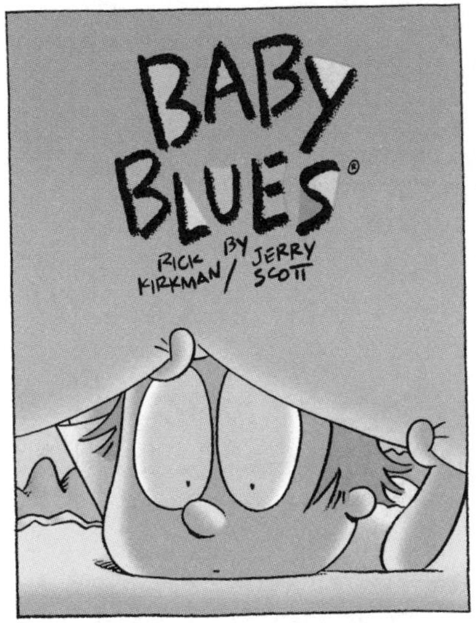
BABY BLUES®
RICK KIRKMAN / BY JERRY SCOTT

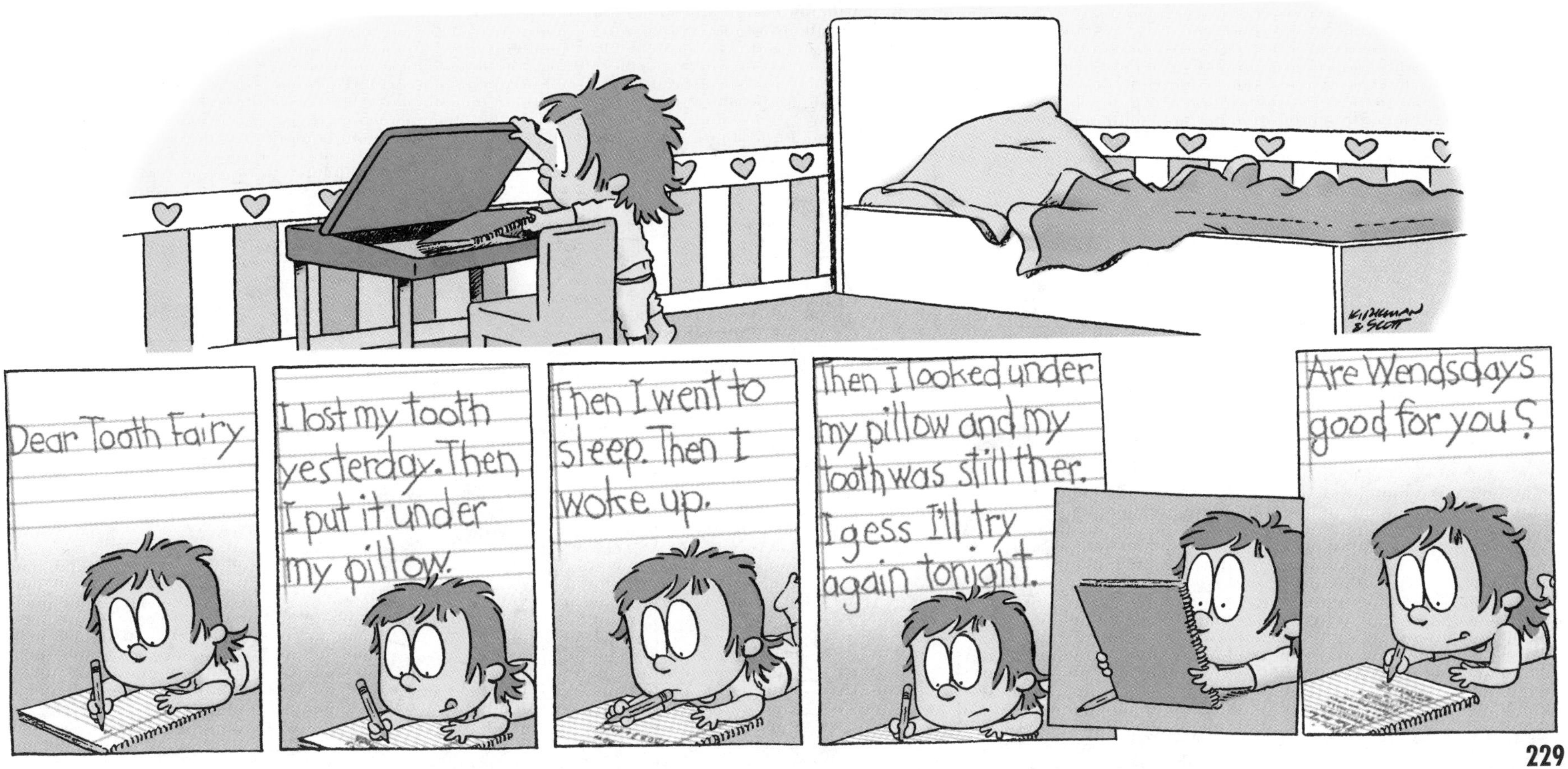
KIRKMAN & SCOTT
Dear Tooth Fairy
I lost my tooth yesterday. Then I put it under my pillow.
Then I went to sleep. Then I woke up.
Then I looked under my pillow and my tooth was still ther. I gess I'll try again tonight.
Are Wendsdays good for you?

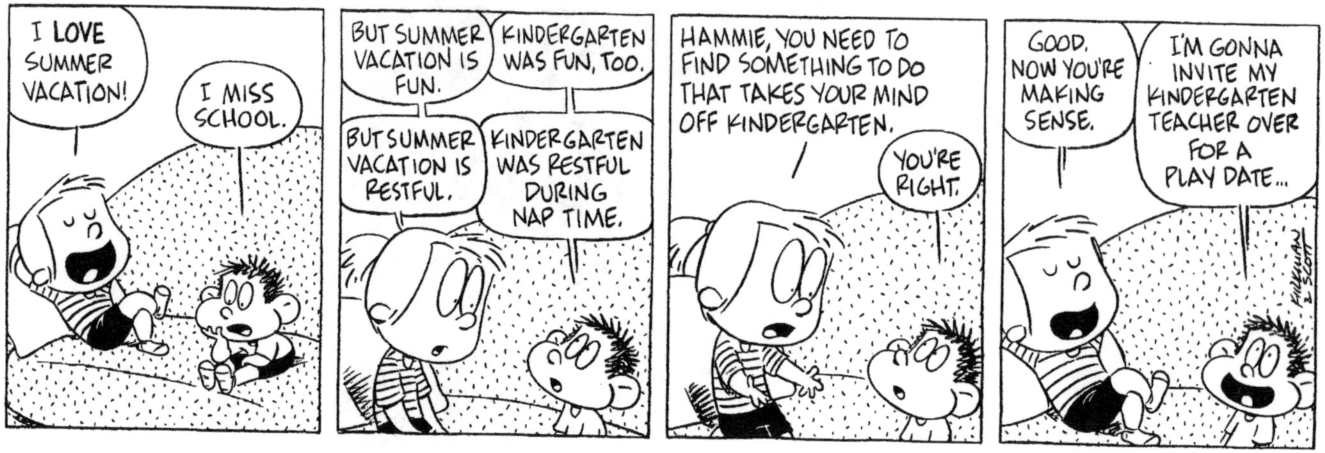
I LOVE SUMMER VACATION!
I MISS SCHOOL.
BUT SUMMER VACATION IS FUN.
KINDERGARTEN WAS FUN, TOO.
BUT SUMMER VACATION IS RESTFUL.
KINDERGARTEN WAS RESTFUL DURING NAP TIME.
HAMMIE, YOU NEED TO FIND SOMETHING TO DO THAT TAKES YOUR MIND OFF KINDERGARTEN.
YOU'RE RIGHT.
GOOD. NOW YOU'RE MAKING SENSE.
I'M GONNA INVITE MY KINDERGARTEN TEACHER OVER FOR A PLAY DATE...
KIRKMAN & SCOTT

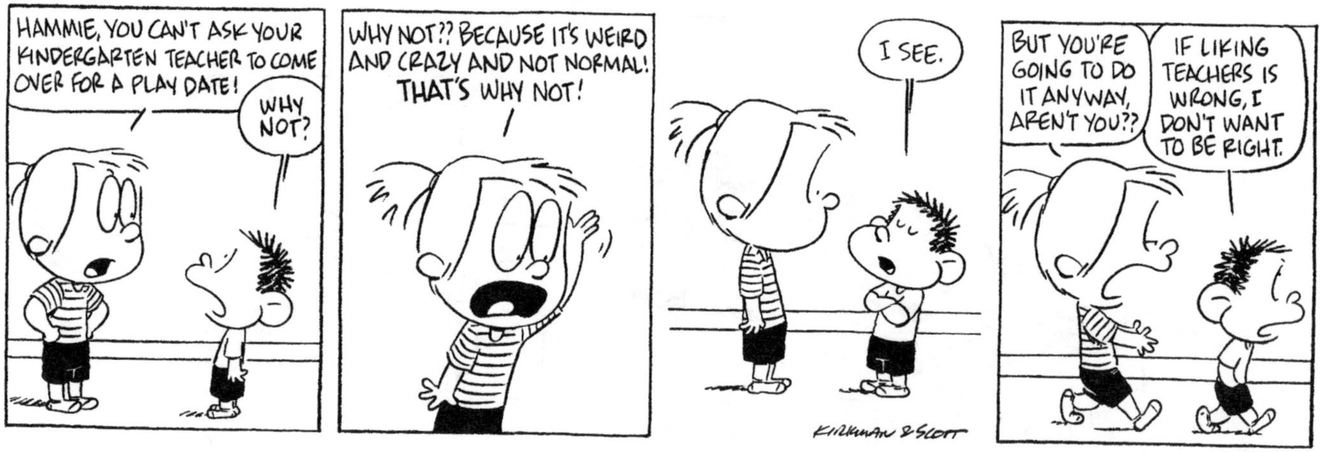
HAMMIE, YOU CAN'T ASK YOUR KINDERGARTEN TEACHER TO COME OVER FOR A PLAY DATE!
WHY NOT?
WHY NOT?? BECAUSE IT'S WEIRD AND CRAZY AND NOT NORMAL! THAT'S WHY NOT!
I SEE.
BUT YOU'RE GOING TO DO IT ANYWAY, AREN'T YOU??
IF LIKING TEACHERS IS WRONG, I DON'T WANT TO BE RIGHT.
KIRKMAN & SCOTT

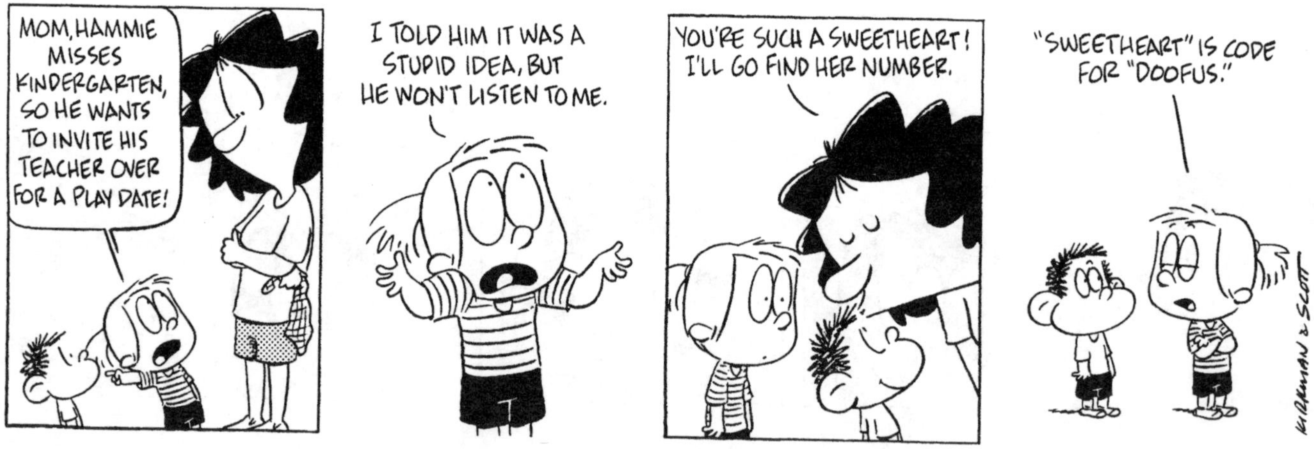
MOM, HAMMIE MISSES KINDERGARTEN, SO HE WANTS TO INVITE HIS TEACHER OVER FOR A PLAY DATE!
I TOLD HIM IT WAS A STUPID IDEA, BUT HE WON'T LISTEN TO ME.
YOU'RE SUCH A SWEETHEART! I'LL GO FIND HER NUMBER.
"SWEETHEART" IS CODE FOR "DOOFUS."
KIRKMAN & SCOTT

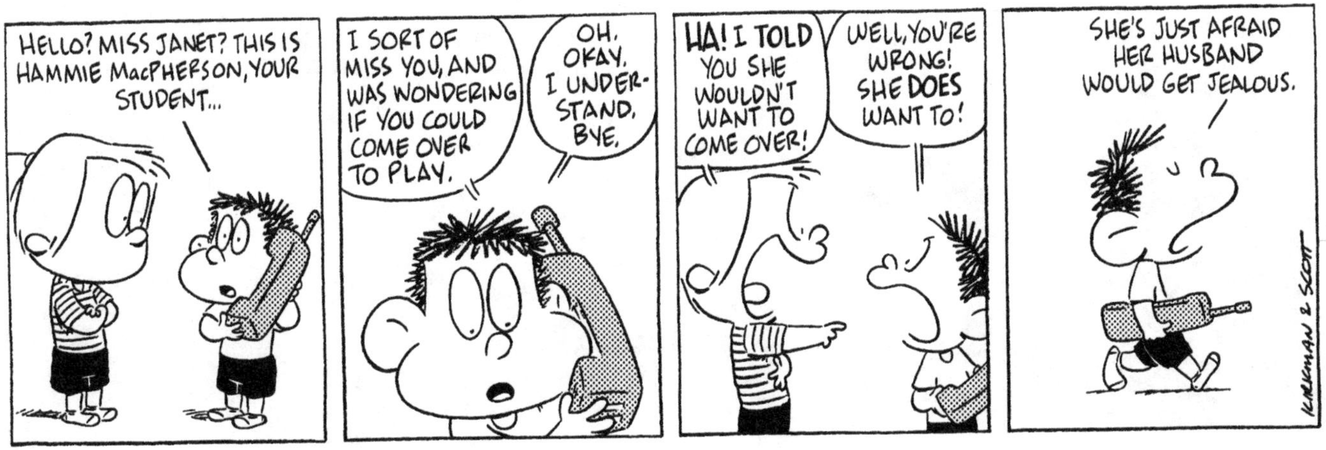
HELLO? MISS JANET? THIS IS HAMMIE MacPHERSON, YOUR STUDENT...
I SORT OF MISS YOU, AND WAS WONDERING IF YOU COULD COME OVER TO PLAY.
OH. OKAY. I UNDERSTAND. BYE.
HA! I TOLD YOU SHE WOULDN'T WANT TO COME OVER!
WELL, YOU'RE WRONG! SHE DOES WANT TO!
SHE'S JUST AFRAID HER HUSBAND WOULD GET JEALOUS.
KIRKMAN & SCOTT

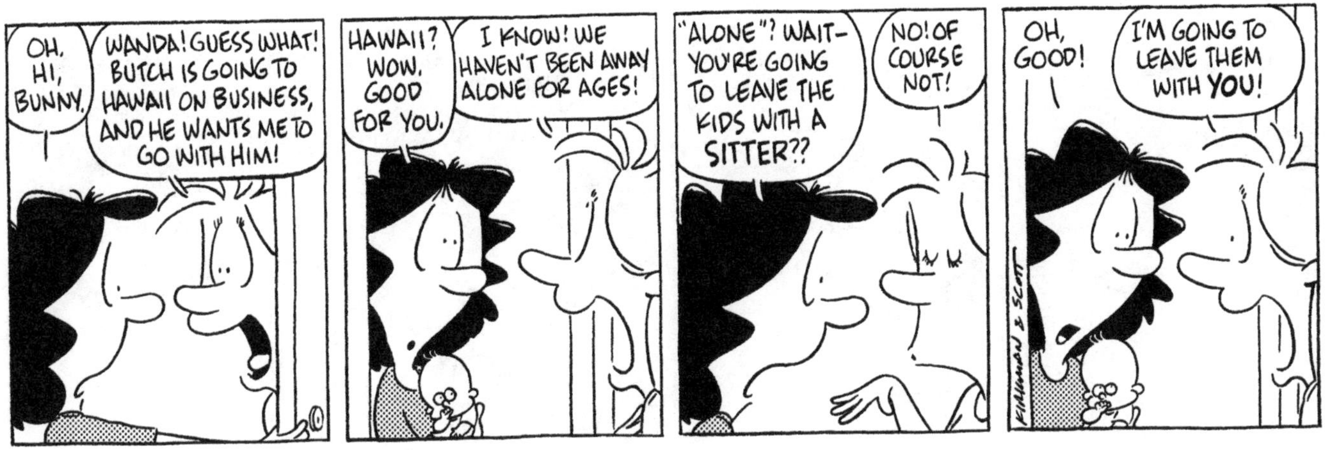
OH. HI, BUNNY.
WANDA! GUESS WHAT! BUTCH IS GOING TO HAWAII ON BUSINESS, AND HE WANTS ME TO GO WITH HIM!
HAWAII? WOW. GOOD FOR YOU.
I KNOW! WE HAVEN'T BEEN AWAY ALONE FOR AGES!
"ALONE"? WAIT— YOU'RE GOING TO LEAVE THE KIDS WITH A SITTER??
NO! OF COURSE NOT!
KIRKMAN & SCOTT
OH, GOOD!
I'M GOING TO LEAVE THEM WITH YOU!

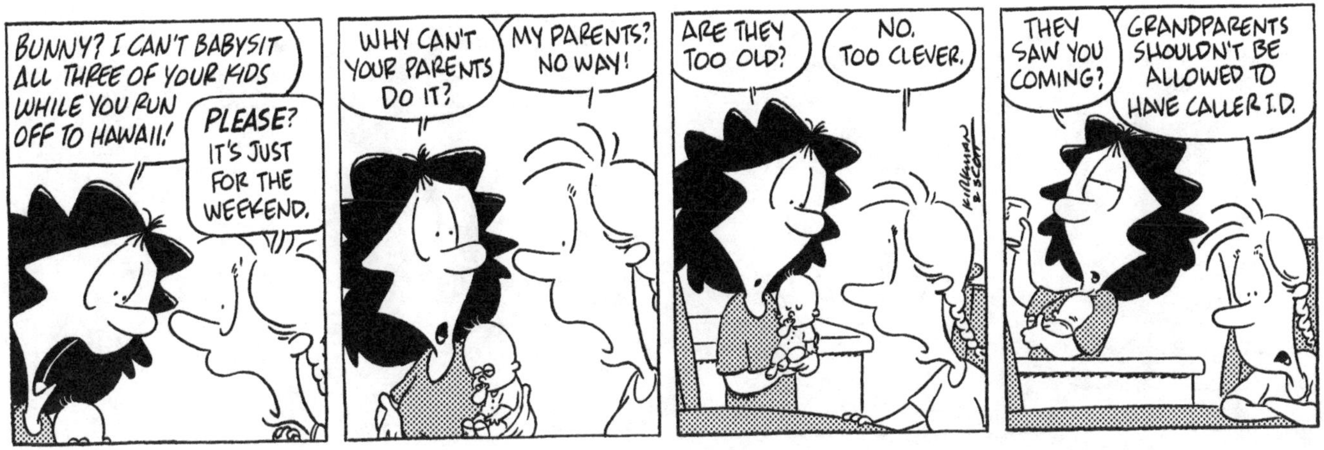
BUNNY? I CAN'T BABYSIT ALL THREE OF YOUR KIDS WHILE YOU RUN OFF TO HAWAII!
PLEASE? IT'S JUST FOR THE WEEKEND.
WHY CAN'T YOUR PARENTS DO IT?
MY PARENTS? NO WAY!
ARE THEY TOO OLD?
NO. TOO CLEVER.
KIRKMAN & SCOTT
THEY SAW YOU COMING?
GRANDPARENTS SHOULDN'T BE ALLOWED TO HAVE CALLER I.D.

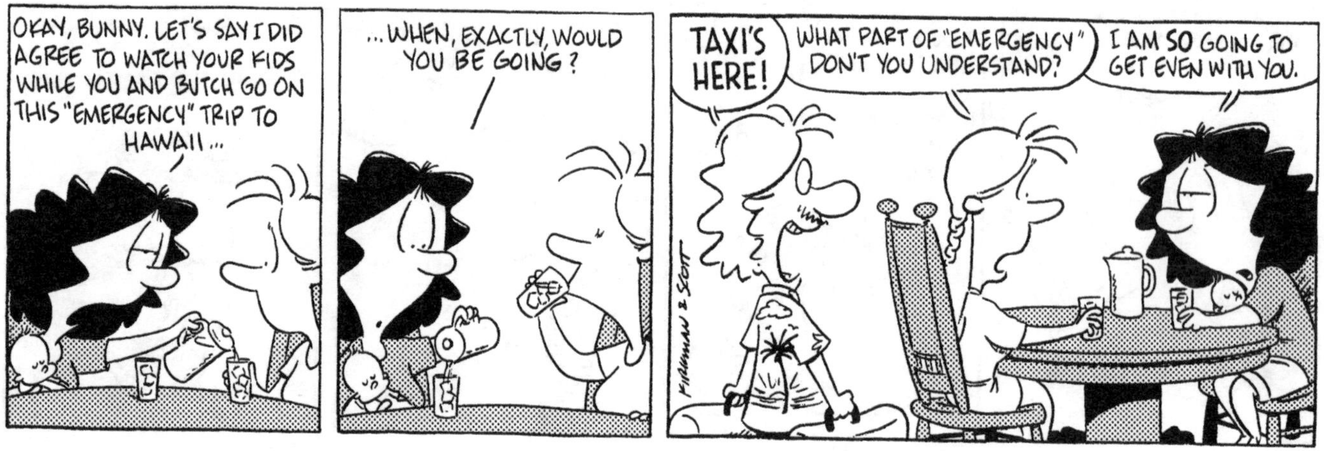
OKAY, BUNNY. LET'S SAY I DID AGREE TO WATCH YOUR KIDS WHILE YOU AND BUTCH GO ON THIS "EMERGENCY" TRIP TO HAWAII...
...WHEN, EXACTLY, WOULD YOU BE GOING?
TAXI'S HERE!
WHAT PART OF "EMERGENCY" DON'T YOU UNDERSTAND?
I AM SO GOING TO GET EVEN WITH YOU.

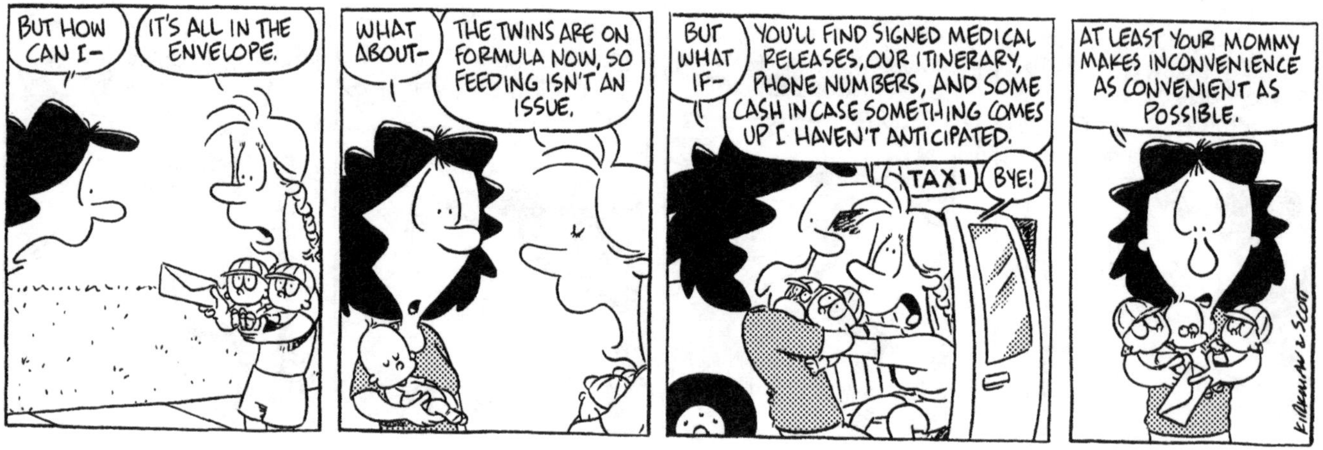
BUT HOW CAN I-
IT'S ALL IN THE ENVELOPE.
WHAT ABOUT-
THE TWINS ARE ON FORMULA NOW, SO FEEDING ISN'T AN ISSUE.
BUT WHAT IF-
YOU'LL FIND SIGNED MEDICAL RELEASES, OUR ITINERARY, PHONE NUMBERS, AND SOME CASH IN CASE SOMETHING COMES UP I HAVEN'T ANTICIPATED.
TAXI
BYE!
AT LEAST YOUR MOMMY MAKES INCONVENIENCE AS CONVENIENT AS POSSIBLE.

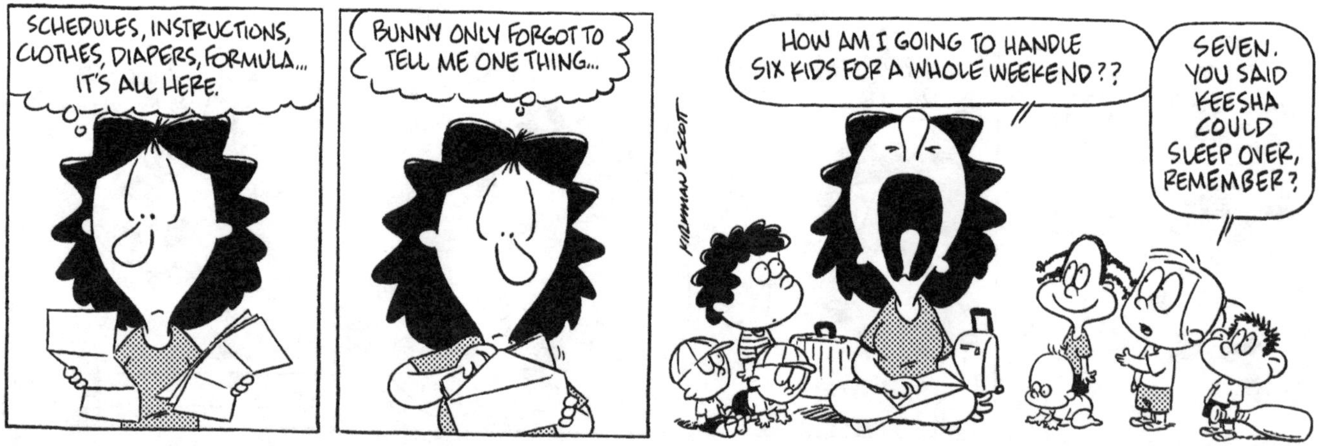
SCHEDULES, INSTRUCTIONS, CLOTHES, DIAPERS, FORMULA... IT'S ALL HERE.
BUNNY ONLY FORGOT TO TELL ME ONE THING...
HOW AM I GOING TO HANDLE SIX KIDS FOR A WHOLE WEEKEND??
SEVEN. YOU SAID KEESHA COULD SLEEP OVER, REMEMBER?

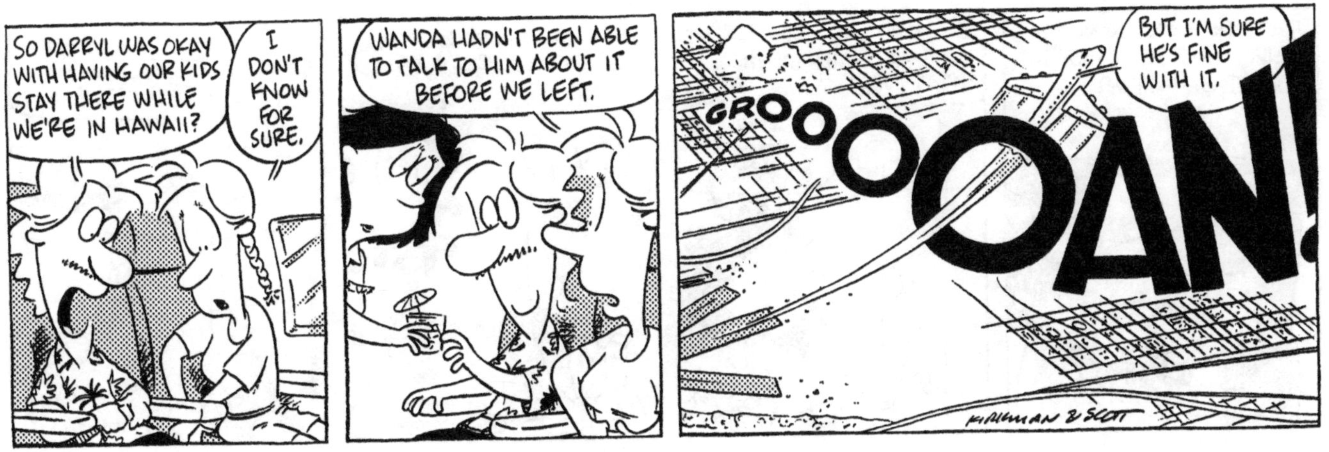
SO DARRYL WAS OKAY WITH HAVING OUR KIDS STAY THERE WHILE WE'RE IN HAWAII?
I DON'T KNOW FOR SURE.
WANDA HADN'T BEEN ABLE TO TALK TO HIM ABOUT IT BEFORE WE LEFT.
BUT I'M SURE HE'S FINE WITH IT.
GROOOOOAN!
KIRKMAN & SCOTT

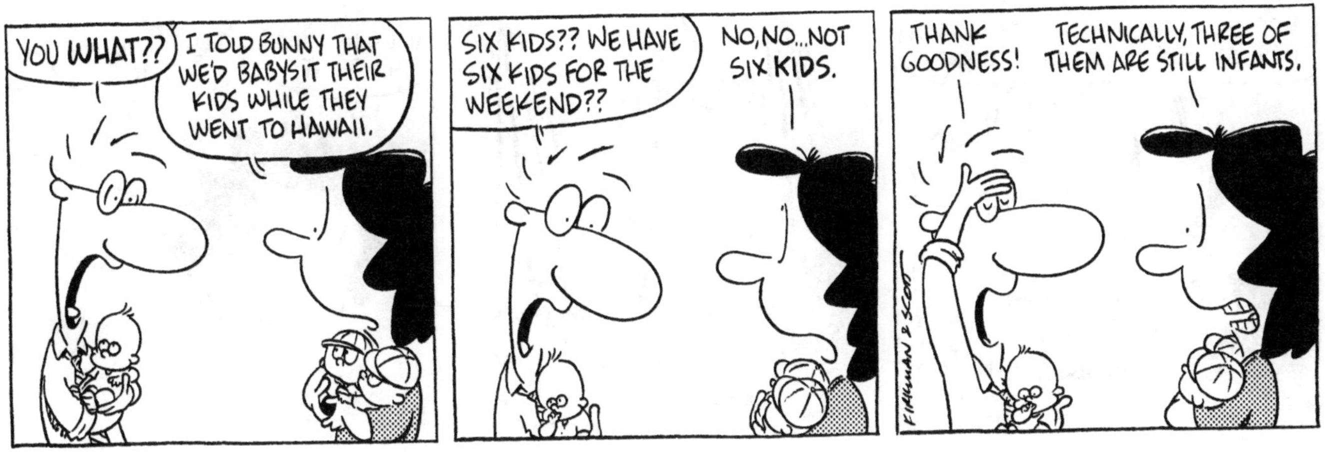
YOU WHAT??
I TOLD BUNNY THAT WE'D BABYSIT THEIR KIDS WHILE THEY WENT TO HAWAII.
SIX KIDS?? WE HAVE SIX KIDS FOR THE WEEKEND??
NO, NO...NOT SIX KIDS.
THANK GOODNESS!
TECHNICALLY, THREE OF THEM ARE STILL INFANTS.
KIRKMAN & SCOTT

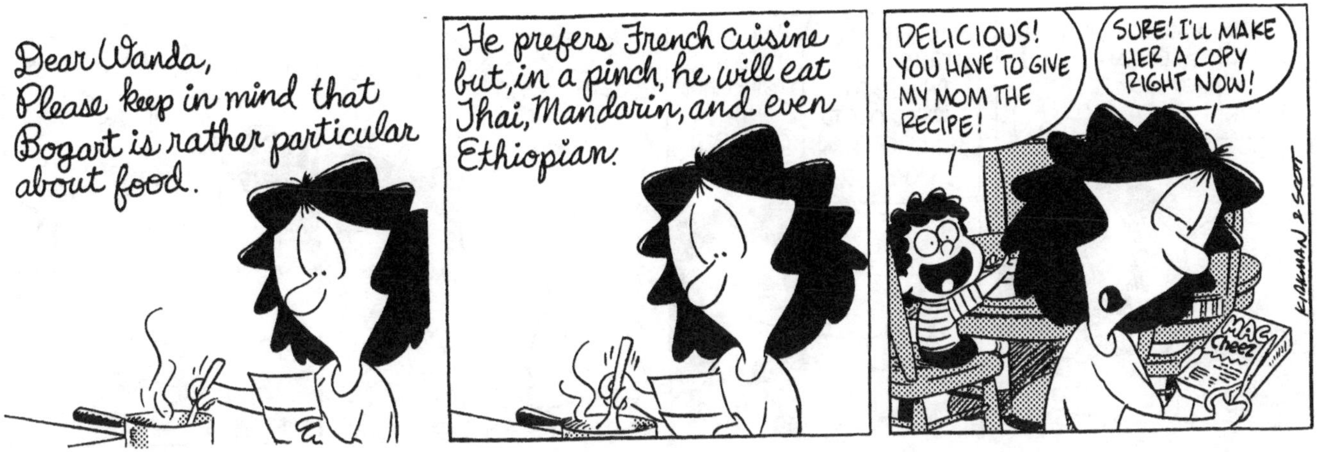
Dear Wanda,
Please keep in mind that Bogart is rather particular about food.
He prefers French cuisine but, in a pinch, he will eat Thai, Mandarin, and even Ethiopian.
DELICIOUS! YOU HAVE TO GIVE MY MOM THE RECIPE!
SURE! I'LL MAKE HER A COPY RIGHT NOW!
MAC Cheez
KIRKMAN & SCOTT

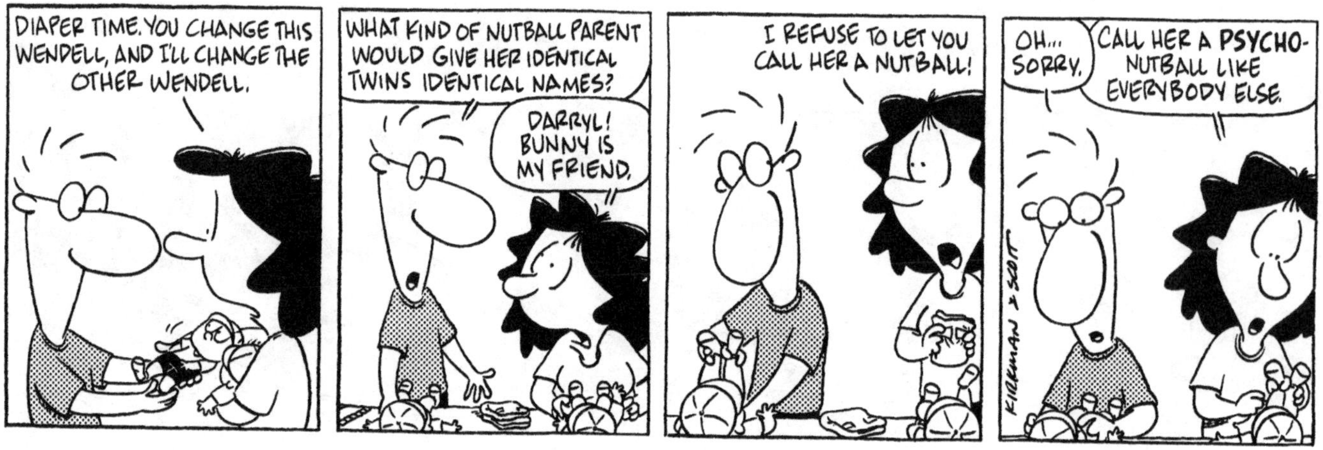
DIAPER TIME. YOU CHANGE THIS WENDELL, AND I'LL CHANGE THE OTHER WENDELL.
WHAT KIND OF NUTBALL PARENT WOULD GIVE HER IDENTICAL TWINS IDENTICAL NAMES?
DARRYL! BUNNY IS MY FRIEND.
I REFUSE TO LET YOU CALL HER A NUTBALL!
OH... SORRY.
CALL HER A **PSYCHO**-NUTBALL LIKE EVERYBODY ELSE.
KIRKMAN & SCOTT

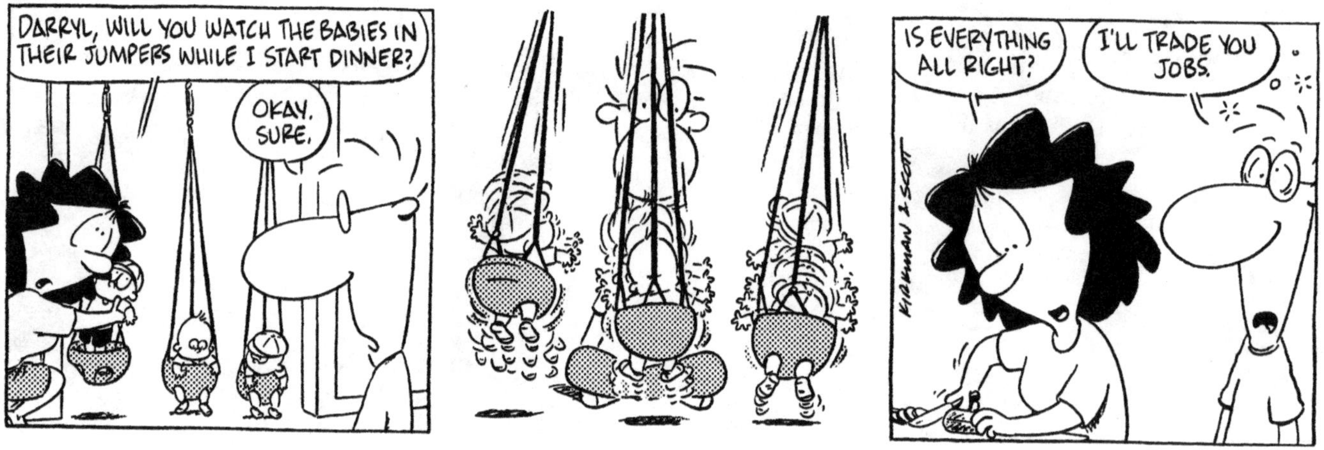
DARRYL, WILL YOU WATCH THE BABIES IN THEIR JUMPERS WHILE I START DINNER?
OKAY. SURE.
KIRKMAN & SCOTT
IS EVERYTHING ALL RIGHT?
I'LL TRADE YOU JOBS.

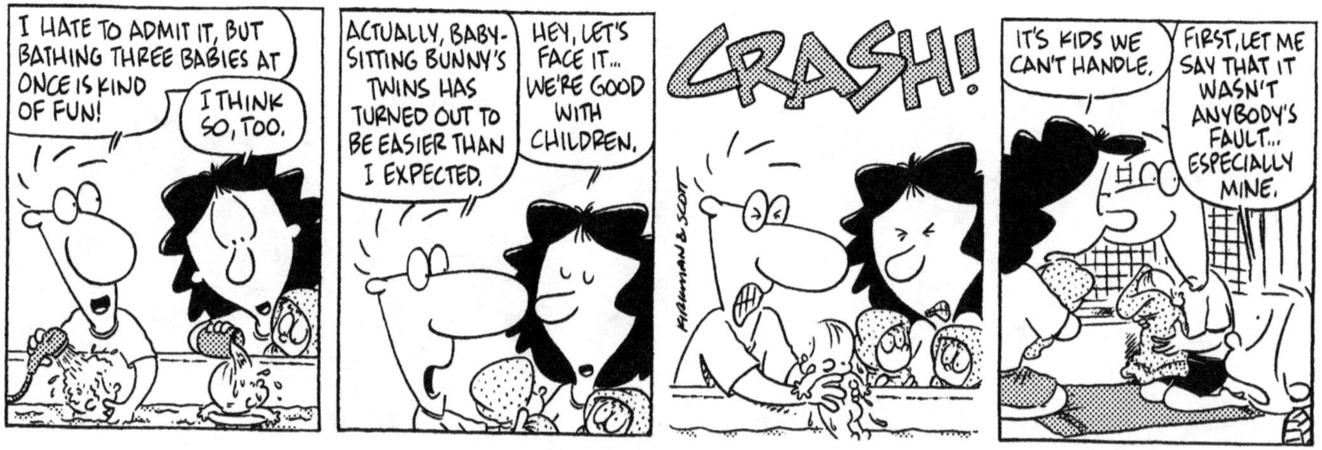
I HATE TO ADMIT IT, BUT BATHING THREE BABIES AT ONCE IS KIND OF FUN!
I THINK SO, TOO.
ACTUALLY, BABY-SITTING BUNNY'S TWINS HAS TURNED OUT TO BE EASIER THAN I EXPECTED.
HEY, LET'S FACE IT... WE'RE GOOD WITH CHILDREN.
CRASH!
KIRKMAN & SCOTT
IT'S KIDS WE CAN'T HANDLE.
FIRST, LET ME SAY THAT IT WASN'T ANYBODY'S FAULT... ESPECIALLY MINE.

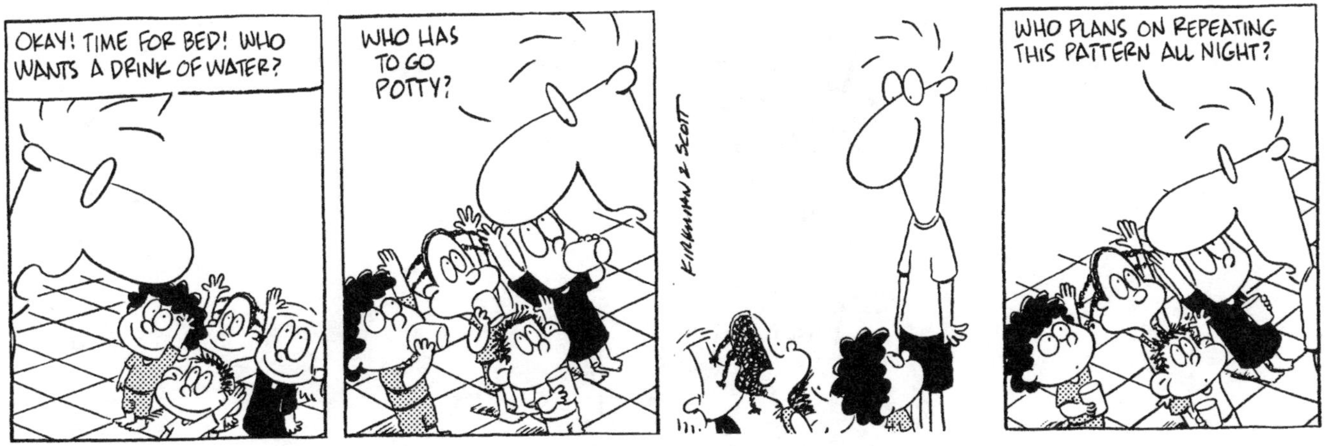
OKAY! TIME FOR BED! WHO WANTS A DRINK OF WATER?
WHO HAS TO GO POTTY?
KIRKMAN & SCOTT
WHO PLANS ON REPEATING THIS PATTERN ALL NIGHT?

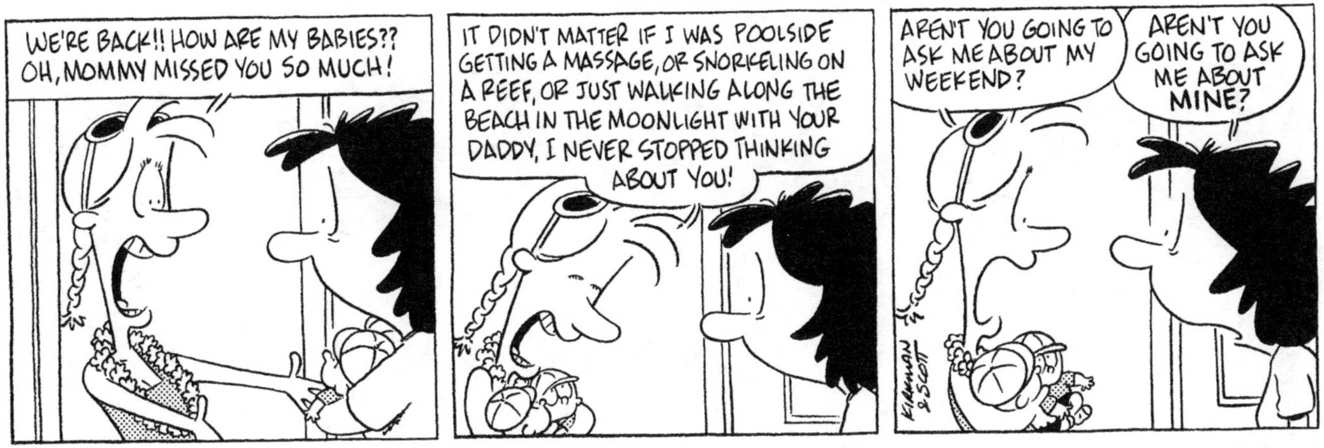
WE'RE BACK!! HOW ARE MY BABIES?? OH, MOMMY MISSED YOU SO MUCH!
IT DIDN'T MATTER IF I WAS POOLSIDE GETTING A MASSAGE, OR SNORKELING ON A REEF, OR JUST WALKING ALONG THE BEACH IN THE MOONLIGHT WITH YOUR DADDY, I NEVER STOPPED THINKING ABOUT YOU!
AREN'T YOU GOING TO ASK ME ABOUT MY WEEKEND?
AREN'T YOU GOING TO ASK ME ABOUT MINE?
KIRKMAN & SCOTT

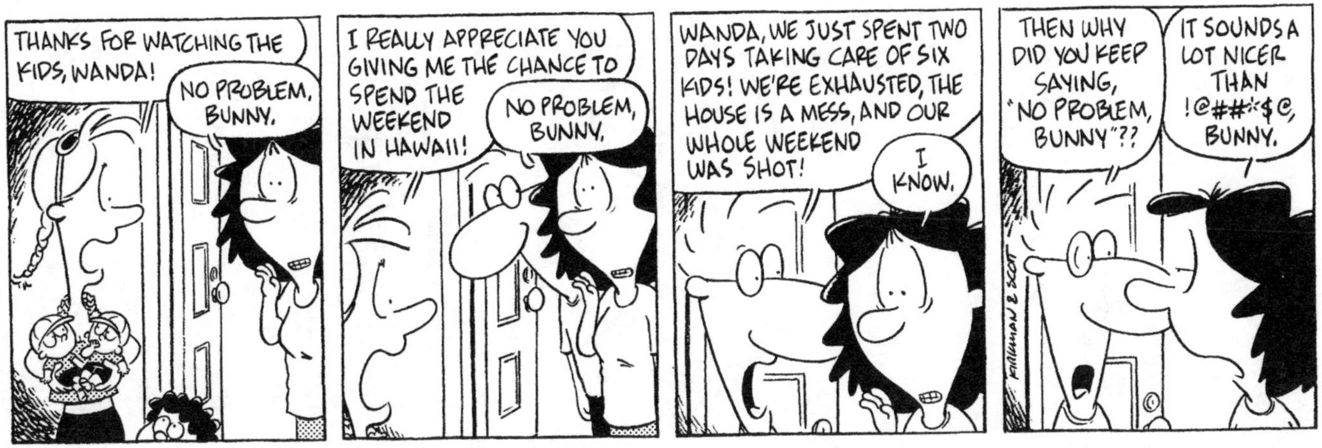
THANKS FOR WATCHING THE KIDS, WANDA!
NO PROBLEM, BUNNY.
I REALLY APPRECIATE YOU GIVING ME THE CHANCE TO SPEND THE WEEKEND IN HAWAII!
NO PROBLEM, BUNNY.
WANDA, WE JUST SPENT TWO DAYS TAKING CARE OF SIX KIDS! WE'RE EXHAUSTED, THE HOUSE IS A MESS, AND OUR WHOLE WEEKEND WAS SHOT!
I KNOW.
KIRKMAN & SCOTT
THEN WHY DID YOU KEEP SAYING, "NO PROBLEM, BUNNY"??
IT SOUNDS A LOT NICER THAN !@##*$@, BUNNY.

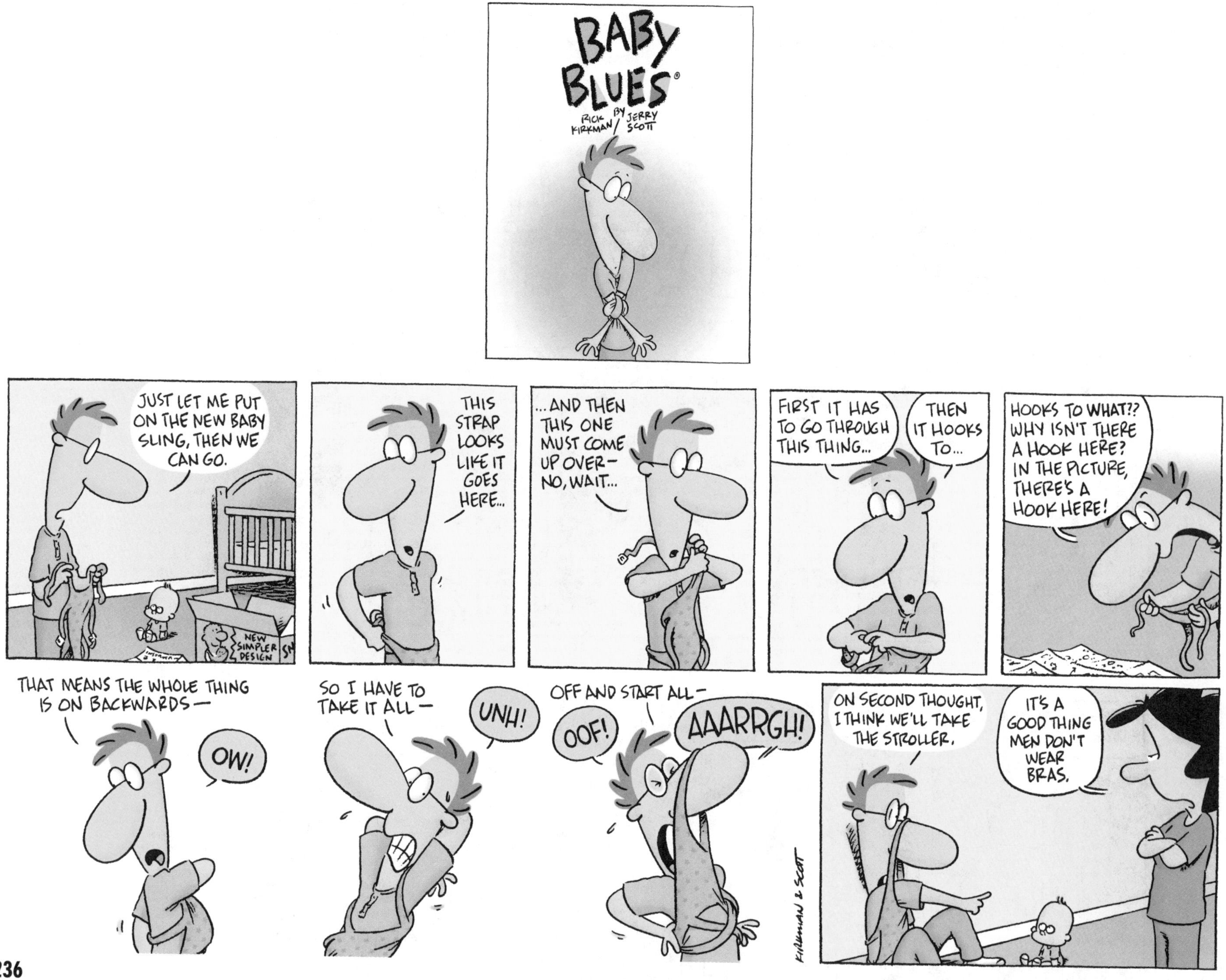
BABY BLUES®
BY RICK KIRKMAN / JERRY SCOTT
JUST LET ME PUT ON THE NEW BABY SLING, THEN WE CAN GO.
NEW SIMPLER DESIGN
THIS STRAP LOOKS LIKE IT GOES HERE...
...AND THEN THIS ONE MUST COME UP OVER— NO, WAIT...
FIRST IT HAS TO GO THROUGH THIS THING...
THEN IT HOOKS TO...
HOOKS TO WHAT?? WHY ISN'T THERE A HOOK HERE? IN THE PICTURE, THERE'S A HOOK HERE!
THAT MEANS THE WHOLE THING IS ON BACKWARDS—
OW!
SO I HAVE TO TAKE IT ALL—
UNH!
OFF AND START ALL—
OOF!
AAARRGH!
KIRKMAN & SCOTT
ON SECOND THOUGHT, I THINK WE'LL TAKE THE STROLLER.
IT'S A GOOD THING MEN DON'T WEAR BRAS.

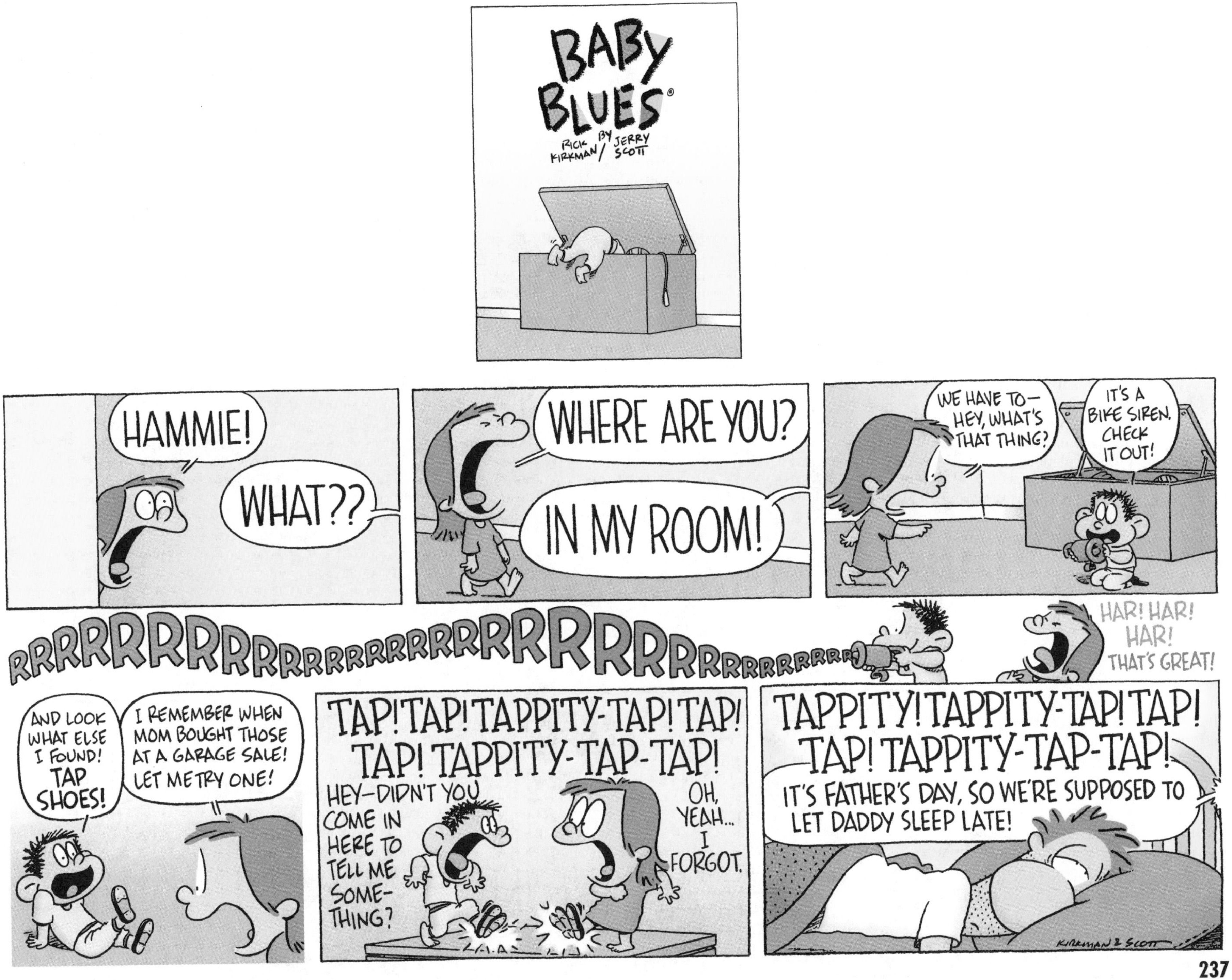
BABY BLUES®
BY RICK KIRKMAN / JERRY SCOTT
HAMMIE!
WHAT??
WHERE ARE YOU?
IN MY ROOM!
WE HAVE TO— HEY, WHAT'S THAT THING?
IT'S A BIKE SIREN. CHECK IT OUT!
RRRRRRRRRRRRRRRRRRRRRRRRRRRRRRRRR
HAR! HAR! HAR! THAT'S GREAT!
AND LOOK WHAT ELSE I FOUND! TAP SHOES!
I REMEMBER WHEN MOM BOUGHT THOSE AT A GARAGE SALE! LET ME TRY ONE!
TAP! TAP! TAPPITY-TAP! TAP! TAP! TAPPITY-TAP-TAP!
HEY—DIDN'T YOU COME IN HERE TO TELL ME SOME-THING?
OH, YEAH... I FORGOT.
TAPPITY! TAPPITY-TAP! TAP! TAP! TAPPITY-TAP-TAP!
IT'S FATHER'S DAY, SO WE'RE SUPPOSED TO LET DADDY SLEEP LATE!
KIRKMAN & SCOTT

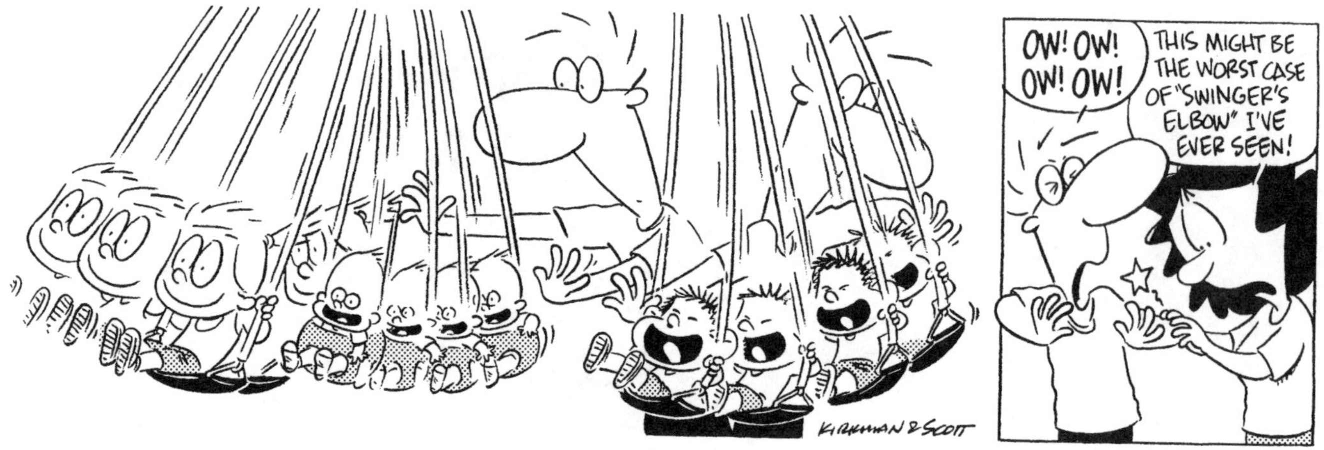
OW! OW! OW! OW!
THIS MIGHT BE THE WORST CASE OF "SWINGER'S ELBOW" I'VE EVER SEEN!
KIRKMAN & SCOTT

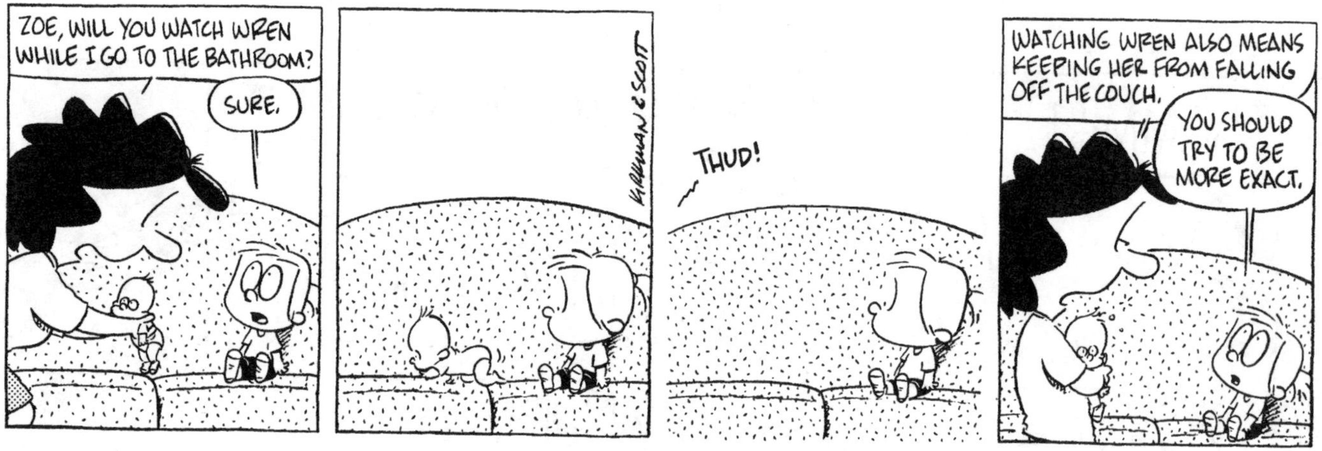
ZOE, WILL YOU WATCH WREN WHILE I GO TO THE BATHROOM?
SURE.
KIRKMAN & SCOTT
THUD!
WATCHING WREN ALSO MEANS KEEPING HER FROM FALLING OFF THE COUCH.
YOU SHOULD TRY TO BE MORE EXACT.

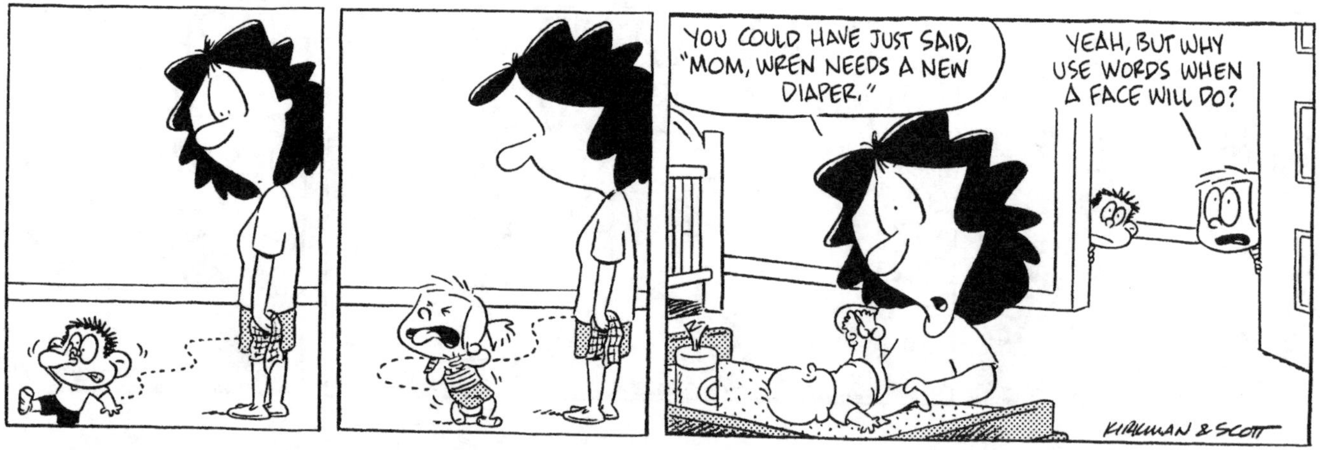
YOU COULD HAVE JUST SAID, "MOM, WREN NEEDS A NEW DIAPER."
YEAH, BUT WHY USE WORDS WHEN A FACE WILL DO?
KIRKMAN & SCOTT

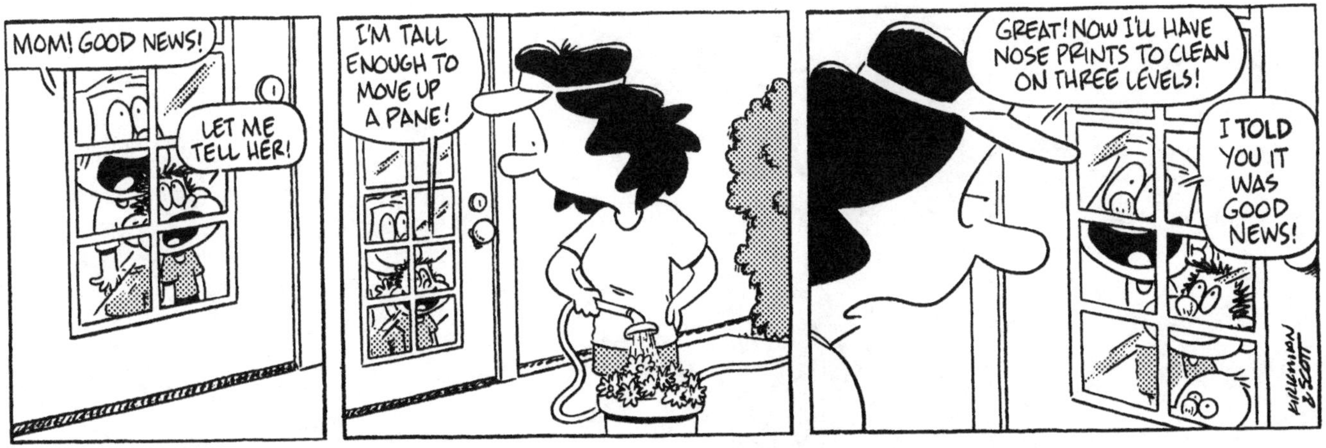
MOM! GOOD NEWS!
LET ME TELL HER!
I'M TALL ENOUGH TO MOVE UP A PANE!
GREAT! NOW I'LL HAVE NOSE PRINTS TO CLEAN ON THREE LEVELS!
I TOLD YOU IT WAS GOOD NEWS!
KIRKMAN & SCOTT

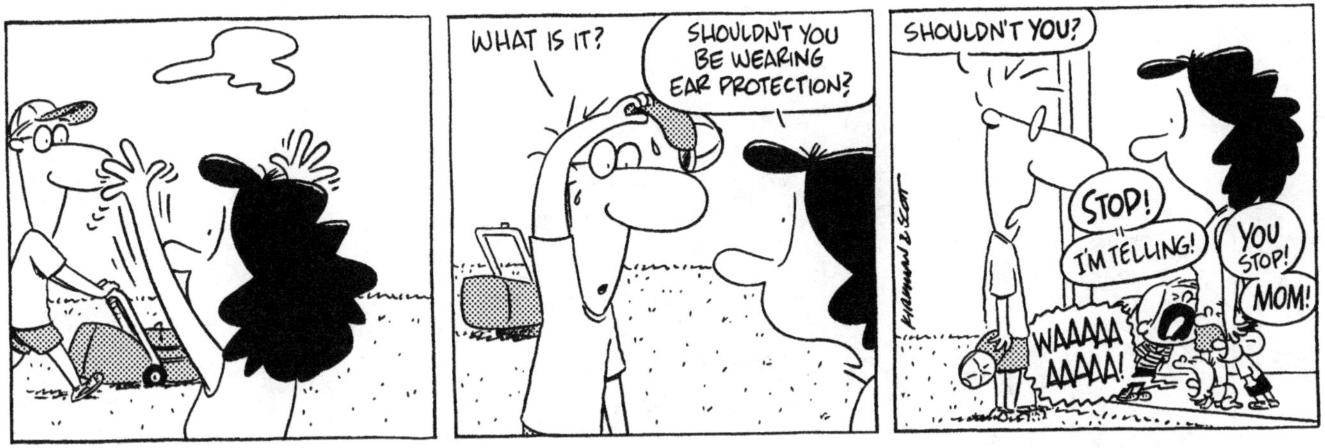
WHAT IS IT?
SHOULDN'T YOU BE WEARING EAR PROTECTION?
KIRKMAN & SCOTT
SHOULDN'T YOU?
STOP!
I'M TELLING!
YOU STOP!
MOM!
WAAAAA AAAAA!

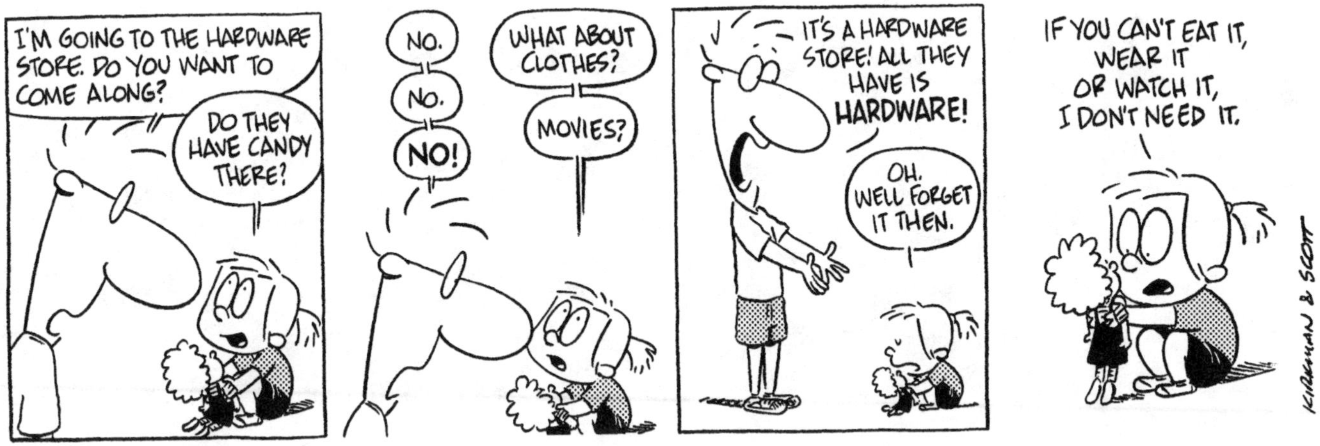
I'M GOING TO THE HARDWARE STORE. DO YOU WANT TO COME ALONG?
DO THEY HAVE CANDY THERE?
NO.
NO.
NO!
WHAT ABOUT CLOTHES?
MOVIES?
IT'S A HARDWARE STORE! ALL THEY HAVE IS HARDWARE!
OH. WELL FORGET IT THEN.
IF YOU CAN'T EAT IT, WEAR IT OR WATCH IT, I DON'T NEED IT.
KIRKMAN & SCOTT

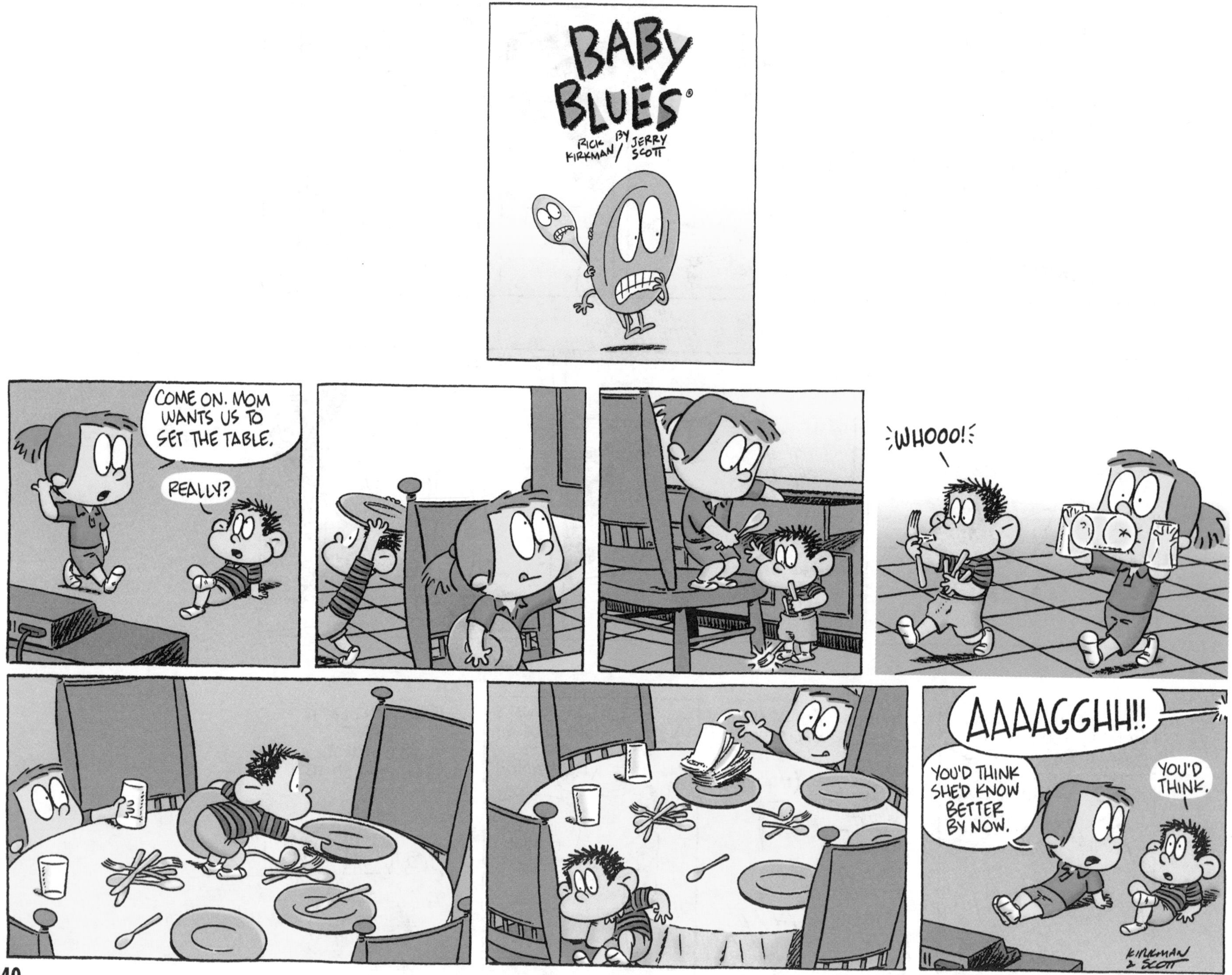

BABY BLUES®
BY RICK KIRKMAN / JERRY SCOTT
COME ON. MOM WANTS US TO SET THE TABLE.
REALLY?
WHOOO!
AAAAGGHH!!
YOU'D THINK SHE'D KNOW BETTER BY NOW.
YOU'D THINK.
KIRKMAN & SCOTT

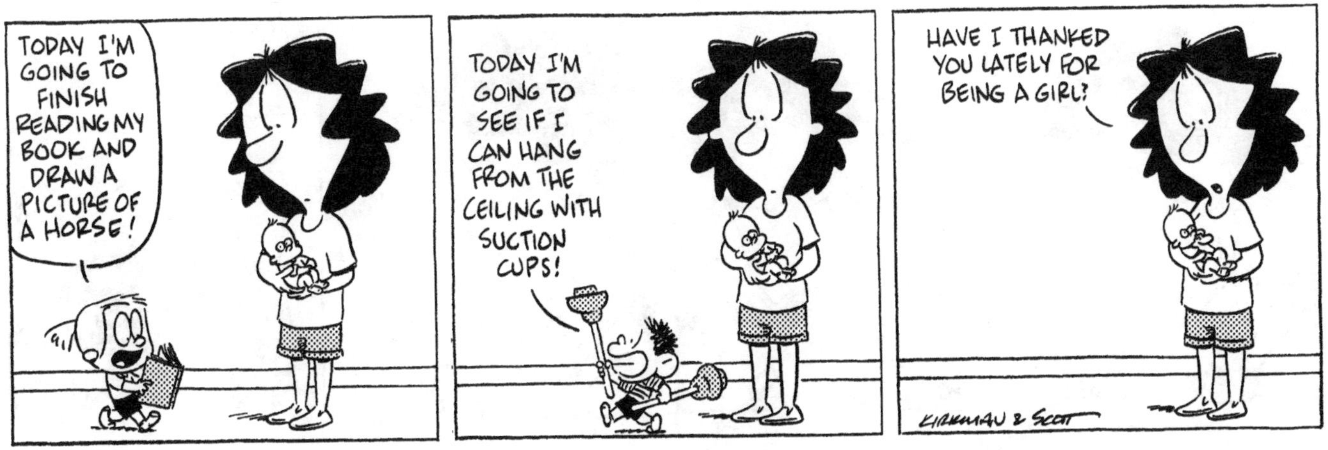
TODAY I'M GOING TO FINISH READING MY BOOK AND DRAW A PICTURE OF A HORSE!
TODAY I'M GOING TO SEE IF I CAN HANG FROM THE CEILING WITH SUCTION CUPS!
HAVE I THANKED YOU LATELY FOR BEING A GIRL?
KIRKMAN & SCOTT

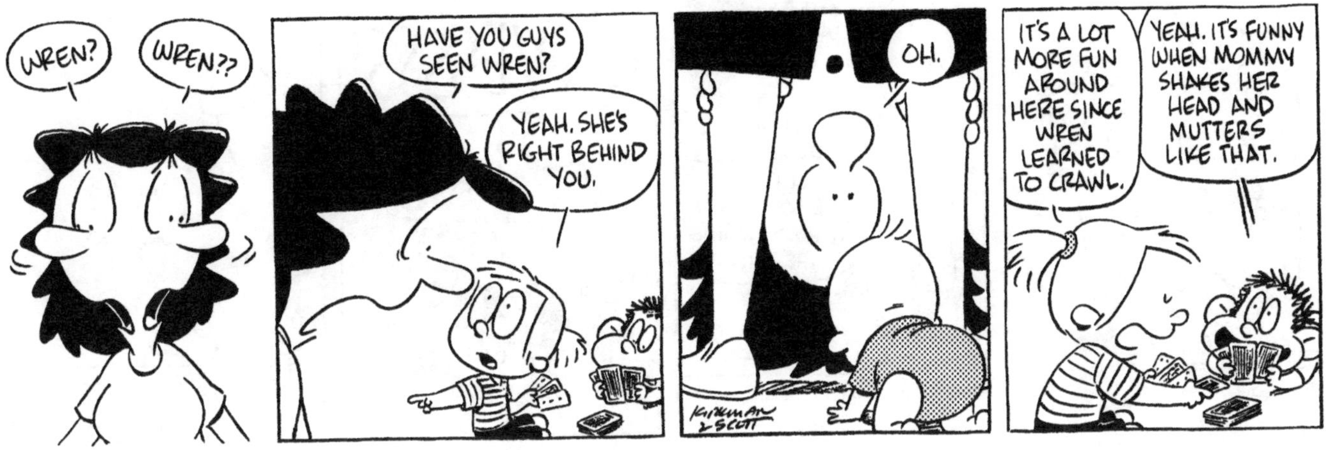
WREN?
WREN??
HAVE YOU GUYS SEEN WREN?
YEAH. SHE'S RIGHT BEHIND YOU.
OH.
KIRKMAN & SCOTT
IT'S A LOT MORE FUN AROUND HERE SINCE WREN LEARNED TO CRAWL.
YEAH. IT'S FUNNY WHEN MOMMY SHAKES HER HEAD AND MUTTERS LIKE THAT.

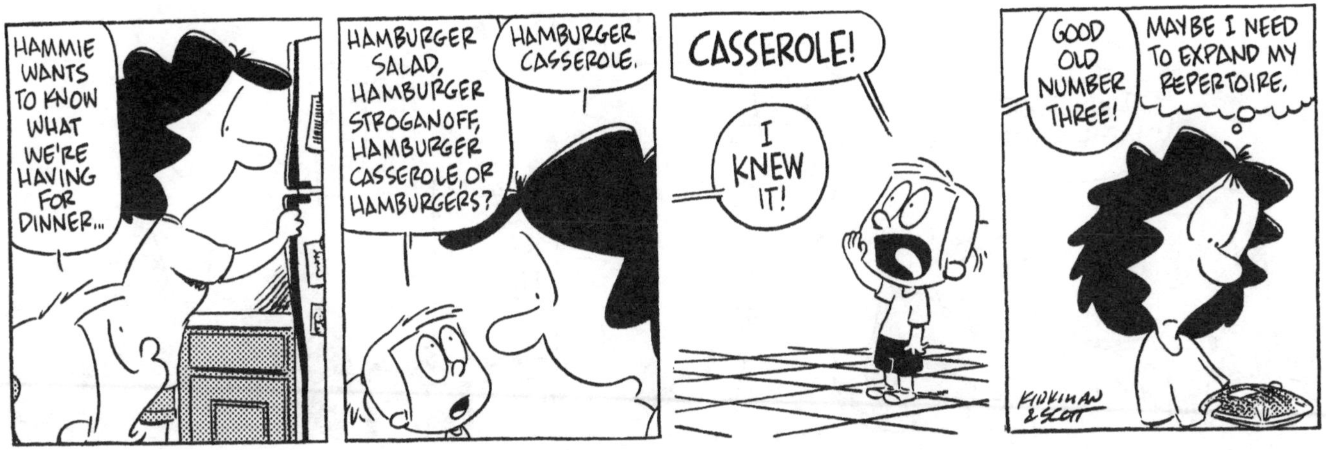
HAMMIE WANTS TO KNOW WHAT WE'RE HAVING FOR DINNER...
HAMBURGER SALAD, HAMBURGER STROGANOFF, HAMBURGER CASSEROLE, OR HAMBURGERS?
HAMBURGER CASSEROLE.
CASSEROLE!
I KNEW IT!
GOOD OLD NUMBER THREE!
MAYBE I NEED TO EXPAND MY REPERTOIRE.
KIRKMAN & SCOTT

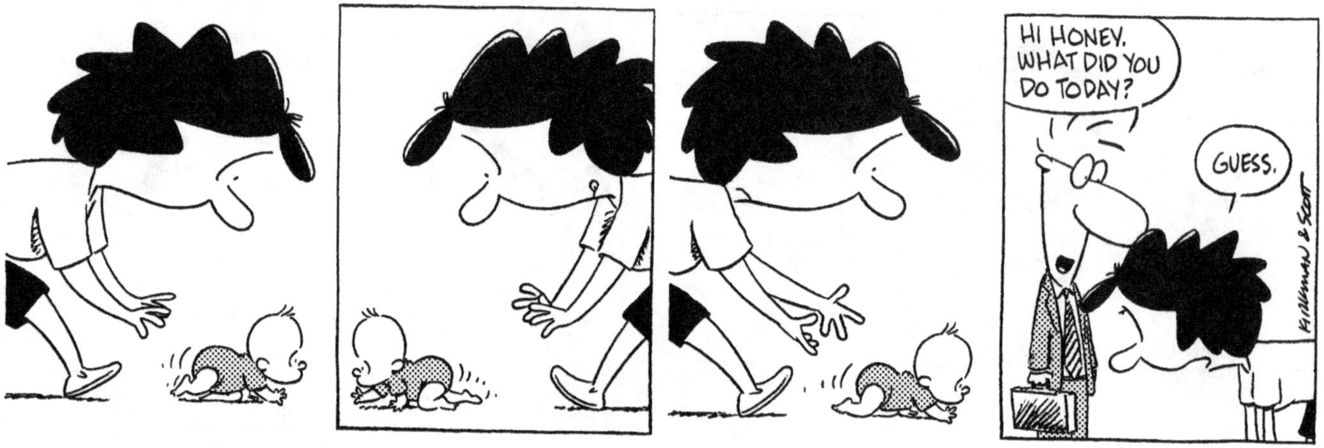
HI HONEY. WHAT DID YOU DO TODAY?
GUESS.
KIRKMAN & SCOTT

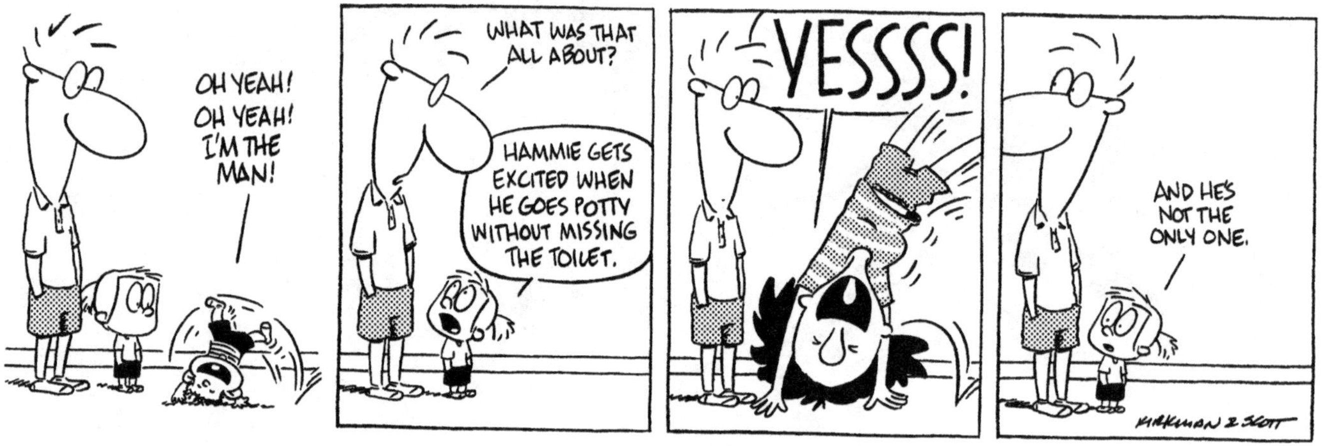
OH YEAH! OH YEAH! I'M THE MAN!
WHAT WAS THAT ALL ABOUT?
HAMMIE GETS EXCITED WHEN HE GOES POTTY WITHOUT MISSING THE TOILET.
YESSSS!
AND HE'S NOT THE ONLY ONE.
KIRKMAN & SCOTT

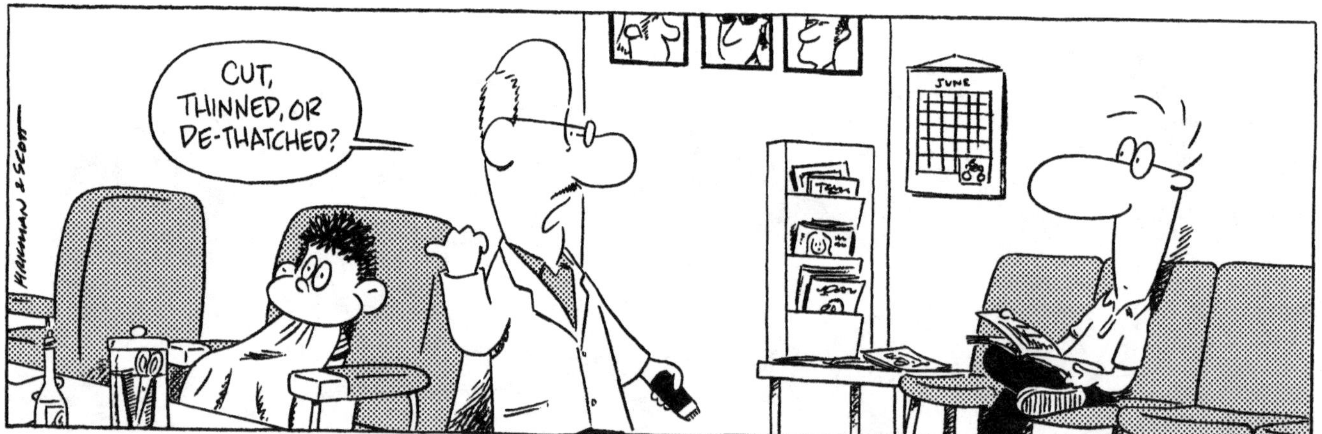
KIRKMAN & SCOTT
CUT, THINNED, OR DE-THATCHED?
JUNE

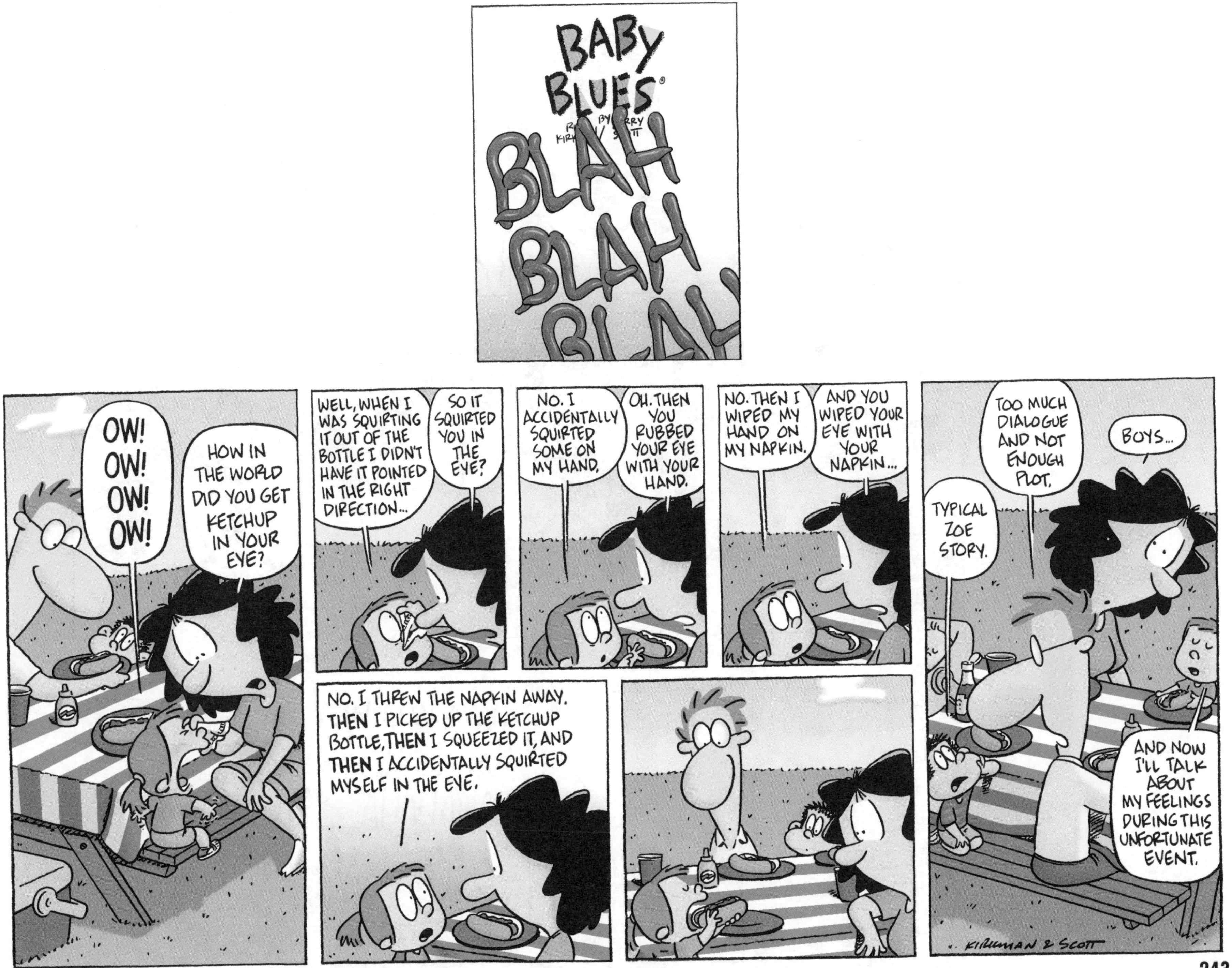
BABY BLUES®
BLAH BLAH BLAH
OW! OW! OW! OW!
HOW IN THE WORLD DID YOU GET KETCHUP IN YOUR EYE?
WELL, WHEN I WAS SQUIRTING IT OUT OF THE BOTTLE I DIDN'T HAVE IT POINTED IN THE RIGHT DIRECTION...
SO IT SQUIRTED YOU IN THE EYE?
NO. I ACCIDENTALLY SQUIRTED SOME ON MY HAND.
OH. THEN YOU RUBBED YOUR EYE WITH YOUR HAND.
NO. THEN I WIPED MY HAND ON MY NAPKIN.
AND YOU WIPED YOUR EYE WITH YOUR NAPKIN...
NO. I THREW THE NAPKIN AWAY. **THEN** I PICKED UP THE KETCHUP BOTTLE, **THEN** I SQUEEZED IT, AND **THEN** I ACCIDENTALLY SQUIRTED MYSELF IN THE EYE.
TYPICAL ZOE STORY.
TOO MUCH DIALOGUE AND NOT ENOUGH PLOT.
BOYS...
AND NOW I'LL TALK ABOUT MY FEELINGS DURING THIS UNFORTUNATE EVENT.
KIRKMAN & SCOTT

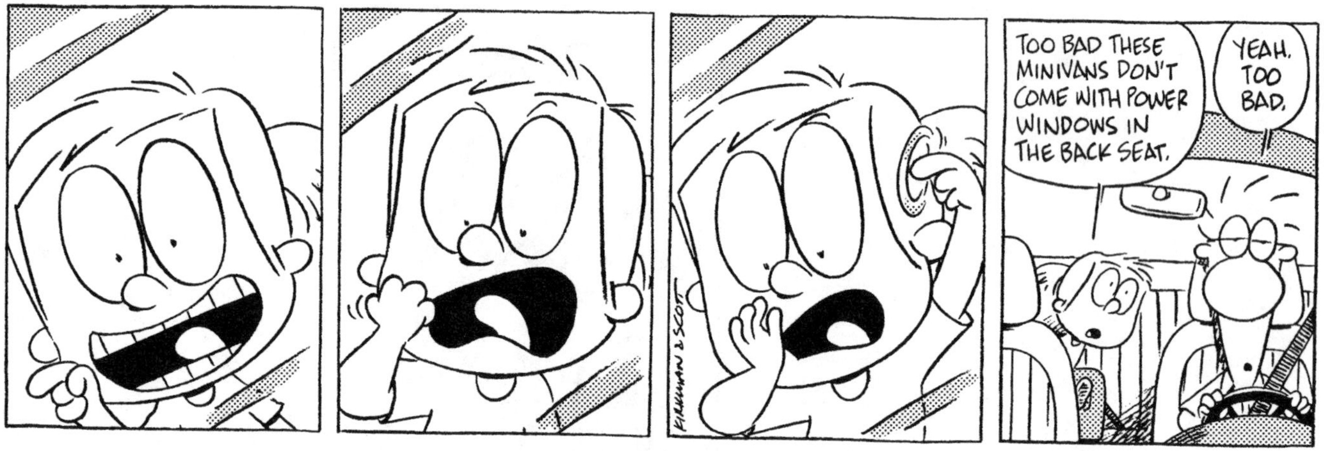
TOO BAD THESE MINIVANS DON'T COME WITH POWER WINDOWS IN THE BACK SEAT.
YEAH. TOO BAD.

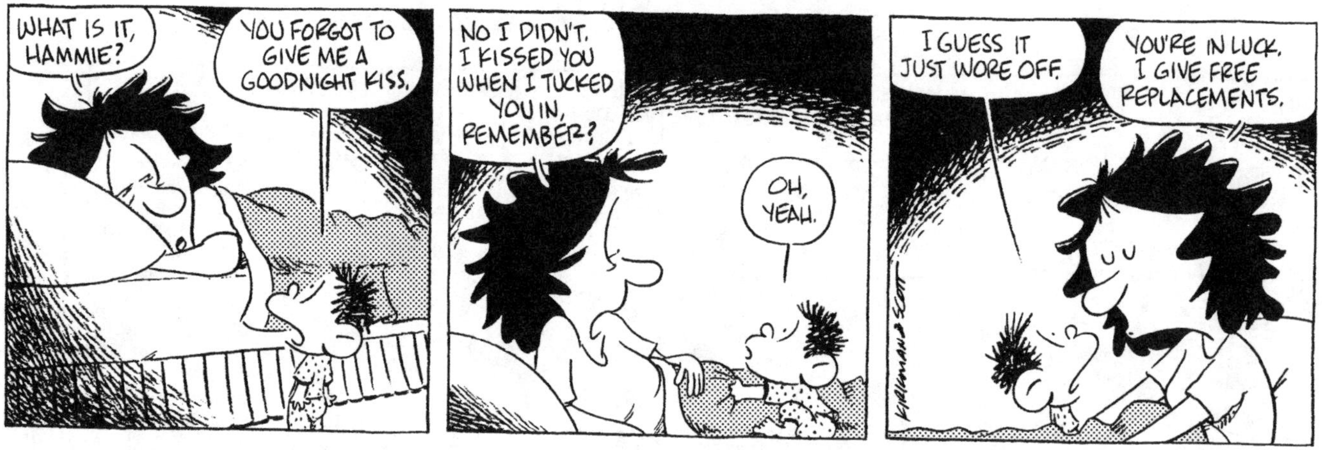
WHAT IS IT, HAMMIE?
YOU FORGOT TO GIVE ME A GOODNIGHT KISS.
NO I DIDN'T. I KISSED YOU WHEN I TUCKED YOU IN, REMEMBER?
OH, YEAH.
I GUESS IT JUST WORE OFF.
YOU'RE IN LUCK. I GIVE FREE REPLACEMENTS.

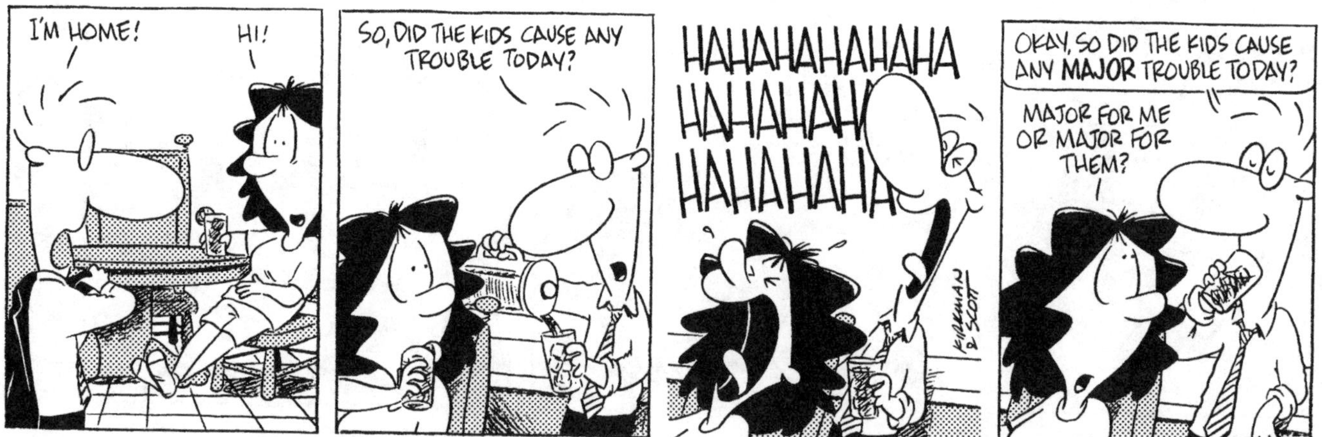
I'M HOME!
HI!
SO, DID THE KIDS CAUSE ANY TROUBLE TODAY?
HAHAHAHAHAHA HAHAHAHA HAHAHAHA
OKAY, SO DID THE KIDS CAUSE ANY MAJOR TROUBLE TODAY?
MAJOR FOR ME OR MAJOR FOR THEM?

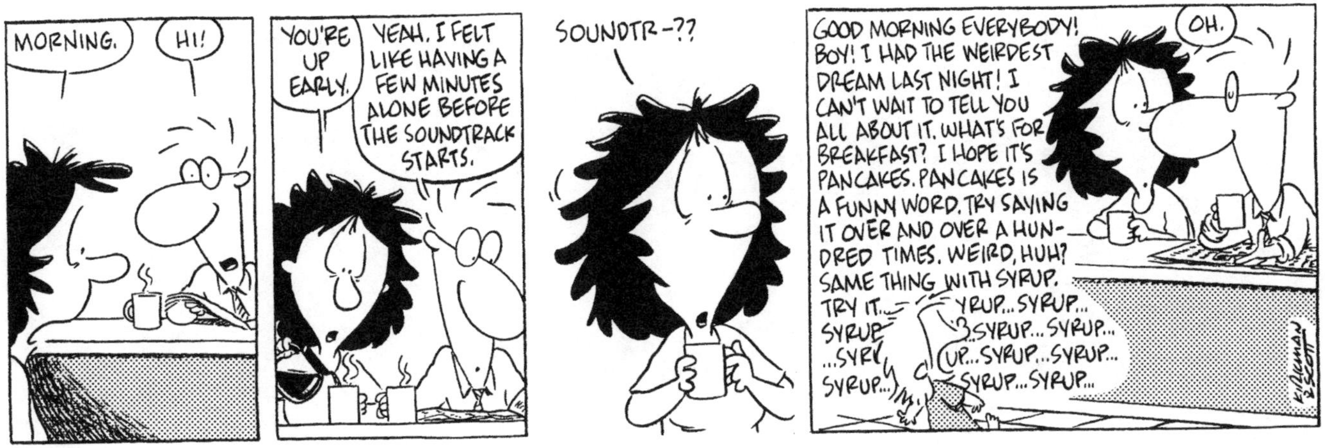
MORNING.
HI!
YOU'RE UP EARLY.
YEAH. I FELT LIKE HAVING A FEW MINUTES ALONE BEFORE THE SOUNDTRACK STARTS.
SOUNDTR-??
GOOD MORNING EVERYBODY! BOY! I HAD THE WEIRDEST DREAM LAST NIGHT! I CAN'T WAIT TO TELL YOU ALL ABOUT IT. WHAT'S FOR BREAKFAST? I HOPE IT'S PANCAKES. PANCAKES IS A FUNNY WORD. TRY SAYING IT OVER AND OVER A HUNDRED TIMES. WEIRD, HUH? SAME THING WITH SYRUP. TRY IT... SYRUP... SYRUP... SYRUP... SYRUP... SYRUP... SYRUP... SYRUP... SYRUP... SYRUP... SYRUP... SYRUP... SYRUP... SYRUP...
OH.
KIRKMAN & SCOTT

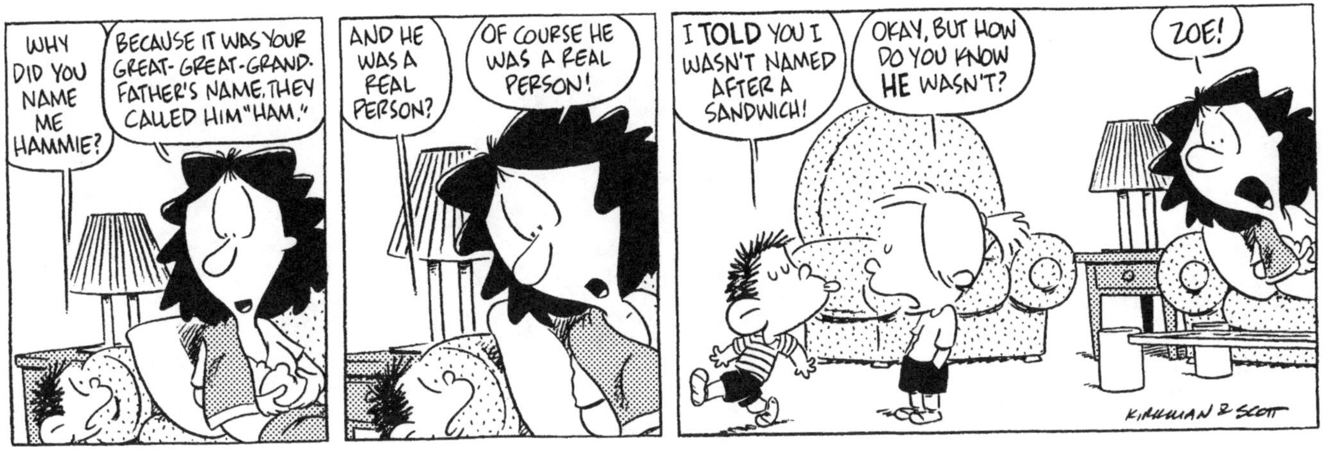
WHY DID YOU NAME ME HAMMIE?
BECAUSE IT WAS YOUR GREAT-GREAT-GRAND-FATHER'S NAME. THEY CALLED HIM "HAM."
AND HE WAS A REAL PERSON?
OF COURSE HE WAS A REAL PERSON!
I **TOLD** YOU I WASN'T NAMED AFTER A SANDWICH!
OKAY, BUT HOW DO YOU KNOW **HE** WASN'T?
ZOE!
KIRKMAN & SCOTT

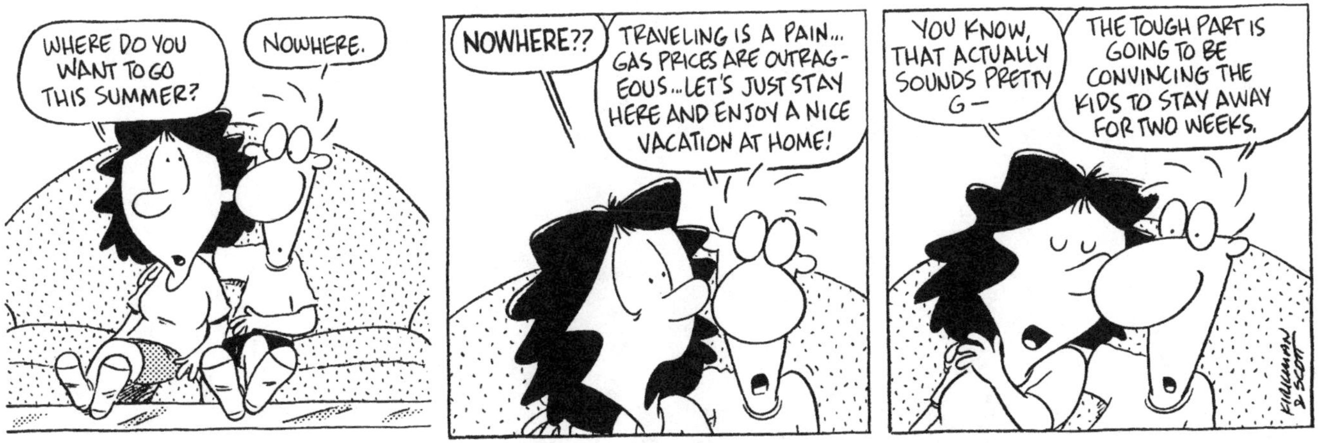
WHERE DO YOU WANT TO GO THIS SUMMER?
NOWHERE.
NOWHERE??
TRAVELING IS A PAIN... GAS PRICES ARE OUTRAGEOUS... LET'S JUST STAY HERE AND ENJOY A NICE VACATION AT HOME!
YOU KNOW, THAT ACTUALLY SOUNDS PRETTY G—
THE TOUGH PART IS GOING TO BE CONVINCING THE KIDS TO STAY AWAY FOR TWO WEEKS.
KIRKMAN & SCOTT

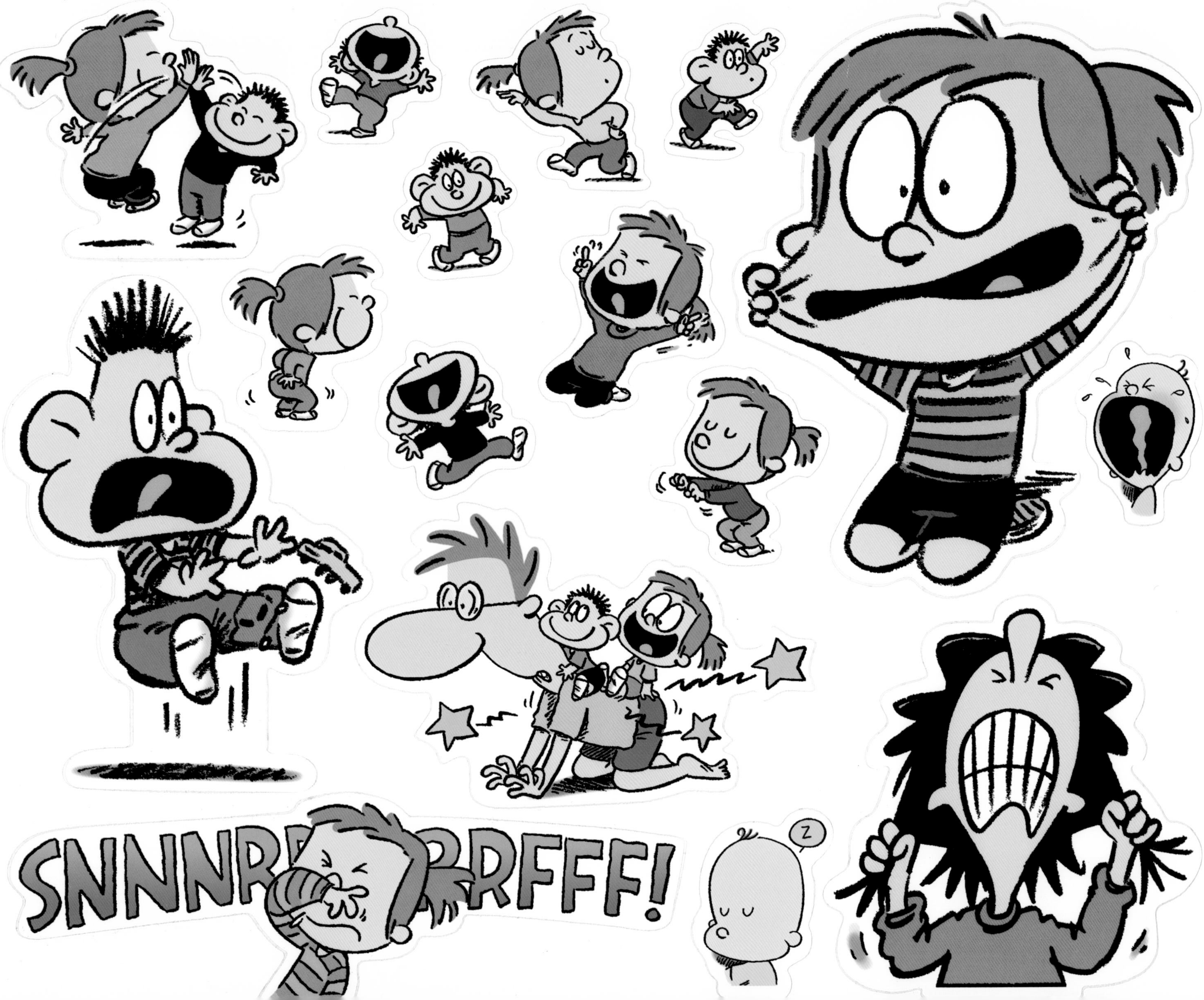
SNNRRRRFFF!

CAUTION:
Driver under the influence of a baby

© 1995, 2005 Baby Blues Partnership. Distributed by King Features Syndicate.

CAUTION:
Driver under the influence of children

© 2005 Baby Blues Partnership. Distributed by King Features Syndicate.